1994?

1947?

1994?

By Harold Camping

Vantage Press, New York

Contents

x   Contents

Preface

The Bible is the greatest book available to mankind even though it is greatly misunderstood by many. It took some fifteen hundred years to prepare and its human authors included many different individuals. But each one was guided by God Himself so that it is perfect in its unity and cohesiveness.

True, its essential message is that of salvation. Yet because it is God's Word it is absolutely accurate in each discipline in which it speaks.

In this study the focus will be on God's timetable of history from the beginning of time to the end of the world. As we look more carefully at the Biblical information pointing to the end of the world, we will discover afresh the perfect unity of the Bible. Moreover, we will discover that the Bible teaches certain absolutes in connection with the end of time.

1. This universe will come to an abrupt end. It will be destroyed and replaced with new heavens and a new earth.

2. At the end Jesus Christ will come to judge all of the people who have ever lived on this earth and who are still unsaved.

3. The unsaved will be judged and removed into Hell to suffer the wrath of God as payment for their sins.

4. The believers in Christ will receive new eternal bodies and will live forever with Christ in the new heavens and new earth.

In this study we will learn from the Bible the many time clues hidden within the Bible that point to the timetable of Christ's first coming. Utilizing the same kind of data and methodology we will learn the timetable of Christ's second coming at the end of the world.

We will discover that even as God created this world in a very precise way, God also designed a very precise and carefully planned timetable for the history and future course of the world. The time line of history is not the rise and fall of political powers. Rather it is the unfolding of God's salvation plan. Thus, events like the circumcision of Abraham or the birth of Jacob, which mean nothing to the world, are in fact very important milestones in the unfolding of history. Thus, too, the rise and fall of the New Testament church is an integral part of this time line.

     We will also discover that we are dramatically close to the end of history. Therefore every reader, with great urgency, must carefully look at his own life to make sure he is ready to meet his maker, the God of the universe.

Introduction

No book ever written is as audacious or bold as one that claims to predict the timing of the end of the world, and that is precisely what this book presumes to do. Actually, however, it is not nearly as audacious or reckless as it first appears. Let us see why this is so.

For more than thirty years I have hosted the Open Forum program on Family Radio. For one and a half hours each evening for five evenings a week I have talked to callers on this live telephone program. Listeners have been invited to call with any questions they had, and I have tried to answer by giving Biblical information that related to the questions.

One of the questions that has been asked repeatedly concerns the timetable of this world's existence. "How close are we to the end of time?" Because these callers had free access to a book I had written, *Adam When?*, which gives the Biblical timetable for the origin of the earth and dates for epochal events such as the time of creation, the year of the flood of Noah's day, the crucifixion of Christ, etc., they asked if the Bible had likewise given me information concerning the timing of the end.

In response to this question my answer has almost always been: "I would be very surprised if the world reaches the year 2000." I would add that the increase of sin in the world, the spiritual decay that is increasingly present in the church world, and the fact that Israel has become a nation were all signs that emphasized our fast approach to the end of the world.

This answer essentially tells our listeners that I believe we are very near the end of time. However, the phrase, "I would be surprised" indicates that even though I am quite certain that all of these signs point to the end of time being very close, the possibility does exist that I could be wrong. Even though such a possibility appears to be quite remote there is always the outside possibility that I am incorrect and this world still does have an unknown number of decades or centuries to run.

The difference between that statement, with which Family Radio listeners are quite familiar, and the publication of a possible month and year of Christ's return, is in one sense very small. In both instances it is insisted that a brief time remains and then the end will be here. In both instances reasons are advanced to show why Christ's coming is believed to be near. In both instances it is indicated that the statements concerning the nearness of the end might be subject to error.

The big difference, however, between the statements "The end of the world in all likelihood will arrive before the year 2000" and "The world in all likelihood will end in a certain month and year" is the amount of Biblical evidence that must be offered to back up each statement. An approximate timetable for the return of Christ can be constructed on fairly general statements. A timetable of a month and year of Christ's return should be constructed on a great amount of Biblical information that focuses on that month and year. Indeed, if a month and year are advanced as a very likely timetable for the end, it better have a great amount of Biblical information to support it. In the past, every attempt to prophesy the date of the end of the world was doomed to failure because of the extreme lack of Biblical data to support it.

We must remember, however, that God does everything in an orderly manner. We see this as we examine the physical universe and in the precise and orderly unfolding of all the major events that relate to God's salvation plan, worked out from the time of creation to the present. Therefore, we know as absolute truth that God has a precise and accurate timetable for the completion of this earth's existence.

Scientists in our day are busy unravelling the complex mysteries of DNA and a great number of other organic and inorganic secrets in the creation that had heretofore been hidden. The big question is: Has God also hidden within the pages of the Bible the secrets of the timing of His return at the end of the world? This is the huge question we will explore in this book.

Expected Reactions to This Book

This book, in which a month and year are going to be offered as the time of the end of this world, is bound to bring on many different reactions in the minds of the readers. Any serious, well-documented book that deals with the future will intrigue a great many people. This is because of man's natural curiosity about the future. Anyone who writes with some conviction about this subject, even with little or no basis, will get a hearing by many people. Reactions will run the gamut from extreme ridicule to serious acceptance. I believe, however, that reaction to this book will be far more intense and agitated. This book seriously faults the churches and denominations of our day. This probably will bring exceedingly strong reactions. Many will be very angry. Some will be outraged. Some will be deeply offended. A great many will react with studied indifference. Ridicule will be commonplace.

Many will criticize those who carefully read and accept the conclusions presented in this book as blind followers of a guru. The fact is, there is nothing secret or mysterious about this study. Each and every facet of it can be examined in the light of the Bible itself.

Moreover, by God's mercy I shall continue to host the Open Forum program. This means that anyone can call and vent their outrage or share their questions in the public marketplace.

Perhaps the chief reason that some readers may feel offended and possibly greatly angered by this book is its insistence that Judgment Day is certain and almost here. It is one thing to say that Christ may come tonight or tomorrow fully realizing that people have been saying that for almost 2000 years. Because He still has not come, the serious possibility of His return in the near future seems very remote; and thus, the idea of His return need not be considered at all.

But when a month and a year are given, and that month and year are very close at hand, and the ascertaining of that month and year is based on a great amount of Biblical data, then it is an entirely different matter. That means I must look at Judgment Day very seriously. Only those who are secure in Christ and confident that their sins have been forgiven dare to face the reality and certainty of Judgment Day. To any one else, a discussion of Judgment Day is far worse than going to a doctor when an individual is quite certain that he has an advanced case of cancer.

Hopefully, sprinkled among the readers will be a few who recognize the terrible predicament they are in if they are still unsaved. By God's mercy some of these will cry to God for mercy as ancient Nineveh did when the prophet Jonah declared that the destruction of

Nineveh was forty days away. It is these people who will be blessed by this book.

It should be noted further that this book was not written to be spectacular, to make money, nor to gain fame for the writer.

This book was written because the information it gives is from the Bible. I feel that any information found in the Bible is to be shared as widely as possible. It must be understood, however, that my knowledge of the Bible is not perfect. Everything written in this book has been carefully taken from the Bible, then cautiously analyzed to produce conclusions. But this does not mean that the conclusions are absolutely true. There still may be something in the Bible that invalidates the conclusions. While such invalidation is extremely unlikely considering the abundance of corroborating information, that possibility does exist. I, like every other human, am a finite being and it is very human to err.

A big advantage gained by publishing this book is the possibility of obtaining further insights from other serious Bible students. This is a blessing I have received through the years as host of the Open Forum program. No individual has a corner on truth. We learn from each other as we share truths we have discovered.

As a matter of fact, a substantial number of Family Radio listeners who have carefully read such books as *Adam When?* and *The Fig Tree* (which are available from Family Radio), have already arrived at the same conclusions as are given in this book. The only addition this book will give to them is the data that further substantiates these conclusions.

One other point that should be emphasized immediately and will be again emphasized in this book: Insofar as our conduct is concerned, as we face the possibility that we are very close to the end of the world, except for making sure of our own salvation, we should continue as if Christ's return is still a hundred years away. As Christians, we should continue to live circumspectly so that our personal lives will be testimonies of the grace of God. Thus, we will be fulfilling God's command to "Occupy till I come" (Luke 19:13). If for some reason we missed something in what we are to understand concerning the timing of the end, and the end does not come in the time we see as a present possibility, we will continue to go forward as witnesses for Christ until death overtakes us or until our Lord returns at some later time.

As we prepare to set forth the Biblical information regarding what we can presently know concerning the timing of Christ's return, we should remember that the Bible is God's book, given to mankind so that we might know His salvation plan. Therefore, the Bible also is the only book that gives us the timetable of history. This is so because the time line of history is the unfolding of God's salvation plan.

This preoccupation with time is seen throughout the Bible. For example, in Genesis 1:1 we read, "In the beginning God created the heaven and the earth."

Genesis 5 and 11 are calendars that cover the first 9000 years of history. Deuteronomy 32:8 underscores that time is governed by God's salvation program:

When the Most High divided to the nations their inheritance, when he separated the sons of Adam, he set the bounds of the people according to the number of the children of Israel.

The New Testament assures us that the children of Israel are those who become saved (Galatians 3:29, 6:16). This is seen in Matthew 24:14 where God indicates that the end of time relates to the sending forth of the Gospel: "And this gospel of the kingdom shall be preached in all the world for a witness unto all nations; and then shall the end come."

Because the Bible is our source of information, we will begin our study by answering the question, "Can the Bible be trusted?"

We should then look at the rapture of the church. In God's time line of history it is the final event that will impact the believers in relation to their life on this present earth. However, because so much incorrect information is being taught concerning the rapture's place in history, we will show that without question it will occur at the end of this world's existence.

Following this we will examine the church as it has existed on the earth throughout time.

Old Testament Israel, which was the only church before the time of Christ, will demand our attention for several reasons.

1. It was the only church in the world before the first coming of Christ.

2. Through it God gave us the Bible so that we can know God's time line of history.

3. From it came Christ who makes possible the salvation plan.

4. It foreshadowed and typified the New Testament church. By studying God's dealings with it, we can learn how God deals with the New Testament church.

Next, we will look with great care at the New Testament church. It is the ultimate unfolding of God's salvation plan. Through the various congregations and denominations that have sprung up throughout the world this salvation plan has become available to the whole human race.

We will then look at the final tribulation period. We will learn that it is the final event in the time line of history during which the era of world evangelization comes to an end. It is a time that signals the end of the world has come. God is finished with His use of the New Testament church since He will have completed the unfolding of His salvation plan. It is a period of great difficulty because it is during this time that God brings to a close His awesome program of bringing the Gospel to the world.

The length of time that the final tribulation occupies in history's time line will next be discovered. We will find that this information is very necessary if we are to know the end of history's time line. Because the final tribulation is a time when churches all over the world will become false churches under the leadership of Satan, we will carefully examine the question, "What is the true Gospel?"

Following that, we will discover the Biblical calendars that permit us to know precisely the timetable of the earth's existence from the creation of the world to the destruction of Israel in 587 B.C.

It might be noted that this calendar of history was developed more than twenty years ago. It was developed without any concern whatsoever for Biblical prophecies that might show the timing of Christ's first coming or second coming. Moreover, since the dates of the Biblical calendar were first made available to the public some twenty years ago, no dates were modified or changed, with one exception. The only change was a date that is not featured in any way in the development of this book, and that is the end of the existence of the ten tribes was changed from 722 B.C. to 709 B.C.

It might also be noted that had the dates in the Biblical calendar of history been even one year different from those shown, it would have invalidated all of the dates used as a basis for the conclusions of this study.

Having established an accurate calendar of history we will then show that by using the Old Testament of the Bible alone we will be able to determine when Christ's first coming would occur. This is so even though the Old Testament was completed about 400 years before Christ came.

Using the same methodology and the same kind of data we will then discover how the Bible discloses to us the timing of Christ's return at the end of the world.

As this book is read it must be kept in mind that the Bible is the revelation to the world of God's salvation plan. In the revealing of that plan the timetable of the earth's existence will be disclosed. This is so because the time line of history is governed by the unfolding of God's salvation plan, and thus we can expect to find the timetable of history within the pages of the Bible.

Therefore, let us begin our study with the question, "Can the Bible be trusted?"

1994?

Chapter 1
Can the Bible Be Trusted?

Before we begin to analyze the Biblical record in an attempt to understand the earth's timetable and the date of man's origin, together with the timing of the end of the world, we must examine the question of the reliability of Scriptures. All Christians agree that the Bible is trustworthy when it speaks on the question of salvation, but there is not always such confidence in the Bible when it speaks in the area of scientific or historical truth. The opening chapters of Genesis are especially suspect to many insofar as historical and scientific accuracy are concerned. If indeed those chapters that purport to give us the history of the beginning of the world are untrustworthy, then surely we can never trust the Bible to give us a timetable for the end of the world.

Science Is Subordinate to the Bible

Increasingly in recent years, geologists, paleontologists, anthropologists, and those committed to other scientific disciplines have been insisting that their research is producing more and more evidence that the concept of long periods of time is the only valid rationale for explaining the existence and condition of our present world. They also conclude that the idea of a universal, earth-inundating flood must be discarded.

Are these scientists correct? Must we reread the Bible from an altogether different point of view than we have in the past? Were our forefathers misguided in believing the six days of creation were six literal days as the Bible evidently teaches? Were they misled into believing that the Bible tells of a literal flood that covered the entire surface of the earth and rose to fifteen cubits above the highest mountain?

Unfortunately, the great majority of those attempting to draw scientific conclusions from evidence being discovered are unsaved men who have no regard for nor any understanding of the Bible. This is true simply because a great majority of all the people in the world are unsaved, including scientists. But the problem of Biblical unbelief arises because a small but significant number of those accepting these conclusions, which are based on long periods of time, are scientists who are born-again Christians. Their accommodation to these conclusions, often by speculations such as theistic evolution, has encouraged acceptance of like truth by an ever increasing number of non- or partially scientifically-oriented Christians. I must confess in my own case, when I was younger I too held the position that the Bible allowed for six long creation periods.

Many serious Christians, however, sense that there is something critically amiss. They may not be able to adequately express their fears in this regard, but they are nevertheless uneasy. Perhaps they fear that acceptance of this new scientific thought can only lead men away from the Bible rather than toward it.

> *Few ministers, theologians, or laymen are*
> *educationally equipped to talk on an equal*
> *level about scientific matters with physicists,*
> *geologists, and other scientists.*

There are a number of valid reasons that may be suggested that have contributed to the development of the acute polarity of opinions concerning the problem of the earth's origins. First of all, few ministers, theologians or laymen are educationally equipped to talk on an equal level about scientific matters with physicists, geologists, and other scientists who are highly trained in their fields. Therefore, communication between the scientific world and the theological world is very poor.

Moreover, our theological posture is cast in the crucible of the Reformation. The reformers were not required to speak in great detail to the questions raised in this discussion, questions which have become so vital in recent years. Thus, our ministers and teachers have not been schooled as well as they should have been to face these questions, and because they have not, none of us sitting at their feet has received adequate Scriptural training. All of us have been trained to think clearly in the areas of sin, salvation, and service, but we have been given no clearly defined framework for understanding the first eleven chapters of Genesis. Therefore, even the Christian who has obtained his doctorate in a scientific field has the same Biblical training as the rest of us; he too is limited in establishing a framework for Biblical truth in the areas of his concern.

Thus, a polarity exists between those who sense that anything but a literal reading of the Genesis account is a direct violation of the rest of the truths of the Bible and those who believe that the widest possible latitude must be given to the interpretation of the Genesis account in order to establish any concordance with scientific truth. Believers on each side of the question are equally sincere in their desire to find truth.

One other point might be raised. In II Peter 3, we read that in the latter days scoffers would arise who would deny the Biblical teaching of the worldwide destructive flood of Noah's day. The reason for this denial is a conscious or subconscious reluctance to accept the certainty of Christ's personal return and judgment. Obviously, the thought of man in some form upon an old world for millions of years does make the concept of the termination of this world, perhaps within our lifetime, appear rather quaint and untenable. If God's judgment on Noah's world was not as extensive and conclusive as Genesis 6 to 9 portrays it, then there is serious doubt as to whether the language of the Bible that relates to the early forthcoming judgment upon this present world is to be taken seriously.

This problem was brought vividly home to me recently when I heard a prominent minister deliver a sermon in which I thought he said that the same trees that we presently see around us could be present after Christ's return. In a discussion with him afterwards, I asked him if he agreed with the statements in II Peter 3 that this world would be destroyed by fire prior to the new heavens and new earth. His reply was very enlightening, "Don't you think this language could be symbolical, and must it necessarily be understood literally?" he asked. In reflecting on his answer to me, the rationale for it is easily seen. If the literal universal flood of Noah did not really happen, then the language of Genesis 6 to 9 must, and the language of II Peter 3 might also, be symbolical or figurative in some sense. Then, too, all statements in the Bible that relate to Christ's coming could be symbolical. The ultimate development of such thinking could lead to a complete denial of the truth of His second coming and judgment. This experience has been cited only to indicate the importance of the question under discussion and the necessity for a clear and forthright stand regarding it.

Speaking to this question, I would like to make a few general observations.

The Bible Is the Ultimate Authority

1. All of the Bible is accurate and authoritative. A modern cliche is often expressed to the effect that the Word of God was never intended to be a textbook of history or science or psychology and that its supreme purpose is to reveal the Creator's wonderful redemptive plan for fallen man through Jesus Christ. This statement in itself is true but unfortunately the impression is often left that the Bible is, therefore, less than accurate when it does speak in the area of science or history. Thus, the authority of the Scriptures is undermined and

> *Unfortunately, the impression is often left that the Bible is less than accurate in the areas of science or history.*

much valuable Biblical truth is disregarded. The fact is that when the Scriptures speak in the area of science or history, or, for that matter, in any other field of learning, they do so with exceeding great care, accuracy, and authority. There are three reasons for this: (1) these subjects are often an integral part of the plan of salvation; (2) they are part of God's message to man; and (3) by reason of His very nature God is accurate when He speaks.

It appears that two events in history are perhaps especially important contributors to the present resistance to the acceptance of the entire Bible as completely authoritative and trustworthy in every detail. The first was the development of the evolutionary theories of Charles Darwin together with the uniformitarian theories of Lyell and others. Darwin and Lyell offered systems of origins that appeared to be substantiated by much evidence from scientific research. Because their theories run counter to the teachings of the Bible a serious question was raised regarding the trustworthiness of the Scriptures.

The second event was the uncovering of the ancient sites of Mesopotamia and Egypt. While the first archaeological effort was begun by Napoleon's expedition in 1798, substantial digging at these sites occurred almost simultaneously with the presentation of the theories of Darwin and Lyell. Not only were ancient cities brought to light but also their primitive libraries were unearthed. After the languages of these bygone civilizations were deciphered, the libraries of clay tablets were read. The archaeologists, many of whom were trained as theologians, discovered many tablets that appeared to disagree with the Bible. Or, they found little evidence that would support the Bible. So immediately the Bible was placed on the same level as that of other ancient writings. It was to be reckoned as one account developed by man but it was not to be regarded as any more authoritative than any other account.

The words of Sir Alan Gardiner, an archaeologist of international fame who regarded Exodus as legendary, tells very succinctly of his feelings:

> I will admit that the lack of logic and imperviousness to facts shown by those who treat the book of Exodus as a good historical document soon ranged me to the other side.[1]

It is true that whenever a Biblical statement was discovered to be true, it was acknowledged. But even this was often done reluctantly.

Because archaeological discovery was of such great interest to Bible scholars, the findings and conclusions of the archaeologists were eagerly read. Unfortunately, however, too few dared to reject the scientific conclusions when such conclusions ran contrary to God's Word. Even in conservative commentaries, questions are raised regarding the trustworthiness of certain parts of the Biblical record. For example, the editors of the highly esteemed "Pulpit Commentary" allowed one of its writers to say:

> The conclusion, therefore, seems to be that, while Scripture does not imperatively forbid the idea of a partial Deluge, science appears to require it, and, without ascribing to all the scientific objections that are urged against the universality of the Flood that importance which their authors assign to them, it may be safely affirmed that there is considerable reason for believing that the 'mabbul' which swept away the antediluvian men was confined to the region which they inhabited.[2]

At a time, then, when the Biblical record is threatened by the secular record we have entered the age of modern science. Scientists in the last several decades have covered themselves with glory as they have made advances in medicine, physics, chemistry, and biological research. Among other discoveries, they have found ways of dating the materials of earth, both inorganic and organic. Their conclusion that the earth must be at least several billion years old seems to agree with the earlier findings of Darwin, Lyell, and others. Because the Bible speaks of creation being completed in six days several thousand years ago, these modern day scientists too have come to the same conclusion as many of the archaeologists: the Bible is untrustworthy in these areas of scientific thought.

> *Some Christians who are scientists have decided that the Bible does not speak at all in areas of history and science and say it is only a book for theologians.*

At the same time, Christians have seriously attempted to harmonize and explain the Biblical account in relation to the scientific evidence and conclusions. Some Christians who are scientists have decided that the Bible does not speak at all in areas of history and science and say it is only a book for theologians. A statement that reflects the current position of many Christians with a scientific background is that which is found in *The Encounter Between Christianity and Science*.[3] In this book, which was written and edited by leading Christians of scientific stature, the premise is set forth that the Bible is trustworthy when it speaks to the questions of God, Jesus, and salvation. They contend that since these are apparently the key subjects of the Bible, the supporting data - the historical, the scientific - need not be necessarily accurate. Consequently, the scientific theories of evolution and uniformitarianism cannot be studied in the light of the Bible but can only be understood in the light of God's natural revelation. In my judgment, such assumptions have led these writers to a kind of neo-orthodoxy that reminds me of the theories of Barth and Brunner. These latter men approached the Bible from a philosophical background whereas those who are scientists approach the Bible with the viewpoint that science is the final authority in its own domain; but both are offering something less than the whole counsel of God.

The point of all this is that believing that the supporting Biblical data is not necessarily accurate and true will lead the believer away from the truth in the so-called spiritual areas. The conclusions of the writers of the book, *The Encounter Between Christianity and Science*, show this trend:

In conclusion, then, the writer takes the following position:

(1) Organic evolution has been verified with sufficient evidence to justify scientific acceptance.

(2) Acceptance of organic evolution does not negate creation or the supernatural. Rather, organic evolution is a natural process accomplishing a supernatural purpose.[4]

> *Without an historical Adam and an historical confrontation between Adam and Satan, the whole purpose of Christ's coming is put into question.*

It seems to me that such conclusions as these effectively destroy the whole purpose of the Bible. Without an historical Adam and an historical confrontation between Adam and Satan, the whole purpose of Christ's coming is put into question. Furthermore, what Scripture can anyone offer to support the conclusions of Dr. Bube? In my judgment, these conclusions may offer the scientist maximum latitude in examining scientific evidence, but this in no sense makes these conclusions true. I believe, for example, it can be shown that the Bible has much to say in the area of evolution theory. I trust that this volume will show how wonderfully God, in His Word, helps us to understand the chronology of mankind. This chronology impinges directly upon the conclusions that are derived from the secular evidence.

For too long many well-meaning Christians have yielded to the temptation to deny the relevancy and wisdom of the Scriptures that relate to these many fields of learning. We must accept all of the Bible as totally accurate and authoritative.

> *One of the most fundamental concepts of Bible exegesis is to let the Bible be its own interpreter.*

Interpret Scripture with Scripture

2. Whenever we have to force a verse or struggle with a verse to make it fit into our idea of what the Word says or will allow, we are on very dangerous ground. One of the most fundamental concepts of Bible exegesis is to let the Bible be its own interpreter. Some subjects

are mentioned in more parts of the Bible than others, and can be interpreted in more ways than others, depending upon the context. But if the Bible does not allow for alternatives, then none can be taken. The Bible must set limits of interpretation. Unless other Biblical evidence of a parallel nature, including but not limited to the context of the verse itself, allows us to do so, we may not take any liberties in trying to understand a verse. What we do not understand, we must simply accept by faith. Later, either in this life or in the life beyond the grave, the Holy Spirit may clarify the verse.

Let us consider, for example, the findings of Sir Leonard Woolley, world renowned archaeologist, concerning the Noachian Flood. After examining evidence obtained during twelve years of excavating at the ancient site of Ur of the Chaldees, Sir Leonard expressed the opinion that the Flood of Noah's day was limited to the Mesopotamia Valley.[5]

The archaeologist had found indisputable proof of a major flood. A deposit of silt to a maximum depth of eleven feet was discovered, with evidence of human dwellings below the level of the silt. In his findings Sir Leonard stated that in his opinion the flood recorded in the Book of Genesis had extended across the flat, low-lying land of Mesopotamia to a depth of twenty-five feet, and over an area of three hundred miles in length and a hundred miles in width.

Viewed under the searchlight of God's Word, however, Woolley's conclusions are invalid. It can be shown that the flood of Noah's day must have been universal if the Scriptures mean what they say. This fact is clearly set forth in the Bible, for when we look at the Scriptures that relate to the flood, we are amazed at the clear language and the repeated emphasis of universality that God uses to describe this flood.

The Bible uses such language as:

And the LORD said, **I will destroy man whom I have created from the face of the earth; both man, and beast, and the creeping thing, and the fowls of the air** (Genesis 6:7)[6].

And God said unto Noah, **The end of all flesh** is come before me; for the earth is filled with violence through them; and, behold, **I will destroy them with the earth** (Genesis 6:13).

And, behold, I, even I, do bring a flood of waters upon the earth, to destroy all flesh, wherein is the breath of life, from under heaven; and **every thing that is in the earth shall die** (Genesis 6:17).

For yet seven days, and I will cause it to rain upon the earth forty days and forty nights; and **every living substance that I have made will I destroy** from off the face of the earth (Genesis 7:4).

And the waters prevailed exceedingly upon the earth; and **all the high hills, that were under the whole heaven, were covered** (Genesis 7:19).

Fifteen cubits upward did the waters prevail; and the mountains were covered (Genesis 7:20).

And all flesh died that moved upon the earth, both of fowl, and of cattle, and of beast, and of every creeping thing that creepeth upon the earth, and every man (Genesis 7:21).

All in whose nostrils was the breath of life, of all that was in the dry land, died (Genesis 7:22).

And every living substance was destroyed which was upon the face of the ground, both man, and cattle, and the creeping things, and the fowl of the heaven; and they were destroyed from the earth: and Noah only remained alive, and they that were with him in the ark (Genesis 7:23).

And the waters decreased continually until the tenth month: in the tenth month, on the first day of the month, **were the tops of the mountains seen** (Genesis 8:5).

Also he sent forth a dove from him, to see if the waters were abated from off the face of the ground; But the dove found no rest for the sole of her foot, and she returned unto him into the ark, **for the waters were on the face of the whole earth: then he put forth his hand, and took her, and pulled her in unto him into the ark** (Genesis 8:8-9).

. . . Neither will I again smite any more every thing living, as I have done (Genesis 8:21).

And I will establish my covenant with you; **neither shall all flesh be cut off any more by the waters of a flood; neither shall there any more be a flood to destroy the earth** (Genesis 9:11).

. . . And the waters shall no more become a flood to destroy all flesh (Genesis 9:15).

> *Could words be more explicit or exact to indicate the **universal** nature of the Flood . . . than the words used in the Genesis account?*

Could words be more explicit or exact to indicate the **universal** character of the Flood, both from the standpoint of the destruction of all flesh and the destruction of the entire face of the earth, than the words used in the Genesis account? To question such positive and clear-cut statements is to impugn the authority of God's Word. Few events in history are as clearly delineated in the Scriptures as is the flood of Noah's day and its inundation of the entire earth. We, therefore, may not assume any different conclusion than that this literally happened. Moreover, the parallel passages in the Bible give no suggestions that these verses are to be taken other than literally; instead they actually reinforce the truth of the nature and extent of the flood (cf. II Peter 3:5-7, Psalm 104:6-9).

In light of the Biblical record of a deluge of cataclysmic proportions, we must carefully appraise many of the conclusions of geologists, anthropologists, and paleontologists of our day. Such men of science frequently base their conclusions on the premise that all change since the beginning of time has continued in a uniform and non-catastrophic fashion. This is an assumption that the Christian cannot accept since all archaeological findings must be examined under the searchlight of God's clear-cut statement that the **whole earth** was destroyed by a flood in one period of history. The Holy Spirit contends with the premise of uniformity in II Peter 3:3-6:

Knowing this first, that there shall come in the last days scoffers, walking after their own lusts, And saying, Where is the promise of his coming? for since the fathers fell asleep, all things continue as they were from the beginning of the creation. For this they willingly are ignorant of, that by the word of God the heavens were of old, and the earth standing out of the water and in the water: Whereby the world that then was, being overflowed with water, perished.

Creation

3. Scientific conclusions regarding the earth's origins are very often based on hypothesis rather than fact.

We might receive the impression that the theory set forth by many scientists that the origins of the world required long periods of time is the only valid one in the light of an abundance of unquestionable evidence. Almost every article written for popular reading on this subject appears to say that the evidence for the conclusions presented is quite free from uncertainty and the supporting evidence is amenable only to that conclusion. However, we find that much of the evidence is fragmentary when we read what scientists write to each other in such scientific journals as the "American Journal of Science." We notice how carefully they indicate the assumptions and hypotheses that they have adopted in arriving at the theories they are offering, and how they carefully state the exceptions and problems that remain, which weaken their conclusions. In other words, they understand that their conclusions must be tentative and subject to radical change if necessary because of the paucity of available data, and the sometimes speculative nature of some of their basic assumptions.

Unfortunately, the layman is seldom given information regarding the tenuous nature of many of these conclusions. In addition, the relevant statements of the Bible are normally not used as basic assumptions upon which the evidence being studied is to be evaluated.

> *The Biblical account of the days of creation . . .*
> *must be recognized before any scientific evidence con-*
> *cerned with origins can be evaluated.*

Yet the Biblical account of the days of creation is a statement that must be recognized before any scientific evidence concerned with origins can be evaluated. Does the Bible suggest or permit long periods of time as a valid option to that of six solar days? The Biblical record of the first day is as follows:

And God said, Let there be light: and there was light. And God saw the light, that it was good: and God divided the light from the darkness. And God called the light Day, and the darkness he called Night. And the evening and the morning were the first day (Genesis 1:3-5).

The first day appropriately begins with the words, "And God said," even as each of the other five days begins with the same words. Let us assume now for the moment that this first day is a long period of time, lasting, say, one million years. This appears to be a valid assumption since the Bible sometimes does use the word "day," the Hebrew "yom," to describe an activity that lasts more than a solar day. Genesis 2:4, for example, speaks of "The day that the LORD God made the earth and the heavens." This particular day probably includes all of the events spoken of in the first chapter of Genesis or as a bare minimum the events of the second and third days. So our beginning assumption that the first day was a long period of time could have Biblical support.

Since the verse speaks of an evening and morning, the first day must have been divided into two periods, each approximately 500,000 years long. Ordinarily the division of day and night is approximately on a fifty-fifty basis inasmuch as the entire Bible was written in an area of the world where this is true. However, for maximum freedom in following this discussion, the hypothetical million years could be divided on almost any basis and the argument will hold. The first was a period of light that was called Day, the second a period of darkness called Night. The "evening" and "morning" must be directly related to the "Day" and "Night" of the same verse. This is the logical and obvious reading of verse 5, with no other relationship intimated.

If we look now at the second and third days of creation, we should conclude that their time spans must be like that of day one. The statements "the evening and the morning were the second day" and "the evening and the morning were the third day" are almost identical to the statement of verse 5, "And the evening and the morning were the first day." Could we not then assume that these days were of like duration to that of day one? Since the second and third days also had an evening and a morning, each must have consisted of a period of light lasting some 500,000 years and a period of darkness lasting some 500,000 years.

> *What was happening to the plants and trees that came into existence the third day during the long night of half a million years?*

The first major problem soon arises, however. What was happening to the plants and trees that came into existence the third day during the long night of half a million years? Since there were no stars and no moon, the darkness must have been total. Surely, no plant life could be sustained during the long night.

On the fourth day, God created the sun, moon, and stars. The greater light (the sun), was to rule over the day. The lesser light (the moon), was to rule over the night. Inasmuch as this, too, was a period of an evening and a morning, this fourth day that lasted some one million years in accord with our initial assumption must also have been divided into a period of 500,000 years of light and 500,000 years of darkness. What about the sun? Was it shining during this long night? The obvious conclusion can be only that this evening and morning lasted the length of a solar day. The fact is that if we start again with Genesis 1:5 and recognize that each day of creation was of twenty-four hours duration and that the "day" of Genesis 1:5a was more specifically the light-time portion of that first day, we will solve all the problems raised above.

The first three days continued twenty-four hours each without the sun. The fourth day continued with the same rhythm but with the sun. Although the light of the first day was the substitute for the sun's light of the fourth, the earth could have been turning on its axis every twenty-four hours the first day even as it does today. The rhythm of twenty-four hours could therefore have been manifested in this phenomenon as well as the alternate light and dark periods of some twelve hours each. Only by this understanding can harmony be provided throughout the entire first chapter of Genesis. Of the some 1480 times that the Hebrew word "yom" is used in the Bible, the preponderant usage is of that suggested above, namely the period of time the sun is shining, or the calendar day of twenty-four hours. These are also the usual ways in which we use the word "day" in our ordinary speech. The concept of solar days for Genesis 1 is not only the most obvious understanding of "yom" in Genesis 1, it is in complete harmony with the entire Bible.

Let us look for a moment at the seventh day when God rested. Doesn't the Bible give support to the concept that this was a long period of time? And if God's cessation from creating is to continue from the end of the six days of creation until the end of the age, doesn't this suggest that the six days were also long periods of time? It is true that at the end of the six days God rested from His work and never again began His initial creation; but did He never more create? Jesus says in John 5:17, "But Jesus answered them, My Father worketh hitherto, and I work." This verse shows God is surely not resting. We cannot conclude then, that there is anything peculiar about the seventh day that automatically makes it longer than any other day. Secondly, whenever the thought is expressed in the Bible that God rested on the seventh day as in Exodus 20:11 and Exodus 31:17, the context never implies a day longer than a solar day. Moreover, while God has completed His initial creation (Genesis 1), can we say that God does not continually create throughout history, as for example, when He brings new lives into existence? We read in Psalms 104:30, "Thou sendest forth thy spirit, they are created: and thou renewest the face of the earth." And in Psalms 102:18, "This shall be written for the generation to come: and the people which shall be created shall praise the LORD." (In this verse, the King James Version most accurately translates the Hebrew word "bara," which is our word for create or created.) In both of these instances, we see that God continues His work of creation as He brings new life into being. Further, such dramatic acts of Jesus as that of multiplying the loaves and fish surely must be considered to be acts of creation. Since His creative work must have continued with the birth of Cain and with the new plants that began to grow in years after the initial creation, the seventh day rest of God may be understood to have been of very short duration. Then the only logical time span for understanding this seventh day must be a solar day. This in turn reinforces the interpretation that insists on six solar days for the days of creation.

We, therefore, see that the logical, harmonious way to understand the verses of Genesis, both in the language of the text itself, in the context of the entire chapter, and in the context of the Bible, is to see creation as an activity that continued for a time period of six days. All scientific evidence should be viewed within this framework.

When God created the universe, He brought it into full operation as if it had existed for many years. Therefore, the various parts of the universe, for example, the stars and the animals, were given an apparent age even though they were created in a moment of time.

> *We know from God's Word that regardless of how much truth appears to be found within these religions, they must be rejected because they are not built upon the foundation which is Jesus Christ.*

4. A false system of knowledge may appear true. In many systems of teaching there appears to be evidence within the system that indicates the validity of the system. Thus, men of high scholarship have adopted Islam and other false religions as true. We know from God's Word that regardless of how much truth appears to be found within these religions, they must be rejected because they are not built upon the foundation which is Jesus Christ. Similarly, many fine thinkers accept Communism as a true and enlightened politico-religious system even though we know it is totally unacceptable because it does not begin with an infinite God and with man created in the image of God.

In the same manner the concept of long periods of time as a solution to the six days of Genesis appears to have much truth within it. We hear a lot about concordant dates, for example, but the whole system must be rejected unless its foundation rests squarely and unequivocally upon the Bible. The seeming internal consistency of parts of this system may be a reward that keeps scientists in pursuit. Ultimate truth can be obtained only when the foundation is trustworthy.

Recently I had the privilege of spending several hours with a scientist who is a serious born-again Christian. He has a lot of training and experience in radioactive isotopes, which are used for dating purposes. He, too, had adopted long periods of time as a valid conclusion and appeared uncertain about the universality of the flood. I must confess that I felt quite uneasy during our discussion because I sensed that somehow there was a tremendously important missing ingredient in his conclusion. We were unable to reach an agreement, even though as fellow born-again Christians we ought to have finally found the same truth.

In analyzing my feelings, I discovered that I felt much like I did when I visited the Mystery Spot in Santa Cruz, California. This is a spot on the side of a hill that does not appear to have the usual direction of the force of gravity. At least the owners make this declaration. Water apparently runs uphill, people on this property often feel ill, and many other curious phenomena are apparent. This is achieved by removing visitors from any known plane of reference. A cabin with an outside wall surrounding it was constructed. All normally horizontal planes, such as floor and ceiling, are constructed to be sloped, and all normally vertical planes and lines, such as walls, door jambs, and window frames, are constructed so that they are not vertical. Obviously, a visitor in this cabin tries to reconcile what his eyes tell him is the direction of the force of gravity, as he relates to normally vertical and horizontal lines, with the direction of the force of gravity that he feels in his own body. This produces a conflict that sometimes makes him ill or uneasy. Moreover, such things as flowing water that appears to run uphill are in evidence. In other words, a system of truth has been developed on the side of this mountain, which appears quite cogent in many respects but is totally erroneous in relationship to the true plane of reference that is found when one leaves this spot. Without the missing ingredient of a true plane of reference, apparent truth poses as real truth.

Faith: The Missing Ingredient

After I left the scientist, I read again the Biblical accounts of the flood, Psalm 104, and other passages. True relief came to me when I read in Hebrews 11:3:

Through faith we understand that the worlds were framed by the word of God, so that things which are seen were not made of things which do appear.

Faith is the element that pervades all aspects of Biblical knowledge and makes the difference between human theories that appear to be true . . . and the Word of God, which is true.

The missing ingredient in our discussion was faith in the plain teachings of the Bible. This is the foundation that must underlie all scientific inquiry if we are to find truth. When Abraham was told to sacrifice his son, Isaac, the command appeared ridiculous. If he killed his son, it would negate all the promises that God had given to him: that he would be the father of a multitude of nations and that in his seed all of the nations would be blessed. Abraham believed that in spite of these inconsistencies God should be obeyed. He obeyed because He had implicit trust in God. This is faith. Faith is the element that pervades all aspects of Biblical knowledge and makes the difference between human theories that appear to be true because of internal agreement, and the Word of God, which is true because He is objectively and absolutely trustworthy.

The point at issue is not the quality or quantity of either my or my scientist friend's faith. Far be it from me to pass judgment upon another. I should be the first to cry out, "I believe, help Thou my unbelief." The point at issue is that we will miss the value and significance of Scriptural truth as it applies to all areas of our observable universe unless we view it consistently with eyes of faith. Without faith the Bible offers no assistance in our understanding of nonbiblical evidence. This applies not only to salvation truth but also to every other area of knowledge that the Bible addresses.

Jesus emphasized the matter of faith by His reference to His purpose for preaching the parables. In Mark 4:2 we read that "He taught them many things by parables." We would immediately speculate that He did this in order to make the Gospel He was preaching more easily understood. The reverse is the case. In Mark 4:11-12 we read:

And he said unto them, Unto you it is given to know the mystery of the kingdom of God: but unto them that are without, all these things are done in parables: That seeing they may see, and not perceive; and hearing they may hear, and not understand; lest at any time they should be converted, and their sins should be forgiven them.

The problem of the Jews was that they were looking for a Messiah who would make logical sense to them. Jesus did not logically fit their idea of what the Messiah ought to be so they rejected Him. Because they were not humbly, with repentant hearts of faith, looking to God's Word, Jesus preached in parables so that even the glimmer of truth that could have come from His Gospel was taken from them. Peter, Mary, Martha, and others, on the other hand, by faith accepted Jesus as the Messiah. Then they were able to see the wonderful logic of God's Word. In similar fashion the Bible's truths are hidden to those who look to it for truth without first humbly trusting it as God's infallible Word.

> *We forget that most of the contributions to scientific inquiry have been made by unsaved men who know nothing of faith.*

I am afraid that in the whole area of knowledge relating to the beginning of man and the earth we have begun to accept a system of truth that appears quite valid and has much internal consistency. Because many elements of this system of truth do not square with the Bible, the Bible appears illogical, and, therefore, is apparently not to be trusted for what it says. We forget that most of the contributions to scientific inquiry have been made by unsaved men who know nothing of faith. We must remember that only when we begin with a deep and abiding faith in the inerrancy of the Scriptures will the beautiful logic of the Bible be revealed to us. We must begin in scientific inquiry with the available evidence set forth in the Biblical record, accepting this by faith as a completely valid foundation for understanding the evidence brought in from other sources.

5. May we dare trust the Bible when it speaks in the area of scientific inquiry? Did not such trust lead an earlier generation of Christians astray as they concluded the earth was flat? It is true that scarcely a millennium ago, as our forefathers considered the flat expanse of their relatively small portion of the globe - the only world they knew - and observed how unerringly the sun travels across the heavens from one end of the land to the other, they were convinced that the earth was shaped like a table whose four ends must come to a sudden halt somewhere beyond the line of ocular vision. And the sun, they concluded, was a ball of fire traveling around the flat earth.

When Christians of much earlier generations reviewed these conclusions, they agreed that the Bible supported the idea that the earth was flat and that the sun was a ball of fire. Sufficient evidence to bolster such conclusions indeed appears to be found in the Scriptures, for God's Word does refer to "the ends of the earth" (Psalm 59:13), "the four corners of the earth" (Isaiah 11:12), and "the rising" and the "going down" of the sun (Psalm 50:1).

However, a more comprehensive study of God's Word would have shown them that their conclusions were erroneous. There are a number of truths that were apparently never considered in earlier days. Nowhere does the Bible state positively that the earth's configuration is flat. On the contrary, a round configuration is indicated in the statement found in Isaiah 40:22, "It is he that sitteth upon the circle of the earth." The Book of Job uses an interesting metonym in reference to the earth: "He has described a circle upon the face of the waters at the boundary between light and darkness" (Job 26:10 Revised Standard). To appear as a circle when viewed from any point above its surface, an object must be spherical in shape. Many other statements are found in God's Word that suggest much more than a flat earth with a flaming ball moving slowly across the sky from one end of the four-cornered table to the other. The following statements clearly say something different.

Proverbs 8:27: When he prepared the heavens, I was there: when he set a compass upon the face of the depth.

Ecclesiastes 1:6: The wind goeth toward the south, and turneth about unto the north; it whirleth about continually, and the wind returneth again according to his circuits.

Job 26:7: He stretcheth out the north over the empty place, and hangeth the earth upon nothing.

We, therefore, must conclude that when all of the Biblical notices concerning the shape of the earth are considered, we cannot say conclusively what its configuration is. It surely does not insist in any way upon a flat earth, and there are many statements that point to a round earth or a sphere. The secular evidence shows us that the earth is a sphere in space; the Bible does not contradict this but actually supports this concept. Thus, we can see how the Holy Spirit guided men to write only that which was accurate and dependable in the Bible.

6. How do we regard the Bible? Some time ago a minister and I were discussing the seeming drift of the Christian community from the Word of God. As we parted, my friend declared, "After all, the Bible is not God!" As I reflected on this assertion, I began to see the serious trouble the church was in, for in this statement I believe we find evidence of its weakened spiritual condition. Let us see why this is so.

Much has been written in recent months and years concerning the infallibility of the Bible. With scholarly rhetoric the writers insist that the Bible is the Word of God and is altogether true and trustworthy when it speaks. It is the final authority because it is inspired by God; it is dependable and accurate.

> *A man can talk forever about his vital and wonderful faith in Christ, but if his works are not showing the evidence of that faith, his faith is dead.*

With all this verbalizing, one wonders if all of us really believe that the Bible is inspired. In the area of salvation God says faith without works is dead. Thus a man can talk forever about his vital and wonderful faith in Christ, but if his works are not showing the evidence of that faith, his faith is dead. Likewise, talking about how one accepts the infallibility of the Bible means nothing unless it translates into concrete substance when the Bible is interpreted. For example, attention is sometimes called to the fact that the parable of the sower, recorded in Matthew 13:3-23, is different from that recorded in Luke 8:4-15. The conclusion is therefore drawn that this is so because the Biblical authors interpret and apply for us the literal words of Jesus. This conclusion makes us wonder if we are then to believe that the quotations found in the Bible are not necessarily verbatim quotes? Does this mean, for example, that the seven statements of Jesus on the cross were not necessarily spoken by Jesus? Is it possible that we have only Spirit-guided interpretation of whatever words He actually spoke?

Since the Bible is its own interpreter, where do we get permission for this kind of reasoning? Where does it say or suggest that the quotations found in the Bible were not actually uttered? How dare we entertain this kind of thinking?

True, there are times when the Bible writer under the inspiration of the Holy Spirit does interpret or change the exact wording of a statement being quoted. This is seen especially in the New Testament quotations of fulfilled Old Testament prophecy. In these cases the Bible gives ample indication that this has occurred. We have both the Old Testament record and the New Testament restatement. These can be compared to discover God's unfolding revelation as He gives additional insights into the intent and purpose of the Old Testament statement. But when similar statements are recorded in slightly different fashion in each of several of the Gospels, the Bible does not say that one Gospel account is a fulfillment or a quotation from the other Gospels. Therefore, we must assume that the precise words found in each Gospel are the actual words spoken. This is readily understood if we realize the Gospel record is but a tiny fragment of all the words spoken (cf. John 21:25). Jesus surely must have frequently repeated the parable of the sower, and each telling must have included different details and therefore each recorded account is slightly different from the others. God follows this same rule as He describes salvation in a great number of different ways in the Bible.

Similarly, for example, the conversation between the rich young man or ruler and Jesus (Luke 10:25-37, Matthew 19:16-22), probably lasted several minutes. One Gospel writer presents some of his actual words and another Gospel writer presents other of his actual words. Combining the two accounts we have an enlarged but probably still incomplete view of the total conversation. The words God wanted us to know about are faithfully recorded for our perusal.

> *We are so ready to accept the conclusions of*
> *secular science that speak to the question of the*
> *origins of man and the world.*

These illustrations (many more of a similar nature could be offered) are sufficient to show the low opinion many have today of the integrity of the Word of God. No wonder we are so ready to accept the conclusions of secular science that speak to the question of the origins of man and the world. In the eyes of most people the Bible has lost its authority. When God says, "For in six days the LORD made heaven and earth, the sea, and all that in them is" (Exodus 20:11a), we set this aside with a wave of the hand, almost as if it does not exist. The fact that this same truth is detailed in Genesis 1 seems to make no impression whatsoever on many of our scientists, who apparently cannot wait to adopt many of the conclusions of their secular colleagues, regardless of how alien those conclusions are to the Bible. No wonder we have arrived at a point where even an account so carefully articulated as that of the Noachian flood (Genesis 6-9) is set aside as so much nonsense. This is effectively what we do when we talk about a Mesopotamia Valley flood rather than a universal flood.

There are other verses that may appear unsolvable. The Bible is the revelation of God, and God is infinite. He is from everlasting to everlasting. Our finite minds cannot possibly begin to grasp all of the truths of the mind of God. At times we must wait for a clearer understanding for God does have a timetable for revealing an understanding of His Word.

Sometimes He does speak symbolically or allegorically, but invariably a careful analysis of the verses, in the context of the whole Bible, will show us how to view these verses. Never may we demean or question the integrity of God's Word.

The fact is, the information I have placed in this book, which encompasses truth found in many parts of the Bible, emphasizes and reinforces that the Bible could be written only by God. The unity, the cohesiveness, the consistency of Biblical language set forth this information, which, we discover, embraces the whole history of mankind from creation to the end of the world. No human author without the Bible could possibly be capable of producing the tremendous truths set forth in this study.

"The Bible is not God," my friend had said. True, the physical Bible that we hold in our hand is not God; it is only paper with ink on it. But when we read the Bible it is as closely related to God as anything can be. It is the voice of God. It is the statement of His perfect will. It is the command of the King. Because it is the voice of God, it may not be changed or altered or questioned as to its authority or veracity. Every word in the original is God's choice, even though it comes from the personality and environment of the human author. No word is accidental or coincidental.

God is a Spirit, so we cannot see Him with our physical eyes. We can see Him in His revelation, the Bible, as God tells us about Himself and His *creative* as well as His redemptive work. His Word is as holy as He is. His Word is to be treated with the same deference, respect, honor, and fear as God Himself. For good reason it is called the "Holy Bible."

The sin of questioning the integrity of God's Word is not an incidental sin. It is one of the first magnitude. God says in Exodus 20:3-5:

Thou shalt have no other gods before me. . . . for I the LORD thy God am a jealous God, visiting the iniquity of the fathers upon the children unto the third and fourth generation of them that hate me.

> *When we put the authority of science above that of the Bible, we have begun to worship science.*

When we put the authority of science above that of the Bible, we have begun to worship science. When we put the authority of a theologian above that of the Bible, we have begun to worship man's mind rather than God. And these sins will bring down the wrath of God.

The ominous phrase "to the third and fourth generation" has eternal implications of the most serious nature. God is declaring that our progeny will be cut off, that Hell is in view. We are reminded of God's Word to Israel in Deuteronomy 4:25-26:

When thou shalt beget children, and children's children, . . . and shall corrupt yourselves, . . . to provoke him to anger: I call heaven and earth to witness against you this day, that ye shall . . . utterly be destroyed.

The scientist can be very helpful in our study of the Bible. However, evidence found by him will never contradict Bible truth. The conclusion of the scientist that is a result of viewing the evidence in the light of his own assumptions must never be accepted unless it agrees with untampered Bible truth.

The views of a theologian may be studied and are surely helpful, but never are we to accept statements from him that show weakness regarding Biblical authority. We should build on theology that is absolutely true to the Bible. We should reject out of hand those ideas that suggest that the Bible is less than absolute truth, even if the theologian who suggests the idea is quite reputable.

What are we to do? I fear that large segments of the church have arrived at a terrible condition. God's wrath is upon us. We have sown the wind and are about to reap the whirlwind. If we do not think this is true, watch what is happening to the thinking of our sons and our daughters, too many of whom are not following in the faith of our fathers.

We are in trouble. We have sinned grievously. When anyone sins there is only one course of action to follow: Beg the Lord to show us mercy as we turn from our sin.

> *This is not the time to defend our faithfulness to God's Word with pious arguments. This is the time to acknowledge our sin.*

This is not the time to defend our faithfulness to God's Word with pious arguments. This is the time to acknowledge our sin. We have impugned the Word. We have begun to worship science. We have spent much too much time listening to Barth and Brunner. We have entertained the unbiblical heresies of Lever and others. No wonder theology (true Bible understanding) is almost at a standstill today.

We ought to put on sackcloth and ashes and cry out for mercy. Perhaps God will protect us as individuals from the judgment He has begun to visit upon us. We ought to repudiate and turn away from those teachings and teachers who are unknowingly leading us to the worship of other gods.

May God have mercy on us.

Fulfilled Prophecy
7. *The Bible proves its veracity by fulfilled prophecy.*

A marvelous feature of the Bible is the fact that repeatedly we discover within its pages records of fulfilled prophecies. For example, in Genesis 6:7:

> And the LORD said, I will destroy man whom I have created from the face of the earth; both man, and beast, and the creeping thing, and the fowls of the air; for it repenteth me that I have made them.

This prophecy was literally fulfilled when God completely destroyed the world of Noah's day.

In Genesis 18 we read of God telling Abraham that He planned to destroy the cities of Sodom and Gomorrah because of their great wickedness. In Genesis 19:24-25 we read:

> Then the LORD rained upon Sodom and upon Gomorrah brimstone and fire from the LORD out of heaven; And he overthrew those cities, and all the plain, and all the inhabitants of the cities, and that which grew upon the ground.

In Joshua 2 God gives us information that the ancient city of Jericho was to be destroyed. In Joshua 6 we read about the destruction of Jericho.

In Joshua 6:26 God pronounced a curse on the one who would try to rebuild the city of Jericho. Joshua 6:26:

> And Joshua adjured them at that time, saying, Cursed be the man before the LORD, that riseth up and buildeth this city Jericho: he shall lay the foundation thereof in his firstborn, and in his youngest son shall he set up the gates of it.

More than 500 years later a man rebuilt Jericho. We read in I Kings 16:34:

> In his days did Hiel the Beth-elite build Jericho: he laid the foundation thereof in Abiram his firstborn, and set up the gates thereof in his youngest son Segub, according to the word of the LORD, which he spake by Joshua the son of Nun.

In Deuteronomy 28:47 God predicted that ancient national Israel would rebel against God after they were given the land of Canaan. He then indicated they in turn would be destroyed by nations whose language they did not understand. Indeed hundreds of years later they were destroyed first by the Assyrians and finally in 587 B.C. by the Babylonians.

Many prophecies were given concerning the Messiah Who would come. It was prophesied that He would be of the tribe of Judah, of the line of David. He would be born in Bethlehem. A most remarkable prophecy is recorded in Daniel 9:24-27, where it is predicted that He would come in the year 7 B.C. In Daniel 12:12 God predicted that His ministry would encompass 1335 days. Later in our study we will look at these prophecies in detail. All of these prophecies were carefully fulfilled.

A prophecy that was made almost 2000 years ago is that the nation of Israel would be reconstituted as a nation. We might recall that national Israel was destroyed in 70 A.D. and for almost 2000 years was scattered among the other nations of the world. In the Bible God typified the nation of Israel as a fig tree and Jesus predicted it would again be in leaf near the end of time. He also predicted that it was to be a nation that would not accept Jesus as their Messiah.

> *Prophecy was dramatically fulfilled*
> *in our day when Israel again became*
> *a nation in 1948.*

Later we will learn how that prophecy was dramatically fulfilled in our day when Israel again became a nation in 1948.

In this study we shall repeatedly see the wonderful cohesiveness and unity of the Bible. Only a book written by God could have such truth. Indeed it is a book that must be listened to with great care. May it be that this study will help show the complete trustworthiness of the Bible.

SUMMARY

1. All of the Bible is accurate and authoritative. Regardless of the field of learning, it is absolutely true and trustworthy in everything it says.

2. The Bible is its own interpreter; we explain the Bible only by the Bible. We must never "force" a statement of the Bible so that we can understand it to say what it has not said.

3. Scientific conclusions concerning the earth's origins are based upon hypothesis rather than fact. Only the Bible is an absolutely trustworthy statement upon which to build truth concerning the earth's origins.

4. If we put the authority of science above the authority of the Bible, we have begun to worship science. If we put the authority of a church or theologian above that of the Bible, we have begun to worship man's mind rather than God.

5. The Bible proves its authority and truthfulness by the fact that the events it has prophesied have come to pass.

Now we should press on toward our goal of discovering the timetable of the end of the world. Next, we will learn what the Bible has to say concerning the rapture of the church in God's timetable.

NOTES

[1] Alan H. Gardiner, "Tanis and Pi-Ramesse: A Retraction," in the "Journal of Egyptian Archaeology" (London, Egypt Exploration Society, Vol. 19, 1933).

[2] Vol. 1, p. 121.

[3] Richard H. Bube, ed., *The Encounter Between Christianity and Science*, William B. Eerdmans, 1968.

[4] *Ibid.*, p. 168.

[5] Sir Leonard Woolley, *Excavations of Ur*, Thomas Y. Crowell Co., 1954.

[6] Scripture references are from the King James Version. Emphasis added by author.

Chapter 2
When Is The Rapture?

As never before in history, there is an increasing preoccupation with the subject of the return of our Lord Jesus Christ. The return of Israel to its land, the tremendous multiplication of knowledge, the potential for massive worldwide destruction by nuclear war, and the rapid increase in communication technology (permitting the Gospel to penetrate everywhere in the world), are some of the phenomena that cause serious students of the Bible to wonder if the end of time is at hand.

Naturally those who have placed their trust in the Bible as the only reliable source of information concerning the future will look to the Bible for information concerning the end-time events.

Two events recorded in the Bible have great importance as the end of the world is contemplated. Before we continue our study to discover the timing of Christ's return, we should look at these two events with great care. One of these is the final tribulation, which will come upon the world just prior to its end. In the next chapter we will examine it in great detail. The other event is the rapture of the church, which we will examine in this chapter.

> *By the word **rapture** we have in mind that moment in history when the believers in Christ who have not experienced physical death will be changed into their glorified bodies.*

One event that gives great comfort to the child of God is the rapture of the believers. By the word *rapture* we have in mind that moment in history when the believers in Christ who have not experienced physical death will be changed into their glorified bodies. At that time they will be caught up in the air to be with Christ, even as I Thessalonians 4:17 declares:

Then we which are alive and remain shall be caught up together with them in the clouds, to meet the Lord in the air: and so shall we ever be with the Lord.

The subject of the rapture of the church is very important for many reasons. One reason is that we must remember that the time line of history is the unfolding of God's salvation plan. The church, and by this we mean the various congregations and denominations in which true believers in Christ are found, is intimately and extensively a part of God's salvation plan. Since the **rapture** is the catching up of believers to be with Christ in the air, it signals the end of the believers on earth. That is, it indicates the church has come to an end on earth. Therefore, we must learn when this will be in relationship to the chronology of history.

A puzzling situation has developed, however, concerning the timing of the rapture. Some hold that it will take place 1,007 years before the end of the world. Others believe the Bible teaches that it will be 1,003.5 years before the end, while still others suggest 1,000 years. Then there are those who teach that this grand event will occur right at the end of time.

One logically, wonders, therefore, whether the Biblical teaching concerning the timing of the rapture is intentionally obscured or whether the language of the Bible is just extremely difficult to understand. Of course one would surely wish that he could understand the Bible clearly on this question, for then one could know more specifically how the believers will relate to the final tribulation of which the Bible speaks. Moreover, a clear understanding of the timing of the rapture would greatly help in understanding many other details relating to the end of time.

Wonderfully, the Bible has much to say about the rapture. It is not an event that is rarely alluded to in the Bible. The timing of the rapture in relation to Judgment Day and the end of time is extremely well documented in the Scriptures. We need have no doubt whatsoever concerning its place in the sequence of events that relate to Christ's return.

The rapture of believers will occur at
the end of time.

In this study we will examine seven different sets of Scriptures that deal with the rapture. As we go through these Scriptures, we will find seven independent paths that lead us to the same inescapable conclusion: **The rapture of the believers will occur at the end of**

time. It will take place at the same time that our Lord comes to judge the world. It will come right at the time that the world is beginning to collapse and when God prepares to destroy it by fire. It will be at the end of the time line of history.

May we be grateful to our Lord for the abundance of Biblical information He has provided on this important matter.

Let us look together at the first of these seven paths.

The Last Trumpet and the Rapture
    In I Corinthians 15:51-53 we read:

Behold, I shew you a mystery; **We shall not all sleep, but we shall all be changed, In a moment, in the twinkling of an eye, at the last trump: for the trumpet shall sound, and the dead shall be raised incorruptible,** and we shall be changed. For this corruptible must put on incorruption, and this mortal must put on immortality.

In these verses God is discussing the fact that not everyone will die. (To fall asleep is Biblical language signifying death.) There will be those who will instantaneously receive their resurrected bodies without first falling asleep. This language is clearly concerned with the rapture, for verse 53 speaks about the believers receiving their immortal bodies.

Then God tells us when this event will occur. Note the language, which declares, **at the sound of the last trump**. This is a time clue. God is effectively saying that when the **last** trumpet sounds the rapture will occur.

Following the Biblical principle that the Bible interprets the Bible, we must now search the Bible to find language that relates to the sound of the last trumpet. If such references can be found, perhaps they will tell us when the last trumpet will sound.

In Revelation 11:15-18 we read:

And the seventh angel sounded; and there were great voices in heaven, saying, The kingdoms of this world are become the kingdoms of our Lord, and of his Christ; and he shall reign for ever and ever. And the four and twenty elders, which sat before God on their seats, fell upon their faces, and worshipped God, Saying, We give thee thanks, O Lord God Almighty, which art, and wast, and art to come; because thou hast taken to thee thy great power, and hast reigned. And the nations were angry, **and thy wrath is come, and the time of the dead, that they should be judged, and that thou shouldest give reward unto thy servants the prophets, and to the saints, and them that fear thy name, small and great; and shouldest destroy them which destroy the earth.**

In this passage God gives us an outline of the events that will accompany the sounding of the seventh or last trumpet. At that time the following becomes a reality:

   a. The time has come for the dead to be judged.
   b. The time for the rewarding of the saints has come.
   c. The time for destroying the destroyers has come.

In other words, the sounding of the seventh trumpet signals that Judgment Day has come. It signals that the time has come for the believers to receive their reward. It is the time that the forces of evil are to be cast into Hell. Therefore, the sounding of the last trumpet must be at the end of time, for it is at the end of time that Judgment Day dawns, and Satan is thrown into the lake of fire.

Returning now to I Corinthians 15:51-53, we will recall that this passage effectively declares that the rapture of believers is to occur at the sound of the last trumpet. Since we have seen from Revelation 11 that at the sound of the seventh trumpet Judgment Day occurs, we can know therefore that the rapture is an event that occurs simultaneously with Judgment Day.

Sodom's Destruction and the Rapture

From I Corinthians 15:51-53 we have seen that the rapture is to occur at the time Christ returns to judge the world. Let us now look at a second path that helps us to better understand the timing of the rapture. In Luke 17:28-37 we read:

Likewise also as it was in the days of Lot; they did eat, they drank, they bought, they sold, they planted, they builded; **But the same day that Lot went out of Sodom it rained fire and brimstone from heaven, and destroyed them all. Even thus shall it be in the day when the Son of man is revealed.** In that day, he which shall be upon the housetop, and his stuff in the house, let him not come down to take it away: and he that is in the field, let him likewise not return back. Remember Lot's wife. Whosoever shall seek to save his life shall lose it; and whosoever shall lose his life shall preserve it. **I tell you, in that night there shall be two men in one bed; the one shall be taken, and the other shall be left.** Two women shall be grinding together; the one shall be taken, and the other left. Two men shall be in the field; the one shall be taken, and the other left. And they answered and said unto him, Where, Lord? And he said unto them, Wheresoever the body is, thither will the eagles be gathered together.

In this passage God is using the destruction of Sodom as a figure or type of the judgment of the last day. We will see that the saving of Lot and his family is a figure of the rapture. God links the rescue of Lot and his family to the rapture in verse 34: "I tell you, in that night there shall be two men in one bed; the one shall be taken, and the other shall be left."

Just before the destruction of Sodom, we can see that God sent heavenly messengers to rescue the family of Lot (Genesis 19). On the heels of this rescue operation God rained down fire and brimstone upon Sodom and the other wicked cities, utterly destroying them.

God declares in Luke 17:30, "Even thus shall it be in the day when the Son of man is revealed." Thus Christ links the destruction of Sodom to Judgment Day.

> *The parallelism . . . between the destruction of Sodom and the end of the world is clearly evident.*

The parallelism that exists between the destruction of Sodom and the end of the world is clearly evident. Sodom, a wicked city ripe for judgment, is populated by two kinds of people. There are the wicked, who are to be destroyed, and there is the church, represented by Lot and his family. It is a tiny little remnant in this wicked city.

So today the world is mostly populated by those who are altogether rebellious against God. Amongst the vast populations of the world there is the church. It consists of only a tiny percentage of the world's population.

Then Judgment Day comes for Sodom. The cup of their iniquity is full. God is to utterly destroy them for their sins, but just ahead of that judgment God rescues Lot. So close in time is the rescue to the poured out judgment of God that Lot's wife is destroyed in the judgment. So it will also be at the end of time. When the nations have become ripe for judgment, God will send His angels to rescue the believers from amongst the unbelievers. Two will be in one bed; one is taken, the other is left. The one that is taken is caught up in the air to be with Christ, even as I Thessalonians 4:17 teaches. The one that is left will stand for judgment even as the wicked of Sodom were left for judgment.

Thus Christ is teaching that the rapture comes simultaneously with Judgment Day. There is complete agreement between the account of Jesus concerning the destruction of Sodom and the I Corinthians 15 account, which speaks of the rapture coming at the sound of the last trumpet.

The Noachian Flood and the Rapture

A third path through the Bible continues to give us vast assurance that the rapture will occur simultaneously with Judgment Day. This is found in the language Jesus utters as He compares the flood and its events to Judgment Day and its events. In Matthew 24:37-41:

> **But as the days of Noe were, so shall also the coming of the Son of man be. For as in the days that were before the flood they were eating and drinking, marrying and giving in marriage, until the day that Noe entered into the ark, And knew not until the flood came, and took them all away; so shall also the coming of the Son of man be.** Then shall two be in the field; the one shall be taken, and the other left. Two women shall be grinding at the mill; the one shall be taken, and the other left.

In this passage God sets up parallel language that relates the flood that destroyed the world of Noah's day to Jesus' return. This parallelism, which indicates that the destruction of the world in the Noachian Flood was a type or figure of Judgment Day, is also set forth in II Peter 3:3-7, where we read:

Knowing this first, that there shall come in the last days scoffers, walking after their own lusts, And saying, Where is the promise of his coming? for since the fathers fell asleep, all things continue as they were from the beginning of the creation. **For this they willingly are ignorant of, that by the word of God the heavens were of old, and the earth standing out of the water and in the water: Whereby the world that then was, being overflowed with water, perished.**

When we look at the flood account in Genesis 7, we see that seven days before the flood, God gave Noah notice that the flood would come in seven days. Therefore, Noah and his family were to go into the ark.

Genesis 7:1: And the LORD said unto Noah, Come thou and all thy house into the ark; for thee have I seen righteous before me in this generation.
Genesis 7:4: For yet seven days, and I will cause it to rain upon **the earth** forty days and forty nights; and every living substance **that I have** made will I destroy from off the face of the earth.

That the flood did indeed come seven days after notice was given, as we read in verse 4, can be learned from the language of Genesis 7:10, "And it came to pass after seven days, that the waters of the flood were upon the earth."
The Bible then records the precise date of the flood, together with the information that Noah actually entered the ark the selfsame day that the flood came. We read in Genesis 7:11-13:
In the six hundredth year of Noah's life, in the second month, the seventeenth day of the month, the same day were all the fountains of the great deep broken up, and the windows of heaven were opened. And the rain was upon the earth forty days and forty nights. In the selfsame day entered Noah, and Shem, and Ham, and Japheth, the sons of Noah, and Noah's wife, and the three wives of his sons with them, into the ark.

Thus Christ teaches that the peoples of Noah's day continued eating and drinking until the day that Noah entered the ark and the flood swept them away. Luke 17:27 reads:

They did eat, they drank, they married wives, they were given in marriage, until the day that Noe entered into the ark, and the flood came, and destroyed them all.

Certainly we can see the parallelisms that exist between the flood and Judgment Day. Noah and his family lived in a world cursed by sin. At Judgment Day the believers, a tiny remnant of people, will exist in a world cursed by sin. When the floods were to begin, Noah and his family entered into the ark, a haven of safety for them. At Judgment Day the believers are raptured while the unsaved are judged and removed into Hell: "Then shall two be in the field; the one shall be taken, and the other left" (Matthew 24:40). The one taken is like Noah. Even as Noah went into the safety of the ark, so the believer is caught up to the safety of Christ. The one left is left for judgment, even as the people outside the ark were left for judgment.

Once again we see clearly that the rapture occurs simultaneously with Judgment Day.

When Christ rose from the grave, He showed the resurrection to be a fact by many proofs (Acts 1:3). Likewise the Bible's teaching concerning the timetable of the rapture is set forth in many places in the Bible. We shall now look at a fourth path in the Bible by which this truth is taught.

The Resurrection of the Dead and the Rapture

In I Thessalonians 4:14-17 we find recorded one of the most frequently quoted passages concerning the rapture. We shall begin with this passage as we discuss a fourth path that shows the timing of the rapture. There we read:

For if we believe that Jesus died and rose again, even so them also which sleep in Jesus will God bring with him. For this we say unto you by the word of the Lord, that we which are alive and remain unto the coming of the Lord shall not prevent [precede] them which are asleep. For the Lord himself shall descend from heaven with a shout, with the voice of the archangel, and with the trump of God: and the dead in Christ shall rise first: Then we which are alive and remain shall be caught up together with them in the clouds, to meet the Lord in the air: and so shall we ever be with the Lord.

> *The rapture . . . occurs simultaneously*
> *with the resurrection of our bodies.*

The first truth that we will look at in this passage is the fact that the rapture will be an event that occurs simultaneously with the resurrection of our bodies. God indicates that at His coming He will bring with Him those who have fallen asleep. Elsewhere (II Corinthians 5:8) God teaches that to be absent from the body is to be present with the Lord. When Christians die, because they were given their resurrected souls at the time of their salvation, in their souls they can go to be with Christ. In this condition they live and reign with Him in Heaven.

At Christ's return all those who have died, that is, who have fallen asleep, and who have been living with Christ in Heaven, will come with Him, as I Thessalonians 4:14 teaches. Then the graves are to be opened and the bodies of those who have died will be resurrected. At the same time the believers who have not died will be given their resurrected bodies. Immediately following this, those resurrected from the graves, together with the believers who have not died but who have instantaneously been given their new bodies, will be caught up in the air to be with the Lord forever. Only the unsaved will remain to face the wrath of God, which will be poured out upon them because of their sins.

All Believers Will Go to be with the Lord

Now we want to look more closely at the fact of the resurrection of these bodies. The Bible teaches the precise time when these bodies will be resurrected, and since, as we have just seen, the rapture occurs simultaneously with the resurrection of the bodies of the believers, the determination of the time of the resurrection of the bodies of the believers will also give us the timetable of the rapture.

> John 6:39: And this is the Father's will which hath sent me, that of all which he hath given me I should lose nothing, but should raise it up again at **the last day**.
> John 6:40: And this is the will of him that sent me, that every one which seeth the Son, and believeth on him, may have everlasting life: and I will raise him up at **the last day**.

John 6:44: No man can come to me, except the Father which hath sent me draw him: and I will raise him up at **the last day**. John 6:54: Whoso eateth my flesh, and drinketh my blood, hath eternal life; and I will raise him up at **the last day**.

The phrase **the last day** is quite significant. It is found only eight times in the whole Bible. Since God chooses words very carefully, we know this phrase has been selected to signify important truth.

Let us look at this phrase for a moment. It is used four times in John 6, as we have seen. The other four references are as follows: John 11:24: Martha saith unto him, I know that he shall rise again in the resurrection at **the last day**. John 12:48: He that rejecteth me, and receiveth not my words, hath one that judgeth him: the word that I have spoken, the same shall judge him in **the last day**. John 7:37: In **the last day**, that great day of the feast, Jesus stood and cried, saying, If any man thirst, let him come unto me, and drink. Nehemiah 8:18: Also day by day, from the first day unto **the last day**, he read in the book of the law of God. And they kept the feast seven days; and on the eighth day was a solemn assembly, according unto the manner.

> *The resurrection of believers is the last day.*

Quickly we see that in John 11:24 God is showing us that Martha understood clearly the truth that is offered in the four verses of John 6. The resurrection of believers is the last day.

From John 12:48, given above, we discover that the last day is Judgment Day. It is then that God will have all the unsaved give account of their sins and remove them into Hell to pay for their sins. Thus we see that the resurrection of believers, which also is to occur the last day (John 6:40), takes place simultaneously with Judgment Day. Since we saw from I Thessalonians 4:14-17 that the resurrection of our bodies occurs simultaneously with the rapture, we can know from these verses that the rapture occurs simultaneously with Judgment Day.

Before we look at the remaining two references to **the last day**, let us continue our thinking a bit longer on John 12:48. If Judgment Day is the last day, then the resurrection of the unsaved must also be the last day, for Revelation 20:13 indicates that the sea "gave up" the dead, and death and Hades "gave up" the dead, and all were judged and cast into the lake of fire. If this is so, then the resurrection of unbelievers occurs on the last day, and there must be one general resurrection of both the saved and unsaved on the last day. Under no circumstances are we to understand that the believers are resurrected at one time and the wicked another.

This is precisely what the Bible teaches. In John 5:28-29 we read:

> Marvel not at this: for the hour is coming, in the which all **that are in the graves shall hear his voice, And shall come forth**; they that have done good, unto the resurrection of life; and they that have done evil, unto the resurrection of damnation.

Everyone will be resurrected at the moment of Christ's return. No one will be left in the grave. In I Thessalonians 4:17 we read that the believers will hear the shout of command. John 5:28-29 shows, however, that the unbelievers too will hear that shout, for our Lord declares, **all that are in the graves shall hear His voice**. This verse cannot possibly be teaching of two resurrections separated by one thousand years, as some would teach. It is speaking of a single time - the hour (singular) is coming.

Those who have done good, that is, those who have had their sins covered by Christ's righteousness, will be resurrected to life.

John 5:29 does add that there are two destinations for these who come forth from the tombs. Those who have done good, that is, those who have had their sins covered by Christ's righteousness, will be resurrected to life. Those who have done evil, that is, the unsaved, those who have not had their sins covered, will be resurrected to damnation in judgment.

We have compared the Scriptures that speak of **the last day** with I Thessalonians 4:14-17 and John 5:28-29, and we have discovered that the Bible clearly teaches that the rapture, the resurrection of believers, the resurrection of unbelievers, and Judgment Day are events that take place simultaneously on the Last Day, which is the end of time. Isn't it marvelous how all these verses fit together so perfectly?

We have looked at six of the eight verses in the Bible that use the phrase **last day**. The remaining two are:

John 7:37: In **the last day**, that great day of the feast, Jesus stood and cried, saying, If any man thirst, let him come unto me, and drink.

Nehemiah 8:18: Also day by day, from the first day unto **the last day**, he read in the book of the law of God. And they kept the feast seven days; and on the eighth day was a solemn assembly, according unto the manner.

We will look also at these to make certain that we are checking everything that relates to the term **last day**.

The Feast Days Relate to the Rapture

These two remaining references are both related to the Feast of Tabernacles. The fact is, both speak of the *last day of* the Feast of Tabernacles.

What does the last day of the Feast of Tabernacles have to do with the rapture or Judgment Day? We shall see that it is intimately involved with these subjects.

Let us first look at the nature of the Feast of Tabernacles. It was a feast to commemorate two events. First, it looked back upon the sojournings of Israel in the wilderness, and secondly it was the time of the completion of the harvest.

In Leviticus 23:42-43 we read:

Ye shall dwell in booths seven days; all that are Israelites born shall dwell in booths: That your generations may know that I made the children of Israel to dwell in booths, when I brought them out of the land of Egypt: I am the LORD your God.

These verses teach that it was a feast that looked back on the wilderness sojourn of Israel, before they entered the Promised Land, the land of rest. So, too, believers today are living in the wilderness of this world. When Christ comes, our rest in Him will be complete. We are strangers and pilgrims now, but when we receive our resurrected bodies we will be forever with Christ (I Thessalonians 4:17). Therefore we can see how this Feast identifies with Christ's return: It is then that we receive our resurrected bodies. It is then that our salvation is complete. It is then that our wilderness sojourn is ended.

The second reason for commemorating the Feast of Tabernacles was the celebration of the end of the harvest.

In Exodus 23:16 we read:

. . . and the feast of ingathering, which is in the end of the year, when thou hast gathered in thy labours out of the field.

This is a surprising verse, for it speaks of the Feast of Ingathering, which is the same as the Feast of Tabernacles, as the end of the year. The Feast of Tabernacles was celebrated during the seventh month (Leviticus 23:39), and the seventh month is many months from the end of the year. Yet God speaks of it as the *end* or *going out* of the year.

When we see how intimately this feast is related to the end of time, we can see why God speaks of it as the end of the year. Jesus speaks in Matthew 13 of His return at the harvest time (Matthew 13:30 and 39):

Matthew 13:30: Let both grow together until the harvest: and in the time of harvest I will say to the reapers, Gather ye together first the tares, and bind them in bundles to burn them: but gather the wheat into my barn. . . Matthew 13:39: . . . the harvest is the end of the world; and the reapers are the angels.

Since the Feast of Tabernacles commemorates the harvest, thus relating it to the end of the year, and since Christ speaks of the end of the world as a harvest time, we can see that a beautiful relationship exists between the Feast of Tabernacles and the end of the world. No wonder then that the term **last day** is found in connection with the resurrection of believers, Judgment Day, and the Feast of Tabernacles. A chart shows these relationships:

Feast of Tabernacles	*End of World*
End of year	End of time
Harvest time for crops	Harvest time for mankind
End of wilderness sojourn for Israel	End of wilderness sojourn for believers
Last day (Exodus 23:16)	Last day (John 6:39-40, 12:48)

No wonder then that in Nehemiah 8:18 and in John 7:37 God uses the term *last day* in connection with the Feast of Tabernacles.

Before we leave the Feast of Tabernacles, one other important fact should be noted, which links the Feast of Tabernacles to the last day or the end of time. In the Old Testament, three times during the year all the men were required to appear before the Lord, as recorded in Exodus 23:14-17:

> Three times thou shalt keep a feast unto me in the year. Thou shalt keep the feast of unleavened bread: (thou shalt eat unleavened bread seven days, as I commanded thee, in the time appointed of the month Abib; for in it thou camest out from Egypt: and none shall appear before me empty:) And the feast of harvest, the firstfruits of thy labours, which thou hast sown in the field: and the feast of ingathering, which is in the end of the year, when thou hast gathered in thy labours out of the field. Three times in the year all thy males shall appear before the Lord GOD.

The first feast was the Feast of Unleavened Bread, that began and was identified with the Passover. This feast began in the evening of the fourteenth day of the first month (Leviticus 23:5), and continued for seven days after the fifteenth day (Leviticus 23:6, Deuteronomy 16:1-3). It was the day that anticipated the shedding of Christ's blood as the Passover Lamb that would take away the sins of the world.

The second was the Feast of Harvest or the Firstfruits or Feast of Weeks. This feast was observed seven full weeks from the morrow after the Sabbath, that is, the Sabbath that occurred during the Passover week (Leviticus 23:15-16, Deuteronomy 16:9). Because this feast day was fifty days after that Sabbath, it was also called Pentecost. It was a day that anticipated the spiritual harvest that would begin as a result of Christ going to the cross.

The third feast during which the males had to appear before the Lord was the Feast of Tabernacles, which was preceded by the Day of Atonement (the tenth day of the seventh month). The Feast of Tabernacles continued from the fifteenth day for eight days of the seventh month (Leviticus 23:27, 34, 39). It was a feast day, as we have seen, that anticipated the completion of the spiritual harvest that would result because God provided salvation through the Lord Jesus Christ.

The awe-inspiring fact that now faces us is that, while these feast days anticipated and pointed to the historical accomplishment of the atonement, on the very same days that the nation of Israel was celebrating these feasts, God brought to pass the spiritual reality to which these days pointed. On the Passover in 33 A.D., while the Jews were keeping the Passover, Jesus hung on the cross as the Passover Lamb.

It was on the Jewish Feast of Pentecost, the Old Testament Feast of Firstfruits, that the Holy Spirit was poured out, and the harvesting of souls began. It was at that time that the firstfruits of the harvest were seen - 3,000 from eighteen nations were saved (Acts 2).

So we see that two of the three most important feasts, those specifically emphasized as times when all Jewish males were to go to Jerusalem, were the occasions when God's program of redemption was being carried out. The Jewish Passover was celebrated the very same day that Christ, the Passover Lamb, was slain. The Jewish Feast of the Firstfruits, Pentecost, was observed the very same day that God poured out His Holy Spirit and the firstfruits of the spiritual harvest were seen.

> *It will be in the fall of the year, at the very same time of year when the Feast of Tabernacles would have been observed by Old Testament Israel, that Christ may come again.*

That leaves one remaining feast day, the Feast of Tabernacles or the Feast of Ingathering. Surely the Bible is suggesting that Christ will return in literal fulfillment of this feast, even as there was literal identification with the two other important feasts. That is, we can believe that it will be in the fall of the year, at the very same time of year when the Feast of Tabernacles would have been observed by Old Testament Israel, that Christ may come again.

No wonder then that God uses the term **last day** in connection with the Feast of Tabernacles. The Feast of Tabernacles is identified with Christ's return on the last day, just as the resurrection of our bodies and Judgment Day are identified with Christ's return on the last day.

We see, therefore, that in all eight places where the term **last day** is found in the Bible, it points to the end of time. It points to the end of this earth's existence, when Christ will return in Judgment.

The Tribulation and the Rapture

We have seen thus far from four separate and distinct Biblical paths that the rapture must be the last day of this world's existence. It must be an event that coincides with the resurrection of all humanity and with Judgment Day, but the Bible has more to say about this. Let us now look at this question from another viewpoint.

In Matthew 24 Christ gives us an outline of the signs or events that must take place just before the end of the world. He declares in Matthew 24:21-31:

> **For then shall be great tribulation, such as was not since the beginning of the world to this time, no, nor ever shall be.** And except those days should be shortened, there should no flesh be saved: but for the elect's sake those days shall be shortened. Then if any man shall say unto you, Lo, here is Christ, or there; believe it not. For there shall arise false Christs, and false prophets, and shall shew great signs and wonders; insomuch that, if it were possible, they shall deceive the very elect. Behold, I have told you before. Wherefore if they shall say unto you, Behold, he is in the desert; go not forth: behold, he is in the secret chambers; believe it not. For as the lightning cometh out of the east, and shineth even unto the west; so shall also the coming of the Son of man be. For wheresoever the carcase is, there will the eagles be gathered together. **Immediately after the tribulation of those days shall the sun be darkened, and the moon shall not give her light, and the stars shall fall from heaven, and the powers of the heavens shall be shaken:** And then shall appear the sign of the Son of man in heaven: and then shall all the tribes of the earth mourn, and they shall see the Son of man coming in the clouds of heaven with power and great glory. **And he shall send his angels with a great sound of a trumpet, and they shall gather together his elect from the four winds, from one end of heaven to the other.**

The rapture not only immediately follows the final tribulation, which believers must endure, but it occurs simultaneously with the end of the world.

As we examine these verses, we shall see that the rapture not only immediately follows the final tribulation, which believers must endure, but that it occurs simultaneously with the end of the world. Thus it must occur simultaneously with Judgment Day.

In verses 21 and 22 God speaks of an increasingly great tribulation that must come upon the earth. For the sake of the elect this tribulation will be shortened. We will not discuss at this time the implication of this tribulation, but we do know it must come. No other passage in the Bible speaks more plainly of it.

We should ascertain who the elect are, who are spoken of in verse 22. God uses the word *elect*, which is the Greek word *eklektos*, some twenty-three times in the New Testament.

Some people teach that the *elect* refers only to believing Jews on the ground that Matthew 24 relates only to the nation of Israel, and not to the Gentiles. According to this reasoning, Matthew 24 is only for the Jews inasmuch as Jesus was speaking to the disciples, who were Jews. By the same token, we could logically argue then that John 3 has no reference to Gentiles, because Christ was speaking to Nicodemus, who was a Jew. On that basis, only Jews are to be born again, to enter the Kingdom of Heaven.

Likewise the Book of Romans has no import for us today because it was addressed to the church at Rome; and the books Isaiah and Jeremiah are of no interest to Gentiles because these prophets were sent primarily to Israel.

On this basis, only certain books of the Bible are to be considered pertinent and authoritative for New Testament believers.

We immediately sense the error of this line of Biblical interpretation. The Bible says that **all** Scripture is profitable for doctrine, for reproof, for teaching, etc. (II Timothy 3:16). **All** the Bible is to be studied and obeyed. Matthew 24 is to be read and studied by Gentiles as well as Jews, and just as carefully as John 3 or any other part of the Bible. The fact is, when we read Matthew 24 carefully, we see that God is discussing the whole world. In verse 13 we read of the **end of the world**. In verse 14 God speaks of the Gospel going to every nation. In verses 28-31 He speaks of His return in power and great glory. He will not return to Jews only. He will return to the whole world. Therefore the warnings of Matthew 24 are to the whole world. The statement of Matthew 24 is as important to Gentiles as I Thessalonians 4:14 or any other passage of the Bible.

Returning now to the word *elect* found in Matthew 24:22, we find that in the King James Bible it is translated as *chosen* or as *elect*. Examining the twenty-three places where the Greek word *eklektos* is used, we see very quickly that the Bible is speaking of those who are elected of God to be believers. This can be seen in such passages as:

Matthew 20:16: So the last shall be first, and the first last: for many be called, but few **chosen**.
Revelation 17:14: These shall make war with the Lamb, and the Lamb shall overcome them: for he is Lord of lords, and King of kings: and they that are with him are called, and **chosen**, and faithful.

Romans 8:33: Who shall lay any thing to the charge of God's **elect**? It is God that justifieth.
Colossians 3:12: Put on therefore, as **the elect of God**, holy and beloved, bowels of mercies, kindness, humbleness of mind, meekness, longsuffering.
Titus 1:1: Paul, a servant of God, and an apostle of Jesus Christ, according to the faith of **God's elect**, and the acknowledging of the truth which is after godliness.

> *Since the believers are the elect, and Matthew 24:22 teaches that the tribulation will be shortened for the sake of the elect, we see that the believers will be present throughout this tribulation.*

Since the believers are the elect, and since Matthew 24:22 teaches that the tribulation will be shortened for the sake of the elect, we see that the believers will be present throughout the tribulation. Thus, on the basis of this verse alone, we would have trouble with a doctrine that teaches that the rapture will occur before this tribulation.

Returning to Matthew 24 we see that God gives us a very careful chronology covering the relationship of the tribulation to the return of Christ. In Matthew 24:29-30 God declares:

Immediately after the tribulation of those days shall the sun be darkened, and the moon shall not give her light, and the stars shall fall from heaven, and the powers of the heavens shall be shaken: And then shall appear the sign of the Son of man in heaven: and then shall all the tribes of the earth mourn, and they shall see the Son of man coming in the clouds of heaven with power and great glory.

This tells us very emphatically that the last event that occurs before the return of Christ is the tribulation spoken of in Matthew 24:21-22. The language **immediately after** does not allow for any passage of time between the tribulation and the events spoken of in verses 29-31.

When we look carefully at the events that immediately follow the tribulation, we see that the sun is darkened and the moon does not give its light. This indicates that it is the end of time. The sun and the moon regulate the passage of time. Now time is no more, for Christ has returned. It is the last day of this world's existence. Then we read that the stars begin to fall from Heaven. This is language of Judgment Day and the destruction of this universe. God gives us further amplification of this event in Revelation 6:12-17, where He declares:

And I beheld when he had opened the sixth seal, and, lo, there was a great earthquake; and the sun became black as sackcloth of hair, and the moon became as blood; And the stars of heaven fell unto the earth, even as a fig tree casteth her untimely figs, when she is shaken of a mighty wind. And the heaven departed as a scroll when it is rolled together; and every mountain and island were moved out of their places. And the kings of the earth, and the great men, and the rich men, and the chief captains, and the mighty men, and every bondman, and every free man, hid themselves in the dens and in the rocks of the mountains; And said to the mountains and rocks, Fall on us, and hide us from the face of him that sitteth on the throne, and from the wrath of the Lamb: For the great day of his wrath is come; and who shall be able to stand?

This can be language only of Judgment Day. We are not surprised to read of the collapse of the universe. In II Peter 3:10-13 we read:

> But the day of the Lord will come as a thief in the night; in the which the heavens shall pass away with a great noise, and the elements shall melt with fervent heat, the earth also and the works that are therein shall be burned up. Seeing then that all these things shall be dissolved, what manner of persons ought ye to be in all holy conversation and godliness, Looking for and hasting unto the coming of the day of God, wherein the heavens being on fire shall be dissolved, and the elements shall melt with fervent heat? Nevertheless we, according to his promise, look for new heavens and a new earth, wherein dwelleth righteousness.

We see that one fact stands out. This universe will be destroyed when Christ comes again. It must be destroyed because it is under the curse of sin. Viruses, earthquakes, tornadoes, and famines are experienced because mankind has rebelled against God. Therefore, not only was man cursed, but the universe over which man ruled was also cursed. We read in Romans 8:20-22:

> For the creature was made subject to vanity, not willingly, but by reason of him who hath subjected the same in hope, Because the creature itself also shall be delivered from the bondage of corruption into the glorious liberty of the children of God. For we know that the whole creation groaneth and travaileth in pain together until now.

The creation looks with eager longing at the revealing of the sons of glory (the believers), because at that time the universe will be made free from the curse. Immediately after the unsaved have been judged and removed into Hell, the destruction of this earth, its redemption and recreation as new heavens and a new earth must take place.

> *A system of teaching that suggests that following the tribulation Christ will return to this sin-cursed earth to set up an earthly throne, offers an impossible situation.*

Therefore we are not surprised to read that the stars will fall from Heaven, and that Heaven will be rolled up when Christ returns. From Matthew 24:29 we know that this immediately follows the tribulation. A system of teaching that suggests that following the tribulation Christ will return to this sin-cursed earth to set up an earthly throne, offers an impossible situation.

We might note the conduct of the unsaved immediately after the tribulation when the universe is collapsing and Christ comes in power and great glory. In Matthew 24:30 we read that all the tribes of earth mourn. In Revelation 6:15-17 we read that all the peoples are in abject terror, calling to the mountains to hide them and the hills to crush them. No wonder they are in great terror. It is the great day of the wrath of the Lamb. It is Judgment Day, at which time they must give an account of their sins and receive the righteous condemnation of God as payment for their sins.

Now let us look more carefully at Matthew 24:31, for there God reveals the first thing that Christ will do when He comes in great power and glory. Note how parallel in language it is to I Thessalonians 4:16-17, which speaks of the rapture.

First we read in the Matthew account that Christ will send His angels with a great sound of a trumpet. I Thessalonians 4:16 speaks of "the voice of the archangel, and with the trump of God." Christ then speaks in Matthew 24 of gathering the elect from the four winds under Heaven. I Thessalonians 4:17 speaks of those who are alive being caught up to be with Christ. As we saw earlier, the elect are the believers who are being raptured from all over the earth. The term *under heaven* could be translated simply *under the sky*. In any case these are the believers living on the earth, whose commonwealth is in Heaven (Philippians 3:20).

So we see that there is parallel language in Matthew 24:31 and I Thessalonians 4:16-17 concerning angel activity, the sound of the trumpet at Christ's return, and the rapture of believers.

Thus in our study of Matthew 24 we can see very clearly that God's timetable for the rapture of believers is at the end of time. It is immediately after the great tribulation and coincides with Judgment Day. How marvelous God is in giving so many proofs concerning the timing of the rapture.

Thus far we have found five very plain and distinctive paths that reveal that the rapture will be at the end of time. Let us now look at a sixth path found in the Bible.

The Man of Sin and the Rapture

In II Thessalonians 2 we discover more information that points to the rapture taking place at the end of time. In this passage God is teaching us that two events must happen before He will be ready to come for His believers. The first is that the rebellion is to take place, and the second is that the man of sin is to be revealed. He will be revealed at the coming of the Lord Jesus Christ, at which time Christ will slay him with the breath of His mouth. That is, the wicked will be cast into Hell. II Thessalonians 2:1-9:

> Now we beseech you, brethren, by the coming of our Lord Jesus Christ, and by our gathering together unto him, That ye be not soon shaken in mind, or be troubled, neither by spirit, nor by word, nor by letter as from us, as that the day of Christ is at hand. Let no man deceive you by any means: for that day shall not come, except there come a falling away first, and that man of sin be revealed, the son of perdition; Who opposeth and exalteth himself above all that is called God, or that is worshipped; so that he as God sitteth in the temple of God, shewing himself that he is God. Remember ye not, that, when I was yet with you, I told you these things? And now ye know what withholdeth that he might be revealed in his time. For the mystery of iniquity doth already work: only he who now letteth will let, until he be taken out of the way. And then shall that Wicked be revealed, whom the Lord shall consume with the spirit of his mouth, and shall destroy with the brightness of his coming: Even him, whose coming is after the working of Satan with all power and signs and lying wonders.

> *Who is the man of sin? . . . he is*
> *Satan as he works through his*
> *emissaries called false prophets or*
> *false christs.*

Who is the **man of sin**? If we see that he is Satan as he works through his emissaries called false prophets or false christs, we find total Biblical validation. We find in these verses that he is worshipped as God. Revelation 13:4 speaks of the dragon, who is Satan, being worshipped:

> And they worshipped the dragon which gave power unto the beast: and they worshipped the beast, saying, Who is like unto the beast? who is able to make war with him?

Thus the language of II Thessalonians 2, which speaks of the man of sin being worshipped, points us to Satan as being the man of sin. How can Satan be called a man? Isn't he indeed a fallen angel? We shall see that he is called a man because he was typified by the king of Babylon who, of course, was a man (Isaiah 14:4).

In Isaiah 14 we read of the fall of Lucifer. From the context we know that this Lucifer is Satan himself, but as Isaiah 14 discusses the fall of Lucifer, God speaks of Lucifer as a man. We read in Isaiah 14:16:

> They that see thee shall narrowly look upon thee, and consider thee, saying, Is this the man that made the earth to tremble, that did shake kingdoms; . . .

As Revelation 18 teaches, Babylon is often used in the Bible as a figure of the kingdom of Satan. Thus we see immediately the parallelism that exists. On the one hand we have Babylon, which is ruled over by the king of Babylon. On the other we have Satan's dominion, ruled over by Satan.

This man of sin, who is Satan, takes his seat in the temple. To what does taking one's seat refer? Jesus is seated at the right hand of God and rules over everything (Ephesians 1:20-22). Thus to take a seat is Biblical language meaning to rule or have authority. The man of sin, Satan, takes his seat or rules in the temple.

To what does the temple refer? Is there to be a literal reconstruction of the temple?

The Temple and the Rapture

To what does the **temple** refer? Is there to be a literal reconstruction of the temple? Nowhere in the Bible do we read of a future reconstruction of the temple. The fact is, since the veil of the temple was rent when Jesus hung on the cross, the temple in Jerusalem ceased to have significance as a holy place. Rather, the Bible speaks of the body of believers as being the temple. We read in Ephesians 2:19-21:

> Now therefore ye are no more strangers and foreigners, but fellowcitizens with the saints, and of the household of God; And are built upon the foundation of the apostles and prophets, Jesus Christ himself being the chief corner stone; In whom all the building fitly framed together groweth unto an **holy temple** in the Lord.

In I Peter 2:5 we read:
> Ye also, as lively stones, are built up a **spiritual house**, an holy priesthood, to offer up spiritual sacrifices, acceptable to God by Jesus Christ.

In I Corinthians 3:16 God emphasizes that the body of believers is the temple, as He declares: "Know ye not that ye are the **temple** of God, and that the Spirit of God dwelleth in you?"

> *The temple is the church, the corporate body of believers. It is here that Satan will operate as the man of sin.*

Therefore we see very clearly that the temple is the church, the corporate body of believers. It is here that Satan will operate as the man of sin. Thus we know that before Christ comes again, the man of sin (Satan), must take his seat (rule) in the temple (the church or body of believers) where he will be worshipped as God. Since he is a spirit, he cannot be seen to literally rule amongst the body of believers. He can rule, however, through false prophets and pseudo-christs who bring a gospel other than the true Gospel. The Bible speaks of this kind of activity in II Corinthians 11:13-14:

For such are false apostles, deceitful workers, transforming themselves into the apostles of Christ. And no marvel; for Satan himself is transformed into an angel of light.

Similarly we read in Matthew 24:24:
For there shall arise false Christs, and false prophets, and shall shew great signs and wonders; insomuch that, if it were possible, they shall deceive the very elect.

These verses emphasize the utter deceitfulness of Satan in this effort. The gospel he brings will be so much like the true Gospel that even the elect would be deceived if that were possible.

Satan will come not only with a gospel so closely patterned after the true Gospel that even the elect would be deceived if that were possible, but he will also give life and vitality to it through signs and wonders.

Note in the Matthew 24 verse that these false prophets will come with signs and wonders. Satan will come not only with a gospel so closely patterned after the true Gospel that even the elect would be deceived if that were possible, but he will also give life and vitality to it through signs and wonders. Even as Jesus came 2,000 years ago with signs and wonders when He brought us the true Gospel, so Satan will attest to the seemingly God-like, Jesus-related character of his gospel by coming with signs and wonders.

The passage we are presently studying, II Thessalonians 2:1-9, also speaks of signs and wonders. The false prophets who represent him will come with signs and wonders even as verse 9 teaches: "Even him, whose coming is after the working of Satan with all power and signs and lying wonders."

We must realize, of course, that these false prophets have been so deceived that they are convinced that they are servants of Christ. Satan is the great deceiver, the father of lies (John 8:44). Moreover, II Thessalonians 2:10-11 teaches that God Himself blinds these who come because they refuse to believe the truth.

Thus we see that God is declaring in II Thessalonians 2 that before Christ comes there must be evidence of the activity of Satan as those who come with signs and wonders, and who in fact are his servants, rule or have authority among the body of believers, where the true Gospel ought to be proclaimed. These false prophets will be convinced that they are true prophets of Christ. Because they are coming with a gospel other than the true Gospel, they will in actuality be causing people to worship Satan. This is the chief nature of the rebellion that must come before Christ returns. The church, consisting of congregations and denominations all over the world, will be infiltrated and finally overrun by those who bring other gospels. The chief characteristic of these false gospels, which serves to help us to immediately recognize this threat, is the focus on signs and wonders.

Restraint of Sin and the Rapture

Returning to II Thessalonians 2, we read in verse 7:

> For the mystery of iniquity doth already work: only he who now letteth will let, until he be taken out of the way.

The word *letteth* is an old English word for restrain. This passage is thus teaching that the one who restrains sin will be taken out of the way.

There are those who teach that the one who restrains is the Holy Spirit. Since the Holy Spirit indwells the believers, they therefore suggest that this verse must be teaching something about the rapture of the church.

They are correct, of course, in teaching that the one who restrains sin is God Himself. We need only recall the event that occurred in Abraham's life. He had left Canaan to dwell in the land of Gerar to escape a famine. While there, for fear of his life he told the king of Gerar that Sarah, his wife, was actually his sister. Consequently the king of Gerar took Sarah into his palace. There he was warned of God not to touch Sarah because she was Abraham's wife. The king of Gerar responded by indicating that he had not touched her. Then God declared, in Genesis 20:6:

> Yea, I know that thou didst this in the integrity of thy heart; for I also withheld thee from sinning against me: therefore suffered I thee not to touch her.

This incident serves to illustrate that God restrains sin. We see God's restraint of sin also through what the Bible declares concerning the nature of mankind. It states that the heart of man is desperately wicked (Jeremiah 17:9). It indicates that out of the heart of man comes murder, adultery, etc. (Matthew 15:19). Only because man experiences this restraint is he able to live a reasonable life and manifest some virtues, such as love between parents and children, kindness and loyalty between friends, and compassion on the underprivileged.

> *The Holy Spirit does His work of restraining sin in the world with or without the presence of believers.*

We must note, however, that this restraint does not take place because of the presence of believers. While God the Holy Spirit does indeed indwell believers, the Holy Spirit is not limited to them. He does His work of restraining sin in the world with or without the presence of believers.

Thus when God speaks in II Thessalonians 2 of taking Him who restrains out of the way, He is not suggesting that the believers will be raptured, for they are not restraining power. Rather He is indicating that He will remove His hand of restraint to permit wickedness to multiply. This is indicated by the context, for in these verses God is speaking of rebellion. Matthew 24 speaks of wickedness being multiplied. Revelation 20 speaks of Satan being loosed. All these passages teach one and the same thing. There will come the time when God will allow the world to become desperately sinful. He will accomplish this by removing His restraint on unsaved man and on Satan and his angels. They will be more wicked than ever.

Returning to II Thessalonians 2:1-11, we see that before Christ returns to receive His own, the man of sin described above must first be revealed. God then declares in this passage that when the man of sin is revealed, Jesus will destroy him by the brightness of His coming. That is, Satan and all the wicked who follow him (the unsaved) will be judged and cast into Hell when Christ comes. It is in Hell that the wicked are punished by eternal destruction.

Notice that II Thessalonians 2:1-3 speaks of the gathering of the believers to meet the Lord Jesus. God is saying that this gathering together of believers to meet Christ will not take place until the man of sin is revealed. Since verse 8 states that when the man of sin is revealed these wicked will be destroyed (that is, judged and cast into Hell) by His coming, we immediately can see the simultaneous timing of the assembling together of the believers to meet Jesus (the rapture) and the destroying of Satan and the wicked (Judgment Day).

Again we find total agreement with all the other passages we have looked at that teach that the rapture comes at the same time as Judgment Day and the end of the world.

Let us now look at one more path that emphasizes the same truth concerning the rapture and its occurrence at the end of the world.

A Thief in the Night and the Rapture
When we seek an understanding of the timing of the rapture, we find more than sufficient information in the Bible to know that it is to occur at the end of time, when Christ returns to judge the nations. Six different paths in the Bible have been examined, and each one gives the same teaching. But before we leave this question, we should look at one more path. It too is intimately concerned with Christ's coming. It too will show us that the believers will be here when Christ returns in judgment.

Repeatedly the Bible speaks of Christ coming as a thief or as a thief in the night. Jesus says in Matthew 24:43 in the context of His discussion concerning His return:

But know this, that if the goodman of the house had known in what watch the thief would come, he would have watched, and would not have suffered his house to be broken up.

God declares in II Peter 3:10, as He discusses the destruction of the universe at the end of time:

But the day of the Lord will come as a thief in the night; in the which the heavens shall pass away with a great noise, and the elements shall melt with fervent heat, the earth also and the works that are therein shall be burned up.

In Revelation 3:3 we read the warning:

Remember therefore how thou hast received and heard, and hold fast, and repent. If therefore thou shalt not watch, I will come on thee as a thief, and thou shalt not know what hour I will come upon thee.

And in Revelation 16:15, as God is speaking of the end of the world, we find:

Behold, I come as a thief. Blessed is he that watcheth, and keepeth his garments, lest he walk naked, and they see his shame.

On the basis of these verses various doctrines have come forth, amongst which are those which suggest that Christ is to come silently. Suddenly and quietly the Christians are to be removed from the earth. This idea certainly appears to be valid in the light of the language of Christ coming as a thief in the night.

Is this really so? I Thessalonians 4:16, which speaks of the rapture of the believers, does not suggest that He will come silently as a thief. There God speaks of the shout of command, of the trumpet of God. That is anything but a silent coming.

Wonderfully, however, the Bible is its own commentary. If we follow the Biblical rule of letting the Bible explain or interpret the Bible, an understanding of the phrase **thief in the night** can be found. We shall discover that the Biblical references that use this phrase are not at all suggesting a silent coming of Christ. Moreover, we shall discover additional support of the clear teaching of the Bible that the occurrence of the rapture must be simultaneous with the timing of Judgment Day.

In I Thessalonians 5:1-9 we read:

But of the times and the seasons, brethren, ye have no need that I write unto you. For yourselves know perfectly that the day of the Lord so cometh as a thief in the night. For when they shall say, Peace and safety; then sudden destruction cometh upon them, as travail upon a woman with child; and they shall not escape. But ye, brethren, are not in darkness, that that day should overtake you as a thief. Ye are all the children of light, and the children of the day: we are not of the night, nor of darkness. Therefore let us not sleep, as do others; but let us watch and be sober. For they that sleep sleep in the night; and they that be drunken are drunken in the night. But let us, who are of the day, be sober, putting on the breastplate of faith and love; and for an helmet, the hope of salvation. For God hath not appointed us to wrath, but to obtain salvation by our Lord Jesus Christ.

> *The day of the Lord is the day when our Lord*
> *Jesus Christ will come on the clouds with*
> *power and great glory.*

In this passage we find a clear reference to the day of the Lord coming as a thief in the night. The day of the Lord is the day when our Lord Jesus Christ will come on the clouds with power and great glory. It is the day when He comes as King of kings and Lord of lords.

In these verses God teaches that day will come as a thief in the night. Is He then teaching that He will come when no one expects Him? Certainly this is true for the unsaved. Verse 3 records:

> For when they shall say, Peace and safety; then sudden destruction cometh upon them, as travail upon a woman with child; and they shall not escape.

> *The unsaved are not looking for Christ to come*
> *in judgment. They may not be looking for His*
> *return at all.*

The unsaved are not looking for Christ to come in judgment. They may not even be looking for His return at all. They may believe, in their evolution theory-blinded minds, that mankind is finding answers to problems of living in this world. These answers may assure them that by exercising careful diligence, mankind can continue a million years or more on this earth. Certainly they are convinced that insofar as a Judgment Day is concerned, if it exists at all, it is probably millions of years away. In their own minds they have concluded that God need not be reckoned with and they are safe and secure to follow their own lustful pleasures.

If among such people are those who relate to the Bible somewhat but are nevertheless unsaved, they also will be quite sure that Judgment Day is of no real concern. After all, they think, God is a loving God; He does not wish that any should perish. Somehow God has a marvelous plan for this earth and its inhabitants that will ensure maximum love for all. In their blindness that stems from their false gospels, which seem so successful and so God-ordained, they will be certain that there is still hope for a utopia on this present earth. Again, as in the case of those who wish to deny God altogether, they will feel that all is secure.

So for the unsaved Christ will come unexpectedly. As a matter of fact, His coming will be a horrible surprise, for those who are not saved will discover that they are to stand for judgment. They will discover that, while perhaps they thought all was well between them and the Lord, they actually had been following a salvation designed to their own liking rather than the salvation designed by the Bible. At Christ's coming it will be a moment of truth. They will realize that they had never served Him as Lord. They had been obeying the Bible only when it was convenient. They had never trusted Christ as the only one who could save them. Rather, they had been seeking a salvation based on the grace of God plus their own meritorious efforts. They had thought they were at peace with God and secure in Christ, but it was a false peace, a false security. At His coming the terrible truth will come to them that they never had been born from above.

> *What will happen to those for whom His coming is as a thief in the night:* **Sudden destruction will come upon them, and there will be no escape.**

For all these, Christ's coming will be as a thief in the night. Notice what will happen to those for whom His coming is as a thief in the night: **Sudden destruction will come upon them, and there will be no escape.**

This is the language of Judgment Day. Remember what happened to the people of Noah's day. Suddenly they were deluged with water and destroyed. Remember Sodom. It, too, experienced sudden destruction. Remember the language Jesus uses as He speaks of Judgment Day in Matthew 7:13:

> **Enter ye in** at the strait gate: for wide is the gate, and broad is the way, that leadeth to destruction, and many there be which go in thereat.

We might recall the warning of Jesus in Matthew 24:37-39.
But as the days of Noe were, so shall also the coming of the Son
of man be. For as in the days that were before the flood they
were eating and drinking, marrying and giving in marriage, until
the day that Noe entered into the ark, And knew not until the
flood came, and took them all away; so shall also the coming
of the Son of man be.

And in II Thessalonians 1:9 God declares:
Who shall be punished with everlasting destruction from the
presence of the Lord, and from the glory of his power.

What an awful moment! What a terrible place to be! No wonder
we read in Revelation 6:16 of men calling upon the rocks to crush them
and the hills to cover them. No experience of trauma that mankind has
ever experienced can approach the sheer terror of Judgment Day.

> *The Bible indicates that there are others for*
> *whom our Lord's coming is not as a thief in*
> *the night: These are the true believers.*

The Bible goes on to disclose other news that relates to this
momentous occasion. It indicates there are others present for whom
our Lord's coming is not as a thief in the night. These are the true
believers. These are the ones who are ready for His coming because
their sins have been washed away in Christ's blood. These are the ones
who are not under the dominion of darkness. They are children of the
day (a synonym for Christ Himself). They are children of the light.
(Jesus is light.) So they are the ones who belong to the Lord.
   I Thessalonians 5:4-5 tells us:
   But ye, brethren, are not in darkness, that that day should
   overtake you as a thief. Ye are the children of light, and the
   children of the day: we are not of the night, nor of darkness.
   We read in these verses that the day of the Lord will not
overtake believers as a thief. They have anticipated His coming and are
ready for it.
   Thus we see that when Christ returns in judgment, the believers
will still be here. Therefore these believers could not have been
raptured earlier. Since Judgment Day is at the end of time, we know

that is when believers will be raptured. In no sense are they to experience judgment, even as I Thessalonians 5:9 declares, "For God hath not appointed us to wrath, but to obtain salvation by our Lord Jesus Christ."

The wrath spoken of in this verse is not the tribulation period, as some would suppose. With the sure knowledge that the rapture will occur simultaneously with Judgment Day, we know that believers will go through the final tribulation period, but that period is not the wrath of God that must be visited upon unbelievers as payment for their sins. The wrath of God is the punishment the unsaved are to experience eternally as a result of their sins. The true believers in no way are to experience this because Christ has covered all their sins by His blood.

Revelation 6:15-17 speaks eloquently of the wrath of God:

> And the kings of the earth, and the great men, and the rich men, and the chief captains, and the mighty men, and every bondman, and every free man, hid themselves in the dens and in the rocks of the mountains; And said to the mountains and rocks, Fall on us, and hide us from the face of him that sitteth on the throne, and from the **wrath** of the Lamb: For the great day of his **wrath** is come; and who shall be able to stand?

This is the wrath from which the saved are free. Praise God for such a wonderful salvation!

SUMMARY

We have seen from I Thessalonians 4:14-17 that the rapture occurs simultaneously with the resurrection of believers, and from John 6, that the resurrection of believers occurs on the last day. From John 12, and from the *last day* references to the Feast of Tabernacles, we have seen that the *last day* is Judgment Day. Moreover, these truths agree precisely with the statement of John 5:28-29, which speaks of one general resurrection at Christ's return.

We have thus seen that I Thessalonians 4, when looked at in the light of John 6 and the other passages that tell us when the resurrection of believers will occur, ties together the rapture, Judgment Day, and the end of time as events that occur simultaneously.

The verses of I Thessalonians 5 can be understood very readily when we recognize that there is a simultaneous occurrence of the rapture and Judgment Day. While Christ comes as a thief in the night to bring judgment upon the unbelievers, the believers are ready for His coming. For believers He does not come as a thief in the night. For them it is the marvelous moment when their salvation is completed; they are raptured to be forever with Christ.

We have looked patiently at seven different paths in the Scriptures concerning the timing of the rapture. Each of them shows us that the rapture of believers occurs simultaneously with Judgment Day. God has indeed given us ample evidence of this.

Because this truth is very clearly documented in the Bible, all other teachings concerning the details of our Savior's return should be studied in the light of this Biblical truth. The fact is, we should find, as we study the Bible to discover aspects of His return, that there is continuous agreement. This is so because the Bible is perfect in its truth and trustworthiness.

We have discovered striking evidence that the time line of history is indeed the unfolding of God's salvation plan. Thus the rapture will conclude the salvation plan on this earth. History will also be concluded and the end of the world will have come.

The big question we all must face is whether or not we are ready for our Lord's return. Have we seen ourselves as the sinners we are? Have we repented of our sins, believing in the Lord Jesus as our sin-bearer? Have we turned from our sins, earnestly desiring to be obedient to Christ?

If we have not, we are not ready for His return. We are still included amongst those who are subject to judgment. Our condition is indeed dangerous.

Praise God for His love, that it is still the day of salvation, that forgiveness is available for any who call upon the Lord. Praise God for such a Savior!

Let us continue to press on. We should now look with great care on the judgment God will put on the church because of its end-time apostasy. This judgment will come during the closing years of the earth's history and is spoken of as a time of great tribulation. We will look at this tribulation in the next chapter.

Chapter 3
The Final Tribulation

We have learned that the end of the world is going to bring to pass the great event of the rapture of the believers. There is another event that is an integral part of the end-time events that is also of extreme importance. As we understand what the Bible has to say about it we will be laying additional groundwork for understanding the timing of the end. That event is the so-called final tribulation.

Any student of the Bible eventually will become interested in the tribulation period that must come prior to the return of Christ. What is this tribulation? When will it come? How long will it continue? How extensive will it be? Will it be a time of worldwide bloodletting? Will believers go through this period? How does it fit into God's salvation program? Will there be events that precipitate this period? How extensively does the Bible speak of this event? Are we close in time to that event? Does it fit into the principle that the time line of history is the unfolding of God's salvation plan?

These are some of the questions that will be examined in this chapter. Hopefully we will gain a clearer understanding of the causes of this period and a better knowledge of the character and nature of this period. We will also learn many things that will help us to discover the timing of Christ's return.

The Bible has much to say about the period of tribulation. God does not assign it a specific title; however, to facilitate our study we will call it "the final tribulation." God has given information in Matthew 24:21 that speaks clearly of this event. There Jesus declares:

> For then shall be great tribulation, such as was not since the beginning of the world to this time, no, nor ever shall be.

> *Tribulation, especially for the believer in Christ, has been normative throughout the history of the world.*

Tribulation, especially for the believer in Christ, has been normative throughout the history of the world. This is shown, for example, in John 16:33 where God declares "in the world you shall have tribulation." It is implied by the words of Matthew 24:21 where God states "tribulation such as was not since the beginning of the world."

The reference in Matthew 24:21 to a greatly intensified tribulation is found in the context of the account of the events that are to take place at the end of the world. Matthew 24:29 informs us:

> Immediately after the tribulation of those days shall the sun be darkened, and the moon shall not give her light, and the stars shall fall from heaven, and the powers of the heavens shall be shaken.

The sun and the moon are the timekeepers that God placed in the heavens to mark the passage of days, months, and years (Genesis 1:14). The darkening of them indicates that time is no more. In other words, immediately after this great tribulation, eternity begins. Thus, we can know that this tribulation is to occur at the end of time.

The Bible has far more to say about the final tribulation than might be realized.

The Final Tribulation: A Well-Documented Event

The Bible has far more to say about the final tribulation than might be realized. In a host of passages it instructs us that just before Judgment Day there will be both an intensification of tribulation and a radical change in the nature of tribulation compared with any tribulation the world previously had endured. Matthew 24:15-28 addresses itself to this matter, especially verses 15-16 and 21-22 and 24:

> When ye, therefore, shall see the abomination of desolation, spoken of by Daniel the prophet, stand in the holy place, (whoso readeth, let him understand:) Then let them which be in Judaea flee into the mountains: **For then shall be great tribulation, such as was not since the beginning of the world to this time, no, nor ever shall be.** And except those days should be shortened, there should no flesh be saved: but

for the elect's sake those days shall be shortened. For there shall arise false Christs, and false prophets, and shall shew great signs and wonders; insomuch that, if it were possible, they shall deceive the very elect.

Matthew 24 is one of the most lucid and detailed Bible passages on the final tribulation period, but many other statements in the Bible relate to it. For example, II Thessalonians 2:1-4 speaks of this period as a falling away.

Now we beseech you, brethren, by the coming of our Lord Jesus Christ, and by our gathering together unto him. That ye be not soon shaken in mind, or be troubled, neither by spirit, nor by word, nor by letter as from us, as that the day of Christ is at hand. Let no man deceive you by any means: for that day shall not come, except there come a falling away first, and that man of sin be revealed, the son of perdition: Who opposeth and exalteth himself above all that is called God, or that is worshipped; so that he as God sitteth in the temple of God, shewing himself that he is God.

Revelation 8 and Revelation 9 speak of it as a period when the third part will be killed. The third part refers to the body of believers within the church, the external body of believers gathered together as congregations and denominations around the world. Revelation 9:15 records:

And the four angels were loosed, which were prepared for an hour, and a day, and a month, and a year, for to slay the third part of men.

In Revelation 11:7-8 God refers to this event when indicating that the two witnesses will be killed:

And when they shall have finished their testimony, the beast that ascendeth out of the bottomless pit shall make war against them, and shall overcome them, and kill them. And their dead bodies shall lie in the street of the great city, which spiritually is called Sodom and Egypt, where also our Lord was crucified.

The two witnesses also refers to the church. Revelation 13:3-8 concerns this dreadful event.

> And I saw one of his heads, as it were wounded to death; and his deadly wound was healed: and all the world wondered after the beast. And they worshipped the dragon which gave power unto the beast: and they worshipped the beast, saying, Who is like unto the beast? Who is able to make war with him? And there was given unto him a mouth speaking great things and blasphemies; and power was given unto him to continue forty and two months. And he opened his mouth in blasphemy against God, to blaspheme his name, and his tabernacle, and them that dwell in heaven. And it was given unto him to make war with the saints, and to overcome them: and power was given him over all kindreds, and tongues, and nations. And all that dwell upon the earth shall worship him, whose names are not written in the book of life of the Lamb slain from the foundation of the world.

Revelation 16 addresses this event in the ominous declaration of verses 13 and 14:

> And I saw three unclean spirits like frogs come out of the mouth of the dragon, and out of the mouth of the beast, and out of the mouth of the false prophet. For they are the spirits of devils, working miracles, which go forth unto the kings of the earth and of the whole world, to gather them to the battle of that great day of God Almighty.

Revelation 17 gives further insight into this traumatic time in verses 12-14:

> And the ten horns which thou sawest are ten kings, which have received no kingdom as yet; but receive power as kings one hour with the beast. These have one mind, and shall give their power and strength unto the beast. These shall make war with the Lamb, and the Lamb shall overcome them: for he is Lord of lords, and King of kings: and they that are with him are called, and chosen, and faithful.

Revelation 20 describes this event as a time when Satan is loosed for a "little season." We read in verses 3 and 7-9:

And cast him into the bottomless pit, and shut him up, and set a seal upon him, that he should deceive the nations no more, till the thousand years should be fulfilled; and after that he must be loosed a little season.

And when the thousand years are expired, Satan shall be loosed out of his prison. And shall go out to deceive the nations which are of the four quarters of the earth, Gog and Magog, to gather them together to battle: the number of whom is as the sand of the sea. And they went up on the breadth of the earth, and compassed the camp of the saints about, and the beloved city: and fire came down from God out of heaven, and devoured them.

Jesus instructs us concerning this event in the prophecy of Luke 21:20-24:

And when ye shall see Jerusalem compassed with armies, then know that the desolation thereof is nigh. Then let them which are in Judaea flee to the mountains; and let them which are in the midst of it depart out; and let not them that are in the countries enter thereinto. For these be the days of vengeance, that all things which are written may be fulfilled. But woe unto them that are with child, and to them that give suck, in those days! for there shall be great distress in the land, and wrath upon this people. And they shall fall by the edge of the sword, and shall be led away captive into all nations: and Jerusalem shall be trodden down of the Gentiles, until the times of the Gentiles be fulfilled.

The Old Testament, too, is replete with references to this awesome period. For example in Daniel 7:23-25 God prophesies:

Thus he said, The fourth beast shall be the fourth kingdom upon earth, which shall be diverse from all kingdoms, and shall devour the whole earth, and shall tread it down, and break it in pieces. And the ten horns out of this kingdom are ten kings that shall arise: and another shall rise after them; and he shall be diverse from the first, and he shall subdue three kings. And he shall speak great words against the Most High, and shall wear out the saints of the Most High, and think to change times and laws: and they shall be given into his hand, until a time and times and the dividing of time.

The same period is in view in Daniel 8:23-25:

And in the latter time of their kingdom, when the transgressors are come to the full, a king of fierce countenance, and understanding dark sentences, shall stand up. And his power shall be mighty, but not by his own power: and he shall destroy wonderfully, and shall prosper and practise, and shall destroy the mighty and the holy people. And through his policy also he shall cause craft to prosper in his hand; and he shall magnify himself in his heart, and by peace shall destroy many: he shall also stand up against the Prince of princes; but he shall be broken without hand.

The Bible anticipates this event in the difficult language of Genesis 19 where God describes the wickedness of the men of Sodom. These men wanted to molest the visitors (who were actually God Himself who had taken on the appearance of men), who came to deliver Lot and his family out of Sodom and its impending destruction.

Genesis 19 is further explicated in Judges 19, which details the killing of the concubine by the men of Benjamin. Both accounts teach aspects of the final tribulation period.

God anticipates this period by His judgments on Israel and Judah. Israel was destroyed by the Assyrians and Judah was destroyed by the Babylonians. Deuteronomy 28:15-68, II Chronicles 36:13-21, and many passages in Isaiah, Ezekiel, and Jeremiah anticipate this dreadful event (these will be studied later).

> *The final tribulation is so frequently alluded to in the Bible that we wonder why it has not become an important part of Christian theology.*

The final tribulation period is not an isolated event with incidental reference to it in the Bible. It is of major importance; it is spoken of repeatedly throughout the Holy Scripture. It is so frequently alluded to in the Bible that we wonder why it has not become an important part of Christian theology.

Ahead of that question, we wonder why God has so much to say about an event that is experienced only by the people of the world who are living near the end of time. We wonder why many final tribulation passages of the Bible are written in such a way that they are difficult to understand. For example, when we analyze the passages mentioned on the preceding pages of this study (a partial listing), we see how obtuse and puzzling the language is. Few of the statements are as plain as Matthew 24:21 where God declares that there will be great tribulation such as this world has never known.

The Final Tribulation Comes at the End of the Church Age
     These questions can be answered if we realize that the chief truth that is hidden in the Biblical language of the final tribulation period is that there comes a time when the work of the church, to evangelize the world, draws to a close. The work of the church is in view for instance in John 20:21, "Then said Jesus to them again, Peace be unto you: as my Father hath sent me, even so send I you," and Mark 16:15, "He said unto them, Go ye into all the world, and preach the gospel to every creature." This work ends only as fewer and fewer of the elect remain to become saved. The end of the work of the church coincides with apostasy within the churches. God's judgment comes upon these churches, the various denominations and congregations throughout the world. This is preliminary to God's judgment upon the whole world at Judgment Day.

> *The dramatic truth that a short time prior to Judgment Day increasingly virtually every congregation and denomination in the world is to become apostate was not to be a concern of the evangelical church.*

     The work of the church to evangelize the world is so important that God did not make the end of the church age a subject for theologians of the New Testament period. While God saves the elect from every nation, he repeatedly warns the churches that He would reject them if they were unfaithful. However, the dramatic truth that a short time prior to Judgment Day increasingly virtually every congregation and denomination in the world is to become apostate was not to be a concern of the evangelical church.

> *The end of the church age and God's judgment upon the*
> *church . . . is apparently antithetical and contrary to*
> *everything the Bible teaches about God's plan of salvation.*

The end of the church age and God's judgment upon the church at the time of the closing of history is apparently antithetical, in opposition, and contrary to everything the Bible teaches about God's plan of salvation. That is why God has written extensively about this event. When it became time for God to reveal these truths to His believers, they would be able to find extensive documentation in the Bible. Therefore, God has hidden the teachings of this dramatic event in some of the most difficult Biblical language. Once we understand the nature and purpose of the final tribulation period, the truths hidden in these passages begin to be revealed, and we see in a fresh and beautiful way the harmony and cohesiveness of the Scriptures.

As has been noted, the final tribulation period is directly associated with the end of the church age, when churches and denominations begin to cease to function as representatives of God to evangelize the world. Therefore, the more we know about the church as it existed throughout the ages, the more qualified we will be to understand the Biblical information concerning the church's end.

> *The final tribulation is the period during which*
> *God's salvation plan comes to an end.*

Remember the principle: The time line of history is the unfolding of God's salvation plan.

In Acts 17:24-27, we read this very significant citation:
God that made the world and all things therein, seeing that he is Lord of heaven and earth, dwelleth not in temples made with hands; Neither is worshipped with men's hands, as though he needed any thing, seeing he giveth to all life, and breath, and all things; And hath made of one blood all nations of men for to dwell on all the face of the earth, and hath determined the times before appointed, and the bounds of their habitation;

That they should seek the Lord, if haply they might feel after him, and find him, though he be not far from every one of us.

> *God insists that He has decreed a very definite time frame for the human race. This time frame has been established for the purpose that mankind may become saved.*

In this very succinct statement in Acts, God is setting forth very important principles that apply to the whole human race. Amongst these we read that God has determined the times before appointed and the bounds of their habitation. By this declaration, God insists that He has decreed a very definite time frame for the human race. This time frame has been established for the purpose that mankind may become saved. (That they should seek the Lord . . . and find Him.)

Thus God is declaring that the timetable for all of mankind is not related to the rise and fall of civilizations. It is not related to political power or to great religions like the Muslim religion which has power in the earth. It is not related to the wearing out of this earth, or to the developments of science. All of these things are under the control of God and are allowed to develop in such a way that they in no manner frustrate God's timetable for the earth. But the markers or milestones of the timetable of history are entirely related to God's salvation plan. Indeed, the time line of history is the unfolding of God's salvation plan.

That is why we want to know how this salvation plan has unfolded. That is why the final tribulation period is so very important: For we are seeing that it is during this period that God must bring His whole salvation plan to an end. And the ending of His salvation plan is very complex, considering it must occur on the heels of the development of congregations and denominations all over the world.

The Old Testament Church

The final tribulation period has been anticipated repeatedly throughout the Scriptures. The Old Testament anticipated it. The New Testament anticipated it. This is an event that has been spoken of in great detail in the Bible. The reason it is well documented is that it is so terrible in nature and purpose.

As we have noted, the chief characteristic of the final tribulation period is God's judgment on the church as God brings to an end the unfolding of God's salvation program. This event is traumatic and contrary to everything that we might expect; God has carefully and extensively written about it so that there might be no misunderstanding.

We will not have an appreciation of the final tribulation unless we understand the Bible's teachings about the church. The mission and character of the church should be of intense concern to every child of God, because he is a part of that church, which is found in every Biblically faithful congregation and denomination. It is Christ's church; He went to the cross to establish it. Therefore, believers want to know all that the Bible teaches concerning the present and the future of the church.

> *As we get an historical perspective of the church, we will get a grasp on the way God unfolded his salvation plan.*

To understand the church, its mission, character, and future, we must understand how God dealt with the nations of the Old Testament (especially national Israel), for they relate to the church's present and future. National Israel, for example, is presented in the Bible as a figure, type, or representation of the church. As we understand how God dealt with Old Testament nations, we will understand that the warnings given in the Old Testament relate to the New Testament church. Let us get a Biblical perspective of the church. At the same time that we get an historical perspective of the church, we will also begin to get a grasp upon the way God unfolded His salvation plan.

The Church from the Fall to Abraham

In the beginning we find that Adam and Eve were created, according to Biblical chronology, about 13,000 years ago, actually in the year 11,013 B.C. (see Chapter 8). From the time of their fall, salvation was possible. Abel, their son, was saved. Possibly Adam and Eve were saved. Noah found grace in the eyes of the Lord. Enoch, who lived a few thousand years before Noah, walked with God and was not because God took him. Indeed, there was salvation from the beginning. From the time that sin came into the world until the present day there has been the possibility of salvation.

During the first 9000 years of the history of the world, people were saved as individuals, just as people today are saved individually. Today we are instructed by God to fellowship together as congregations. In those early years, God does not speak of a collective body assembling together. God does not speak of a congregation; God does not speak of a church. Nevertheless, their salvation was identical to our salvation and to the salvation of believers throughout time. We do not find that they were admonished to be a part of a congregation. It was not God's plan in those early days to have a great body of believers nor to assemble believers together in congregations.

> *At the time of the flood, only eight people were saved out of a population of perhaps a million people.*

The number of believers at any time was exceedingly few. At the time of the flood, for instance, only eight people were saved out of a population of that day of perhaps a million people. During the 9000 years from the fall of Adam and Eve until the time of Abraham, there was no structured body of believers called a congregation or church.

The Church from Abraham to Christ

When Abraham came on the scene about 4000 years ago, it was the beginning of a change. He headed the first official congregation, i.e., the nation of Israel. The approximately 9000 years that had gone before are recorded in the first eleven chapters of Genesis. In Genesis Chapter 12 God begins to deal with Abram. He was not a Jew. He was a Gentile who trusted God just as we must trust God. He was saved exactly as we are saved.

The time line of history is the unfolding of God's salvation plan. In Abraham's day the unfolding of this plan was focussed very narrowly on Abraham and his family. Therefore, the Bible gives us much information so that we can accurately date various experiences in his life.

In the year 2092 B.C. Abram was called out of Ur of the Chaldees, a Gentile nation, and into the land of Canaan (which today is the land of Israel). At that time Abram was 75 years of age. Twenty-four years later, in the year 2068 B.C. (see page 297), Abram and his family received circumcision as a sign that they were in the covenant.

The covenant was the agreement God made within the Godhead, on behalf of those who were to become saved, that God would save a people for Himself. Theologically speaking it is called the "Covenant of Grace" or the "Covenant of Redemption." Those who become saved as part of God's covenant plan become eternal citizens of the Kingdom of God. This covenant is closely associated with the Kingdom of God. The word "covenant" is actually a synonym for the "Gospel."

God began to identify His Kingdom with a visible body of believers by the sign of the covenant, circumcision. The fact that all males in Abraham's family and servants and slaves in Abraham's household were circumcised indicates that God was beginning to deal with a congregation.

> *Israel was the official congregation that*
> *represented the Kingdom of God in a visible,*
> *corporate, and institutional way.*

Abraham fathered Isaac, who fathered Jacob. Jacob fathered sons who headed the twelve tribes (actually there were thirteen) that became national Israel. Again and again in the Bible national Israel is spoken of as the congregation. They looked to their roots; they looked to their progenitor Abraham as the beginning because he was brought to the land of Canaan, to the land of Israel, by God. It was in this land that the congregation of Israel lived for most of the 2,000 years from Abraham to the time of the cross. Israel was the official congregation that represented the Kingdom of God in a visible, corporate, and institutional way. From what we read in the Bible, there was no other congregation in the world. Israel alone was the congregation. God unfolded His salvation plan through the people of Israel.

There was salvation among the Ninevites after Jonah came on the scene. You can read about them in the Book of Jonah. You will not read that the believing Ninevites became a congregation. They are a special case that God put in the Bible for other purposes, for example, to illustrate that it was not God's intention that salvation be confined to the nation of Israel. Their salvation emphasized that it was possible for Gentiles to be saved. There are other reasons why God gave us the Book of Jonah, but there is no intimation that God is teaching that congregations other than the nation of Israel existed in the world prior to the coming of Christ. The saving of the people of Nineveh tells us much about God's salvation plan, and later we will discover it also assists us with the timetable of history.

God's Congregation - The Nation of Israel
The only congregation that existed in the world from the fall of man until Christ came to die for our sins was the nation of Israel. (See Acts 13:43, I Chronicles 28:8, Joshua 22:12-16.) This congregation was to be separated from the world. It was to have a distinct and unique identification that showed it was God's congregation. In Exodus 12, for example, if a Gentile (a stranger to national Israel), wanted to partake of the Passover, he and his household were to be circumcised (Exodus 12:48). In other words, if someone became saved, he was to identify with the nation of Israel by a particular sign placed on him. If a member of the congregation rebelled against God, he was to be cut off, which was frequently signified by stoning. The congregation was to be kept as pure as possible.

This congregation was so important and so intimate with God, that He declared that national Israel was His wife, to whom He was married (Jeremiah 3:1, 8-10, Isaiah 50:1). In this intimate relationship God lavished blessing after blessing upon Israel. No political nation has ever enjoyed the special favors that were experienced by Israel.

However, for long periods in its history it appeared that Israel was under the wrath of God rather than under the blessing of God. It enjoyed exceptional blessings of God, but Israel did not always show the evidence of these blessings. Therefore God's judgments repeatedly fell on Israel.

During the days of King David and King Solomon, Israel was in its flower; it existed as a beautiful nation. There was no division within its ranks, but that condition was tentative. Solomon worshipped other gods in his old age and as a penalty God destroyed Israel. Actually, He divided Israel. In the year 931 B.C., He took ten tribes, the largest part of Israel, and gave them into the hands of a foreign king. He left only Judah and Benjamin under the rulership of Solomon's son. This was a tremendous judgment of God upon Israel.

Two hundred and twenty-two years later, in the year 709 B.C., the ten tribes, also called the northern kingdom, were destroyed by the Assyrians because they were rebellious against God. One hundred and twenty-three years after the ten tribes were destroyed the remainder of Israel, called Judah or the southern kingdom, was destroyed by the Babylonians, in the year 587 B.C. (See page 310.)

That was not the end of national Israel, even though they were in captivity in Babylon for a long time. In spite of the apostasy that had prevailed, a remnant came out of Babylon. God still recognized the nation of Israel as His congregation, as the corporate body. A remnant came out of Babylon, returned to Jerusalem, and there the nation of Israel was slowly rebuilt.

> *By examining ancient Israel we will be able to discover the unfolding of God's salvation plan during the period from their beginning to the cross.*

Up to and including when Christ came on the scene, Israel continued as the external official representation of the Kingdom of God on earth. Anyone who identified with the God of the Bible and salvation would have been a part of the congregation in national Israel. The nation of Israel continued until the time of Christ to be an integral part of God's visible church. By carefully examining ancient Israel, we will be able to discover the unfolding of God's salvation plan. Remember that it is the time line of history during the period that extended from their beginning until the time of the cross.

Ancient Israel Relates to the New Testament Church

We are interested in ancient Israel because it gives us insights into New Testament congregations; as we see how God dealt with ancient national Israel, we get insights as to how God deals with the church of our day. It identifies with New Testament congregations from many vantage points.

> *The Israel of God is the body of true believers.*

Ancient Israel was a nation that God used as a type or figure of the Israel of God that came into existence later in history. It shall be seen that it was revealed later in history that the Israel of God is the body of true believers, from the beginning up to the present day and till Christ returns.

> *Another tremendous blessing we received from national Israel is the Lord Jesus Christ.*

Ancient Israel served many purposes in God's salvation plan in addition to that of being a type of the Israel of God. During their era they served as the visible, external representation of the Kingdom of God. They served a marvelous purpose in that God used the Jews, the blood descendants of Abraham, as the people to write the Bible; possibly the whole Bible was written by official members of the congregation of the nation of Israel.

Another tremendous blessing we received from national Israel is the Lord Jesus. Jesus was a Jew. He was a blood descendant of Abraham, of the tribe of Judah, of the house of David. We can be grateful to national Israel that humanly speaking they produced the Christ.

The nation of Israel was the progenitor of the New Testament church. Christ came from Israel, and the New Testament church came from Christ; therefore, the New Testament church came from national Israel. God used them in marvelous ways.

Another purpose in God's plan for national Israel was that He used them to bring Christ to crucifixion. The Sanhedrin (the Jewish rulers), the High Priest, and the Pharisees plotted the death of the Lord Jesus, which was an important part of God's plan. If Jesus had not been crucified, there would be no salvation for us. We are grateful that He was crucified. The nation of Israel, particularly the leaders of the nation of Israel, were incensed against Jesus. They were convinced that He was of Satan and therefore they wanted Him killed. They induced the Roman Governor Pontius Pilate to have Him crucified - a necessary part of God's salvation plan.

The apostles, who played an important part in the formation of the New Testament church, also came from national Israel. The twelve apostles were Jews. They were members of the synagogue, the church of the Jews. They were the men whom God used to begin the New Testament church. We owe much to national Israel. It was used in a profound and wonderful way by God to prepare our salvation.

National Israel was a corporate, visible, institutional, external body intimately related to God. God brought magnificent blessings upon them.

This does not imply that every man of national Israel was saved. There were true believers within national Israel, but as a nation they remained unsaved. Since the nation itself was the church, it can be said that many people within the church of that day were unsaved. Nevertheless, God loved them as a corporate body. Only those who were truly saved have eternal life. Those who were unsaved, even though they were members of the corporate body, remain under the wrath of God. They must pay for their sins the same as anyone else in the world who remains unsaved. Salvation through the shed blood of Christ was as essential for them as it is for us today. We read that Noah found grace in the eyes of the Lord (Genesis 6:8). Likewise, we read that Job declared, "I know that my redeemer liveth" (Job 19:25).

> *The unfolding of God's salvation program shifted from ancient national Israel to the New Testament church.*

Israel's Era Comes to an End

The era when national Israel served as the external representation of the Kingdom of God on earth ended in a dramatic way when Jesus hung on the cross. The end of that era opened the way for the Kingdom of God to be externally represented by the New Testament church. The unfolding of God's salvation program shifted from ancient national Israel to the New Testament church.

The end of national Israel will be studied in some detail to be certain of this conclusion. Before the cross (throughout the Old Testament period), sacrifices and blood offerings were made. Burnt offerings were made on the altar. These sacrifices pointed to the Lord Jesus Christ, the Lamb of God, who was sacrificed for our sins.

The physical focus of these sacrifices was the temple in Jerusalem. In the temple was the Holy of Holies; it was the most holy place. It was separated from the major part of the temple by a huge veil or curtain behind which no one ever saw. Behind the veil was the ark. In this ark were the two tablets of stone on which the ten commandments were written. The ark represented Christ. Once a year, on the Day of Atonement, the high priest entered the veil to sprinkle blood on the mercy seat which covered the ark. When he went behind the veil, everyone else left the temple. No one could look behind the veil because the Holy of Holies, which was the room behind the veil, represented God. The Bible speaks of it as the place where God came down to man. It was the most holy place that made the temple the most holy building in the world. The temple was in Jerusalem, and Jerusalem therefore became the holy city.

When Christ hung on the cross, the veil of the temple was rent (Matthew 27:51). God, as it were, took His finger and tore the veil from top to bottom. The huge curtain, which as near as we can determine was more than fifty feet high, was rent by God; no longer was the Holy of Holies a hidden place. No longer was it a place into which no one could look. It was wide open, and that meant that it was no longer the holy place. Since it no longer was the holy place, the temple was no longer the holy building. Since the temple was no longer the holy building, Jerusalem was no longer the holy city. This marked the end of the era of national Israel.

> *Christ's suffering on the cross was the fulfillment of all the Old Testament sacrifices.*

Christ's suffering on the cross was the fulfillment of all the Old Testament sacrifices. He was the Lamb to which all the previously slaughtered lambs pointed. His death, therefore, marked the end of the observance of the ceremonial laws. The end of the ceremonial law brought the end of national Israel as God's official representation of the Kingdom of God on earth.

God formed national Israel in the year 2068 B.C., the year Abraham was circumcised. Exactly 2,100 years later, in the year 33 A.D., national Israel stopped being the official representation of the

Kingdom of God on earth. (THERE IS NO YEAR ZERO. TO DETERMINE THE PASSAGE OF TIME FROM AN OLD TESTAMENT DATE TO THE NEW TESTAMENT DATE, THE TWO PERIODS MUST BE ADDED TOGETHER AND THEN ONE (1) IS SUBTRACTED FROM THE TOTAL TO OBTAIN THE ACTUAL YEARS THAT TRANSPIRED BETWEEN THE TWO DATES. THUS THE PERIOD 2068 B.C. TO 33 A.D. EQUALS 2101 CALENDAR YEARS BUT 2100 ACTUAL YEARS: 2068 + 33 - 1 = 2100.) From that time forward, if anyone wanted to know something about Jehovah God, if he wanted to know about the Bible, or the Lord Jesus Christ, he did not go to national Israel. We do not go to Jerusalem today to find out about the Christ. We go to the churches and the congregations that sprang up subsequent to the cross. God's action of tearing the veil as Christ hung on the cross ended the era of national Israel because they were the stewards or the custodians of the ceremonial law.

During the first 9,000 years of world history there was no congregation. During the last 2,100 years of the Old Testament era there was a congregation - and that congregation was national Israel. Its land was the land of Israel; Jerusalem was its capital. The Lord Jesus Christ came out of that congregation. The crucifixion of Christ ended the era.

The Bible says that God would have one more thing to do with national Israel; it is another subject. Briefly, it is: God speaks of Israel as a sign that we are near the end of time. The Bible indicates that when the fig tree is in leaf, you know that summer is nigh. When you see these things happening, you know that Christ is at the very door (Matthew 24:32-33). The fig tree, which typifies national Israel in the Bible, is again in leaf and that tells us that we are very close to the end.

This is of great importance and will be studied later in detail. It impinges heavily on the timing of the final tribulation period.

The Beginning of the New Testament Church

As we are beginning to see, it was at the cross that the unfolding or revealing of God's salvation plan shifted from the nation of Israel to the New Testament church. God's timetable or time line was now to be determined by the time duration of these churches.

The beginning of the New Testament church was as dramatic as the end of the era of the Old Testament church. Jesus told His apostles in John 16:7-8:

Nevertheless I tell you the truth; It is expedient for you that I go away: for if I go not away, the Comforter will not come unto you; but if I depart, I will send him unto you. And when he is come, he will reprove the world of sin, and of righteousness, and of judgment.

> *The Comforter is God the Holy Spirit who would begin His program to evangelize the world immediately after Christ returned to heaven.*

The Comforter is God the Holy Spirit, who would begin His program to evangelize the world immediately after Christ returned to heaven. This grand event, which was promised in many places in the Old Testament, ushered in the continuation of God's time line of history as God would unfold His salvation program in the New Testament church. One phrase used by God to describe this new program is that the Holy Spirit would be poured out. In Joel 2:28, for example, God decreed that "it shall come to pass afterward, that I will pour out my Spirit upon all flesh." This prophecy was fulfilled at Pentecost in 33 A.D. It was then that the Holy Spirit was poured out.

The pouring out of the Holy Spirit does not indicate that God, who is the Holy Spirit, can be physically poured out. He is not a quantity that can be treated this way. God uses "pouring out" to identify with the Biblical concept that the world before the coming of Christ was a spiritual desert; few had been saved. The spiritual desert was to be turned into a fruitful field. Spiritual forests would grow, and the wilderness would bring forth green vegetation. It is as though copious quantities of water were poured out on the spiritual desert. The water is a figure or type of God the Holy Spirit beginning His program to evangelize the world. The language that the Holy Spirit was poured out simply means that God the Holy Spirit had begun His evangelistic commission. This was the fulfillment of hundreds of Old Testament promises that indicated that believers would come to God from every nation.

To further build on the figure of water being poured on the desert, God used the term "filled with the Spirit" to indicate that New Testament believers were qualified to be witnesses. The picture God paints is that the Holy Spirit, like great quantities of water, is poured out and fills every believer; out of their bellies as out of Christ Himself, flow rivers of living water (John 7:38). The world, which had been a spiritual desert, would blossom with new believers in Christ, as God worked through believers to evangelize the world.

The program of worldwide evangelization began fifty days after Christ hung on the cross. Ten days before Pentecost, Jesus had gone back to heaven. At Pentecost God indicated that His work of atonement had been completed in the sense that it was time to begin God's program to evangelize the world.

> *Pentecost in 33 A.D., fifty days after Christ was crucified, was the beginning of God's salvation program whereby people from every nation were to be saved.*

Pentecost in 33 A.D., fifty days after Christ was crucified, was the beginning of God's salvation program whereby people from every nation were to be saved. National Israel no longer represented the Kingdom of God. The congregations that began to spring up all over the world became the external representation of the Kingdom of God. At Pentecost 3,000 were saved from eighteen different nations. These people went back to their nations and they became the church of God. They were not identified with the temple in Jerusalem. They were not identified with the synagogues.

It is true that the apostles still went to synagogues to teach; that is where the Jews were. That is where they assembled in religious worship. God had commanded the apostles to go first to the Jews to make sure that they heard the Gospel of the Lord Jesus Christ. The apostles no longer belonged to the synagogues. The church had begun afresh, apart from the church of the Old Testament. It began with the apostles who came out of the church of the Old Testament.

The Bible teaches that Christ went to the cross for more reasons than to save the elect, even though that was the most important reason. Our Lord Jesus went to the cross, first, to save all who would believe on Him. He went to the cross to save David, to save Elijah, to save Moses, to save Enoch. The impact of the cross reached back to the beginning so that these men were saved anticipating the shed blood of the Lord Jesus Christ. Jesus is called Jesus because He saves His people from their sins: That is the big task God placed upon Him on the cross. He had become sin for every one of God's elect.

Jesus Went to the Cross to Establish the External Church

One may not normally think of this, but nevertheless it is Biblical: Jesus also went to the cross to establish the congregations, the visible, external church.

The Old Testament church had an external corporate character. For example, we read in Acts 7:38 that national Israel was the church in the wilderness. The institutional, visible body consisted of the whole nation of Israel and the Gentiles who joined by circumcision. Within the church were found the true believers who had eternal life. They had personally had their sins paid for by the Messiah who was to come. They had been chosen or elected by God to become saved. This election process had taken place before God created the world (Ephesians 1:4). Those who were elected by God are the only ones who would ever believe in Christ and become saved.

National Israel was important to God as a corporate, institutional body. This was seen, for example, in the wilderness after they had come out of Egypt. They were saved from the bondage of enslavement to Egypt. They came through the Red Sea in a miraculous way. God was present with them in the pillar of fire by night and the cloud by day. God cared for them; He brought to them the heavenly bread, manna. God gave them water out of the rock; they had plenty of water to drink. Their shoes did not wear out; their feet did not swell. God cared for them in marvelous ways even though individually most of them were unbelievers. God was tremendously involved with them as an external and visible body.

> *In the New Testament, also, God is involved with the external, visible body.*

In the New Testament also, God is involved with the external, visible body. Every congregation is identified with Christ. Christ went to the cross to establish these congregations. In II Peter 2:1 God declares that false prophets will arise from among you "even denying the Lord that bought them." These false prophets are members of the visible body, but they are not eternal members. They are not saved; they are in the congregation and they deny the Lord who bought them. The phrase "bought them" guides us to understand the corporate body's relationship to the cross.

God did not "buy them" in the sense that He paid for their sins. If this were so, then they would have been saved; they would not have been false prophets. God bought them in the sense that Christ went to the cross to establish the congregations as visible, corporate representations of the Kingdom of God on earth. The unsaved, false prophets were members of the congregation; in that respect, God bought them. God expected Old Testament believers to belong to a visible body called national Israel, and God expects New Testament believers to belong to a visible body.

The relationship of Christ to the visible body is seen in Revelation 2 and 3. The seven churches of Asia, which included Ephesus, Philadelphia, Smyrna, and Laodicea are named. Each of these congregations was represented in heaven by a candlestick, and Christ walked among these candlesticks. Yet, in these congregations there were many unbelievers. There was a Jezebel in one of them and there were the Nicolaitans who were in rebellion against God. Grievously bad things were going on in some of these congregations. Nevertheless, God repeatedly spoke of the fact that they were His congregations. They were each represented by a candlestick in heaven. God as Christ went to the cross to establish these congregations. Christ went to the cross not only to save individual believers but also to bring into existence the corporate, external body called the church. In the corporate sense it can be said that Christ bought the unsaved members of the church. This can be seen, for example, in the fact that the false prophet of II Peter 2:1 has been bought by Christ.

God's relationship to the New Testament congregation is not quite like it was to the Old Testament congregation, national Israel. The Old Testament congregation became the wife of God. God entered into that intimate relationship, but the New Testament does not say that Christ is married to the corporate, external congregation. God does not use that language when speaking of the New Testament congregation.

Christ was able to divorce the Old Testament congregation because God included in the ceremonial laws (Deuteronomy 24:1), that if a husband found that his wife was guilty of some unclean thing, that is, she was guilty of fornication, then he could write her a bill of divorcement and put her away. This is the law, or the principle, that God exercised to put away national Israel because of the Israelites' continuing infidelity. They continued to rebel against Him and go after other gods; therefore, God divorced them.

When Christ came on the scene, the possibility of divorce was rescinded. In Matthew Chapter 19, verse 8, the Bible declares that from the beginning it was not so (that a man could divorce his wife for fornication). It was never God's intention that a man could divorce his wife, so the principle in the ceremonial law of Deuteronomy 24 no longer stands. If a man finds that his wife has been engaged in fornication, he cannot divorce her.

God never speaks of having a wife-husband relationship with the New Testament institutional or corporate body. If He were married to her, to the corporate body, the institutional church, in the light of Matthew 19:8, He could not put her away. He is not married to it; He can separate Himself from it because there never has been a marriage. Later we shall see how God intends to separate Himself from the New Testament congregations.

In the New Testament God does speak of a marriage relationship. Instead of a marriage relationship to the corporate, external body (as in the Old Testament with national Israel), in the New Testament the relationship is with the eternal body, the invisible body of believers, which is found in every congregation that is reasonably true to the Word of God.

The difference must be underscored. In the New Testament when God speaks about His church, He may be speaking about the external, visible, institutional, corporate body that is called the Lutheran church or the Presbyterian church or the Mission Covenant church, etc. This is the external, visible congregation just as national Israel in the Old Testament was the visible congregation - the external representation of the Kingdom of God on earth. The Bible reveals that God has a tremendous interest in the corporate, external body of believers. When we join a church, corporately we become identified with the Kingdom of God. This is true even if we are unsaved, as were the false prophets spoken of in II Peter 2 who were members of a church.

The Bible declares many good and important things about the corporate body, the external institution, which is called the First Baptist Church or the First Presbyterian Church or the Episcopal Church, or whatever it may be called. However, under no circumstances are we saved because we belong to a congregation. Under no circumstances do we look to that church to save us. We must be extremely clear on this. Our salvation comes through a personal relationship with the Lord Jesus Christ. He personally has to wash away our sins.

> *We are not saved by the church. We*
> *are saved by the blood of Christ.*

Our salvation is entirely independent of our congregation. We may have been saved before we were aware that there were congregations. Many people are saved this way. We may have been saved after being invited to visit a congregation and hearing the preaching of the Word, in which case God blessed that preaching to our hearts, cleansed us from our sins, and we became saved. Nonetheless, we are not saved by the church. We are saved by the blood of Christ. We are saved by what Christ did for us on the cross.

The external church, the institutional church to which we belong, is the place where we gather to encourage one another in the Word and to worship. Worship is a large part of our relationship with Christ. As we pray and sing songs together, we worship Him. We can worship individually, but we are also to worship collectively. God has admonished us, if at all possible, to belong to a congregation. This is very important. The eternal church is made up of only true believers. The invisible church is eternal in character. It is the church that will be the bride of Christ eternally.

The Eternal Church Within the External Church
Within the external body there are those who are true believers. They should be found in the congregations that are reasonably true to the Word of God, because God commands us, if possible, to be a part of a congregation.

The invisible church is invisible because only God knows who are the saved ones. You and I, who are saved, can know in our own hearts that we are children of God. God certainly gives us that assurance as we read the Scriptures and our faith is built up. Faith comes by hearing and hearing by the Word of God (Romans 10:17).

One cannot know who else is saved. One cannot know the heart of another person. God knows who they are. Within any congregation there are those who are saved and those who are not saved. Insofar as the elders, the deacons, and the pastor desire, hopefully everybody within the congregation is saved. However, in the seven churches of Revelation 2 and 3, there were members, called Jezebel and Nicolaitans, who were running after another gospel. Therefore, it is certain that in virtually every congregation there are those who are unsaved.

Of prime importance to God is the invisible body, the eternal church, made up of those who have truly become saved, who have personally received their resurrected souls. These were named by God from before the foundation of the world. They are named in the Lamb's Book of Life. They are the elect of God who were predestinated to be saved. They are the individuals named in God's will and to whom God has obligated Himself to give the eternal inheritance. These are the ones that the Bible speaks of as, "Thou shalt call His name JESUS: for He shall save **His** people from their sins" (Matthew 1:21). These are the ones that Jesus spoke about when He said in John 6:37, "All that the Father giveth me, shall come to me." These are in the eternal Kingdom of God.

> *When we truly become saved, when we become children of God, then we are members of the eternal Kingdom of God.*

When we truly become saved, when we become children of God, then we are members of the eternal Kingdom of God. The eternal Kingdom of God is found in every congregation that is reasonably true to the Word of God. This is the Israel of God. This is the eternal Israel that has trusted in the Lord Jesus Christ. This is the seed of Abraham in the spiritual sense: people who have had their sins covered by the blood of Jesus - these are the bride of Christ.

In Revelation Chapter 21 God tells us about the holy city, the New Jerusalem, coming down out of heaven, prepared as a bride for her husband. The holy city is not the institutional church. The New Jerusalem is not the external congregation. The bride of Revelation 21 consists only of those who are born from above, those who are part of the eternal, invisible church; God alone knows its total extent.

In Ephesians Chapter 5 there is an interesting statement concerning this bride relationship. Jesus commands husbands in verses 25-26: "Husbands, love your wives, even as Christ also loved the church, and gave himself for it; That he might sanctify and cleanse it with the washing of water by the word."

Christ does not cleanse the external congregation; it can go deeper and deeper into sin and finally, God cuts it off. He cuts it off because He is not married to it. He need not divorce it as He had to divorce ancient Israel. He is not married to the New Testament corporate, institutional body, so He simply cuts it off. He destroys it. He removes the candlestick.

The invisible church - the eternal body of believers, which is found within the institutional congregation - is the bride of Christ. Christ is married to it. He is the husband of the true believers, and He says that we are to love our wives as Christ loved the church. God uses the husband-wife relationship to give us an idea of the intimacy that exists between Christ and His body of believers. He declares that His purpose is to sanctify and cleanse it with the washing of water by the Word. Those who are eternally saved have been cleansed by the blood of Christ. He will present them to Himself, a glorious church, not having spot or wrinkle or any such thing, that it should be holy and without blemish.

The external congregation, the Baptist denomination, or the Reformed denomination, or the Presbyterian denomination, or the Methodist denomination, will never be without spot or wrinkle. No denomination will ever be without spot or wrinkle. No denomination nor local congregation is the bride of Christ: It is the external representation of the Kingdom of God, as has been seen, but it will fall away in time, just as churches throughout history have fallen away.

> *True believers within the congregations are the eternal church. They are the Israel of God; they are the bride of Christ.*

True believers within the congregations are the eternal church. They are the Israel of God; they are the bride of Christ. It is they whose sins have been washed away. They are the ones who are presented to God without having spot or wrinkle; God has covered them with His blood. God gave them, first of all, resurrected souls when they became saved. When He completes their salvation, He will give each of them a resurrected body in which they will never sin again. This is the most important aspect of the church. These individuals are indwelt by the Holy Spirit. They are the legitimate ambassadors of Christ, and as ambassadors of Christ, they are qualified (by being filled with the Spirit), to be Christ's witnesses to the world.

> *Christ can never divorce this church because what God has joined together let not man put asunder. God will not violate this rule.*

Christ can never divorce this church because what God has joined together let not man put asunder. God will not violate this rule. God has guaranteed that we will be His bride throughout eternity. What a blessed, blessed promise this is!

The Eternal Church Includes the Old Testament Believers
The eternal church, the invisible body of believers, includes not only those who have been saved since the establishment of the New Testament church, it also includes those who were saved in the Old Testament days. It includes those who lived in the nation of Israel and those who lived before the nation of Israel, for example, Noah, who "found grace in the eyes of the LORD" (Genesis 6:8). He lived almost 3,000 years before the founding of the nation of Israel. The Pharisee, Nicodemus, whom Jesus talked to in John 3 is an Old Testament believer. Christ here speaks on the Old Testament side of the cross, and yet He tells him, "Ye must be born again." He must be born from above, otherwise, he cannot see or enter the Kingdom of God. This is the same language the Bible uses in reference to New Testament salvation.

God's purposes for the nation of Israel, the corporate, external, institutional body for 2,100 years before the cross, ended when Christ hung on the cross. Unfortunately, it will be seen that the external visible body, our congregation, whatever the name may be, will also end before Judgment Day. Only the invisible church, which is made up of those who are true believers in the Lord Jesus Christ, will go on into eternity and forever be the bride of Christ.

Those who make up the invisible church, those who are saved, are also called a "remnant" or a "remnant chosen by grace." They represent a small percentage of all the people of the earth. As individual congregations become more apostate, as they become more rebellious against God, true believers will be a smaller and smaller percentage of the members of the congregations.

This is not surprising. In national Israel, at any time in its history, the true believers, members of the invisible, eternal church, were a tiny percentage of the whole nation of Israel.

The same is frequently true in our congregations. Ideally, the congregation consists of only those who are true believers. In practice, particularly as a church becomes more and more interested in the world and tries to achieve success by rapidly adding members, it begins to let down the bars. To some degree, this church begins to redesign God's laws as laid down in the Bible. The rulers do this to make it easier for people to become members of their congregation. Finally, it gets to the point where the number of true believers in that church (and only God knows who they are), is a remnant of the congregation.

Throughout history the number of true believers was a remnant compared with the totality of all people. The number of people in the world who are true believers is a small percentage of the whole.

Nevertheless, the totality of all those who have believed on Him is a vast company. In Revelation 7, for example, God declares that the totality of true believers is a vast company which no man could number. The building of the church, the invisible, eternal church, of which we become a part when we become saved, has been going on throughout history, particularly during the last 1950 to 2000 years. A tremendous number of people have become believers.

As we study the church and see how God has worked out His program to bring the Gospel, I surely hope that you are a child of God. In all likelihood you have membership in a congregation. Because you have been baptized, have membership in a congregation, teach a Sunday School class, faithfully go to church, and pray, does not guarantee that you are a child of God. None of these things guarantees that you are the bride of Christ, that you are part of the eternal body that will go on eternally.

> *Only if you have begun to find it more and*
> *more distasteful to sin, and if you have*
> *repented of your sins, is there evidence that*
> *God is doing a work of grace in your heart.*

If you have come to the Lord with a broken and a contrite heart, if you have looked upon yourself with the stark knowledge that you are a sinner under the wrath of God, and if you have begun to trust in Christ as your only sin bearer, as your Savior, you can know that you are on the path of salvation. Only if you have begun to find it more and more distasteful to sin, and if you have repented of your sins, is there evidence that God is doing a work of grace in your heart. Only then can you know that you are a member of the true church.

It is my desire that each one who reads this book might indeed know that he or she is a member of Christ's glorious eternal church.

> *The era of the New Testament church will end,*
> *as did the Old Testament church, the*
> *nation of Israel.*

The Task of the Church

In this study of the final tribulation period, it will be discovered that the things thus far learned fit precisely into God's end-time program of bringing judgment upon the church. Because of the church's increasing apostasy near the end of time, the era of the New Testament church will end, as did the Old Testament church, the nation of Israel. This fits precisely into the unfolding of God's salvation plan, which, as we have learned, is the time line of history. When the New Testament church era ends, history will have come to an end.

To appreciate and understand the end of the New Testament church, one must understand the task of the church. The external church is the body within which the true believers are found. Therefore, all of the tasks that are assigned to them individually are assigned to the church. What is the major task of the institutional church, the visible representation of the Kingdom of God?

First of all, the task is to nourish and feed believers within the congregation. Those who have become members of the body of Christ, who truly have been saved, assemble and worship together as a body. This is an important function for the believer and is not to be taken lightly. The Bible teaches that we are not to neglect the assembling together of the saints, particularly as the day draws nigh (Hebrews 10:25). The Bible speaks of those in the congregation who rule over us (I Peter 5:1-3). It is God's plan that we are to be members of congregations. One task of the church is that within our congregation we are to be exhorted. We are to be taught the Word of God. We are to become more qualified to get on with the task that God has assigned to each of us: The task of sending the Gospel into the world.

> *We are mandated by God to send the Gospel*
> *into the world, that many more might be saved.*

The other major task of the church, and it is a major task, is that we are mandated by God to send the Gospel into the world, that many more might be saved. God does not expect the secular community, nor the business community, nor the political community, to evangelize the world. They have nothing to do with the true Gospel. They have no mandate of any kind to send the Gospel into the world.

The congregations and denominations that have sprung up during the New Testament period, which have within them the true believers who are filled with the Spirit, have the task of evangelizing the world. They are to marshall their resources so that the Gospel might go forth. As the Gospel goes forth, and this one is saved and that one is saved, it is the congregation, the official representation of the Kingdom of God, that welcomes the saved ones into the body of believers. They are baptized within the congregation. They fellowship within the congregation, commune together in the communion service, and anticipate the oneness that eternally exists in the body of believers.

God has assigned to the congregations the important task of bringing the Gospel to a lost world. Each congregation, while it labors at the task of evangelizing the world, is responsible to God to be a faithful representative of the Kingdom of God. If they are unfaithful, if they become apostate, and go after gospels other than the true Gospel, then God removes the candlestick. That is, God cuts them off; they are no longer His church.

> *There is hardly any substantial Christian presence in the nation of Turkey today. Their candlesticks were removed because they did not remain faithful.*

Throughout New Testament history, this falling away has happened again and again and again. For example, the seven churches of Revelation 2 and Revelation 3 were located in the part of the world that is now called Turkey. The churches that were in Turkey no longer exist; there is hardly any substantial Christian presence in the nation of Turkey today. Their candlesticks were removed because they did not remain faithful.

Denominations have risen, they have become apostate, and they are no longer the church of Jesus Christ. The moment that a denomination or a congregation begins to have as its authority something other than the Bible alone and in its entirety, it is no longer a congregation of Jesus Christ. However, as this happened throughout the New Testament period, God raised up more faithful congregations.

It is the church's responsibility to send out God's Word. Jesus declared, "as my Father hath sent me, so send I you" (John 20:21). The church as a corporate body can officially send out missionaries and use other methods to send forth the Gospel. Individual members of the church can exercise their responsibility by personally witnessing to others, handing out tracts, and joining with other Christians in ministries such as Family Radio. The Lord's command to every believer is to go into all the world making disciples. This is the grand and important task of the church. By this means God has sought out and saved His lost sheep.

What is the end of the church, the corporate, external, institutional body? Before that question is answered, Satan's relationship to the body of believers, or to the church, will be examined. Satan must be kept in view when trying to gain a Biblical perspective of what happens in the world that leads to the end of the church and Judgment Day. True believers once were slaves of Satan and Satan still tries to claim them. Satan is constantly trying to destroy the church. As we near the end of time, God is actually allowing Satan to destroy the corporate church as its task is completed.

Who Is Satan?

From everything read in the Bible, we must conclude that Satan was a created angel, along with legions of other angels. However, he wanted to be like God. He wanted to be a king in his own right. In Isaiah 14:12b-14 God speaks of him:

> ... O Lucifer [Lucifer simply means "shining one"], son of the morning! how art thou cut down to the ground, which didst weaken the nations! For thou hast said in thine heart, I will ascend into heaven, I will exalt my throne above the stars of God: I will sit also upon the mount of the congregation, in the sides of the north: I will ascend above the heights of the clouds: I will be like the Most High.

> *Lucifer aspired to be a king . . . he rebelled against God and many other angels rebelled with him.*

God created the angels to be ministering spirits, used of the Lord on behalf of those who were to be saved (Hebrews 1:14). God knew before He created anything that man would rebel against Him and come under the wrath of God. In anticipation of this, God created the angels to be used on behalf of those who were being saved. They were servants of God. One of the angels, Lucifer, aspired to be a king in his own right. He rebelled against God and many other angels rebelled with him.

Lucifer saw an opportunity to be a king when God created the earth and Adam and Eve, whom God gave rule of the earth. God created mankind, and He gave them dominion over this creation (Genesis 1:28). Lucifer reasoned something like this, "If I can get Adam and Eve to obey me, rather than God, then by right of conquest I become their master. Then, if God is just, He has to allow me to rule over them."

Whether he actually reasoned this out in his heart in this language is unknown, but this is the way it worked out. He came in the form of a serpent, the most wise of all the animals that were created in the Garden of Eden. He tempted Eve to disobey God - to eat of the forbidden fruit (Genesis 3). Adam also ate of the tree, and both Adam and Eve rebelled against God and began to be enemies of God. By rebelling against God, they indicated their enslavement to Lucifer. Therefore, God allowed Lucifer, who is Satan, who is also called the serpent, to have spiritual rule over mankind. Ever since that time the heart of unsaved man is under the rule of Satan.

At no time in history was Satan allowed to do anything that would frustrate God's eternal plan for the world and its inhabitants.

This does not mean that God totally abandoned His rule of man. At no time in history was Satan allowed to do anything that would frustrate God's eternal plan for the world and its inhabitants. God did allow Satan to have spiritual rule over unsaved man.

Satan's Rule Over the World Before the Cross

Until Christ came as Savior, that is, for the first 11,000 years of the history of this world, Satan's rule over mankind was great; few became saved. Most people were kept in the darkness of sin. Only occasionally in the Bible do we read of anyone becoming saved. In the days of the flood, for example, when there may have been as many as a million people living, only eight people entered the ark to escape God's judgment; that was a tiny percentage of the world's population.

When Sodom and Gomorrah were to be destroyed, Abraham pleaded with God that they would not be destroyed if there were ten righteous people in these cities (Genesis 18:32). The only way one can become righteous is to be saved. The heart of man is desperately wicked (Jeremiah 17:9), and there is none righteous, no, not one (Romans 3:10). It is obvious that the only way one can become righteous is to be redeemed from the wrath of God. The wrath of God is rightly deserved by all mankind because of their sins. Abraham effectively asked God to spare these cities if only ten were saved within them.

Thousands of people lived in Sodom and Gomorrah; ten was a tiny percentage of the people, so few were saved within these cities. God faithfully promised, "I will not destroy it for ten's sake" (Genesis 18:32b).

He did destroy those cities, and fewer than ten people were saved. Actually only Lot and possibly his two daughters were saved.

The spiritual darkness of Sodom and Gomorrah existed all over the world on the Old Testament side of the cross. In places like China, the South Pacific, and North and South America, no one was saved. Everyone was completely under the rule of Satan. They were blinded by sin. In national Israel, which had been set apart to represent the Kingdom of God on this earth, only a small percentage was saved. For example, during the forty years that they were in the wilderness, after they came out of Egypt to go to the land of Canaan, virtually the whole nation perished because of unbelief (Hebrews 3:19). How could this be? These were God's special people. They were "the apple of His eye" (Deuteronomy 32:10).

During the period from the fall of Adam and Eve until the time of the cross, Satan was allowed to bind and blind the hearts of men to such a degree that they were kept in the darkness of sin. This was coincidental with God's elective program. God elected a small number to salvation from these early nations. Had He elected more than this number, God would have had to make provision for their salvation, but that was not God's program. Therefore, to a high degree, He allowed Satan to control the hearts of unsaved men.

Evidence of Satan's control over the hearts of men is seen, for example, when in the days of Elijah only 7,000 were saved (I Kings 19:18), out of a nation of possibly two million people. This is about one-third of one percent. The nation of Israel was the only nation where people were becoming saved, with a few exceptions such as Rahab the harlot, Ruth the Moabitess, the Queen of Sheba, and the city of Nineveh. These are notable exceptions.

During the 11,000 year period before Christ came, Satan had great freedom. He was audacious in his freedom. He was allowed to go into heaven. God tells us in Job Chapter 1 verse 6 that Satan appeared among the sons of God. While there he said to God that Job remained faithful because God had put a hedge around him. Satan said Job was faithful to God only because God had bestowed so many blessings upon him. He was the accuser of the brethren. He enjoyed this freedom throughout time - until Christ came on the scene.

In Satan's rebellion against God he took many angels with him. These are called devils or fallen angels or evil spirits. The Bible records that evil spirits were in the hearts of people, particularly when Christ walked on earth (Luke 4:33), and in the Old Testament one may read of evil spirits (I Samuel 19:9).

Satan's Rule Over Mankind Was Never Total

During the 11,000 year Old Testament period, Satan's spiritual rule over unsaved men's hearts was not total. He had not become king of kings and lord of lords as God is King of kings and Lord of lords. God restrains sin in unsaved men's hearts.

The restraint on sin of the unsaved is seen, for example, in Genesis 20 when Abraham fled to Gerar to escape the famine of the land. While there, Abraham became frightened that the king of Gerar would kill him to have Sarah for his wife. This was a low point in Abraham's life. He did not trust God sufficiently. Abraham was an individual like each of us, and he had sinful moments. He lied to Abimelech, the king of Gerar, and said of Sarah, "She is my sister" (Genesis 20:2). Actually, this was a half truth because Sarah was his half sister, but the intent of his statement was that she was not his wife.

God came to Abimelech in a dream (verse 3 of Genesis 20), and said to him, "Thou art but a dead man, for the woman which thou hast taken: for she is a man's wife." In other words, "You are in great danger. You have taken a man's wife into your home." Abimelech had not come near her, and he said,

> Lord, wilt thou slay also a righteous nation? Said he not unto me, She is my sister? and she, even she herself said, He is my brother: in the integrity of my heart and innocency of my hands have I done this (verses 4-5).

He had not committed adultery, although he would have in time. He had not yet taken nor tried to take Sarah as his wife, but he had taken her into his home. He argued with God that he had had no adulterous intentions toward her. He argued with God that this had been done innocently, that he did not realize she was a man's wife.

God says in verse 6 of Genesis 20:

> And God said unto him in a dream, Yea, I know that thou didst this in the integrity of thy heart; for I also withheld thee from sinning against me: therefore suffered I thee not to touch her.

> *Abimelech was an unsaved man, in the blackness of*
> *Satan's spiritual rule, and yet God restrained*
> *sin in Abimelech's life.*

God gives us tremendous insight here. Abimelech was an unsaved man, in the blackness of Satan's spiritual rule, and yet God restrained sin in his life. Abimelech did nothing that God did not want him to do.

God teaches that the heart of man is desperately wicked (Jeremiah 17:9) and out of the heart comes all manner of evil things (Matthew 15:19). The reason that mankind is not more sinful than he is, is because God restrains sin. Satan's rule is not total. Satan rules only insofar as God will allow him to rule.

The evil spirits and the wicked who were under the spiritual control of Satan were frequently used to accomplish God's purposes. When God wanted to destroy Israel, He allowed the wicked Babylonians to come and destroy them. When it served God's purposes for Saul to rule in accordance with Saul's desires, which resulted in Saul reigning as a bad king, God took His Spirit from him and gave him an evil spirit. This does not make God guilty of sin. If God removes His hand of restraint, the evil will come in. The nature of man's heart is desperately wicked. Satan always looks for an opportunity to rule more heavily over men's hearts. The moment that God removes His hand of restraint the evil spirits will be there, and the wicked will be more wicked.

Until Christ came on the scene, this was the nature of the world; few people were being saved. The world was in bondage to sin as it has never been since Christ came.

Satan Is Bound so that Christ Can Build the New Testament Church

A drastic change took place when Christ came as the Savior. It was a change of such stupendous proportions that Satan was tremendously affected by it, and the world was greatly influenced. The Bible tells about this change in many different ways; for example, in the account of Jesus when He welcomed the seventy who had been sent out with the Gospel: the Savior is on the scene. The shadow of the cross is brilliant. God is preparing the believers for the beginning of the New Testament church, and when the seventy came back (Luke 10, verse 17), they "returned again with joy, saying, Lord, even the devils are subject unto us through thy name."

Jesus then said, "I beheld Satan as lightning fall from heaven" (verse 18). In other words, Satan will be conquered and he will lose his right to go into heaven. This is a drastic change in Satan's freedom.

Further commentary on this is in Revelation 12:7-9:

And there was war in heaven: Michael and his angels fought against the dragon; and the dragon fought and his angels, And prevailed not; neither was their place found any more in heaven. And the great dragon was cast out, that old serpent, called the Devil, and Satan, which deceiveth the whole world: he was cast out into the earth, and his angels were cast out with him.

Satan was cast out of heaven. Careful study of Revelation 12 reveals that the casting out of Satan occurred because of Christ's victory over Satan. This was accomplished by Christ going to the cross. Because of Christ's victory, Satan could no longer approach God and accuse the brethren as he did in the time of Job.

God has more to say about Satan. This is seen in the impact of the cross on Satan's actions: God had begun to deal with Satan; Satan will not frustrate God's plan to save people from all over the world.

> *Christ bound Satan so that God's program of building the church could take place.*

Christ bound Satan so that God's program of building the church could take place. Jesus alludes to this in Matthew 12, where He speaks of Beelzebub (another name for Satan). In Matthew 12:27-29:

And if I by Beelzebub cast out devils, by whom do your children cast them out? therefore they shall be your judges. But if I cast out devils by the Spirit of God, then the kingdom of God is come unto you. Or else how can one enter into a strong man's house, and spoil his goods, except he first bind the strong man? and then he will spoil his house.

In these verses, Jesus speaks of Satan as the strong man. Our Savior declares that Satan, the strong man, must be bound and his house plundered.

Who is in Satan's house? Unfortunately, the whole world. All of the unsaved, to a high degree, are under Satan's spiritual power. God's intention from the beginning was that Christ came as the Savior of a vast company of believers from every nation. To accomplish this, Satan was bound; he cannot frustrate God's plan to evangelize the world. God's intention was to plunder the spiritual house of Satan, i.e., Christ rescued those who were to be saved.

God gives additional information in the Bible about the change in Satan's condition. For example, in Hebrews 2:14, God speaks of Satan being destroyed as a result of Christ's victory on the cross:

> Forasmuch then as the children are partakers of flesh and blood, he also himself likewise took part of the same; that through death he might destroy him that had the power of death, that is, the devil.

Satan in principle has been destroyed, although he is allowed to continue to rule over the hearts of unsaved men to some degree. A fantastic thing happened at the cross: Satan and his fallen angels were consigned to hell.

Jude verses 5 and 6 prove this:

> I will therefore put you in remembrance, though ye once knew this, how that the Lord, having saved the people out of the land of Egypt, afterward destroyed them that believed not. And the angels which kept not their first estate, but left their own habitation, he hath reserved in everlasting chains, under darkness, unto the judgment of the great day.

The fallen angels, those who rebelled against God, were consigned to hell by Christ's victory on the cross.

The fallen angels, those who rebelled against God, were consigned to hell by Christ's victory on the cross. They have not yet actually been put in hell. Hell is the place where people and Satan and the fallen angels will be placed on Judgment Day, at the end of time.

They will be put there after they have been arraigned and tried before the judgment throne of God, and their sins have been exposed. In principle Christ has consigned Satan to hell; therefore, the Bible often speaks of him as being in a pit or being in hell, even though he continues to rule over the hearts of unsaved men with varying degrees of success. He will be allowed to rule over the hearts of the unsaved until the end of the world because he won this right when he defeated mankind (headed by Adam and Eve) in the Garden of Eden. Christ's victory on the cross guarantees that Satan will spend eternity in hell. As a result, God uses language, in passages such as Jude 5 and 6, that seems to indicate he is already in hell.

Another passage that speaks of the change in Satan's rule over mankind because of Christ's victory on the cross is Revelation 20:3:

> And cast him into the bottomless pit, and shut him up, and set a seal upon him, that he should deceive the nations no more, till the thousand years should be fulfilled: and after that he must be loosed a little season.

This language is parallel to Jude 5 and 6 and to II Peter 2:4 where the binding of Satan is discussed.

As a result of the cross, there was a fantastic change in Satan's relationship to the world.

Before Christ went to the cross, Jesus as eternal God was a preacher of the Gospel (Luke 4:18, 43-44). He was the perfect Preacher; He preached for over three years and yet there was only a handful of believers when He returned to heaven. Then at Pentecost something wonderful happened: Peter preached one sermon and 3,000 from eighteen nations were saved. As a result of the cross, there was a fantastic change in Satan's relationship to the world. God's plan was to save people from every nation, and Satan was bound to the degree that he could do nothing to frustrate the plan.

Satan Is Bound but He Still Rules the Unsaved

The binding of Satan was not total. He continues to rule the hearts of unsaved men. For example, in Ephesians Chapter 2 God discusses salvation in the New Testament after Satan had been bound. He discusses those who have been saved, and indicates that before they were saved they were enslaved to Satan. Ephesians 2:2:

> Wherein in time past ye walked according to the course of this world, according to the prince of the power of the air, the spirit that now worketh in the children of disobedience.

To walk under Satan's rule is to walk, "according to the prince of the power of the air." He continues to go about tempting believers. In Ephesians 6:11 God declares, "Put on the whole armour of God, that ye may be able to stand against the wiles of the devil," that is, so that Satan, the devil, cannot overcome you. "For we wrestle not against flesh and blood [that is, against human beings], but against principalities, against powers, against the rulers of the darkness of this world, against spiritual wickedness in high places" (verse 12).

Satan is referred to as the ruler of the darkness of this world. He is spoken of as the one who engages in spiritual wickedness in high places. In other words, he is still able to deceive. He is still able to assault the believers. I Peter 5:8 says that Satan goes about as a roaring lion seeking whom he might devour. Satan is present in this world, and his deception is terrible; it is magnificent at the same time because it is total deception. II Corinthians 11 says that he comes as an angel of light and that his ministers come as ministers of righteousness. This condition applies throughout the New Testament period.

> *Satan's rule is not so complete that he can frustrate God's plan to evangelize the world. When God intends to save someone, that person will be saved.*

Satan's rule is not so complete that he can frustrate God's plan to evangelize the world. When God intends to save someone, that person will be saved. Once we are saved, we are taken out of the dominion of darkness and translated into the Kingdom of His dear Son (Colossians 1:13). This is guaranteed for every believer.

Satan could NEVER stop God.

Satan to be Used of God to Bring Wrath on the Church

There will be another change in Satan's relationship to the church and to the world. God plans to use Satan as a means to bring His wrath on the church - the corporate, institutional body - when it becomes increasingly apostate before Judgment Day, which is the end of the world. That is, God will use Satan to bring the unfolding of God's salvation plan to an end.

For example, in Matthew 24:15-16 God warns:

> When ye, therefore, shall see the abomination of desolation, spoken of by Daniel the prophet, stand in the holy place, (whoso readeth, let him understand:) Then let them which be in Judaea flee into the mountains.

God is anticipating a time when the institutional church, called the "holy place" in this context, will be overrun by the abomination of desolation. God speaks of this in Matthew 24:24:

> For there shall arise false Christs, and false prophets, and shall shew great signs and wonders; insomuch that, if it were possible, they shall deceive the very elect.

He speaks of this dreadful change in the church in II Thessalonians 2:3 "that man of sin" (another name for Satan, Isaiah 14:16) will take his seat in the temple and be worshipped as God. These things will happen. After the institutional body has been used by God in His salvation program, then the church will become increasingly apostate and God will bring judgment on the church. This will be examined in great detail. For now: the Bible teaches that a time will come when God will remove the strictures on Satan so that increasingly the unsaved will be in bondage to sin as never before in history.

We have looked at Satan's relationship to the body of believers from the time of Adam and Eve until just before the beginning of the final tribulation period. From the fall of Adam and Eve until the time of the cross, Satan's rule over mankind was so complete that at any one time only a small trickle of believers came into the eternal body of Christ.

True believers cannot lose their salvation.
They will never fall away.

True believers cannot lose their salvation. They will never fall away; they have been given eternal life. Nothing can snatch them out of the hand of Christ.

The external, corporate body called the congregation or denomination is another matter. Does the Bible say anything about God's expectation concerning its faithfulness? Is the future conduct of the corporate body totally unknown? Is it true that God knows the end from the beginning and, therefore, knows precisely what the church will do, including during the end time? If God knows the future, does He in any way disclose in the Bible what the future will be? Does He declare in the Bible His expectation concerning the future faithfulness or faithlessness of the church? These questions will be examined as we continue our study.

God's expectation for the corporate body is seen as it existed in the Old Testament. The nation of Israel was the external representation of the Kingdom of God in the Old Testament era. It also served as a type or figure of the New Testament church; therefore, studying God's expectation for the end of Israel teaches something about God's expectation for the New Testament church.

God's Expectation Concerning National Israel's Apostasy

The nation of Israel began with Abraham and Isaac and Jacob. Abraham was a man who dearly loved the Lord. Isaac was a man who loved the Lord. One would think, therefore, that the nation of Israel was a people for whom God had high aspirations and ideals, and God could expect the utmost faithfulness.

God called them, as His own people, out of the land of Egypt; He delivered them with a mighty hand from the Egyptians and slew all the Egyptians' firstborn. He cared for them in the wilderness with miraculous water that came out of the rock and miraculous manna from heaven. He was in their presence in the pillar of fire by night and in the cloud by day. He was with them in miraculous ways when He parted the waters of the Red Sea, and the water stood as a wall on either side, and they passed through on dry ground. God did the same thing when they crossed the Jordan River.

> *In spite of these marvelous accomplishments, God's expectation of the faithfulness of national Israel was not good.*

In spite of these marvelous accomplishments, God's expectation of the faithfulness of national Israel was not good. God declares the future infidelity of Israel in the words of Deuteronomy 31:16. The context is that God is speaking to Moses just before his death:

> And the LORD said unto Moses, Behold, thou shalt sleep with thy fathers; and this people will rise up and go a whoring after the gods of the strangers of the land, whither they go to be among them, and will forsake me, and break my covenant which I have made with them.

What a dreadful expectation! God is speaking of the nation of Israel. These are not my words. They are God's words.

God says in verse 20:

> For when I shall have brought them into the land which I sware unto their fathers, that floweth with milk and honey; and they shall have eaten and filled themselves, and waxen fat; then will they turn unto other gods, and serve them, and provoke me, and break my covenant.

This is a terrible expectation for the nation of Israel!

In verse 27 of Deuteronomy 31 (please read the whole chapter to get the full flavor of what the Bible is teaching), Moses addresses Israel:

> For I know thy rebellion, and thy stiff neck: behold, while I am yet alive with you this day, ye have been rebellious against the LORD; and how much more after my death?

Then he declares unto them (verses 28-29):
> Gather unto me all the elders of your tribes, and your officers, that I may speak these words in their ears, and call heaven and earth to record against them. For I know that after my death ye will utterly corrupt yourselves, and turn aside from the way which I have commanded you; and evil will befall you in the latter days; because ye will do evil in the sight of the LORD, to provoke him to anger through the work of your hands.

Ugly, is it not? - yet these are the disclosures God makes in the Bible of His expectations for ancient Israel.

He had done many great and wonderful things to bring Israel into existence, but the people were in constant rebellion against God. They went their own way, and God expected this.

The Bible's Expectation for the New Testament Church
What is God's expectation for the New Testament church and for New Testament congregations? Does He expect that they, too, will fall away, that they, too, are going to follow in the shoes of national Israel?

In the New Testament church there will always be some unfaithfulness.

The Bible does not teach that the New Testament church will continuously rebel against God as ancient Israel did throughout most of its history. The Bible does teach that in the New Testament church there will always be some unfaithfulness. This is seen in many ways; for example, in Jude 17-19 God declares:

> But, beloved, remember ye the words which were spoken before of the apostles of our Lord Jesus Christ; How that they told you there should be mockers in the last time, who should walk after their own ungodly lusts. These be they who separate themselves, sensual, having not the Spirit.

The context indicates that He is speaking of those within the congregation. The phrases, "last days," "the latter days" and "the last time" as used in the Bible refer to the whole New Testament period, which ends at Judgment Day. God here indicates that He expects mockers within the congregation during the last time.

II Peter Chapter 3, verse 3, says: "Knowing this first, that there shall come in the last days scoffers, walking after their own lusts."

This prophecy could be addressed to those outside the congregation. There are scoffers out there, but is it possible within the congregation? The first three verses of II Peter Chapter 2 emphasize the possibility. There God declares:

But there were false prophets also among the people, even as there shall be false teachers among you, who privily shall bring in damnable heresies, even denying the Lord that bought them, and bring upon themselves swift destruction. And many shall follow their pernicious ways; by reason of whom the way of truth shall be evil spoken of. And through covetousness shall they with feigned words make merchandise of you: whose judgment now of a long time lingereth not, and their damnation slumbereth not.

This is a statement of God concerning New Testament congregations. It speaks the same way as does II Peter 3:3. One may be appalled at these words, but they are the words that God gave to us. They are not isolated statements found in only one or two places; God is emphasizing that we can expect unbelief to arise in New Testament congregations. There are numerous other statements similar to those that have been read.

II Timothy Chapter 4 verses 3 and 4:

For the time will come when they will not endure sound doctrine; but after their own lusts shall they heap to themselves teachers, having itching ears; And they shall turn away their ears from the truth, and shall be turned unto fables.

I Timothy Chapter 4 verses 1 and 2:

Now the Spirit speaketh expressly, that in the latter times some shall depart from the faith, giving heed to seducing spirits, and doctrines of devils; Speaking lies in hypocrisy; having their conscience seared with a hot iron.

God says this about New Testament congregations. It is similar, is it not, to what was read in Deuteronomy 31?

This is a dreadful situation! Christ is talking about the church, the institutional body: the First Baptist Church of your city, or the First Methodist Church, or the First Presbyterian, or the Third Christian Church, or whatever the name may be. The potential exists within every congregation; it is God's expectation. He expects this to happen. God warns about it, but He expects it to happen. He does not say that it might happen; He says that it will happen.

This is not surprising in view of what God says of the seven churches in Revelation 2 and 3. These seven churches are in the latter days. They have members who are compared to Jezebel in the Old Testament; they are grievous, adulterous members. Some people in these congregations are like Balaam, the wicked soothsayer who wanted to curse Israel. Within these seven congregations are those who are called the synagogue of Satan. This language depicts a terrible development!

> *The expectation of unbelief, unfaithfulness, and spiritual harlotry in the New Testament church is declared in the Scriptures.*

The expectation of unbelief, unfaithfulness, and spiritual harlotry in the New Testament church is declared in the Scriptures. It is a gigantic warning. No congregation can pull its holy rags around itself and say, "We are such a wonderful congregation. That could not happen to us. We study the Bible so faithfully. We have such a marvelous set of doctrines; we have such a tremendous confession; we have such a faithful seminary." Regardless of what they rest their laurels on, they are not speaking correctly if they say, "this cannot happen in our denomination, in our congregation." These statements are addressed to every congregation, and God says that they will occur.

They must occur because eventually history must come to an end. Given the Biblical principle that the time line of history is the unfolding of God's salvation plan, there must come a time when that plan has been completed. When that plan has been completed, that is, when everyone who is to be saved has become saved, then history will have come to its end. However, at that time simultaneous with the end of time, the church will have become apostate.

Because the church has been used of God throughout the New Testament era to reveal God's salvation plan to the world, it is shocking to the highest degree that it will finally have served its purpose and will come to an end as an instrument of God to evangelize the world. That is one reason why the Bible speaks so extensively and intensively of the final tribulation period and the rapture of believers, which follows immediately after the final tribulation. These events are the end of the unfolding of God's salvation plan and therefore are also the end of history.

How Can a Church Become Apostate?

If the elders and the pastor have carefully introduced and brought into a congregation only those who are saved, how can that church become apostate?

Pastors, elders, and deacons cannot know the hearts of those who become members. They may interrogate a person who wants to become a member, and investigate as best they can whether this person is truly a child of God. Based on the confession they hear and what they see in the person's life, they may decide, "This person is indeed a child of God. He should be taken into full communicant membership with the congregation." This is proper; it is expected of the rulers of the congregation.

If they bring into the congregation someone who is unsaved, someone who gave the appearance of being saved and yet was not, these unsaved members of the congregation will eventually depart from the truth. They do not understand the truth. They do not know what salvation is. They may have an intellectual idea of what it is. They may know some verses from the Bible, but in actuality, they have no idea what it is. God the Holy Spirit has not opened their spiritual eyes.

> *They will begin to lead the congregation into spiritual adultery.*

They may become increasingly dominant in the congregation. This may be because they speak well, or because of their warm personalities, or winning smiles, or because more and more of them come into the congregation. They may be rulers in the congregation: the pastor or elders. They will begin to lead the congregation into spiritual adultery. This has happened in congregation after congregation.

The measure of a congregation's faithfulness to the Word of God depends upon the percentage of the congregation that is born from above. God has faithfully built His church - His congregation, His institutional body - and it consists of congregations in cities and nations around the world. Because it is God's expectation that there will be spiritual adultery, churches occasionally lose their place with God. They no longer have a candlestick in God's presence (God warns of this in Revelation Chapter 2). Consequently, they are no longer a congregation of the Lord Jesus Christ. They may still speak about a relationship with Christ, but they have no relationship with Him.

> *The potential exists for any congregation to go in the direction of apostasy.*

Therefore, the potential exists for any congregation to go in the direction of apostasy. Every congregation can become spiritually adulterous and come under the judgment of God. These Biblical statements are addressed to every congregation because the potential for apostasy exists in every congregation.

Even more ominously, the Bible indicates that as the end of time approaches, spiritual apostasy will envelop churches all over the world. In Matthew 24:15-16 God declares:

> When ye therefore shall see the abomination of desolation, spoken of by Daniel the prophet, stand in the holy place, (whoso readeth, let him understand:) Then let them which be in Judaea flee into the mountains.

This statement is further developed in verse 24:

> For there shall arise false Christs, and false prophets, and shall shew great signs and wonders; insomuch that, if it were possible, they shall deceive the very elect.

The elect are the true believers. They are found ordinarily in congregations that are reasonably true to the Word of God. In this solemn verse, God warns that false prophets will teach and preach in churches. They will come with a gospel that is so close to the true Gospel that believers would be deceived - if that were possible. False prophets use Biblical phrases that true believers know. They speak of salvation, heaven, hell, the Holy Spirit, being born again, sin, etc. They declare some doctrines that are Biblical. If God did not teach true believers they could be easily deceived into following false teachers.

Later it will be shown: 1) that God guarantees that true believers cannot be deceived by false prophets, and 2) how to recognize false prophets. Matthew 24:24 teaches that false prophets will come with signs and wonders; this truth will be developed in detail.

In II Thessalonians 2:1-4 God restates the expectation for the church near the end of time:

> Now we beseech you, brethren, by the coming of our Lord Jesus Christ, and by our gathering together unto him. That ye be not soon shaken in mind, or be troubled, neither by spirit, nor by word, nor by letter as from us, as that the day of Christ is at hand. Let no man deceive you by any means: for that day shall not come, except there come a falling away first, and that man of sin be revealed, the son of perdition; Who opposeth and exalteth himself above all that is called God, or that is worshipped; so that he as God sitteth in the temple of God, shewing himself that he is God.

These verses teach the same truth that was learned from Matthew 24:15-24. Whereas Matthew 24:24 spoke of emissaries of Satan called false christs or false prophets, II Thessalonians 2 speaks of Satan himself (called "man of sin") coming to rule (taking his seat) in the congregations (the temple of God). He accomplishes this through preachers and rulers in the congregation who no longer follow the true Gospel. These men and women are deceived by Satan, but they are convinced that they are faithfully serving Christ.

These dreadful things will happen. There is no suggestion that "maybe" or "possibly" this falling away will occur. God declares that it will happen, and Satan will rule in the church.

Both in the case of ancient Israel and New Testament congregations, God's expectation is they will eventually become apostate.

It must be concluded, therefore, that both in the case of ancient Israel and New Testament congregations, God's expectation is they will eventually become apostate.

God Warned Ancient Israel

Let us look in the Old Testament to examine the question of God's warnings concerning Old Testament Israel. We saw in Deuteronomy 31 God's expectation concerning what would happen to them. God's warning to them may be read in many passages. Two have been selected because they are representative of Old Testament warnings.

In Deuteronomy Chapter 8 verses 19 and 20 God declared to the congregation that was ancient Israel:

And it shall be, if thou do at all forget the LORD thy God, and walk after other gods, and serve them, and worship them, I testify against you this day that ye shall surely perish. As the nations which the LORD destroyeth before your face, so shall ye perish; because ye would not be obedient unto the voice of the LORD your God.

This is the warning. God warned them that if they were unfaithful, they would perish. Deuteronomy 31 states God's expectation that they would become spiritually adulterous. In Deuteronomy 8, God says that if they did become spiritually adulterous, they would perish. God declared with startling clarity what was to happen. Indeed, the Bible declares how God destroyed them.

In Deuteronomy 28 God gives a long warning. In the first fourteen verses He has good things to say to the congregation of ancient national Israel.

He enunciates blessing after blessing that can come to Israel as a nation. Beautiful statements are made, like verses 9-11:

The LORD shall establish thee an holy people unto himself, as he hath sworn unto thee, if thou shalt keep the commandments of the LORD thy God, and walk in his ways. And all the people of the earth shall see that thou art called by the name of the LORD; and they shall be afraid of thee. And the LORD shall make thee plenteous in goods, in the fruit of thy body, and in the fruit of thy cattle, and in the fruit of thy ground, in the land which the LORD sware unto thy fathers to give thee.

God emphasized that His blessings would be upon ancient Israel if they remained faithful. If they were unfaithful, another set of conditions applied. In Deuteronomy 28:15-17 God declares:

> But it shall come to pass, if thou wilt not hearken unto the voice of the LORD thy God, to observe to do all his commandments and his statutes which I command thee this day; that all these curses shall come upon thee, and overtake thee: Cursed shalt thou be in the city, and cursed shalt thou be in the field. Cursed shall be thy basket and thy store.

> *Read Deuteronomy 28:15-68. Read and weep. Read and be warned.*

Please read Deuteronomy 28, verses 15 through 68. Read and weep. Read and be warned. The warning goes on and on. Dreadful things were to happen to the congregation of Israel if they were unfaithful.

They did not heed the warning and God's expectation was realized; they became apostate and consequently perished. The New Testament congregation has also been warned.

God Warns New Testament Congregations

When God speaks of the seven churches in Revelation 2 and 3, He says of the church of the Laodiceans, "I will spue thee out" (Revelation 3:16), which means: I will vomit you out. This is ugly language. He says of another of the seven congregations, if they are unfaithful, "I . . . will remove thy candlestick" (Revelation 2:5). Each congregation was represented in heaven by a candlestick. To have their candlestick removed means they have ceased to be a congregation of the Lord Jesus Christ. In these statements, God warns our congregations of what will happen to them if they are unfaithful.

In John 15:1-5 the Lord declares that Christ is the vine and we are the branches. He says in verse 2, "Every branch . . . that beareth not fruit He taketh away." He could be speaking of an individual who has joined the congregation and is not a true believer, but the principle applies to the entire congregation.

God's warning to the congregation that dreadful things will happen to the unfaithful church is seen in Revelation 6 when the seals are opened. The first horseman goes forth; this is a statement of the victorious nature of the cross. The second horseman goes forth; God calls our attention to Satan's opposition to the Gospel being spread into all the world.

The third seal is opened, and the third horseman appears. In Revelation 6:5-6 God declares:

> And when he had opened the third seal, I heard the third beast say, Come and see. And I beheld, and lo a black horse; and he that sat on him had a pair of balances in his hand. And I heard a voice in the midst of the four beasts say, A measure of wheat for a penny, and three measures of barley for a penny; and see thou hurt not the oil and the wine.

Exercise the Biblical principle of interpreting the Bible with the Bible, and it is discovered that the truth in these verses reiterates God's warnings to ancient Israel. For example in Ezekiel 5:11-16:

> Wherefore, as I live, saith the Lord GOD; Surely, because thou hast defiled my sanctuary with all thy detestable things, and with all thine abominations, therefore will I also diminish thee; neither shall mine eye spare, neither will I have any pity. A third part of thee shall die with the pestilence, and with famine shall they be consumed in the midst of thee: and a third part shall fall by the sword round about thee; and I will scatter a third part into all the winds, and I will draw out a sword after them. Thus shall mine anger be accomplished, and I will cause my fury to rest upon them, and I will be comforted: and they shall know that I the LORD have spoken it in my zeal, when I have accomplished my fury in them.

> Moreover I will make thee waste, and a reproach among the nations that are round about thee, in the sight of all that pass by. So it shall be a reproach and a taunt, an instruction and an astonishment unto the nations that are round about thee, when I shall execute judgments in thee in anger and in fury and in furious rebukes. I the LORD have spoken it. When I shall send

upon them the evil arrows of famine, which shall be for their destruction, and which I will send to destroy you: and I will increase the famine upon you, and will break your staff of bread.

Breaking the staff of bread signifies that God is hiding the truth of the Gospel. The bread represents the Word of God. The ominous implication of breaking the staff of bread is that God will take away the truth, the Word of God. The breaking of the staff of physical bread signifies famine, and the breaking of the staff of the Word of God signifies spiritual famine. Physical famine results in death and destruction, and spiritual famine results in spiritual death and destruction. Thus, this passage warns that God will destroy the spiritually unfaithful.

Revelation 6:6 declares: "hurt not the oil and the wine." The oil and the wine represent true believers within the congregation, those who cannot come under God's judgment. The oil signifies the Holy Spirit; He indwells the true believers. The wine signifies the blood of Christ, with which all believers identify. Their sins are covered by Christ. Therefore, they cannot suffer any further penalty for their sins.

> *God can cut off the congregation as a corporate body even though it tries to identify with the Kingdom of God.*

God can cut off the congregation as a corporate body even though it tries to identify with the Kingdom of God. The spiritually unfaithful church or denomination will come under God's wrath. The same warning is found in Leviticus 26:21-26 where God declares:

And if ye walk contrary unto me, and will not hearken unto me; I will bring seven times more plagues upon you according to your sins. I will also send wild beasts among you, which shall rob you of your children, and destroy your cattle, and make you few in number; and your high ways shall be desolate. And if ye will not be reformed by me by these things, but will walk contrary unto me; Then will I also walk contrary unto you, and will punish you yet seven times for your sins. And I will bring a sword upon you, that shall avenge the quarrel of my covenant:

and when ye are gathered together within your cities, I will send the pestilence among you; and ye shall be delivered into the hand of the enemy.

And when I have broken the staff of your bread, ten women shall bake your bread in one oven, and they shall deliver you your bread again by weight: and ye shall eat, and not be satisfied.

"They shall deliver you your bread again by weight," is the warning restated in Revelation 6:5-6 when the rider of the third horse carries a balance in his hand. It is a solemn warning to the congregations to remain faithful to the truth or come under the wrath of God.

This warning is reinforced and underscored when the fourth seal is opened and the fourth horseman appears, in Revelation 6:8:

And I looked, and behold a pale horse; and his name that sat on him was Death, and Hell followed with him. And power was given unto them over the fourth part of the earth, to kill with sword, and with hunger, and with death, and with the beasts of the earth.

God is speaking more plainly of death, hell, and destruction. A further development of this verse is in Ezekiel 14:13:

Son of man, when the land sinneth against me by trespassing grievously, then will I stretch out mine hand upon it, and will break the staff of the bread thereof, and will send famine upon it, and will cut off man and beast from it.

Verses 19-21:

Or if I send a pestilence into that land, and pour out my fury upon it in blood, to cut off from it man and beast; Though Noah, Daniel, and Job, were in it, as I live, saith the Lord GOD, they shall deliver neither son nor daughter; they shall but deliver their own souls by their righteousness. For thus saith the Lord GOD; How much more when I send my four sore judgments upon Jerusalem, the sword, and the famine, and the noisome beast, and the pestilence, to cut off from it man and beast?

The four judgments of verse 21, the sword, the famine, the beasts, and the pestilence, are parallel to the judgments in connection with the rider of the fourth horse in Revelation 6. The fourth rider was given power to kill with the sword, with hunger, with death, and with the beasts. Revelation 6, therefore, restates the Ezekiel 14 warning that His destruction comes because of the apostasy of the congregation. In these passages, God warns of the awful certainty that His judgment is coming upon the congregations that are not faithful to the truth.

> *The Bible teaches that God had terrible warnings for the Old Testament church, and He also has terrible warnings for the New Testament church.*

Dearly beloved, the Bible clearly teaches that God had terrible warnings for the Old Testament church, and He also has terrible warnings for the New Testament church. In Deuteronomy 31 God talks about the fact that Israel would become apostate. He warns in verse 29, "ye will utterly corrupt yourselves, and turn aside from the way which I have commanded you; and evil will befall you in the latter days." "Latter days" in the Bible refers to the time of the New Testament church. Therefore, Deuteronomy 31:29 applies as much to the New Testament congregation as it did to the Old Testament congregation.

Compare the warnings of Leviticus 26, Ezekiel 5, and Ezekiel 14 with the language of Revelation 6, and it is obvious that the Old Testament warnings apply equally to ancient national Israel and to the New Testament congregations.

SUMMARY

In this chapter, we have learned that the Bible speaks of a time of great tribulation that will come upon the world just prior to its end. The chief focus of the tribulation will be a judgment upon the churches and congregations because they have fallen away from the truth.

This falling away coincides with God's timetable of history. When the unfolding of God's salvation plan has come to an end, history will also be at an end. Since the New Testament churches are the means by which God unfolds His salvation plan, the church age will end at the same time the world ends.

We have examined the development of the church from the beginning of time. We have learned that before the first coming of Christ, national Israel was the church, and that era ended when Christ went to the cross. Following this, the church expanded into congregations and denominations all over the world.

We have discovered that throughout history those individuals who became saved were found within the external corporate church. These individuals are in the eternal church because every believer has been given eternal life and will never come under the wrath of God. The big task of the church is to send the Gospel into all the world; through the Gospel, God saves those who are to be saved.

We have learned that the chief enemy of God is Satan. Satan was an angel who rebelled against God, and who now rules over the unsaved. During the Old Testament era, very few became saved because Satan ruled over mankind with great strength. However, Christ went to the cross and conquered Satan. Christ spiritually bound Satan so that throughout the New Testament era many people from every nation are to be saved.

God prophesied long before it happened that the Old Testament church, national Israel, would eventually fall away from God. Likewise, the Bible predicts that the time will come when the New Testament churches will fall away and rebel against God's authority. God predicted this apostasy and also warned about the resultant punishment.

In the next chapter, the sins which led to the destruction of the Old Testament congregation will be studied and compared with the sins of the New Testament congregations. It will be seen how history repeats itself.

Chapter 4
God Begins to Judge the Church

To understand the final tribulation period, we have sought an objective Biblical perspective of God's plan of salvation as it unfolded throughout the history of ancient national Israel and continues to unfold in the New Testament churches. This perspective is extremely important if we are to understand the final tribulation period, because the final tribulation, which comes at the end of time, is intimately associated with the churches that are in existence at that time. It is the time when God brings to an end the unfolding of His salvation plan. It, therefore, is the time when history will come to its close.

> *It is the time when God brings to an end the*
> ***unfolding*** *of His salvation plan . . . history will*
> *come to its close.*

God formed the New Testament congregations. They were brought into existence all over the world. But we have learned that even as God formed the New Testament congregations, He expected them to become adulterous. The seeds of spiritual adultery were in these congregations, as the same seeds were in the congregation of national Israel. God expected them to go contrary to His will, and they did; that expectation is the same for the New Testament churches. According to the Bible this falling away from the truth is to especially characterize the congregations that are in existence right near the end of time.

God warned the Old Testament congregation, the nation of Israel, and He also warns the New Testament congregations of what will happen if and when the church becomes unfaithful. God declares He will remove His candlestick. He will vomit that church out. He will bring terrible things against it and destroy it, as He brought terrible things against the Old Testament congregation, national Israel.

How these judgments against the New Testament churches are to be carried out, and what is to happen to these churches will be studied as we develop a greater understanding of the final tribulation period.

To look at the churches and congregations in their historical perspective is not too difficult. There have been traumatic times when Christians were persecuted and churches were assaulted by heresy from within. In spite of this, the movement of the church to evangelize the world has persistently continued. The rider on the white horse, to use the analogy of Revelation 6, has continued to go forth conquering and to conquer.

Biblical Basis that God Will Judge the Church
        The conclusion that the time has descended upon us when the church is increasingly ceasing to function as the instrument of God to evangelize the world and is to be judged requires a basis in Biblical authority.
        Jesus promised He would build His church, and the gates of hell would not prevail against it (Matthew 16:18). Satan was defeated at the cross. He could not frustrate God's plan to evangelize the world; therefore, how could anyone dare suggest anything other than a glorious future for the church - a future that will continue till the last day of this world's existence?
        As we have learned, some verses clearly teach that God expects the church to become adulterous. It may be argued: That does not imply that the end of the church age is upon us; or, that does not prove that God will reject His corporate body, the external church, which Jesus also went to the cross to establish; it's true, some denominations are not as faithful to the Bible as they should be, but this has been the situation throughout the history of the church.
        In view of these arguments, great care must be exercised before drawing conclusions that there will be an end of the church age, that there will come a time when, as a judgment of God, virtually all churches will be increasingly overrun with false gospels so that fewer and fewer are becoming saved. This is precisely why God has given us the Bible. Under no circumstances do we trust our sin-tainted minds. Personal speculations and philosophies have no value. The Bible is God's Book. It is perfect in its presentation of truth. Things written in the Bible may be disliked but obedience to God's Word is required.
        Biblical passages that speak of God's past or future judgments are not exciting to read. It is a happier situation to focus one's eyes and mind on Biblical declarations of God's love and grace and be content with the fact that whatever God's judgments are, they will be tempered

by God's love, compassion, patience, and forgiveness. To some people, this is a happier and more acceptable part of the Gospel.

> *We cannot pick and choose what we like to study and forget the rest of the Bible.*
> *If the Bible brings us to a conclusion that is unacceptable because it is negative or ominous, . . . we must ask God for His mercy and grace to accept it and react obediently.*

All of the Bible is God's Word. We cannot pick and choose what we like to study and forget the rest of the Bible. We cannot stick our heads in the sand like the proverbial ostrich and hope that the danger of God's judgments will go away. All Scripture is given by inspiration of God and is profitable for doctrine, for reproof, for correction, and for training in righteousness (II Timothy 3:16). We must be ready, therefore, to carefully, prayerfully, and obediently examine and study everything in the Bible. If the Bible brings us to a conclusion that is unacceptable because it is negative, ominous, or because it is something we have never before been taught, we must ask God for His mercy and grace to accept it and react obediently.

Is it right to look at the experiences of ancient Israel, Babylon, and Egypt as guidelines for the future of the church? Repeated references to these ancient nations have been made in this study in an attempt to understand the future of the New Testament churches.

Biblical references to these nations cannot be accidental or incidental. God says that all Scripture is inspired by God. This principle cannot be set aside. God wrote extensively of these ancient nations to instruct us in the will of God. The Bible also answers the question of how Biblical information about these nations can instruct us today.

God's Judgments on Old Testament Nations Teach Us What to Expect

God recorded the experiences of Old Testament nations to serve as warnings to us today. In I Corinthians 10:1-11 God speaks of ancient Israel when they sojourned in the wilderness after they came out of Egypt to go to the land of Canaan. They were a people especially blessed by God as indicated by the language of I Corinthians 10:1-4:

Moreover, brethren, I would not that ye should be ignorant, how that all our fathers were under the cloud, and all passed through the sea; And were all baptized unto Moses in the cloud and in the sea; And did all eat the same spiritual meat; And did all drink the same spiritual drink: for they drank of that spiritual Rock that followed them: and that Rock was Christ.

The blessings did not protect them from God's judgment, for the next verse says, "But with many of them God was not well pleased: for they were overthrown in the wilderness."

Verse 6 explains why God instructs us in His dealings with ancient Israel. There we read, "Now these things were our examples, to the intent we should not lust after evil things, as they also lusted."

God emphasizes the point of verse 6 with specific examples of sins that ancient Israel committed, sins which brought God's judgments upon them. Verses 7-10 admonish us:

Neither be ye idolaters, as were some of them: as it is written, The people sat down to eat and drink, and rose up to play. Neither let us commit fornication, as some of them committed, and fell in one day three and twenty thousand. Neither let us tempt Christ, as some of them also tempted, and were destroyed of serpents. Neither murmur ye, as some of them also murmured, and were destroyed of the destroyer.

The historical account of these sins and God's judgments upon Israel is in Numbers 16:41-50, Numbers 21:5-9, and Numbers 25:1-9. To clarify God's purpose in writing about these events, He says in verse 11 of I Corinthians 10:

Now all these things happened unto them for ensamples: and they are written for our admonition, upon whom the ends of the world are come.

God declares that His dealings with ancient national Israel anticipate how He will deal with the New Testament church.

Jude 5 also warns New Testament congregations:

I will therefore put you in remembrance, though ye once knew this, how that the Lord, having saved the people out of the land of Egypt, afterward destroyed them that believed not.

God again instructs us to look into the Old Testament to learn from His dealings with those ancient peoples.

Jesus, who is eternal God, is the
same yesterday, today, and forever.

The import of Jude 5 is ominous. In that single sentence God informs us that He destroyed His own people. God is not speaking of a wicked, heathen nation like Babylon, Moab, or Egypt. He is speaking of the nation that is the apple of God's eye, the nation that God had set apart for Himself. This warning should cause any congregation to tremble. God does not speak any more lovingly of New Testament congregations than He does of ancient Israel. Jesus, who is eternal God, is the same yesterday, today, and forever. He reacted to the sin of His beloved ancient Israel by destroying them, and He will react the same way to sin in New Testament congregations.

Further Biblical evidence that New Testament congregations are warned by God's actions in regard to His ancient people is in Hebrews 3:8-9:

> Harden not your hearts, as in the provocation, in the day of temptation in the wilderness: When your fathers tempted me, proved me, and saw my works forty years.

He warns us not to harden our hearts like they did - like the people of ancient Israel did when they were in the wilderness. He says in verses 15-17:

> ... To day if ye will hear his voice, harden not your hearts, as in the provocation. For some, when they had heard, did provoke: howbeit not all that came out of Egypt by Moses. But with whom was he grieved forty years? was it not with them that had sinned, whose carcases fell in the wilderness?

God is again directing our attention to what happened to ancient Israel. This must be understood if we are is to understand what to expect for the New Testament congregations.

We have learned that there was an expectation in the Bible of shattering unfaithfulness in the Old Testament congregation, national Israel; and there is an expectation that New Testament congregations will be shattered. Therefore, it must be concluded that there is to be judgment on New Testament congregations as judgment came upon the Old Testament congregation.

Old Testament Israel: Not a Perfect Picture of the New Testament Church

The concept of national Israel as a picture of the New Testament church is limited. It is not a perfect picture. The reason is that the era of national Israel was followed by the era of the New Testament church, while the era of the New Testament church - congregations from Pentecost to the present - will be followed by the end of the world and Judgment Day.

This sequence makes a difference. The difference is that grace would shine through the worst condemnations of the national Israel of the Old Testament. One of many Old Testament examples is Ezekiel 20. In this chapter God speaks of His wrath which is to come upon ancient Israel; Israel is to be destroyed by the Babylonians. However, in verses 41-44a He says:

> I will accept you with your sweet savour, when I bring you out from the people, and gather you out of the countries wherein ye have been scattered; and I will be sanctified in you before the heathen. And ye shall know that I am the LORD, when I shall bring you into the land of Israel, into the country for the which I lifted up mine hand to give it to your fathers. And there shall ye remember your ways, and all your doings, wherein ye have been defiled; and ye shall loathe yourselves in your own sight for all your evils that ye have committed. And ye shall know that I am the LORD, when I have wrought with you for my name's sake.

God is emphasizing that grace will come. Beautiful things are going to happen to Israel in the future.

The fulfillment of these promises is the Lord Jesus Christ, who is of national Israel, of the tribe of Judah. He is the head of the new nation of Israel, the Israel of God, which is made up of congregations that come from every nation.

In Hosea Chapter 1 God says ugly things to national Israel. Israel is being taken captive by the Assyrians, and God says in verse 2 of Chapter 2, "She is not my wife, neither am I her husband; let her therefore put away her whoredoms out of her sight, and her adulteries from between her breasts." God goes on to say many ominous things because His wrath is upon national Israel.

However, Chapter 2 verses 14-19 have some of the most loving and most beautiful language of the Bible. God says:

Therefore, behold, I will allure her, and bring her into the wilderness, and speak comfortably unto her. And I will give her her vineyards from thence, and the valley of Achor for a door of hope; and she shall sing there, as in the days of her youth, and as in the days when she came up out of the land of Egypt.

And it shall be at that day, saith the LORD, that thou shalt call me Ishi, and shalt call me no more Baali [Ishi means husband; Baali means lord]. For I will take away the names of Baalim out of her mouth, and they shall no more be remembered by their name.

And in that day will I make a covenant for them with the beasts of the field, and with the fowls of heaven, and with the creeping things of the ground: and I will break the bow and the sword and the battle out of the earth, and will make them to lie down safely. And I will betroth thee unto me for ever; yea, I will betroth thee unto me in righteousness, and in judgment, and in lovingkindness, and in mercies.

God has in view here the only bride that Christ is married to forever - the body of believers that has come into existence all through time. It is for the most part believers who have come into the congregations - into a saving relationship with Christ - during the New Testament period. This softens Old Testament statements about the wrath of God and the utter destruction of national Israel - Grace is going to shine through.

When (as the Bible warns) the final destruction of New Testament congregations, which corporately represent the Israel of God, comes, then there can be no future blessings on the congregations. Old Testament Israel had a promise of future blessing; in this respect, it is not a perfect type of the New Testament church.

There is, however, a parallel between a future blessing of Old Testament Israel and the New Testament church. When God's judgment is poured out on the congregations, true believers will have a beautiful future. They will receive their resurrected bodies; they will receive the new heavens and the new earth. This is somewhat of a parallel between the blossoming of the Gospel and the end of the era of ancient Israel.

God's Judgment on the New Testament Church Will Parallel His Judgment on the Old Testament Church
In God's judgments there is a closer parallel. God's judgments on ancient Israel because of their sins parallel the judgments that will fall on the end-time New Testament congregations because of apostasy.

> *God expected apostasy to cause the destruction of ancient Israel . . . God expects the New Testament churches to fall away.*

God expected apostasy to cause the destruction of ancient Israel. The Bible also indicates that God expects the New Testament churches to fall away and warns that they, too, will be destroyed.

Because of the parallelism, the nature of Israel's sins will be compared with the sins that plague the congregations of today. We will study in greater detail how God responded to Israel's sins, and thus understand what our congregations can expect.

Ancient Israel's Sins
A host of verses refer to Israel's sins, but just a few verses are needed to give an idea of what was going on. Equally explicit accounts of their sins are recorded in Deuteronomy, Isaiah, Ezekiel, Hosea, and other Old Testament passages and some New Testament passages. Jeremiah will be studied because Jeremiah was being written while the Babylonians were beginning to destroy Israel; it was the end of national Israel as a free and independent nation. It was a time of severe judgment on national Israel. This judgment typifies the judgment that is going to come against the congregations of the New Testament.

Jeremiah 5, verses 30 and 31:

A wonderful and horrible thing is committed in the land; The prophets prophesy falsely, and the priests bear rule by their means; and my people love to have it so: and what will ye do in the end thereof?

This is a terrible indictment of the spiritual rulers. The prophets and the priests were commissioned and mandated by God to bring the truth of God's Word to the congregation. They taught and preached in the name of Jehovah God; therefore, they should have been sure they were not bringing their own ideas or philosophies. They should have repeatedly checked their messages against the written Word that they had in their day.

> *They should have made sure they were not bringing their own ideas or philosophies.*

They did not check the Bible; they taught their own doctrines. They brought messages that suited their fancy and pleased the congregation. The phrase "my people love to have it so," indicts them for preaching lies and bearing false witness. They ruled according to their own pleasure rather than in accordance with the will of God.

"And what will ye do in the end thereof?" is a rhetorical question that indicates that the spiritual rulers and the congregation will come into judgment for their conduct. They will forever suffer in hell for their rebellion against God.

In Jeremiah 6:14-16 God takes the prophets to task over the Old Testament congregation. He warns:

They have healed also the hurt of the daughters of my people slightly, saying, Peace, peace: when there is no peace. Were they ashamed when they had committed abomination? nay, they were not at all ashamed, neither could they blush: therefore they shall fall among them that fall: at the time that I visit them they shall be cast down, saith the Lord. Thus saith the LORD, Stand ye in the ways, and see, and ask for the old paths, where is the good way, and walk therein, and ye shall find rest for your souls. But they said, We will not walk therein.

The indictment against national Israel is that the prophets were saying something like: "Everything is well. God is not going to bring judgment against national Israel. We are God's people. We are God's congregation. We are the chosen ones. We will never come under terrible judgment from God. Jeremiah, you speak falsely when you say that the Babylonians are going to destroy us. There is peace in our day."

Jeremiah 6 speaks about walking in the old ways or in the old paths. The old paths have to do with the Scriptures, which is where truth is found.

> *Ancient Israel was not satisfied with the Gospel that the prophets offered from the Scriptures.*

Ancient Israel was not satisfied with the Gospel that the prophets offered from the Scriptures. They wanted a more contemporary gospel. They wanted a gospel that dealt with the issues of the day and recognized that the Assyrians and Babylonians also had wonderful altars and prophets and worship services, and they wanted Israel to learn from them.

In Jeremiah 7:8 God accuses Israel: "Behold, ye trust in lying words, that cannot profit." Some Old Testament prophets did not speak what God had given them; some prophets spoke of ideas that came out of their own hearts. They said what they thought would please the congregation: They were lies because God had not said so.

Jeremiah 16, verses 10-11 say:

And it shall come to pass, when thou shalt shew this people all these words, and they shall say unto thee, Wherefore hath the LORD pronounced all this great evil against us? or what is our iniquity? or what is our sin that we have committed against the LORD our God? Then shalt thou say unto them, Because your fathers have forsaken me, saith the LORD, and have walked after other gods, and have served them, and have worshipped them, and have forsaken me, and have not kept my law.

> *The prophets began to speak from their own minds, and sin followed sin until ancient Israel worshipped other gods.*

When the prophets began to bring their lies, they began to neglect the truth that God had put in the old paths from the beginning, when He spoke through Moses and Abraham. The prophets began to speak from their own minds, and sin followed sin until ancient Israel worshipped other gods.

God speaks plainly about the sin of ancient Israel and the indictments He brought against them. History is repeating itself in that the same sins are in the congregations of our day.

The Bible discloses God's response to Israel's sin.

God Blinds Israel

The Bible reveals that a number of things happened to Israel because of their continuing rebellion. First, God began to blind them (Isaiah 6). This judgment was declared almost 800 years before the end of the era of the nation of Israel as the external representation of the Kingdom of God. Isaiah prophesied about 750 B.C. Already in Isaiah's day, Israel had gone deeply into sin.

Isaiah 6:10 tells of this indictment:
Make the heart of this people fat, and make their ears heavy, and shut their eyes; lest they see with their eyes, and hear with their ears, and understand with their heart, and convert, and be healed.

This is dreadful! God is speaking of His people Israel. They have rebelled against God; they have gone their own way. God gets involved and actually begins to blind them, which is what God calls for in Isaiah 6. Romans 11, verse 8 is a commentary on this:

(According as it is written, God hath given them the spirit of slumber, eyes that they should not see, and ears that they should not hear;) unto this day.

This indictment was brought against Israel because of their sins: God began to blind them. It was bad that they were already blinded in their sin and in the perverseness of their hearts. It was bad that they were blinded by Satan who rules over the hearts of unsaved men. When God began to deal with Israel, He declared that He would blind them. This is emphasized in Isaiah 29:10-12:

For the LORD hath poured out upon you the spirit of deep sleep, and hath closed your eyes: the prophets and your rulers, the seers hath he covered. And the vision of all is become unto you as the words of a book that is sealed, which men deliver to one that is learned, saying, Read this, I pray thee: and he saith, I cannot; for it is sealed: And the book is delivered to him that is not learned, saying, Read this, I pray thee: and he saith, I am not learned.

God says here that He blinds the rulers of the church when the church begins to rebel against Him. As the church becomes increasingly wicked and rewrites the rules to please men rather than to faithfully follow God's rules, God begins to blind the spiritual rulers and they can no longer see the truth.

God Removes the Truth

Another of God's actions in response to the sin of ancient Israel was that He removed the truth. He took the truth away from them. This is implied in that He blinded the rulers.

Almost 800 years before the end of the era of the nation of Israel, Isaiah Chapter 3 verses 1-5a were written:

For, behold, the Lord, the LORD of hosts, doth take away from Jerusalem and from Judah the stay and the staff, the whole stay of bread, and the whole stay of water. The mighty man, and the man of war, the judge, and the prophet, and the prudent, and the ancient, The captain of fifty, and the honourable man, and the counsellor, and the cunning artificer, and the eloquent orator. And I will give children to be their princes, and babes shall rule over them. And the people shall be oppressed, every one by another.

> *When God takes away the staff, the Gospel is no longer available . . . because God has blinded the prophets.*

God here is taking away the stay and the staff. The staff has to do with the bread of life - the Gospel. When God takes away the staff, the Gospel is no longer available. It is not available because God has blinded the prophets. They are no longer able to bring truth. This is the judgment that comes upon the church as it becomes contrary to the Word of God.

The breaking of the staff is seen also in Ezekiel 4 where God tells about His judgment on ancient Israel; it was to be destroyed by the Babylonians. God indicates in verse 17 of Ezekiel 4: "That they may want bread and water, and be astonied one with another, and consume away for their iniquity."

This verse was previously examined in view of the third horseman of Revelation 6. It relates to the fact that the Gospel was no longer available. God had removed the truth. This verse teaches the same sad truth that Isaiah 6 teaches.

God Rejects Israel

God blinded the people of Israel, removed the truth from them, and He rejects them. A number of verses speak of this, but one verse in particular is Hosea Chapter 4, verse 6:

> My people are destroyed for lack of knowledge: because thou hast rejected knowledge, I will also reject thee, that thou shalt be no priest to me: seeing thou hast forgotten the law of thy God, I will also forget thy children.

The people of God (the congregation of Israel) were married to God in the Old Testament, but they were not listening to the Word of God. They did not want to be obedient to the Word of God. They wanted what was in their own minds. They wanted their own kind of gospel.

To be rejected of God is terrible. The nation of Israel had been the apple of God's eye. God had carefully nurtured the congregation while He miraculously brought them out of bondage in Egypt, through the Red Sea, across the Jordan River, and delivered them into the land of Canaan. He defeated nations and conquered cities on their behalf. He gave them principles whereby they could know the way of God and know God. But they rebelled against Him; therefore, God blinded them. He took the truth away from them, and He rejected them. They are no longer His congregation.

Earlier in the study it was seen that this rejection is stated in the language, He divorced them. The divorce became final in 33 A.D. when Christ hung on the cross. God's reaction to sin in the congregations is dynamic.

God Destroys the Congregation

Another result of Israel's sin is that God brought judgments upon them. The judgments were of such nature that Israel was destroyed. The end result of a rebellious congregation is that God destroys it.

In the case of the nation of Israel the destruction came by wicked nations that were under the power of Satan. God warned Israel that if they disobeyed Him they would be destroyed by heathen nations. God warned the congregation of Israel before they came into the promised land, the land of Canaan, in Deuteronomy 28:47-48a:

> Because thou servedst not the LORD thy God with joyfulness, and with gladness of heart, for the abundance of all things; Therefore shalt thou serve thine enemies.

In language of today, God is effectively saying, "You are not content with the principles I have laid down for you: you want your own salvation program." God, therefore, declares in verse 49:

> The LORD shall bring a nation against thee from far, from the end of the earth, as swift as the eagle flieth; a nation whose tongue thou shalt not understand.

It was a nation whose tongue they did not understand that was to destroy them. The remaining verses of Deuteronomy 28 describe how that nation was to destroy Israel.

Isaiah 28 presents the same truth, where God speaks particularly about the end of the ten tribes of the northern kingdom, which were separated from Judah upon the death of Solomon. God declares in Isaiah 28:7 that He is going to destroy Israel because of their sins:

> But they also have erred through wine, and through strong drink are out of the way; the priest and the prophet have erred through strong drink, they are swallowed up of wine, they are out of the way through strong drink; they err in vision, they stumble in judgment.

God uses wine and strong drink in this context to speak of running adulterously after other gospels.

God uses wine and strong drink in this context to speak of running adulterously after other gospels. Earlier in Isaiah 28 He says, "Woe . . . to the drunkards of Ephraim" (verse 1). The prophets drunkenly run after gospels or religions of nations whose language they do not understand.

God declares in verse 11 of Isaiah 28, "For with stammering lips and another tongue will he speak to this people." He concludes in verse 13, "that they might go, and fall backward, and be broken, and snared, and taken." This echoes the warning of Deuteronomy 28 that God would bring judgment upon Israel by a wicked nation whose language they did not understand. As will be seen, Assyria was the wicked nation that destroyed the ten tribes of Israel and the capital in Samaria.

One hundred and twenty-three years later (587 B.C.), the nation of Judah, the part of Israel that had its capital in Jerusalem, came into judgment because of its sins. God says in Jeremiah 5:15-17a:

> Lo, I will bring a nation upon you from far, O house of Israel, saith the LORD; it is a mighty nation, it is an ancient nation, a nation whose language thou knowest not, neither understandest what they say. Their quiver is as an open sepulchre, they are all mighty men. And they shall eat up thine harvest, and thy bread.

Destruction again was upon Jerusalem and Judah by a nation whose language they did not understand. This is the language God used to declare He would destroy the congregation of Israel because of wickedness.

In the laboratory of God's Word, one can investigate what God says about the future of churches and congregations.

In the laboratory of God's Word, one can investigate what God says about the future of churches and congregations of today. In this investigation flashes of insight have indicated that there are ominous things on the horizon. All will not continue in a happy and wonderful way until Judgment Day.

Wonderfully, one can study the Word of God and know what is going to happen. There is no need to speculate and be left in doubt. Faithfully read the Bible with a view to being obedient to what is found there.

In summation: God dealt with ancient Israel, the congregation of the Old Testament (the whole nation was the congregation), when they sinned and rebelled against God. The end of ancient Israel provides insight as to what can be expected for congregations of today.

God's response to the sin of the congregation of Israel was, first, He blinded them. He closed the eyes of their prophets; they were unable to bring the truth.

Second, He removed the truth from them. They did not have the full staff of the bread of life. They did not have all that was necessary to know truth. What a dreadful thing this was; it left most of ancient Israel in unbelief.

Third, He rejected them. They rejected knowledge and did not want to obey His law; thus, God declared in the most certain terms that He rejected them.

Fourth, He destroyed them. They were destroyed by wicked nations whose language they did not understand. The nations whose language they did not understand provided God's testing program for them.

The concept that God establishes testing programs bears heavily on the events that lead up to the end of the church age. Therefore, we will look at testing programs as they especially relate to ancient Israel. Later in our study we will focus on God's testing program that relates to the congregations that exist at the end of time.

God's Testing Programs

God sets up testing programs through which He accomplishes His overall plan for the human race. There was a testing program in the Garden of Eden. Adam and Eve had not sinned; there was no thought of rebellion against God. Everything was sweetness and light. God saw everything that He had created and it was very good (Genesis 1:31).

God planted a tree in the Garden of Eden, which He called the tree of the knowledge of good and evil. This was the testing arena. What kind of tree it was is immaterial. They were not to eat of that tree. They could eat of every other tree of the garden - beautiful trees with beautiful fruit - but of that tree they could not eat. That is where mankind was destroyed. That is where mankind failed the test.

Into this arena came Satan (the angel Lucifer). He wanted to be like God; he wanted to be a king in his own right. He came as the serpent, the wisest of all the animals; and he tempted Eve. He told her half-truths, and she obeyed the serpent, Satan, rather than God. She ate of the tree of the knowledge of good and evil. This was the testing program whereby mankind came into destruction: Adam and Eve failed the test. They disobeyed God.

The testing program was not a judgment of God because of previous sin. This is the way in which God deals with mankind, who was created in the image of God: He sets up testing programs.

When the nation of Israel was in the wilderness God set up a testing program. Moses left Israel for forty days and forty nights. In his absence, the people were unfaithful to God. They wickedly turned from God after Moses left them.

The Bible tells us they failed the test. They caused Aaron to make a calf, and they fell down and worshipped before the calf. They began to worship other gods, as Adam and Eve did when they obeyed the serpent. By obeying Lucifer they had begun to worship Satan rather than God.

Testing programs are constantly with and to be expected for mankind and congregations. Believers are surrounded by the wicked world: by the blandishments and enticements of other gospels, by the deception of sin and the deceitfulness of Satan. God allows testing programs. Are we going to fail the test or are we not?

Assyria and Babylon - Tests for Israel and Judah
In the case of Israel, God set up a final testing program in which He brought Assyria close to the ten tribes. Israel became interested in the gods and idol worship of ancient Assyria.

Ezekiel 16, verse 28 says:

Thou hast played the whore also with the Assyrians, because thou wast unsatiable; yea, thou hast played the harlot with them, and yet couldest not be satisfied.

This speaks of Israel: "Thou hast played the whore," that is, you are a harlot, an adulterous woman. The Assyrians came with their idol worship and heathen altars, and Israel wanted the same thing.

King Ahaz was King of Judah, but he mimicked what Israel did. After he saw an altar that had been built by the Assyrians, he had his priests make a copy of it and put it in the city of Jerusalem. This is dreadful spiritual harlotry.

The nation of Judah later began to engage in spiritual harlotry with the Babylonians. Ezekiel 16, verses 29-32:

Thou hast moreover multiplied thy fornication in the land of Canaan unto Chaldea [Chaldea is another word for Babylon]; and yet thou wast not satisfied herewith. How weak is thine heart, saith the Lord GOD, seeing thou doest all these things, the work of an imperious whorish woman; In that thou buildest thine eminent place in the head of every way, and makest thine high place in every street; and hast not been as an harlot, in that thou scornest hire; But as a wife that committeth adultery, which taketh strangers instead of her husband!

God is weeping over Israel because it is His wife and they are taking strangers as does an adulterous wife.

In these verses, God is, as it were, weeping over Israel because it is His wife and yet they are taking strangers as does an adulterous wife - the worst kind of harlotry.

A similar reference is found in Ezekiel 23, and it is ugly. However, it is the Word of God, and it must be read; it refers to the congregation of the Old Testament. In Ezekiel 23 God typifies the nation of Israel (the ten tribes with their capital in Samaria), by a woman named Aholah. He names Jerusalem, or Judah (Judah had its capital in Jerusalem), Aholibah. God says of Aholah (ancient Israel), in Ezekiel 23, verses 5-7:

And Aholah played the harlot when she was mine; and she doted on her lovers, on the Assyrians her neighbours, Which were clothed with blue, captains and rulers, all of them desirable young men, horsemen riding upon horses. Thus she committed her whoredoms with them, with all them that were the chosen men of Assyria, and with all on whom she doted: with all their idols she defiled herself.

The Israelites saw the Assyrians and their apparent success, their fine young men and their beautiful clothing, and they were convinced that the Assyrians were prosperous because their gods were powerful gods. Consequently, they ran after the gods of the Assyrians; for this reason, God speaks of Israel as a harlot.

Ezekiel 23:11-12 declares:

And when her sister Aholibah [Judah with its capital in Jerusalem] saw this [saw the adultery of Israel], she was more corrupt in her inordinate love than she [than Aholah, or Israel], and in her whoredoms more than her sister in her whoredoms. She doted upon the Assyrians her neighbours, captains and rulers clothed most gorgeously, horsemen riding upon horses, all of them desirable young men.

Verses 16-17:
And as soon as she saw them with her eyes, she doted upon them, and sent messengers unto them into Chaldea. And the Babylonians came to her into the bed of love, and they defiled her with their whoredom, and she was polluted with them, and her mind was alienated from them.

God is speaking of the dreadful whoredoms of Israel: whoredoms committed with the Assyrians and the Babylonians. The Israelites found these wicked nations with their gorgeously apparelled and handsome horsemen very desirable. They did not like the true Gospel. They did not like what God had spiritually given them. They wanted something more exciting. They wanted that which was apparently wonderful in Assyria and Babylon.

God set up these nations as testing programs for ancient Israel: to determine whether they would be in rebellion against these nations or fall into damnation by running adulterously after them. God's purpose when sin surrounds us is that it is a testing program to discover whether or not we will remain faithful.

> *God's purpose when sin surrounds us is that it is a testing program to discover whether or not we will remain faithful.*

The nations with which Israel played spiritual harlotry were the nations that destroyed Israel. In Ezekiel 23 God speaks of Aholah (the ten tribes, Israel). They were destroyed in the year 709 B.C. by the Assyrians, with whom Israel had played spiritual harlotry. In verse 10 of Ezekiel 23 God says: "These discovered her nakedness," which means they saw the spiritual nakedness of Israel and engaged with her in spiritual harlotry. Also, "they took her sons and her daughters, and slew her with the sword; and she became famous," which means she became a name among women. The verse ends with: "for they had executed judgment upon her." The nation with which Israel had played spiritual harlotry (a heathen nation, a nation whose language she did not understand), destroyed Israel. This is a fulfillment of Deuteronomy 28 and Isaiah 28, where God warned that He would destroy Israel with a nation of stammering lips, a nation whose language they did not understand; He would make them fall backward and they would be snared and be taken.

This is the judgment that God placed upon the church in the Old Testament: He destroyed them.

This is the judgment that God placed upon the church in the Old Testament: He destroyed them. He blinded them. He took the truth away from them. He rejected them. Prior to destroying them, He set up a testing program. The testing program involved a nation whose men rode on beautiful horses, who were desirable, and who were gorgeously apparelled, a nation whose language Israel did not understand. God used that nation as a judgment against Israel; it brought destruction to ancient Israel.

Judah was the two tribes to the south; their capital was in Jerusalem. In Ezekiel 23 they are called Aholibah. In Ezekiel 23:22 God says: "Therefore, O Aholibah [Judah, capital in Jerusalem], thus saith the Lord God; Behold, I will raise up thy lovers against thee." Her lovers were the Babylonians and Chaldeans, whose language they did not understand, whose riders were gorgeously apparelled, and the men were desirable young men.

Ezekiel 23:23-29:

The Babylonians, and all the Chaldeans, Pekod, and Shoa, and Koa, and all the Assyrians with them: all of them desirable young men, captains and rulers, great lords and renowned, all of them riding upon horses. And they shall come against thee with chariots, wagons, and wheels, and with an assembly of people, which shall set against thee buckler and shield and helmet round about: and I will set judgment before them, and they shall judge thee according to their judgments. And I will set my jealousy against thee, and they shall deal furiously with thee: they shall take away thy nose and thine ears; and thy remnant shall fall by the sword: they shall take thy sons and thy daughters; and thy residue shall be devoured by the fire. They shall also strip thee out of thy clothes, and take away thy fair jewels. Thus will I make thy lewdness to cease from thee, and thy whoredom brought from the land of Egypt: so that thou shalt not lift up thine eyes unto them, nor remember Egypt any more. For thus saith the Lord GOD; Behold, I will deliver thee into the hand of them whom thou hatest, into the hand of them from whom thy mind is alienated: And they shall deal with thee hatefully, and shall take away all thy labour, and shall leave thee naked and bare: and the nakedness of thy whoredoms shall be discovered, both thy lewdness and thy whoredoms.

God is indicating: "Judah, my congregation, the congregation that I love, because you have rejected me, and you have not obeyed my law, I have begun to blind you. I have taken the truth away from you. I have rejected you. I have set up a testing program to discover where you stand and you have committed whoredom. You have gone after other nations whose language you do not understand, and they are going to destroy you. They are going to take you captive. They are going to wipe you out."

That is exactly what happened. In the year 709 B.C., the Assyrians came against the ten tribes and destroyed them. One hundred and twenty-three years later (587 B.C.), and actually for the previous twenty-three years, God brought destruction against Judah: First, by the Egyptians, and then by the Babylonians. By 587 B.C. the ancient nation of Judah was removed from God's sight. He destroyed Jerusalem. He destroyed the temple. They were taken into captivity by Babylon. That was the end of the Old Testament congregation.

It was discovered earlier, however, that even though these judgments came upon ancient Israel, God had a future for national Israel. Christ came out of the nation of Israel, and God brought into existence the New Testament church. So there was a sequel: God eventually brought them back to the land, they became a nation again, out of that nation came Christ, and from Christ come the tremendous blessings of the New Testament church. In this way, ancient Israel is not an exact type or figure of the New Testament church. Insofar as concerns God's judgment upon them, it is a picture of the way God will deal with the New Testament church. This is true even though the end of Israel as the external representation of the Kingdom of God on earth did not occur until Christ hung on the cross.

All of this relates to our congregations today. Israel succumbed in the midst of the final testing program. God destroyed them by means of the nations of Assyria and Babylon, with whom they had played spiritual harlotry.

Sins of the New Testament Church

The Bible also speaks of the New Testament church and the end of these congregations.

> *God's program for the New Testament church has many parallels with the Old Testament church.*

When we examine God's program for the New Testament churches, we discover many parallels with the Old Testament church. Without question, God placed many facts in the Bible concerning the beginning, the development, and the end of the Old Testament church, which identifies with ancient national Israel, because these facts teach us what to expect in the New Testament churches. This is so in view of the fact that ancient Israel is used by God as a type or figure of the New Testament church.

Therefore, we should return to our examination of the New Testament church, particularly as it exists in our day, when there is so much evidence that we are near the end of the world.

The final tribulation period comes just prior to Judgment Day, and therefore at the end of the New Testament church age. In Chapter 6 we will more fully study the final tribulation period. It is intimately associated with the end of congregations and denominations that have existed throughout the last 2000 years.

As we have already noted, there are distinct parallels between the congregation of the Old Testament, national Israel, and the New Testament church. A study of Israel and its end have given insights into God's plan for the end of the New Testament church.

The nation of Israel, which typifies the New Testament church, became increasingly apostate. Increasingly, they went after other gods. God had indicated that He had expected them to do this, and God brought destruction upon them by the Assyrians and the Babylonians.

God also described the nature of the sin of New Testament churches. There is an expectation in the Bible that they, too, will fall into grievous sin. The nature of the sin that finally brings the wrath of God and the end of the era of the institutional church will be determined.

The sin that will envelop the congregations is disclosed, for example, in I Timothy 4:1-2:

> Now the Spirit speaketh expressly, that in the latter times some shall depart from the faith, giving heed to seducing spirits, and doctrines of devils; Speaking lies in hypocrisy; having their conscience seared with a hot iron.

The New Testament church is seduced by gospels that are under the power of Satan.

The New Testament church is seduced by gospels that are under the power of Satan. Many in the church heed these seducing spirits.

II Timothy 3:1-5:

> This know also, that in the last days perilous times shall come. For men shall be lovers of their own selves, covetous, boasters, proud, blasphemers, disobedient to parents, unthankful, unholy, Without natural affection, trucebreakers, false accusers, incontinent, fierce, despisers of those that are good. Traitors, heady, highminded, lovers of pleasures more than lovers of God; Having a form of godliness, but denying the power thereof: from such turn away.

This is a description of the terrible sins that will overcome many within the church and finally the church itself. The situation is reprehensible; the charges are serious. It is speaking of the church because verse 5 says they have a form of godliness, but deny the power thereof. The secular world does not have a form of godliness. Only the church wishes to appear godly.

If a congregation is ruled by those who are unsaved, or has many members who are unsaved, then these charges will apply. The church could be overrun with those who are lovers of pleasure more than lovers of God, who are covetous, proud, blasphemers, unholy, false accusers, and traitors. This may be, even though the outward appearance is that of a viable, holy body of believers.

There is a total distinction between the child of God (a citizen of God's Kingdom) and the unsaved (those who are under the dominion of Satan). An antithesis exists between the two.

God's man:	*Satan's man:*
Has an earnest desire to be holy	Is still under the power of sin
Loves God above all	Loves himself
Walks very humbly	Is very proud
Is thankful to God for every gift	Is convinced he is entitled to what he receives
Is faithful to God	Is a traitor to God
Loves God above the pleasures of this world	Has no love for God but eagerly desires the pleasures of the world

This list could cover every phrase in II Timothy 3:1-5. The point is that a church filled with unsaved people - people who think they are saved because they went through a ritual like baptism or publicly confessing their faith before the congregation - will be a church patterned after these verses. Their sin is not that they have been baptized or made confession of faith (true believers do this), rather, their sin is that they make these acts the basis for their salvation.

> *Salvation has to do with a broken and contrite heart . . . a childlike trust in Christ, which is manifested in an earnest desire to please Him.*

They experienced these rituals, and they believe they have become saved. They have not actually become saved, and the same desires exist in their lives (those which exist in the unsaved). Therefore the sins listed in II Timothy will find expression in their lives. They fail to realize that salvation has to do with a broken and contrite heart. Salvation has to do with a childlike trust in Christ, which is manifested in an earnest desire to please Him.

How Much of the World Is in Today's Church?

An honest look at today's churches reveals that these conditions do exist. Few pastors preach on such passages as James 4:4, which warns:

> Ye adulterers and adulteresses, know ye not that the friendship of the world is enmity with God? Whosoever therefore will be a friend of the world is the enemy of God.

Few sermons are heard on Galatians 6:14, where God admonishes:

> But God forbid that I should glory, save in the cross of our Lord Jesus Christ, by whom the world is crucified unto me, and I unto the world.

Few teach I John 2:15-17:

> Love not the world, neither the things that are in the world. If any man love the world, the love of the Father is not in him. For all that is in the world, the lust of the flesh, and the lust of the eyes, and the pride of life, is not of the Father, but is of the world. And the world passeth away, and the lust thereof: but he that doeth the will of God abideth for ever.

Frequently church members love the world as much as unsaved people do. They find joy and security in things that money will buy just as their unsaved neighbors do. The church member may follow certain forms and practices expected by the church, but where is his heart? Jesus warns in Matthew 6:21: "For where your treasure is, there will your heart be also."

> *How many children of so-called Christian parents grow up in homes where the holiness of God . . . and the lifestyle of the parents enable the children to see the difference between the Kingdom of Christ and the dominion of Satan?*

I often wonder how many children of so-called Christian parents grow up in homes where the holiness of God, where the authority of the Bible, and where the lifestyle of the parents are so all-pervasive that the children recognize from a very young age the tremendous difference between the Kingdom of Christ and the dominion of Satan.

"Carnal Christians"

Many denominations have come forth with the doctrine that there are three kinds of people: First, the unsaved; second, the saved, those who love the Lord and want to be obedient to Him; and third, carnal Christians, those who are saved but for whom Christ has not yet become Lord of their lives. This is such a convenient doctrine because the third class of people can have Christ and also the world. They are reasonably active church members, and they can live in the world much like the unsaved; however, this doctrine is contrary to the Bible. In I John 2:3-5 God warns:

> And hereby we do know that we know him, if we keep his commandments. He that saith, I know him, and keepeth not his commandments, is a liar, and the truth is not in him. But whoso keepeth his word, in him verily is the love of God perfected: hereby know we that we are in him.

In Matthew 6:24 our Savior declares:

> No man can serve two masters: for either he will hate the one, and love the other; or else he will hold to the one, and despise the other. Ye cannot serve God and mammon.

The doctrine that there are three kinds of people is widely taught in the evangelical community of our day, which demonstrates that the sinful conditions spoken of in II Timothy 3:1-5 exist far too frequently in the church. Surely God's judgments will fall upon the church.

A statement in the Book of Daniel relates entirely to the final tribulation period and speaks of the spiritual condition in the church that brings the judgment of God upon it. God speaks of the little horn; the little horn can be shown to be Satan. He is the one who is loosed at the end of time. Daniel 7:25:

And he shall speak great words against the most High, and shall wear out the saints of the most High, and think to change times and laws: and they shall be given into his hand until a time and times and the dividing of time.

This verse will be developed only insofar as what Satan, the little horn, will do. He will "think to change times and laws." This condition is virulent and present in so many congregations and denominations that it is extremely probable that we are in the final tribulation period. Certainly this is so based on a consideration of the number of doctrines that churches have written and adopted to suit the carnal desires of members. A few unbiblical contemporary doctrines will be examined.

Divorce - Changing Biblical Rules

When I was growing up (and that was quite a few years ago), we never thought of the possibility of anyone getting a divorce. Divorce was contrary to the Bible. Since then, the church has attempted to change the law of God, which says there is to be no divorce, and after divorce there is to be no remarriage. The church (virtually all denominations) has rewritten the law, and most pastors teach, "Oh, yes, you can have a divorce if there has been fornication. Oh, yes, if you have been divorced under certain circumstances you can be married again." Even deacons, elders, and pastors are divorcing and remarrying. They have changed the law of God to suit the carnal desires of men. We are reminded of the old nursery rhyme:

Humpty Dumpty sat on the wall,
Humpty Dumpty had a great fall,
And all the king's horses and all the king's men
Couldn't put Humpty Dumpty together again.

Humpty Dumpty represents an egg that once broken, can never be put together again. So, too, the marriage institution that has existed for 13,000 years as a God-ordained institution has been fatally shattered.

The amazing fact is that virtually every denomination has made provision for divorce. Some people attempt to sugarcoat it by speaking of it as an annulment. But it is still divorce. Consequently great effort is put forth to deal with the problems resulting from the ever-increasing divorce syndrome. Broken homes, mixed-up children, single parents, etc., demand greater and greater attention.

> *How can we stop the divorce plague and return to the sanctity of marriage?*

But no denomination is dealing with the root problem, namely, how can we stop the divorce plague and return to the sanctity of marriage? The evidence clearly shows that the marriage institution has been fatally shattered. And when the family unit has been seriously fractured, it means that society has been seriously fractured. It can only mean that mankind is on the verge of destroying itself.

Birth Control - A Change in God's Law

Another example of rewriting God's law is in the matter of birth control. Presently, most pastors teach that birth control is acceptable. They say: God has given us minds of wisdom to make these decisions.

They fail to realize they are teaching people to disobey God's commands, such as Genesis 9:1: "And God blessed Noah and his sons, and said unto them, Be fruitful, and multiply, and replenish the earth."

Psalm 127:3-5:
Lo, children are an heritage of the LORD: and the fruit of the womb is his reward. As arrows are in the hand of a mighty man; so are children of the youth. Happy is the man that hath his quiver full of them: they shall not be ashamed, but they shall speak with the enemies in the gate.

Psalm 128:3-4:
Thy wife shall be as a fruitful vine by the sides of thine house: thy children like olive plants round about thy table. Behold, that thus shall the man be blessed that feareth the Lord.

Psalm 104:30:
Thou sendest forth thy spirit, they are created: and thou renewest the face of the earth.

Isaiah 42:5:
Thus saith God the LORD, he that created the heavens, and stretched them out; he that spread forth the earth, and that which cometh out of it; he that giveth breath unto the people upon it, and spirit to them that walk therein.

In these verses, God says that He creates the baby in the womb. For those who are children of God, children are an immense blessing from God. However, when man rewrites the law of God, people are instructed that man makes these decisions, and they are not to trust that God knows exactly what size every family ought to be.

The Bible teaches that God utilizes the family to bring forth Godly seed (Malachi 2:14-15). Satan, on the other hand, tries to prevent this: For example, when Israel was in Egypt and all the boy babies of Israel were to be killed (Exodus 1), and when Jesus was a young child and the babies in Bethlehem were killed.

> *Satan has planted the rebellious idea in people's minds that they are the decision makers concerning the size of their family.*

Today, Satan is up to the same tricks. Through the success of birth control devices, he has planted the rebellious idea in people's minds that they are the decision makers concerning the size of their family. Even church rulers have decided that man knows more than God about the number of children that should be in a family. They do not realize that no baby is conceived unless God Himself has taken action to create that baby in the womb. Little do they realize that they have become pawns of Satan. Little do they realize that the practice of birth control is a negation of the principle that one must trust God in all aspects of life.

God's laws have not changed. The church, which should be the custodian of the law and carefully guard and hold it and resist teaching that which is contrary to the will of God, is now changing these laws.

The Place of Women in the Church

Women's place in the church is another example of the decision to change God's law to suit man's ideas. There is tremendous pressure to accept women in the pulpit and to permit women to rule and have authority in the church. This is absolutely contrary to the law of God (I Corinthians 14:34, I Timothy 2:12).

> *There have been changes in God's law so that men can do what they want to do.*

In many areas of life, the Bible is no longer the authority. Learned theologians talk about the inerrancy and infallibility of the Bible, but where the rubber meets the road - that is, where the congregation or pastor wants their own way about something - there have been changes in God's law so that men can do what they want to do.

Today in many churches those who stand for Biblical truth and want to do things God's way are considered to be oddballs even by many within the church. They are thought to have an "holier-than-thou" attitude and an inflated spiritual ego. There is no longer an intense desire in many congregations to live faithfully by the law of God. In effect, they say: "Let us change the laws so that they are more convenient for our lifestyle." This is the desire of many in the congregations.

Salvation Is by Grace Alone

The law of God has been changed in that it is widely taught that salvation is not altogether dependent on God's grace alone. It is taught that God has provided for the salvation of every individual in the human race and that salvation thus depends upon man to be the decision maker. Of his own free will, some say, man can accept or reject salvation. Thus, salvation would ultimately be a joining of Christ's work on the cross and man's work in accepting Christ - both would have contributed to the individual's salvation.

This perverse teaching disregards all kinds of laws of the Bible. No recognition is given to the Bible's teaching that man is spiritually dead and has no desire to seek God (Ephesians 2:1-5, Romans 3:10-11). It denies the truth that Christ went to the cross to save *His* people from their sins, and the rest of the world must stand at Judgment Day and give an account of their sins. This teaching fails to face statements such as Revelation 17:8, which teaches that only some people have their names written in the book of life from the foundation of the world.

Moreover the Bible tells us to believe on the Lord Jesus Christ; that is, we are to trust Him for all that He has done for our salvation, and that includes the fact that from the foundation of the world, God chose those whom He would save, and therefore has obligated Himself to save those whom He has chosen (Ephesians 1:4-10).

> *Those who believe that man has a free will effectively are indicating that they do not trust Christ to save them in His time and in His manner.*

Those, however, who believe that man has a free will effectively are indicating that they do not trust Christ to save them in His time and in His manner. They want a salvation in which they, themselves, are the guarantor; that is, they can become saved any time they wish by simply reaching out and accepting Christ. In this way they do not have to wait for God to act. Thus, effectively they do not trust God at all. But if they do not trust Christ who is eternal God then they are not saved, for they do not believe on Him. To believe on Him means that our will is broken and we trust everything in the Bible that God has declared concerning salvation.

To some degree, the pernicious teaching of free will has plagued the church throughout New Testament history, but in our day it has invaded almost every congregation. Thus these congregations no longer have God's salvation plan. The salvation they offer is designed by men and will save no one from the wrath of God. What a terrible situation the church has come into.

Today's Gospel - A Social Gospel
All people have three aspirations: 1) political freedom, 2) economic security, and 3) freedom from disease. All of mankind desires these blessings, and pastors and teachers increasingly incorporate these desires into their gospels. The social gospel, which has great concern for the physically hungry, is becoming the number one priority. Preachers say that the Christian ethic demands that all men have political freedom. In the social gospel, it is believed that the church must do all it can to provide medicine and doctors to the world, and it is also believed that the church can expect God to provide good health (even miraculous healings), to those who claim the name of Jesus.

These aspirations have nothing to do with the Gospel of the Bible. This is proven by the parable of the rich man and Lazarus (Luke 16). The rich man with all his money could buy many, many freedoms that were denied others. He could afford the finest doctors and medicines. Certainly he had economic security.

Lazarus, on the other hand, was a beggar. He had sores that were licked by dogs. He had no economic security, and he had poor health. His political freedom was of no consequence.

> *God strips aside the curtain of eternity and the rich man is seen in hell and Lazarus is seen in Abraham's bosom, which signifies heaven.*

Which of these two men most badly needed the Gospel? According to today's social gospel it is obvious that Lazarus had the greater need, but did he? They equally need the Gospel. God strips aside the curtain of eternity and the rich man is seen in hell and Lazarus is in Abraham's bosom, a figure which signifies heaven. The beggar, Lazarus, had everything in this life because he was saved. The rich man had nothing because he was unsaved. Surely this teaches that the social-political gospel has nothing to do with the Gospel of salvation.

The Gospel is concerned with the spiritual needs of mankind. Only within the congregation does the Gospel concern itself with physical needs.

Many doctrines and practices that are prevalent today present evidence that the church has rewritten the laws of the Bible. Indeed, congregations are being encouraged to follow a salvation program different from that which is found in the Bible.

The Changing of Times

Daniel 7:25 advises that not only are the laws changed but also the times. The changing of times is increasingly present in the evangelical community.

The Bible is clear that it is appointed unto men once to die and then the judgment. Judgment is the last day; all the graves will open and everyone will either stand for judgment or be caught up to be forever with Christ (John 5:28-29). The Bible is clear about this, and yet many churches and denominations have reconstructed the Word of God and devised an entirely different time scheme. They say, for example, that Judgment Day is at least 1000 years in the future. That is convenient because man does not want to talk about Judgment Day. It is a relief to know that it cannot come for at least another 1000 years. In spite of the fact that the Bible repeatedly asserts that this is the last generation, they teach that God has another plan for this present world. However, their timetable is not what the Bible teaches. That which is spoken of in Daniel 7 is coming to pass all around us. We are approaching the end of time, the time when the corporate body, the institutional church will be judged.

It must be noted also that in our generation Sunday is no longer God's Holy Day. Fifty years ago Sunday was a day set aside for worship. It was a day when all but the most necessary secular activity ceased. Thus Sunday was set aside for the spiritual activity of worship, of Bible study, of singing God's praises, of visiting the sick, etc. Today the focus of Sunday to a very high degree is on man's pleasure, on shopping, on ball games, etc. Sunday as God's Holy Day has been almost completely repudiated. This can only bring God's judgment upon the church.

Unhappy Pastors

These teachings may offend many pastors. They may be disturbed. They may profess to love their congregations, and they are sure that they are Christ's church. If someone warns of God's judgment on the institution of the church, he speaks in their home territory. He speaks of the place where they minister. This is unacceptable to them and makes them unhappy.

The same thing happened in the nation of Israel when Jeremiah, Ezekiel and others prophesied that Babylon was going to destroy them because of their sin. The false prophets in Israel were unhappy with Jeremiah and the few prophets that dared to predict that judgment was coming. After all, they thought, Israel was the apple of God's eye. Israel was God's chosen people. God would never destroy Israel.

Jeremiah, Ezekiel, Hosea, Amos, and the other prophets whose statements are recorded in the Bible were carefully reading the Word of God - more carefully than the prophets who did not want to see God's judgment coming. The true prophets looked at the Word of God carefully and realistically. They did not stick their heads in the sand. They did not hope that it would all go away.

God Blinds the Church

In II Thessalonians 2 God teaches that He will blind those who reject His Word. In this passage God warns what will happen when Satan is loosed and God brings judgment on the church. Verses 3-4:

Let no man deceive you by any means: for that day shall not come, except there come a falling away first, and that man of sin be revealed, the son of perdition: Who opposeth and exalteth himself above all that is called God, or that is worshipped; so that he as God sitteth in the temple of God, shewing himself that he is God.

Verses 9b-12 speak of Satan coming with:
all power and signs and lying wonders, And with all deceivableness of unrighteousness in them that perish; because they received not the love of the truth, that they might be saved. And for this cause God shall send them strong delusion, that they should believe a lie: That they all might be damned who believed not the truth, but had pleasure in unrighteousness.

This is speaking of the church. One might ask, "How can that be, when these statements apply to the unsaved? The unsaved are damned." It must be realized that, obviously, not everyone in the church is saved.

Hell and Damnation
One frightening thing is that there is so little conversation about hell and damnation, which is what we are saved from. All kinds of salvation messages are being presented with the general theme of God's love, the idea being that it would be salutary and wise to become identified with the Lord Jesus Christ. These messages imply that by accepting Him, things are going to go well and life will have purpose and meaning.

How can anyone become saved if he does not know what he is being saved from? How can he know what he is saved from unless it is thoroughly discussed and diligently taught that because of sins he is under the wrath of God. He is subject to eternal damnation. To repent of sins, turn to the Lord Jesus Christ, and be saved in accordance with God's salvation plan, he must know what he is being saved from.

God did not place multitudinous references in the Bible as to the awfulness and certainty of His wrath just to fill up space.

One can rightly fear eternal damnation only if the Bible's disclosures of the awful nature of hell are taught from the pulpit. God did not place multitudinous references in the Bible as to the awfulness and certainty of His wrath just to fill up space. These warnings are to be read, taught, and discussed; they are there to instill fear in mankind. If these passages are neglected, it is not the whole counsel of God. It will be man's and not the true Gospel.

God Removes the Truth from the Church

The sad and terrible truth is that the congregations and denominations are heading for disaster. As they become increasingly unfaithful to the Word of God, His wrath descends upon them. Ancient Israel finally came under the judgment of God; God blinded them, removed the truth from them, rejected them, and last of all He destroyed them.

Many New Testament congregations are becoming increasingly apostate.

Many New Testament congregations are becoming increasingly apostate. Spiritual blindness is descending on these congregations, which means that the truth has been removed from them.

God is deeply concerned about the corporate, institutional, external body of believers called the church. The era of the external body called national Israel came to an end at the time of the cross, and the era of the New Testament external body is ending as apostasy develops all over the world.

God's judgment on the institutional church does not include true believers within it, those who are born from above. They do not come into judgment, even though they go through the tribulation, affliction, and difficulties as God's judgment is visited upon the New Testament corporate church.

We have seen that as the church becomes more rebellious against God - it changes laws and times, men's love grows cold, and it preaches a gospel of men rather than the Gospel of God - God blinds. A dynamic activity operates whereby God actually causes theologians and church leaders to see less and less truth. What truth they had is taken away from them because they do not bow their knees before God.

They are not ready to acknowledge that the Bible alone and in its entirety is the Word of God. They will not submit to it as the Word that is to be studied and obeyed. Therefore, God blinds them.

The blinding of ministers in the congregations is intimately associated with the removal of truth from the congregations. The institutional body, the church, is where truth ought to be found. The church is the custodian of the Word. Since Christ went to the cross and the Holy Spirit was poured out on Pentecost day in 33 A.D., the Old Testament congregation, Israel, has not had truth. Their era ended. Throughout the New Testament period, one expects to find truth in congregations and denominations that are reasonably true to the Word of God.

As God's judgment comes against the corporate, institutional body because of its rebellion, truth is increasingly difficult to find. God blinds those who have been unfaithful in their presentation of the Gospel. Pastors and others who have been taught truth in their younger years are repudiating one aspect of truth after another. Sometimes it seems they can hardly wait to get on the bandwagon of teachings and practices that are contrary to the Word. The more they depart from the Word, the less truth they have to offer. Through their teaching and preaching, truth is removed from the congregation.

> *The term "latter days" in Jeremiah*
> *23 does not refer to national Israel.*

Learn from the Old Testament

The removal of truth from New Testament churches is emphasized in the Old Testament and in the New Testament. Jeremiah 23 is an excellent example of this. Let the warnings of the Bible seep deeply into our souls. Jeremiah 23:20 relates to us today because God teaches, "In the latter days ye shall consider it perfectly." The term "latter days" in the Bible points to the New Testament period. Sometimes it points to the whole New Testament period and sometimes it refers particularly to the end of the New Testament period. Thus, we know that the term "latter days" as found in Jeremiah 23 does not refer to national Israel. There are many Old Testament references to the final demise of national Israel and their sin (as was seen earlier in this study), but Jeremiah 23 speaks principally of the New Testament body of believers - the church. Chapter 23 sums up many teachings of the potential apostasy that exists in the New Testament church; therefore, this chapter of the Bible will be closely studied.

Jeremiah 23 emphasizes that God's wrath will be visited upon the institutional, external church, because of growing apostasy. Verse 14:

> I have seen also in the prophets of Jerusalem an horrible thing: they commit adultery, and walk in lies: they strengthen also the hands of evildoers, that none doth return from his wickedness: they are all of them unto me as Sodom, and the inhabitants thereof as Gomorrah.

Jerusalem is another name for the body of believers, typified, of course, by Old Testament Jerusalem. The prophets in the first instance are the preachers who declare the Word of God. In a wider sense, the prophets include all who are in the congregation, for every member of the congregation is mandated to be a witness.

God is teaching that these prophets have become false witnesses. They run after other gospels. They hold as the ultimate authority things and ideas other than the Bible. In their spiritual fornication, God likens them to Sodom and Gomorrah, which were destroyed because of wickedness.

God declares in Jeremiah 23 verse 15a: "Therefore thus saith the LORD of hosts concerning the prophets, Behold, I will feed them with wormwood." Wormwood is probably a synonym for hemlock and hemlock is poisonous. In other words, He gives them poison to drink. The congregation no longer receives the pure water of the true Gospel; it receives the poisonous water of false gospels. Verses 15b-17:

> And make them drink the water of gall: for from the prophets of Jerusalem is profaneness gone forth into all the land. Thus saith the LORD of hosts, Hearken not unto the words of the prophets that prophesy unto you: they make you vain: they speak a vision of their own heart, and not out of the mouth of the LORD. They say still unto them that despise me, The LORD hath said, Ye shall have peace; and they say unto every one that walketh after the imagination of his own heart, No evil shall come upon you.

God here outlines the nature of the sin that causes the institutional church to come under His judgment. False prophets say to congregations, "All is well. We don't want to talk about hell and damnation. We don't want to talk about God's judgment. We want to speak of loving, joyful things that fill our hearts with peace."

> *These are unacceptable to some preachers*
> *because they emphasize doom and gloom, and*
> *that is not what people want to hear.*

Dearly beloved, these verses have been in the Bible since the Bible was completed, and yet for most of the history of the church, few people have paid attention to them. If you talk to most pastors, perhaps if you look at your own life, you will discover that little is known about the prophecies of Jeremiah, Hosea, Malachi, and prophecies of a similar nature. These are unacceptable to some preachers because they emphasize doom and gloom, and that is not what most people want to hear.

These prophecies deal expressly and explicitly with conditions that exist today. They are being fulfilled in our day because we are so near the end of time.

The Church Must Engage in Self-Examination

God is forcing each of us to look at where we are in the church, in the corporate, institutional body. God is addressing us right where we are, and we had better heed His warning. Spiritual rulers have an especially weighty responsibility, but every believer in the congregation should listen to God's warnings, so that he does not fall into those sins.

The verses of Jeremiah 23 have taught us that there will be churches that teach "Peace, peace" when there is no peace. Some will say, "All is well, God is not going to bring evil on the church. Hasn't Christ declared that 'I will build my church; and the gates of hell shall not prevail against it'? (Matthew 16:18) Isn't God true to His promise? How can you say that God will let Satan win a victory over the church, the institutional body?"

The reason that God will, is because God has so decreed. As the churches complete their work of evangelization and the last of the elect are being saved (by that time the church will have become almost completely apostate), then God is going to bring His judgment upon it, whether we like it or not.

He has given ample evidence of this. It is seen in the nation of Israel, the congregation of the Old Testament, and what happened to them. Therefore, we had better heed His warnings. Many pastors today say, "Oh, we're just a wonderful body of believers, and we rejoice in the Lord. Praise God this and praise God that, but don't talk about these ugly things that relate to God's damnation or God's judging the church. We don't want to hear it." This attitude is precisely what God is anticipating in Jeremiah 23:18:

> For who hath stood in the counsel of the LORD, and hath perceived and heard his word? who hath marked his word, and heard it?

This is a rhetorical question and indicates that the congregations are not standing in the counsel of God. They are not perceiving and hearing His Word. They are bringing their own word, which is what they like to hear. Verse 19:

> Behold, a whirlwind of the LORD is gone forth in fury, even a grievous whirlwind: it shall fall grievously upon the head of the wicked.

That is the judgment that is coming on the church, the corporate, institutional body. Verses 20-21:

> The anger of the LORD shall not return, until he have executed, and till he have performed the thoughts of his heart: in the latter days ye shall consider it perfectly. I have not sent these prophets, yet they ran: I have not spoken to them, yet they prophesied.

> *God teaches that the church will be*
> *overrun with those who say they have*
> *been sent by God.*

God teaches that the church will be overrun with those who say they have been sent by God. They will insist that they have been called by God, but in truth they have not been called by God. Anyone who brings his own gospel rather than the Gospel of the Bible is not sent by God. This is true regardless of how his gospel may identify with the Bible. True prophets are those who maintain the utmost fidelity to the Word of God.

The Church Is Overrun with False Prophets

The prophets who are presented to us in Jeremiah 23 have not been spoken to by God. They do not have a message from God. They have been blinded. They bring their own gospel, a gospel that leaves people feeling fine. They have gospels that stress the power of positive thinking. Their gospels stress the idea that we need not worry about God's judgment falling upon us. They emphasize the idea that God will do increasingly wonderful works in our day and manifestations will develop here and there.

God says in Jeremiah 23:22:

But if they had stood in my counsel, and had caused my people to hear my words, then they should have turned them from their evil way, and from the evil of their doings.

One who brings the truth of the Word of God, as ominous and negative as it may sound, causes those who listen and who are touched by that Word, to turn from their evil deeds and to Christ. An outstanding example of this, of course, is Jonah, when he went to Nineveh with the Word that God was going to destroy them. Ugly, but they listened and they repented.

> *God has in view the congregations*
> *and denominations with the highest*
> *percentages of the body of believers.*

Few contemporary preachers say that God's judgment rests on the corporate, institutional body. The cults and sects that continuously flourish in the world are not in view here. God has in view the congregations and denominations with the highest percentages of the body of believers. God declares that His judgment will come upon them as they go more and more against the Word of God.

God Rejects His Church

Within the corporate body are the true believers. They are the invisible, eternal church. The invisible body, those who are truly children of God (wherever they may be and in whatever congregation or denomination they are), do not come into judgment. True believers who are living on earth as God brings the corporate, institutional body into judgment will suffer grievous tribulation because God's judgments are coming on the congregations to which these true believers belong.

It has been seen that there is an expectation in the Bible that the church will become increasingly wicked, and that as wickedness multiplies, God will begin to take action. He will blind the church. He will give them the spirit of unbelief to make them believe a lie. He will begin to remove the truth from that church.

In Jeremiah 23:20-21 and 25-28 we read:

The anger of the LORD shall not return, until he have executed, and till he have performed the thoughts of his heart: in the **latter days** ye shall consider it perfectly. I have not sent these prophets, yet they ran: I have not spoken to them, yet they prophesied.

I have heard what the prophets said, that prophesy lies in my name, saying, I have dreamed, I have dreamed. How long shall this be in the heart of the prophets that prophesy lies? yea, they are prophets of the deceit of their own heart; Which think to cause my people to forget my name by their dreams which they tell every man to his neighbour, as their fathers have forgotten my name for Baal. The prophet that hath a dream, let him tell a dream; and he that hath my word, let him speak my word faithfully. What is the chaff to the wheat? saith the LORD.

This passage warns of apostasy in our day, not in Israel's day. When God tells us, "In the latter days ye shall consider it perfectly," the "latter days" are the New Testament period, even though it was written in the time of national Israel. Therefore, we must listen carefully.

> *This can be a problem in a congregation where the pastor wants to have a so-called successful ministry.*

Prophets who prophesy lies think their dreams are truth from God. This is a problem that will increase in the church, as will be discovered. This also could be a reference to church leaders' dreams, fantasies, or imaginations of what they would like the church to be. This can become a problem in a congregation where the pastor wants to have a so-called successful ministry. He can be tempted to introduce unbiblical practices and doctrines into his church in an effort to please people.

This study is not meant to encourage anyone to despise pastors nor to despise the church. I, personally, belong to the church. I have been a member of the church all of my years. My children belong to the church. We believe that this is where we must be because God has so declared: "Not forsaking the assembling of ourselves together, as the manner of some is; but exhorting one another: and so much the more, as ye see the day approaching" (Hebrews 10:25). The day is drawing nigh. Judgment Day is close, but be careful not to leave the church earlier than necessary. The question of when true believers should leave the church is pursued later in this study.

The Task of the Pastor

In the light of Jeremiah 23, it appears that many pastors today have as their first interest a large, successful congregation (there are exceptions - praise God for the exceptions). As a result, the church becomes entertainment: movies are shown and "gifted" singers are brought in. Events are scheduled that titillate the fancies of the congregation. The preaching becomes increasingly pinched off and bland. It does not get into the heaven-hell question. It ignores the matter of eternal life versus eternal damnation. It does not mention God's judgment because it is preaching to keep the congregation happy. The pastor preaches from his own mind. These are reprehensible ideas.

One sad thing that happens in our day is that many pastors get their sermons from what others have written. They trust church fathers or certain theologians. Unhesitatingly, they proclaim what their authorities have written; they never bother to check what they have read against the Bible to see if it is Biblical. One theologian simply teaches what another theologian teaches, who in turn teaches what another theologian teaches, until it becomes increasingly difficult to find a foundation in the Word of God.

> *These pastors fail to realize that the theologians*
> *they trust . . . are not always trustworthy.*

These pastors fail to realize that although the theologians they trust may have in many ways declared true doctrine, they are not always trustworthy. No teacher, no preacher is without error. This is simply because no one has a perfect understanding of the Bible. Throughout a teacher's lifetime he should constantly search the Bible for truth. He should persistently and faithfully correct and refine the doctrines he teaches.

Great havoc is created in the church if teachers or theologians implicitly trust an earlier theologian. God has enabled each generation of theologians to personally go to the fountainhead of truth, the Bible.

The Bible says in Jeremiah 23, verse 28, "He that hath my word, let him speak my word faithfully." Faithfully means to search the Word. It takes a lot of time to search. Word studies have to be made; Scripture must be compared with Scripture to determine what God has in view in a given verse. Conclusions arrived at by studying one part of Scripture must be checked against everything else in Scripture that might possibly relate to it to ensure that the conclusion is in harmony with all Scripture.

> *To ferret out truth from the Bible*
> *requires great diligence.*

To ferret out truth from the Bible requires great diligence. Teachers have to "burn the midnight oil," so to speak. Teachers must deny themselves things with which other people attempt to satiate themselves, i.e., hours of nightly watching television, many trips, and long vacations. They have to diligently apply themselves to the Word; otherwise, they will not bring the Word faithfully, and they bring chaff rather than wheat. The Bible asks, what is the chaff to the wheat? and answers, the chaff is nothing.

Jeremiah 23:29: "Is not my word like as a fire? saith the LORD; and like a hammer that breaketh the rock in pieces?" In other words, the Word of God is powerful. The Word of God is penetrating. The Word of God, brought faithfully, pierces into the heart of man and breaks down the toughest sinner until he cries out, "Oh, God, have mercy on me. I'm a sinner. I don't want to go to hell."

Verse 30 of Jeremiah 23 ominously declares: "Therefore, behold, I am against the prophets, saith the LORD, that steal my words every one from his neighbour." God is declaring that some pastors negate the Word of God and encourage their congregations to turn from those who faithfully bring truth.

God goes on in verse 31, "Behold, I am against the prophets, saith the LORD, that use their tongues, and say, He saith." Many preachers wave their Bibles and say, "This is the Word of God and God says . . . ," and they proceed to offer doctrines and philosophies that have no more basis in the Word of God than any other secular philosophy. Their ideas come from their own minds and what they think is truth.

God warns in verse 32:

Behold, I am against them that prophesy false dreams, saith the LORD, and do tell them, and cause my people to err by their lies, and by their lightness; yet I sent them not, nor commanded them: therefore they shall not profit this people at all, saith the LORD.

God is disclosing information about the dreadful situation that develops when pastors and teachers in a church do not faithfully bring the Word of God. Rather than bearing the truth, they bring lies. If it is not truth, it is a lie. They bring chaff for that congregation, and it will not profit them. How terrible to realize that much preaching today is merely from thoughts of men rather than a careful presentation of the Word of God. How dreadful to contemplate that a pastor stands before his congregation and preaches lies. Unfortunately, this is the present situation in many churches.

God Forsakes His Church

As has been seen in ancient Israel, God spiritually blinded the congregation of that day, then He removed the truth from them, and following this, He rejected them. God will also forsake New Testament churches as they go deeper into apostasy.

Jeremiah 23:33 declares:

And when this people, or the prophet, or a priest, shall ask thee, saying, What is the burden of the LORD?

[substitute the word "message" to understand this phrase, "What is the message of the Lord?"]

thou shalt then say unto them, What burden?

["What message?"]

I will even forsake you, saith the LORD.

God is declaring what His action will be as unfaithful preaching develops in the church. When pastors preach from their own minds rather than the Bible, God warns them with this message: "I will forsake you. I will reject you. I am going to bring you to an end." This is the last step before judgment.

> *Even though they use Biblical language and quote verses, if what they teach is not firmly based in the Word of God, then it is lies.*

When the pastor and the teachers in a congregation teach the ideas of men, even though they may use Biblical language and quote verses, if what they teach is not firmly based in the Word of God, then it is lies. It is of men, and God warns, "I will forsake you." As for the prophet, priest, and people who shall say, "The burden [the message] of the Lord, I will even punish that man in his house" (Jeremiah 23:34). In other words, damnation will come upon them and their households because they are blind leaders of the blind.

God solemnly continues in Jeremiah 23:35-36:

Thus shall ye say every one to his neighbour, and every one to his brother, What hath the LORD answered? and, What hath the LORD spoken? And the burden of the LORD shall ye mention no more: for every man's word shall be his burden; for ye have perverted the words of the living God, of the LORD of hosts our God.

They will no longer be able to find the Word. Every man's message will be his own word; it will not be the Word of the Bible.

Dearly beloved, you might ask, "Is that the condition in the church today?" It is not the situation in every congregation, but in many congregations, this is the situation. It must be concluded that currently in many congregations, the truth is reprehensible and there is no desire to hear Biblical preaching. The people want what is pleasing to their ears rather than that which is faithful to God's Word.

This is not to imply that I or that anyone has perfect truth. We all have to admit that we are learning. We all have to admit that we have feet of clay. One who is bringing the truth has an earnest and ongoing desire to continue to search out the Word and to change if something from the Word of God is contrary to what has been taught.

God threatens in verses 39-40:

Therefore, behold, I, even I, will utterly forget you, and I will forsake you, and the city that I gave you and your fathers, and cast you out of my presence: And I will bring an everlasting reproach upon you, and a perpetual shame, which shall not be forgotten.

God is not talking about Communism nor wicked people in the political arena. He is not referring to sects and cults that obviously are under the power of Satan. God is talking about the institutional church from which the Gospel has been going forth throughout New Testament history, but to a high degree has become apostate. It is no longer faithful to the Word of God, and God is declaring what He will do to that church. He ends the solemn discourse of Jeremiah 23 with the declaration that He is going to reject them and cast them out. This is what happened to national Israel, the church of the Old Testament, when they increasingly rejected God's truth. God is declaring that this same rejection is to occur to New Testament congregations that are unfaithful.

Jeremiah 23 is an eye opener to anyone who is serious about Bible truth. One may not like God's threats and warnings but they are true. The language of this chapter and of so many other passages of this study are contemporary.

> *If one finds he has been going down*
> *the wrong path, he has time to repent*
> *and turn from wrong ways.*

Wonderfully, God has given ample warning. Thus, even if one finds he has been going down the wrong path, he has time to repent and turn from wrong ways. It is still the day of salvation. Even if one's congregation is rejected, individual believers cannot expect rejection.

Praise God that we can know that we have eternal life, and we can know that nothing can snatch us out of our Savior's hand.

The last things that came upon ancient Israel were God's judgments. The Israelites experienced these dreadful events at the hands of the Assyrians and the Babylonians.

SUMMARY

We have learned that God warned ancient Israel that they would rebel against God and that God would bring His judgments upon them. We are to carefully examine God's dealings with ancient Israel to find clues concerning God's plans for the New Testament congregations when they fall away from the truth. We have learned that as a result of ancient Israel's constant rebellion, God first blinded them, then He removed truth from them, then He rejected them and finally destroyed them.

As we continued our study, we found that the New Testament church is walking in the same shoes as ancient Israel. Increasingly the congregations are departing from the Bible and introducing doctrines and practices that show rebellion against God. These sins, which are so much in evidence in our day, are being followed by the blinding of the church and the removal of truth from the church. Thus the congregations and denominations that are rebelling against the teachings of the Bible, which is God's law book for the church, are coming under God's judgment.

What judgment will come on New Testament congregations following their rejection by God? This question will be answered in the next chapter.

Chapter 5
God Will Destroy the External Church

The Old and the New Testaments give ample evidence that the New Testament corporate, external body will come under the wrath of God and be destroyed just as ancient Israel came under God's wrath and was destroyed.

Israel's era ended after Christ came forth from them and was crucified. It is God's purpose to evangelize the world by means of the New Testament church; thus, the New Testament church era cannot end until the last of God's elect are saved. Only then will God's salvation plan, which is the time line of history, come to an end.

No one knows the day nor the hour when the last of the elect will be saved because no human being knows who the elect are. Only God knows who they are. The church must continue to witness to the world through the faithful proclamation of the Word and trust that God will save the elect.

A significant body of truth relates to the future of the church. It can be known that when congregations and denominations become apostate, God will reject and destroy them. This warning is applicable to any congregation of New Testament history; however, it becomes a far more significant warning as the end of the world draws close.

National Israel Returns to their Land - A Sign that We Are Near the End

One of the most important signs that the world's history is about to close is Israel's return to their land. Jesus declares in Matthew 24:32-33:

> Now learn a parable of the fig tree: When his branch is yet tender, and putteth forth leaves, ye know that summer is nigh: So likewise ye, when ye shall see all these things, know that it is near, even at the doors.

Careful study of the Bible reveals that the only nation that meets the criteria of being the fig tree is the nation of Israel. After almost 2000 years, they are again in their own land; this is truly a sign that we are near the end of time. The Lord Jesus Christ must soon come on the clouds in judgment.

Israel as a political nation remains steadfast in its rejection of Christ as Messiah. This identifies perfectly with the prophecy of Matthew 24 where God declares the fig tree will have leaves. Significantly, no fruit is anticipated, and except for a tiny trickle of believers from Israel, no spiritual fruit is seen in that nation.

Knowing that we might be near the end of time, we must become even more interested and concerned about what is happening in the churches today. If indeed we are near the end of time, then nearly all of God's elect have become saved. If this is so, then the era of the New Testament church must be almost to an end.

The era of the Old Testament church ended as a direct result of national Israel's apostasy, their unfaithfulness to God. The Biblical language for the New Testament church and its potential for apostasy is parallel to that which was declared for ancient Israel. Therefore, if the end of time is near, substantial evidence of apostasy will be seen within congregations.

This is precisely what has been discovered in this study. In the Bible, God repeatedly describes the nature of the sin of the church. Much that is unbiblical goes on in congregations and denominations today. This is not apostasy in sects and cults, which obviously are under the power of Satan; rather, it is in evangelical, Bible-related churches. To our utter consternation, these sins apply to a high degree to the most conservative contemporary churches and denominations.

Opportunities to study the Bible do not produce
great fidelity to the Word of God.

Bibles are available to more literate people than ever before in history. Opportunities to study the Bible do not produce greater fidelity to the Word of God. Instead, increasing unfaithfulness to the Bible is developing all over the world.

This is not because God's promise that His Word will not return void has failed. It is because mankind is not reading, studying, and believing the Word as he should. His trust has shifted to science, social structures, and man's philosophies.

Ancient Israel was destroyed by political nations: Assyria, Babylon, and Rome. Will the church of today be destroyed by a political nation?

God warns that the New Testament institutional corporate body will be destroyed, and He uses the figure of political bodies, particularly Babylon, to illustrate how it will be destroyed. Babylon does not exist today, of course, but could a Communist philosophy be used by God to destroy the churches?

Through the years I have been trying to more fully understand prophetic statements such as Daniel, Revelation, II Thessalonians 2, I Thessalonians 4, and Matthew 24. For a long time I wondered, "What is the role of Communism, the dynamic ideology that is so satanic in nature and which has swept the world during the last seventy years?"

In its anti-God stance, it appeared that it must have a significant role to play. It is predominantly a political ideology, although in its anti-God posture it has religious overtones. Will God use it to silence the Gospel as a judgment upon the church? Or will God bring the institutional, corporate church into great and terrible trouble by some other political action, for example, a United States president so anti-Gospel that he persecutes the church and brings judgment against it?

It is significant that Satan, working through Communism, has done his best to destroy the cause of Christ. Communism has made life difficult for the institutional church, and by this means, Satan has hoped that true believers would cease to exist. But we know as history unfolds in our day, Communism has not won. True believers continue to exist in every Communist country.

> *In the Bible, we can learn how God plans to destroy the church. . . . It will not be by an ideology like Communism.*

In the Bible, however, we can learn how God plans to destroy the church. It will not be by political action. It will not be by an ideology like Communism. It will be by satanic activity working through false gospels that look so much like the true Gospel that even the elect would be deceived, if that were possible. We shall now examine this idea in greater detail.

God Uses Satan to Destroy

The Bible discloses that right near the end of time, Satan will become the dominant ruler within the congregations. In II Thessalonians 2, God speaks of the man of sin taking his seat in the temple. It will be seen that the man of sin can be only Satan. Matthew 24, verse 24:

> For there shall arise false Christs, and false prophets, and shall shew great signs and wonders; insomuch that, if it were possible, they shall deceive the very elect.

In Revelation 13, verse 7, God informs us:

> And it was given unto him to make war with the saints, and to overcome them: and power was given him over all kindreds, and tongues, and nations.

Revelation 13 speaks of the beast that comes out of the earth. This can be only Satan and his dominion, as he rules through false gospels. By this means, he is able to destroy the churches that are under the judgment of God. Thus, he is able to overcome the saints - the true believers - within the congregations.

Destruction of the New Testament church is not through political action but through the action of the church itself as it becomes apostate. Clues and guidance as to how this will materialize can be learned from God's dealings with ancient Israel, because Israel is a type, figure, or representation of the New Testament church. What happened in the nation of Israel gives insight as to what will happen to the congregations of our day.

Remember that God had set up a testing program for ancient Israel. The testing program involved contemporary nations. During the days of the demise of the ten tribes, it was the nation of Assyria. The nation of Israel looked with longing at the beautiful horses and the beautiful apparel of the Assyrians and decided that their gods must be victorious gods. They began to play spiritual harlotry with Assyria. They began to run after the gods of the Assyrians, a nation whose language they did not understand. It was the Assyrians that God used to destroy Israel.

Then the nation of Judah began to play spiritual harlotry with the gods of the Babylonians and the Assyrians. They looked at the success of these nations (the beautiful horses and the beautiful apparel), and all that went along with it, and Judah began to lust after their gods. Babylon, too, was a nation whose language they did not understand. It was this nation that destroyed Judah in 587 B.C. This is the scenario that God gives to guide us into truth concerning the destruction of the New Testament church.

God's Long-Term Testing Program for the Church

As we learned in the last chapter, God sets up testing programs for mankind. If man fails the test, terrible things happen to him. If he is victorious through the test, great blessings will result.

The principle of a testing program is found repeatedly in the Bible. Israel, for example, was tested by God when Moses left them for forty days to receive the tables of the law on Mt. Sinai. Israel failed the test by making and worshipping the golden calf. As a result, God's wrath came upon them and about 3000 men were killed (Exodus 32).

The number 40 in the Bible, or a multiple of ten of the number 40 such as 400, may be a clue that a testing program is in progress. Israel was in the wilderness forty years after coming out of Egypt. They failed the test; few of them trusted in God. Therefore, the Bible records in Joshua 5:6:

> For the children of Israel walked forty years in the wilderness, till all the people that were men of war, which came out of Egypt, were consumed, because they obeyed not the voice of the LORD: unto whom the LORD sware that he would not shew them the land, which the LORD sware unto their fathers that he would give us, a land that floweth with milk and honey.

Significantly, it can be shown that there were exactly 400 years from the time when Israel came out of Egypt (1447 B.C.), and Saul became king over Israel (1047 B.C.). The latter occurred in the days of Samuel, who was the last of God's prophets to judge Israel. When Samuel was old, Israel came to him and asked for a king to rule over them. I Samuel 8:4-7:

> Then all the elders of Israel gathered themselves together, and came to Samuel unto Ramah, And said unto him, Behold, thou art old, and thy sons walk not in thy ways: now make us a king to judge us like all the nations. But the thing displeased Samuel, when they said, Give us a king to judge us. And Samuel prayed unto the LORD. And the LORD said unto Samuel, Hearken unto the voice of the people in all that they say unto thee: for they have not rejected thee, but they have rejected me, that I should not reign over them.

Saul became king exactly 400 years after Israel, under the direct rule of God, came out of Egypt. They failed the test in that they did not want God to rule over them directly.

Another interesting testing program in relation to the number forty is in the Book of Jonah. Jonah was instructed to cry against Nineveh because of their wickedness (Jonah 1:2). In Jonah 3:4 are these significant words:

> And Jonah began to enter into the city a day's journey, and he cried, and said, Yet **forty days**, and Nineveh shall be overthrown.

Wonderfully, the people of Nineveh were victorious in their test. Jonah 3:5 and 10 report:

> So the people of Nineveh believed God, and proclaimed a fast, and put on sackcloth, from the greatest of them even to the least of them.
>
> And God saw their works, that they turned from their evil way; and God repented of the evil, that he had said that he would do unto them; and he did it not.

Perhaps the greatest testing program of all occurred in the New Testament, when the Lord Jesus Christ took on a human nature and was tested. Luke 4:1-2:

> And Jesus being full of the Holy Ghost returned from Jordan, and was led by the Spirit into the wilderness. Being **forty days** tempted of the devil. And in those days he did eat nothing: and when they were ended, he afterward hungered.

The first Adam was tested in the Garden of Eden, and the second Adam, Christ, was also tested. The first Adam failed the test by disobeying God and thus plunged the human race into sin, but our Lord was victorious in the test. He remained entirely obedient to God. His perfect obedience has made the incomprehensible Kingdom of God a reality for all who believe on Him. Obviously, the principle that God tests the human race is firmly established in the Bible.

> *The end-time church is faced with a testing program. Unfortunately, the Bible reveals it will fail.*

The end-time church, too, is faced with a testing program. Unfortunately, the Bible reveals that the end-time church will fail its testing program, just as Adam and Eve failed in their day and as ancient Israel repeatedly did. The church will fail the test and will come under God's wrath, just as God's judgment came when Adam and Eve failed the test.

God's Final Testing Program

The testing program that identifies with the end-time church will be focused on a nation whose language the congregation does not understand. Because of the dynamic importance of this truth, we will study it in some detail.

God gives at least two prominent clues in the Old Testament as to the nature of the final testing program. The first is in Deuteronomy 13:1-3 where God informs us:

> If there arise among you a prophet, or a dreamer of dreams, and giveth thee a sign or a wonder, And the sign or the wonder come to pass, whereof he spake unto thee, saying, Let us go after other gods, which thou hast not known, and let us serve them; Thou shalt not hearken unto the words of that prophet, or that dreamer of dreams: for the LORD your God proveth you, to know whether ye love the LORD your God with all your heart and with all your soul.

God clearly says that He is proving, that is, testing the congregation through the activity of a false prophet within their midst. One should know the character of this prophet and the nature of his teaching.

The introduction to Chapter 13 of Deuteronomy is the last verse of Deuteronomy 12, where God admonishes the congregation: "What thing soever I command you, observe to do it: thou shalt not add thereto, nor diminish from it."

> *To believe that there is an additional*
> *source of divine information, . . .*
> *effectively is worshipping a god*
> *other than the God of the Bible.*

In this admonishment God says that man shall not add to nor take away from the Word of God. To recognize the Word of God as His Word and have an intense desire to be obedient to it, is in fact worshipping God as the giver of the Word. On the other hand, to believe that there is an additional source of divine information (to believe that it is from God when indeed it is not), that effectively is worshipping a god other than the God of the Bible.

God gives the same warning in the New Testament, in Revelation 22:18-19:

> For I testify unto every man that heareth the words of the prophecy of this book, If any man shall add unto these things, God shall add unto him the plagues that are written in this book: And if any man shall take away from the words of the book of this prophecy, God shall take away his part out of the book of life, and out of the holy city, and from the things which are written in this book.

This book can be only the Bible. The Bible alone and in its entirety is the Word of God. An additional articulated, verbalized message from God which is delivered through a dream, vision, or by any other means, would be an addition to the Bible. If one listens to these messages and believes they are of God, he effectively is worshipping a god other than the God of the Bible. God warns in verse 18 that anyone who commits this sin is subject to the plagues written in the Bible; that is, he is subject to eternal damnation.

Deuteronomy 13 says the false prophet is a dreamer of dreams, that is, he is convinced that what he hears in his dreams is of God. The sign or the wonder, the prophetic statement of his dream or vision, comes to pass. He, therefore, has received a supernatural visitation, but because the message he received was not from God, it had to be from Satan. When he teaches that the message he received in a dream or vision was from God and, therefore, is the Word of God, he is encouraging the people to go after a god other than the God of the Bible.

This is a deadly serious sin within the congregation. Deuteronomy 13 says that this prophet is to be put to death even if he is the dearest loved one of someone in the congregation.

The key phrases in these verses in Deuteronomy 13 are, "for the Lord your God proveth you" (or tests you) and "to know whether ye love the Lord your God with all your heart and with all your soul." These phrases teach something about God's final testing program for the church. God clearly says that He will test the congregation by allowing those who say they declare the Word of God but who are in fact false prophets (because their source is other than the Bible), to be within the congregation.

I Corinthians 14 Gives a Clue Concerning the Final Testing Program

The second Old Testament clue to the final testing program that will come against the church is that which came against ancient Israel. The signpost to this clue is in the New Testament, I Corinthians 14:21:

> In the law it is written, With men of other tongues and other lips will I speak unto this people; and yet for all that will they not hear me, saith the Lord.

To understand this clue, one must know the setting in which it is found. I Corinthians 14 discusses the phenomenon of tongues, which was present in the church at Corinth. Certain individuals there received from God, as a gift of the Holy Spirit, messages in a language (a tongue), which neither they nor anyone else in the congregation could understand. In I Corinthians 14:2 God speaks of these as "in the spirit he speaketh mysteries."

Additionally, within that congregation God gave certain individuals the gift of interpretation. By means of this God-given gift, the message received in the tongue was made understandable to the congregation. I Corinthians 14:5 informs us that when the tongues message was interpreted, it edified the congregation.

This was a valid spiritual event in the church at Corinth. They had only that part of the Bible which is now called the Old Testament. God was still breaking the silence between the supernatural and the natural when He gave messages to Paul, John, Peter, and Agabus (Acts 11:28). Because these messages were from God, they were an addition to the Word of God. The New Testament had not yet been completed; even with these additions, the churches of that day had an incomplete Word of God.

> *During the same time that it was possible for*
> *the apostles to receive direct messages from*
> *God, individuals in the church of Corinth*
> *received messages from God in a tongue.*

During the same time that it was possible for the apostles to receive direct messages from God, there were individuals in the church of Corinth who received messages from God in a tongue. The messages could have been in the form of a prayer, praise, or a revelation. Howbeit, it was a message from God, therefore, it was an addition to the written Word of that time.

In the center of the discourse on the phenomenon of tongues (I Corinthians 14, verse 21), is a reference to the law wherein God had written that through tongues He would speak to the people and they would not listen. This is a reference to the law of the Old Testament. God speaks about tongues in Deuteronomy 28, as examined earlier in the study. Moses addressed Israel when they were about to enter the Promised Land. He warned them that they would not be content with the Gospel he brought them (Deuteronomy 28:47):

> Because thou servedst not the LORD thy God with joyfulness, and with gladness of heart, for the abundance of all things.

The result of their rebellion against God was punishment. This is declared in the remaining verses of Deuteronomy 28; however, verses 48 and 49 summarize the warning:

> Therefore shalt thou serve thine enemies which the LORD shall send against thee, in hunger, and in thirst, and in nakedness, and in want of all things: and he shall put a yoke of iron upon thy neck, until he have destroyed thee. The LORD shall bring a nation against thee from far, from the end of the earth, as swift as the eagle flieth; a nation whose tongue thou shalt not understand.

The enemy that was to destroy them was a nation whose tongue they could not understand. Therefore, this is the passage of law referred to in I Corinthians 14 in regards to the tongues phenomenon.

As we learned earlier, the ten tribes of Israel were destroyed by the nation of Assyria after Israel had engaged in spiritual harlotry with the Assyrians. As a result of their spiritual rebellion, God caused the nation of Assyria, a nation whose language Israel did not understand, to destroy them.

God gave a final warning of this a few years before it happened. The warning is found in Isaiah 28:11-12.

> For with stammering lips and another tongue will he speak to this people. To whom he said, This is the rest wherewith ye may cause the weary to rest; and this is the refreshing: yet they would not hear.

The sequel to God's judgment on Israel occurred 123 years later. The nation of Judah ran like a harlot after Babylon, a heathen nation whose language they did not understand, and Babylon is the nation that destroyed Judah in the year 587 B.C. A few years earlier they had been warned by the prophet Jeremiah. Jeremiah 5:15-17:

> Lo, I will bring a nation upon you from far, O house of Israel, saith the LORD; it is a mighty nation, it is an ancient nation, a nation whose language thou knowest not, neither understandest what they say. Their quiver is as an open sepulchre, they are all mighty men. And they shall eat up thine harvest, and thy bread, which thy sons and thy daughters should eat: they shall eat up thy flocks and thine herds: they shall eat up thy vines and thy fig trees: they shall impoverish thy fenced cities, wherein thou trustedst, with the sword.

God is focusing on a nation "whose language thou knowest not." This passage, too, is referred to in the ominous language of I Corinthians 14:21.

Deuteronomy 13, Deuteronomy 28, I Corinthians 14, and God's judgment are tied to the end-time church when one considers the two important principles learned earlier.

> *God's judgment on Israel for spiritual adultery*
> *sheds light on the nature of God's judgment on*
> *the New Testament church.*

The first principle is that ancient Israel was a picture or type of the New Testament church. God's judgment on Israel for their spiritual adultery sheds light on the nature of God's judgment on the New Testament church for its spiritual rebellion.

The second principle is that God sets up testing programs for mankind. In Deuteronomy 13 it is seen that within the church a testing program will involve false prophets who receive supernatural messages. These false prophets will encourage the congregations to go after other gods by revealing their supernatural experiences, which come from a source other than God. These two Biblical principles give understanding as to how God judges the end-time church.

Tongues: End-Time Testing Program

The question might be raised: Why does God write extensively in I Corinthians 12, 13, and 14 about the phenomenon of tongues? One might be surprised to read in the Bible about this temporary phenomenon. A few decades after this phenomenon occurred in the church in Corinth, the visions of the Book of Revelation were received by the Apostle John on the Island of Patmos. This book closed with the warning that anyone who added to its words would be subject to plagues; therefore, there could be no further revelation from God by visions, voices, tongues, or anything else. Thus, the phenomenon of tongues that occurred in the church at Corinth would also have come to an end. From that time to the present day, do not expect God to bring a message by these means or by any other means. The Word of God is complete. The Bible alone and in its entirety is the Word of God.

It appears that the phenomenon of tongues from God was short-lived and confined only to the church at Corinth. It was an incidental matter even in that day; thus, the question persists: Why did God write extensively about it?

The answer lies in the realization that these three chapters of I Corinthians discuss the matter of tongues as God's testing arena for the end-time church. God planted the tree of the knowledge of good and evil in the Garden of Eden, and it was the testing arena of our first parents. Satan saw his opportunity in that testing program to tempt man into sin and thus enslave him. In the warning and testing program of Deuteronomy 13, God allows a false prophet to deceive some people within the congregation. God sets up the testing programs, but it is Satan who uses the tests as opportunities to lead people astray.

> *God established the phenomenon of tongues as a testing arena for the end-time church.*

It is the phenomenon of tongues, recorded in I Corinthians 12, 13, and 14, that God established as a testing arena for the end-time church. God gave the true gift of tongues briefly in the church at Corinth so that the end-time churches' fidelity to the Word of God could be discovered.

Adam and Eve were permitted to eat of every tree of the garden except one. In these trees there were lavish blessings of God; they provided fragrant and delicious fruits to satisfy the physical needs of man. Lucifer wanted man to serve Satan rather than God, and he tempted Adam and Eve into thinking they were missing something important if they did not taste the fruit of the one tree that had been placed off-limits.

The church is repeatedly reminded throughout the Bible of the lavish blessings that attend salvation. They are far more than anyone deserves. They are so wonderful that our hearts should continuously praise God.

The one minor blessing that was briefly enjoyed by a few people in the church at Corinth was an incidental blessing (being able to receive an additional message from God in an unknown language), before the magnificent blessings of the whole Word of God were available.

God maximized His communicative blessings to mankind by giving us the entire record of His will (the New Testament and the Old Testament), and He placed off-limits the minor blessing enjoyed by the church at Corinth. It was no longer to be expected in view of the fact that God had given His larger blessing - the entire Bible.

God, in His wisdom, retained the record; indeed He prominently displayed the record of the phenomenon of tongues in the Bible. Its placement there makes it a testing arena for the end-time church, as the tree of the knowledge of good and evil was the testing arena for the beginning of the human race.

> *Satan defeated Adam and Eve by encouraging them to eat of the forbidden tree in the Garden of Eden.*

Satan Uses Tongues to Destroy

It is precisely this testing arena that Satan uses as his final opportunity to win a decisive victory over Christ by defeating the external church. He defeated Adam and Eve by encouraging them to eat of the forbidden tree in the Garden of Eden. Likewise, he encourages the end-time church to enjoy the forbidden gift of tongues.

When God set up the testing arena in the Garden of Eden, He used language that made it easy - or at least paved the way - for Lucifer to tempt Eve. God did not give the forbidden tree a foreboding name like "forbidden" tree. God gave this tree the intriguing name "the tree of the knowledge of good and evil." Certainly, such a title would cause Adam and Eve to wonder what mysterious power the fruit of this tree possessed. This is evidenced by Eve's reaction to Satan's enticements, in Genesis 3:6:

> And when the woman saw that the tree was good for food, and that it was pleasant to the eyes, and a tree to be desired to make one wise, she took of the fruit thereof, and did eat, and gave also unto her husband with her; and he did eat.

Satan stimulated Eve's lustful thinking by making reference to the name God had given the tree. In Genesis 3:5 Satan declared to Eve:

> For God doth know that in the day ye eat thereof, then your eyes shall be opened, and ye shall be as gods, knowing good and evil.

Note his words, "your eyes shall be opened, and ye shall be as gods, knowing good and evil." Surely in giving this tree the name "the knowledge of good and evil," God gave Satan a theme that he could use to stimulate our first parents into sin.

God, of course, is not the author of sin, nor is He in any way guilty of sin. God did, however, design an insistent and valid testing program, in that the fruit appeared to be especially luscious ("the tree was good for food, and that it was pleasant to the eyes," verse 6), and in the name that the tree was given.

God also made the testing arena for ancient Israel quite intensive. The ten tribes of the northern kingdom, called Israel, were destroyed by the Assyrians, a nation whose language they did not understand. While Israel was failing the test, God blessed the nation of Assyria: they conquered Syria (II Kings 16:9), and appeared to be the nation with all the answers. Ezekiel 23:5-6:

And Aholah played the harlot when she was mine; and she doted on her lovers, on the Assyrians her neighbours, Which were clothed with blue, captains and rulers, all of them desirable young men, horsemen riding upon horses.

As previously mentioned, "Aholah" is another name for the capital of Israel, which was in Samaria. Assyria and its political successes and worldly achievements appeared to be the nation to emulate. Similarly, Judah, the southern kingdom with its capital in Jerusalem, was enamored by the beauty, power, and successes of both the Assyrians and the Babylonians.

> *The beauty, power, and political*
> *successes of Assyria and Babylon*
> *were the results of God's blessings.*

The beauty, power, and political successes of Assyria and Babylon were the results of God's blessings. These wicked nations were in total rebellion against God, yet God brought them to power and made them attractive merely to serve as testing programs for Israel and Judah.

Israel Goes to Assyria for Help

The Bible gives a vivid illustration of how God allowed a wicked nation like Assyria to appear to Israel to be a success story. During the days of Isaiah, Jerusalem was threatened by Israel and Syria. The situation was grave. II Chronicles 28 discloses the wickedness of Judah's King Ahaz, and the resultant punishment God brought upon Judah by Israel and Syria. II Chronicles 28:5-6:

Wherefore the LORD his God delivered him into the hand of the king of Syria; and they smote him, and carried away a great multitude of them captives, and brought them to Damascus. And he was also delivered into the hand of the king of Israel, who smote him with a great slaughter. For Pekah the son of Remaliah slew in Judah an hundred and twenty thousand in one day, which were all valiant men; because they had forsaken the LORD God of their fathers.

The king of Judah, a wicked man named Ahaz, and all of Judah should have cried to God for help. They should have repented in sackcloth like Nineveh did when Jonah preached to them. They should have cried out to God as King Jehoshaphat did when the Moabites and the Ammonites came to destroy Judah (II Chronicles 20). Instead the Bible records that Judah went to Assyria for help. II Kings 16:7:

> So Ahaz sent messengers to Tiglath-pileser king of Assyria, saying, I am thy servant and thy son: come up, and save me out of the hand of the king of Syria, and out of the hand of the king of Israel, which rise up against me.

They could not have more dramatically displayed their complete lack of trust in God. God rescued sinful Judah by wicked Assyria, as II Kings 16:9 declares:

> And the king of Assyria hearkened unto him: for the king of Assyria went up against Damascus, and took it, and carried the people of it captive to Kir, and slew Rezin.

Assyria conquered Syria. Until recent times, Syria had not been an independent nation. God used Assyria to destroy the ten tribes; they no longer existed as an independent kingdom. These two nations, Syria and the northern kingdom of Israel, therefore were removed as a threat to Judah by the strength of the heathen nation Assyria.

> *The successes of Assyria and Babylon suggested that their gods were more powerful and more trustworthy than Jehovah God.*

The point of this information is that God brought successes to Assyria to intensify the testing program that was coming against Judah. The successes of Assyria in its flower, and Babylon in its flower, suggested that their gods were more powerful and more trustworthy than Jehovah God. God, for His divine purposes, gave Assyria the victory, but Judah was convinced that the superiority of the Assyrian gods made them victorious. This spiritual mentality is seen in the citation of II Chronicles 25:14 where another king of Judah, Amaziah, worshipped the gods of an enemy called Edom or Seir. This verse declares:

Now it came to pass, after that Amaziah was come from the slaughter of the Edomites, that he brought the gods of the children of Seir, and set them up to be his gods, and bowed down himself before them, and burned incense unto them.

II Chronicles 28:22-23 records similar action by the wicked King Ahaz:

And in the time of his distress did he trespass yet more against the LORD: this is that king Ahaz. For he sacrificed unto the gods of Damascus, which smote him: and he said, Because the gods of the kings of Syria help them, therefore will I sacrifice to them, that they may help me. But they were the ruin of him, and of all Israel.

> *God strengthens the test by His choice of words or by allowing the enemies of God to appear to be successful.*

God Intensifies the Final Testing Program

When God sets up a testing program, He strengthens the test by His choice of words or by allowing the actions of enemies of God to appear to be successful. The same principles apply to God's final testing program for the end-time church: in relation to God's Word, the Bible, and in relation to the successes that God allows the enemies of the Gospel to enjoy.

Three examples of words that God uses to indicate the severity of the test for the end-time church are offered. First God says that those who spoke in tongues in the Corinthian church were edified as they spoke these mysteries in the Spirit (I Corinthians 14:2-4). Surely anything that serves to edify or build up the faith of the individual believer is to be sought after but the context in which these words are found warns the reader to be careful.

Secondly, God declares in I Corinthians 14:39, "forbid not to speak with tongues." Does this teach that speaking in tongues is sinful?

The third example requires more explanation. In three of the four gospels, Matthew, Mark, and John, the sin called blasphemy against the Holy Spirit is mentioned. It is also referred to in I John 5 as a "sin unto death." This sin is unusual in that those who commit it can never have forgiveness; that is, they can never become saved. Moreover, it is unusual in that God protects mankind from it to the point that it is virtually impossible to find anyone who has ever committed this sin.

However, the scribes of Jesus' day committed this sin. Mark 3:22 says of them:

> And the scribes which came down from Jerusalem said, He hath Beelzebub, and by the prince of the devils casteth he out devils.

In response to this grievous sin Jesus declares in Mark 3:28-29,

> Verily I say unto you, All sins shall be forgiven unto the sons of men, and blasphemies wherewith soever they shall blaspheme: But he that shall blaspheme against the Holy Ghost hath never forgiveness, but is in danger of eternal damnation.

In verse 30 He explains that the sin of blasphemy against the Holy Spirit is to believe that Christ was under the power of Satan rather than under the power of the Holy Spirit. The scribes who hated Jesus and desired His death had committed this dreadful sin; they were convinced that He was of Satan. They had no desire to look upon Him as their Messiah.

Those who have committed this sin . . . will never worry about Christ being their Savior.

The Bible mentions only that the scribes in Mark 3 and Matthew 12 have committed this sin. The most hardened sinner of today ordinarily would not become convicted that Jesus received His power from Satan. There may be those in the world who have committed this sin, but if they have they will never worry about Christ being their Savior. Anyone who has the slightest interest in Jesus as Savior could not have committed this dreadful sin.

One might ask: Why did God put an extensive record of this sin in the Bible? Its presence in the Bible has produced much sorrow for true believers who have been incorrectly taught that the sin of blasphemy of the Holy Spirit is to reject Christ. Many true believers when young repeatedly rejected Christ. They have become saved in their later years, but are haunted by the question: Can they be saved? One reason for the recording of this sin in the Bible is to increase the severity of the testing program of the end-time church.

The correct understanding of the sin of blasphemy against the Holy Spirit is to believe that Jesus, when He came as the Savior, was under the power of Satan.

By a simple extension of this idea, it could wrongly be concluded that anyone who believes that a church is actually under the power of Satan, has committed this terrible sin. In other words, it might be said that if someone examines a particular gospel or church and decides that it is of Satan, by that judgment he is in danger of having committed blasphemy against the Holy Spirit. This conclusion is erroneous, but it is widely taught by those who believe in tongues. Few dare to make the judgment that a "tongues gospel" is of Satan. Almost no one dares to conclude that a gospel can be a product of Satan when it claims that Christ is the Savior. As a result, the "tongues gospel" is protected from criticism even by those who want to remain true to the Bible. In fear of blaspheming the Holy Spirit, they are forced to acknowledge that even though they disagree with many doctrines of the "tongues gospel," it must be considered an aspect of the true Gospel. This, in turn, encourages many people to follow the "tongues gospel." God, thus, has built characteristics into the tongues testing program that make it appear safe in its identification with the true Gospel.

> *The tongues movement, also called the charismatic movement, is sweeping through churches like wildfire.*

The Success of the Tongues Movement

An ever-increasing number of individuals and congregations all over the world fail this end-of-time testing program. The tongues movement, also called the "charismatic movement," is sweeping through churches like wildfire. Virtually every denomination has churches that have welcomed it with open arms.

For generations attempts have been made to unify various faiths and denominations; however, no attempt has made progress like the charismatic movement. Roman Catholics, Lutherans, Presbyterians, Methodists, Baptists - all gospels that identify with the Christian ethic - find brotherhood under the charismatic banner. To those who embrace the tongues phenomenon, it appears to be a wonderful and certain demonstration of the power of the Holy Spirit.

The Bible guides us into truth; we can know the facts. The church has become apostate. Consequently, God is blinding people so that they believe this movement is of the Holy Spirit. They do not realize that it is of Satan. By means of this phenomenon, Satan appears to be defeating the true Gospel to a degree never before realized.

Indeed, God brought judgment on the Old Testament church (Israel and Judah), by nations whose language Israel did not understand, nations with whom Israel had engaged in spiritual harlotry. God used these nations to destroy Israel and Judah. Likewise, churches and denominations of today are engaging in grievous spiritual harlotry by blindly running after gospels that feature an unknown language called "tongues." These false gospels are being used of God as a judgment on the church. Expect to see the church destroyed by them.

Congregations will continue to exist. They may appear to be more vibrant and spiritually successful than ever. It may appear that the cause of Christ is advancing all over the world: Crusades attended in ever-increasing numbers, churches filled to capacity, seminaries with more prospective preachers. Nevertheless, it must be realized that the church is under God's judgment. The abomination of desolation increasingly stands in the holy place. The man of sin increasingly takes his seat in the temple. The era of the New Testament church has almost ended.

Two important characteristics always appear to be present in the tongues movement: First, acceptance of the principle that God is still speaking today. Additional revelation, it is believed, may be revealed through an unknown language called tongues, a vision, a dream, or by hearing a voice. Invariably where there is an interest in dreams and visions, there is an interest in tongues. Likewise, wherever there is an interest in tongues, there is an interest in dreams and visions.

The insistence on the principle that God is speaking today automatically proves that the tongues movement is a false gospel. Its authority is a different authority than that of the true Gospel.

Signs and Wonders

The true Gospel is circumscribed by its authority - the Bible alone and in its entirety. The "tongues gospel" has as its authority the Bible plus the messages that supposedly come from God in a tongue, dream, vision, or voice. It is easy to know that it is not the true Gospel, and if it is not the true Gospel, it is a false gospel.

> *There is a pronounced interest in signs and wonders. There is a conviction that God is performing miracles today, as our Lord and the twelve apostles did signs and wonders.*

Secondly, in the tongues movement, there is a pronounced interest in signs and wonders. There is a conviction that God is performing miracles today, as our Lord and the twelve apostles did signs and wonders. Miraculous healing is most commonly expected. The sign of people falling backward - being "slain in the spirit," as some call it - is evidence of a supernatural event. While so-called miraculous healing can be explained in earthly, physical terms, falling backwards appears to be unexplainable from an earthly, physical vantage point.

The phenomena of someone appearing to receive a message from God in a tongue or vision, etc., may actually have a physical explanation. It could be the result of an hallucination or it could be related to the individual's subconscious mind. Also, it could be supernatural activity induced by Satan; he captivates the hearts of those who are not content with the true Gospel. When it is a supernatural activity it should be called a sign or a wonder because God calls the activity of speaking in tongues a sign in I Corinthians 14:22.

> *The Bible makes reference to "signs and wonders" in connection with the end of time. . . . these references have nothing to do with the true church.*

Significantly, the Bible makes reference to "signs and won-ders" in connection with the end of time. Of great importance is the fact that these references have nothing to do with the true church. Every reference relates to satanic activity. For example, in Matthew 24:24:

> For there shall arise false Christs, and false prophets, and shall shew great signs and wonders; insomuch that, if it were possible, they shall deceive the very elect.

This verse indicates that false prophets will come with a gospel that is so much like the true Gospel that even the elect would be deceived, if that were possible. The elect are the true believers - chosen by God to salvation. They cannot be deceived because God will hold them fast. False prophets can be recognized by their signs and wonders.

In II Thessalonians 2:9 God warns of the man of sin who will take his seat in the temple: "Even him, whose coming is after the working of Satan with all power and signs and lying wonders."

In Revelation 13, in reference to Satan coming as a false prophet, God warns in verses 13-14:

And he doeth great wonders, so that he maketh fire come down from heaven on the earth in the sight of men, And deceiveth them that dwell on the earth by the means of those miracles which he had power to do in the sight of the beast; saying to them that dwell on the earth, that they should make an image to the beast, which had the wound by a sword, and did live.

In Revelation 16, verse 14, God is speaking of satanic activity just before Judgment Day:

For they are the spirits of devils, working miracles, which go forth unto the kings of the earth and of the whole world, to gather them to the battle of that great day of God Almighty.

God shows in these references that as He brings His judgment on the end-time church, it is through gospels that feature miracles. Do not be surprised that signs and wonders are prominent in churches with false gospels. When Christ came with the true Gospel He attested to its genuineness by performing miracles. John 20:30-31:

And many other signs truly did Jesus in the presence of his disciples, which are not written in this book: But these are written, that ye might believe that Jesus is the Christ, the Son of God; and that believing ye might have life through his name.

Satan comes with his false gospels that feature tongues and attempts to attest to their genuineness with signs and wonders.

As Satan comes at the end of time with his false gospels that feature tongues he, too, attempts to attest to their genuineness with signs and wonders. As was seen earlier, only two miracles are credited to him in the Bible. These are: First, his ability to break the silence between the supernatural and the natural with messages in tongues and visions; and second, he can supernaturally cause people to fall backward. To add further credence to these gospels, Satan comes with lying signs and wonders; that is, his adherents will claim to do miracles and believe miracles have been done, when there has been no miracle.

Modern means of communication such as television enhance the spread of these false gospels. People who worship in churches that are reasonably faithful to the true Gospel may become familiar with the blandishments and enticements of false gospels in the privacy of their homes. With no one knowing, they drink deeply of this poisoned water, and as the plague enters their churches, they are prepared to accept it as an aspect of the true Gospel.

> *Right before our eyes, church after church capitulates to gospels that do not consider the Bible alone and in its entirety to be the Gospel.*

One can see the reality of God's judgment on the church because of growing apostasy. Right before our eyes, church after church capitulates to gospels that do not consider the Bible alone and in its entirety to be the true Gospel.

The destruction of the church, to a high degree, is accomplished through the testing program of tongues. In blindness, a church will fail the test as Satan deceives the congregation into accepting the false gospels of tongues and signs and wonders. Thus, congregations will continue to exist during the final tribulation period, but they will be increasingly false. True believers will either voluntarily leave or they will be asked to leave when the congregation begins to follow a false gospel. Those who remain within the congregations in reality will be serving Satan even though they think they are serving Christ.

We have seen, therefore, that the final tribulation period is God's judgment on the church because of its apostasy. It is a judgment on the world in the sense that the possibility of salvation is rapidly coming to an end.

Who Is the Antichrist?

A great many theologians and pastors speak much about the antichrist who will come. They constantly focus on this individual or that individual as a likely candidate to be the antichrist. They have convinced themselves that Satan will rule through an outstanding religious-political individual who will have tremendous power in the world. In fact, if they would read I John 4:3 more carefully, they would learn that the antichrist cannot be a human being. This verse declares:

> And every spirit that confesseth not that Jesus Christ is come in the flesh is not of God: and this is that spirit of anti-christ, whereof ye have heard that it should come; and even now already is it in the world.

If the antichrist were alive about 2000 years ago when this verse was written, and if he is coming much later in history, he cannot be a human being. He can be only Satan. Christ heads up the Kingdom of God wherein His subjects are called Christians. Satan, the antichrist, heads up the dominion of darkness with his subjects being called false prophets and antichrists.

Satan is the master deceiver. He is
the antichrist.

Satan is the master deceiver. He is the antichrist. All kinds of churches are looking for the antichrist to come as an outstanding religious-political figure, but he has already overcome many churches as they have become false gospels.

In II Corinthians 11, God describes how Satan works in the churches. He does not come with a forked tail and a red suit. Rather he comes looking holy and righteous. II Corinthians 11:13-15:

> For such are false apostles, deceitful workers, transforming themselves into the apostles of Christ. And no marvel; for Satan himself is transformed into an angel of light. Therefore it is no great thing if his ministers also be transformed as the ministers of righteousness; whose end shall be according to their works.

Many people have the naive notion that if they use language like "pleading the blood of Christ," Satan will flee from them. The fact is, however, that Satan himself uses this kind of language as he speaks through ministers and church leaders who are following a false gospel rather than the true Gospel. Satan is the father of lies. As such, he has blinded countless people into thinking they are serving Christ when in actuality they are serving Satan.

Believers Are Killed When Satan Rules in the Church

We have learned from the Bible that the New Testament church era will end, just as the era of ancient Israel came to an end. The end of the New Testament church results from increasing worldwide apostasy within the church and God's judgment upon it. That judgment is totally involved with the final tribulation period.

Few verses thus far quoted in this study suggest that the final tribulation period is a time of massive bloodletting. If other verses allude to this ugly possibility, perhaps they will teach more about the character of the final tribulation period.

Because of the important teaching of Matthew 24:21 and because the time has come when this verse has come to fulfillment, it will be studied again. In Matthew 24:21 God declares:

> For then shall be great tribulation, such as was not since the beginning of the world to this time, no, nor ever shall be.

This verse says that the character of the final tribulation period will be different from any that has ever come on the face of the earth. Physical persecution is not the chief characteristic of the final tribulation period; persecution by bloodletting has happened throughout history. However, this will be different; it will be something the world has not previously known.

The context of Matthew 24:21 gives some clues as to what this tribulation will be. Verses 15-16 instruct:

> When ye therefore shall see the abomination of desolation, spoken of by Daniel the prophet, stand in the holy place, (whoso readeth, let him understand:) Then let them which be in Judaea flee into the mountains.

As was noted earlier, the only Biblical holy place, after Christ went to the cross, is the body of believers. The homeland of the corporate body is the congregation or church. The abomination of desolation is the incursion of Satan into the heart of the church. The phrase "spoken of by Daniel the prophet" identifies with Daniel 8:13:

> Then I heard one saint speaking, and another saint said unto that certain saint which spake, How long shall be the vision concerning the daily sacrifice, and the transgression of desolation, to give both the sanctuary and the host to be trodden under foot?

In this verse God speaks of the sanctuary being trodden under foot. The "sanctuary" like the "holy place" in Matthew 24:15 can identify only with the body of believers. Therefore, the phrase "trodden under foot" in the Daniel account gives the same information as the phrase "stand in" in the Matthew account.

During the final tribulation period, congregations and denominations worldwide will be increasingly overrun with satanically inspired gospels.

Satan Rules in the Church

When Satan stands in the holy place - when he rules in the church - then the sanctuary will be trodden under foot; the external church will have become vanquished by Satan. Daniel 8:13 and Matthew 24:15 speak of the same sad event. Thus, it can be fairly safely asserted that these verses teach that during the final tribulation period, congregations and denominations worldwide will be increasingly overrun with satanically inspired gospels. It is God's plan that the churches will come under this judgment. The chief characteristics of the final tribulation period will be Satan's spiritual leadership in the congregations and the binding of the hearts of the unsaved, so that in all probability there is a great slowing down of the number of people becoming saved. One reason for this is that as fewer and fewer churches faithfully bring the true Gospel, there are fewer and fewer people hearing the truth. In our day, it is surprising how few evangelists and preachers faithfully preach the whole counsel of God or even understand salvation.

Satan's leadership and character in the church are known from verses that follow Matthew 24:21. Verse 24 declares:

For there shall arise false Christs, and false prophets, and shall shew great signs and wonders; insomuch that, if it were possible, they shall deceive the very elect.

Our Lord could not make plainer the fact that the congregations will be grievously troubled by Satan during the final tribulation period. This truth is in evidence in II Thessalonians 2:1-4:

Now we beseech you, brethren, by the coming of our Lord Jesus Christ, and by our gathering together unto him, That ye be not soon shaken in mind, or be troubled, neither by spirit, nor by word, nor by letter as from us, as that the day of Christ is at hand. Let no man deceive you by any means: for that day shall not come, except there come a falling away first, and that man of sin be revealed, the son of perdition: Who opposeth and exalteth himself above all that is called God, or that is worshipped; so that he as God sitteth in the temple of God, shewing himself that he is God.

These instructive verses show that the man of sin will take his seat in the temple and be worshipped as God. Satan is called the man of sin; he is typified by the king who reigned over ancient Babylon in Isaiah 14. In this chapter, God discusses Babylon and its king and directs attention to the fall of Satan. In the same paragraph, with no transition whatsoever, the Bible discloses both events: The destruction of Babylon and the fall of Satan. The reason is that Babylon is a type or figure of Satan's kingdom, and the king of Babylon is a type or figure of Satan.

God declares in Isaiah 14, verses 16 and 17:

They that see thee shall narrowly look upon thee, and consider thee, saying, Is this the man that made the earth to tremble, that did shake kingdoms; That made the world as a wilderness, and destroyed the cities thereof; that opened not the house of his prisoners?

Satan is called the man of sin; he is typified by the king who reigned over ancient Babylon in Isaiah 14.

Satan made the world as a wilderness by tempting Adam and Eve into sin. He desires to hold the inhabitants of the world in spiritual bondage and refuses to let anyone out of his prison house. Praise God, our Savior bound Satan by going to the cross and set His prisoners free.

In these verses Satan is called "a man." Satan, of course, is not a man. He is called a man because he was typified by a man: The king who had ruled over ancient Babylon.

In II Thessalonians 2:3, Satan is called "that man of sin." Undoubtedly God deems it appropriate in this passage to call him a man because God is emphasizing Satan's kingship as he rules in the external church. The type of Satan, the king of Babylon, ruled over Babylon; and Satan will rule as a king within the church. Verse 4 bears this out; it speaks of him sitting in the temple of God and showing himself as God. "To sit" Biblically connotes reigning. Jesus sat down at the right hand of God and was given authority over all things (Ephesians 1:20-22). God alone reigns as King of kings and Lord of lords.

But we discover in II Thessalonians 2:4 that Satan will be allowed to rule in the temple. The temple can be only the congregations where the true believers should worship.

> *Satan does not wear a red suit with a forked tail. He comes as an angel of light.*

As was noted earlier, Satan does not wear a red suit with a forked tail. He comes as an angel of light, and his ministers come as ministers of righteousness (II Corinthians 11:13-15). Those who remain in congregations with false gospels have been deceived by the master deceiver. They think they are worshipping the Lord Jesus Christ. Instead, they are worshipping Satan. This is suggested in Revelation 13, where God says that the beast that comes out of the earth will cause those who follow him to make an image of the beast which had the wound by a sword and did live. Verses 13 and 14 show us this dramatic truth:

> And he doeth great wonders, so that he maketh fire come down from heaven on the earth in the sight of men, And deceiveth them that dwell on the earth by the means of those miracles which he had power to do in the sight of the beast; saying to them that dwell on the earth, that they should make an image to the beast, which had the wound by a sword, and did live.

The beast that was wounded by a sword is Satan. Hebrews 2:14:

> Forasmuch then as the children are partakers of flesh and blood, he also himself likewise took part of the same; that through death he might destroy him that had the power of death, that is, the devil.

Christ destroyed Satan in principle by going to the cross. Christ endured the equivalent of eternal damnation in the cross experience, which guarantees that all the wicked, including Satan, are subject to the second death, eternal damnation.

Satan lives in that he is allowed to continue to reign over the hearts of unsaved men during the final tribulation period. However, on Judgment Day the second death with all its force will overtake Satan and he will be thrown into hell.

According to Revelation 13:14, Satan is worshipped. The phrase "make an image" in this verse is drawn from the Old Testament. Israel was frequently snared into false religions that featured idol gods. Therefore, to make an image refers to the development of false gospels. Those within these gospels think they are serving the Lord Jesus Christ. Revelation 13:11 pictures the beast with two horns like a lamb. Christ is the Lamb who took away the sins of everyone who believes on Him. Thus, verse 11 teaches that Satan comes with the appearance of Christ.

Revelation 13:15 indicates that the adversaries of the beast will be killed:

> And he had power to give life unto the image of the beast, that the image of the beast should both speak, and cause that as many as would not worship the image of the beast should be killed.

This verse parallels Revelation 11:7, which says that the two witnesses who bring the Gospel eventually will be killed by Satan. The two witnesses will be killed after their testimony has been finished. God has written, in Revelation 11:7:

> And when they shall have finished their testimony, the beast that ascendeth out of the bottomless pit shall make war against them, and shall overcome them, and kill them.

The Two Witnesses

A study of Revelation 11 reveals that the two witnesses who must be killed (verse 7), refer to the body of believers, those mandated by God to bring the Gospel. In Revelation 11:4 they are called "two olive trees" and "two candlesticks standing before the God of the earth." God speaks of the body of believers as an olive tree into which the individual believer is grafted. The number two is commonly used in the Bible as a figure of the church, for example, when God sent the seventy out two by two. They are a picture of the church as it proclaims the Gospel. Moreover, it is out of the mouths of two or three witnesses that every word is established. Thus, both from the standpoint that the olive tree represents the body of believers and from the standpoint that the number two signifies the church, the two olive trees represent the church as it brings the Gospel.

In Revelation 1:20 God speaks of the seven churches represented in heaven by seven candlesticks. God uses the term "candlestick" as a synonym for a congregation. Thus, the phrase "two candlesticks" as used in Revelation 11 describes the two witnesses who represent the New Testament congregations that go forth with the Gospel.

Revelation 13:15 and Revelation 11:7 seem to contradict the premise that the final tribulation period will not be a time of grievous bloodletting, the chief characteristic of persecution throughout history. The conclusion might be reached that these verses speak of physical violence. However, a fundamental principle of Scripture is that spiritual things must be compared with spiritual; that is, test all conclusions against the rest of the Bible to see if they are in harmony with everything else the Bible teaches.

That physical bloodletting is not the major focus of the final tribulation period is strongly suggested in Matthew 24:21 where Jesus declares that it will be a tribulation like no other. Matthew 24:15 and 24:24 and II Thessalonians 2:1-9 indicate that the final tribulation period will be a time when false gospels that feature signs will be present in the churches. The success of false gospels that closely resemble the true gospel points to the absence of physical persecution. Physical persecution is not currently limited to those who hold the true Gospel. Persecution, if in vogue, is against all who call themselves Christian. In Muslim countries, for example, the true Gospel and every false gospel that includes the idea of Christ as Savior are the enemy. This is true also in Communist countries where any gospel called Christian, or any religion regardless of its character, is an enemy of the state.

Thus, if the false gospels mentioned in Matthew 24 and II Thessalonians 2 are to flourish as indicated, their environment cannot oppress any gospel that calls itself Christian. Therefore, we should not expect special bloodletting during the final tribulation period.

The Bible indicates that the final tribulation period is a time of substantial world peace. It is business as usual. Matthew 24:37-39 says:

> But as the days of Noe were, so shall also the coming of the Son of man be. For as in the days that were before the flood they were eating and drinking, marrying and giving in marriage, until the day that Noe entered into the ark, And knew not until the flood came, and took them all away; so shall also the coming of the Son of man be.

Similarly, in Luke 17:28-30, God compares world conditions at the time of Christ's return to the situation in Sodom when it was destroyed:

> Likewise also as it was in the days of Lot; they did eat, they drank, they bought, they sold, they planted, they builded; But the same day that Lot went out of Sodom, it rained fire and brimstone from heaven, and destroyed them all. Even thus shall it be in the day when the Son of man is revealed.

The final tribulation period does not include physical persecution of true believers, but Revelation 11:7 and 13:15 speak of killing. However, the Bible says that those who hate are, in fact, murderers. I John 3:15 says: "Whosoever hateth his brother is a murderer: and ye know that no murderer hath eternal life abiding in him."

I John 3:13 emphasizes the fact that the true believer will be hated by the world, "Marvel not, my brethren, if the world hate you." In Matthew 10:22 Jesus emphasizes the world's hatred for the believer: "And ye shall be hated of all men for my name's sake; but he that endureth to the end shall be saved."

Satan wanted Jesus killed when Jesus came as Savior, and Satan wants the citizens of Jesus' Kingdom killed.

The basis of this hatred is, of course, that the people of this world are enslaved to sin and Satan. They are citizens of Satan's dominion, and Satan is the bitter foe of Christ. Satan wanted Jesus killed when Jesus came as the Savior, and Satan wants the citizens of Jesus' kingdom killed.

Satan has two options whereby he can cause the death of the true believers: First, he can subject them to physical death. This longstanding method has been employed often by the forces of evil. Satan's difficulty with this murder method is its long-time failure to accomplish his desired goal, which is stamp out the Kingdom of Christ. Physical bloodletting actually tends to build the church. The blood of the martyrs becomes the seed of the church.

Satan's alternative method of attempting to neutralize the Kingdom of God is to kill those within the church, which is a two-sided method, as we shall see later (page 202). This method appears eminently successful. In John 16:2 we read: "They shall put you out of the synagogues: yea, the time cometh, that whosoever killeth you will think that he doeth God service."

> *True believers within the congregations are killed in the sense that they are driven from these congregations.*

In this verse we find that being put out of the synagogues is equivalent to being killed. Thus when congregations embrace false gospels, or become so apostate that they approximate a false gospel, the true believers within them are killed in the sense that they are driven from these congregations either voluntarily or by force.

Moreover, if Satan can cause a person to turn from the true Gospel to a false gospel, he effectively will have killed that person, who remains under the condemnation of God. He is subject to the most awesome death mankind will ever know: eternal damnation. Satan is the essence of destruction; his goal is to draw people away from Christ, who is life, and into the path that leads to destruction. An unsaved person is spiritually dead because he is under the wrath of God.

There is what seems to be an apparent contradiction: Verses that suggest "business as usual" during the final tribulation period and verses that speak of Satan killing believers. Revelation 13:15 teaches that those who do not worship the beast (that is, true believers), must be killed. A true believer is not subject to eternal damnation; therefore, this kind of killing cannot be in view in this verse. Other verses teach that physical persecution will not be a major factor of the final tribulation period.

The solution is found in Revelation 13:7:

And it was given unto him to make war with the saints, and to overcome them: and power was given him over all kindreds, and tongues, and nations.

In this revealing verse God assures us that Satan will win in a sense. In the warfare Satan has assaulted the church again and again, but Satan cannot win until the last of the elect have become saved. Christ will build His church and the gates of hell cannot triumph.

After the last of the elect have become saved (the temple, consisting of true believers, has been built), then God will have ended the saving of the elect and it will appear that Satan has won. No one else will become saved.

Satan: The Little Horn

Similar language discusses the fourth beast, the ten horns, and the little horn, in Daniel 7:7-8:

After this I saw in the night visions, and behold a fourth beast, dreadful and terrible, and strong exceedingly; and it had great iron teeth: it devoured and brake in pieces, and stamped the residue with the feet of it: and it was diverse from all the beasts that were before it; and it had ten horns. I considered the horns, and, behold, there came up among them another little horn, before whom there were three of the first horns plucked up by the roots: and, behold, in this horn were eyes like the eyes of man, and a mouth speaking great things.

Who or what is the little horn before whom three of the first horns were plucked up by the roots, and which had eyes like the eyes of man and a mouth speaking great things? Verse 21 says that the horn made war on the saints and prevailed against them: "I beheld, and the same horn made war with his saints, and prevailed against them."

The same truth is revealed in Revelation 13:7 where God says that Satan will overrun the churches with false gospels. Thus, the little horn of Daniel 7 is Satan. The ten horns represent the completeness or finality of Satan's rule at the end of time, that is, the final tribulation period. Revelation 17:12-14 addresses this subject:

> And the ten horns which thou sawest are ten kings, which have received no kingdom as yet; but receive power as kings one hour with the beast. These have one mind, and shall give their power and strength unto the beast. These shall make war with the Lamb, and the Lamb shall overcome them: for he is Lord of lords, and King of kings: and they that are with him are called, and chosen, and faithful.

Ten is the number of completeness. Satan's rule will be completed, or finalized, during the final tribulation period as he wars against the Lamb. The Lamb, of course, is Christ. Satan's war with Christ will be directed against the body of Christ, the church, in that he will overrun it with other gospels.

Three of the horns plucked up by the roots can be understood if one bears in mind that ancient Israel and its end typified and anticipated the New Testament church. Israel was destroyed by Babylon in 587 B.C., and Babylon is a type or figure of the kingdom of Satan. The destruction of Israel by Babylon is a picture of the end-time when Satan will be victorious over the external church. It is in connection with the destruction of Israel by Babylon that the putting down of the three horns can be understood. When Babylon conquered Israel, Babylon removed the last three kings that ruled over Israel: Jehoiakim (II Chronicles 36:5-8), Jehoiachin (II Chronicles 36:9-10), and Zedekiah (II Kings 25:1-7). These three kings did evil in the sight of God. Therefore, they, like Babylon, were instrumental in causing the demise of Israel. This is summed up in II Chronicles 36:14-17.

> Moreover all the chief of the priests, and the people, transgressed very much after all the abominations of the heathen; and polluted the house of the LORD which he had hallowed in Jerusalem. And the LORD God of their fathers sent to them by his messengers, rising up betimes, and sending; because he had compassion on his people, and on his dwelling place: But they mocked the messengers of God, and despised his words, and misused his prophets, until the wrath of the LORD arose against his people, till there was no remedy. Therefore he brought upon them the king of the Chaldees, who slew their young men with the sword in the house of their sanctuary, and

had no compassion upon young man or maiden, old man, or him that stooped for age: he gave them all into his hand.

The final three kings of Israel, like Babylon, became intimately associated with wickedness. Therefore, they relate to the reign of Satan at the end of time. God does the relating in the language of Daniel 7, where He declares that the little horn plucks up three of the horns.

The description (Daniel 7:7-8) of the little horn is significant. It had the eyes of man and a mouth speaking great things. The phrase "eyes of man" undoubtedly relates to Isaiah 29:10:

For the LORD hath poured out upon you the spirit of deep sleep, and hath closed your eyes: the prophets and your rulers, the seers hath he covered.

This verse teaches that the eyes represent the prophets who ministered to Israel. Thus, God teaches that the little horn represents Satan and his rule in the church through false prophets and false Christs. This conclusion harmonizes with Matthew 24:24, where God teaches:

For there shall arise false Christs, and false prophets, and shall shew great signs and wonders; insomuch that, if it were possible, they shall deceive the very elect.

The "eyes of man" represent false prophets - emissaries of Satan - as does the phrase "a mouth speaking great things" (Daniel 7:8, 20). Daniel 7:25:

And he shall speak great words against the most High, and shall wear out the saints of the most High, and think to change times and laws: and they shall be given into his hand until a time and times and the dividing of time.

> *As part of the apostasy . . . God allows pastors to rewrite the rules of the Bible.*

As part of the apostasy that will develop in the church and cause God's judgment to fall upon it, God allows pastors to rewrite the rules of the Bible, as this verse teaches. God emphasizes that this is the character of Satan's rule (the little horn's rule), over the church. Satan will rule in the manner described in II Corinthians 11:13-15, where God warns:

For such are false apostles, deceitful workers, transforming themselves into the apostles of Christ. And no marvel; for Satan himself is transformed into an angel of light. Therefore it is no great thing if his ministers also be transformed as the ministers of righteousness; whose end shall be according to their works.

These verses show that Satan is so deceptive as he rules in the churches during the final tribulation period that his followers are convinced they are serving Christ.

The dominant and all pervasive goal of the church is to send forth the Gospel so that the temple of God can be built. The church has become spiritually destroyed when it is no longer used of God to save people. It has become a dead church, and it shows itself to be spiritually dead because it is overrun by gospels fostered by Satan. Thus, true believers are killed in a two-fold sense: The church to which they belonged has become spiritually dead, and true believers are being driven from the church. The two witnesses have been killed (Revelation 11:7); the church is no longer a fountainhead of life. Rivers of living water no longer flow from them to bring spiritual life to the unsaved.

> *Hope for the salvation of the lost will be gone.*

The second way in which the final tribulation is different from any other tribulation is that there has never been a time when people could not be saved. Even in that dark and terrible day when Christ hung on the cross, the thief was saved. There has always been the hope of salvation, but increasingly during this period, fewer and fewer people come to salvation. By the time the final tribulation period comes to an end, hope for the salvation of the lost will be gone. Satan will appear to have won. True believers will exist as though they have been killed. The unsaved will be in bondage to sin and Satan.

The Hope of Salvation

The world does not recognize the hope of salvation. The unsaved do not want salvation, but without their awareness, there is in the world the hope of salvation. Salvation is being free of eternal damnation; it is the hope for the world. The existence of the possibility of salvation is the highest blessing this world can know, and the removal of the possibility of salvation will be the most traumatic event. When hope is taken away and there is no program of salvation, then the world has experienced the most grievous tribulation.

The awful nature of this truth can now be only sensed. Today, and throughout history, believers witness to and pray for unsaved loved ones. The hope is always present that God in His magnificent mercy will save them. If a loved one dies apparently unsaved, one clings to the possibility that, unknown to living relatives, there may have been a death-bed conversion. Thus, to live in the world with no hope of salvation is the most serious of traumas, but this is what to expect at the close of the final tribulation period.

This truth is suggested by the language of Matthew 24:15, as it speaks of the abomination of desolation overrunning the church. It is suggested by II Thessalonians 2, where God speaks of the man of sin taking his seat in the temple. It is taught by Revelation 11:7, which says that the two witnesses must be killed. Revelation 13:7 teaches the same truth when it declares the saints will be overcome. In John 9:4, Jesus declares: "I must work the works of him that sent me, while it is day: the night cometh, when no man can work."

Revelation 7 and the Final Tribulation

In Revelation 7, God speaks of the nature of the final tribulation period in the parabolic language of Revelation 8 and 9. The two latter chapters describe the final tribulation period in the most traumatic language, and they speak of massive devastation. It may appear that these chapters point to massive bloodletting as the chief characteristic of the final tribulation period, but the key to understanding them is that God is speaking in parabolic language. The earthly story, described in all its horror, points to the spiritual meaning of God's judgment on the church. In this context He prophesies in Revelation 7:2-3:

> And I saw another angel ascending from the east, having the seal of the living God: and he cried with a loud voice to the four angels, to whom it was given to hurt the earth and the sea, Saying, Hurt not the earth, neither the sea, nor the trees, till we have sealed the servants of our God in their foreheads.

The four angels and their activity of destruction are also spoken of in Revelation 9:15:

And the four angels were loosed, which were prepared for an hour, and a day, and a month, and a year, for to slay the third part of men.

The Bible is its own interpreter; thus, it must be learned what the Bible means by the phrase "the third," which is frequently found in these chapters.

The third part of men is a parabolic phrase which points to the church. The number is taken from Zechariah 13 where God indicates that the world is symbolically divided into two groups of people. The unsaved are typified by the number two thirds and the saved by the number one third. Zechariah 13:8-9:

And it shall come to pass, that in all the land, saith the LORD, two parts therein shall be cut off and die; but the third shall be left therein. And I will bring the third part through the fire, and will refine them as silver is refined, and will try them as gold is tried: they shall call on my name, and I will hear them: I will say, It is my people: and they shall say, The LORD is my God.

The one third are God's people. They have been refined in that Christ has endured hell for them. Thus, they are clean before God. In Revelation 8 and 9 the one third are pictured as being dead. This truth is seen in Revelation 11:7, 13:7, and 13:15. The true believers have been killed in that the church to which they belonged is no longer the fountain of life. They have been killed in that the external, corporate representation of the body of Christ (the church) has been overrun with false gospels; it is spiritually dead. They have been killed in the sense that they have been driven from the church.

The Third Part

Revelation 8 and 9 can be understood only when it is realized that references to one third in the earthly story point to the body of believers in the heavenly meaning. God points in Revelation 8 to:

The third part of the:	In verse:
trees	7
sea	8
creatures	9
ships	9
rivers	10
waters	11
sun	12
moon	12
stars	12
day	12

Revelation 9:15 speaks of the third part of men. In each reference to the third part, death and destruction are in view. The figures of speech (trees, sea, creatures, ships, rivers, etc.), can be shown in their context to represent the body of believers, which is called the church. These two chapters can be understood only when it is realized that they discuss the final tribulation period, as the church is being judged and no one can become saved within the dead congregations. The death of the third part of man must be understood in the same way as the death of the two witnesses in Revelation 11:7.

In Revelation 9:15, "an hour, and a day, and a month, and a year" means that this will be accomplished in the fullness of time. The figure is similar to that in Galatians 4:10, where reference is made to the ceremonial law: "Ye observe days, and months, and times, and years."

The ceremonial laws pointed to the first coming of Christ. Our Savior was to come at a special moment in history, called the fullness of time (Galatians 4:4).

Remember, the time line of history is governed by the unfolding of God's salvation program. Thus, the end of the final tribulation that signifies that the Gospel presentation has come to an end and all the elect have become saved, is also the end of time. There is a predecreed time when the world will come to its end. It is in the fullness of God's timetable for the saving of people.

Time is of the essence in God's salvation plan.

Time is of the essence in God's salvation program. Rigorous laws dictated when feast days were to be observed. These precise times anticipated God's precise timetable for the coming of Christ. For example, when Jesus hung on the cross as the Passover Lamb, the priests in the temple were killing the lambs that were to be eaten as part of the Passover feast. When God poured out the Holy Spirit to begin His program to evangelize the world, it was on the same day that the nation of Israel celebrated the Feast of Pentecost, which was a feast pointing to the pouring out of the Holy Spirit.

Revelation 7:2 and 3 indicate the chronology of events using somewhat different language:

And I saw another angel ascending from the east, having the seal of the living God: and he cried with a loud voice to the four angels, to whom it was given to hurt the earth and the sea, Saying, Hurt not the earth, neither the sea, nor the trees, till **we have sealed the servants of our God in their foreheads.**

In these verses, God is saying that the events of Revelation 8 and 9 cannot take place until all of God's servants have been sealed on their foreheads. The servants of God are the believers. They became bondservants of Christ the moment they were saved. They are called the twelve tribes of Israel because they are typified by Old Testament Israel. There is a vast number of believers who throughout time have come from every nation (Revelation 7:9). The number twelve in Revelation 12 signifies the fullness of all believers.

To be sealed on the forehead means to be saved. In Ephesians 1:13 God declares:

In whom ye also trusted, after that ye heard the word of truth, the gospel of your salvation: in whom also after that ye believed, ye were sealed with that holy Spirit of promise.

Sealing is on the forehead, as the Father's name is written on the forehead of the 144,000 (a number that symbolizes the full and complete number of all who are to be saved), in Revelation 14:1. The forehead signifies that the mind has been renewed. The person has become born again; he has become a child of God.

Thus, Revelation 7:2-3 teaches that the terrible event recorded in Revelation 8 and 9 cannot take place until those who are to be saved have been saved. During the final tribulation, church after church becomes apostate because it no longer brings the true Gospel. As a church becomes apostate it comes under the judgment spoken of in these chapters. By the time of the end of the final tribulation this will characterize almost every church in the world. This same truth was learned from other passages.

Matthew 24, II Thessalonians 2, Revelation 13, and other passages teach that the special trauma of the final tribulation period will be twofold. First, the churches, which historically have been the bastions of the true Gospel, will be overrun by false gospels and true believers will flee from them. By the end of the final tribulation period, it appears that churches that follow the true Gospel will be very hard to find.

Second, by the time the final tribulation period draws to a close, all of the elect will have become saved. Consequently, during the final tribulation period fewer and fewer will become saved. This will bring spiritual trauma to the world as never before experienced.

AIDS: An End of the World Sign?

For the last several years the eyes of the world have been increasingly riveted on a deadly plague, a disease that has been named "Acquired Immuno-Deficiency Syndrome" or AIDS. It is an awful disease, and there is little likelihood of a cure in the foreseeable future. It appears to have been diagnosed in the past as a rare disease, but in the last few years it has afflicted people by the thousands.

AIDS particularly afflicts homosexuals and through homosexuals it appears to have spread to many parts of the world. It is exceedingly contagious. It has spread from homosexuals to many who are sexually promiscuous, to some who have received transfusions of AIDS-tainted blood, and to some from infected needles. Babies of diseased parents are vulnerable. As with all plagues, the innocent suffer with the guilty.

Disease resulting from sexual misconduct is not a new phenomenon. For hundreds of years, venereal diseases have scourged mankind. AIDS is unique in that it has been heavily identified with homosexual behavior. Because of its terrible nature, it has received a lot of publicity. In the United States, it has such a high profile that virtually every citizen is aware of it.

> *The AIDS plague has come when*
> *many signs seem to indicate that the*
> *end of the world is close at hand.*

The AIDS plague has come when many signs seem to indicate that the end of the world is close at hand. One cannot help but wonder if it is related to the final tribulation period. Does the Bible contain language that identifies a disease like AIDS as an important ingredient of the final tribulation period?

Many Biblical passages describe the character of the final tribulation period, but insofar as can be determined, none of these passages has language that specifically describes a plague like AIDS. The focus of Bible prophecy concerning the final tribulation is on the church. The AIDS plague is only incidentally in the church. AIDS is a dreadful plague that particularly assaults those outside the church where sexual perversion is rampant and where the drug culture flourishes. However, one passage in the Bible appears to contain prophecy concerning this disease, and this passage will be carefully studied to discover its relationship to end-time events.

Romans 1 discusses the fact that mankind does not want to worship God as the Creator of the universe. Verses 22 and 23:

> Professing themselves to be wise, they became fools, And changed the glory of the uncorruptible God into an image made like to corruptible man, and to birds, and four-footed beasts, and creeping things.

The result of rebellion against God has dire consequences. Verses 24 and 25 declare:

> Wherefore God also gave them up to uncleanness through the lusts of their own hearts, to dishonour their own bodies between themselves: Who changed the truth of God into a lie, and worshipped and served the creature more than the Creator, who is blessed for ever. Amen.

More specifically in verses 26 and 27 God says:

For this cause God gave them up unto vile affections: for even their women did change the natural use into that which is against nature: And likewise also the men, leaving the natural use of the woman, burned in their lust one toward another; men with men working that which is unseemly, and receiving in themselves that recompence of their error which was meet.

Verses 28 through 32 complete the list of sins for which God gives people over as a result of their continuing and insistent rebellion against Him:

And even as they did not like to retain God in their knowledge, God gave them over to a reprobate mind, to do those things which are not convenient: Being filled with all unrighteousness, fornication, wickedness, covetousness, maliciousness; full of envy, murder, debate, deceit, malignity; whisperers, Backbiters, haters of God, despiteful, proud, boasters, inventors of evil things, disobedient to parents, Without understanding, covenantbreakers, without natural affection, implacable, unmerciful: Who knowing the judgment of God, that they which commit such things are worthy of death, not only do the same, but have pleasure in them that do them.

The prediction of Romans 1, that God gives the wicked over to dreadful sins, has been fulfilled throughout history. At any time in the history of mankind any or all of the twenty-four sins named could be found. The heart of man is desperately wicked; mankind by nature is enslaved to sin and Satan, and the potential to grievously sin is ever present. However, God in His mercy restrains sin in the human race; ordinarily, these dreadful sins are not on display. Neighbors who may have no interest in Christ as Savior may be decent, moral, and law abiding. This does not mean that their hearts are not wicked; it is simply evidence that God restrains sin in mankind. If He did not, sin would be so rampant that mankind would destroy themselves. God in His mercy restrains sin so that the world can continue to its predestined end.

When God has given people up, or given them over to awful sin, then an end is in view.

Romans 1 Points to the End of the World

When the Bible uses language that God has given people up, or given them over to awful sin, then an end is in view. When ancient Israel began to be exceedingly sinful, God was about to send judgments upon them, and He did when He destroyed them by the Assyrians and the Babylonians. When the world of Noah's day became dreadfully wicked, the judgment of the flood came upon them.

In II Thessalonians 2 God speaks of the final tribulation period as a time when people will be so deceived that they will think they are serving Christ, but they will be serving Satan. In that context God indicates that He will give them a strong delusion so that they will believe a lie (II Thessalonians 2:4-12). There is evidence in the Bible that when sin multiplies, God's judgment cannot be long in coming. Thus, when God declares that He gives up the wicked to gross sin (Romans 1), it means that an end is very close. The language of Romans 1 can apply to many situations throughout history, but it especially applies to the final tribulation period.

A prophecy in these verses indicates that they are focused on the final tribulation period. Verses 26 and 27 speak of the sin of homosexuality. God indicates that there will be serious consequences in the lives of those who are guilty of this sin. He declares that they will receive "in themselves that recompence [payment] of their error [sin] which was meet [deserved]."

Ordinarily God warns that those who continue in sin will be blinded and go deeper into sin or He warns that they will come into judgment if they continue in sin. However, it is unusual for God to single out a sin and indicate a specific judgment upon those who commit that sin. It is a warning that something special is in view.

One might wonder if the sin of homosexuality is greater than any of the other sins that are named. It is a repugnant sin, but so are fornication and murder. God does not indicate a natural consequence of such sins as fornication and murder which relate to the sin itself. Homosexuality is a terrible sin, but God is not highlighting it as an especially awful sin.

This world has existed for about 13,000 years. Except for the present time, God has not brought a specific sin-related judgment on the homosexual. Judgments of venereal diseases such as syphilis and gonorrhea have existed, but these diseases may result from any sexual immorality. They are not focused on the homosexual.

There are increasing signs that we are near the end of the world, including the fact that a homosexual runs a great risk of receiving the AIDS virus: The prophecy of Romans 1 comes alive. Practicing homosexuals are at the forefront of those under the judgment of AIDS. The warning prophecies of Romans 1 have had relevancy at any time in history. They have particular and insistent relevancy at a time when other signs indicate that the final tribulation period is probably here.

Romans 1 Predicts the Plague of AIDS

Romans 1:26 and 27 describe a judgment on the sin of homosexuality that has not been in evidence until this decade. AIDS, with its major focus on the sin of homosexuality, is a terrible plague; it is evidence that the world is very close to Judgment Day.

All the sins named in Romans 1, including fornication and murder, are in greater evidence now than at any time in history.

All the sins named in Romans 1, including fornication and murder, are in greater evidence in the world now than at any time in history. Sexual promiscuity is rampant in all the world today. When the great empire of Rome fell, a large contributing factor was the debauchery of the upper classes, but there is no clear evidence that debauchery characterized the masses. Today sexual debauchery cuts through every level of society.

Was there a time when a highly educated people, with a Judeo-Christian heritage, such as our nation, ruthlessly murdered more than one million babies a year? When Egypt attempted to murder all the male children of the people of Israel, they were only a step from Judgment Day. When the first-born of Egypt were killed it was a picture of Judgment Day. The murder of babies in the womb emphasizes that Romans 1 points to the end of the world. Likewise, the plague of AIDS, which increasingly ravages the world, is in all likelihood an end-time phenomenon even though the major Biblical focus is judgment upon the churches as they become increasingly apostate.

Homosexuality and the End of Time

Two historical parables in the Bible that point to the end of time and the final tribulation period focus on homosexuality. The first is in Genesis 19 where God describes His judgment on Sodom and Gomorrah. The destruction of these cities typifies the final judgment on the world. God speaks of the men of the city demanding the right for homosexual conduct with the men who came to warn Lot of impending judgment. God is surely focusing on homosexuality in connection with the final judgment.

The second account is in Judges 19, where the man of Ephraim and his concubine, who are on their way home, are overtaken by darkness. They find shelter in the home of an aged man of the tribe of Benjamin, but, as the men of Sodom desired homosexual relations with Lot's visitors, the men of this town of Benjamin demanded homosexual conduct with this visitor. Judges 19:22:

> Now as they were making their hearts merry, behold, the men of the city, certain sons of Belial, beset the house round about, and beat at the door, and spake to the master of the house, the old man, saying, Bring forth the man that came into thine house, that we may know him.

This sad account in Judges 19 can be shown to be an historical parable that points to the final tribulation period, as are the activities in and around Lot's home before the destruction of Sodom. The final consequence of Sodom's sin was the destruction of Sodom. The final consequence of the land of Benjamin's sin in Judges 19 was the almost total destruction of the tribe of Benjamin (cf. Judges 20:44-48 and Judges 21:1-3).

The sin of homosexuality has distinct end-time significance. This sin is singled out for special mention in Romans 1, and it is featured in a context wherein God gives people up so the sin will be more sinful. These are definite reasons to believe that an end-time judgment is in view.

Judgment Day Is Coming

God warns throughout the Scriptures that Judgment Day is coming and will eventuate in eternal damnation for all unsaved sinners. Believers know that the great judgment will come at the end of the world.

To emphasize the certainty of His wrath at the end of the world, God has given examples of judgment predicted and realized. For example, God told Noah that He was going to destroy the entire world by the flood, and He did. God told Abraham that He was going to destroy Sodom, and Sodom was destroyed. God warned Israel that He was going to destroy Israel by the Assyrians; this prophecy also came true.

> *For almost 2000 years, no specific judgment*
> *related to gross sin has occurred.*

The problem is that for almost 2000 years, no specific judgment related to gross sins has occurred. Mankind in general pays no attention to the ancient judgments.

The statement of Romans 1 - that specific judgment will come upon the homosexual - has been unfulfilled during the almost 2000 years since it was written in the Bible. Mankind gives no heed to the multitudinous warnings in the Bible that Judgment Day is coming.

A dramatic break in the apparent inaction of God to fulfill prophecy is that the prophecy of judgment upon homosexual behavior is being fulfilled. Mysteriously, several years ago, the terrible disease AIDS appeared. God raised it up and all the world knows about it.

The explosion of AIDS, in precise agreement with the Scriptures, is a giant reminder to the world that when God predicts judgment in the Bible, judgment will come. AIDS is a case in point; it demonstrates that God means what He says.

Be assured that as this judgment on homosexual activity is taking place, so, too, all of the prophecies concerning Judgment Day will take place. Mankind attempts to mock God and contends that eternal damnation cannot be real, but the plague of AIDS demonstrates in no uncertain terms that eternal damnation is coming.

> *The AIDS plague dramatically warns that the*
> *end is near and that Judgment Day and eternal*
> *damnation are real.*

The plague of AIDS serves at least two important functions. First, it is evidence that the end of time is near. Second, it is a dramatic warning to the world that Judgment Day and eternal damnation are real.

Marvelously, there is another half of the story: God has told of the astonishing and wonderful plan that whosoever believes on Christ as Savior and Lord will escape the awful judgment of hell.

However, time is fast running out. Throughout the history of mankind, as long as a person was alive, there was the possibility of salvation. That possibility will end when the final tribulation ends. Many current events indicate the end of time is near. It is imperative that people everywhere become right with God by beseeching God for salvation. In the short days that lie ahead, it is imperative that Christians marshal every means to warn the world that Judgment Day is coming.

Woe unto anyone who treats the subject of the final tribulation and the end of the world as an academic matter that has no reality. Woe unto anyone who rebelliously continues to go his own way and serves the world and his own lusts. Woe unto those who will not cry out to God for mercy while there is time for salvation.

Oh, that many will heed the warnings
of the Bible.

Many additional passages of the Bible offer evidence to prove the conclusions of this study. The Biblical passages that have been offered should be sufficient to warn us that the world is in a terrible predicament. Oh, that many will heed the warnings of the Bible.

SUMMARY

In this dreadful chapter we have learned that immediately before the end of the world, God brings judgment upon the church. We have learned that that judgment signals that the unfolding of God's salvation plan has come to an end. That is, history has drawn to a close. Remember that the time line of history is the unfolding of God's salvation plan.

In many ways, that judgment resembles the judgment that came upon ancient Israel. God tested the faithfulness of ancient Israel by raising up the nations of Assyria and Babylon whose language Israel did not understand. He gave these heathen nations many successes in order to discover if Israel would remain faithful to God or desire the gods of these nations. Israel failed the test and was destroyed by these nations.

Likewise, God tests the congregations of our day by speaking extensively in the Bible about a gift of tongues that had been given to the church of Corinth. Increasing numbers of people in our day want that gift even though later in the Bible God indicates that He had completed the Bible, and we are to seek no other revelation. The churches of our day increasingly fail the test as they seek for additional revelation from God. The Bible indicates that Satan, as he comes with gospels that feature visions and signs and wonders, is being used as a judgment against these rebellious churches. Thus they become false churches with Satan ruling over them even though those within these churches believe they are serving Christ.

We have learned that Satan is the antichrist; he is the little horn of Daniel 7; he is the one who comes as an angel of light to destroy the churches during the final tribulation period. True believers within these churches are killed in the sense that they are driven out. This permits the churches to become even more apostate. Moreover, as this happens increasingly throughout the world, fewer and fewer churches bring the true Gospel. Thus fewer and fewer people become saved. The world is under great tribulation because it is increasingly difficult to find the true Gospel inasmuch as churches are increasingly becoming apostate. It is a time of great tribulation because to a high degree God is destroying the churches that allowed Satan to rule where Christ should rule.

Two events will develop simultaneously in preparation for Judgment Day. The first event is that the time of the final tribulation will arrive, and, as we continue this study, we will discover that in all probability we are already in that period. The nature of the final tribulation period is that comparatively few will become saved during that time; thus, it cannot begin until almost all of the elect have become saved.

The second event is the end of the era of the corporate church as the external representation of the Kingdom of God on earth. The steps that lead to the end of the church era are well defined in the Bible, as we have learned. Let us repeat these steps once more because they are so important.

First, churches and denominations increasingly rewrite the laws of the Bible.

Second, God begins to blind the churches and they stumble into greater apostasy.

Third, God removes the truth from them as they are increasingly under His judgment.

Fourth, God rejects them and allows sin to multiply within the congregations.

Fifth, God destroys them in that they are no longer an external representative of the Kingdom of God.

But now we should ask the question: "How long will the final tribulation continue?" Does the Bible give us information about this?

Chapter 6
How Long Is The Final Tribulation?

A period of affliction more severe than this world has ever known frightens many people. They think of tribulation as a time of great physical suffering, i.e., nuclear war or physical persecution. No one enjoys physical suffering; therefore, they cling to the idea that a good God will not let His children suffer; He will rapture them before the final tribulation period. They fail to realize, however, that when tribulation comes into the world, believers experience it as readily as the unsaved. When Jerusalem was destroyed, in horrible fashion, by the Babylonians, believers experienced the trauma of the event just as the unsaved did. Today when an earthquake, tornado, war, or famine strikes, believers experience the same hurt as the unsaved. If persecution comes, believers will frequently experience the trauma and many unbelievers will not.

Jesus says in John 16:33 "In the world ye shall have tribulation." Anyone who thinks that because he believes in Jesus Christ he will be safe from grievous affliction, is not reading the Bible carefully enough.

The Bible clearly indicates that believers will be present on earth when Christ returns at the end of the world. II Thessalonians 2:1: "Now we beseech you, brethren, by the coming of our Lord Jesus Christ, and by our gathering together unto him." If believers are to meet Jesus when He comes, then they must be on earth. In John 6 God declares four times that believers will be resurrected the last day. John 6:44: "No man can come to me, except the Father which hath sent me draw him: and I will raise him up at the last day." Verses 39, 40, and 54 repeat the assertion that believers will be resurrected the last day. John 12:48 says that the last day is Judgment Day.

> He that rejecteth me, and receiveth not my words, hath one that judgeth him: the word that I have spoken, the same shall judge him in the last day.

I Thessalonians 4:17 teaches that the rapture of believers will be simultaneous with the resurrection of believers.

Then we which are alive and remain shall be caught up together with them in the clouds, to meet the Lord in the air: and so shall we ever be with the Lord.

The resurrection of believers is the last day; therefore, the rapture is the last day. Thus, believers will be present on earth until the last day.

Tribulation Is Not God's Wrath

Thus far, nothing has even hinted that the final tribulation takes place after the believers are raptured from this earth. However, two verses that are used to attempt to prove that believers will be raptured before the final tribulation are I Thessalonians 5:9 and Revelation 3:10. These verses will be studied.

In I Thessalonians 5:9 God declares: "For God hath not appointed us to wrath, but to obtain salvation by our Lord Jesus Christ."

Some theologians attempt to equate God's wrath, spoken of in this verse, with the final tribulation. They fail to realize that the wrath of God is eternal damnation. Most believers have lived and died and were never threatened by the final tribulation. Until saved, they were threatened by eternal damnation. This is the awful calamity from which believers in the Lord Jesus Christ are saved. The closing verses of Revelation 6 disclose the truth of the awful moment at the end of time when the unsaved must face "the wrath of the Lamb: For the great day of his wrath is come" (verses 16-17). I Thessalonians 5:9 cannot be speaking of the final tribulation period.

Revelation 3:10 informs us:

Because thou hast kept the word of my patience, I also will keep thee from the hour of temptation, which shall come upon all the world, to try them that dwell upon the earth.

Theologians may carelessly equate the "hour of temptation" with the final tribulation period, but they fail to realize that the Greek word *pierasmos*, translated "temptation" and "try" in this verse, is never translated "affliction" nor "tribulation" nor "trouble." It is always translated "temptation" or "trial" or "testing." The Greek word *thlipsis*, translated "affliction" or "tribulation" or "trouble" is never translated "testing" nor "temptation" nor "trial." Thus, the final tribulation period cannot be in view in this verse.

The "hour of temptation" is Judgment Day. If someone is charged with a crime, he is brought to trial, where his guilt or innocence is determined. Judgment Day is the hour of trial when all the unsaved must stand trial. Revelation 3:10 would be more easily understood had it been translated "hour of trial." Believers are not brought to trial. John 5:24 declares that believers do not come into judgment. The Greek word *krisis*, translated "condemnation" in John 5:24 is also translated "judgment" in Matthew 12:18, 20, 36, and 41. Romans 8:1 assures believers that there is no condemnation for those who are in Christ Jesus.

This same truth is in the prayer Jesus taught the disciples. The petition "lead us not into temptation, [Greek *pierasmos*] but deliver us from evil" (Matthew 6:13), is a prayer for salvation, i.e., deliver me from the terrible event of Judgment Day which I so rightly deserve. Also deliver me from the evil of my bondage to sin and to Satan. Of course, deliverance is an accomplished fact in the life of the believer.

Matthew 24:29-31 teaches that the final tribulation is the last event this world faces before Judgment Day. God emphasizes that immediately after the final tribulation, the sun will be darkened, the moon will not shine, and the stars will fall from heaven. The sun and the moon were placed in the sky to regulate time. When they are darkened, they can no longer govern time - time will be no more. Stars falling from heaven indicates that the universe is collapsing. These events signal the end of the world's existence.

Is Seven Years the Time Period?

Many theologians teach that the final tribulation period will continue for seven years. They base their conclusion on Daniel 9:27:

> And he shall confirm the covenant with many for one week: and in the midst of the week he shall cause the sacrifice and the oblation to cease, and for the overspreading of abominations he shall make it desolate, even until the consummation, and that determined shall be poured upon the desolate.

These theologians believe the seventieth seven of Daniel 9:27 is a final tribulation period that will come after Christ reigns for 1000 years on earth. However, careful Bible study reveals that both of the suppositions are false: Christ will not reign on earth for "1000 years" and the seventieth seven of Daniel 9:27 cannot be the final tribulation period. It cannot be the final tribulation period because in the middle of the seventieth seven, sacrifice and offering cease.

For 11,000 years, beginning with Cain and Abel, sacrifices were offered. These sacrifices were types and shadows of the Lord Jesus Christ. When He offered Himself as the sacrifice, the system of sacrifices ended. Jews continued to offer sacrifices at least until 70 A.D. when Jerusalem was destroyed, but the sacrifices had no meaning. The great sacrifice that ended all sacrifices was Jesus, when He went to the cross in 33 A.D. Therefore, the middle of the seventieth week - when sacrifices and offerings ended - can be only 33 A.D. Regardless of anything else taught by Daniel 9:27, the middle of the seventieth seven must be 33 A.D. This period of time cannot be the final tribulation. (See Chapter 12 for an enlarged discussion of Daniel 9:25-27.)

> *The Bible does give information on*
> *the duration of this traumatic event.*

The Bible does give information on the duration of this traumatic event. It would be profitable to search this out in the Bible.

When we study the Bible for clues concerning the duration of the final tribulation period, we find two periods of time of special interest. The first is seventy years and the second is twenty-three years. We shall look at the seventy year period first.

Israel: Seventy Years Under God's Wrath

In Leviticus 26:14-29 God is warning that God's wrath will be visited upon His people if they do not obey Him. Among other things He warns in Leviticus 26:33-34:

> And I will scatter you among the heathen, and will draw out a sword after you: and your land shall be desolate, and your cities waste. Then shall the land enjoy her sabbaths, as long as it lieth desolate, and ye be in your enemies' land; even then shall the land rest, and enjoy her sabbaths.

In Jeremiah 25 God speaks of this prophecy of God's wrath upon His people as having become an actuality because of their sins. Israel was to be destroyed by the Babylonians. They were to be punished by the Babylonians during a period of seventy years. We read in Jeremiah 25:11:

And this whole land shall be a desolation, and an astonishment; and these nations shall serve the king of Babylon seventy years.

This terrible punishment is further spoken of in II Chronicles 36:20-21:

And them that had escaped from the sword carried he away to Babylon; where they were servants to him and his sons until the reign of the kingdom of Persia: To fulfil the word of the LORD by the mouth of Jeremiah, until the land had enjoyed her sabbaths: for as long as she lay desolate she kept sabbath, to fulfil threescore and ten years.

This historical event actually took place, as follows. Prior to 931 B.C., the kingdom of Israel was in its flower. David ruled for forty years and then his son Solomon reigned, until his death. But Solomon in his old age began to worship other gods; therefore, upon his death in 931 B.C., God divided Israel into two kingdoms. Ten tribes became Israel with their capital in Samaria. Two tribes, Judah and Benjamin, with their capital in Jerusalem, became the nation of Judah.

Israel was ruled over by a succession of twenty kings, all of whom did evil in the sight of God. Consequently they were destroyed in 709 B.C. by the Assyrians. The remnants from those ten tribes joined the nation of Judah and from 709 B.C. on, Judah was in fact Israel.

Although Judah was repeatedly warned by God that they were not to follow in the wicked ways of Israel, they nevertheless persisted in doing so. Finally God began to bring His judgments on them. In 609 B.C. their last good king, Josiah, was killed in battle and they became subjugated by the Egyptians. Four years later, in the year 605 B.C., Egypt's armies were defeated by the Babylonians and Israel came under subjugation to the Babylonians.

This sad state of affairs continued until 587 B.C. at which time the Babylonian armies destroyed Jerusalem, including the most important building of all, the temple. This ended the existence of Israel as a nation.

During the twenty-three inclusive years from 609 B.C. to 587 B.C., many of the Israelites, like Daniel and his friends, were taken as slaves into Babylon.

In 539 B.C., seventy years after the beginning of Judah's subjugation, Babylon was conquered by the Medes and the Persians. Almost immediately the Persian king Cyrus issued a decree permitting a number of the Israelites to return to their homeland. This ended the seventy years that had been prophesied by God in Leviticus 26 and Jeremiah 25.

> *Israel was punished and scattered for apostasy and the church at the end of the New Testament era is punished for its apostasy.*

This seventy year period therefore foreshadowed the final tribulation period. Even as Israel was punished and scattered for its growing apostasy, so the church at the end of the New Testament era is punished for its growing apostasy. As we saw earlier in this study, the final tribulation is a judgment of God on the church for their growing apostasy as we near the end of time.

In the citation of II Chronicles 36:20-21 God speaks of the seventy years from 609 B.C. to 539 B.C. as a Sabbath. This seventy year Sabbath is a type or figure of the final tribulation period, which must be the reference God has in view in Matthew 24:20, when He warns, "But pray ye that your flight be not in the winter, neither on the sabbath day." The word "Sabbath" identifies with the seventy year Sabbath of Israel and indicates that a period of seventy years should be considered as a possibility for the duration of the final tribulation period.

The Final Tribulation Should Encompass Twenty-Three Years
The next possibility we must consider as God's timetable for normal expectation of the final tribulation period is the time span twenty-three years. This is the period from 609 B.C. to 587 B.C. inclusive. As noted, upon the death of King Josiah in 609 B.C., Israel lost its independence and the enemy began to rule them. It was a picture of the church that has lost its standing as the representation of the Kingdom of God on earth and has come increasingly under Satan's rule. Finally, twenty-three years later Israel is destroyed by Babylon (a figure of the kingdom of Satan). So, too, the apostate church at the end of the final tribulation period comes into judgment and ceases to exist.

This twenty-three year period has as its beginning the same point in time, the same occasion for, and the same character of God's judgment on Israel as the seventy year period.

The seventy year period follows that judgment all the way to the restoration when the first contingent of Israelites returned to Jerusalem. The twenty-three year period stops at the point when the temple was destroyed and Israel ceased to be a nation.

> *The number twenty-three is used to typify judgment.*

The number twenty-three is used a number of times in the Bible to typify judgment. As we have seen, the final twenty-three years of the nation of Israel was a time when God's judgment was upon the nation of Israel. There was another time when God's judgment was upon Israel and in that connection the number twenty-three is prominently featured. We read in I Corinthians 10 about a tragedy that enveloped ancient Israel when they were to cross the Jordan River and go into Canaan, the promised land. Their entrance into the promised land typifies the completion of salvation. The forty years that Israel wandered in the wilderness is a picture of the believer's life on earth. Believers are strangers and pilgrims, waiting for the completion of salvation, which will occur at the end of the world. Israel wandered in the wilderness, waiting for the time when they could enter the land of Canaan, which was to be their permanent home.

Before they entered the promised land, a terrible tragedy occurred. Numbers 25 indicates that 24,000 died in the plague. I Corinthians 10:8 states: "Neither let us commit fornication, as some of them committed, and fell in one day three and twenty thousand." The startling information in this statement is the number 23,000. In Numbers 25:9 God informs us: "And those that died in the plague were twenty and four thousand."

There is, of course, no contradiction. The I Corinthians 10 citation says that 23,000 died in one day (obviously the worst day of the plague), and the next day 1000 died, for a total of 24,000.

God calls attention to the number twenty-three in I Corinthians 10. The judgment of God upon ancient Israel, before they entered the promised land, parallels the final tribulation, when God will judge the church before our salvation is completed. Therefore, God definitely identifies the number twenty-three with the final tribulation period and with judgment.

Twenty-Three Kings

In I Samuel 8 we read of the desire of ancient Israel to have a king to rule over them. Until the year 1047 B.C. they had been a true theocracy; that is, God was their king. God ruled over them through prophets and judges such as Moses, Joshua, and Gideon, but they wanted a king like the other nations. The prophet Samuel was greatly troubled by this because he thought they were rejecting him. God informed Samuel in I Samuel 8:7:

> And the LORD said unto Samuel, Hearken unto the voice of the people in all that they say unto thee: for they have not rejected thee, but they have rejected me, that I should not reign over them.

It marked the time when there was a serious break in the relationship between Israel and God.

In other words, the beginning of the reign of the kings over Israel marked a most decisive period in Israel's history. From God's vantage point it marked the time when there was a serious break in the relationship between Israel and God. "They have rejected me," God declared. Immediately we sense a relationship to the final tribulation period when there is to be a great falling away as the congregations increasingly reject Christ's authority and seek their own authority.

With this thought in mind let us see how many kings actually ruled over Israel. Before they were divided into two kingdoms, three kings ruled over them: Saul, David, and Solomon. Then they were divided into two kingdoms: Israel with its capital in Samaria and Judah with its capital in Jerusalem. Amazingly, each of these two nations had exactly twenty rulers rule over them. And right after the rule of the twentieth king they were destroyed: The nation of Israel by the Assyrians in 709 B.C. and the nation of Judah by the Babylonians in 587 B.C. The list of rulers is as follows.

Combined Israel
Saul
David
Solomon

Judah	Israel
Rehoboam	Jeroboam
Abijam	Nadab
Asa	Baasha
Jehoshaphat	Elah
Jehoram	Zimri
Ahaziah	Tibni
Athaliah[1]	Omri
Joash	Ahab
Amaziah	Ahaziah
Azariah (Uzziah)	Jorom
Jotham	Jehu
Ahaz	Jehoahaz
Hezekiah	Jehoash
Manasseh	Jeroboam
Amon	Zachariah
Josiah	Shallum
Jehoahaz	Manahem
Jehoiakim	Pekahiah
Jehoiachin	Pekah
Zedekiah	Hoshea
20 kings	20 kings

When we add the twenty rulers of Judah to the first three kings - Saul, David, and Solomon - we find that twenty-three rulers ruled. Likewise we get the same result when we add the twenty kings of Israel to the initial three kings. After these twenty-three rulers both Israel and Judah ceased to exist as nations.

> *The beginning of the reign of Saul is marked by God's observation that Israel had rejected God, . . . the reign of kings over Israel typifies the final tribulation period.*

Remembering now that the beginning of the reign of Saul is marked by God's observation that Israel had rejected God, we see that in a real sense the period of the reign of kings over Israel typifies the final tribulation period. The final tribulation period begins with the break in the relationship between God and the external church and ends with the elements of the church that are in rebellion going into eternal damnation. The parallelism is as follows.

National Israel	*The Church*
Israel rejects God as king	The church rejects Christ as king as it is overrun by false gospels
23 kings rule	23 years follow
Israel is destroyed	The church is condemned to eternal damnation. (True believers of course have increasingly been driven from the external church.)

We thus see that in a very interesting way the number twenty-three is utilized to point to the final tribulation period.

A Shipwreck Points to the Final Tribulation Period

Sometimes the Bible focuses very directly on the number twenty-three so that we cannot miss it. At other times it is slightly veiled, as we have seen in connection with the twenty-three kings that ruled over Israel. There are also instances in which the number twenty-three is being featured but is not readily seen. Such is the situation in relation to a shipwreck spoken of in Acts 27.

In Acts 27 the Bible gives an account of a shipwreck in which the Apostle Paul was involved. Statements in this account show that it is an historical parable that typifies the final tribulation period. The Bible informs us that the Apostle Paul and other prisoners, soldiers, and sailors were en route to Rome. They arrived in a seaport near the city of Lasea at the beginning of winter (verse 8). This haven was not a good place to spend the winter, and even though it had become dangerous to sail (verse 9), they sailed on. They hoped to reach a better port, Phenice, where they would stay for the winter (verses 12-13). While at sea a great storm, called *Euroclydon*, arose and caused the ship to be wrecked. However, not one of the 276 men aboard was lost; all were saved.

The ship is a picture of the church during the final tribulation period. Spiritually the church has no haven because God is bringing judgment against it. Spiritually the church is in winter, because it is a time when little new vegetation (new believers) will come forth. The word tempest, in verse 20, "no small tempest lay on us," is the same Greek word in Matthew 24:20, where it is translated winter. By the word "winter," God is tying Acts 27 to the final tribulation period. This is so because in Matthew 24:20 God associates the word "winter" with the final tribulation period.

The Storm Typifies Satan's Attack on the Church

The storm, *Euroclydon*, identifies with the Greek word *eurochoros*, which is used only in Matthew 7:13, and is translated "broad": "broad is the way, that leadeth to destruction." A storm came up on the Sea of Galilee and caused the disciples to fear their ship would sink. Jesus stilled the storm on the Sea of Galilee. Both storms are a figure of Satan attempting to destroy the church. However, Satan cannot frustrate God's plan to build His church as typified by Christ stilling the storm. In Acts 27 the storm was not stilled because it is the "broad" way by which God, during the final tribulation period, will allow the external church to be destroyed.

Historical parables incorporated into Acts 27 are: 1) the ship was destroyed even as the era of the New Testament church will end with the final tribulation period. 2) None of the 276 people on board lost their lives in the shipwreck, and not one true believer in the church will be spiritually lost during the final tribulation period.

The number 276, which God carefully includes in the Biblical account, is a significant number and has an unusual characteristic. Few numbers in the Bible have this unusual characteristic. One that does is the number 153, which we will examine later in our study. But now we want to look at the number 276. Why is it special?

Some Biblical Numbers Are Extra Special

In the Bible one can find hundreds of numbers. Among them are seven that have special properties. Their special characteristic is that each of these numbers can be broken down into two numbers. The sum of all the numbers coming before and including one of these numbers equals the beginning number. For example the number six is also 2 x 3, and 1 + 2 + 3 = 6. The number six is found rather frequently in the Bible, notably in connection with the six days of the week when God worked and when man worked. These special numbers are derived from the equation:

$$\Sigma n = n \text{ times } \frac{n + 1}{2}$$

Wherein n = any odd number,
    and Σn = the sum of all the integers preceding and including n.

Thus when n = 3, the sum of $1 + 2 + 3 = 3$ times $\frac{(3 + 1)}{2}$

$$6 = 3 \times 2$$

The second number with this special characteristic is fifteen.

In the number 15, n = 5.

$$5 \frac{(5 + 1)}{2} = \text{ the sum of } 1 + 2 + 3 + 4 + 5$$

Therefore $5 \times 3 = 15$ and $1 + 2 + 3 + 4 + 5 = 15$.

It is found a few times in the Bible, notably in connection with the flood of Noah's day when the waters stood fifteen cubits above the highest mountain of that day.

The third number is the number twenty-eight.

$7 \times 4 = 28$ and $1 + 2 + 3 + 4 + 5 + 6 + 7 = 28$.

It is found a few times in the Bible, but in all cases, in seemingly unimportant usage.

The fourth number is forty-five.

$9 \times 5 = 45$ and $1 + 2 + 3 + 4 + 5 + 6 + 7 + 8 + 9 = 45$.

It is found a few times in the Bible, for example, once in connection with the construction of the tabernacle and once in connection with a building constructed by Solomon.

The fifth number that has this characteristic is the number sixty-six.

$$11 \times 6 = 66 \text{ and } 1 + 2 + 3 + 4 + 5 + 6 + 7 + 8 + 9 + 10 + 11 = 66$$

To my knowledge it is not found in the Bible. The fact that our English Bible is divided into sixty-six books cannot be looked upon as divine truth.

The sixth number is ninety-one.

$$13 \times 7 = 91 \text{ and } 1 + 2 + 3 \ldots + 12 + 13 = 91.$$

To my knowledge it is not found in the Bible.

The seventh number is 120.

$$15 \times 8 = 120 \text{ and } 1 + 2 + 3 \ldots + 14 + 15 = 120.$$

It is found a few times in the Bible, notably in giving us Moses' age when he died, in God's declaration of Genesis 6, that man's days on earth were to be 120 years, and in Acts 1 where we are taught that there were about 120 people in the upper room.

In all the Bible to my knowledge there are only two additional numbers that bear the special characteristics of these special numbers. One is the number 153.

$$17 \times 9 = 153 \text{ and } 1 + 2 + 3 \ldots + 16 + 17 = 153.$$

Later in our study we will look at this number very carefully.

The other number is 276. It is the number that we want to examine carefully because it bears heavily on our study.

The Number 276 Is An Extra Special Number

As we have learned, the number 276 is special. It is found only once in the Bible and that is in the unusual setting of the storm and shipwreck that Paul endured as recorded in Acts 27. God carefully let us know that there were 276 people on board and none were lost. What spiritual truth can be discovered in the number 276?

The number 276 is equal to 12 x 23. This also can be written 2 x 2 x 3 x 23 or 4 x 3 x 23. The number two signifies the body of believers, the number three the purpose of God, the number four universality, i.e., four points on the compass, and the number twelve signifies the fullness of whatever is in view in the context.

The number twenty-three is especially highlighted, both in the fact that 12 x 23 = 276 and that 1 + 2 + 3 ... + 21 + 22 + 23 = 276. We are learning that it is the number twenty-three in the Bible that especially identifies with God's judgment on the church. But as we learned, in this setting, God is emphasizing that none of the 276 - that is, none of the 12 x 23 - were lost even though the ship was totally destroyed. Thus we may read 2 x 2 x 3 x 23 to mean: It is the purpose of God that during the final tribulation period, when the church as a corporate body will be increasingly under God's judgment, none of the true believers will lose their salvation.

Or we can read the number as 3 x 4 x 23, which spiritually indicates that it is the purpose of God that as judgment comes on the church all over the world, not one true believer will be lost. Or we can read the number as 12 x 23, which spiritually indicates that as the fullness of God's judgment descends on the church, true believers are safe.

> *Nothing, not even the end of the church, can separate the believer from the love of God.*

Surely, during the final tribulation, the era of the New Testament church will end, i.e., the ship will be entirely destroyed. True believers within the church, who are represented by the 276 people aboard the ship, are saved. Not one aboard the ship was lost. Salvation is eternal; nothing, not even the end of the church, can separate the believer from the love of God.

322 Soldiers

The Bible records another instance in which the number twenty-three is being featured but is not readily seen. Such is the situation in relation to an historical event recorded in Genesis 14. God speaks there of the capture of the nephew of Abram, named Lot, together with Lot's family and many other people living in Sodom, the city in which Lot lived.

We read in Genesis 14:12-15:

And they took Lot, Abram's brother's son, who dwelt in Sodom, and his goods, and departed. And there came one that had escaped, and told Abram the Hebrew; for he dwelt in the plain of Mamre the Amorite, brother of Eshcol, and brother of Aner: and these were confederate with Abram. And when Abram heard that his brother was taken captive, he armed his trained servants, born in his own house, three hundred and eighteen, and pursued them unto Dan. And he divided himself against them, he and his servants, by night, and smote them, and pursued them unto Hobah, which is on the left hand of Damascus.

From this citation we learn that Abram had 318 trained men who were prepared to fight, and he himself went, which made a total of 319 men. He was a confederate of Mamre, Eshcol, and Aner, who were not of Abram's household. Genesis 14:24 records that these three men also assisted in the fight, "the men which went with me, Aner, Eshcol, and Mamre." Thus the total number of men who banded together to rescue Lot were:

Trained men of Abram's household	318
Abram	1
Aner, Eshcol, and Mamre	3
Total	322

The number 322 is not an extra special number like 153 or 276, but it is a very significant number because it breaks down to 2 x 7 x 23. As we have already learned, if these numbers have any spiritual significance, it must be as follows:

2 is the number of the church
7 is the number of perfection
23 is the number of judgment

When Abram returned from the rescue operation, Christ as a theophany, the high priest Melchizedek, met him. Melchizedek brought out bread and wine (Genesis 14:18) and to him Abram gave tithes (verse 20). This indicates that the whole historical event is pointing to Jesus our Savior, who broke His body as the bread of life and who shed

His blood that we might be freed from our enemies. While it is not our purpose to develop this in this study, the tithes represent the people who become saved as we assault Satan's dominion with the Gospel. Significantly, Melchizedek told Abram in Genesis 14:20, "Blessed be the most high God, which hath delivered thine enemies into thy hand.

> *The historical event points to Jesus our Savior, who broke His body as the bread of life and who shed His blood that we might be free.*

And he gave him tithes of all." Thus we learn that the number 322 or 2 x 7 x 23 is intimately identified with the bringing of the Gospel. In bringing the Gospel, salvation is provided for those who believe but judgment is brought against those who remain enemies of Christ. Because it is the body of believers who are called the church and who bring the Gospel, we can see why the number two is featured. Because the enemy was vanquished, we can see why the number twenty-three, which stands for judgment, was featured. Because the sending forth of the Gospel is guided perfectly by the Holy Spirit, we can see why the number seven, the number of perfection, is featured.

The Three and One Half Days of Revelation 11
Thus far we have learned that the final tribulation period can be seventy years duration, as was typified by the seventy years of Israel's experiences during the years 609 B.C. to 539 B.C. Or it can identify with twenty-three, as we discovered by numerous citations. This is particularly so because the number twenty-three is identified with judgment.

Another time period in the Bible that apparently identifies quite dramatically with the duration of the final tribulation period is found in Revelation 11. God presents two witnesses who witness for 1260 days. These two witnesses represent the church as it brings the Gospel throughout the New Testament era. The time 1260 days, which equals three and a half years, is a figure taken from Daniel 9:27, where the middle of the seventieth seven was the time of the cross, when sacrifice and offering ceased. (See Chapter 12 for a full discussion of this.) The last half of Daniel 9:27 says that the end of the seventieth seven relates to "the overspreading of abominations he shall make it desolate, even until the consummation, and that determined shall be poured upon the desolate." The overspreading of abominations surely refers to the final tribulation and the consummation can refer only to the end of the world and Judgment Day. Thus, the entire New Testament era, from the time of the cross to Judgment Day, is typified by 1260 days or three and one half years. During this time the church witnesses.

Revelation 11 instructs us that after the two witnesses have finished their testimony, they will be killed and "their dead bodies shall lie in the street of the great city, which spiritually is called Sodom and Egypt, where also our Lord was crucified" (verse 8). At the end of the three and one half days, they became alive again and ascended up into heaven.

> *The death of the two witnesses will signify that the final tribulation is in progress.*

It was discovered earlier in this study that the death of the two witnesses will signify that the final tribulation is in progress. Almost all of the elect have become saved. Increasingly the church becomes apostate as indicated by the language that they are called Sodom and Egypt. The Lord was crucified outside the wall of Jerusalem. Jerusalem is used in the Bible as a representation of the church. But now it has become like Sodom, that is, it has become spiritually adulterous. Like Egypt, which spiritually is used of God to represent being in bondage to sin, the church, too, is in bondage to sin. It is the means that God uses to curtail the proclamation of the true Gospel.

The resurrection of the two witnesses signifies the end of the world when believers are raptured to be with Christ. Thus, the three and one half days, during which the two witnesses are dead, represent the final tribulation period, which ends with the raising up of the two witnesses. This surely points to the rapture of the believers at the end of the world.

When they are killed we are told in Revelation 11:9-12:
And they of the people and kindreds and tongues and nations shall see their dead bodies three days and an half, and shall not suffer their dead bodies to be put in graves. And they that dwell upon the earth shall rejoice over them, and make merry, and shall send gifts one to another; because these two prophets tormented them that dwelt on the earth. And after three days and an half the Spirit of life from God entered into them, and

they stood upon their feet; and great fear fell upon them which saw them. And they heard a great voice from heaven saying unto them, Come up hither. And they ascended up to heaven in a cloud; and their enemies beheld them.

This succinct description tells us that during the final tribulation period, which ends with the rapture of the believers, the denominations and congregations will rejoice because they can increasingly have a gospel of their own making, a gospel that is not the true Gospel.

> *Denominations and congregations will rejoice because they can increasingly have a gospel of their own making.*

The curious fact, however, is that this period is set forth as a period of three and a half days. This obviously cannot be a literal period of time. Why did God choose three and a half days?

The first reason is that in one sense it identifies with the "time and times and the dividing of time," spoken of in Daniel 7:25, where God says of the final tribulation period:

And he shall speak great words against the most High, and shall wear out the saints of the most High, and think to change times and laws: and they shall be given into his hand until a time and times and the dividing of time.

This passage is speaking of Satan who is loosed during the final tribulation period. As he increasingly overcomes the external church, it appears that he is overcoming the believers. It will appear that he has won. In Daniel 7 God speaks of this period as three and a half times. By the figure of three and a half the tribulation period of Revelation 11 is tied together with the same tribulation period of Daniel 7:25.

Final Tribulation - Forty-Two Months

One other time reference to the duration of the final tribulation should be noted. In Revelation 11:1 we read:

And there was given me a reed like unto a rod: and the angel stood, saying, Rise, and measure the temple of God, and the altar, and them that worship therein.

The setting of this verse is the measurement of "the temple," "the altar," and "them that worship therein." This can be shown to indicate that God has a very precise number of people who are chosen from eternity to become saved. They are built into a spiritual temple. The implication is that when the temple is completed, the end will come. This identifies with the premise found all through the Bible; the time line of history is the unfolding of God's salvation plan.

Verses 3 and 4 of Revelation 11 then record:

And I will give power unto my two witnesses, and they shall prophesy a thousand two hundred and threescore days, clothed in sackcloth. These are the two olive trees, and the two candlesticks standing before the God of the earth.

As we have learned, these two witnesses represent the church as it brings the Gospel throughout the New Testament era. The "thousand two hundred threescore days" (1260 days) are the whole New Testament era.

In Revelation 11:2 we read:

But the court which is without the temple leave out, and measure it not; for it is given unto the Gentiles: and the holy city shall they tread under foot forty and two months.

This verse can be shown to indicate that time is not measured by the number of people upon the earth. The Gentiles or nations are the unsaved on the earth who are ruled over by Satan. It is they who will trod under foot the holy city. Remember we have learned that the holy city, like the temple, is a figure that represents the believers, who are normally found in churches. To tread under foot is a figure that points to the fact that the time will come when Satan, utilizing the unsaved, will rule over the churches. This is especially true during the final tribulation period. In verse 2 God shows that the time when the unsaved will occupy the holy city is to be forty-two months. While forty-two months is three and one half years, it is a different period from the 1260 days of the next verse. God indicates this difference by using the term forty-two months.

The same forty-two month period is in view in Revelation 13 wherein God describes how Satan is being worshipped. Revelation 13:4-7 declares:

And they worshipped the dragon which gave power unto the beast: and they worshipped the beast, saying, Who is like unto the beast? who is able to make war with him? And there was given unto him a mouth speaking great things and blasphemies; and power was given unto him to continue **forty and two months**. And he opened his mouth in blasphemy against God, to blaspheme his name, and his tabernacle, and them that dwell in heaven. And it was given unto him to make war with the saints, and to overcome them: and power was given him over all kindreds, and tongues, and nations.

Please note that this passage also gives a time of forty-two months. It also is speaking of the final tribulation period. We wonder why forty-two months, since we will learn that the actual time of the final tribulation is 2300 days. The reason for this undoubtedly is the fact that the final tribulation period is typified by the time when Jesus ministered on earth. We learned that from the time He was baptized until He went into Jerusalem to be crucified was exactly three and one half years (see page 408 ff.).

The conditions in the church in Jesus' day and the conditions in the church during the final tribulation have many similarities. In both instances:

1. Satan is loosed. Remember he was bound when Christ went to the cross.

2. The church is increasingly apostate.

3. The number of people becoming saved is diminishing.

The big difference between these two periods is, of course, that during Christ's ministry there was great hope for future salvation. It was God's plan to open up the whole world to salvation. During the final tribulation there is progressively decreasing hope for salvation as the true Gospel is silenced. Only Judgment Day is left for the world at the end of the final tribulation period.

Nevertheless God uses the forty-two months of Jesus' ministry as a figure of the final tribulation period.

This also gives us another reason why God uses three and one half days to represent the final tribulation period. Utilizing a day for a year, three and one half days equals three and one half years, which was the time Jesus ministered on earth.

The three and a half days like the forty-two months have a unique identification with seventy years and twenty-three years: In these four numbers there is a very important common denominator. The common denominator is forty-two, which is also the number 2 x 3 x 7. Seven, the number of perfection, times three, the number of purpose times two, the number that signifies the church. Thus the final tribulation period is the perfection of the purpose of God's plan for the end of the church.

How does forty-two relate to these four numbers, which seem to be so unrelated to each other? Let us see how this is.

Each day has twenty-four hours. Thus three and a half days equals 3½ x 24 or eighty-four hours and 2 x 42 = 84. That is quite easy to see.

Likewise each year has twelve months. Thus seventy years equals 70 x 12 or 840 months and 2 x 10 x 42 = 840 months.

So far, we see the occurrence of forty-two in both three and a half days and in seventy years. Both hours and months are time divisions repeatedly referred to in the Bible. Thus, we can be very comfortable with this means of identifying the three and a half days and forty-two with seventy years.

But what about twenty-three years? How can the number forty-two relate to twenty-three years? Are you surprised that there are precisely 8400 days in twenty-three years? Yes, there are!

Let's see the truth of this. According to the most exact astronomical information there are 365.2422 days in a year. If we multiply 365.2422 by 23 the product is 8400.57 days. Drop the fraction and we have left 8400 whole days. We thus have before us:

$$3½ \text{ days} = 84 \text{ hours}$$
$$70 \text{ years} = 840 \text{ months}$$
$$23 \text{ years} = 8400 \text{ days}$$

> *God has interrelated the periods 3½ days, 42 months, 23 years, and 70 years by the common denominator 42.*

And 8400 days equals 2 x 42 x 100. Isn't this a startling piece of information? Surely God has interrelated the periods of three and a half days, forty-two months, twenty-three years, and seventy years by the common denominator forty-two.

Thus far, then, four numbers point to the time duration of the final tribulation period: seventy years, twenty-three years, forty-two months, and three and a half days. It must be learned which, if any, of these time periods is the actual duration of the final tribulation.

To assist in answering that question we should look at Daniel 8 where God gives us important information.

Another Look at the Little Horn of Daniel 8
God has given another citation that relates to the time duration of the final tribulation in Daniel 8. Earlier in the study, reference was made to the little horn of Daniel 8. Daniel 8:8 refers to a great horn that becomes broken. Verse 21 teaches that this symbolizes the first king of Greece, Alexander the Great, whose brilliant leadership resulted in Greece becoming a worldwide power. He died about 300 years before Christ, but God continues to recognize the Greeks as representative of all the nations of the world until the end of the world. This is seen in verses 21 and 22:

> And the rough goat is the king of Grecia: and the great horn that is between his eyes is the first king. Now that being broken, whereas four stood up for it, four kingdoms shall stand up out of the nation, but not in his power.

The number four indicates universality, or the entire world. The New Testament recognizes this Grecian reference to all the kingdoms of the world, it repeatedly uses the phrase Jews and Greeks (cf. Acts 14:1, 18:4, 19:10, 19:17, 20:21, I Corinthians 1:22-24), to distinguish between the blood descendants of Abraham and the rest of the world. For centuries the Roman empire was the dominant nation of the world, but God does not use the phrase Jews and Romans. In agreement with the prophecy of Daniel 8, God uses the phrase Jews and Greeks.
Daniel 8 explains that the little horn, who is Satan, comes out of the nations of the world. Verse 9 declares "out of one of them came forth a little horn." God explains who this little horn is and when he will appear, in verse 23:

> And in the latter time of their kingdom, when the transgressors are come to the full, a king of fierce countenance, and understanding dark sentences, shall stand up.

"When the transgressors are come to the full," can refer only to the end of time when God comes in judgment. God explains that this little horn, Satan, will be a king of fierce countenance who understands dark sentences. To understand dark sentences is a phrase that identifies with understanding the Bible. For example, Psalm 78:1-3 declares:

Give ear, O my people, to my law: incline your ears to the words of my mouth. I will open my mouth in a parable; I will utter dark sayings of old; Which we have heard and known, and our fathers have told us.

> *The little horn comes through preachers and theologians who have a substantial understanding of the Gospel.*

Thus, the little horn, the king of fierce countenance, comes through preachers and theologians who have a substantial understanding of the Gospel. The little horn, Satan, comes through teachers that present a gospel that is so close to the true Gospel that even the elect would be deceived if that were possible. II Corinthians 11:14-15 addresses Satan's activities with false gospels:

And no marvel; for Satan himself is transformed into an angel of light. Therefore it is no great thing if his ministers also be transformed as the ministers of righteousness; whose end shall be according to their works.

It Looks Like Satan Will Win

Daniel 8 explains Satan's apparent success in causing the true Gospel to suffer defeat. Verses 24 and 25 prophesy:

And his power shall be mighty, but not by his own power: and he shall destroy wonderfully, and shall prosper, and practise, and shall destroy the mighty and the holy people. And through his policy also he shall cause craft to prosper in his hand; and he shall magnify himself in his heart, and by peace shall destroy many: he shall also stand up against the Prince of princes; but he shall be broken without hand.

This is the situation during the final tribulation period, as Satan ravages the churches with gospels that feature signs and wonders (Matthew 24:24). Satan's success in his warfare against the true Gospel is further explicated in Daniel 8:10-12:

And it waxed great, even to the host of heaven; and it cast down some of the host and of the stars to the ground, and stamped upon them. Yea, he magnified himself even to the prince of the host, and by him the daily sacrifice was taken away, and the place of his sanctuary was cast down. And an host was given him against the daily sacrifice by reason of transgression, and it cast down the truth to the ground; and it practised, and prospered.

In the phrase "daily sacrifice," in the King James Bible, the word sacrifice is *italicized*, which means that it was not in the original language of the Bible. It was inserted by the translators because they believed that sacrifice was the daily activity that was taken away by the antichrist or the little horn. However, the word sacrifice cannot be a correct understanding, because sacrifice ended when Christ hung on the cross. He was the completion and the fulfillment of every sacrifice.

> *Sacrifice ended when Christ hung on the cross.*

The Daily Candlestick
The "daily" that will be taken away by the activity of Satan is the daily candlestick. It is important to understand this because it will give understanding of the duration of the final tribulation period. The Hebrew word for 'daily' in Daniel 8 is the word '*tamid.*' It is translated into the word "continually" in Leviticus 24:2-4:

Command the children of Israel, that they bring unto thee pure oil olive beaten for the light, to cause the lamps to burn continually. Without the veil of the testimony, in the tabernacle of the congregation, shall Aaron order it from the evening unto the morning before the LORD continually: it shall be a statute for ever in your generations. He shall order the lamps upon the pure candlestick before the LORD continually.

> *The Gospel was to go into the world without ceasing . . . until the elect become saved.*

The candlestick that was to burn continually or daily in the temple represented the light of the Gospel. The temple was a picture of the church, or body of believers, that Christ came to build. Believers are assigned the task of being lights in the world; they share the Gospel. The Gospel was to go into the world without ceasing, that is, it was to go into the world continuously, until the elect become saved. Then, according to God's plan, the light would go out. This is what Daniel 8:11 means. Satan, the little horn, the antichrist, working through gospels that feature signs and wonders as well as through churches that no longer look to the Bible as their ultimate authority, will increasingly overwhelm the church so that fewer and fewer of them will bring the true Gospel. The era of the New Testament church will have come to an end. In the churches that have false gospels, the abomination of desolation will be standing in the holy place.

Two Thousand Three Hundred Days
Daniel 8, verses 13 and 14 declare:
Then I heard one saint speaking, and another saint said unto that certain saint which spake, How long shall be the vision concerning the daily sacrifice, and the transgression of desolation, to give both the sanctuary and the host to be trodden under foot? And he said unto me, Unto two thousand and three hundred days; then shall the sanctuary be cleansed.

In this time reference the number 2300 is identified as the period of time when the sanctuary is trodden under foot. Since the sanctuary is a figure that points to the body of believers, we can readily see that this verse speaks of the final tribulation period. As was learned, the number twenty-three is intimately associated with the final tribulation period. Therefore, it is not surprising to see the number of days is 2300 because the number twenty-three is again featured. It must be determined whether this is a symbolic number or a real number. A period of 2300 days is approximately six years and four months. In the phrase "two thousand three hundred days," the Hebrew word translated days is actually a word that should be translated "evening morning." This is reinforced by the language of verse 26:
And the vision of the evening and the morning which was told is true: wherefore shut thou up the vision; for it shall be for many days.

The phrase "the evening and the morning" is fairly unusual in the Bible. Ordinarily when the Bible speaks of the passage of a day, the morning is put before the evening; a day progresses from morning to evening. God reversed this order in Daniel 8 and mentioned evening ahead of morning. The word "daily" as it is found in Daniel 8:11-12, explains why. We have learned that the "daily" had reference to the candlestick that burned continuously in the temple. Leviticus 24:3-4 also speaks about the candlestick burning continuously in the temple, and in the same sequence: the evening precedes the morning:

> Without the veil of the testimony, in the tabernacle of the congregation, shall Aaron order it from the **evening unto the morning before the LORD continually**: it shall be a statute for ever in your generations. He shall order the lamps upon the pure candlestick before the LORD continually.

> *The focus of evening to morning is that the lamp was to burn through the night . . . into a world that is under the dominion of darkness.*

In the historical context, the focus of evening to morning is that the lamp was to burn through the night. Spiritually this is an important focus. The light of the Gospel is to go into a world that is under the dominion of darkness. Numerous New Testament verses bear on this concept (cf. John 1:4-9, Colossians 1:12-13). When the candlestick is taken away, the unsaved world remains in the darkness of sin and the darkness of Satan's dominion.

The point is that the candlestick was to burn in the temple each and every day. The passage of a day encompasses twenty-four hours; therefore, we can understand that the 2300 evening mornings of Daniel 8 represent 2300 days, each twenty-four hours long.

Evening and Morning Days of Creation

An important reference to further substantiate the idea that "evening morning" points to literal twenty-four hour days is Genesis 1:3-5:

And God said, Let there be light: and there was light. And God saw the light, that it was good: and God divided the light from the darkness. And God called the light Day, and the darkness he called Night. And the evening and the morning were the first day.

God's words, "let there be light" and "the evening and the morning were the first day," teach that light was created on the first day of creation. Spiritually this historical event was looking forward to the time when Jesus would come as the light of the world and to the New Testament era when the light of the Gospel would be sent into all the world.

The word "evening" before the word "morning" is the same sequence as in Leviticus 24 and Daniel 8. This can be expected because all three passages spiritually relate to the Gospel going into the world: Genesis 1 anticipates the Gospel going into the world. Leviticus 24 indicates the Gospel is to go forth continuously. Daniel 8 says there will be a time when the Gospel light will be extinguished.

The evenings and mornings referred to in Genesis 1 were twenty-four hour days. This is known because on the fourth day God created the sun and the moon to serve as the timekeepers. Therefore, each day had to be twenty-four hours in length. Moreover, if the third day, when the vegetation was created, had been a period longer than twenty-four hours, then plants could not have survived through the long night that would have followed. If the evening and morning of Genesis 1 was twenty-four hours, and if the evening and morning of Leviticus 24 was twenty-four hours, then the evening and morning of Daniel 8 must also be twenty-four hours.

In fact, God gives us an unusual confirmation of the 2300 evening mornings of Daniel 8:13-14 by the language of verse 26: "The vision of the evening and the morning which was told is true."

> *In all likelihood it is to be a period of 2300 days, which is a little more than six years.*

Thus it would appear that the duration of the final tribulation period is not to be seventy years, nor twenty-three years, nor forty-two months, nor three and a half days. Rather, in all likelihood it is to be a period of 2300 days, which is a little more than six years. Later in our study we will see how this 2300 day period fits exactly into God's end-time plan.

The final tribulation period that the church and the world must face before the end of the world has been examined in detail, including its purpose, its chief character, and the time span it will encompass. Two additional questions are relevant to this study: Will we know when we have actually come into the final tribulation period? Will there be conclusive evidence that we have indeed entered this final traumatic period, which immediately precedes the end of the world and Judgment Day?

Carefully Continue to Send Forth the Gospel
I feel compelled to warn that we must be very careful. The Bible instructs the believer to "occupy till I come" (Luke 19:13), that is, continue to witness the true Gospel as long as possible, till the last day of this earth's existence. God appears to have disclosed to us that during the last 2300 days on earth, the earth will experience a final tribulation. We may have already come into the final tribulation period, as indicated by the present development of events in the church and in the world. However, we must not risk trying to be wiser than God. God has given considerable Biblical evidence that may indicate that the end is near, but conclusions as to the timing of the end of the world are partially based on circumstantial evidence. No statements in the Bible plainly and unequivocally tell of the arrival of the final period.

Wonderfully, the closing events of the end of the world are in God's hand. God has cared for the world - and especially for those who have become His children - since its creation approximately 13,000 years ago. We can be sure that God will care for this world and His children to the last day.

SUMMARY

In this chapter we have learned that believers do indeed go through the final tribulation period that will come upon the earth just prior to the end.

This, of course, is to be expected since we have learned that the unfolding of God's salvation is the time line of history. Believers are an integral part of God's salvation plan. Only when history has come to an end will there no longer be people becoming saved. The final tribulation period is that time when the churches increasingly become apostate and fewer and fewer people are becoming saved. God brings judgment upon the churches by allowing them to become false churches with gospels other than the true Gospel.

We have also learned that this terrible period was typified by the closing experiences of ancient Israel. Thus a period of seventy years could be the time duration of this tribulation, but even more insistently, twenty-three years could be the length of this trauma. We have begun to see that the number twenty-three is definitely associated with judgment.

However, when we analyzed much more Biblical data, we discovered that the duration of the final tribulation is in all likelihood 2300 days. We must keep this in mind as we continue to study.

> *As we obtain a clear picture of what the true Gospel is, we will be better qualified to see how greatly Satan is ravaging the churches in our day.*

What is the true Gospel to which we repeatedly refer? Given the fact that there are many gospels vying for the attention of the world, how can we really know that we have found the true Gospel? As we obtain a clear picture of what the true Gospel is, we will be better qualified to see how greatly Satan is ravaging the churches in our day. This in turn will assist us in seeing the reality of the Biblical timetable for the end of the world. It is, therefore, very desirable that we spend some time on this question.

NOTE

[1] Athaliah was actually a queen who usurped the throne. However, she reigned as the sole ruler over Judah from 841 B.C. to 835 B.C.

Chapter 7
What Is the True Gospel?

What is the true Gospel of Jesus Christ, who alone can save men and women from their sins? There is no question that is of greater importance facing the world today. This is so because only the true Gospel will provide the answer that can save us from spending eternity under the wrath of God. Therefore, as we seek to identify the true Gospel, we will endeavor to discover answers to the following questions: What is the divine authority that structures and determines the true Gospel? What is the message of the true Gospel? What is the mandate of the true Gospel? Every gospel is structured and determined by its authority, so when the authorities differ, the gospels themselves differ.

We are living in a day when false gospels are proliferating. Everywhere we turn we find different kinds of gospels. Indeed, we wonder, how can I really know I am following the true Gospel?

We hear sermons of various kinds; we read the Bible here and there; we generally hear a lot of good things about the Gospel. We hear about how we are to walk as Christians; we see rules in the Bible that God has given to us for the good of mankind. But, we begin to wonder, what is the essential structure of the Gospel of the Lord Jesus Christ? Can we strip away the peripherals and get right down to the very substance, the inner core of the true Gospel?

The Authority that Structures and Determines the True Gospel

In order to know what the Gospel actually is, we must first of all determine the authority that structures and determines what it is. This is necessary because the nature of the true Gospel is defined and established by its divine authority. In fact, the nature of every religion, gospel, and ideological system is defined and established by its recognized authority.

A Muslim, for example, may wish to know how to live as a good Muslim. So he carefully consults the Koran, a book in which Muslims believe God has spoken. The Koran, therefore, is the written authority that establishes the Islamic gospel, that is, the Muslim religion. An orthodox Jew has a different authority. It includes what we call our Old authority. It includes what we call our Old Testament, along with the writings of the church fathers that are considered to be divinely inspired. That is the authority that establishes the nature and character of the Jewish religion. On the other hand, a Mormon has as his divine authority the Bible, plus the Book of Mormon, which is believed to be divinely inspired. Because the Book of Mormon came later than the Bible, it has become a shadow that lies over the Bible. That is, someone who follows the Mormon gospel examines everything he reads in the Bible in the light of what is found in the Book of Mormon.

Similarly, the Roman Catholics follow still another gospel. The authority that structures and determines their gospel begins with the Bible, but the apocrypha books are also a part of that authority, as are the visions of Joan of Arc, the visions of Fatima, and the so-called infallible utterances of the Pope. All of these are looked upon as divine, and together they make up the authority that establishes the character of the Roman Catholic gospel.

Likewise, the charismatic gospel has its authority. It believes that the Bible is the Word of God, but it also believes in divine revelation through visions, voices, or tongues, which expands its authority beyond the Bible. Therefore, it has as its authority the Bible, *plus* the messages presumably received from God through dreams, visions, and tongues. This widened authority structures and determines the character of the charismatic gospel.

> *Every time we have a different authority, we*
> *also have a different gospel.*

Bear in mind that every time we have a different authority, we also have a different gospel. One definition sometimes offered to describe the true Gospel is set forth in I John 4:2. There we read that if we confess that Christ has come in the flesh, then we are of God. Yet as we read in Luke 4:34, the demons also admit that Jesus Christ has come in the flesh, and they are still under God's wrath. So that particular definition standing alone may not be adequate in every case. We must, therefore, discover the divine authority that structures and determines the character and nature of the true Gospel.

The Bible indicates that it alone and in its entirety is the authority that establishes the Gospel of the Lord Jesus Christ. Revelation 22:18-19 says it best:

> For I testify unto every man that heareth the words of the prophecy of this book, If any man shall add unto these things, God shall add unto him the plagues that are written in this book: And if any man shall take away from the words of the book of this prophecy, God shall take away his part out of the book of life, and out of the holy city, and from the things which are written in this book.

By that statement God establishes the parameters of the true Gospel. It is circumscribed by the Bible alone.

> *The Bible is the true divine authority*
> *. . . that establishes the Gospel of our*
> *Lord Jesus Christ.*

The Bible, therefore, is the true divine authority. It is the only complete authority that establishes the Gospel of our Lord Jesus Christ. Because it is the divine authority, because it is from God, it is to be entirely authoritative in our lives. We must eagerly read it; we must eagerly study it with a view to being obedient to it. If we discover in our lives any kind of practice, or any kind of doctrine that is contrary to the Word of God, then as children of God, there will be within us an earnest desire to change that practice or that doctrine so that we will become more faithful to the Word of God.

If we follow an authority that is narrower or wider than the Bible alone and in its entirety, we are not following the Gospel of the Bible. Regardless of how holy it may appear to be, such a gospel will not lead to salvation.

The Central Message of the True Gospel

What is the central message of the true Gospel? We could say that the Gospel is God's love letter to mankind whereby we can become righteous, know the love of God, come into the more abundant life, or learn to live to God's glory. We can think of a lot of verses in the Bible that describe and perhaps even crystallize the essential nature of the Gospel.

Actually, however, we can find summed up in John 3:16 the core meaning of the Gospel. This verse strips away everything else and gets right down to the essential message. There we read, "For God so loved the world, that he gave his only begotten Son, that whosoever believeth in him should not perish, but have everlasting life."

Ordinarily, theologians focus on the first part of the verse: "For God so loved the world . . . ." And that is a glorious phrase that introduces us to the amazing truth that God in His magnificent love has provided salvation to all who believe in the Lord Jesus Christ. But the love of God and the salvation He has so generously provided cannot be fully understood unless we also understand the meaning of the word "perish" found later on in this verse. Only too seldom do we hear a sermon on that statement, " . . . shall not perish . . . ." The phrase "shall not perish" is an integral part of the Gospel.

> *The wages of sin is death. The living death is*
> *to exist throughout eternity in hell.*

When we search the Scriptures, we find that the word "perish," as it is used in John 3:16, does not mean "annihilation." In our English language when we say, "I will perish," we think of dying, of ceasing to exist. In the Bible the word "perish" has another definition. The Bible tells us that the wages of sin is death (cf. Romans 6:23). The living death that God has in view is to exist throughout eternity in hell. That is the predicament of rebellious mankind. That is what it means to perish.

The terrible problem of mankind is that we are sinners. Remember Romans 3:10-11: "As it is written, There is none righteous, no, not one: There is none that understandeth, there is none that seeketh after God." The heart of man by nature is desperately wicked, as we read in Jeremiah 17:9.

Because we sin - even a single sin - we will perish. Because we have been created in His image, God holds each one of us completely accountable to Himself for the conduct of our lives. God has appointed a day at the end of the world when we are to be judged. The Bible says in Hebrews 9:27, " . . . It is appointed unto men once to die, but after this the judgment." Because all of us are sinners, without the Gospel we are all on our way to hell.

This terrible truth cannot be seen with our physical eyes because we cannot look into the future. But what we see with our physical eyes is not the whole story. In fact, it is a very shallow and incidental part of the whole story. For example, we may have had a friend who died. We have seen him as a man who lived out his life well regarded by his fellowman. Then he died. He was eulogized at his funeral as one of the greatest, and then we all went about our business and forgot about Brother Jones. But if Brother Jones died without the Gospel, that is, without being saved, the next thing he will be aware of is that he is standing before the Judgment Throne of God, where he must answer for every sin he ever committed; and these will be multitudinous. Any one of these sins could condemn him to eternal damnation. There is no escape; there is no reprieve, no parole. There is no way out.

> *Every day almost 200,000 people die unsaved and the next conscious thing they will know is that they are standing before the Judgment Throne of God.*

Every day approximately 200,000 people die all over this earth. When we realize that most of these 200,000 people die unsaved and that the next conscious thing they will know is that they are standing before the Judgment Throne of God, subject to eternal damnation, we become aware of a horror story of magnificent proportions.

We sometimes hear about an earthquake in which 50,000 people are killed. We hear about wars in which 700,000 or 800,000 people are killed. We hear about man's inhumanity to man. We hear about famines that kill many thousands. None of these tragedies holds a candle to the most dreadful tragedy of all, the dreadful, daily trauma that faces mankind.

The horrors of man's inhumanity to man, the horrors of famine, of war, or of whatever the trauma, result only in physical death, but physical death in itself is not the horror story. The horror story is that after death there is the judgment. God's perfect justice demands eternal damnation as payment for sins.

Unfortunately we do not hear this part of the Gospel preached very frequently. It is so reprehensible, so sorry, so serious. It is so terrible that we want to forget about it. We would rather just talk about the love of God. We would rather talk about moral living. We prefer to talk about all kinds of things rather than this very important teaching of the Gospel.

> *The truth that hell is waiting for the human race is not the whole story.*

Wonderfully, the truth that hell is waiting for the human race is not the whole story. If God had written the Bible simply to tell us that we are going to hell, we could still praise God that at least He warned us. That knowledge would not do us much good, because we are all sinners, and we would still end up in hell. But woven into the fabric of the Gospel of the Lord Jesus Christ, like a golden thread running through the entire Bible, is the message of hope. This is the message: That we can know the love of God by trusting in the Lord Jesus Christ as our Savior. That is the other side of the Gospel coin, the central part of the Gospel presentation: "For God so loved the world, that he gave his only begotten Son, that whosoever believeth in him should not perish, but have everlasting life" (John 3:16).

Why is it that if we believe on Him we will not go to hell? The Bible tells us that it is because Christ became sin for us! We read in II Corinthians 5:21, "For he hath made him to be sin for us, who knew no sin; that we might be made the righteousness of God in him." Or, as Isaiah 53:6 puts it, "the LORD hath laid on him the iniquity of us all" (that is, all who will hang their lives on Him).

> *All of us who cry out to the Lord Jesus Christ for mercy and hang our lives on Him can know freedom from hell.*

That is the central message of the Gospel. There is no other news that can compare to this. It begins with the terrible truth that mankind is sinful and heading for hell, but additionally it is the wonderful news that all of us who cry out to the Lord Jesus Christ for mercy and hang our lives on Him can know freedom from hell because He became sin for us. Laden with our sins, as our substitute, He stood before the Judgment Throne of God when He stood before Pontius Pilate. He was found guilty for our sins, and God poured out His condemnation upon Him to the degree that it was the equivalent of every one of us who would believe on Him spending an eternity in hell. In this way He paid for all of our sins. He satisfied God's perfect justice that demands eternal damnation as punishment for sin. Since our sins have been paid for, hell no longer threatens us. We are no longer under the law that decrees that we are to go to hell. We are now under grace. By God's grace we have become children of God. We have left the dominion of Satan (which we were in before we were saved), and we have become citizens of the Kingdom of the Lord Jesus Christ.

The pathetic fact, however, is that to a high degree, the church of today is no longer aware of this message. This has been true to some degree throughout history, but it is particularly true today. Obviously, there are exceptions. Praise God for the exceptions! But to a high degree, the church has lost its sensitivity to the central nature of the Gospel. Too many preachers no longer talk about hell. In fact, I once heard a theologian from a reputable seminary publicly say that hell is like being in an airplane and just going round and round and round. In other words, he was ridiculing hell. He had better read Deuteronomy 28 again. He had better read Revelation 14 again, where it says "the smoke of their torment ascendeth up for ever and ever" (verse 11). He had better read Matthew 13, Mark 9, and Matthew 25 again where Jesus says things like "there shall be wailing and gnashing of teeth" (Matthew 13:42), and "their worm dieth not" (Mark 9:44), and where He speaks of eternal damnation (cf. Matthew 25:46). The only reason that we do not often read those passages is because they are so frightening. We had better be frightened if we are not saved, because hell is real.

What Does Mankind Want from the Gospel?

If someone does not want to face the central message of the Bible because he does not want to talk about hell, then what is he going to do with the Gospel? Unfortunately, we find that theologians begin to change the message of the Gospel to satisfy their own desires. They begin to make the Gospel political or economic. They say, for example, "Christianity has to do with being free from political oppression." Or, they begin to teach an economic gospel by saying that Christianity has to do with having enough food to eat and having economic security. Or, they make it a physical well-being gospel by saying that the goal of the gospel is good health and happy lives here on this earth.

None of these aspirations has any direct relationship to the Gospel of the Lord Jesus Christ.

These three aspirations: Political freedom, economic security, and good health, are sought by every man. All mankind seeks for these in one way or another. We do not have to call ourselves Christians to have these kinds of goals. The fact is that none of these aspirations has any direct relationship to the Gospel of the Lord Jesus Christ, that is, to the true, spiritual Gospel. Let us see why this is so.

In Luke 16 God gives us the parable of the rich man and Lazarus. Reference to this parable was made earlier, but because it is so pertinent and helpful to the question we are now studying, we will look at it again. The Bible reveals that the rich man had all that money could buy. Certainly we would assume that, because he had all that money, he must have had a lot of political freedom. Also, he had at his command the finest doctors and the finest nutritionists so that he could enjoy maximum good health. Without a doubt, he had economic security and everything that goes along with it. If anyone appeared to have no need for the message of the Gospel, it was this rich man. He apparently had everything going for him.

On the other hand, God talks about Lazarus. Lazarus had nothing; he was a beggar. He had no economic security. He could not afford a doctor, even though he greatly needed one. Perhaps he slept out on the streets and was getting insufficient food or the wrong kind of food. In any case, his body was laden with sores. He had very poor bodily health. Certainly, as a beggar who would be kicked by everyone who walked by, he had no political security. He was considered to be riffraff. He was nothing. If anyone had a need for an earthly gospel, it would have been Lazarus. As the story continues, we learn that both Lazarus and the rich man died.

Suddenly God strips away the curtain and gives the true picture of these two men as they are to live throughout eternity. What do we find? We find that Lazarus, who had none of the essential desires of mankind, is resting forever in Abraham's bosom. This figure of speech indicates that he is in the place of the highest good, the highest blessing. It is a picture of being saved and being forever in the Kingdom of the Lord Jesus Christ.

On the other hand, where do we find the rich man who on earth had everything a man could want? In this parable, we see him in hell, piteously crying out to Father Abraham to "send Lazarus, that he may dip the tip of his finger in water, and cool my tongue; for I am tormented in this flame" (Luke 16:24). It is a picture of the utterly terrible nature of hell, and this rich man is to be there forever.

Which of these two men really needed the Gospel? Which of these men was really in need?

If you had come to Lazarus with a political gospel or a social gospel, trying to give him medicine and offering him economic security, would that have changed his position in Heaven? The answer is no. He had no need insofar as the true, eternal Gospel is concerned. Surely, as a human being, he could have stood a little food. As a human being, he could have stood a little compassion. But insofar as his relationship to God was concerned, which is the real need of mankind, he himself had no need.

> *Identifying the Gospel message with political, economic, or cultural aspirations has caused the "Christian Gospel" to be especially reprehensible to the leaders of many nations.*

Identifying the Gospel message with political, economic, or cultural aspirations has caused the "Christian Gospel" to be especially reprehensible to the leaders of many nations. When we send a message forth, tailored according to the desires of mankind, which has nothing to do with the Gospel of the Lord Jesus Christ, we enter into areas of activity that threaten political rulers. I am sorry to say that in the past (and it is still happening today), missionaries often went to China and to many other countries spreading a gospel heavily flavored by their Western culture. Thus the gospel message they brought became identified to a great extent with physical prosperity or some kind of political freedom. That is not the Gospel of the Bible. These missionaries, unfortunately, were giving the wrong signals. They had begun meddling in the affairs of the nations to which they were sent, affairs in which they had no business and which had nothing to do with the true Gospel message.

The fact is that the Gospel is unconcerned with the kind of rulers that a nation has. It is unconcerned with the political system under which a people lives. It does declare, however, that it is God who puts up and puts down rulers. It does warn that the citizens of any country are expected to be obedient in all things to those who rule over them. It does not indicate that one kind of government is to be obeyed more than another.

The Bible is not concerned about the economic situation of those who hear the Gospel. In the day that Jesus ministered, and as the disciples went out, did man's inhumanity to man exist? Indeed, it did. There were slaves who were piteously beaten and mistreated. Was there economic uncertainty? Indeed, there was. It was a day when there were no mercy ships. Certainly there were people dying of starvation. Were there people who desperately needed a healing who did not receive it? Indeed, there were.

> *Christ did not come with a gospel that promises good health. He did those miracles of healing as proofs that He was God and as parables.*

Some people misunderstood Jesus' mission when He healed the sick. Christ did not come with a gospel that promises good health. He simply did those miracles of healing as proofs that He was God and in order to give us historical parables through which we can see the spiritual nature of the Gospel. They were earthly stories with a heavenly meaning. Once Christ went to the cross and the apostles died, we do not find any further statements in the Bible regarding physical healing. The Gospel is concerned with spiritual healing: ". . . by whose stripes ye were healed. For ye were as sheep going astray . . . " (I Peter 2:24-25). The Gospel has to do with the healing of our sin-sick souls. The message of the Gospel is that mankind is on its way to hell, but that anyone can know God's love by trusting in Christ as Savior.

When we become saved, we are transferred out of the dominion of Satan, which encompasses all the unsaved people of the world, wherever they are found, in whatever political system they are found. We are translated into the Kingdom of the Lord Jesus Christ, which is a spiritual nation made up of those who are born-again believers, regardless of political ideology, or cultural differences, or whatever.

Many theologians fracture the truths of the Bible concerning the nature of the Gospel when they attempt to understand the meaning of Christian unity. Ephesians 4:4-5 teaches us that: "There is one body, and one Spirit, even as ye are called in one hope of your calling; One Lord, one faith, one baptism." What kind of unity does God have in view? Well-meaning but misguided theologians, in attempting to explain this unity, have tried to introduce concepts into the Gospel that are foreign to it. They effectively believe we are one in "One Lord, one faith, one baptism" only when we have equal political freedom or equal economic prosperity.

The true Gospel looks far beyond political activity, economic desires, and desires for good health. When we have the true Gospel, whether we live in Russia, China, Germany, Peru, the United States, or any other country, there is one Lord, one faith, one baptism. It is a spiritual unity. It is a faith wherein we understand that our sins are washed away. Spiritually we have become right with God. Spiritually we know that we are not sentenced to hell and that we have eternal life. Spiritually we have become one body, even though politically or economically or culturally we have no relationship at all to each other.

We must not fall into the snare that many fall into. In the Old Testament they read about all the gold and silver of Solomon, and they read about the riches of Abraham, as well as many other statements about great physical prosperity. They conclude, "You see, that is what happens when we become saved. We are to have similar physical expectations when we become saved." They fail to realize that God has set up types and figures in the Bible. Old Testament Israel was part of an earthly story, an historical picture pointing to the spiritual meaning of what the New Testament church was to be, that is, what it means to be a child of God. The physical prosperity of Old Testament Israel was an earthly story pointing to the heavenly meaning that believers in Christ become spiritually prosperous, copiously feeding their souls on the Bread of Life, which is Jesus Himself. The wine vats that were filled to overflowing in the Old Testament were a dramatic earthly story pointing to the plenteous flowing of the blood of Christ for the complete payment for all of our sins. Whatever historical freedoms ancient Israel had represented the fact that in Christ we are free from the bondage to sin and Satan.

The problem is, however, that our sin-tainted minds prefer to go to these historical antecedents (which are meant by God to be just figures and types) and make them the very essence of the Gospel. That caters to our sensual nature. That caters to what all men want: political freedom, economic freedom, and good health.

> *If we try to make the Gospel fit the physical characteristics of the Old Testament figures, then we must also offer the sacrifices.*

If we try to make the Gospel fit the physical characteristics of the Old Testament figures, then we must also offer the sacrifices that were to be offered by the Old Testament believers. In other words, we are effectively denying the fact that Christ has come! In the New Testament we do not find any references teaching political freedom, economic security, or good health. The whole essence of the Gospel is spiritual freedom in Christ. Freedom from what? It is freedom from the wrath of God! It has nothing to do with the politics of this world! Simply stated, we have been translated out of the dominion of Satan. The law no longer can send us to hell. We are free in Christ. We have eternal life. That is the nature of the Gospel. That is the only message that we are to proclaim.

The Mandate of the Gospel

Now we have come to the third point that needs to be examined. We have already looked at the authority that structures and determines the Gospel, and we have looked at the message of the Gospel. Now we should examine the mandate of the Gospel.

In the most lucid fashion, God has decreed that we are mandated to bring the Gospel message to all the world: "Go ye into all the world, and preach the gospel to every creature" (Mark 16:15). Jesus commanded this; it is not an option. It is not something we can do if it is convenient or if we feel like doing it. It is an imperative command of the Bible that we are to go out into the world and preach the Gospel. We are Christ's ambassadors to this sin-sick world - Christ, as it were, makes His appeal through us.

Remember, Jesus said that He came to seek and to save that which was lost (cf. Luke 19:10). He has people in China whom He has come to seek and to save. He has people in America whom He has come to seek and to save. He has people in Germany and in Russia and in every nation of the world whom He has come to seek and to save. We do not know who they are, but we know from the Bible that they are people who were already named in the Lamb's Book of Life from the very foundation of the world. We know that God has obligated Himself to save these people.

> *True ambassadors for Christ are the born-again believers, who understand the real nature of the Gospel.*

The true ambassadors for Christ are the born-again believers, who understand the real nature of the Gospel. They have come face-to-face with the reality of hell because they have learned to trust the Bible implicitly. They have been given the marvelous task (which is a mandate as well as a fantastic privilege) to send the Gospel into the world. There are no alibis. We must do it by whatever means the Lord has made available to us.

> *Let us be very certain that we are bringing the*
> *Gospel of the Bible and not the gospel of the*
> *United States or Mexico.*

Let us be very certain that we are bringing the Gospel of the Bible and not the gospel of Europe, or the gospel of the United States, or the gospel of Mexico, or any other perverted gospel. As long as we focus on the basic fundamentals, the true Gospel is absolutely common to every nation. It makes no difference what nation we are in. We all have the exact same spiritual need for the exact same spiritual antidote. We need to be set free from sin through the blood of Christ. Once we are free from sin, knowing that Christ has endured hell for us, then, even if we must live out the rest of our lives in a concentration camp, dying of beatings and starvation, we still have everything. Whether we are to merely exist like Lazarus as a beggar with only the dogs to lick our sores, or whether we live in a palace with all the blessings of this world, makes no difference. If we are saved, we know that we have the greatest good that we could ever have.

The Bible says that we are to love our neighbor as ourselves (Luke 10:27). What does it mean to love our neighbor as ourselves? In John 13:34 Jesus says, "A new commandment I give unto you, That ye love one another; as I have loved you, that ye also love one another." That establishes the nature of the love we are to have for others. We are to love our fellowman as Christ has loved us.

What was the nature of Christ's love for you and me? Did He come to bring us economic security or political freedom or good health? Did He do any of those things for Lazarus (cf. Luke 16)? The answer is no. Absolutely not. In His love for us, He laid down His life. He endured the wrath of God, the equivalent of spending an eternity in hell, in order that we might have eternal life and not go to hell ourselves.

Jesus exhorts, "love one another; as I have loved you" (John 13:34). If Christ has desired eternal life for me to the extent that He went to the cross and endured the wrath of God that I might be saved, if that desire was the focal point of His love, then that desire must be the focal point of my love for others as well.

> *Hell is grasping out for the unsaved
> of the world.*

The Gospel Only Is Needed

When we look at the world, the one thing we should see, the one terrible specter that should grip our souls, is hell grasping out for the lives of the unsaved of the world. Because most people die unsaved, at a rate of almost 200,000 a day, hell is getting its due. That is the truth that we should see. That is the truth that Christ saw when He went to the cross. In our love for our fellowman, we want to warn them: "Don't you see it? Because of your sins, hell is coming and hell is real, but there is a wonderful way of escape through the Lord Jesus Christ. In my love for you, I want the very best for you. Sure, I could spend some money to help you in many ways, but if you die unsaved, even though your life may have been extended because you were given some antibiotics, what difference does it make? You are still going to die, and after death comes the judgment. Can't you see it? If you will only become a believer in Christ, then your physical situation, your political situation, your health situation, is altogether unimportant. You are like Lazarus. You can still have the very highest good. You, too, can have salvation." To desire this for others is true love.

Notice that Jesus says, "Love your neighbor as yourself." How do I love myself? What is the highest good that I could possibly desire for myself? Is it that I might have more physical prosperity? Is that the highest good for me? Not in any sense at all. In fact, it may even tempt me away from serving the Lord the way I ought. Well then, is it to be famous? Is it to have a name? Is it any of the things to which the world aspires? The answer is no. None of those things are the highest good. The highest good for me is what I should desire for others. So what is it? The one thing I need to be sure of is that I have been saved. That is, I must be sure that my sins have been paid for so there is no possibility of going to hell when I die.

Can anyone living on the face of the earth possibly think that he is going to escape death? This world has been around for about 13,000 years and, with only two exceptions (Enoch and Elijah), every human being that has ever walked the face of the earth has died or will die - every one. No one can escape. This is in accordance with the Biblical rule that it is appointed unto men once to die and then comes the judgment (Hebrews 9:27). This means that that is going to happen to me - unless, of course, the Lord comes first. Therefore, if I truly love myself, I am not going to aspire for more of this world's goods. I am not going to aspire to have a better place in this world. Because, in the measure that I desire those things, I am going away from the path that is the very best for me. My first and all-important concern must be that I am absolutely certain that I am a child of God, that I am saved. Only then will I realize that all these other things are unimportant. It really makes no difference how many clothes I have, what kind of car I drive, whether I even own a car, or what kind of situation I live in. These things have no lasting value.

As a matter of fact, God declares in Romans 12:1, "I beseech you therefore, brethren, by the mercies of God, that ye present your bodies a living sacrifice, holy, acceptable unto God, which is your reasonable service." In the Old Testament the Israelites were commanded to tithe, that is, give ten percent of their income. That is the way the priestly offices were supported. In the New Testament God wants everything. The Old Testament tithe was just an example to us pointing to the fact that God wants everything. God is simply saying, "I want all of you, all of your possessions, all of your money, all of your energy, in order that your task as ambassadors of Christ may be done." That task is to present the precious Gospel of salvation to a world that is headed for hell.

> *The golden thread that runs through the Bible is the message of salvation.*

Can we begin to see the truth more clearly? The golden thread that runs through the Bible is the message of salvation. Any time we lose sight of that thread, or that focus, we can be sure we no longer have the Gospel of the Bible. We will have a gospel that has been designed in the minds of men, and we are going to get into trouble as we try to bring it to other nations of the world. A gospel that wrongly talks about economics or politics is going to be resisted, particularly by political authorities who rightly feel their rule is being threatened by political or social gospels.

The true Gospel will also be resisted.
It is reprehensible to man.

Obviously, the true Gospel will also be resisted. It is reprehensible to man. Mankind does not like to be told that he is going to hell. No one wants to hear that. It is reprehensible to the mind of natural man to hear that there is nothing he can do to save himself. Such resistance can be changed in the hearts of only those who become saved by crying out to God: "O God, have mercy on me, a sinner!" It involves a child-like trust in Jesus Christ, who walked the face of the earth a couple of thousand years ago. It means my ego must be shattered. It shatters my self-respect.

That is the only reason the Gospel should be reprehensible. May it never be that the gospel we present is resisted by the political authorities because we are preaching the culture and politics of a political nation. Such a gospel cannot be the Gospel of the Bible.

We read in John 5:24 that those who believe on Him do not come into judgment, but have passed from death unto life. In our love for others, that is the good we should earnestly desire for them. That is the message God has mandated us to faithfully bring to the whole world.

As believers, faithfully obeying the
command to bring the Gospel to the
world, the Bible insists that we are to
walk very humbly.

As we live our lives as believers, faithfully obeying the command to bring the Gospel to the world, the Bible insists that we are to walk very humbly. Our example is the Lord Jesus Christ; we read of Him that He was meek and lowly. So it is that we should be ready to be reviled without reviling back again, be ready to patiently take whatever is brought against us, and be ready to give credit to anybody who wants it. Let someone else have the worldly honor. The child of God, who has become a citizen of Christ's Kingdom, is to walk humbly.

Why? Why are we to walk humbly? First of all, because God has so commanded. Jesus, our example and our King, was meek and lowly. He emptied Himself of all His heavenly glory and took on the form of man - sinful, rebellious man. Then He became laden with our sins. Nobody has ever humiliated himself like the Lord Jesus Christ, as He established His Kingdom by going to the cross. We, who believe in Him, are in His Kingdom, and He is our King. He rules over us and commands us to walk honestly and humbly. We also are to be ready to be humiliated. We are to walk as the most humble people on this earth.

Besides that, we are to walk very humbly because we cannot take any credit for our salvation. It is nothing we can boast about. We cannot say, "Well, you know, the real story is that God saw me and saw that I was a little bit better than somebody else, and therefore, He decided to save me." No way! As Ephesians 2:1-3 indicates, we were dead in our sins. We were followers of Satan and after the lusts of the flesh like the rest of mankind. It is only by God's mercy, it is only by God's grace that He saved us. So we live out our Christian lives saying, "Oh my, how is it possible that I can be a child of God, that I can have eternal life, so that I fear no man? No matter what happens to me, I know that the moment I die, I am going into the heavenly palaces, into glory with the Lord Jesus Christ, and I have got everything going for me. All I want to do is live out my life in service to Him. I want to sacrifice my life, to lay it down on the altar of sacrifice. I am consumed with passion that others might hear the Gospel so that they, too, can know the wonderful salvation which God has so richly provided."

Don't we have a wonderful Savior? Don't we have a wonderful Gospel, when we see what the Gospel really is? We can just stand amazed before the glory of God as He glorifies Himself through His Gospel. Let's be sure that we keep the Gospel message in the forefront of our thinking and in our hearts. If we find that at any time the gospel we bring begins to differ from the true Gospel, let us cry out to God, "O God, forgive me that I might have had something else in my head when I was trying to bring the Gospel, that I was trying to tailor it to my own lustful desires." The true Gospel is this: I want this wonderful salvation for everybody else, and because I know I have become saved, there is nothing else in this world I need for myself.

Now we should lay some additional groundwork as we seek to know more about the timing of the end of the world. We must discover what the Bible says about God's timetable for the world, beginning with creation.

SUMMARY

The true Gospel is the only gospel that can save men and women and children from spending eternity under the wrath of God. The true Gospel is found in the Bible, the Bible only, and the entire Bible, from Genesis to Revelation.

All gospels are determined by their source or sources of authority. If a gospel is structured and determined by less than the Bible or by sources other than but in addition to the Bible, it is a false gospel.

The central message of the true Gospel is found in John 3:16, which tells both sides of God's Word, the two-edged sword, that we either believe on the Lord Jesus Christ and spend eternity in heaven, or we do not believe and spend eternity in hell. The mandate of the Gospel is that we go into all the world and preach the Gospel, and that we are not to confuse the issue with economic, political, or financial matters.

Chapter 8
Guideposts in the Sacred Text

The goal of this book is to discover as much as we can in the Bible that may give us clues to the timing of the return of our Lord Jesus Christ. We will know much about the timing of Christ's first coming as we see history unfolding. That is, when we know about key dates of historical events and project them forward we will become aware of the timetable of historical events that relate to the unfolding of God's Gospel program. Indeed, we will discover that God timed the various historical events in a very precise fashion. By projecting the time relationships of the past into the future, we will find that we can determine the timing of some future events.

Therefore, we should learn what the Bible can tell us about the timetable of the past. We have discovered the principle that the time line of history is God's plan of salvation. Therefore, we will discover that the key milestones or markers of the passage of time are intimately associated with some aspect of God's salvation plan. God has given detailed information concerning the timing of these events so that we can know precisely how each one fits chronologically into the timetable of history.

We must begin this search with the study of the genealogical record of Genesis 5 and 11. If further light could be given to arrive at a proper understanding of these important chapters, a great stride forward would be taken toward the development of a consistent statement regarding the exact date of Adam, the Flood, and other phenomena of history. This in turn would greatly help in understanding and evaluating the evidence being brought by scientific discovery. Such new information and interpretation would point up anew the orthodox Christian's belief in the total accuracy and authority of the Bible, especially with regard to the early chapters of Genesis, which have long been open to dispute.

> *We will receive enlightenment from*
> *God's Word only when we recognize*
> *it as His infallible revelation.*

Again, I must emphasize that as a fundamental starting point, one basic fact must be acknowledged as a presupposition upon which this study rests. It is that we will receive enlightenment from God's Word only when we recognize it as His infallible revelation. "For the prophecy came not in old time by the will of man: but holy men of God spake as they were moved by the Holy Ghost" (II Peter 1:21; see also II Timothy 3:16). The Bible must be accepted as God's inerrant word to man and is, therefore, entirely trustworthy.

Inspired Verbs

The first marker given in the Bible related to chronological history is the genealogical record found in Genesis 5 and 11. As we examine this record we might ask, is there anything distinctive in the language pattern used that might give us a clue to the understanding of these chapters? The verses do seem similar to each other. Although there are two that are definitely different from the others, and we will consider those in a moment, all the other genealogical notices in this chapter follow the same pattern: namely, when 'A' had lived 'x' years, he begat 'B.' For example, we read in Genesis 5:15-16, "And Mahalaleel lived sixty and five years, and begat Jared. And Mahalaleel lived after he begat Jared eight hundred and thirty years, and begat sons and daughters." There is no indication that Mahalaleel gave his son the name Jared. The passage simply says he begat Jared.

Now let us look more intently at these two passages that stand apart from the usual pattern. The first is Genesis 5:3, which records the genealogical descent of Seth from Adam. It records that Adam begat a son, and *called his name* Seth. The second is verses 28 and 29, which tell us about the relationship of Lamech to Noah. It records that Lamech begat a son and *called his name* Noah.

It is this phrase *called his name*, which is the Hebrew "qara shem," that gives us help with at least a few of the names in these chapters. A search of the Bible reveals no instance where such a phrase is used in connection with the naming of a person, where the person named was not an immediate child or was not immediately related to the person doing the naming. Many examples might be given to show this. "Abraham called the name of his son . . . Isaac" (Genesis 21:3). "So they *called his name* Esau" (Genesis 25:25). This phrase is used in describing the births of all the sons of Jacob: for example, "And she *called his name* Reuben" (Genesis 29:32). It is also used in Genesis

38 where the five sons of Judah are noted (verses 3-5, 29-30). This particular indisputable father-son relationship is underscored in I Chronicles 2:4 by the statement, "Judah had five sons in all." Interestingly, the same phrase, "qara shem," is used in Isaiah 7:14, where God prophesied that a virgin would bear a son and *call his name* Immanuel. It is used also in Genesis 5:2, where God called the man "Adam." We know, of course, from other Biblical data that there were no humans before Adam. From all this evidence we therefore can be quite sure that wherever this "clue" phrase, "qara shem" occurs, we may be certain that an immediate son is being described and not a grandson or some more remote descendant.

> *Wherever this "clue" phrase occurs, we may be certain that an immediate son is being described and not a grandson.*

Returning to the Genesis account with this knowledge concerning the Bible's use of the clue phrase *called his name*, we discover in Genesis 4:25 and in Genesis 5:3 that Seth was undoubtedly an immediate son of Adam, for in both of these verses *"qara shem"* is used. We find, too, in Genesis 4:26, "To Seth, to him also there was born a son; and he called his name Enos." Thus, we can know that Enos was an immediate son of Seth. Likewise, on the same grounds we can know that Noah was the immediate son of Lamech (Genesis 5:28-29).

We thus may conclude on the basis of the information found in the verses cited above that when Adam was 130 years old, Seth was born to him. When Adam was 235 years old and Seth was 105, Enos, the grandson of Adam was born. Similarly, when Lamech was 182 years of age, Noah was born.

Noah's and Terah's Sons

Two other generations are named in the genealogical accounts of Genesis 5 and 11 that can be shown to be of an immediate father-son relationship. In neither of these is the clue phrase *called his name* used, but sufficient information is given in other Biblical references so that we can know this.

The first of these is in relationship to Noah's son, Shem. In Genesis 5:32 we read, "And Noah was five hundred years old: and Noah begat Shem, Ham, and Japheth." We can know that these must be immediate sons by the testimony of Genesis 9:18, which reads, "the sons of Noah, that went forth of the ark, were Shem, and Ham, and Japheth." Genesis 7:13 states that Noah, Shem, Ham, and Japheth, together with their wives, entered the ark. We also read in I Peter 3:20 that there were "eight souls" in the ark. These verses lead us to the inescapable conclusion that Shem was an immediate son of Noah and not a grandson or later descendant.

The other generation that can be known to represent an immediate father-son relationship is that of Terah and Abram. Genesis 11:26 declares, "And Terah lived seventy years, and begat Abram, Nahor, and Haran." The verses that follow give additional information, which points conclusively to the relationship that existed. Genesis 11:27-28 declares:

> Now these are the generations of Terah: Terah begat Abram, Nahor, and Haran; and Haran begat Lot. And Haran died before his father Terah in the land of his nativity, in Ur of the Chaldees.

Verse 31 continues:

> And Terah took Abram his son, and Lot the son of Haran his son's son, and Sarai his daughter in law, his son Abram's wife; and they went forth with them from Ur of the Chaldees, to go into the land of Canaan; and they came unto Haran, and dwelt there.

This language surely makes reference to an immediate family relationship. Thus, Abram could only have been the son of Terah and not his grandson or some later descendant.

Some further clarification might be helpful at this point. Although Genesis 11:26 would seem to indicate that all three of Terah's sons, Abram, Nahor, and Haran, were born when he was 70 years old, this cannot have been the case unless they were triplets. Verse 32 clearly states that Terah died in Haran at the age of 205 years. Upon his father's death, Abram left Haran at the age of seventy-five

(Acts 7:4, Genesis 12:4). We must therefore conclude that **Terah was actually 130 years of age at the time of Abram's birth**, and that either Nahor or Haran was the oldest of the three brothers, one having been born when his father was seventy. In the genealogies, Abram is probably mentioned first because he was the important figure in God's redemptive plan for man.

Returning to the sons of Noah, we are led to a similarly interesting conclusion. We find that Genesis 5:32 declares that Noah was 500 years old when he became the father of Shem, Ham, and Japheth, yet in the tenth verse of Genesis 11 we are told that "Shem was an hundred years old, and begat Arphaxad two years after the flood." Since Noah was 600 years old at the time of the flood, **Shem must have been born when Noah was 502.** And since Genesis 10:21 refers to Shem as "the brother of Japheth the elder," we can know that Japheth was born before Noah was 502 years old. Thus, Shem was not the oldest son even though he was named first when the three sons are named. We may, therefore, reasonably conclude that Shem was born when his father was 502, and that he lived an additional 502 years after the flood, with his father his contemporary for 350 years of that time (Genesis 9:28, Genesis 11:10-11). Again, as in Abram's case, Shem's name probably appears first in the Bible record because of his place in God's great plan.

> *Seth, Enos, Noah, Shem, and Abram were all immediate sons of their fathers named in Genesis 5 and 11.*

Thus far then we have established that Seth, Enos, Noah, Shem, and Abram were all immediate sons of their fathers named in the record of Genesis 5 and 11. Now, we are left with the remaining names in these two chapters. Are they immediate sons or are they later descendants? The phrase *qara shem* is not used anywhere in the Bible in connection with these names to indicate an immediate father-son relationship. Neither is there other evidence in Scripture that conclusively suggests this kind of relationship. Is there Scriptural evidence to indicate that these verses are speaking of anything other than a father-son relationship? There is indeed, as we shall see.

Patriarchal Periods

An analysis of the language used in Genesis 5 and 11 reveals a pattern that is unique only to these chapters. A typical verse is that of Genesis 5:15-17:

And Mahalaleel lived sixty and five years, and begat Jared: And Mahalaleel lived after he begat Jared eight hundred and thirty years, and begat sons and daughters: And all the days of Mahalaleel were eight hundred ninety and five years: and he died.

This verse sets forth truth that might be written as the principle: "When 'A' was 'x' years old, he begat a son 'B,' he then lived 'y' years after he begat 'B' and begat other sons and daughters." This language pattern is used to describe men from Adam all the way to Terah, the father of Abraham. The account of Genesis 5 adds that thus all the days of 'A' were $(x + y)$ years and he died. This was added probably because of the extreme longevity of these ancients. By this added phrase there could be no misunderstanding regarding these long life spans.

How are we to understand these verses? Is 'B' the son of 'A' or is he a later descendant of 'A'? The word "begat" does not help us. In some cases it is used in the Bible where unquestionably an immediate father-son relationship is in view. Such is the case in I Chronicles 1:34, for example, where we read that "Abraham begat Isaac." On the other hand, "begat" sometimes is used where a later descendant other than an immediate son is in view. In Matthew, for example, we read that Joram begat Ozias (Matthew 1:8), but Ahaziah, Joash, and Amaziah should come between Joram and Ozias. Thus, in this case "begat" could have reference only to a descendant later than a son.

Furthermore, in Matthew 1:11 we read that "Josias begat Jechonias," as if Jechonias was an immediate son of Josias. Yet there is abundant Biblical evidence that Jechonias was the grandson of Josias.

Additionally, we read in Ruth 4:18-22:

Now these are the generations of Pharez: Pharez begat Hezron, And Hezron begat Ram, and Ram begat Amminadab, And Amminadab begat Nahshon, and Nahshon begat Salmon, And Salmon begat Boaz, and Boaz begat Obed, And Obed begat Jesse, and Jesse begat David.

The nine generations represented by this citation encompass about 850 years of time inasmuch as it is clear that Pharez, who was the immediate son of Judah, would have been born approximately 1890 B.C. while David was born in the year 1037 B.C. If all these "begats" represent immediate father-son relationships, on the average the father was about ninety-five years older than the son. This, of course, is impossible since during most of this time the life expectancy of mankind was 70 years or at most 80 years (Psalm 90:10). Thus we know the "begats" represent lineage but not necessarily immediate father-son lines. In fact, the Bible discloses that in the above line: Ram was not the immediate son of Hezron for we read in I Chronicles 2:25, "And the sons of Jerahmeel the firstborn of Hezron were, Ram the firstborn, and Bunah, and Oren, and Ozem, and Ahijah." In this verse God details for us that while Hezron begat Ram, Ram was a grandson of Hezron.

A casual comparison of Genesis 11:16-17 with Genesis 10:25 would seem to offer a solution. In Genesis 11:16-17, which follows the typical language pattern of Genesis 5 and 11, we read that:

> Eber lived four and thirty years, and begat Peleg: And Eber lived after he begat Peleg four hundred and thirty years, and begat sons and daughters.

In Genesis 10:25 we find recorded, "And unto Eber were born two sons: the name of one was Peleg." Do these verses say that Peleg was an immediate son of Eber? If this is so, in Genesis 11:16-17 the word "begat" must necessarily be understood as a reference to an immediate father-son relationship. Since at first this appears to be true for Genesis 11:16-17, we would suspect that this would be true of all the other verses of Genesis 5 and 11 that follow the same language pattern.

Yet the problem with this reasoning is that other language found in Genesis 10 indicates that the reference to "sons," as it is used in Genesis 10:25, does **not at all** ensure that an immediate father-son relationship is in view, i.e., that Peleg was the immediate son of Eber. In the same chapter, for example, we read "these are the sons of Shem" (Genesis 10:31). In this verse "sons" has reference to all of the descendants of Shem. Thus the word "sons" does not prove that a reference is made to the immediate son of the father. It might be noted that Matthew 1:1 also illustrates this truth, for there we read of "Jesus Christ, the son of David, the son of Abraham."

Moreover, when we look at Eber and Peleg more carefully we will discover evidence that suggests very strongly that Peleg **could not** have been the immediate son of Eber. In Genesis 10:25 we read, "And unto Eber were born two sons: the name of one was Peleg; for in his days was the earth divided." This statement is repeated in I Chronicles 1:19, which suggests that God appears to be calling definite attention to these facts as if they are of great importance. From Genesis 11:16-19 we discover that Eber begat Peleg, and Peleg begat Reu. Let us now assume for the moment that Peleg was an immediate son of Eber and that Reu was an immediate son of Peleg. Since according to Genesis 11:16-18, Eber was 34 years old when Peleg was born and presumably thirty years later begat Reu, the result would look like this:

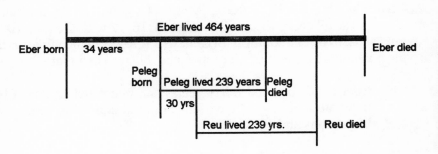

Thus we can immediately see from the diagram that these three men must have been contemporaries, with Eber the oldest. If Eber had actually been born earlier than Peleg and Reu, and if he had outlived both Peleg and Reu (as the diagram shows), so that **he** was the patriarch of the clan, so to speak, we would surely think it would have been a matter of divine record that he, instead of Peleg, lived when the earth was "divided" (Genesis 10:25). We thus are led again to the conclusion that the term "begat" as used in Genesis 5 and 11 must, at least in some instances, make reference to relationships other than that of an immediate father-son.

The Arphaxad-Cainan-Salah Connection

In fact, God gives us clear proof that the "begats" of Genesis 5 and Genesis 11 do not necessarily indicate an immediate father-son relationship. We read in Genesis 11:12-13:

And Arphaxad lived five and thirty years, and begat Salah: And Arphaxad lived after he begat Salah four hundred and three years, and begat sons and daughters.

If we are to understand that "begat" means a father-son relationship, then we are to understand that at one time in history there lived a man named Arphaxad. When he was 35 years old, a son named Salah was born to him.

God Himself shows us that this was not so. We read in Luke 3:35-36:

> . . . which was the son of Sala, Which was the son of Cainan, which was the son of Arphaxad, which was the son of Sem, which was the son of Noe, which was the son of Lamech.

In these verses God clearly shows us that in the genealogical line Arphaxad had a son or descendant named Cainan. Cainan in turn had a son or descendant named Salah. Thus under no circumstances could Salah have been born to Arphaxad when Arphaxad was 35 years old. It had to be Cainan or the father or grandfather, etc., of Cainan who was born to Arphaxad at that time. This son became the progenitor of Salah through Cainan.

Immediately we must realize, therefore, that all attempts that have been made to date the beginning of the world by assuming that the "begats" of Genesis 5 and Genesis 11 indicate an immediate father-son relationship are in error. We have learned from Luke 3 that Salah is not the immediate son of Arphaxad as Genesis 11 appears to indicate.

How then are we to understand the statement of Genesis 11 that at the age of 35 Arphaxad begat Salah? Obviously, because this information is in the Bible, it must be accurate. First of all this has greatly helped us to define the term "begat." Since Salah was not the immediate son of Arphaxad and yet Arphaxad "begat" Salah, we know that the Bible's use of the "begat" refers to being the "progenitor of." Arphaxad was the progenitor of Salah.

How then are we to understand that Arphaxad was 35 years old when he became the progenitor of Salah? Since according to Luke 3 Cainan was definitely in the genealogical line between Arphaxad and Salah, could it be that Cainan was born to Arphaxad when Arphaxad was 35 years old? If that were so, how old was Cainan when Salah was born to Cainan? The Bible does not tell us. Thus, the information that Arphaxad was 35 years old when he begat Salah appears to be meaningless.

But nothing in the Bible is meaningless. What are the possible solutions to an understanding of the fact that at the age of 35 Arphaxad "begat" Salah, when the Bible clearly teaches that Cainan came between Arphaxad and Salah in the genealogical line. The only way this can make sense is that the word "begat" must be understood to mean "to be the progenitor of." Thus, tying Genesis 11 together with Luke 3, we can know that when Arphaxad was 35 years of age, he was the progenitor of Cainan who in turn was the progenitor of Salah, thus making Arphaxad the progenitor of Salah. But we will discover that this information still has no meaning unless we understand that Salah was born the year of the death of Arphaxad. As we go on in our study we will see this more clearly.

> *Could the calendars of ancient*
> *peoples have been tied to the life*
> *spans of certain individuals?*

The Calendar Referenced to Noah

Two additional passages must be examined. These suggest an answer to our problem that can be shown to make abundant sense. The first is that of Genesis 7 and 8 where the dates of the flood events are referenced to the age of Noah. Genesis 8:13 records, "In the six hundredth and first year, in the first month, the first day of the month, the waters were dried up from off the earth." Genesis 7:6 indicates that the 600 years was the age of Noah when the Flood came. This leads us to an important question: Could the calendars of ancient peoples have been tied to the life spans of certain individuals?

The second passage is in the New Testament where Christ declares in Matthew 24:34, "Verily I say unto you, This generation shall not pass, till all these things be fulfilled." In this reference, Christ is speaking of events that will take place just before His return. He was, therefore, insisting that "this generation" will continue at least for almost 2,000 years, for this much time has now elapsed and all of the events of which He prophesies in Matthew 24 have not yet happened.

As a matter of fact, this present generation is the generation of Jesus Christ.[1] We speak of today's years as A.D., which means *the year of our Lord.* The events of today are dated exactly as they were in Noah's day: by reference to the birth date of a person.

Since this method of dating events, which was practiced in Noah's day, was suggested by Jesus Himself, and is actually the practice used today, could not this have been the method described in Genesis 5 and 11? If so, then Eber, Peleg, and Reu were patriarchs who followed each other in history. Each in turn was the reference patriarch of his period or generation in history. This would make abundant sense and provide for continuity and clarity in historical reckoning.

Thus we see that when the Bible records that Eber was 34 years old when Peleg was born and lived 430 years after the birth of Peleg, fathering other sons and daughters (Genesis 11:16-17), it means literally that when Eber was 34 years of age, a son was born to him. Significantly, the Bible does not record that Eber *"called his name Peleg"* because as a point of fact Peleg was not born until about the time Eber died. The son born to Eber at age 34 was an ancestor of Peleg, but his name is non-essential insofar as God's record is concerned. The important fact to remember is that the patriarchal successor to Eber was Peleg. Peleg was a direct descendant, and Eber at 34 was the progenitor of the Peleg line. The result should look like this:

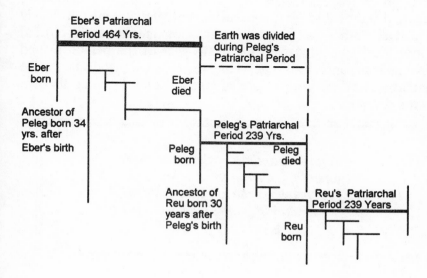

We are suggesting at this point in our study that the language of Genesis 5 and 11 that follows the equation: " 'A' lived 'x' years and begat 'B' and 'A' lived after he begat 'B' for 'y' years" is actually a calendar. Exceptions to the patriarchal calendar are introduced, namely, Adam begetting Seth, Seth begetting Enos, and Lamech begetting Noah. Yet these exceptions are distinguished by the phrase "called his name," thus showing Seth, Enos, and Noah to be immediate sons. Of course some of our conclusions are still tentative; but as we consider more and more data, we will discover how close to the truth we are.

Patriarchal Periods on the Family Tree

In our study thus far we have seen that when the phrase "called his name," the Hebrew "qara shem," is used in the Bible, it has reference to an immediate son. Thus we know that Seth was the immediate son of Adam, Enos was the immediate son of Seth, and Noah was the immediate son of Lamech. We have also determined that in two cases where this key phrase is not used in connection with close relatives there is sufficient evidence in other parts of the Bible to assure us that they are related to each other on an immediate father-son basis. Thus, we know with certainty that Shem was an immediate son of Noah and that Abraham was an immediate son of Terah. Finally, we discovered that the other individuals named in the genealogical records of Genesis 5 and 11 probably are not related as immediate descendants. In fact, we have seen that the Bible offers some evidence that they were not closely related at all. Rather we offered the suggestion that the year of birth of one individual coincided with the death year of the person named before him in the ancestral table. Thus, we proposed that each of these remaining characters are patriarchal leaders, each heading his own ancestral division.

> *An understanding of the Israelites'*
> *genealogy during their sojourn in*
> *Egypt provides the key that confirms*
> *our understanding of Genesis 5 and 11.*

Though it may seem a bit removed from our discussion, it develops that an understanding of the Israelites' genealogy during the time of their sojourn in Egypt provides the key that confirms our understanding of Genesis 5 and 11. For when we study the genealogical descent of Levi who entered Egypt as a son of Jacob, we find additional evidence that substantiates our patriarchal calendar. We will show that during the Egyptian sojourn a kind of calendar existed that was referenced to descendants of Levi, with each of his descendants being the reference patriarch during his entire lifetime.

To develop this point, let us now examine the various Biblical references that relate to the descendants of Levi, who entered Egypt with his brothers and his father Jacob, when Joseph was prime minister. These references are as follows.

Genesis 46:11: And the sons of Levi; Gershon, Kohath, and Merari.

Exodus 2:1-2, 10: And there went a man of the house of Levi, and took to wife a daughter of Levi. And the woman conceived, and bare a son: and when she saw him that he was a goodly child, she hid him three months. . . . And the child grew, and she brought him unto Pharaoh's daughter, and he became her son. And she called his name Moses: and she said, Because I drew him out of the water.

Exodus 6:16-20: And these are the names of the sons of Levi according to their generations; Gershon, and Kohath, and Merari: **and the years of the life of Levi were an hundred thirty and seven years**. The sons of Gershon; Libni, and Shimi, according to their families. And the sons of Kohath; Amram, and Izhar, and Hebron, and Uzziel: **and the years of the life of Kohath were an hundred thirty and three years**. And the sons of Merari; Mahali and Mushi: these are the families of Levi according to their generations. And Amram took him Jochebed his father's sister to wife; and she bare him Aaron and Moses: **and the years of the life of Amram were an hundred and thirty and seven years**.

Exodus 7:7: And Moses was fourscore years old, and Aaron fourscore and three years old, when they spake unto Pharaoh.

Numbers 3:15-20: Number the children of Levi after the house of their fathers, by their families: every male from a month old and upward shalt thou number them. And Moses numbered them according to the word of the LORD, as he was commanded. And these were the sons of Levi by their names; Gershon, and Kohath, and Merari. And these are the names of the sons of Gershon by their families; Libni, and Shimei. And the sons of Kohath by their families; Amram, and Izehar, Hebron, and Uzziel. And the sons of Merari by their families; Mahli, and Mushi. These are the families of the Levites according to the house of their fathers.

Numbers 3:27-28: And of Kohath was the family of the Amramites, and the family of the Izeharites, and the family of the Hebronites, and the family of the Uzzielites: these are the families of the Kohathites. In the number of all the males, from a month old and upward, were eight thousand and six hundred, keeping the charge of the sanctuary.

Numbers 26:57-59: And these are they that were numbered of the Levites after their families: of Gershon, the family of the Gershonites: of Kohath, the family of the Kohathites: of Merari, the family of the Merarites. These are the families of the Levites: the family of the Libnites, the family of the Hebronites, the family of the Mahlites, the family of the Mushites, the family of the Korathites. And Kohath begat Amram. And the name of Amram's wife was Jochebed, the daughter of Levi, whom her mother bare to Levi in Egypt: and she bare unto Amram Aaron and Moses, and Miriam their sister.

I Chronicles 6:1-3: The sons of Levi; Gershon, Kohath, and Merari. And the sons of Kohath; Amram, Izhar, and Hebron, and Uzziel. And the children of Amram; Aaron, and Moses, and Miriam. The sons also of Aaron; Nadab, and Abihu, Eleazar, and Ithamar.

I Chronicles 6:16-18: The sons of Levi; Gershom, Kohath, and Merari. And these be the names of the sons of Gershom; Libni, and Shimei. And the sons of Kohath were, Amram, and Izhar, and Hebron, and Uzziel.

The Time Bridge

Some interesting observations that impinge on our study can be noted about these references to the descendants of Levi:

1. The phrase "called his name" (qara shem) is not used in these references except in Exodus 2:10 where the child of this passage is named Moses by the Egyptian princess.

2. It is very clear from the detail given in Exodus 2:1-10 as well as the use of the phrase "qara shem" that Moses was the son of the unnamed man and woman of Exodus 2:1.

3. With all the other detail given in Exodus 2:1-10 it is significant that Amram and Jochebed are not named as the father and mother of Moses as Exodus 6:20 would appear to indicate. Why are Amram's and Jochebed's names omitted from the detailed account of Exodus 2:1-10 if they were indeed Moses's father and mother?

4. There is no evidence of an immediate father-son relationship in any of these accounts except in the Exodus 2:1-10 account, which relates Moses to an unnamed father and mother.

5. The life span of Levi and only two of his descendants are noted as are the ages of Moses and Aaron at the time of the Exodus (Exodus 6:16-20, Exodus 7:7). Doesn't this appear rather strange? What purpose could God have in mind in giving us the ages of just these men? Is there possibly in these **verses a time bridge built across the period from Jacob's descent into Egypt to the Exodus?**

6. If Kohath is the father of Amram and Amram is the father of Moses, how can we account for the reference of Numbers 3:27-28 that indicates the number of male descendants of Kohath to be 8600 persons? Since the census of Numbers 3 was taken at Mount Sinai (Numbers 3:1) when Moses, the apparent grandson of Kohath, was about 82 years old, there could not possibly have been this many descendants in such a short period of time.

Parents and Patriarchs

We shall begin to answer these difficult questions by attempting to arrive at the age of Levi when he entered Egypt. This information is essential if we are to correlate the various time notices given in the Bible that refer to the Israelites' sojourn in Egypt. In particular, if we can relate Levi's age to that of his father Jacob who was 130 years old (Genesis 47:9) when he entered Egypt, we will have the correlation we are seeking.

We do know that Levi's younger brother Joseph was probably 39 when Jacob was 130. For Joseph was 30 when he was made ruler over Egypt (Genesis 41:46); and it was during the second year of the famine, or nine years later, that he revealed his identity to his brothers (Genesis 45:4-6). Thus we also know that Jacob was 91 years of age when Joseph was born (130 - 39 = 91).

Can we now discover how much younger Joseph was than Levi? The solution to this question depends upon whether Jacob spent twenty years or forty years in Haran with his Uncle Laban. If he spent twenty years, the time sequence would work out something like this: Jacob worked seven years for Rachel (Genesis 29:20). Deceived into marriage with Laban's older daughter, Leah, Jacob was forced to serve another seven years for Rachel, whom he apparently married at the beginning of this second seven years (Genesis 29:30). Since Jacob worked six years for the flocks he received from Laban (Genesis 31:41), and these six years followed the birth of Joseph (Genesis 30:24ff), all of Jacob's children, with the exception of Benjamin, must have been born during the period he was working a second seven years for Rachel. With Levi being the third son and Joseph the last born during this period, Levi must have been at least four years older than Joseph.

For a number of reasons this conclusion appears untenable, however. For instance, we know Jacob was 91 when Joseph was born, and if we assume Jacob spent only twenty years in Haran, he must have been about 84 or 85 when Reuben, his first son, was born and he must have been 77 when he came to Haran. Although this is possible, it seems a bit difficult to believe. Abraham, for example, at the age of 86 was so concerned about being childless at his advanced age that he fathered Ishmael by the Egyptian maid, Hagar, to be sure that somehow God's promise would be carried out (Genesis 16:16). When Abram was 100 the Bible says he was old and advanced in years (Genesis 18:11).

Because of this deep concern of the patriarchs concerning God's promises, which were to be fulfilled in their descendants, it does not seem at all reasonable that Jacob would have waited until he was an old man of 84 before he married. It is also noteworthy that none of the records leading back to Shem mention a man being 84 at the birth of his firstborn. Abraham is the obvious exception.

Furthermore, to conclude that so many children were born to Jacob during the second seven year period while he was working to pay for Rachel is also difficult. Presumably during this period Leah bore four children, none of whom were twins (Genesis 29:31-35); she then ceased bearing (Genesis 29:35) and because she ceased bearing she gave Zilpah, her maid, to Jacob to father two sons (Genesis 30:9-13) and finally she bore two more sons and a daughter (Genesis 30:16-21). To conclude that all of these events occurred during a seven year period seems impossible.

Also, if Jacob's time with Laban in Haran had been restricted to twenty years, the events related in Genesis 38 concerning Judah's family would have been well nigh impossible. Chapter 38 records events that lead up to the birth of twin sons to Judah by his daughter-in-law, Tamar. Genesis 46:12 indicates that these sons of Judah, Pharez and Zerah, went into Egypt with Jacob. On the presumption of a twenty year Haran sojourn, Jacob could not have been less than 88 or 89 when Judah was born. Since Jacob was 130 when he entered Egypt, Judah could not have been older than 41 or 42 years when he entered Egypt. During this forty-one or forty-two years Judah would have had to grow from a baby to manhood, and additionally, all of the events of Genesis 38 would need to have taken place. These events are as follows:

> 1) Judah married a Canaanite woman called the daughter of Shua. She gave him three sons, Er, Onan, and Shelah. Er grew up and married Tamar. Er died without seed (it could have been soon after marriage). Onan was slain by God because he refused to marry Tamar upon Er's death.

> 2) Judah promised his youngest son, Shelah, to Tamar as a husband, but she had to wait until he grew up.

> 3) Shelah grew up but was not given to Tamar.

4) Tamar, rebuffed at Judah's broken promise concerning Shelah, enticed Judah to commit adultery with her. Twin sons, Pharez and Zerah, were born from this union. These sons, together with Shelah, entered Egypt with Judah.

Quite obviously all of these events could not have taken place within that period of forty-two years unless Judah and his son Er had both married as young as 12 to 14 years of age, but this is completely improbable and has no Scriptural validation. Only if we understand that Jacob sojourned in Haran longer than twenty years does this record make historical sense.

Jacob: Forty Years in Haran

What alternative to a twenty year sojourn in Haran does the Bible offer? Genesis 29:18-30 clearly indicates that Jacob worked the first fourteen years as payment for Rachel and Leah. Genesis 30:25-32 indicates that following Joseph's birth Jacob made a contract with Laban to work in return for spotted and speckled sheep. Genesis 31:41 summarizes his work for Rachel and Leah and indicates that he worked for a period of six years for his flocks.

> Thus have I been twenty years in thy house; I served thee fourteen years for thy two daughters, and six years for thy cattle: and thou hast changed my wages ten times.

Since Jacob left Haran immediately after he had obtained his flocks, the only time during his Haran sojourn when he could have added to the twenty years named in Genesis 31:41 is the time between his contract to obtain Rachel and Leah and his contract to obtain his flocks. In other words, he must have worked for wages of some kind for a period of time following the expiration of his second seven year agreement to obtain Rachel. During this wage-earning period his family continued to grow until Joseph was born. Then he wished to leave but was induced to stay in Haran in return for all the oddly marked sheep.

How long was this wage earning period? The only clue the Bible offers is the notice of Genesis 31:38-39.

> This twenty years have I been with thee; thy ewes and thy she goats have not cast their young, and the rams of thy flock have I not eaten. That which was torn of beasts I brought not unto

thee; I bare the loss of it; of my hand didst thou require it, whether stolen by day, or stolen by night.

Since twenty years is also named here as a time span, some would conclude this is the identical period named in verse 41 of the same chapter. But this cannot be, for, as we have seen, we must assume his total stay was more than twenty years. Moreover that these were different twenty year periods is suggested by the language of verse 39 where the Bible indicates that Jacob had to pay for animals stolen or killed by beasts, and of verse 38, which implies that he had to pay for any animals killed for his own food. These conditions may have been a part of his contract with Laban when he acquired Rachel and Leah, but the Bible gives no indication of this. Moreover, these do not appear to be the kinds of conditions that one would expect as part of a contract for a man's daughter. They would be too petty and would tend to demean the value of the daughters. On the other hand, they would be very logical clauses in a contract in which money is paid for services rendered. [The phrase "thou has changed my wages ten times" in verse 41 clearly has reference to the last six years when Jacob received his flocks (see Genesis 31:7-8) and therefore, does not relate to any other time except this six year period. These six years followed the twenty years recorded in Genesis 31:38-39.] We therefore must conclude that the twenty years of Genesis 31:38 were in addition to the twenty years of Genesis 31:41, which makes a total of forty years. They followed the second seven-year contract for Rachel and ended with the beginning of the new six-year contract for the speckled sheep.

Returning now to Levi, we remember that he could not have been less than four years Joseph's senior, but with this added twenty year period he may have been as many as twenty-four years his senior.

The Bible does appear to indicate that Joseph was probably much closer to twenty-four years younger than Levi than to four years younger. According to Genesis 29:31-35, Leah bore four children without ceasing to bear. Thus Levi, the third child, could well have been born in the third year after Jacob's marriage or the tenth year after Jacob arrived in Haran. If his birth was not in this third year, it probably was very close to it. Joseph, on the other hand, was born in the year just prior to the last six years (Genesis 30:25) or at most, a few years earlier than the last six years.

The Book of Maccabees (7:27) suggests a child was weaned at the age of three years. In II Chronicles 31:16 we read that the age of three was the minimum age for males to enter the house of the Lord for service. In I Samuel 1:22-24 we read that Hannah brought young Samuel to the house of the Lord immediately following his weaning. Thus, by relating these two passages together we receive the impression that weaning took place at the age of three, which indicates the reliability of the Maccabees account on this point even though Maccabees is not divinely inspired as is the Bible. It is therefore quite probable that Joseph was weaned at three years. Jacob was then ready to leave Haran. It was at this time that he began his last six years with Laban.

In summary, we must conclude that the period between the births of Levi and Joseph could not have been more than twenty-four years. Moreover, it seems very likely that this period could not have been less than a few years short of twenty-four years. A twenty-one year age differential between Levi and Joseph is most probable. This is the result of assuming that Levi was born in the tenth year after Jacob arrived in Haran, and that Joseph was born when Jacob was 91 years old, nine years before Jacob left Haran. Since he lived forty years in Haran he would have arrived there when he was 60 years old, thirty-one years before Joseph's birth. This conclusion establishes the following sequence of events:

1. Jacob arrives in Haran at the age of   60

2. He works seven years for Rachel and is then
   married to Leah and Rachel. He is then   67

3. Reuben is born to Leah the following year,
   when Jacob is   68

4. Simeon is born next to Leah, when Jacob is   69

5. Levi is born next to Leah, when Jacob is   70

6. Jacob finishes his second seven year contract
   for Rachel when he is   74

7. He works for wages for twenty years. In the
   17th year of this period, Joseph is born. Jacob is   91

8. At the end of this twenty year period, Joseph is
   weaned and Jacob wishes to leave Haran. He is　　94

9. He works six years longer for his flocks and
   leaves Haran at the age of　　　　　　　　　100

Interestingly, there is a bit of circumstantial evidence that gives further credence to the possibility of Jacob being 60 years of age when he arrived in Haran. The situation that precipitated Jacob's leaving for Haran was the threat that his brother Esau would kill him for stealing the blessing (Genesis 27:41). The blessing was given exactly at this time because undoubtedly his father Isaac feared he would soon die. Isaac's own words indicate this: "And he said, Behold now, I am old, I know not the day of my death" (Genesis 27:2). If Jacob was 60 years old at this time, Isaac was 120; for Jacob and Esau were born when Isaac was 60 years old (Genesis 25:26). Now Isaac lived to the ripe old age of 180 years (Genesis 35:28). He, therefore, was a long way from being near death when he wanted to give the blessing. What could have induced him to do this so many years before he actually died? Let us recall that God made a significant statement to Noah before the flood. He said in Genesis 6:3, "And the LORD said, My spirit shall not always strive with man, for that he also is flesh: yet his days shall be an hundred and twenty years." Could it not have been that faithful Isaac, fully aware of this notice of death to Noah, decided in his 120th year that it was time to straighten out his affairs? Therefore, he immediately set into motion the events that ended with Jacob's flight to Haran. This is a possibility and it fits into the chronological timetable.

Returning to our timetable, we see that all of the Biblical conditions are met if we consider that Levi was 21 years older than Joseph. While the Bible does not give exact information that points to this twenty-one year age differential between Levi and Joseph, we know it cannot be more than two or three years in error. The circumstantial evidence based on the weaning of a child at three years and the reasons for Jacob's flight to Haran, as outlined above, point to this twenty-one years as a logical and Biblical answer.

The Perfect Tally

One other piece of evidence points precisely to this 21 year age differential and also shows us how time was reckoned during the Egyptian sojourn. In fact, it also gives us the Biblical evidence for understanding the language of Genesis 5 and 11.

We previously saw that Joseph was 39 when Jacob and his family entered Egypt. Since Levi, as we have seen, must have been 21 years older than Joseph, he would have been 60 when Jacob's family entered Egypt. Since Levi died at the age of 137 (Exodus 6:16), 77 years (137 - 60) of his life would have been spent in Egypt.

> *In the absence of evidence that the Genesis genealogies specifically indicate an immediate father-son relationship, we may assume the relationship to be one that interrelates individual patriarchs living their entire lifetimes as the family heads.*

Let us recall now the premise that we established: in the absence of evidence that the Genesis genealogies specifically indicate an immediate father-son relationship, we may assume the relationship to be one that interrelates individual patriarchs living their entire lifetime as the family head. Let us apply this principle to the family of Levi. In Exodus 6:16-20 we saw the genealogical sequence of Levi. His 137 years were followed by Kohath's 133 years, which in turn were followed by Amram's 137 years; Amram was followed by Aaron. Since we know Levi lived 77 years in Egypt (if our twenty-one year assumption is correct), and since the Bible indicates that Aaron was 83 years old at the time of the Exodus (Exodus 7:7), all of the ingredients are available to establish the chronological sequence during the Egyptian sojourn. Remember that the death year of one patriarch coincides with the birth of the next, and the result looks like this:

Levi's time in Egypt   77 years (137 - 60)

Kohath's period of patriarchal
leadership   133 years

Amram's period of patriarchal leadership	137 years
Aaron's age at the time of the Exodus (Exodus 7:7)	<u>83</u> years
Total	<u>430 years</u>

This sum tallies exactly with Exodus 12:40-41 where Israel's sojourn in the land of Egypt is given as 430 years.

Exodus 12:40-41: Now the sojourning of the children of Israel, who dwelt in Egypt, was four hundred and thirty years. And it came to pass at the end of the four hundred and thirty years, even the selfsame day it came to pass, that all the hosts of the LORD went out from the land of Egypt.

Thus, we see that our assumption is correct: in certain situations there existed a patriarchal calendar with the one patriarch living his entire lifetime as the family head. God indicates to us that the generation or patriarchal period of Kohath followed the period of Levi and commenced in the year that ended Levi's period. Similarly, Amram's generation followed Kohath's. Aaron's generation began at the death of Amram. In this way the Bible gives us a time bridge that covers the Israelites' sojourn in Egypt that is identical to the 430 years of Exodus 12:40.

It could be argued that this genealogical proof is based upon the assumption that Levi was 21 years older than Joseph and, therefore, is not necessarily valid. Yet if we look at the alternatives, we can see the validity of this assumption. We saw that in any case Levi could not have been more than 24 years older than Joseph and probably not less than a few years short of 24 years older than Joseph. Thus, the period of Levi's residence in Egypt could have been as much as three years more or less than the 77 years arrived at in this study. There would, therefore, have been either a cumulative gap or cumulative overlapping in the genealogical timetable of Levi to Aaron of not more than possibly two or three years. Even though this is possible it makes no apparent sense in any kind of patriarchal dynastic system or calendar system. If any kind of gap or overlap occurred, one would expect a far greater number of years than these few, inasmuch as in that event the time spans would probably begin when each patriarch was old enough to assume leadership. In addition, the Biblical record of the births in rapid succession of Reuben, Simeon, Levi, and Judah to Leah, which is followed by the statement that then she ceased to bear, agrees very well with the timetable of Levi being born in Jacob's tenth year in Haran. Furthermore, the Maccabee's account of a Jewish child being weaned at three years focuses the birth of Joseph as being nine years before Jacob left Haran. Since he lived in Haran a total of forty years, twenty-one years would have elapsed between the births of Levi and Joseph. This, of course, is the exact figure that agrees with the genealogical proof under discussion.

> *The family of Levi . . . to Aaron was*
> *the patriarchal family selected to*
> *establish the calendar during the 430*
> *year bondage in Egypt.*

While Exodus 6:16-19 refers to the generations of Levi by name, significantly Kohath and Amram are the only two patriarchs of all those named whose ages have been written into the genealogical record. Obviously the family of Levi from Kohath to Amram and finally to Aaron was the patriarchal family selected to establish the calendar during the 430 year bondage in Egypt. The method of doing this would have been similar to that done by their forefathers before Abraham.

> *Amram and Jochebed were not the*
> *immediate parents of Moses.*

This is surely the reason why the ages of Levi, Kohath, and Amram have been recorded, and one of the reasons why we are given so many details that relate to the ages of both Joseph and Moses. It is why the parents of Moses are not named Amram and Jochebed in Exodus 2:1, when so many other details concerning the birth of Moses are given. *Amram and Jochebed were not the immediate parents of Moses.* Moses was of the patriarchal family of Amram; Amram must have died the year of Aaron's birth.

We can now see how the descendants of Kohath (Amramites, the family of Izharites, the family of Hebronites, and the family of Uzzielites) numbered 8600 men at the time of Mount Sinai (Numbers 3:27-28). Kohath had died 220 years before the Exodus. These 220 years are sufficient for his male descendants to number as many as 8600.

> *Levi was the first, Kohath was second, Amram was third, and Aaron fourth in the prophetic sequence.*

It also throws a great spotlight of revelation upon God's prophecy to Abram in Genesis 15:13-16 where He tells Abram that his descendants would be oppressed for 400 years in a land that was not theirs, and that they would return to their own land in the **fourth** generation. **Levi was the first, Kohath was second, Amram was third, and Aaron the fourth in the prophetic sequence.**

Thus, God in His wonderful wisdom has placed in our hands a key that unlocks the hitherto perplexing genealogies of Genesis 5 and 11. This key is the chronological record of the Israelites' sojourn in Egypt. By properly understanding the timetable of the Egyptian sojourn we establish the evidence for understanding Genesis 5 and 11. God gave considerable information about the Egyptian sojourn so that this key could be found.

Genesis 5 and 11 Are a Calendar

To return to the disputed genealogies of Genesis 5 and 11, we have already pointed out that in the cases of Adam and Seth, Enos and Lamech, Noah and Shem, and finally Terah and Abraham, the Bible indicates conclusively the existence of immediate father-son relationships. **All of the other names recorded, we must assume, were the patriarchal heads of families and followed each other chronologically even as they did in the case of Levi, Kohath, Amram, and Aaron.**

> *This is the generation or patriarchal*
> *period of Jesus Christ.*

When we reflect on the foregoing study we discover that Genesis 5 and 11 are actually a kind of calendar. Think for a moment of our present calendar. We speak of an event that happened in the year 1950. What we mean is that this event occurred in the year of our Lord 1950 or that 1950 is the 1950th year after the "birth of Christ." This is the generation or patriarchal period, if you will, of Jesus Christ. Jesus, the Lord of all history, in Matthew 24:34 used the language of man's earliest history when He described the certainty of God's plan until the end of the age. We read in Matthew 24:34, "Verily I say unto you, This **generation** shall not pass, till all these things be fulfilled."

This was the situation that existed in man's early history. The time was divided into patriarchal periods or generations even as the New Testament period is the generation of Jesus Christ and as the Egyptian sojourn was so divided. Thus, for example, when Methuselah died, bringing to an end his generation, a man who was born in the year of Methuselah's death was selected to be the next reigning patriarch or at least the next man for calendar reference. After Methuselah it was Lamech. None of the conditions of his selection are given except that he had to be a descendant of Methuselah. Therefore, the Bible indicates that Methuselah was 187 years old when he begat Lamech; that is, when he was 187, the forefather of Lamech was born to Methuselah (Genesis 5:25). This notice establishes the certainty of Lamech's blood descent from Methuselah by showing where his forefather tied into the life of Methuselah.

The selection of the next patriarch had to include a birth date that coincided with Methuselah's death date to ensure a rational history. Had he been born one or more years earlier than the year Methuselah died, an overlap would have occurred that would have blurred history. If Lamech had been born one or more years later than Methuselah's death, a gap would have occurred that would have confused history. Therefore, when a citizen of the world of that day spoke of an event that occurred in the year Methuselah 950, only one year in history answered to this date. Again, if he spoke of the year Lamech 2, only one year answered to this date, and he knew precisely how many years transpired from Methuselah 950 to Lamech 2.

At the beginning men were comparatively scarce. Thus, it seems apparent that when Adam died there was no one born that year who was qualified to become the next reference patriarch. When Seth died 112 years later the same situation prevailed. God alerts us to these facts by use of the phrase "qara shem" in connection with Seth and Enos. When Enos, the grandson of Adam, died ninety-eight years after Seth, a child who was a descendant of Enos was born in the same year and was eventually named the next reference patriarch. This was Kenan. Kenan's life span thus became the calendar reference for that period of history. The calendar was continued in this fashion until Methuselah died and Lamech was born.

The Bible does not disclose how the next calendar reference patriarch was chosen in the event two or more sons were born the same year the previous calendar patriarch died. Perhaps, and it certainly seems logical, the son that was born closest to the death date of the previous patriarch would automatically have been the next patriarch. In any case, when Lamech was born he was the one to whom the calendar was referenced. His descendant who was born the year of Lamech's death and who should have become the next patriarch died in the Flood. This can be known easily for Lamech died five years before the Flood and only Noah and his immediate family survived the Flood. Noah, who was an immediate son of Lamech, of necessity became a substitute calendar reference. Thus, the Flood events are all dated by the life span of Noah (Genesis 7:6, 11; Genesis 8:4-5, 13-14).

When Noah died 350 years after the flood the same situation prevailed that existed when Adam died. Few people lived upon the earth and no one met the conditions required to become the next reference patriarch. When Shem died 152 years after Noah, the child Arphaxad, a descendant of Shem, was born the same year and he became the next patriarch. The calendar was then continued in this same fashion until Terah was born.

Speaking about Arphaxad, remember we had learned that in Genesis 11:12-13 God declares that when Arphaxad was 35 years old he begat Salah, but in Luke 3:35-36 the Bible informs us that the genealogical line was not Arphaxad-Salah. Rather it was Arphaxad-

Cainan-Salah. Thus Salah definitely could not have been the immediate son of Arphaxad. (See page 274.)

Now we know what God was saying in Genesis 11. When Arphaxad was 35 years of age, a son was born to him who was the progenitor of Cainan who in turn was the progenitor of Salah. Salah was born the year Arphaxad died, and thus became the next calendar reference patriarch after Arphaxad. Only with this understanding does the language that "Arphaxad lived five and thirty years, and begat Salah" (Genesis 11:12) make sense.

Continuing with the Bible chronology we know that after Terah was born, he was the reference patriarch. During his life span God brought into being the nation of Israel through Terah's immediate son, Abram. Thus the descendant of Terah who was born the year of Terah's death was outside the Messianic line and outside of God's chronological purposes. God effectively had narrowed men down to the family of Abram. The normal method of calendar keeping was set aside in the absence of patriarchs who qualified.

When Abraham died no descendant of his was born the year of his death. When Isaac, the immediate son of Abraham died, the same situation prevailed. This was repeated when Jacob, the immediate son of Isaac, died. But in the year that Levi, the immediate son of Jacob, died, a descendant of Levi was born whose name was Kohath and he apparently met the qualifications of a reference patriarch. Thus, he continued the calendar line as we have seen. Amram followed Kohath, and Aaron followed Amram.

Significantly the calendars we have been examining in Genesis 5 and 11, Exodus 6, and in other references, are entirely related to the unfolding of God's salvation plan. The line from Seth, the son of Adam, through Enoch, who was raptured, to Noah who found grace in the eyes of the Lord (Genesis 6), is the line of believers. The line from Noah to Abraham and from Abraham to Aaron is the line through which God was unfolding His salvation plan. Indeed we are learning afresh the principle that the time line of history is the unfolding of God's salvation plan.

The Timetable of Man Revealed

We are now ready to set forth the calendar of history beginning with creation. If our modern calendar is used, we would learn, for example, that the division of the nation of Israel into two kingdoms upon the death of Solomon occurred in the year 931 B.C. Since Solomon reigned for forty years (I Kings 11:42) and began to build the temple in the fourth year of his reign (I Kings 6:1), this building began in the year 967 B.C.

God gives us the time bridge from the Exodus to the building of the temple in I Kings 6:1:

> And it came to pass in the four hundred and eightieth year after the children of Israel were come out of the land of Egypt, in the fourth year of Solomon's reign over Israel, in the month Zif, which is the second month, that he began to build the house of the LORD.

In a later chapter we shall discover another Biblical time bridge that substantiates this time span. A time span of 480 years brings us to 1447 B.C. as the date of the exodus. If we work from this date back to Adam we arrive at a date for Adam of 11013 B.C. Again we should take note of the important principle: The time line of this chronology is the unfolding of God's salvation plan. It is not governed by the rise and fall of political powers. Thus, a seemingly insignificant event such as the circumcision of Abraham becomes an important part of the chronological development of history. The following table shows this chronology beginning with Adam inasmuch as he was the first man.

Event	*B.C.*
Creation of Adam	11013
Birth of Seth. Adam was 130 when Seth was born (Gen. 5:3)	10883
Birth of Enosh. Seth was 105 when Enosh was born (Gen. 5:6)	10778
End of Enosh's period 905 years after his birth (Gen. 5:11), which is the year Cainan was born and which began his period	9873
End of Cainan's period 910 years after his birth (Gen. 5:14). This is the year Mahaleel was born and the beginning of his period	8963

End of Mahaleel's period 895 years after his birth
(Gen. 5:17). This is the year Jared was born and
the beginning of his period   8068

End of Jared's period 962 years after his birth
(Gen. 5:20). This is the year Enoch was born
and the beginning of his period   7106

End of Enoch's period 365 years after his birth
(Gen. 5:23). This is the year Methuselah was
born and the beginning of his period   6741

End of Methuselah's period 969 years after his
birth (Gen. 5:27). This is the year Lamech was
born and the beginning of his period   5772

Birth of Noah. Lamech was 182 when Noah
was born (Gen. 5:28-29)   5590

The flood. Noah was 600 when the flood came
(Gen. 7:6)   4990

Death of Shem 502 years after the flood (Gen.
11:10-11). This is the year Arphaxad was born
and the beginning of his period   4488

End of Arphaxad's period 438 years after his
birth (Gen. 11:12-13). This is the year Salah was
born and the beginning of his period   4050

End of Salah's period 433 years after his birth
(Gen. 11:14-15). This is the year Eber was born
and the beginning of his period   3617

End of Eber's period 464 years after his birth
(Gen. 11:16-17). This is the year Peleg was born
and the beginning of his period   3153

The Tower of Babel incident must have occurred
between 3153 and 2914 (Gen. 10:25).

End of Peleg's period 239 years after his birth (Gen. 11:18-19). This is the year Reu was born and the beginning of his period	2914
End of Reu's period 239 years after his birth (Gen. 11:20-21). This is the year Serug was born and the beginning of his period	2675
End of Serug's period 230 years after his birth (Gen. 11:22-23). This is the year Nahor was born and the beginning of his period	2445
End of Nahor's period 148 years after his birth (Gen. 11:24-25). This is the year Terah was born and the beginning of his period	2297
Birth of Abram to Terah. Terah was 130 years old when Abram was born (pp. 270-271)	2167
Circumcision of Abraham when he was 99 years old (Gen. 17:1, 23-24)	2068
Birth of Isaac. Abraham was 100 years old when Isaac was born (Gen. 21:5)	2067
Birth of Jacob. Isaac was 60 years old when Jacob was born (Gen. 25:26)	2007
Jacob's name changed to Israel when Jacob was 100 years old	1907
Jacob's family arrived in Egypt when Jacob was 130 years old (Gen. 47:9)	1877
Exodus from Egypt 430 years later (Exo. 12:40)	1447

Entrance into Canaan 40 years later (Exo. 16:35)	1407

Solomon's temple construction is begun 480 years after Exodus (I Kings 6:1)	967

Division of kingdom at death of Solomon 36 years later (I Kings 12, II Chron. 10)	931

Thus Adam was created about 13,000 years before our present time.

> *From Exodus 6 we have discovered that these ancient peoples kept track of time by referencing the passage of time to the life spans of key individuals.*

By analyzing the data offered in Exodus 6 concerning the life spans of Levi, Kohath, and Amram, we have discovered that these ancient peoples kept track of time by referencing the passage of time to the life spans of certain key individuals. These individuals were selected on the basis of at least two qualifications:

1. Their birth year had to coincide with the death year of the previous reference patriarch.

2. They were to be in the same blood line as the previous reference patriarch.

By analyzing all of the Biblical data concerning Levi, Kohath, Amram, and Aaron, we have discovered that they met these two qualifications.

We then applied our understanding of this ancient method of calendar keeping to the genealogical accounts of Genesis 5 and 11, where the life span of each reference patriarch is given. Additionally, the age of each reference patriarch is given at the point when the next reference patriarch tied into his blood line. The formula that is used in each case is, "when 'A' was 'x' years old he begat 'B.' 'A' lived after he begat 'B' 'y' years and had other sons and daughters." The sum of (x + y) indicates the life span of the reference patriarch 'A.' He was 'x' years old when the progenitor of the next reference patriarch 'B' was born to him. The giving of the value of 'x' assured that 'B' was indeed of the blood line of 'A.'

There were periods in history when the rules for calendar keeping could not be strictly kept. Such was the situation when men were just beginning to multiply on the earth. This was the situation after the flood of Noah's day and the special time when God limited his people to the family of Abraham.

God uses two methods to guide our thinking through these special periods in history. In the first place, He indicates that wherever the clue phrase "qara shem" is used, which indicates a parent named his child, we can be sure the child in question is the immediate son of the parent. Such was the case of Adam-Seth, Seth-Enosh, and Lamech-Noah. In the second place, God at times gives other Biblical information to indicate an immediate father-son relationship. Such was the case with Noah-Shem, Terah-Abram, Abram-Isaac, Isaac-Jacob, Jacob-Levi, and the history of man following Aaron. By applying these principles we have been able to develop an accurate calendar of ancient man beginning with Adam at 11013 B.C.

Our God is indeed a wise and all-sufficient God. Often when He gives us truth, He gives us an abundance of evidence to support that truth. When Christ rose from the dead, He showed Himself by many proofs (Acts 1:3) so there was no possibility of believers misunderstanding this wonderful event. When He gave us the facts of His earthly sojourn, God gave us four Gospels so that these truths would be especially clear. So, too, God has given us additional evidence in His Word that appears to substantiate and validate the correctness of the chronology outlined in this chapter. This evidence will increasingly come into view as we continue our study.

Chronology of the Judges

The chronological chain presented in this study has one link in it that looks very fragile. In I Kings 6:1 we read that there was a passage of 480 years of time from the exodus from Egypt until the fourth year of Solomon's reign. Since this is a long period of time covering the wilderness sojourn, the claiming of the land of Palestine by Joshua, the period of the Judges and the kingdoms of Saul and David, one cannot help wondering if some additional Biblical evidence might be available to support this one lonely statement.

Earlier in this chapter we saw that the 430 year Egyptian sojourn was supported by the genealogical timetable of Levi, Kohath, Amram, and Aaron. Can we find similar Biblical data to support the 480 years under question? We will find that there is great value in doing this because in the process we will discover precise dates for at least two events that are also markers in the development of the historical time line. The first of these two events is the death of Gideon in 1207 B.C., and the second is the timetable when the ark was captured by the enemy in 1068 B.C. Knowing the time of each of these events contributes to our understanding of God's methodology in working out history.

Let us begin to examine this question by first establishing the chronology of Saul, David, and Solomon. We shall discover that there is definitely another time bridge, in addition to that in I Kings 6:1, that links the Exodus to the time of Solomon. We shall also discover the precise chronology of the period of Judges. Additionally, we will be taught afresh the perfect harmony of the Bible. This will in turn help us to realize that all of the chronological notices in the Bible are absolutely trustworthy. This is very important to us because the truths we will be discovering concerning the timing of the end of the world are altogether dependent upon the trustworthiness of the chronological notices found in the Bible.

A David and Solomon Coregency
Let us begin this part of our reconstruction by discovering the precise time sequence of the first three kings of Israel: Saul, David, and Solomon. To establish this time sequence we must first of all discover if there was a coregency between Saul and David or between David and Solomon. While the prophet Samuel anointed David king when he was but a lad, the Bible shows in unmistakable fashion that David's reign began after the death of Saul. The first two chapters of II Samuel should be consulted to verify this. We therefore can know that Saul's reign of forty years (Acts 13:21) was followed by David's reign of forty years (II Samuel 5:4). Thus a period of eighty years transpired from the end of the period of the Judges until the end of David's reign.

---

*Solomon began to reign four years
before David's death.*

When did Solomon begin to reign? Was it upon David's death or was it earlier? We shall discover that Solomon began to reign four years before David's death so that the fourth year of Solomon's reign coincided with the end of David's reign.

The Bible shows a coregency of David and Solomon of four years. The reason for the coregency is easily found. First, Absalom aspired to be king when David was old (II Samuel 15:1-8). A few years later another son of David named Adonijah declared that he would be king (I Kings 1:5). Upon this turn of events, Nathan the prophet instructed Bathsheba, mother of Solomon, to remind King David of his promise that Solomon was the heir to the throne (I Kings 1:11-14). David, thereupon, before he died and ceased to reign, declared Solomon king (I Kings 1:32-37) in order to remove any doubt about who was his successor.

David had one constant and consuming concern in the closing years of his life. The object of this concern is the event that ties the reigns of David and Solomon together and gives the evidence upon which the length of the coregency can be determined. This concern was that the temple should be constructed. David was not permitted to build the house of God, we are told in I Chronicles 28:3: "But God said unto me, Thou shalt not build an house for my name, because thou hast been a man of war, and hast shed blood." But David made all kinds of provision for this building. He made the decision of where it was to be located (I Chronicles 22:1). He put stonecutters to work to prepare stones for the temple (I Chronicles 22:2); he provided great stores of nails, bronze, and cedar for the temple (I Chronicles 22:3-4); he provided for the operation of the temple (I Chronicles 23:4-5); he had all the plans drawn for the construction (I Chronicles 28:11-19); he provided all the gold, silver, and precious stones required for the temple construction (I Chronicles 29:2); and he provided for the financing of the temple (I Chronicles 29:3-9). In other words, David performed every possible preparation for the actual construction to begin.

The Bible gives David a prominent part in this preparation, but it was actually a joint venture of David and Solomon. In I Chronicles 22:2-4 we read:

And David commanded to gather together the strangers that were in the land of Israel; and he set masons to hew wrought stones to build the house of God. And David prepared iron in abundance for the nails for the doors of the gates, and for the joinings; and brass in abundance without weight; Also cedar trees in abundance: for the Zidonians and they of Tyre brought much cedar wood to David.

In I Kings 5 we read how Solomon contracted for timbers from Hiram, King of Tyre, and from the Sidonians. In I Kings 5:17 the notice is given that Solomon was in charge of the quarrying of the foundation stones. The information of I Kings 5:13-18 indicates that it was Solomon who was in charge of the building. All of these references relate to building activity before the laying of the foundation in the fourth year of Solomon.

David then charged Solomon, in I Chronicles 22:14-16:

Now, behold, in my trouble I have prepared for the house of the LORD an hundred thousand talents of gold, and a thousand thousand talents of silver; and of brass and iron without weight; for it is in abundance: timber also and stone have I prepared; and thou mayest add thereto. Moreover there are workmen with thee in abundance, hewers and workers of stone and timber, and all manner of cunning men for every manner of work. Of the gold, the silver, and the brass, and the iron, there is no number. Arise therefore, and be doing, and the LORD be with thee.

And in I Chronicles 28:10:

Take heed now; for the LORD hath chosen thee to build an house for the sanctuary: be strong, and do it.

Not only did he lay this charge upon Solomon to begin the construction but he also gave a similar charge to the leaders of the people. I Chronicles 22:17-19:

David also commanded all the princes of Israel to help Solomon his son, saying, Is not the LORD your God with you? and hath he not given you rest on every side? for he hath given the inhabitants of the land into mine hand; and the land is subdued before the LORD, and before his people. Now set your heart and your soul to seek the LORD your God; arise therefore, and build ye the sanctuary of the LORD God, to bring the ark of the covenant of the LORD, and the holy vessels of God, into the house that is to be built to the name of the LORD.

> *The laying of the foundation may not take place as long as David is living.*

The picture that emerges from the Bible is one of great activity centered around construction of the temple. At first David as the father-King guides his young son, King Solomon, in the multitudinous preparations as well as being directly active in these preparations himself. All of this activity points to the moment when the actual construction will begin at the building site, but the laying of the foundation may not take place as long as David is living.

Then David dies, and Solomon reigns alone. The command to "arise and build" still rings in his ears and the ears of the people. The great moment, which David, Solomon, and all Israel had been eagerly anticipating, arrives. With David's death, no obstacle stands in the way; and the laying of the temple foundation begins. All the preparations of the past several years now become reality.

The fourth year of Solomon's reign, when the foundation of the temple was laid, must have coincided with the fortieth year of David's reign. The last four years of David's reign, during which he reigned as coregent with Solomon, were years of preparation for temple construction.

We may therefore conclude that since Saul reigned forty years and David reigned forty years, Saul's reign must have begun eighty years earlier than Solomon's fourth year. Since the fourth year of Solomon was 967 B.C., eighty years earlier was the year 1047 B.C. at which time Saul became king. Therefore, the year 1047 B.C. must be regarded as the year that ended the period of the Judges.

We have previously determined that the Exodus occurred in 1447 B.C. We know that they entered Canaan forty years later (Exodus 16:35, Numbers 14:34, Numbers 32:13, Joshua 5:6-12), which was the year 1407 B.C. And since, as we have just discovered, Saul began to reign in 1047 B.C., a time span of 360 years was the duration of the period of the Judges (1407 - 1047 = 360).

Is this 360 years borne out by other Biblical information? Many scholars have felt that it is impossible to establish a precise chronology for this time, because the Biblical information seems to be confused and sketchy. When we analyze the Biblical notices more carefully, we will see that they show that the period of the Judges was indeed 360 years.

The following are time notices set forth in the Bible beginning with the entrance into Canaan and ending with the last time notice before the reign of Saul.

Verse	Event	Years
Judges 3:8	Israel served Cushanrishathaim 8 years	8
Judges 3:11	Land had rest 40 years	40
Judges 3:14	Israel served Eglon, King of Moab, 18 years	18
Judges 3:30	Land had rest for 80 years	80
Judges 4:3	Israel oppressed by Jabin, King of Canaan, 20 years	20
Judges 5:31	Land had rest for 40 years	40
Judges 6:1	Israel in hand of Midian 7 years	7
Judges 8:28	Gideon judged 40 years	40
Judges 9:22	Abimelech ruled Israel for 3 years	3
Judges 10:2	Tola judges Israel 23 years	23
Judges 10:3	Jair judges Israel 22 years	22
Judges 10:8	Philistines oppressed Israel 18 years	18
Judges 12:7	Jephthah judged Israel 6 years	6
Judges 12:9	Ibzan judged Israel 7 years	7
Judges 12:11	Elon judges Israel 10 years	10
Judges 12:14	Abdon judges Israel 8 years	8
Judges 13:1	Israel in hand of Philistines 40 years	40
Judges 15:20	Samson judged Israel 20 years	20
I Sam. 4:18	Eli judged Israel 40 years	40
I Sam. 6:1	Ark was in Philistines' hands 7 months. This figure rounded off to years equals 1 year	1
I Sam. 7:2	From the time ark is returned until next event a period of 20 years passes. Since no other time notices are given until I Sam. 13:1, which speaks of the length of	

King Saul's reign, we must assume this 20
year period ends with the beginning of
Saul's reign as king   <u>20</u>

Total years   471

Inasmuch as the figure 471 years is 111 years longer than the 360 years that appears to be the correct figure for this period of time, we could assume with many other scholars that some of the judges ruled as contemporaries, and since we do not know who they were and when they ruled, we cannot determine an exact chronology for this period of history.

The fact is, however, that a very exact chronology can be determined. When we look again at the above references, we see there are two kinds. One describes the passage of time with respect to the land of Israel or to the rule of an Israelite judge. The other describes oppression or subjugation by a heathen power or king. If we separate this last kind from the total list, we discover a very exact chronology.

Israel Chronology		*Oppression By Heathen Power*	
		Israel served Cushanrishathaim	8 years
Land had rest	40 years		
		Israel served Eglon	18 years
Land had rest	80 years		
		Israel oppressed by Jabin	20 years
Land had rest	40 years		
		Israel in hand of Midian	7 years
Gideon judged	40 years		
Abimelech rules	3 years		
Tola judged	23 years		
Jair judged	22 years		
		Philistines oppressed Israel	18 years
Jephthah judged	6 years		
Ibzan judged	7 years		
Elon judged	10 years		
Abdon judged	8 years		

(Israel Chronology continued)		(Oppression)	
		Israel in hand of	
		Philistines	40 years
Samson judged	20 years		
Eli judged	40 years		
Ark captured	1 year		
Final period of			
Samuel	20 years		
Total	360 years		111 years

The 360 years agrees precisely with the period we have already established as the time span from the entrance into Canaan in 1407 B.C. until Saul became king in 1047 B.C. As we shall see, the oppression at various times, which added up to 111 years, really occurred during these 360 years.

We thus have established that even as in the case of the two time bridges from Jacob to Moses, the Bible also offers two time bridges from the Exodus to Solomon. The first is the 480 years of I Kings 6:1. The second is found in the Books of Joshua, Judges, I and II Samuel, I Kings, I Chronicles, and Acts.

Let us now set forth this chronology in greater detail and establish some absolute dates. The Exodus occurred Nisan 15, 1447 B.C. as we saw earlier in our study. Joshua 5:6-12 indicates that the entrance into Canaan was exactly forty years later, which was the year 1407 B.C. The next chronological notice is that given in Judges 3:11, which declares, "The land had rest forty years." This would be the period 1407-1367 B.C. At the beginning of this time the initial period of the conquest of Canaan took place. This occurred during the first seven years (Joshua 14:7-10, Deuteronomy 2:14). During this forty year period the people served Cushanrishathaim, King of Mesopotamia, for a period of eight years (Judges 3:8). Their deliverer was Othniel, son of the younger brother of Caleb (Judges 3:9).

The next chronological notice concerning Israel is that in Judges 3:30, "And the land had rest fourscore years." This was the period from 1367 B.C. to 1287 B.C. During this period Israel served Eglon, King of Moab, for eighteen years (Judges 3:14). Their deliverers were Ehud (Judges 3:15) and Shamgar (Judges 3:31).

The next chronological notice is that of Judges 5:31, "And the land had rest forty years." This was the period from 1287 B.C. to 1247 B.C. During this period Israel was oppressed by Jabin, King of Canaan, who reigned in Hazor and oppressed the Israelites for twenty years (Judges 4:3). Israel's deliverers were Deborah and Barak (Judges 4 and 5).

The next notice is found in Judges 8:28, "And the country was in quietness forty years in the days of Gideon." This was the period from 1247 B.C. to 1207 B.C. Near the beginning of this period, Israel was given into the hands of Midian for seven years (Judges 6:1). Their deliverer was Gideon (Judges 7:14). His death in 1207 B.C. ended this period. This is a very important date in our study as we shall see later.

Abimelech, a son of Gideon by a concubine (Judges 8:31), reigned as king for three years (Judges 9:22). This was the period from 1207 B.C. to 1204 B.C. To ensure his reign he killed his seventy brothers (Judges 9:5). He was killed by a millstone dropped upon him by a woman (Judges 9:53). Abimelech's evil and short-lived kingship was followed by the judgeship of Tola who judged Israel for twenty-three years: 1204 B.C. to 1181 B.C. (Judges 10:1-2).

After Tola came Jair, the Gileadite, who judged Israel for twenty-two years (Judges 10:3), 1181 B.C. to 1159 B.C. Apparently during this period Israel was oppressed for eighteen years by the Philistines and the Ammonites (Judges 10:7-8).

Jair was followed by four judges who ruled successively.

Jephthah	6 years (Judges 12:7)	1159-1153 B.C.
Ibzan	7 years (Judges 12:9)	1153-1146 B.C.
Elon	10 years (Judges 12:11)	1146-1136 B.C.
Abdon	8 years (Judges 12:14)	1136-1128 B.C.

The next chronological notice is that of Judges 15:20 where we read that Samson judged Israel twenty years, 1128 B.C. to 1108 B.C. We read in Judges 13:1 that during this time in Israel's experiences, "the LORD delivered them into the hand of the Philistines forty years." Probably this oppression began sometime during the era of the judges Ibzan, Elon, and Abdon. Samson's birth was predicted to his mother and she was told that her son would begin to deliver Israel from the hand of the Philistines, who were probably their oppressors at that time (Judges 13:5)

For our next chronological notice we must leave the Book of Judges, which closes with no more information of this nature, and go to the Book of I Samuel. In I Samuel 4:18 we receive information that Eli judged Israel for forty years. This was the period from 1108 to 1068 B.C.

The Bible gives us sufficient information about Eli and his contemporaries that we are able to insert a few bits of interesting information into our study. These are interesting but not in themselves important to our study. We know, for example, that since Eli was 98 years old at death, he was born in the days of Jair, possibly even before Samson's birth. He must have been priest in Shiloh at the time Samson was judge. He is first introduced in the Bible as a priest in I Samuel 1-3, when Hannah came to the temple at Shiloh to pray. Eli could well have been 50 or more at the time Samuel was born inasmuch as Eli's two sons already officiated as priests (I Samuel 1:3). He became official judge of the land at the age of 58. This was probably about the time Samuel came to the temple as a weaned child, for it is reported that Samuel was an old man at the time Saul became king (I Samuel 8:5). We shall see that Saul became king about sixty years after Eli became judge. Eli's judgeship came to a tragic end when the Philistines routed the Israelites, killed his two sons, and captured the ark. The news of the captured ark was the tidings that resulted in Eli's death (I Samuel 4:18).

Returning to the chronological sequence, we next discover that the ark was in the hands of the Philistines for seven months (I Samuel 6:1). This was seven months of the year 1068 B.C. or seven months beginning the latter part of 1068 B.C. and continuing into the early part of 1067 B.C. For our chronological sequence all other notices from the entrance into Canaan until David are given in years only. We, therefore, may round off this seven month period to one year, 1068-1067 B.C., to follow the pattern established by the previous chronological notices.

In I Samuel 7:2 we read the final chronological notice. The ark was returned to Israel at Kirjathjearim at the end of the seven month period. In this verse we read that twenty years passed after this event and "all the house of Israel lamented after the Lord." Since the next major event in Israel's history is the selection of Saul as king, and the beginning of his reign is the next Biblical chronological notice (I Samuel 13:1), we can conclude this twenty years was the period when Samuel judged Israel. His judgeship, of course, ended when Saul became king. This twenty year period is thus 1067 B.C. to 1047 B.C.

The forty year reign of Saul was from 1047 B.C. to 1007 B.C., when David came to the throne. David's forty year reign covered the period 1007 B.C. to 967 B.C. In the year 967 B.C. David died and the foundation of the temple was laid, as determined earlier in this chapter.

Thus, we have seen once again how the Scriptural record provides precise and adequate information to permit a very exact chronology, even through the troubled period of the judges.

The following is the chronology timetable from the Exodus to the destruction of Israel by the Babylonians.

Event	*Years*
The Exodus	1447 B.C.
Entrance into Canaan	1407 B.C.
Initial 40 year period in Canaan	1407-1367 B.C.
During this period the conquest of Canaan occurred under Joshua and Othniel delivered Israel	
Next 80 year period in Canaan	1367-1287 B.C.
During this period Ehud and Shamgar delivered Israel	
Next 40 year period in Canaan	1287-1247 B.C.
Deborah and Barak were deliverers during this period	
Gideon judged	1247-1207 B.C.
Abimelech rules	1207-1204 B.C.
Tola judged	1204-1181 B.C.
Jair judged	1181-1159 B.C.
Jephthah judged	1159-1153 B.C.
Ibzan judged	1153-1146 B.C.
Elon judged	1146-1136 B.C.
Abdon judged	1136-1128 B.C.
Samson judged	1128-1108 B.C.
Eli judged	1108-1068 B.C.
Ark in Philistines' hands	1068-1067 B.C.
Samuel judged	1067-1047 B.C.
Saul reigned as king	1047-1007 B.C.
David reigned	1007-967 B.C.
Solomon reigned	971-931 B.C.
Foundation of temple laid in fourth year of Solomon's reign	967 B.C.

Division of kingdom of Israel	931 B.C.
End of northern kingdom of Israel	709 B.C.
Israel comes under dominion of Egypt	
upon Josiah's death	609 B.C.
Israel destroyed by Babylon	587 B.C.
Babylon conquered by Medes and Persians	539 B.C.

SUMMARY

We have seen thus far that God has provided in His marvelous Word a calendar that reaches back all the way to the first man, Adam.

Additionally, we have been able in very precise fashion to set forth the chronological dates during which the judges ruled. As we carefully worked through the Biblical references that pertain to this period of time we learned how precise the Bible is in giving chronological notices. Moreover, we discovered the dates when the ark was in the Philistines' hands (1068-1067 B.C.). Later in our study we will become aware of the importance of these dates.

We also have discovered that the timetable of history is not governed by the rise and fall of great nations or political powers. These events are certainly important for God Himself raises up and puts down nations. However, the time line that establishes the chronology of history is the unfolding of God's salvation plan. Since the Bible is the only book that sets forth perfectly accurately God's plan for salvation, it also is the only source wherein we can determine an accurate record of the chronology of history.

Now we should press on toward our goal: What about the future? Can we know the timetable? The information we have discovered in this chapter will help us greatly in that quest.

NOTE

[1] The word "generation" in this verse (Matthew 24:34) is from the Greek word *genea.* It is translated generation, age, and nation in the King James Version. It could have reference in this verse to the nation of the Jews who would endure until Christ's return. More likely, *genea* refers to the generations of evil that have existed throughout history and will exist until the end of time.

Chapter 9
All Biblical Information Must Be Shared

We have come to that place in our study where we are almost ready to entertain a search of the Bible to try to discover the timetable of the end of the world. Again it should be asked, *Do we dare do this?*

Writing a book on the timing of Christ's return and the end of the world is a difficult and dangerous task. Anyone who dares to write such a book should do so with great fear and trepidation.

> *Predicted dates passed by and the*
> *world continues to exist . . . Thus the*
> *prophets who made the predictions*
> *have been shown to be without*
> *authority and without wisdom.*

This is true because every attempt to do so (and there have been many attempts), has proven to be altogether futile. Each predicted date passed by and the world continues to exist right up to the present day. Thus, the prophets who made the predictions have been shown to be without authority and without wisdom. In addition, they could have become the laughingstock of those who never trusted their prognostications in the first place.

Peoples' lives can be seriously affected by such predictions. There have been those who have sold their homes and businesses in anticipation of the end of the world. (Although one wonders about the value of such activity when it is realized that upon Christ's return this world will be destroyed by fire. Thus, our possessions, whether they are money or property, will be totally consumed.) Nevertheless, the blind followers of blind prophets, who dared to give a date for the end of the world, have frequently been seriously hurt by such forecasts.

The most important problem that must be faced by anyone who dares to suggest that he knows the timing of Christ's return is the warning in Scripture. In the Bible, God emphasizes that, "Of that day and hour knoweth no man" (Matthew 24:36). Also, in Acts 1:7, "It is not for you to know the times or the seasons." These are God's statements that must be viewed as being absolutely authoritative. What is one to do?

Search the Scriptures

Some twenty years ago I began to discover the information contained in this book, which is completely derived from the Bible. During this twenty-year period there has been a nagging feeling that truth obtained from the Bible must be shared. It is God's Word to mankind and, therefore, should be made as available as possible to mankind.

One might argue, of course, that if it is truth that must be shared, then God would certainly have made it clear in the Bible so that many could read and understand it. The difficulty with this assumption is that God did not place truth in the Bible so that anyone could understand it. Dramatic truths such as the nature of the Covenant of Grace, the place of national Israel in end-time history, and the timing of creation and the flood have been denied to most generations throughout history. However, after careful examination of all Scripture, we find that God gives specific and detailed information concerning these truths. One of the principles that must be recognized in approaching God's Word for truth is that we must *search* the Scriptures. God has carefully written His Word so that those who read it carelessly or without faith in the absolute authority of the Bible as the Word of God, will be left not only in unbelief but also will be convinced of doctrines that are contrary to truth.

Moreover, God has a timetable for the revelation of truths set forth in His Word. For example, the Old Testament is replete with references to the fact that God would save people from every nation once the Messiah had come. Yet the Apostle Paul speaks in Ephesians 3:3 of this truth as a mystery that has been revealed to him; and the Apostle Peter required a dramatic vision concerning the eating of unclean animals to prepare him for this concept.

As God is giving information concerning the end of the world, He tells us in Daniel 12:4:

> But thou, O Daniel, shut up the words, and seal the book, even to the time of the end: many shall run to and fro, and knowledge shall be increased.

He further declares in Daniel 12:8-9:

And I heard, but I understood not: then said I, O my Lord, what shall be the end of these things? And he said, Go thy way, Daniel: for the words are closed up and sealed till the time of the end.

There is much more in the Bible concerning the timing of the return of Christ than most theologians realize.

There is much more in the Bible concerning the timing of the return of Christ than most theologians realize. It can be shown that we are very near the end of time; and therefore, it is time for additional understanding concerning Christ's return to be realized by the careful and faithful student of the Bible. God declares in Amos 3:7, "Surely the Lord GOD will do nothing, but he revealeth his secret unto his servants the prophets."

When God was ready to destroy Sodom and Gomorrah, He first disclosed it to the believer Abraham. Similarly, I believe that since Judgment Day is close at hand, we can expect that God will reveal much more concerning this event to those who implicitly trust in Him.

We must realize, of course, that God's full and complete revelation is the Bible. Therefore, our only source (and it is a complete source) of divine truth is the Bible. We may look only to the Bible in our search for truth concerning the timing of Christ's return. We, therefore, will begin our quest by first considering the question, "What are we to do with those passages that apparently conclusively teach that we are not to look for a precise timetable of our Lord's return?"

Dare We Look for the Timetable of the End?

In this book we have embarked on a search which at first blush appears to be quite contrary to the teaching of the Bible. The Bible declares in Matthew 24:36, "But of that day and hour knoweth no man, no, not the angels of heaven, but my Father only."

Matthew 24:42 emphasizes, "Watch therefore: for ye know not what hour your Lord doth come."

Luke 12:40 further informs us, "Be ye therefore ready also: for the Son of man cometh at an hour when ye think not."

When the disciples raised a question concerning the timing of the restoration of Israel, our Savior instructed them in Acts 1:7, "And he said unto them, It is not for you to know the times or the seasons, which the Father hath put in his own power."

Don't these passages clearly tell us that we cannot know, and in fact are not to know, the timetable of Christ's return? And, therefore, we should stop any further pursuit of an answer to the question of the timing of His return? If we proceed with this question, are we not acting rebelliously against our Lord?

While some people may be ready to adopt this attitude (based on the preceding verses), before we abandon any further search on the subject of the timetable of the end of the world, we must ask: Have we rightly understood the meaning of these verses? Have we examined them in the light of everything else in the Bible? Is the conclusion, based on these verses, that we cannot know and are not to attempt to know anything that concerns the timetable of Christ's return, in harmony with everything else the Bible teaches?

What are we to do, for example, with Matthew 24:32-33, where we are advised:

Now learn a parable of the fig tree; When his branch is yet tender, and putteth forth leaves, ye know that summer is nigh: So likewise ye, when ye shall see all these things, know that it is near, even at the doors.

Doesn't this verse instruct us that as we approach the end there will be certain signs that show us that we have almost arrived there? If this is so, then isn't God saying that we *can* know something about the timetable of His return?

Also, what are we to do with I Thessalonians 5:1-5 where we read:

But of the times and the seasons, brethren, ye have no need that I write unto you. For yourselves know perfectly that the day of the Lord so cometh as a thief in the night. For when they shall say, Peace and safety; then sudden destruction cometh upon them, as travail upon a woman with child; and they shall not escape. But ye, brethren, are not in darkness, that that day should overtake you as a thief. Ye are all the children of light, and the children of the day: we are not of the night, nor of darkness.

Verse 4 explicitly declares that for the true believer the return of the Lord will not come as a thief. This implies that perhaps we can know something about the timing of the return of Christ.

Moreover in Amos 3:7 God promises, "Surely the Lord GOD will do nothing, but he revealeth his secret unto his servants the prophets."

As noted in our introduction, when God was about to destroy Sodom and Gomorrah, He visited Abraham and declared, in Genesis 18:17, "And the LORD said, Shall I hide from Abraham that thing which I do . . . ?"

In addition, God informed Noah of the timetable of the destruction of the world of his day. We read in Genesis 6:3:

And the LORD said, My spirit shall not always strive with man, for that he also is flesh: yet his days shall be an hundred and twenty years.

God followed this with the pertinent language of Genesis 6:13:

And God said unto Noah, The end of all flesh is come before me; for the earth is filled with violence through them; and, behold, I will destroy them with the earth.

Moreover, in Hebrews 10:25 we read:

Not forsaking the assembling of ourselves together, as the manner of some is; but exhorting one another: and so much the more, as ye see the day approaching.

This verse clearly implies that the believers will know when the end is very near.

Remember, too, that God repeatedly warned Judah by the prophets Ezekiel and Jeremiah that the time was coming for its destruction by the Babylonians, as recorded in Jeremiah 38:14-28 and Jeremiah 25:1-11 and elsewhere.

Thus, the verses quoted from the New Testament are not necessarily so simplistic that we can conclude they teach that we can know nothing about the timing of Christ's return. Perhaps it would be well if we looked at those New Testament verses more carefully to determine what they teach.

No Man Knoweth the Day or the Hour
Let us begin with Matthew 24:36-37:

> But of that day and hour knoweth no man, no, not the angels of heaven, but my Father only. But as the days of Noe were, so shall also the coming of the Son of man be.

A further development of this verse is found in Mark 13:32 where our Lord discloses: "But of that day and that hour knoweth no man, no, not the angels which are in heaven, neither the Son, but the Father."

Please note the similarity of these verses. Also note the phrase in Mark 13:32, "neither the Son." This is indeed a remarkable addition. It is easy to imagine that created beings such as mankind and angels do not know the day nor the hour of Christ's return. But, can it be that the Lord Jesus Christ, Who is eternal God, Who is the creator of the universe, Who knows the end from the beginning, does not know the timetable of the end? Surely that is an impossible idea. After all, all who are to be saved were given to Him by the Father (John 6:37), and when all the elect have become saved, then we know that the end will be upon us. Revelation 7 teaches that the plagues of Revelation 8 and 9, which are word pictures of the final tribulation, cannot take place until all of the servants of God have been sealed in their foreheads (Revelation 7:3). To be sealed in the forehead is language that speaks of salvation, and Jesus Himself is the advocate Who intercedes with the Father on behalf of those who are to be saved.

What then are we to do with Mark 13:32? When we look at this verse more carefully we see that it speaks of knowing the day or the hour. The word "day" and the word "hour" could be time references, but they also can be references to Judgment Day. The Bible speaks repeatedly of Judgment Day as "the day" (Hebrews 10:25) and as "the day of the Lord" (I Thessalonians 5:2). In Revelation 18:10 and 17 God speaks of Judgment Day and uses the phrase "one hour." Thus the phrase "to know the day or the hour," rather than referring to the time of Christ's return, could refer to the matter of experiencing Judgment Day.

This agrees with the rest of Mark 13:32. Please note that there are three categories of those who do not know the day nor the hour: Mankind; the angels; and Christ Himself. At the time that Jesus spoke these words, had mankind or the fallen angels, both of whom are subject to eternal damnation because of their rebellion against God, experienced eternal damnation? The answer is, "Of course not." They are to experience Judgment Day at the end of time. That conclusion agrees with Mark 13:32, which asserts that of that day and hour knoweth no man, no not the angels which are in heaven. (Remember, Satan and his angels were not banished from heaven until Christ went to the cross.)

> *Was the Lord Jesus to experience*
> *Judgment Day? Indeed He was.*

What about the Lord Jesus? Was He also to experience Judgment Day? Indeed He was. He had become sin for all who believe on Him. At the cross He experienced the wrath of God to pay for the sins of believers. When Jesus spoke these words of Mark 13:32, at that time, He did not know the day and the hour. That is, He had not yet experienced Judgment Day. In fact, we can now gain some insight into the difficult words of Hebrews 5:8 where we read: "Though he were a Son, yet learned he obedience by the things which he suffered."

Jesus Suffered Judgment Day at the Cross

How can Jesus, Who never ceased to be eternal God, have to learn something? This can be understood only if we realize that He had to experience the cup of God's wrath that God would pour on Him.

We are told in Mark 13:32 that God the Father knew the day and the hour. Does this mean that God had experienced Judgment Day? That, of course, is an impossible idea. God the Judge poured out His wrath on the Son, and as the Judge He determined precisely how grievous the suffering of Jesus was to be so that our sins would be forever expiated. Jesus, the Son, learned how great this suffering was as He experienced the suffering. God as Judge knew exactly how much suffering by Christ was required. We read in John 18:11 the declaration of Jesus, "The cup which my Father hath given me, shall I not drink it?" And in Hebrews 5:8 God informs us, "Though he were a Son, yet learned he obedience by the things which he suffered." The distinction that Christ looked to the Father as His Judge appears to be strengthened by His plea in Gethsemane when He prayed three times, "O my Father, if it be possible, let this cup pass from me" (Matthew 26:39, 42, and 44). The idea that Christ was learning the full extent He must suffer the wrath of God is also suggested by the words wrenched from Jesus as He hung on the cross, "My God, my God, why hast thou forsaken me?" (Matthew 27:46).

In John 12:27 Jesus gives us this information: "Now is my soul troubled; and what shall I say? Father, save me from this hour: but for this cause came I unto this hour." This verse definitely ties experiencing the suffering of the wrath of God to the word "hour," an hour that Jesus must experience.

Therefore, the explanation of Mark 13:32, that "of that day and that hour knoweth no man" refers to the fact that no one who is to experience Judgment Day has yet experienced Judgment Day, appears to meet all the requirements set forth in Mark 13:32. It appears to be in harmony with everything else the Bible teaches concerning its subject matter.

However, it is not important to our present discussion whether or not we have adequately understood Mark 13:32. While this explanation takes Matthew 24:36 and Mark 13:32 out of contention insofar as teaching that we are not to seek to know the timetable of Christ's return, what about the other verses that seem to say plainly that we cannot know the time? Does not Matthew 25:13 say, "Watch therefore, for ye know neither the day nor the hour wherein the Son of man cometh."

In the parable of the wise and faithful servant as opposed to the evil servant, Christ declares in Matthew 24:50, "The lord of that servant shall come in a day when he looketh not for him, and in an hour that he is not aware of."

One might think that surely both of these verses are without question a reference to time. Surely both of them, therefore, teach that we cannot know the day nor the hour when Christ will come.

In Principle Christ Comes When One Dies
To what does the coming of Christ refer? We must realize that insofar as any human being is concerned, regardless of when he lived in history, in a sense Christ's coming for that person is at the moment of his death. If he is a believer in Christ, at the moment of his death he will be translated into heaven to live and reign with Christ. He will go

to be with Christ because he is ready. He is saved. Regardless of when Christ comes to take him home to glory, he is ready.

The moment of the death of an unbeliever is also in one sense effectively the time of Christ's coming. True, he does not see Jesus at that moment, but in his next conscious moment after death, he will see Jesus on the clouds of glory. This is because at death his soul goes to a place of silence (Psalm 115:17). Revelation 20:5 teaches that the rest of the dead lived not (did not have conscious existence) until the thousand years (the completeness of God's plan) were ended. We know from Revelation 20 and John 5:28-29 that the unbelievers are resurrected at Judgment Day. Thus, effectively for them, the moment of their death is the coming of Christ. In their next conscious moment they will be standing before the Judgment Throne at the end of time.

Can any man predict the day or hour of his death? If he is dying of terminal cancer, he might be able to predict the year or even the month of his death. However, he cannot know what day or what hour of the day will be his last. Even the man who commits suicide cannot know because if it were God's will that the suicidally inclined person not die on the day or the hour selected by him or her, God can use many means to interrupt or frustrate his suicidal plans. Indeed no one knows the day or the hour of the coming of the Lord Jesus because no one knows the day or the hour he will die. Each one of us must be ready. We must watch. That is, each of us must make sure that we are saved so that whenever God takes us in death (whether by means of an accident, illness, or by any other means), we are ready. I Thessalonians 5:1-6 teaches that Christ will not come as a thief in the night for the believer. We who are saved are children of the light. We are ready for His coming at the moment of physical death when He will take us home to heaven.

For the unsaved, the moment of Christ's coming will be like a thief in the night. This is because the unsaved are not ready to meet Him. They still have their sins and, therefore, Christ's coming will guarantee eternal damnation for them.

That bears repeating: These verses, which speak of no one knowing of the day and the hour of Christ's coming, may in a sense be speaking about the time of any individual's death. There is, however, a primary meaning to these statements in that they are pointing to the timetable of the return of Christ on the clouds of glory. Indeed, we shall see that even though there will come a time when the believers will know considerably more about the timing of the coming of Christ, they will not know the day nor the hour of His return.

> *Indeed, we shall see that even though there will come a time when the believers will know considerably more about the timing of the coming of Christ, they will not know the day nor the hour of His return.*

We are still faced with Acts 1:7. The disciples asked the question in verse 6: "Lord, wilt thou at this time restore again the kingdom to Israel?"

Regardless of what the disciples had in mind when they asked this question, we know from the context as well as from everything else the Bible teaches that effectively God had them ask, "Lord, wilt thou very presently complete your work of saving all of the elect, of completing your plan of salvation in the world?" We know because this verse echoes a beautiful prophecy of Isaiah 49:6 where God promises:

> And he said, It is a light thing that thou shouldest be my servant to raise up the tribes of Jacob, and to restore the preserved of Israel: I will also give thee for a light to the Gentiles, that thou mayest be my salvation unto the end of the earth.

We know that this verse refers to the whole salvation plan that God instituted by Christ going to the cross. Israel consists of both Jews and Gentiles who enter the Kingdom of God by trusting in the Lord Jesus Christ. When Christ comes on the clouds of glory to complete our salvation by giving us our resurrected bodies and by giving us the new heaven and new earth, then the restoration of the kingdom of Israel will be complete in every sense of the word.

This wonderful truth is seen in Jesus' response to the disciples' question in Acts 1:6. Jesus declares in Acts 1, verses 7 and 8:

> And he said unto them, It is not for you to know the times or the seasons, which the Father hath put in his own power. But ye shall receive power, after that the Holy Ghost is come upon you: and ye shall be witnesses unto me both in Jerusalem, and in all Judaea, and in Samaria, and unto the uttermost part of the earth.

Times and Seasons

By this answer Jesus is saying that believers ordinarily are not to know the timing of the return of Christ (at which time the restoration of Israel - the body of believers - will be completed). They are to be busy witnessing to the world concerning the Gospel of Christ. Of course when they witness, they are being used of God to build up the body of believers, who are the Israel of God.

The phrase "times or the seasons" requires special attention. In Genesis 1:14 we read:

And God said, Let there be lights in the firmament of the heaven to divide the day from the night; and let them be for signs, and for seasons, and for days, and years.

In this verse God indicates that He placed the sun and the moon in the heavens to be the means of marking time. Days and years and seasons are measured by the interrelationships that exist between the sun and the moon and the earth. When Christ comes on the clouds of glory, the first thing that will happen is the sun and the moon will cease to function. Matthew 24:29 declares:

Immediately after the tribulation of those days shall the sun be darkened, and the moon shall not give her light, and the stars shall fall from heaven, and the powers of the heavens shall be shaken.

This verse teaches us that when Christ returns, time will be no more. There will no longer be a sun or moon to mark out times and seasons.

Therefore, in Acts 1:7 Jesus is effectively answering the question of the previous verse that it is not for the disciples to know the time of Christ's return. Instead, they are to get busy with the task assigned to the church: Go into all the world with the Gospel.

In I Thessalonians 5:1, God makes reference to the same truth with the words: "But of the times and the seasons, brethren, ye have no need that I write unto you."

In the following verses of I Thessalonians 5, He emphasizes that while Christ will come as a thief in the night for the unbelievers (because they are not ready for His coming in view of the fact that they are still unsaved), we believers need not concern ourselves with this timetable because He will not come as a thief in the night for us. We are ready for His coming whenever that may be.

But this conclusion indicates that we are to stop right now in this book. We are not to try to discover the timing of the second coming of Christ. Rather, we are to expend every effort to get on with the task of sending forth the Gospel.

Is this the end of the matter? Is there nothing else in the Bible that indicates we are to be concerned about the timing of Christ's return and which is to be carefully considered by the believer?

> *We will find that many new truths*
> *will be revealed to believers very*
> *near the end of time.*

Indeed there is. As we go on in our study, we will discover that the believers will know much about both the spiritual condition of the church as well as the timetable of the end. In other words, as we apply all of the Bible references we will find that many new truths will be revealed to believers very near the end of time.

As we continue, let us look again at a great judgment that was a type of the judgment that will take place at the end of the world.

The Judgment of the Flood

Reference has already been made to the judgment that came upon the world of Noah's day. Did this judgment come with no specific warning to the world of that day? The Bible tells us that Noah was a preacher of righteousness (II Peter 2:5). The Bible also assures us that Noah found grace in the eyes of the Lord (Genesis 6:8). Therefore, we know that Noah became saved in the way we become saved. He, therefore, had to be quite aware of the fact that as a result of sin we are under the wrath of God, and that is why we need salvation.

God was going to bring judgment on the earth because of sin, so He told Noah to build the huge ark. The building of that 450-foot boat by the preacher of righteousness was, in dramatic language, telling the world of Noah's day that:

1. Judgment on the world would not come until the boat was finished.

2. At any time after the ark was finished, judgment would come.

Then God gave specific information concerning the timetable of judgment. God told Noah in Genesis 7:1-4:

> And the LORD said unto Noah, Come thou and all thy house into the ark; for thee have I seen righteous before me in this generation. Of every clean beast thou shalt take to thee by sevens, the male and his female: and of beasts that are not clean by two, the male and his female. Of fowls also of the air by sevens, the male and the female; to keep seed alive upon the face of all the earth. **For yet seven days**, and I will cause it to rain upon the earth forty days and forty nights; and every living substance that I have made will I destroy from off the face of the earth.
>
> Either before or during these seven days, Noah and his family were assembling the animals and taking them into the ark. Regardless of how much time it took to gather and board the animals, it could not have been done secretly. We can be sure that all kinds of people were knowledgeable of the oddball shipbuilding project, and they were also aware of the final preparations of taking the animals into the ark. Without question, Noah, a preacher of righteousness, was warning people of that day that God was about to destroy the world. We read in I Peter 3:19-20 that Christ, in His Spirit, preached through Noah to the spirits in prison (that is, to the unsaved), while the longsuffering of God waited in the days of Noah until the ark was prepared. Indeed, even if the world of Noah's day did not know the day nor hour of judgment, they were made especially aware of the nearness of judgment as the ark was closer to completion.
>
> The judgment on the world of Noah's day is a dramatic type or reminder of the judgment of the last day of this world's existence. We read in II Peter 3:3-7:

> Knowing this first, that there shall come in the last days scoffers, walking after their own lusts, And saying, Where is the promise of his coming? for since the fathers fell asleep, all things continue as they were from the beginning of the creation. For

this they willingly are ignorant of, that by the word of God the heavens were of old, and the earth standing out of the water and in the water: Whereby the world that then was, being overflowed with water, perished: But the heavens and the earth, which are now, by the same word are kept in store, reserved unto fire against the day of judgment and perdition of ungodly men.

There can be no question that the people of Noah's day were adequately warned of imminent judgment. Moreover, the timetable for this judgment became increasingly clear each day as the building of the ark approached completion and as the animals were being assembled to be placed in the ark.

Nineveh Will Be Destroyed

Even more insistent is the Biblical account of another huge potential judgment of a people when a precise timetable was given. We read in Jonah 1:1-2:

Now the word of the LORD came unto Jonah the son of Amittai, saying, Arise, go to Nineveh, that great city, and cry against it; for their wickedness is come up before me.

Then we read in Jonah 3:2-4:

Arise, go unto Nineveh, that great city, and preach unto it the preaching that I bid thee. So Jonah arose, and went unto Nineveh, according to the word of the LORD. Now Nineveh was an exceeding great city of three days' journey. And Jonah began to enter into the city a day's journey, and he cried, and said, Yet forty days, and Nineveh shall be overthrown.

> *God gives a precise timetable: Nineveh is to be destroyed in forty days.*

Here we find that God is about to destroy the great city of Nineveh because of their wickedness. Amazingly, God gives a precise timetable: Nineveh is to be destroyed forty days after Jonah began to preach.

It is true that the city was not destroyed. We read further in the Book of Jonah that the people repented of their sins and God spared them. However, we can be absolutely certain that had they not repented, God would have destroyed them at the prescribed time. The world of Noah's day did not repent and they were destroyed. As we go on in this study, we will discover that the world of our day will not repent as we approach Judgment Day. Therefore, whatever is disclosed by the Bible as the timetable for Judgment Day and the end of the world, will take place.

The World Must Be Warned

As we think of the final judgment and the end of this world, we might be reminded of what we are told in Ezekiel 33:1-9:

> Again the word of the LORD came unto me, saying, Son of man, speak to the children of thy people, and say unto them, When I bring the sword upon a land, if the people of the land take a man of their coasts, and set him for their watchman: If when he seeth the sword come upon the land, he blow the trumpet, and warn the people; Then whosoever heareth the sound of the trumpet, and taketh not warning; if the sword come, and take him away, his blood shall be upon his own head. He heard the sound of the trumpet, and took not warning; his blood shall be upon him. But he that taketh warning shall deliver his soul. But if the watchman see the sword come, and blow not the trumpet, and the people be not warned; if the sword come, and take any person from among them, he is taken away in his iniquity; but his blood will I require at the watchman's hand. So thou, O son of man, I have set thee a watchman unto the house of Israel; therefore thou shalt hear the word at my mouth, and warn them from me. When I say unto the wicked, O wicked man, thou shalt surely die; if thou dost not speak to warn the wicked from his way, that wicked man shall die in his iniquity; but his blood will I require at thine hand. Nevertheless, if thou warn the wicked of his way to turn from it; if he do not turn from his way, he shall die in his iniquity; but thou hast delivered thy soul.

> *The Gospel presentation is not only*
> *that salvation can be obtained through*
> *the Lord Jesus Christ, but also that the*
> *wrath of God is upon all the unsaved.*

The task of being a watchman to warn of impending judgment is assigned to every believer. The Gospel presentation is not only that salvation can be obtained through the Lord Jesus Christ but also that the wrath of God, which will result in eternal damnation, is upon the unsaved; both are integral parts of the Gospel message.

The sword that is coming upon mankind is the eternal damnation that will follow Judgment Day, which will come at the end of the world. The rest of the Gospel presentation is the wonderful news that we can escape that awful judgment by trusting in the Lord Jesus Christ as our Savior.

We Constantly Give Timetables As We Witness

When we tell individuals and groups of individuals about the Gospel, possibly without realizing we are doing so, we are presenting a timetable regarding the timing of judgment. The timetable is tied to the anticipated remaining life of those to whom we witness. The Bible teaches that when an unsaved person dies, while his body is placed in a grave or cremated, his soul or spirit essence goes to a place of silence; however, that is not the end of that individual. The Bible records in John 5:28-29:

> Marvel not at this: for the hour is coming, in the which all that are in the graves shall hear his voice, And shall come forth; they that have done good, unto the resurrection of life; and they that have done evil, unto the resurrection of damnation.

This will happen because God sets forth this principle in Hebrews 9:27, "And as it is appointed unto men once to die, but after this the judgment."

Thus, the next conscious awareness of an individual who dies unsaved is that of standing before the Judgment Throne of God at the end of the world.

> *We should warn them that if they die*
> *unsaved the Bible guarantees that*
> *they will come into judgment.*

When we tell the unsaved about the Gospel, we should warn them that if they die unsaved the Bible guarantees that they will come into judgment. Since no one knows for sure that he will be alive tomorrow (almost 200,000 people die within every twenty-four hour period), we must warn as many people as possible that effectively Judgment Day could be as close as tomorrow. If we witness to someone who is terminally ill, effectively we may be telling him that Judgment Day is as close as two years away or six months away, etc. If we witness to someone on his deathbed, effectively we may be warning him that Judgment Day is only a few days away.

Without realizing it, therefore, when we share the Gospel with the world we are constantly giving timetables.

It is one thing to tell the Gospel to a terminally-ill individual or someone sentenced to the electric chair and warn that the sword of God's wrath is close; it is quite different to tell the same Gospel to the whole world and indicate a timetable for Judgment Day and the end of the world.

Or is it different? When we share the Gospel with a terminally ill individual who will probably die within the next month, do we not give him all the Biblical information we know that might help him to see his need for a Savior? This could include reference to the expected approximate time of his death.

When Jonah went to Nineveh he preached to that great city and gave the citizens of Nineveh all the information that God had given him. This information included the fact of their wickedness and the certainty of being under the wrath of God. It included the God-given information that destruction was to come in forty days.

What about any God-given information concerning the destruction of the whole world? Is that a different matter? To answer these questions, we should first ask the question: Why did God write the Bible? Was it written so that faithful, studious believers could know certain significant or interesting facts about God, His salvation plan, and other subjects treated in the Bible, for his own personal enjoyment? Is it like a man who discovers a process that will produce something very valuable and very salable, and to gain as much personal wealth as he can, he keeps the process a secret? Of course, we know that this example is not at all analogous to what we do with information from the Bible. One of the rewards of teaching from the Bible is that the teacher can and should share anything and everything he has learned. There are to be no secrets. In Philippians 2:13 God declares that "it is God which worketh in you both to will and to do of his good pleasure." A fundamental principle of the Bible is that what can be known by faithful study of the Bible is a gift and is to be gladly and freely shared. God says in Matthew 10:8, "freely ye have received, freely give."

The Bible Instructs Us to Share

The question we have been struggling with, "Should all the information we have learned concerning the time of the end be shared with all who will listen?" is answered for us in Daniel 12. The Book of Daniel was written with many difficult passages that obviously relate in some way to the end of the world. In regards to this God tells us in Daniel 12:4:

> But thou, O Daniel, shut up the words, and seal the book, even to the time of the end: many shall run to and fro, and knowledge shall be increased.

This verse assures us that at the time of the end knowledge shall be increased. This knowledge is in the Bible, but the knowledge was to be sealed up until the end. When we examine God's use of the Hebrew word that is translated "knowledge" (*daath*) we find that it is used more than eighty times. In every case it is used in a context that signifies spiritual knowledge, that is, knowledge that comes from the study of the Bible. The knowledge does not appear to envision secular knowledge that the world develops as it learns more and more about this earth and the universe through science.

Secondly, God is indicating that the knowledge of this information would be hidden in the Bible until the time of the end. The information that was hidden in the Bible, and that would become available as knowledge was increased, has to do with the end-time itself.

> *This information would not become available to believers until near the end of time.*

This information would not become available to the believers until near the time of the end, when they would be given spiritual eyes so that they could understand it.

We can see why God's spiritual economy has been established in this way. God has assigned to the believers the task of evangelizing the world. They are to marshal all of their energies to carry out this task throughout the New Testament era. They are not to become sidetracked by being concerned about the details relating to the end of time. God has commanded in Acts 1:7 that it was not for the believers "to know the times or the seasons."

To make sure that the believers would not turn their attention away from the task assigned to them, God sealed within the Bible all kinds of information that relates to the end of the world. Thus, theologians, regardless of how godly they were or how diligently they studied verses and chapters that obviously related to the end of the world, were denied truth. God simply did not open their spiritual understanding concerning these passages.

When we come to the end of time it is an entirely different matter. Knowledge will increase. That is, God will begin to open believers' spiritual understanding. Daniel 12:10 declares:

Many shall be purified, and made white, and tried; but the wicked shall do wickedly: and none of the wicked shall understand; but the wise shall understand.

The wise spoken of in this verse can be only the believers. They will understand these truths that had been hidden in the Bible. God will open up their understanding as they face the final tribulation and all the special traumas that relate to the end.

> *This is why God has given the information*
> *written in this book . . . because we are living*
> *in a time close to the end.*

This is why God has given the information written in this book. Very little of it can be found in any commentary or theological treatise. It is not because the writer of this book is smarter or more intelligent than anyone else; it is simply because we are living in a time close to the end.

Because verse 10 declares that the wise will understand, we know that any knowledge given to believers must be shared.

True, verse 10 tells us that the wicked - that is, the unsaved - will not understand. They, of course, will ridicule information that God reveals in the end time context.

> *Could it be that as a result of warning the*
> *world of the month and year of judgment,*
> *many might still become saved?*

Verse 10 also declares that many will be purified and made white and tried. This surely implies that as this end time knowledge is made available there will be those who will become saved. The Hebrew word that is translated "tried" (*tsaraph*) means to "refine" or "purge." Every believer is refined in the sense of Zechariah 13:9 where the same Hebrew word is translated as "refine" and "refined."

> And I will bring the third part through the fire, and will refine them as silver is refined, and will try them as gold is tried: they shall call on my name, and I will hear them: I will say, It is my people: and they shall say, The LORD is my God.

This verse describes what is required in order that we may be saved. While Christ as our substitute or stand-in has endured hell in our place, in principle the believer has gone through the fires of hell, fully meeting the penalty demanded by the law of God. Thus, Daniel 12:10 indicates that even as the believers are given the information that has been sealed up until the time of the end, there will still be people becoming saved. All three words used in Daniel 12:10 - "purify," "white," and "tried" - are synonyms for salvation. No blessing is greater than that of salvation. Indeed may that be accomplished in the lives of many by the setting forth of the information in this book. When Jonah cried to Nineveh that in forty days destruction would come, the whole city was saved. *Could it be that as a result of warning the world of the month and year of judgment, many might still become saved?*

SUMMARY

In harmony with these verses, we have come to the following conclusions:

1. The coming of the Lord Jesus Christ for the peoples who have lived and died throughout time was the moment of their death. No one can be certain of the day or hour of his death.

2. Throughout the New Testament period the church was not to concern itself with the timetable of Christ's return. Therefore, God would not give them any help to learn the timetable of His return. They were to focus all of their attention on the task of sending forth the Gospel into the world.

3. When the world is near the end of time we are to expect more understanding of the nature and timing of Christ's return.

4. This information is to be shared so that all believers will have more understanding.

5. This information is to be widely shared so that it may be used of God as a means to bring many to repentance and salvation.

Now we can see why it was necessary to write this book. There is ample evidence that we are very near the end of time; therefore, God will give believers who carefully study the Bible more and more evidence concerning this timetable. Where will this evidence and understanding come from? We have learned that it is hidden within the Bible. Daniel 2:21 and 22 tell us:

> And he changeth the times and the seasons: he removeth kings, and setteth up kings: he giveth wisdom unto the wise, and knowledge to them that know understanding: He revealeth the deep and secret things: he knoweth what is in the darkness, and the light dwelleth with him.

In these verses God informs us that understanding of the deep and hidden things comes from God. Since the Bible is the Word of God, it is the Bible from which we will gain our understanding.

That we can expect further understanding is also seen in the promise, which we looked at earlier, in Amos 3:7:

> Surely the Lord GOD will do nothing, but he revealeth his secret unto his servants the prophets.

Therefore, we are on very safe Biblical ground to investigate the question of the timing of Christ's return.

Not surprisingly, when we have completed our study we will know much about God's timetable for the history of the world. *But we will not know the day and hour of the actual end of the world when Christ is to come the second time.*

Chapter 10
The Timing of Christ's First Coming Unfolds

We have seen that the signs dramatically point to the fact that we must be very near the time of the return of Christ. Is it possible that we can have more definite information concerning this from the numbers of the Bible? After all, God frequently indicated very specific time periods for future events.

Did God set forth information in the Bible that gave the timetable for the first coming of Christ?

Was it possible that believers like Simeon and Anna could have known the timetable of the first coming of Christ?

> *We may be able to find clues concerning the timing of the second coming of Christ and the end of the world.*

If we can find strictly within the Old Testament information that gives us clues concerning the timing of the first coming of Christ, then utilizing the whole Bible and following the same methodology and the same kind of data, we may be able to find clues concerning the timing of the second coming of Christ and the end of the world.

When Jesus at the age of 40 days was brought by Joseph and Mary to the temple to become ceremonially purified, how did the aged Simeon and the widow Anna know that He was the Messiah? (Luke 2:25-30) True, the Bible tells us in verse 26 that the Holy Spirit had revealed to Simeon that he would not see death until he had seen the Lord's Christ. And it is possible that they had heard of the shepherds' experience forty days earlier when they were visited by the angelic hosts at the time of Christ's birth. This is likely in view of the fact that the shepherds "made known abroad the saying which was told them concerning this child" (Luke 2:17).

To find an answer to this question let us go back in time and try to walk in the shoes of a devout Jew who lived just prior to the birth of Christ. We know that their Bible consisted of our Old Testament. Therefore, based on the Old Testament alone what can we find that might suggest a timetable for the coming of Christ?

Since, as we have learned, the time line of history is the unfolding of God's salvation plan and since the Bible is God's gift to mankind, in which He sets forth His salvation plan, we know that only the Bible can give us information that would permit an understanding of the chronological history of the world.

The first thing we do is to set forth all of the historical dates and time periods of consequence that can be determined from the Old Testament. This was done in the book *Adam When?* and is repeated in Chapters 8 and 9 of this book. The believer who lived just before Jesus' birth would have a different base year for his calendar (and therefore his dates would read differently), nevertheless, the time intervals between the various historical events would have been exactly as set forth in this book. This, of course, would be true only if the compilation is altogether faithful to the Word of God and if the believer of that day was altogether faithful to the Word of God.

While the historical dates were obtained strictly from Biblical data, with no view toward using them to discover the timing of Christ's return, the time relationships found from a study of these dates that point first to the timing of the first coming of Christ and secondly to the timing of the second coming of Christ, greatly encourage me that these dates are trustworthy. More than twenty years ago, while researching and writing *Adam When?*, in which all of these historical dates were established, I had no thought of using them to try to discover the timetable of Christ's return. Only after the information found in *Adam When?* had been substantially completed did I begin to wonder if God had hidden timetable information within the Bible that points to Christ's return. The fact that these dates harmonize with many paths that lead to a very possible knowledge of the timing of both Christ's first coming and second coming gives me great assurance that I had accurately done the Biblical research as set forth in *Adam When?*

Let us return to the devout believer who lived at or prior to the birth of Christ. The historical dates set forth in this book are the dates he could have known strictly from a study of his Bible, which is our Old Testament.

The Mythical Nathanael

We are going to spend the next couple of chapters walking in the shoes of a Jewish believer (let's name him Nathanael), who lived a few decades before the birth of the Lord Jesus Christ. This believer had at his disposal a copy of the Bible, which at that time in history consisted of what we today call the Old Testament.

> *Nathanael implicitly believed that everything he read in the Bible was absolutely trustworthy and authoritative.*

Nathanael not only was a diligent student of the Word of God, but he also implicitly believed that anything and everything he read in the Bible was absolutely trustworthy and authoritative.

Because Nathanael trusted the Bible with his whole life, he knew that the Messiah was coming. He knew that He was to come as a root out of dry ground (Isaiah 53:2); that is, He would come even when Israel had become so apostate that it looked like there was no hope for Israel.

Nathanael knew the Messiah would be born in Bethlehem Ephratah (Micah 5:2). He was certain He would be of the tribe of Judah (Genesis 49:8-12) and of the family line of King David.

But Nathanael often wondered: "With so much information in the Bible concerning the Messiah who was to come, were there any clues in the Bible that might suggest the time of His coming?" He was encouraged to think about this because God often had given time information before great events happened. Hadn't God told the patriarch Abram that Israel would be under oppression for four generations and for 400 years? And hadn't that come to pass? The four generations were Levi, Kohath, Amram, and Aaron (see Chapter 8) and the 400 years were the major part of a total of 430 years (Exodus 12:40) that Israel spent in Egypt. True, 400 years is not 430 years, but neither was Israel under oppression the entire 430 years. They had gone into Egypt as free men. It was later that the oppression began.

Hadn't God instructed Jonah to preach to Nineveh that in forty days God would destroy Nineveh? And in connection with the Flood of Noah's day didn't God insert a time of 120 years? (Genesis 6:3).

And didn't God predict in Jeremiah that Israel would remain under oppression for seventy years? This was from the time King Josiah was killed in 609 B.C. until 539 B.C., when Israel began to return to the land of Israel under the benevolent rule of the Medo-Persian King Cyrus, who conquered the Babylonian oppressors of Israel.

Nathanael was, of course, tremendously encouraged when he was able to discover, using the Biblical data alone, important dates such as the creation of the world, the timing of the flood of Noah's day, the timing of the Tower of Babel and the division of the continents, and the year of the official beginning of the nation of Israel (see Chapter 8). Nathanael was encouraged in that, since God had included all this dramatic information in the Bible, perhaps there was Biblical information that would give him a clue to the time of the coming Messiah.

So Nathanael studied and studied. And he prayed that God would give him wisdom. Could he know something from the Bible that would indicate whether the Messiah would come in his lifetime or was it an event that was still hundreds of years in the future?

Nathanael had carefully studied the Bible to know all that he could about God's salvation plan, and he had studied diligently to find Biblical historical dates. Now, Nathanael began to search the Scriptures for clues that might suggest the timetable for the coming of the Messiah. Nathanael realized that he would have to look in the Bible for those passages that specifically relate to the coming Messiah, and that his analysis of Bible references must be only in the framework of the Bible. In other words, he must always have Biblical sanction for any ideas or conclusions derived from the Biblical data. Only in this way could he be assured of truth. Keeping these principles in mind, he carefully began his search.

The Seventy Sevens of Daniel 9

The first passage that Nathanael was attracted to was Daniel 9:24-25. In this provocative statement God had declared:

> Seventy weeks are determined upon thy people and upon thy holy city, to finish the transgression, and to make an end of sins, and to make reconciliation for iniquity, and to bring in everlasting righteousness, and to seal up the vision and prophecy, and to anoint the most Holy. Know therefore and understand, that from the going forth of the commandment to restore and to

build Jerusalem unto the Messiah the Prince shall be seven weeks, and threescore and two weeks: the street shall be built again, and the wall, even in troublous times.

As Nathanael concentrated on these verses, he realized that seventy weeks or seventy sevens could easily relate to a period of 490 years, for 70 x 7 = 490. Because he was well trained in the salvation message of the Bible, he also knew that the end of 490 could be describing the coming of the Messiah. For the language of verse 24 had everything to do with the work the Messiah would accomplish. He would finish transgression by paying for the sins of those who trusted Him. He would make reconciliation for iniquity. He would bring in everlasting righteousness. This had to be a very important verse.

What was the beginning point of these 490 years - if indeed years were in view? He felt comfortable with the idea of years because so much of the Bible spoke of years in describing the passage of time.

Verse 25 seemed to strongly indicate that the beginning of the 490 years was the time when a command was given to restore and build Jerusalem. Because Nathanael knew his Jewish history very well, he knew that King Cyrus had commanded the rebuilding of God's house in Jerusalem. In II Chronicles 36:23 the Bible declared:

Thus saith Cyrus king of Persia, All the kingdoms of the earth hath the LORD God of heaven given me; and he hath charged me to build him an house in Jerusalem, which is in Judah. Who is there among you of all his people? The LORD his God be with him, and let him go up.

This surely was a possible beginning for the 490 years.

From secular history Nathanael knew that Cyrus had begun to rule over the Persian empire in 559 B.C. Later he conquered the Medes and began to rule over them in 550 B.C. Still later in 539 B.C. he conquered the Babylonians, and it was at this time he became acquainted with Israel. The Bible showed that Israel had come under oppression in the year 609 B.C., and continued under this oppression right up until Babylon was conquered by Cyrus.

Nathanael was also aware that the Bible prophesied that Israel would be oppressed for seventy years. In II Chronicles 36:20-21 we read:

And them that had escaped from the sword carried he away to Babylon; where they were servants to him and his sons until the reign of the kingdom of Persia: To fulfil the word of the LORD by the mouth of Jeremiah, until the land had enjoyed her sabbaths: for as long as she lay desolate she kept sabbath, to fulfil threescore and ten years.

Since the year that Cyrus began to reign over Babylon was the year 539, and since it was also the year that ended the period of seventy years beginning with the death of the king of Israel, Josiah, at which time Israel came under oppression, it surely was a year that could be the beginning of the 490 years called for in Daniel 9:24. So Nathanael calculated: 539 - 490 = 49 B.C. (Nathanael, of course, was using different numbers because he knew nothing of our calendar today. In this study we are taking the years he would have used and giving them in relation to our calendar.) The year 49 B.C. could have a relationship to the time of the Messiah.

There was more. Nathanael was a careful student. He knew from his study of the Bible that almost 100 years after Cyrus had given the command to build Jerusalem another man was instrumental in causing the walls of Jerusalem to be rebuilt. That man was Nehemiah, the cupbearer of King Artaxerxes, the king who ruled the Medo-Persian empire some time after King Cyrus. Nathanael knew that in the twentieth year of Artaxerxes - the year 445 B.C. - Nehemiah had been given permission to rebuild the wall of Jerusalem. True, this was by permission of the king and not a command and, therefore, it did not meet the prescription of Daniel 9:25 perfectly where it speaks of **a command** to build, but it had to be considered a possibility. So again Nathanael calculated - 445 B.C. minus 490 years equals 46 A.D. (remember we are transposing the calendar Nathanael used to fit our calendar, 445 + 46 - 1 = 490). So far, therefore, two dates look interesting: 49 B.C. and 46 A.D.

But Nathanael wasn't through with his study. He also realized that God frequently spoke in parables. That is, sometimes God cloaked the truth He was teaching by using figures of speech in an allegorical language. He was aware of Psalm 78, which is a recounting of many historical events that had happened to Israel. He knew they were historical parables because the opening verses of Psalm 78 declare:

Give ear, O my people, to my law: incline your ears to the words of my mouth. I will open my mouth in a parable: I will utter dark sayings of old: Which we have heard and known, and our fathers have told us.

Ezra Brings the Law of God to Jerusalem

Nathanael knew, for example, that God had promised that Abraham was to inherit the land of Canaan. Like Abraham, he knew this referred to the Kingdom of God. God tells us in Hebrews 11:13-16 that Abraham dwelt as a stranger and pilgrim in the world and that he was looking for a heavenly city. Abraham realized the city of God is obtained through salvation. Even though he did not have the Hebrews 11 citation, Nathanael, too, realized that Daniel 9:25, which speaks of the building of Jerusalem, could refer to salvation. That is, the building of the Jerusalem could refer to the teaching of the Word of God whereby men would become saved.

With this in mind Nathanael recalled another event written about in the Bible that could be significant. He realized that the good priest Ezra in the year 458 B.C. had been given the command to reestablish the law in Israel. In the book of Ezra these verses identified with the question at hand:

Ezra 7:21: And I, even I Artaxerxes the king, do make a decree to all the treasurers which are beyond the river, that whatsoever Ezra the priest, the scribe of the law of the God of heaven, shall require of you, it be done speedily.

Ezra 7:23: Whatsoever is commanded by the God of heaven, let it be diligently done for the house of the God of heaven: for why should there be wrath against the realm of the king and his sons?

Ezra 7:25: And thou, Ezra, after the wisdom of thy God, that is in thine hand, set magistrates and judges, which may judge all the people that are beyond the river, all such as know the laws of thy God; and teach ye them that know them not.

Ezra 7:26: And whosoever will not do the law of thy God, and the law of the king, let judgment be executed speedily upon him, whether it be unto death, or to banishment, or to confiscation of goods, or to imprisonment.

The language of these verses fits the prescription of Daniel 9:25, which speaks of the command to build Jerusalem. So Nathanael calculated again - 458 B.C. minus 490 years equals 33 A.D. (458 + 33 - 1 = 490). He now has found three years that might be significant - 49 B.C., 33 A.D., and 46 A.D.

A Jubilee Period

Before Nathanael left Daniel 9:24-25 to look elsewhere in the Bible he saw another possible clue. Daniel 9:25-26 declared that from the going forth of the command to restore and build Jerusalem until the Messiah the Prince, shall be seven weeks and sixty-two weeks and after the sixty-two weeks Messiah would be cut off. Then in Daniel 9:27 God declared that in the middle of the seventieth week sacrifice and offering would be cut off.

How was all of this to be understood? Nathanael realized that seven weeks or forty-nine years was a very important time period. It was the period between two jubilee years. In Leviticus 25 God had decreed that every seventh year was to be a Sabbath year when the land was to lie fallow. It was not to be planted, cultivated or harvested. After seven of these periods of seven years there was the most important year of all - the jubilee year. That was the year when everyone was to receive his inheritance. In Leviticus 25:10 God declared:

> And ye shall hallow the fiftieth year, and proclaim liberty throughout all the land unto all the inhabitants thereof: it shall be a jubile unto you; and ye shall return every man unto his possession, and ye shall return every man unto his family.

So Daniel 9:25, which spoke of seven weeks, surely could have a jubilee period in view. Nathanael began to search to determine which years were jubilee years. Leviticus 25:2 states:

> Speak unto the children of Israel, and say unto them, When ye come into the land which I give you, then shall the land keep a sabbath unto the LORD.

Nathanael knew because of his previous careful study of the Bible that the year 1407 B.C. was the year Israel came into the land of Canaan. So that was the year Leviticus 25:2 had in view. Then he read Leviticus 25:8-9:

And thou shalt number seven sabbaths of years unto thee, seven times seven years; and the space of the seven sabbaths of years shall be unto thee forty and nine years. Then shalt thou cause the trumpet of the jubile to sound on the tenth day of the seventh month, in the day of atonement shall ye make the trumpet sound throughout all your land.

These verses state that the year 1407 B.C. was a Sabbath year. This was to be followed by forty-nine years to cover a period of seven weeks of years. The next year after these forty-nine years was to be a jubilee year. This would be the year 1357 B.C. Thus, the year 1407 B.C., which was the year Israel came into the land of Canaan, was a jubilee and every fiftieth year thereafter was a jubilee year.

With this information in hand Nathanael looked again at Daniel 9:25. There in connection with the coming of the Messiah it spoke of seven weeks, which was a jubilee period. But which jubilee period? Did any of the dates he had been examining concerning the command to restore and build Jerusalem relate to a jubilee period? The year 539 B.C., when Cyrus gave the command to rebuild Jerusalem, did not so relate for the jubilee years were 557 B.C. and 507 B.C.

The year 49 B.C., which terminated the 490 years after 539 B.C., was not a jubilee year; the closest jubilee years were 57 B.C. and 7 B.C.

When he examined the possibilities relating to Nehemiah he again found no help. The closest jubilee year to 445 B.C. when Nehemiah began to build the wall was 457 B.C. And on the other end, 490 years after 445 B.C., which came to the year 46 A.D., missed the jubilee year that would have come in the year 44 A.D.

When he examined the question from the vantage point of Ezra going forth to reestablish the law he found something very interesting. The year 458 B.C., when Ezra was commanded to reestablish the law was a Sabbath year, a Sabbath year just prior to a jubilee year for the year 457 B.C. was a jubilee year. This was an exciting piece of information because this then could have been the beginning of the seven weeks of Daniel 9:25.

Nathanael calculated: The command was given to Ezra to build the spiritual house of Jerusalem in the Sabbath year 458 B.C. The next fifty years was the jubilee period spoken of in Daniel 9:25 by the language of seven weeks. It would, therefore, be the period from 457

B.C. to 407 B.C. Following this, Daniel 9:25 spoke of a period of sixty-two weeks or 434 years that would go on in unbroken fashion.

The next year after the initial jubilee period (457 B.C. to 407 B.C.) was 406 B.C. Going 434 years from 406 B.C. brought him to 29 A.D. (406 + 29 - 1 = 434). According to Daniel 9:26-27 it was, therefore, after this year that the Messiah was to be cut off. Moreover, the next year, 30 A.D., would be the beginning of the seventieth week of years. According to Daniel 9:27 it was in the middle of the seventieth week that sacrifice and offering would cease. This would have to be the year 33 A.D. or 34 A.D. One half of seven is three and one half. Thus, 29 A.D. plus 3½ years must end either in 33 A.D. or 34 A.D.

Nathanael realized that the cutting off of the Messiah and the cessation of sacrifice and offering would be the same event. In the Bible the phrase "cut off" points to eternal damnation. It points to the penalty the coming Messiah had to pay in order to be the Savior of Nathanael and all other believers.

He also realized that all of the ceremonial laws that deal with sacrifices and burnt offerings pointed to the sacrifice that somehow must be paid by the Messiah in order to free us from our sins. Therefore, he knew that 33 A.D. or 34 A.D. could be the year in which the Messiah was to be cut off and when sacrifice and offering would cease because the Messiah had become the eternal sacrifice.

Nathanael wondered if he was about to discover something. He remembered that earlier he had found that 490 years after 458 B.C. had also brought him to 33 A.D. The pieces of the puzzle were beginning to focus on 33 A.D.

Was there more to this jubilee period that marked the beginning of the second path to the coming of the Messiah? The year 33 A.D. was not a jubilee year. The years that were near 33 A.D. were 7 B.C. and 44 A.D. Could either of these years be significant in some way? If the Messiah was to be cut off in 33 A.D., could He be born into this world in the jubilee year 7 B.C.?

At this point Nathanael could see that he did not have enough information for a clearer understanding of Daniel 9:24-27. He could not figure out what to do with the last half of the seventieth week. He would have to search for additional clues elsewhere in the Bible.

David Becomes King

Nathanael realized that King David was a great figure or type of the coming Messiah. He knew from the Bible that the Messiah was to sit on the throne of David and that the Messiah was to be a descendant of David. The life of David, therefore, could be significant.

> *The year 1007 B.C. was exactly 1000 years from the jubilee year 7 B.C.*

Nathanael had worked out the Biblical dates very accurately, and he knew that David was born in the year 1037 B.C., ascended the throne upon the death of King Saul in the year 1007 B.C., and reigned forty years. Therefore, David died in the year 967 B.C. When Nathanael examined these dates he saw something that looked interesting: 1007 B.C. was exactly 1000 years from the jubilee year 7 B.C., which he had been attracted to in his study of Daniel 9:24-27. He also knew that the number 1000, if it symbolized anything spiritual, signified the completeness of whatever was in view in the context. He knew, for example, that the Bible spoke of God's love continuing for a thousand generations. He had read in Deuteronomy 7:9:

> Know therefore that the LORD thy God, he is God, the faithful God, which keepeth covenant and mercy with them that love him and keep his commandments to a thousand generations.

And in Psalm 105:8 he had read:

> He hath remembered his covenant for ever, the word which he commanded to a thousand generations.

Since Psalm 105:8 declares that God's covenant is eternal, Nathanael knew that he must understand the phrase "thousand generations" to mean the completeness of God's plan rather than a literal one thousand generations. God's mercy on those who love Him continues everlasting (a thousand generations), which is the completeness of God's plan. Likewise, God's Word was to go to all peoples throughout time (a thousand generations), which is the completeness of God's plan for the sending forth of the Gospel.

Nathanael read in Psalm 105:9-11:

Which covenant he made with Abraham, and his oath unto Isaac; And confirmed the same unto Jacob for a law, and to Israel for an everlasting covenant: Saying, Unto thee will I give the land of Canaan, the lot of your inheritance.

As he read these verses Nathanael recalled that Abraham had entered the promised land when he was 75 years of age (Genesis 12:4), and that he died at the age of 175 (Genesis 25:7). Thus, he had lived in Canaan one hundred years. He also knew that Abraham had been promised the land eternally (Genesis 17:8). Yet Abraham had never owned any land except the cave in which he buried Sarah. Therefore, Nathanael realized that the land of Canaan was a type or figure of the eternal blessings that go with salvation. The one hundred years of Abraham's sojourn in the land of Canaan typifies eternity. Abraham lived in Canaan 100 years, which typified eternity (the completeness of God's plan). The number one hundred symbolized the same truth as the number 1000 - the completeness of God's plan.

> *The land of Canaan was a type or figure of the eternal blessings that go with salvation.*

With this concept in mind Nathanael looked again at King David, who ascended the throne in the year 1007 B.C. One thousand years later (the completeness of God's plan) could surely relate to the coming Messiah who was typified by David. He realized, too, that 1007 B.C. was a jubilee year. Since David was a great type of the coming Messiah, surely Nathanael had additional reason to believe that the jubilee year must relate to the Messiah. The jubilee year, 7 B.C., that came exactly 1000 years (the completeness of God's plan) after the jubilee year 1007 when King David ascended the throne, surely must be significant.

Nathanael was aware that King David was born in the year 1037 B.C. and 1000 years after this event was the year 37 B.C. Therefore, 37 B.C. must at least be kept in mind as a possibly significant date.

The Death of David

However, when he looked at the year that King David died, Nathanael again began to tingle with excitement. David died in the year 967 B.C. One thousand years later (the completeness of God's plan) was the year 34 A.D. (967 + 34 - 1 = 1000). He remembered that earlier in his study he had found that 34 A.D. had appeared to be a significant date. Since David - a great type of the Messiah - had died in 967 B.C., could it be that the Messiah at the completeness of God's plan, 1000 years after David's death, would be cut off for the sins of those to be saved? Could it be that the Messiah would be born in the year 7 B.C. and would be cut off in some way in the year 34 A.D.?

As Nathanael continued to look at the dates of King David, he noticed something else that looked very significant. King David had ruled forty years (I Kings 2:11). The number of years from 7 B.C. to 34 A.D. was also forty years (7 + 34 - 1 = 40). Could this have further bearing on the importance of the years 7 B.C. and 34 A.D. in connection with the timetable of the coming of the Messiah? Even as King David reigned forty years, would the coming Messiah live on this earth a period of forty years?

The Laying of the Foundation of the Temple

Nathanael was struck by another important fact: King David died in the year 967 B.C., which pointed to the possibility of 34 A.D. being related to the coming Messiah, but 967 B.C. was a year in which another event occurred that was intimately related to the coming of the Messiah. In the year 967 B.C. the foundation of the temple was laid. Nathanael knew that King David had aspired to build the temple (I Chronicles 22:7), but God would not allow David to be the builder (I Chronicles 22:8). Rather, it was his son Solomon who was to be the builder (I Chronicles 22:9-19).

Nathanael also knew that David had made abundant preparation for the building of the temple (I Chronicles 22:5, 14-16). Moreover, David had carefully instructed Solomon to build the temple and he was to build with great urgency (I Chronicles 22:16).

Nathanael discovered when he worked out the chronology of the world and ancient Israel (see Chapter 5), that Solomon laid the foundation of the temple in the same year that David died - the year 967 B.C. The laying of the foundation of the temple was intimately related to the coming Messiah. The Bible provided sufficient information to show that the temple was a picture of those who were to believe on Him. In I Kings 9:3 he had read:

> And the LORD said unto him, I have heard thy prayer and thy supplication, that thou hast made before me: I have hallowed this house, which thou hast built, to put my name **there for ever**; and mine eyes and mine heart shall be there perpetually.

How could God put His name forever in a literal temple of stone and cedar and gold and silver? Surely nothing of this earth could last forever. Furthermore, Nathanael knew that God had declared in I Kings 6:12-14:

> Concerning this house which thou art in building, if thou wilt walk in my statutes, and execute my judgments, and keep all my commandments to walk in them; then will I perform my word with thee, which I spake unto David thy father: And **I will dwell among the children of Israel**, and will not forsake my people Israel. So Solomon built the house, and finished it.

These verses showed that there must have been a very close relationship between the temple and the children of Israel. Nathanael recalled, as he read these verses, that God would dwell in the temple. In II Chronicles 6:2 Solomon declared:

> But I have built an house of habitation for thee, and a place for thy dwelling **for ever**.

He realized that some kind of house other than a literal physical house would be required if God was to dwell there forever. He recalled that in Ezekiel 36:25-27 God had declared:

> Then will I sprinkle clean water upon you, and ye shall be clean: from all your filthiness, and from all your idols, will I cleanse you. A new heart also will I give you, and a new spirit will I put

within you: and I will take away the stony heart out of your flesh, and I will give you an heart of flesh. And **I will put my spirit within you**, and cause you to walk in my statutes, and ye shall keep my judgments, and do them.

> *The idea of God's Spirit indwelling the one who had been cleansed of his sins matched the idea of God dwelling in a temple forever.*

The idea of God's Spirit indwelling the one who had been cleansed of his sins matched the idea of God dwelling in a temple forever, that is, if the temple is considered a type of the body of believers. Believers believed only because the coming Messiah would provide for their salvation. Therefore, the laying of the foundation of the temple indeed could be related to the coming of the Messiah.

If this were true, then for another reason 34 A.D. appeared to be a very important date in relation to the coming Messiah - 34 A.D. was exactly 1000 years after 967 B.C., when the foundation of the temple was laid.

One Thousand Years - The Completeness of God's Plan

There were other interesting and significant events recorded in the Bible that were separated by exactly 1000 years. Nathanael knew that the nation of Israel was officially formed in the year 2068 B.C., when Abraham was circumcised (Genesis 17). Exactly 1000 years later in the year 1068 B.C. the ark, which represented God Himself, was taken captive by the Philistines (I Samuel 4:11). The capture of the ark symbolized that God had left Israel. The formation of the nation of Israel in 2068 B.C. signified that God had come to Israel.

The 1000 years between these two dramatic events surely pointed to the completeness of God's plan in His dealings with national Israel. At the very least it showed that important events did not happen in random fashion.

This conclusion was again in evidence when Nathanael compared the date of the birth of Isaac with the recovery of the ark from the Philistines. The birth of Isaac was a dramatic fulfillment of God's promise that Abraham would be given a seed through whom all of the Messianic blessings would flow, and the restoration of the ark signified the coming of God to Israel. These striking events were also separated by 1000 years for Isaac was born in the year 2067 B.C. while the ark was restored in the year 1067 B.C. (I Samuel 6).

Reflecting on these time relationships, Nathanael saw that dates 1000 years after the birth of King David, 1000 years after he ascended the throne, and 1000 years after he died, when the foundation of the temple was laid, could all be significant dates. They could indeed be giving the timing of the coming of the Messiah.

Twenty-One Days Equals Twenty-One Hundred Years

As Nathanael studied afresh the events pertaining to Abraham and Isaac, he noted another important time relationship. The year 2068 B.C., when Abraham was circumcised and the nation of Israel was formed, was exactly 2100 years earlier than 33 A.D. (2068 + 33 - 1 = 2100), and the number 2100, like the number 1000, had great importance. The number 1000 signified the completeness of God's plan. The number twenty-one, which is the multiple of the two numbers three and seven (3 x 7 = 21), signified the perfection (seven) of the purpose (three) of God's plan.

Nathanael knew that in the tenth chapter of Daniel, God had made specific reference to a time span of twenty-one days. When he read Daniel 10 again he saw that not only did the twenty-one days represent a much longer period of time than twenty-one days but that it also was a time period that seemed to be related to the coming Messiah. In Daniel 10:1 he read, "And the thing was true, but the time appointed was long."

Verses 2 and 3 speak of a period of twenty-one days during which Daniel mourned. This mourning came to an end when Daniel ate flesh and drank wine and anointed himself at the end of the twenty-one days. These verses declare:

> In those days I Daniel was mourning three full weeks. I ate no pleasant bread, neither came flesh nor wine in my mouth, neither did I anoint myself at all, till three whole weeks were fulfilled.

Further commentary on these twenty-one days is found in Daniel 10:13 where we read:

> But the prince of the kingdom of Persia withstood me one and twenty days: but, lo, Michael, one of the chief princes, came to help me; and I remained there with the kings of Persia.

Nathanael wondered. During all of the history of Israel the great spiritual promises given throughout the Bible (our Old Testament) had not come to fruition. They all seemed to point to the glorious day when the Messiah would come. In the meanwhile Israel mourned. Because of their continuous rebellion against God, God's judgments came repeatedly upon them. Even in Nathanael's day (a few decades before the birth of Christ), Israel appeared to have little hope. They were under the heel of the Roman empire. True believers could hardly be found. Indeed Israel was in mourning.

Daniel 10:3 indicated that at the end of twenty-one days - a long or great period of time according to Daniel 10:1 - Daniel ended the time of mourning. Did this signify that the hope of Israel, the Messiah, had come? Furthermore, verse 13 indicated that Michael, one of the chief princes, came at the end of twenty-one days. Could Michael, whose name means "who assuredly is God," be the Messiah, who is one person of the triune God, who rules as king? This seemed possible to Nathanael, especially when he saw that in Daniel 12:1-2, where God talked about the final salvation of His people and the resurrection of the just and the unjust, God spoke of Michael as the great prince which stands for the children of thy people. These two verses declare:

> And at that time shall Michael stand up, the great prince which standeth for the children of thy people: and there shall be a time of trouble, such as never was since there was a nation even to that same time: and at that time thy people shall be delivered, every one that shall be found written in the book. And many of them that sleep in the dust of the earth shall awake, some to everlasting life, and some to shame and everlasting contempt.

Surely Michael, the Messiah Himself, would come after twenty-one days of mourning.

Nathanael continued to study. He realized that during the wilderness journey of Israel, as they went from Egypt to Canaan, one day symbolized a year (Numbers 14:34). He knew, too, that in Psalm 90:4 the Bible declared that "a thousand years in thy sight are but as yesterday."

Could it be that each day of the twenty-one days of Daniel 10 represented one hundred years? Surely it appeared that 2100 years ending with the coming of the Messiah must be possible.

What significant events in Israel's history related to the Messiah? Was Abraham's arrival in the land of Canaan in 2092 B.C. important? A period of 2100 years after that event would be the year 9 A.D. (2092 + 9 - 1 = 2100). Could 9 A.D. relate to the coming Messiah?

An even more important event was the year of the formation of the nation of Israel. As we have already noted, this was the year 2068 B.C. Because it was the year that Abraham was circumcised, it was a year that in a sense marked the ratification of God's covenant. As Genesis 17 indicates, the sign of the covenant was circumcision. Genesis 17:10-11:

> This is my covenant, which ye shall keep, between me and you and thy seed after thee; Every man child among you shall be circumcised. And ye shall circumcise the flesh of your foreskin; and it shall be a token of the covenant betwixt me and you.

As we have already seen, 2100 years after 2068 B.C. is the year 33 A.D. Surely this year, 33 A.D., must have a vital relationship to the coming of the Messiah. Here was tremendous agreement with the information he discovered in his study of the seventy weeks of Daniel 9.

Nathanael was aware that the next year, 2067 B.C., was also an exceedingly important year insofar as the Messiah was concerned. God had promised Abraham a seed with whom God would establish His covenant as an everlasting covenant. In Genesis 17:19 Nathanael read:

> And God said, Sarah thy wife shall bear thee a son indeed; and thou shalt call his name Isaac: and I will establish my covenant with him for an everlasting covenant, and with his seed after him.

Since God spoke in this verse of an everlasting covenant, it had to relate to the coming Messiah. Nathanael realized that only in the coming Messiah would God's everlasting promises find their fulfillment. Since Genesis 17:19 related Isaac to the everlasting covenant, surely the birth of Isaac as the seed of Abraham had to be anticipating the coming of the Messiah. And 2100 years after the birth of Isaac in 2067 B.C. was the year 34 A.D. (2067 + 34 - 1 = 2100).

Surely, Nathanael thought, 33 A.D. and 34 A.D. must relate to the coming Messiah for repeatedly they came into focus.

While Nathanael was considering the importance of Abraham's circumcision and the birth of Isaac, he remembered another Bible statement. Isaiah 53:2 declared that the Messiah would come like a root out of dry ground. In other words, His coming would be a miraculous event that would take place when there would appear to be no possibility of His appearing: Even as Isaac was born as a miraculous baby long after Sarah was capable of bearing children. More and more Isaac appeared to Nathanael to be a figure or type of the coming Messiah.

Moreover, Nathanael discovered that Isaac was born when Abraham was 100 years old. Nathanael saw that again the completeness of God's plan was in view. He had seen it earlier when he had discovered that Abraham had lived exactly one hundred years in the land of Canaan. This added weight to his earlier evaluation of the 1000 years (the completeness of God's plan) from the beginning of the reign of David in 1007 B.C. to 7 B.C. and from the death of David in 967 B.C. to 34 A.D.

As Nathanael continued to reflect on Isaac as a type or figure of the coming Messiah, he recalled that the temple was constructed on the very site where Abraham had been ready to sacrifice his son Isaac. In II Chronicles 3:1 the Bible showed that the temple was built on Mount Moriah. Nathanael knew that this was the same place where Abraham began to offer Isaac as a sacrifice. Therefore, the temple had to be related in some sense to the coming Messiah.

191-1910

Nathanael knew that Israel had entered Egypt to come under the care and safety of Joseph in the year 1877 B.C. This rescue of Israel appeared to relate somehow to the coming Messiah. The condition of Israel was critical. They would die if they did not find food. And a son of Israel - Joseph - had become a great ruler in a land where there was plenty of food. Surely this event would typify the coming of the great prince - the Messiah who would supply all the spiritual food necessary to save people from spiritual death.

Nathanael noted that 191 years transpired between 2068 B.C., the year Abraham was circumcised, and 1877 B.C., the year Jacob and his family entered Egypt. He then noted that the same period of time - multiplied by ten - would elapse between 1877 B.C. and 34 A.D. (1877 + 34 - 1 = 1910). Again he was struck by the repeated appearance of 34 A.D. as a date that was likely to relate to the coming Messiah.

While the number 191 has no apparent spiritual significance in the Bible, the number ten does have spiritual significance. As we learned, it signifies completeness. Two important signs pointing to salvation were 191 years apart. The fulfillment of these signs pointing to salvation was 10 x 191 years after the second sign.

190-1900

Because Nathanael wanted to consider all possibilities he noted, too, that 190 years transpired between 2067 B.C., the year Isaac was born, and 1877 B.C. And 1900 years after 1877 B.C. brought him to the year 24 A.D. We know that Isaac was a miracle baby because he was born to Sarah long after she could normally bear children. Isaac's birth fulfilled God's promise that through Abraham's seed the Messiah would come. Thus, the year 24 A.D. also must be kept in mind in relation to the timing of the coming of the Messiah.

While Nathanael was reflecting on the possible significance of 190 or 1900 years he thought of another patriarch who had had a very significant role in relation to the coming Messiah. This was the patriarch Jacob. Jacob was the seed of Abraham, the father of the twelve tribes of Israel, surely he bore an important relationship to the coming Messiah. Jacob's name became Israel - prince of God - Nathanael remembered. So the coming Messiah was the Prince of God. Didn't Isaiah 9:6 declare that the Messiah who would be born a son would be the Prince of Peace?

Nathanael knew from Genesis 32 that Jacob's name was changed to Israel at the time he returned to Canaan from the land of Haran, which must be a significant date because such a significant event occurred that year. Nathanael had worked out the dates that relate to this event and had found that Jacob was then 100 years old (amazingly the completeness of God's plan shines through again). The year was 1907 B.C., but what date would the passage of 1900 years bring? The year 7 B.C. Nathanael realized that 7 B.C., like 33 A.D. and 34 A.D., was appearing again and again. Again the significant number was not 190. Rather it was the fact that 190 years separated two important events that were signs pointing to God's salvation plan, but 190 multiplied by 10, the number of completeness, gave the number 1900 years. And 1900 years was a time period from an important event that signified the coming of the Messiah.

Nathanael knew, from his diligent searching of the Bible, that the Messiah would be born as a baby. Isaiah 9:6 declared this. Could it be that 7 B.C. was the year in which the Messiah was to be born, while 33 A.D. and 34 A.D. somehow related to the fact that the Messiah would be cut off, that God would pour out His wrath on Him even as Isaiah 53 declared?

Because Nathanael wanted to cover all possibilities he took note of the fact that 1910 years after 1907 B.C. was the year 4 A.D. (1907 + 4 - 1 = 1910). This year, too, must be kept in mind in his study of the possible year of Christ's coming.

Nathanael was aware that 1907 B.C. was an important date. It was not only the year Jacob's name was changed to Israel, but it was also the year Jacob purchased a piece of land in Shechem for one hundred pieces of silver. Genesis 33:19 records this purchase. Surely, Nathanael thought, this significant purchase must point in some way to the coming Messiah. Jacob who had just been called a prince of God bought a piece of land for one hundred shekels (one hundred, the completion of God's plan of a purchase price). What land could be in view? Nathanael knew that God would provide a land as an everlasting inheritance (Genesis 17:8). Was that land typified by the land Jacob - a type of the coming Messiah - bought? Did the purchase price of one hundred shekels typify the completion of the price the coming Messiah must pay as He bore the sins of those who were to be saved by Him?

Two Thousand Years

Nathanael noted that Jacob was born in the year 2007 B.C., exactly 2000 years earlier than the tantalizing year 7 B.C. that kept coming into view. As he searched the Bible for clues that might indicate that 2000 years was a significant time span, Nathanael found the interesting statement of Joshua 3:4.

> Yet there shall be a space between you and it, about two
> thousand cubits by measure: come not near unto it, that ye may
> know the way by which ye must go: for ye have not passed this
> way heretofore.

The setting of this verse is most striking for Israel was about to
cross the Jordan River into Canaan, the promised land. God declared
there were to be about 2000 cubits between the priests and the nation
of Israel. Nathanael didn't understand what all of this signified. But he
did realize that somehow 2000 was an important number insofar as the
coming of the Messiah was concerned. He knew the land of Canaan was
intimately related to the covenant promises of Genesis 17, and the
crossing of the Jordan River somehow related to the entrance into that
covenant. Beyond that he could not figure it out.

The importance of the number two or 2000 was also brought
home to him when he recalled that each tribe brought their offering to
the dedication of the altar, and each offering consisted first of all of a
charger weighing 130 shekels and a silver bowl weighing seventy
shekels, so the combined weight was 200 shekels (Numbers 7).
Nathanael had already concluded that the temple somehow involved
the coming Messiah, and he knew that the altar in the temple was
entirely related. It was on the altar that the sacrifices were offered,
anticipating the sacrifice that would be made by the coming Messiah.
Therefore, Nathanael was quite sure that the offering totaling 200
shekels of silver, which was made at the dedication of the altar, was an
important number.

Because Nathanael wanted to leave no stone unturned insofar
as Biblically suggested dates for the coming Messiah, he noted that
2068 B.C. - 2000 = 68 B.C. And 2067 B.C. - 2000 B.C. = 67 B.C.
These two dates, 68 B.C. and 67 B.C., must also be noted as possible
important dates.

Please note that from time to time in this book, we pursue an
idea suggested by Biblical data which proves to be futile in helping to
discover God's timetable for the world. For example, in this chapter we
investigated some information that suggested that 4 A.D. or 9 A.D.
might be important, and even though we know these dates do not
identify with the question being studied, the information has been

presented to demonstrate two ideas that have guided my thinking as I wrote this book.

One idea is that I wish to demonstrate that I have attempted to be as thorough and complete as possible in my analysis of the Bible. I have tried to face all possible ways of thinking about Bible passages even if they led to wrong conclusions. Only after looking at the Bible passages from *all* possible angles and dismissing the wrong views, after having checked them out, can I be confident that the path I finally end up with is correct.

The second idea is that I wish to demonstrate that I have attempted to be as submissive to the Bible as possible. If a way of thinking about a Bible passage turns out to be wrong, I have been willing to face that fact honestly. Only by making sure that I abandon wrong views and do not force a view when it does not seem to work, will I have the confidence that the understanding I finally adopt is correct.

SUMMARY

While Nathanael's search of the Bible for evidence suggesting a date for the coming of Christ was not complete, he thought it would be interesting to summarize what he had found thus far.

Cyrus began to reign 539 B.C. - 490 years later	= 49 B.C.
Nehemiah built the wall 445 B.C. - 490 years later	= 46 A.D.
Ezra taught the law of God 458 B.C. - 490 years later	= 33 A.D.
Middle year of Daniel's 70th week	33 A.D.
OR	34 A.D.
Jubilee year	7 B.C.
Jubilee year	44 A.D.
David ascended throne 1007 B.C. - 1000 years later	= 7 B.C.
David born 1037 B.C. - 1000 years later	= 37 B.C.
David died 967 B.C. - 1000 years later	= 34 A.D.
Foundation of temple laid 967 B.C. - 1000 years	= 34 A.D.
David ruled 40 years - 40 years after 7 B.C.	= 34 A.D.

Nation of Israel formed 2068 B.C. - 2100 years later   = 33 A.D.
Isaac born 2067 B.C. - 2100 years later   = 34 A.D.
Abraham entered land of Canaan 2092 B.C. - 2100 years = 9 A.D.
Israel saved by Joseph 1877 B.C. - 1910 years later   = 34 A.D.
Isaac born 2067 B.C. - 190 = 1877 B.C. - 1900   = 24 A.D.

Jacob's name changed to Israel 1907 B.C. - 1900 years = 7 B.C.
Jacob buys land for 100 shekels 1907 B.C. - 1900 years = 7 B.C.
Jacob's name changed to Israel 1907 B.C. - 1910 years = 4 A.D.
Jacob buys land for 100 shekels 1907 B.C. - 1910 years = 4 A.D.
Jacob born 2007 B.C. - 2000 years later   = 7 B.C.

Abraham circumcised 2068 B.C. - 2000 years later   = 68 B.C.
Isaac born 2067 B.C. - 2000 years later   = 67 B.C.

Nathanael reviewed the dates that he had come to thus far and was struck by the fact that three dates stood out: 7 B.C. five times; 33 A.D., three times; and 34 A.D., five times.

The date 4 A.D. appeared twice. All other dates appeared once, but 7 B.C., 33 A.D., and 34 A.D. appeared to be especially significant.

Was there more Biblical information? Was there further evidence that should be considered? In our next chapter we will look at Nathanael's further study.

Chapter 11
The Timing of Christ's First Coming Revealed

We are patiently attempting to discover if a careful Bible student who lived a few decades before Christ was born could have ascertained from the Bible (the Old Testament only would have been available to him), the possible date of the coming of the Messiah.

We, therefore, are trying to walk in the shoes of a mythical believer named Nathanael. What could he find in his Bible that would give him a clear idea as to when the Messiah would come?

Thus far in our study we have found that Nathanael would have been interested especially in three dates: 7 B.C., 33 A.D., and 34 A.D. (Remember that we are adjusting his calendar so that it agrees with ours.)

Nathanael found the year 7 B.C. especially exciting because it was a jubilee year; and 33 A.D. was especially significant because it identified with a provocative prophecy of the Old Testament - the seventy weeks of Daniel 9. The year 34 A.D. was especially outstanding because on six different occasions his calculations led to this year.

Nathanael was a careful and diligent student of the Bible. Therefore, he continued to come up with information. He was meticulous in his efforts to have Biblical authority for his conclusions. He began at important Biblical events that in themselves pointed to the coming Messiah and from there arrived at possible dates.

Nathanael knew, too, that Israel had entered the land of Canaan forty years after they left Egypt, in 1407 B.C., and that the entrance into the land of Canaan must be a picture of salvation or of entering the Kingdom of God. Therefore, the year 34 A.D. again showed itself to be important in connection with the dating of Messiah's coming for 34 A.D. was exactly 1440 years after 1407 B.C. (1407 + 34 - 1 = 1440).

Nathanael realized, too, that 1407 B.C. was 1400 years earlier than the jubilee year 7 B.C. He had learned from the Bible that the number seven symbolized the perfection of God's plan. The seven days of the week, for example, and the number seven was used in many ways in the temple service. He wondered, therefore, if the number fourteen, seven plus seven, symbolized the perfection of God's plan - even as twelve plus twelve symbolized the fullness of God's plan. It appeared that this could be true because the jubilee year 7 B.C. was exactly 1400 years after Israel entered the land of Canaan.

> *In enumerations of the tribes, one tribe was normally omitted so that the number twelve would result rather than the number thirteen.*

The Number Twelve

Nathanael was fully aware of the importance of the number twelve in the Bible, and he began to wonder if the number twelve played a role in providing a clue to the timing of the coming of the Messiah. Perhaps the most significant and important usage of the number twelve in the Bible was in connection with the tribes of Israel. Jacob was the father of the twelve sons after whom the tribes were named. Jacob's son Joseph was given a double inheritance so the tribe of Joseph became the two tribes of Ephraim and Manasseh. Thus, there were in actuality thirteen tribes. In enumerations of the tribes, one tribe was normally omitted so that the number twelve would result rather than the number thirteen. Most commonly the tribe left out of enumerations was the tribe of Levi from which the temple servants came; occasionally Levi was named and another tribe was omitted. As a result, the number twelve became symbolic of the fullness of God's plan, and in the case of the tribes of Israel, it indicated the fullness of believers.

Nathanael was aware that in Genesis 6, when God was getting ready to destroy the world with the Flood of Noah's day, God declared that the days of man were to be 120 years. Nathanael did not know whether this meant that 120 years after God made this pronouncement He would destroy the world or whether it had some other, deeper meaning. Nathanael did realize, however, that the statement was in character with the idea that the days of mankind on earth will be in accord with the fullness of God's plan.

He knew, too, that the number twelve either as twelve standing alone or as twelve plus twelve to give twenty-four was a common number and was utilized in connection with the temple service. For example, there were twenty-four courses of priests (I Chronicles 24), twenty-four courses of singers (I Chronicles 25), and of course, there were twelve months in the year (I Chronicles 27:1-15).

Nathanael became particularly interested when he discovered that Israel had left the land of Egypt in the year 1447 B.C. He knew that at the time Israel went out of Egypt the Passover was instituted. He knew, too, that the Passover pointed to the Messiah who was to come to offer Himself for the sins of the believers.

The year 1447 B.C. was 1440 years earlier than the jubilee year 7 B.C., and 1440 is made up of the numbers twelve times twelve times ten. Therefore, it was highly suggestive that in the fullness of time the Savior who would be the Passover Lamb would come. Indeed 7 B.C. continued to be a significant date for the coming of the Messiah.

Nathanael continued to ponder the significance of the number twelve as it related to the fullness of time, and he became intrigued by the timing of the death of Gideon, who judged Israel for forty years. Upon his death all but two of his seventy sons were ruthlessly killed by one of his sons, named Abimelech. Abimelech aspired to be king and killed his brothers so there would be no competitors for the throne. Effectively this act symbolized that Israel was dead. Israel appeared to be without hope, without a ruler or a redeemer. It was one of the darkest moments in the history of Israel. He had calculated from the Biblical information that Gideon died in the year 1207 B.C. (see page 307 ff).

Exactly 1200 years later - in the fullness of time - was the year 7 B.C. Again Nathanael realized that God could be showing that the jubilee year 7 B.C. was the year for the coming of the Messiah. In the perfection of time the Messiah would come.

Eleven Days' Journey

Nathanael became interested in a strange verse in Deuteronomy. The verse was Deuteronomy 1:2, which reads: "There are eleven days' journey from Horeb by the way of mount Seir unto Kadesh-barnea."

This was a puzzle. Mount Horeb was located in the Sinai wilderness. Kadesh-barnea was about 500,000 cubits (150 miles) north of Mount Horeb. What did the Bible mean that there was an eleven days' journey between these two points?

The verse was not speaking of a straight line between Mount Horeb and Kadesh-barnea. It spoke of going between these two points by way of Mount Seir. Mount Seir was Edom where the descendants of Esau dwelt. Therefore, it would be difficult to know with any accuracy what distance God had in view. When Nathanael searched the Bible to see if Israel travelled from Mount Horeb to Kadesh-barnea, he found that they had, but not in eleven days. If all the events that took place between these two points were considered, they must have taken many weeks or even several months to travel between these cities.

God does not make mistakes. Everything recorded in the Bible has a purpose. Surely a caravan could travel a distance of sixty or seventy thousand cubits (about twenty miles) a day, even if it probably was impossible for a nation of two or three million people with their cattle to travel anywhere near this distance.

As Nathanael pondered this verse he began to realize that perhaps God was teaching another truth by means of this verse. Mount Horeb was another name for Mount Sinai, and the law was given at Mount Sinai. God's law was not first enunciated on Mount Sinai, it was first enunciated in the Garden of Eden at the beginning of time. Mankind (Adam and Eve) were to care for the garden; they were to be fruitful and multiply. Negatively, they were to refrain from eating of the tree of knowledge of good and evil. Mount Sinai or Mount Horeb was where God enlarged on His law by making it more specifically applicable to the nation of Israel.

Kadesh-barnea, Nathanael knew, was the place just south of the land of Israel from where the twelve spies had been sent forth. Therefore, it was the place from which Israel was to enter the promised land (Deuteronomy 9:23). It identified with the coming Messiah since spiritually believers enter the promised land through the Messiah. Mount Seir, another name for Edom or the descendants of Esau, represented the people of the world who troubled and harassed the believers on the way to the promised land.

What about the eleven days? Nathanael realized that Psalm 90:4 said, "a thousand years in thy sight are but as yesterday." Could eleven days represent 11,000 years? Was God teaching in this verse that there were 11,000 years from creation to the coming of the Messiah? Was God saying that there were 11,000 years (eleven days) from creation (Horeb, where the law was given) to the Messiah (Kadesh-barnea, where Israel was to enter the promised land), by way of the world (Mount Seir)?

> *The passage of 11,000 years (from creation) came to 13 B.C. Was 13 B.C. a date to be remembered?*

Nathanael had previously discovered that the date of creation was 11,013 B.C. The passage of 11,000 years came to 13 B.C., which was surprisingly close to 7 B.C. Was 13 B.C. a valid date that must be considered or must something more be known?

Twenty-Three Years

Nathanael looked at another important date in relation to the creation date 11,013 B.C. It was the date of the flood that devastated the earth in the days of Noah. The flood began in the year 4990 B.C., 6023 years after creation. The event was so close to an even 6000 years from creation and yet it was twenty-three years off. Could it be that the twenty-three years was significant?

At the same time he noted that the flood date 4990 B.C. was so close to a multiple of an even 1000 years from the dates that kept appearing as dates for the coming of the Messiah. An even 5000 years after 4990 came to 11 A.D. Was this date significant?

The flood came 6023 years after creation. What would be the result if even as there were twenty-three years more than 6000 years from creation to the flood, twenty-three years were added to an even 5000 years following 4990 B.C., the year of the flood? What year was 5023 years after the flood? To his amazement he found that 5023 years after 4990 B.C. was the year 34 A.D. (4990 + 34 - 1 = 5023). He knew by this time that 34 A.D. had to be involved with the timetable of the coming Messiah.

If 34 A.D. did relate to the time of the coming Messiah, what did the twenty-three years represent? He had now discovered that from creation to the Flood equalled 6000 plus twenty-three years and from the flood to 34 A.D., which appeared to be involved with the coming of the Messiah, was 5000 plus twenty-three years. Could it be that he should add twenty-three years to 11,000 years to get another date for the coming of the Messiah? When he subtracted 11,023 years from 11,013 B.C. he came to 11 A.D. (11,013 + 11 - 1 = 11,023). Was 11 A.D. an important date in relation to the timing of the coming Messiah?

Nathanael began to search for more information concerning a time span of twenty-three years or concerning the number twenty-three. He found one outstanding place where twenty-three years was the end of an era: The end of the nation of Israel when they were destroyed by the Babylonians. In the year 609 B.C. the good king Josiah was killed. Immediately Israel became subjugated, first by Egypt and then by Babylon. Finally, in the year 587 B.C. Israel was destroyed; the temple was razed and the people were taken captive into Babylon.

The twenty-three years from 609 B.C. to 587 B.C. inclusive thus represented the final tribulation that the nation of Israel had to undergo before God's judgment upon them became complete.

In his study of the Book of Daniel, Nathanael had read about a future time when God's house would be destroyed and trodden under foot. Daniel 8:9-12:

> And out of one of them came forth a little horn, which waxed exceeding great, toward the south, and toward the east, and toward the pleasant land. And it waxed great, even to the host of heaven; and it cast down some of the host and of the stars to the ground, and stamped upon them. Yea, he magnified himself even to the prince of the host, and by him the daily sacrifice was taken away, and the place of his sanctuary was cast down. And an host was given him against the daily sacrifice by reason of transgression, and it cast down the truth to the ground; and it practised, and prospered.

In Daniel 8:23-25 Nathanael discovered who this little horn was. There God taught:

> And in the latter time of their kingdom, when the transgressors are come to the full, a king of fierce countenance, and understanding dark sentences, shall stand up. And his power shall be mighty, but not by his own power: and he shall destroy

wonderfully, and shall prosper, and practise, and shall destroy the mighty and the holy people. And through his policy also he shall cause craft to prosper in his hand; and he shall magnify himself in his heart, and by peace shall destroy many: he shall also stand up against the Prince of princes; but he shall be broken without hand.

The little horn was, therefore, a king who would come at the end of time. By comparing verses 9-12 with 23-25 Nathanael was assured that his earlier understanding that the sanctuary or temple was a figure or picture of believers was accurate.

Even more significantly these verses were teaching that at some future time - apparently right at the end of time when transgressions had reached their fullness - God would in some sense allow the congregations to be destroyed by this little horn. Thus Nathanael saw that history was to repeat itself. Israel was subjugated and destroyed by Babylon when the time ended for it to be an independent nation of God's people; and at the end of time, God's people will be destroyed by a king of fierce countenance.

Nathanael had read earlier of a king of fierce countenance in Deuteronomy 28. In Deuteronomy 28:49-51 he read:

The LORD shall bring a nation against thee from far, from the end of the earth, as swift as the eagle flieth; a nation whose tongue thou shalt not understand; A nation of fierce countenance, which shall not regard the person of the old, nor shew favour to the young: And he shall eat the fruit of thy cattle, and the fruit of thy land, until thou be destroyed: which also shall not leave thee either corn, wine, or oil, or the increase of thy kine, or flocks of thy sheep, until he have destroyed thee.

Nathanael knew that this prophecy was fulfilled in regard to the nation of Israel when the Babylonians - a nation whose tongue Israel did not understand - destroyed Israel in 587 B.C. They had been called a nation of fierce countenance.

In Daniel 8:23 God spoke of a king of "fierce countenance" who was to come. Therefore, Nathanael saw that the final destruction of the believers by a king of fierce countenance was typified by the final destruction of Israel by the Babylonians.

Nathanael wondered about this future event and noted that Daniel 8:13-14 gave a clue concerning the duration of time that God's people were to be subjugated by this king of fierce countenance, who was typified by Babylon. Nathanael read these verses:

Then I heard one saint speaking, and another saint said unto that certain saint which spake, How long shall be the vision concerning the daily sacrifice, and the transgression of desolation, to give both the sanctuary and the host to be trodden under foot? And he said unto me, Unto two thousand and three hundred days; then shall the sanctuary be cleansed.

The time God had decreed for the end-time tribulation was to be 2300 evening-mornings or 2300 days. Daniel 8:26 underscored that this was an accurate and literal duration of time, for there God informs:

And the vision of the evening and the morning which was told is true: wherefore shut thou up the vision; for it shall be for many days.

Nathanael recalled that God used the phrase evenings and mornings in Genesis 1 where He gave details of creation. Nathanael also knew from his previous study of the chronology of the beginning of the world (Chapter 1), that these were literal twenty-four hour days. Therefore, he knew, too, that he must understand the 2300 evenings-mornings of Daniel 8 to be literal days.

Nathanael immediately saw that the 2300 days furnished an additional link between the final destruction of national Israel and the final destruction of the body of believers at the end of time. The twenty-three in the twenty-three years during which Israel's final subjugation by Babylon took place identifies with the twenty-three that is found in the final 2300 days when the body of believers are trodden underfoot at the end of time.

Nathanael summarized what he had learned from Daniel 8 as it related to the final destruction of Israel by Babylon.

Israel's final subjection ended in 587 B.C.	The believers' final subjection at end of time
By a nation of fierce countenance (Deuteronomy 28:50)	By a king of fierce countenance (Daniel 8:23)
Time duration 23 years	Time duration 2300 days

When Nathanael calculated the duration of 2300 days, he saw that it was a little more than six years (about six years and four months). Thus the period of twenty-three years was intimately related to a period of six years (when 2300 days is rounded off to the nearest whole year).

With this in mind he looked again at the time relationships he had discovered that pointed to the coming of the Messiah. He saw that from the creation to the flood of Noah's day there were exactly 6000 plus twenty-three years. That is, there were even multiples of 1000 years plus the time span when God's final judgment would come on Israel.

Then Nathanael saw something that greatly excited him. When he went 11,000 years from creation in 11,013 B.C. and added to this the 2300 days - six years - that was symbolized by the twenty-three years of Israel's final tribulation, he came to the year 7 B.C., and 7 B.C. was the jubilee year that appeared to be the year in which the Messiah would be born.

Summarizing this data he could show that:

1) **Creation (11,013 B.C.) to the Flood (4990 B.C.) =**

6000 + 23 years

2) **Creation to the coming Messiah (7 B.C.) =**

11,000 years + 2300 days (6 years)

3) **Flood (4990 B.C.) to the coming Messiah (34 A.D.) =**

5000 years + 23 years

Surely God was focussing on the dates 7 B.C. and 34 A.D. by these number relationships.

The Number Eleven Again

While Nathanael continued to pray for wisdom concerning these number relationships as they related to the possible timing of the coming Messiah, he noted another special emphasis on the number eleven. God at times revealed the death ages of some of the patriarchs. Abraham died at the age of 175 (Genesis 25:7), Isaac at 180 (Genesis 35:28), Jacob at 147 (Genesis 47:28), Levi at 137 (Exodus 6:16), Moses at 120 (Deuteronomy 34:7), and Aaron at 123 (Numbers 33:39). These death ages were given with only one Biblical reference, but Nathanael discovered that there were two important men whose death ages were mentioned twice and both of these men lived equally long. Surely this must be significant.

It is true that in the accounts that gave the histories of the kings of Israel he found that many of the death ages of the kings were mentioned twice. This was because two kingdoms, Judah and Israel, existed simultaneously. One account detailed the history of these nations from Judah's perspective, and the other from Israel's perspective so there was duplication of information in I Kings through II Chronicles.

However, there were two men who lived at different times before Israel was divided into two kingdoms who not only had the unique distinction that their life spans were given in the Bible, but they had the even more unique distinction that their life spans were given twice. When Pharaoh dreamed about the seven fat and the seven thin cows and then about the seven fat and the seven thin ears of corn, Joseph, under the inspiration of the Holy Spirit, declared in Genesis 41:32:

And for that the dream was doubled unto Pharaoh twice; it is because the thing is established by God, and God will shortly bring it to pass.

Thus the doubling of the naming of the life spans of these two men appears to be significant.

The first man was Joseph. Nathanael discovered that in many ways Joseph appeared to be a figure or type of the coming Messiah. He was the one who saved Israel when they would have died of starvation. He was the one who had come out of prison to become the prime minister of Egypt, second only to Pharaoh, the highest ruler of the land. So, too, Nathanael knew that the coming Messiah would endure the wrath of God - the eternal prison of hell - and then would be highly exalted as King. Joseph's death age or life span is recorded in Genesis 50:26, where God declares:

So Joseph died, being an hundred and ten years old: and they embalmed him, and he was put in a coffin in Egypt.

And in Genesis 50:22 we read:

And Joseph dwelt in Egypt, he, and his father's house: and Joseph lived an hundred and ten years.

The second man whose death age was recorded twice in the Bible was Joshua. Nathanael realized that Joshua, too, must be a great figure or type of the coming Messiah. Joshua, whose name means "savior," was the leader who brought Israel through the Jordan River and into the promised land.

Nathanael found that Joshua, too, lived to be 110 years old and this fact was noted twice in the Bible. In Joshua 24:29 we read:

> And it came to pass after these things, that Joshua the son of Nun, the servant of the LORD, died, being an hundred and ten years old.

And we read in Judges 2:8:

> And Joshua the son of Nun, the servant of the LORD, died, being an hundred and ten years old.

Nathanael realized that this information concerning Joseph and Joshua had to be very important. Surely it could not be incidental nor accidental that two men, both of whom appeared to be types or figures of the coming Messiah, died at the age of 110, and in both instances their death age was given twice. This strongly suggested that whatever their death age represented, it surely was established by God and was certain to come to pass. Actually Nathanael realized that God had provided a double doubling:

> Joseph 110 years - twice given
> Joshua 110 years - twice given

God was truly calling attention to the 110 years as signifying the certainty of whatever God had in view.

When Nathanael remembered the eleven days of Deuteronomy, he knew the number eleven must relate to the coming Messiah. He knew from previous study of the number eleven that two years stood out importantly.

Creation (11,013 B.C.) less 11,000 years = 13 B.C.

Creation (11,013 B.C.) less (11,000 years + 2300 days) = 7 B.C.

The date 7 B.C. frequently appeared as Nathanael worked through the number patterns of the Bible to find clues that might relate to the time of the coming of the Messiah. Could it be that through the death ages of Joseph and Joshua, God was pointing to the timing of Messiah's coming? By doubling the record was He pointing to the certainty of the coming of the Messiah? Could it be that the life spans of these two men, who were types or figures of the coming Messiah, were utilized by God to provide a clue to the time of the coming of the Messiah?

While Nathanael thought about the significance of the number eleven, he noticed another interesting relationship. He remembered that the ark was taken into enemy hands in the year 1068 B.C. (See page 304.) This was an extremely terrible incident in the life of ancient Israel. The ark of the covenant, which was to be kept in the Holy of Holies in the tabernacle, was the most holy object Israel ever had. For it to have been captured by the Philistines was equivalent to God having left Israel. Exactly 1100 years later was the year 33 A.D. (1068 + 33 - 1 = 1100). Was this year somehow related to the Messiah being rejected of God as spoken of in Isaiah 53?

On the other hand 1100 years after the year 1067 B.C. when the ark was restored to Israel brings us to the year 34 A.D. Does the restoration of the ark relate in some way to the successful completion of the Messiah's work of saving Israel? Thus both the years 33 A.D. and 34 A.D. are again featured as years that possibly relate to the coming Messiah.

Nathanael now summarized the data he had gathered thus far. He discovered that he had arrived at (see page 356):

(see page 356)

The jubilee year 7 B.C. five times
The year 33 A.D. three times
The year 34 A.D. five times
The year 4 B.C. two times

Additionally, he found the following patterns:

Passover instituted 1447 B.C. - 1440 years later		= 7 B.C.
Israel entered Canaan 1407 B.C. - 1440 years later		= 34 A.D.
Israel entered Canaan 1407 B.C. - 1400 years later		= 7 B.C.
Gideon died 1207 B.C. - 1200 years later		= 7 B.C.
Creation 11,013 B.C. - 11,000 years later		= 13 B.C.
Creation 11,013 B.C. - 11,000 + 23 years later		= 11 A.D.
Creation 11,013 B.C. - 11,000 + 6 years later		= 7 B.C.
Flood 4990 B.C. - 5000 years later		= 11 A.D.
Flood 4990 B.C. - 5000 + 6 years later		= 17 A.D.
Flood 4990 B.C. - 5000 + 23 years later		= 34 A.D.
Ark taken 1068 B.C. - 1100 years later		= 33 A.D.
Ark restored 1067 B.C. - 1100 years later		= 34 A.D.

As Nathanael reviewed these dates, he saw that the jubilee year 7 B.C. was pointed to four more times, the year 33 A.D. one more time, and the year 34 A.D. three more times. Additionally the year 11 A.D. was pointed to twice.

When he added this summary to his previous summary of dates he saw the following:

7 B.C. a jubilee year	9 times
34 A.D.	9 times
33 A.D.	4 times
4 B.C.	2 times
11 A.D.	2 times

Additionally by means of his study of the number eleven he had found that he had considerable assurance that his previous study of the chronology of history was accurate. The unusual and mysterious verse 2 of Deuteronomy 1 especially assured him of this. In this verse God speaks of eleven days' journey from Horeb to Kadesh-barnea by way of Mount Seir. The verse became meaningful when he understood it to be teaching that the time span from creation to the coming of the Messiah was 11,000 years. Indeed these conclusions appeared to give added support to his previous Biblical conclusion that creation occurred in the year 11,013 B.C.

Nathanael's Analysis

Nathanael was now prepared to assess and interpret the data he had discovered that appeared to relate to the timetable of the coming Messiah.

First he saw that the earliest date, 7 B.C., was exceedingly prominent. Nine times the Bible had brought him to this year. Moreover, in itself this was an important year because it was a jubilee year. Surely this must be the year in which the Messiah was to be born. With so many paths coming to 7 B.C., and every path utilized Biblical data that in itself was related to the coming Messiah, there was no escape from the conclusion that 7 B.C. must be the year in which the Messiah was to be born.

Even if two or three of the paths Nathanael had analyzed should prove to be invalid for some reason, the remaining evidence was pervasive; it was clear and conclusive. Surely 7 B.C. was the year that the hope of Israel, the Messiah, would be born in Bethlehem as prophesied in Micah 5:2.

The second date that Nathanael reflected upon was 4 B.C. Two of his paths had come to this date, so it had far less significance than 7 B.C. If the Messiah were to be born in the year 7 B.C., then in 4 B.C., He would be three years of age. Would there be an important event in the life of the Messiah when He was three years of age?

The third date that Nathanael believed to be of possible significance was the year 11 A.D. He felt that this might be significant because it had appeared twice, as had the year 4 B.C. In the year 11 A.D. the Messiah would be 17 years of age. Was something special going to happen in His life at that age, as something very special (and very dreadful) had happened in the life of Joseph at that age? (See Genesis 37.)

The fourth date that Nathanael believed had great significance was the year 33 A.D. Four times it had appeared in his search. Because it identified directly and clearly with the timing of the coming Messiah as set forth in the seventy sevens of Daniel 9, he believed that this must be a date of great importance.

How was it important? The Messiah would become 39 years of age this year. That was the age of Joseph when he saved his brethren and his father Israel from starvation. Could it be that 33 A.D. somehow related to the actual Messiahship of the Messiah? That is, was 33 A.D. the year that the Messiah was to be cut off? Was it to be the year that

God would pour out His wrath on the Messiah because God had laid on Him our sins and iniquities? (See Isaiah 53:6.)

There was one more date that Nathanael had discovered concerning the timetable of the coming Messiah. It was the year after 33 A.D., the year 34 A.D. It had appeared nine times in Nathanael's search. How did it relate to the time of the coming Messiah? Was it possible that the Messiah would be cut off in 33 A.D. and return to heaven in 34 A.D.? Or was the punishment the Messiah was to endure for the sins of His people to encompass two years, 33 A.D. and 34 A.D.?

Nathanael could not find answers to these questions. In his search he was unable to discover why both 33 A.D. and 34 A.D. appeared so prominently. Possibly, he reasoned, it had something to do with a pattern God sometimes used in Bible revelation. For example, in Amos 2:1 God used the expression:

Thus saith the LORD; For three transgressions of Moab, and for four, I will not turn away the punishment thereof; because he burned the bones of the king of Edom into lime.

And in Proverbs 6:16 He states:

These six things doth the LORD hate: yea, seven are an abomination unto him.

Could it be that 33 A.D. and 34 A.D. were to be related to each other in some similar fashion?

Or was there to be something in 33 A.D. that would emphasize the saving character of the coming Messiah while something in 34 A.D. gave understanding of His kingdom?

Nathanael puzzled over these probabilities without coming to an answer. However, he knew that he had made many conclusive discoveries about the timetable of the coming Messiah.

First, he was certain that the Messiah would be born in the jubilee year 7 B.C.

Second, he was certain that by the year 34 A.D. the Messiah's atoning work would be finished.

Nathanael was certain of these conclusions because no significant date earlier than 7 B.C. had appeared, and no significant date later than 34 A.D. had appeared. Moreover a tremendous amount of the Biblical data had focused on 7 B.C., 33 A.D., and 34 A.D.

Furthermore, he knew that in his search he had been faithful to the Scriptures. He had not introduced any secular evidence. He had faithfully allowed the Bible to be its own interpreter.

He was assured that he knew what year the Messiah would come. He was content to know that no later than the fortieth year of the Messiah, His atoning work would be complete.

Nathanael's Conclusions Very Accurate

In our desire to discover if the Bible gives any clues concerning the timetable of the return of Christ, we have tried to learn all that we could from the Bible relative to the first coming of Christ.

To facilitate this study we have attempted to walk in the shoes of a mythical Jew named Nathanael who lived a few decades before the first coming of Christ. He was a serious and diligent student of the Bible (our Old Testament). He discovered conclusively that the Messiah would be born in the year 7 B.C. From our vantage point of having the New Testament as well as the Old Testament, we know that this conclusion was totally accurate. Let us see why this is so.

The Bible does not give us concrete evidence concerning the birth date of Jesus, but it gives us sufficient evidence to know the year it must have been. Even though we speak of the year 1980 A.D. as if Jesus was born 1980 years ago, we know that this cannot be. In Matthew 2:16, the Bible speaks of a Herod who, in his attempt to kill the baby Jesus, killed all the children of Bethlehem. The secular evidence is quite clear that this Herod died in the year 4 B.C.; therefore, Jesus must have been born before 4 B.C.[1]

Moreover, this Herod killed all the babies two years old and under, in accordance with the time he had ascertained from the magi as to when they first saw the star in their homeland. This indicates that Jesus could have been born two years earlier than the time the magi spoke to Herod. Thus the birth of Jesus could have been at least two years earlier than 4 B.C. Also, a period of time may have elapsed between the killing of the babies by Herod and his death. Thus, we may be reasonably certain that on the basis of this evidence concerning Herod, Jesus must have been born between 9 B.C. and 6 B.C.

From Biblical data discovered in previous chapters that repeatedly focused on 7 B.C., we know that Jesus must have been born in the year 7 B.C. The data is in accord with Daniel 9:25, which seems to imply that the Messiah would come in a jubilee year. Indeed, Nathanael had discovered the year that the Messiah would come by using only Biblical data.

Nathanael's concern for the years 4 B.C. and 11 A.D. had no basis. Nothing we can discover in the New Testament relates to Jesus at the age of 3 nor the age of 17. These two dates have no special significance for the coming of the Messiah.

What about 33 A.D. and 34 A.D., dates that were of great importance in Nathanael's study? We can be certain from the New Testament record that Jesus was crucified on the Passover in 33 A.D., and that forty days later He ascended to heaven. Therefore, 34 A.D. bears no relation to the actual coming of Christ.

Does this mean that our methodology of attempting to find Biblical clues concerning the return of Christ must be abandoned? Since much Old Testament data focuses on 34 A.D. as being importantly related to the first coming of Christ and yet Christ ascended to heaven in 33 A.D., does that invalidate the method we are using to discover clues to the timing of the return of Christ? It might appear to be so.

We cannot deny that Nathanael's study accurately predicted 7 B.C., and it was accurate concerning the importance of 33 A.D. Therefore, we are reluctant to conclude that our entire study is of no consequence. What are we to do with all this Biblical data that points to 34 A.D.?

> *The solution would not have been available to Nathanael but it is available to us.*

What About 34 A.D.?

Actually, there is a beautiful solution to this puzzle. The solution would not have been available to Nathanael but it is available to us. Let us discover what this is.

When the Julian calendar was prepared, two drastic errors were made. They are errors of such great magnitude that today we wonder how they could have occurred. The first is the fact that the timing of the birth of Christ was moved by seven years; the second is that in going from the Old Testament dates to the New Testament dates the year 0 was not included. By leaving out the year 0 it is impossible to have continuity between Old Testament and New Testament dates.

When we want to know the years that have passed between two dates we simply subtract to arrive at the answer. Thus, the number of years from 1940 to 1960 is twenty (1960 - 1940 = 20).

Likewise we would expect that to go from an Old Testament year to a New Testament year we would simply add the Old Testament date to the New Testament date. Thus we might expect that from 10 B.C. to 15 A.D. would be twenty-five years (10 + 15 = 25). But because there is no year 0, the actual number of years from an Old Testament date to a New Testament date is one year less than the calendar years. Therefore, an event that occurred in 10 B.C. happened twenty-four years before an event that took place in 15 A.D. (25 - 1 = 24). To put it another way, the last day in the year 1 B.C. is followed by the first day in the year 1 A.D.

These two errors were not isolated so that they impacted a small part of the world for only a brief period of time. The Julian calendar gave way to the Gregorian calendar, which has become the standard calendar for most of the world. Certainly every nation that has the Bible uses the Gregorian calendar. Therefore, these two errors are intrinsically identified with Bible chronology.

> *How is it possible that virtually the entire world is under the control of a calendar that has such blatant and obvious errors?*

How is it possible that virtually the whole world is under the control of a calendar that has such blatant and obvious errors as these two errors? How is it possible that such obvious errors were made?

When we realize that God rules the world, these difficulties can be explained. I am certain that these errors were incorporated into the calendar that most of the world uses because of the express intent of God.

Let us look for a moment at error number one, that Jesus was born in the year 0 instead of the year 7 B.C.

We have learned that David was a great type of Christ. He ruled over Israel for forty years, but there was a division in his ruling. The Bible informs us that he ruled for seven years in Hebron over a part of Israel. At the beginning of these seven years many people of Israel were still aligned with the house of Saul, who was the previous king. During these seven years David consolidated his rule until in the eighth year, when he was able to begin to rule over all of Israel from the holy city Jerusalem. He thus reigned for seven years from Hebron over part of Israel and for thirty-three years from Jerusalem over all of Israel.

This is a dramatic picture of the reign of Christ. Before the cross Christ ruled over a relatively small number of believers. After the cross Christ's rule extended to believers in every nation of the world.

Thus the period beginning with 7 B.C. and ending with 1 B.C. represents the Old Testament side of the cross. The period that begins with 1 A.D. and ends with 33 A.D. represents the rule of Christ on the New Testament side of the cross. Only because of the error that is built into our calendar do we see this significant relationship.

We see a similar relationship in connection with the circumcision of a Jewish baby. The baby was unclean for a period of forty days. This forty-day period was divided into two periods; one seven days long and one thirty-three days. This was because on the eighth day the baby was circumcised. This circumcision pointed specifically to the circumcision - the cutting off, the shedding of the blood - of the Lord Jesus Christ. Thus in the way that God guided and allowed our calendar to be developed, He emphasized this distinction between the Old Testament side of the cross and the New Testament side.

The following is a summary of the points that concern calendar error number one.

Old Testament side of Jesus' life	New Testament side of Jesus' life
7 B.C. to 1 B.C. inclusive	1 A.D. to 33 A.D.
David ruled from Hebron over part of Israel: 7 years	David ruled from Jerusalem over all of Israel: 33 years
Jesus ruled over few believers on Old Testament side of the cross	Jesus rules over believers from every nation on New Testament side of the cross

| Jewish baby unclean 7 days | Jewish baby unclean 33 days but at the beginning of these days he was circumcised |

We thus see that this error that was built into our calendar was not accidental nor incidental. It was part of God's plan by which He demonstrates His truths.

There is one other error in our calendar that is also there so that certain Biblical truths can be highlighted. It is the fact that there is no year 0.

The impact of this error is such that we are enabled to have two methods by which the passage of time between an Old Testament event and a New Testament event can be calculated.

As we have already seen there are twenty-four actual years between the time of an event that occurred in 10 B.C. and an event that occurred in 15 A.D. But there are twenty-five calendar years between these two events: ten years on the B.C. side and fifteen years on the A.D. side.

> *The actual years versus the calendar years provide the solution to the puzzle of both 33 A.D. and 34 A.D. appearing to be significant concerning the coming of the Messiah.*

The condition of actual years versus calendar years provides the solution to Nathanael's puzzle as to why 33 A.D. and 34 A.D. appeared to be significant years concerning the timing of the coming of the Messiah.

The paths that led Nathanael to focus on 34 A.D. actually focussed on 33 A.D. when calculated as calendar years. For example, the year 34 A.D. is actually 2100 years after the birth and circumcision of Isaac, which occurred in 2067 B.C. Nathanael had calculated correctly, but because there is no year 0 to obtain the actual passage of time from an Old Testament event to a New Testament event, the two years should be added together and then one is subtracted from the sum (2067 + 34 = 2101; 2101 - 1 = 2100 years).

To obtain the passage of 2100 *calendar* years, the Old Testament date is simply added to the New Testament date. Thus, since 2067 + 33 = 2100, we can see that from a calendar vantage point 2100 years after 2067 B.C. is 33 A.D.

The importance of this principle is very great. We saw that Nathanael had found three or four paths that led to 33 A.D. as the year that Christ was to be cut off. This was an accurate and correct calculation, for Christ was crucified in 33 A.D.

There were eight or nine paths that led Nathanael to 34 A.D. This year is not accurate because, as we know from our vantage point, no part of the atonement occurred in 34 A.D.

However, if we recognize that these eight or nine paths are to be understood as *calendar* years rather than actual years, then all of these paths come to 33 A.D. Add the eight or nine paths to the three or four paths that are based on *actual* years, and we have a total of eleven or twelve separate and distinct paths or sets of Biblical dates that assure us that the Messiah died in 33 A.D.

By allowing the development of a calendar with no year 0 between the Old Testament and the New Testament dates, God greatly increased the number of clues that point to the timing of the atonement. Let us once again set forth the data that can be found in the Bible.

Ezra taught the law of God in 458 B.C.
Seventy sevens or 490 actual years later   = 33 A.D.

Middle year of Daniel's 70th week   = 33 A.D.

David died 967 B.C.; 1000 calendar years later   = 33 A.D.

The foundation of the temple was laid 967 B.C.
1000 calendar years later   = 33 A.D.

David ruled for 40 years; 40 calendar years
after Jesus' birth in 7 B.C.   = 33 A.D.

Nation of Israel formed 2068 B.C.;
2100 actual years later   = 33 A.D.

Isaac born 2067 B.C.; 2100 calendar years later   = 33 A.D.

Israel entered Canaan 1407 B.C.;
1440 calendar years later   = 33 A.D.

Flood of Noah's day, 4990 B.C.;
5000 + 23 calendar years later   = 33 A.D.

Ark taken by Philistines in 1068 B.C.;
1100 actual years later   = 33 A.D.

Ark restored to Israel in 1067 B.C.;
1100 calendar years later   = 33 A.D.

We must note that each and every one of the above references identify with the unfolding of God's salvation plan. None has to do with the rise or fall of political empires or powers. Each time reference has a unique and important reference to some aspect of God's salvation plan. Even the duration of time that separates events has spiritual significance. Given the fact that:

The Number:	*Spiritually Signifies:*
2	the church
3	the purpose of God
4	universality
5	grace and judgment
7	perfection
10, 100, 1000	completion
11	the certainty of salvation coming
12	fullness
13	super fullness
21	3 x 7, which signifies the perfection of God's purpose
23	judgment
40	testing

How beautifully God controls the affairs of men so that His Biblical plans will work out! We have seen that God placed within the Old Testament tremendous clues, helps, and guideposts so that a thorough and careful student of the Bible could have known with great precision the year of Christ's birth. Moreover, the careful student could have known with an error of not more than one year the year of Christ's death.

The Bible declares that Jesus came in the fullness of time. Galatians 4:4-5 declares:

> But when the fulness of the time was come, God sent forth his Son, made of a woman, made under the law, To redeem them that were under the law, that we might receive the adoption of sons.

We have learned that in God's precise time line of history, by which God's salvation plan unfolds, there was to be a very definite time when Jesus would come. That could be only in the fullness of time; that is, it could be only at the moment that fit perfectly into God's program of history. That is why Christ came in the fullness of time.

Now we come to the big question. It is the question that we approach extremely carefully and extremely cautiously. Does the Bible likewise give clues and helps and guideposts that will tell us the year of Christ's return?

As further preparation for that study, we should come to an understanding of Daniel 12:12, which appears to relate to end time timing. As preparation for an understanding of that verse, we will look at Daniel 9:24-27. Our mythical Nathanael made reference to this passage earlier in our study. Now we want to explore these verses.

SUMMARY

We have learned how the years 7 B.C. and 33 A.D. relate to Christ's first coming. In the year 7 B.C., Jesus was born in Bethlehem; in 33 A.D., He went to the cross. The year 34 A.D. actually has no relation to the cross and is a miscalculation.

We have learned how several numbers in the Bible signify various truths. For example, the number twelve is symbolic of the fullness of God's plan and is illustrated in the twelve tribes of Israel. Numbers can be used in the Bible with certain variations to expand on the same truth, for instance, twelve plus twelve or twenty-four or 120.

The numbers eleven and twenty-three have also been studied to learn how they relate to major themes of the Bible. We have looked at Daniel 8 and discovered a lot of information about the little horn and evenings and mornings in relation to literal twenty-four hour days.

We have seen twelve paths that led from Old Testament events to 33 A.D., when Christ completed the atonement. The Old Testament events were milestones in the history of ancient Israel.

We have learned how God allowed two errors to be incorporated into our Gregorian calendar from the Julian calendar: The first is that the timing of Christ's birth was moved by seven years, and the second is that in going from the Old Testament dates to the New Testament dates the year 0 was not included. By leaving out the year 0 it is impossible to have continuity between Old Testament and New Testament dates.

As a result of all these discoveries, it has been shown that several decades before our Savior was born, a careful student of the Old Testament could have known when the Messiah was to come and when He would die. God has wonderfully placed these clues in His Word.

NOTE

[1] Jack Finegan, *Handbook of Biblical Chronology* (Princeton, New Jersey: Princeton University Press, 1964), 231.

Chapter 12
The Seventy Weeks of Daniel 9

One of the most intriguing passages of the Bible is Daniel 9:24-27. In this fascinating passage God presents to us a vision that He gave to Daniel declaring that certain events would take place during a period of seventy weeks. Scholars have worked long and hard to discover the import of these verses because they seem to offer a timetable concerning the coming of the Lord Jesus Christ.

Every student of the Bible who has any interest at all in prophecy has spent time trying to understand the seventy weeks of Daniel 9. Somehow we all sense that these verses have great significance in regard to the coming of the Lord Jesus Christ.

In understanding God's teachings in any part of the Bible, we know we have not arrived at a satisfactory conclusion until every phrase of the passage in question can be understood. It may be possible to find a solution that aligns with a few of the key phrases in a passage, but the conclusion is unsatisfactory if it does not harmonize with all the phrases of the passage. Moreover, the conclusion must harmonize with the other teachings of the Bible that relate in any way to the passage in question.

In this study we will suggest a solution to the seventy weeks that we believe meets the above criteria. Every phrase in these verses finds its logical place within this solution. The solution as a whole agrees with everything else the Bible offers insofar as the nature of God's salvation program is concerned, including the coming of Christ.

A most serious problem in interpreting this passage is to discover the meaning of the words of Daniel 9:25:

> Know therefore and understand, that from the going forth of the commandment to restore and to build Jerusalem unto the Messiah the Prince . . .

This event of the setting forth of a commandment to build Jerusalem appears to be the beginning point of the seventy weeks or sevens. (The Hebrew word translated "week" can also be translated "seven.") In order to obtain any light from the rest of the passage, we must determine when this commandment was given.

Who Built Jerusalem?

Most Bible students, theologians, and writers of commentaries understand the language of restoring and building Jerusalem to refer to a physical rebuilding of the literal city of Jerusalem. However, as we shall see, this kind of understanding is not required by the Bible nor is it possible to find a solution to the seventy weeks by this means. We shall discover that the key to the seventy weeks is to understand that the Bible frequently uses Jerusalem as a figure or type of Christ's body of believers. The command to restore and to rebuild, therefore, will be found to mean that the Word of God was proclaimed so that believers could come into the Kingdom of God. We shall develop this as we work out this study.

Is Nehemiah a Candidate?

One of the most commonly accepted beginning points for the seventy weeks is the year 445 B.C., when Nehemiah, who was the cup bearer for the Persian King Artaxerxes, asked the king for permission to go to Jerusalem to rebuild the walls; and in a period of fifty-two days he indeed did rebuild the walls of Jerusalem.

Nehemiah, however, is not a possible answer to our question as to when the seventy sevens were to begin. First of all, while King Artaxerxes gave Nehemiah permission to build the walls, he did not command the rebuilding of the walls. Moreover, nowhere do we read that God gave such a command either to the Persian king or to Nehemiah. Therefore, Nehemiah cannot be related to Daniel 9:25 where God states that a command was given. Furthermore, no matter how we try, we cannot go through the seventy sevens from a time standpoint and arrive at anything that properly relates to the coming of the Lord Jesus Christ.

There is one solution, beginning with Nehemiah, that has been suggested; namely, that we take all the days between 445 B.C. and 32 A.D., assuming 365¼ days in a year, and then divide this product by 360 days. By following this computation, we get exactly sixty-nine sevens, or 483 years of 360 days, from 445 B.C. to 32 A.D. One can read about this in almost any study on the seventy weeks of Daniel 9.

While this solution may seem interesting and intriguing, it does not appear valid. There is no place in the Bible where this kind of computation, wherein time is first calculated on the basis of 365¼ days in a year and then divided by 360 days, is utilized. Therefore, we have no Biblical authority for it.

Christ Was Crucified in 33 A.D.

Moreover, Christ was not crucified in 32 A.D. We know from the Bible that He was crucified in 33 A.D. In Luke 3:1, as God describes the preaching of John the Baptist, at the time Jesus was baptized, we read:

> Now in the fifteenth year of the reign of Tiberius Caesar, Pontius Pilate being governor of Judaea . . .

This piece of information gives us an historical time clue. We know from very accurate secular records that Tiberius Caesar began to reign alone in the year 14 A.D.[1] His fifteenth year was, therefore, 29 A.D. We also know, as we go carefully through the Gospel of John, that Jesus actually preached for about three and one half years. Since He was crucified at the Passover, which was observed in the spring of the year, His baptism would have been in the fall of a previous year. Thus, three and one half years following 29 A.D. brings us to 33 A.D., when He was crucified.

Furthermore, because of the moon phases that governed the timing of the Jewish feasts, the year 32 A.D. could not possibly have been the year He was crucified. The timing of the Passover Feast was related to the full moon. Only 30 or 33 A.D. were possible years that would agree with the timing of the Passover observed at the time Jesus was crucified.[2] Therefore, the Biblical evidence appears to point to 33 A.D. as the year that Christ was crucified. When we understand the seventy sevens of Daniel 9, we will see that it also shows us that 33 A.D. was the year of His crucifixion.

> *We must reject Nehemiah's activity in Jerusalem as being a solution to our problem.*

For all of the foregoing reasons, therefore, we must reject Nehemiah's activity in Jerusalem as being a solution to our problem.

Is King Cyrus a Possibility?

A second solution has been suggested by some. While it appears to be attractive in some ways, it also will not meet all the criteria demanded by Daniel 9. This solution involves a predecessor of Artaxerxes, a king named Cyrus, who defeated Babylon in 559 B.C. We read about him in II Chronicles 36:22-23:

> Now in the first year of Cyrus king of Persia, that the word of the LORD spoken by the mouth of Jeremiah might be accomplished, the LORD stirred up the spirit of Cyrus king of Persia, that he made a proclamation throughout all his kingdom, and put it also in writing, saying, Thus saith Cyrus king of Persia, All the kingdoms of the earth hath the LORD God of heaven given me; and he hath charged me to build him an house in Jerusalem, which is in Judah. Who is there among you of all his people? The LORD his God be with him, and let him go up.

Indeed, in 537 B.C. about 50,000 Israelites who had been captives in the land of Persia, as a result of the command given by God to Cyrus to rebuild His house in Jerusalem, did return to Jerusalem; and they did lay the foundation of the temple.

Significantly, this activity of Cyrus was predicted almost 200 years earlier by Isaiah. Under the inspiration of the Holy Spirit, he declared in Isaiah 44:28:

> That saith of Cyrus, He is my shepherd, and shall perform all my pleasure: even saying to Jerusalem, Thou shalt be built; and to the temple, Thy foundation shall be laid.

Thus we see that Cyrus meets two qualifications demanded by Daniel 9:25, namely, that the command was of the Lord and that the command concerned itself with the rebuilding of Jerusalem.

Unfortunately, for his candidacy to be considered as the beginning of the seventy weeks, there is one flaw. There is no possible way to relate the year 537 B.C., on a seventy week basis, with the Lord Jesus, who was baptized in the year 29 A.D. and crucified in the year 33 A.D. Thus Cyrus, as well as Nehemiah, must be set aside as a solution to Daniel 9:24-27.

Ezra Returns to Jerusalem

Now we must consider a third possibility, which, we shall see, meets all the requirements of Daniel 9. This solution relates to the return of Ezra to Jerusalem in the seventh year of King Artaxerxes. This was the year 458 B.C., at which time Ezra returned to Jerusalem to reestablish the law. While preaching the Word of God or teaching the law of God seems quite unrelated to building a city, we will see that the Bible does show us an intimate relationship between these two activities. Therefore, we will examine the Scriptures to show that a command to reestablish the law was indeed equivalent to a command to build Jerusalem.

Let us look at Cyrus again. As we study the language concerning him we will begin to see the close relationship that exists between the physical building of Jerusalem and the sending forth of the Gospel. While he was commanded to build Jerusalem and lay the foundation of the temple, the prophecy of Isaiah 44:28 quoted above speaks of Cyrus as God's shepherd. King Cyrus was not a shepherd. He was a king. When the Bible speaks of a shepherd, we immediately think of the Lord Jesus Christ, who was the Good Shepherd.

The fact is, while God is using the name Cyrus in Isaiah 44 and 45, and while in a physical sense the prophecy of Isaiah concerning Cyrus was fulfilled when the foundation of the temple was laid about 537 B.C., in another sense the language is pointing altogether to the Lord Jesus Christ. God is using Cyrus as a type or figure of Christ. Even as Cyrus, the king of the Persians, destroyed Babylon in 539 B.C., so Christ, typified by Cyrus, destroyed the kingdom of Satan by going to the cross. We know, of course, from such passages as Revelation 18, that the kingdom of Satan is typified by Babylon.

As Cyrus was commanded by God to build a literal house of God, so Christ was commanded by God to build a spiritual house. The temple and the city that He came to build is His body. We already see this in Isaiah 45:13 as God, in speaking of Cyrus, declares: "He shall build my city, and he shall let go my captives, not for price nor reward, saith the LORD of hosts." He goes on in verse 17: "Israel shall be saved in the LORD with an everlasting salvation."

Thus God is equating the building of a city with salvation, which is everlasting. We see, therefore, that when God speaks in the Book of Isaiah about Cyrus building a city and a temple, in its spiritual fulfillment God has in mind the Lord Jesus Christ, who builds Christ's body.

---

*The temple of God and Jerusalem
are figures of the body of Christ.*

The Body of Christ - A Temple and A City

The concept that the temple of God and Jerusalem are figures of the body of Christ is amply seen in the Bible. We read, for example, in Isaiah 60:14, where God speaks of Israel and the fact that peoples from the world will come to build its walls, "they shall call thee, The city of the LORD, The Zion of the Holy One of Israel." In this passage God equates Israel with a city.

In the New Testament we see the same truth as God uses the word Jerusalem. In Revelation 21 God presents the picture of the bride of Christ coming down out of heaven. Revelation 21:2 declares:

And I John saw the holy city, new Jerusalem, coming down from God out of heaven, prepared as a bride adorned for her husband.

The bride is called the Holy City, the New Jerusalem. The bride of Christ is a people - the people who are the body of Christ. The bride cannot be a physical city, and yet it is portrayed in Revelation 21 as a city with foundations, gates, and a wall.

Moreover, in the New Testament God speaks about building walls and building the ruins in the context of sending forth the Gospel. In Acts 15, for example, we have the account of the leaders of the New Testament church puzzling and wondering about what to do with the Gentiles who were coming into the body of Christ. Therefore, they held a council in Jerusalem to discuss this problem. Finally, it was James who stood up to speak on the phenomenon of the Gentiles coming in. He said in verses 15-17:

And to this agree the words of the prophets; as it is written,
After this I will return, and will build again the tabernacle of
David, which is fallen down; and I will build again the ruins
thereof, and I will set it up: That the residue of men might seek
after the Lord, and all the Gentiles, upon whom my name is
called, saith the Lord, who doeth all these things.

James, under the inspiration of the Holy Spirit, rightly saw that
the inclusion of the Gentiles in the body of Christ was a fulfillment of
Old Testament prophecies that spoke about the rebuilding of the walls
and the ruins of Jerusalem. The bringing of the Gospel is an effort to
build the city of Jerusalem.

We see the same figure in Ephesians Chapter 2, which speaks
of the believers as building blocks in the temple of God. We are not a
physical temple, of course, but in Ephesians 2:20-22, this is what we
read about the body of Christ:

And are built upon the foundation of the apostles and prophets,
Jesus Christ himself being the chief corner stone; In whom all
the building fitly framed together groweth unto an holy temple
in the Lord: In whom ye also are builded together for an
habitation of God through the Spirit.

In I Peter 2:4-5 God speaks of believers as lively stones in the house
of God.

> *This is the clue to help us break open
> the meaning of the seventy sevens of
> Daniel 9.*

In the Bible, God distinctly uses the figures of Jerusalem and
the temple as references to the body of believers. I believe this is the
clue with which we can break open, under the guidance of the Holy
Spirit, the seventy sevens of Daniel 9. This is the key to the correct
solution of these seventy weeks.

Unfortunately, most theologians get tangled up looking for a
command to rebuild a literal city. So often, in relation to salvation and
in relation to God's salvation program, we keep our eyes on this sin-
cursed world, and we do not look beyond it. We do not look at the true

nature of salvation. Salvation is concerned with something far more precious and exciting than this sin-cursed world. It has to do with the people of God, a salvation that is eternal in character. We are going to find that Daniel 9:25, in which God speaks about rebuilding Jerusalem, relates to bringing the Gospel. Then the seventy sevens can be understood in every detail.

Ezra's Bringing the Law Equals Building the City

Returning now to Ezra, you will recall that Ezra was commanded by King Artaxerxes, in the year 458 B.C., to reestablish the law in Jerusalem. We read in Ezra 7:12-13, 23, and 26 that King Artaxerxes declares:

> Artaxerxes, king of kings, unto Ezra the priest, a scribe of the law of the God of heaven, perfect peace, and at such a time. I make a decree, that all they of the people of Israel, and of his priests and Levites, in my realm, which are minded of their own freewill to go up to Jerusalem, go with thee.
>
> Whatsoever is commanded by the God of heaven, let it be diligently done for the house of the God of heaven: for why should there be wrath against the realm of the king and his sons?
>
> And whosoever will not do the law of thy God, and the law of the king, let judgment be executed speedily upon him, whether it be unto death, or to banishment, or to confiscation of goods, or to imprisonment.

Ezra 7:10 supplies the additional information: "For Ezra had prepared his heart to seek the law of the LORD, and to do it, and to teach in Israel statutes and judgments."

To reestablish the law is the equivalent of bringing the Gospel, and bringing the Gospel is the equivalent of building the city.

To reestablish the law is the equivalent of bringing the Gospel, and bringing the Gospel is the equivalent of building the city, as we have just seen. Therefore, God, through the king, had effectively given a command to Ezra to rebuild the city. This command agrees with the statement of Daniel 9:25, which places the beginning of the seventy weeks as the time when the command was given to rebuild the city. We therefore are on very safe Biblical ground to begin the seventy weeks at the year 458 B.C., when Ezra was given the command to reestablish the law in Jerusalem.

The fact is, that even Ezra himself, under the inspiration of the Holy Spirit, relates the teaching of the law to a literal building activity. While the foregoing verses in Ezra 7 indicate that Ezra, the priest of God, was first concerned with teaching the law of God, we might note that in Ezra 9:9, in his prayer concerning this command of God through King Artaxerxes, Ezra uses language that relates to normal building activity:

> For we were bondmen; yet our God hath not forsaken us in our bondage, but hath extended mercy unto us in the sight of the kings of Persia, to give us a reviving, **to set up the house of our God, and to repair the desolations thereof, and to give us a wall in** Judah and in Jerusalem.

From the foregoing we see that the command of God to King Artaxerxes, to send Ezra to reestablish the law in the year 458 B.C., meets all the requirements of Daniel 9:25, where it speaks about a command going forth to restore and to build Jerusalem.

Returning to Daniel 9, we read in verse 24:

> Seventy weeks are determined upon thy people and upon thy holy city, to finish the transgression, and to make an end of sins, and to make reconciliation for iniquity, and to bring in everlasting righteousness, and to seal up the vision and prophecy, and to anoint the most Holy.

We have learned thus far that the Holy City referred to is actually the people of God, but to what do the other phrases in this verse refer, and when do they find fulfillment?

An Exact Path Is Found to Satisfy Daniel 9:24

By answering the question as to when the phrases of Daniel 9:24 find fulfillment, we will also discover to what they refer. When did God finish the transgression on behalf of those who are being saved? When did He make an end of our sins? When did He make reconciliation for iniquity?

Immediately you say, "Why, it was at the cross, of course. Christ hung on the cross to pay for our sins. Anyone knows that. This verse is speaking about the cross." Yes, indeed, this verse is pointing to the cross. At the cross, Christ did make reconciliation for iniquity. He did make an end of our sins. He did undergo the judgment of God in order that we might be saved.

Does the timing of the crucifixion of Christ in 33 A.D. relate to 458 B.C.? Indeed it does! If we go from 458 B.C., when Ezra was mandated by King Artaxerxes to go to Jerusalem to reestablish the law (that is, to take the Gospel there or to build the spiritual city), to 33 A.D. when Christ hung on the cross to make atonement for sins, we will find that precisely 490 years are required. Let us see how this computation works out.

In going from the Old Testament to the New Testament, we must add the Old Testament years to the New Testament years, and subtract one to get the actual number of years between the two events.

Ezra to the Cross Equals Seventy Weeks

Ezra went to Jerusalem to build a city, that is, to reestablish the law, in the year 458 B.C. Christ hung on the cross in 33 A.D. If we add 458 to 33, the sum is 491. Subtract one from 491, and we end up with 490 actual years from the going forth of the command to rebuild the city to the time of the cross when Christ brought in everlasting righteousness, when He made reconciliation for iniquity, when He finished the transgression. It was at the cross that God put His seal on the vision and prophecy. And 490 years equal seventy weeks; that is, $70 \times 7 = 490$ years. Immediately we see the precise fulfillment of Daniel 9:24-25.

The phrase "seal up [or seal] the vision and prophecy [or prophet]" can be understood to mean that when Christ hung on the cross, God put His seal on the whole program of salvation and upon Christ as the Savior. It was the official declaration that God's salvation program was absolutely certain. The phrase "anoint the most holy" points to the cross, at which time Christ established His Kingship. The "most holy" is a phrase identified with the "holy of holies." Inasmuch as Christ is the sanctuary (John 2:19: Jesus answered and said unto them, Destroy this temple, and in three days I will raise it up), He is the One who is anointed in the sense of officially being our King as well as the everlasting Prophet and High Priest.

> *We see a direct path from when Ezra was commanded to reestablish the law, that is to rebuild the city, to when Christ hung on the cross.*

Four hundred and ninety years equal seventy sevens, as called for in Daniel 9:24. Therefore, we see a direct path from 458 B.C., when Ezra was commanded to reestablish the law, that is, to rebuild the city, until Christ hung on the cross. Thus we have discovered one certain solution to the seventy weeks of Daniel 9.

A Second Path to Christ

In Daniel 9:25-27, we are going to see that we have another path that leads to Christ. This time it does not lead to Christ hanging on the cross, but it leads to Christ coming in judgment at the end of time. This path begins at the same point as the first path, that is, at 458 B.C., when the command was given to reestablish the law. This path is more complicated because it is impossible to chart two events separated by almost 2,000 years by following a path that deals only with seventy sevens of years. There must be something more mysterious about this second path. Let us begin our study of these verses. In verse 25 of Daniel 9 we read:

Know therefore and understand, that from the going forth of the commandment to restore and to build Jerusalem unto the Messiah the Prince shall be seven weeks, and threescore and two weeks: the street shall be built again, and the wall, even in troublous times.

Immediately the question surfaces: Why does God divide this path into two parts, into seven weeks, which would be forty-nine years, and into sixty-two sevens, which would be 434 years? Why doesn't He simply say sixty-nine sevens? God does nothing accidentally. Everything in the Bible is carefully put there by God and has a very definite purpose. So we puzzle about this initial seven sevens and wonder what is significant about it.

> *All debts were canceled, . . . the land*
> *went back to its proper owners, and*
> *every Israelite was set free.*

First a Jubilee Period
The thought came to me years ago that seven sevens signifies a jubilee period. In Leviticus 25 we read about the jubilee year, which was to occur every fifty years. Thus between successive jubilee years there existed a period of forty-nine years, which is equal to seven weeks of years. The jubilee year was the year when all debts were canceled. It was the time when the land went back to its proper owners, and every Israelite who had been enslaved to another was set free. Since a period of seven sevens or forty-nine years was the period between two jubilee years, immediately I began to wonder: Is God saying that in this second path from 458 B.C. when Ezra went to Jerusalem to reestablish the law, that is, to build the spiritual city, the first period of time to be considered is a jubilee period? Is He using the phrase "seven weeks" to signify the period from one jubilee year to the next, so that we are to begin the next period of threescore and two weeks the year after a jubilee year?

Let us examine this possibility by first looking at the Biblical timetable of the jubilees. We shall see how this meshes with the language of Daniel 9:25, which suggests a jubilee period as the initial part of the second path leading from 458 B.C. to the second coming of Christ.

Let us determine which calendar years were jubilee years and then see how that relates to Ezra's return to Jerusalem. To determine which years were jubilee years, we must go back to the initial jubilee year. In Leviticus 25:2 God indicates that, at the time the nation of Israel was to come into the land of Canaan, they were to keep a Sabbath unto the Lord. He then continues in verse 8 that they were to "number seven times seven years," for a total period of forty-nine years. In Leviticus 25:10 God declares: "And ye shall hallow the fiftieth year, . . . it shall be a jubile unto you." Thus the fiftieth year after they entered Canaan would have been a jubilee year. With this knowledge, if we can determine the calendar year that Israel entered the land of Canaan, we will know which calendar years were jubilee years.

As we learned earlier (see Chapter 8), Israel left Egypt in the year 1447 B.C. and entered the land of Canaan in the year 1407 B.C. Remembering what we learned from Leviticus 25:2-10, we can therefore ascertain the date of the first jubilee year. Leviticus 25:2 declares that the year of entrance into Canaan was to be a Sabbath year. We have now determined that year to be the year 1407 B.C. This was to be followed by seven sevens of years, with the following year becoming the first jubilee year. That would have been the year 1357 B.C. (1407 - 50 = 1357). Thereafter, in every century, every year that ended in 07 or 57 was a jubilee year. For example, jubilee years would have been 1357, 1307, 1257, 1207, etc.

The Year Immediately Following Ezra's Return a Jubilee Year

Because we are interested in the period of time around 458 B.C. when Ezra returned to Jerusalem, when did the closest jubilee year occur? Of course, it was the year 457 B.C., which immediately followed 458 B.C. This certainly is encouraging to our study, is it not?

Since the last year of each seven of the seven sevens of years that made up the forty-nine years between two jubilee periods was a Sabbath year, we know that the year before each jubilee year was a Sabbath year. Thus the year 458 B.C. would have been a Sabbath year, while the year 457, which was a year ending in 57, would have been a jubilee year. Therefore, the concept that the initial period spoken of in Daniel 9:25 is to be considered a jubilee year is greatly strengthened by the discovery that Ezra returned to Jerusalem in a Sabbath year just before a jubilee period. Thus the seven weeks spoken of in Daniel 9:25 fits very logically with the idea of an initial jubilee period.

Going from the jubilee year of 457 B.C. to the next jubilee year, which would have been seven sevens of years or forty-nine years later, we come to 407 B.C. as the next jubilee year. The next period of sixty-two weeks would then have begun the next year after the jubilee year of 407 B.C. That would have been the year 406 B.C.

A Period of 434 Years Follows a Jubilee Period

The Bible speaks of a period of threescore and two sevens, or sixty-two times seven years. There is no suggestion of a break during this sixty-two sevens, which is a period of 434 years. Therefore, if we go in unbroken fashion through history for 434 years from the next year, 406 B.C., which immediately followed the jubilee period considered above, we come to the year 29 A.D. This arithmetic can be checked. First add the 406 years of the Old Testament to the 29 years of the New Testament. This sum equals 435. Then subtract one, because there is no year 0, and we arrive at 434 years, which is sixty-two times seven.

Thus far we have seen that God is giving us a path that begins with the command by King Artaxerxes to Ezra to reestablish the law in the year 458 B.C. God is saying that until the coming of the Messiah the Prince there should be seven sevens and sixty-two sevens. The seven sevens is a jubilee period, which follows 458 B.C., a Sabbath year. The first jubilee period signified by seven sevens is therefore the period beginning in the year 457 B.C. and ending in 407 B.C. Beginning then in the next year, 406 B.C., and going for 434 years, that is, for sixty-two sevens, we arrive at 29 A.D. as the year that ended the sixty-two sevens and begins the seventieth seven.

> *Christ was baptized 29 A.D. in the*
> *River Jordan.*

Jesus Was Baptized in 29 A.D.

This is becoming increasingly interesting because 29 A.D. is the year that Christ was baptized in the River Jordan. Thus we are already beginning to see that the computation called for in Daniel 9 identifies very clearly with the historical fact of the coming of the Lord Jesus Christ. You will remember when we followed the first path (in verse 24), without a break for seventy sevens or 490 years, we arrived at the year 33 A.D. as the end of the seventy sevens. Christ was crucified in the spring, that is, on Passover Day, in the year 33 A.D. He preached for approximately three and one half years, so it was three and one half years earlier that He was baptized in the River Jordan. At this time He officially began His role as High Priest, to offer the sacrificial lamb, which He Himself was. Going back three and one half years from the spring of 33 A.D. will take us to the fall of 29 A.D. But this is the same year that ends the sixty-two sevens, in accordance with the second path we have found in Daniel 9. You see how it is all beginning to tie together now? Verse 25 of Daniel 9, therefore, takes us to 29 A.D. Then verse 25 declares: "The street shall be built again, and the wall, even in troublous times."

God is indicating that there is going to be a rebuilding of Jerusalem. The Gospel is going forth again. Remember in this passage that the language referring to the building of Jerusalem is not speaking of a physical building; it is talking about building the body of Christ, the spiritual temple. Christ, of course, came not only as our sin bearer but also as a preacher of the Gospel (Luke 4:43-44).

In Daniel 9, verse 26, we read: "And after threescore and two weeks shall Messiah be cut off, but not for himself."

We know that three and one half years after 29 A.D. was 33 A.D., when Christ was crucified. Remember, 29 A.D. was the year that ended the sixty-two sevens. Then it was indeed after the sixty-two sevens, or after 29 A.D., that the Messiah was "cut off." In the language of the Bible, being "cut off" refers to being under God's judgment. Any time we read the phrase "cut off" in the Bible, we can be sure that it is speaking about being under the judgment of God.

Phrase by phrase, verse by verse, this is all beginning to identify precisely with the coming of the Lord Jesus Christ. He was not cut off for Himself; He was cut off on behalf of you and me. He came under judgment because of our sins. Christ was cut off, that is, He experienced God's wrath for our sins, in the year 33 A.D. This was after the year 29 A.D., which was the last year of the sixty-two weeks of Daniel 9:25.

Christ Crucified
Verse 26 goes on to say: "And the people of the prince that shall come shall destroy the city and the sanctuary." A lot of theologians think this refers to the destruction of Jerusalem in 70 A.D. because, as we saw before, they have in mind a physical, literal city, but remember, the key to this passage is that the city in view is not a literal city; it is the body of believers.

> *The Prince is the Messiah . . . the
> Prince of Peace.*

This passage speaks of the people of the Prince. The Prince that is referred to is the Messiah. He came as the Prince of Peace. He came as the King to die for our sins. When He hung on the cross, a sign over His head said: "JESUS OF NAZARETH THE KING OF THE JEWS" (John 19:19). Indeed He was the King. He established His Kingdom by going to the cross. The people of the Prince, that is, the Jewish nation, are the ones who made the decision to put Him to death. We might recall that it was the high priest Caiaphas who made the decision that Jesus must be crucified. In John 11:50, as he condemned Jesus to be crucified, he declared: "That it is expedient for us, that one man should die for the people, and that the whole nation perish not."

Christ Is The City and The Sanctuary

What are the city and the sanctuary that were to be destroyed by the people of the Prince who was to come? Maybe you have never thought of this before, but remember when Jesus was talking to the pharisees, He said, "Destroy this temple, and in three days I will raise it up" (John 2:19). What was Jesus speaking about when He said that? Did He have the physical temple in view? That is what the Jews thought. They said: "Forty and six years was this temple in building, and wilt thou rear it up in three days?" (John 2:20).

> *Jesus was speaking of His own body.
> He is the temple of God that was to
> be destroyed and rebuilt.*

Jesus was speaking of His own body. He is the temple of God that was to be destroyed and rebuilt. We do not want to fall into the same snare that the Jews fell into when Jesus talked about Himself being the temple. We do not want to begin to look for a physical temple here. It says in Daniel 9:26: "The people of the prince that shall come shall destroy the city and the sanctuary." Jesus said that He is the sanctuary. He is the temple that was to be destroyed and rebuilt in three days. Thus Daniel 9:26 is disclosing to us that the Jews, who were the people of Christ, would destroy Christ. Christ was the Prince that was to come. Christ was the Sanctuary that was to be destroyed.

Verse 26 also refers to the destruction of the city. To what or whom does this refer? Is this also a reference to Jesus? Indeed it is, as we shall see.

Remember that even as Christ calls Himself the temple, He calls His body, the believers, the temple. Our bodies are temples of the Holy Spirit. We are built into a holy temple, as we read in Ephesians 2. That is easy to say, is it not? He is the head of the church, the body of believers; and if He is the temple, we are the temple.

By the same token, since He is the head of the body of believers, if the believers are a city of God, He is the city of God. We have already seen that the Bible speaks of believers as being the city of God. This is shown dramatically in Revelation 21, where God speaks of the whole body of believers, the bride of Christ, as the Holy City, the New Jerusalem.

If we are the city of God, then Christ as our head is the city. He is the temple; we are the temple. He is the city; we are the city. If we are a city and we are "in Christ" as we read so frequently in the Bible, then Christ is also a city. See, too, Isaiah 62:12, where Christ is called "A city not forsaken." Thus verse 26, of Daniel 9, which speaks of the city being destroyed, also points to the crucifixion of Jesus.

Daniel 9:26 Predicts Christ's Death on Our Behalf

We can see now how we are to understand Daniel 9:26. "After threescore and two weeks," that is, after the 434 years that ends in the year 29 A.D., "Messiah shall be cut off." That is, He was crucified after He was baptized in 29 A.D. It was three and one half years later, three and one half years after the 434 years. He was cut off by "the people of the prince," that is, the pharisees, the Sanhedrin, and the high priest, who headed up the nation of Israel. It was they who would "come and destroy the city and the sanctuary." They caused Jesus to be crucified.

Verse 26 of Daniel 9 also declares, "but not for himself," or not because of His sins. He was crucified on our behalf. He took upon Himself our sins. Therefore, He had to come under the wrath of God.

Daniel 9:26 then declares: "And the end thereof shall be with a flood, and unto the end of the war desolations are determined." When the Bible talks about a flood, it is talking about the wrath of God being poured out. We see this figure in Genesis, Chapters 7 and 8, where God details the flood of Noah's day. Then God's wrath was poured out by the flood, through which He brought judgment against the wicked of that day. Likewise, when Christ hung on the cross, God poured out His wrath on Him to pay for our sins. Judgment Day at the cross was typified by the flood of Noah's day.

The phrase "unto the end of the war" of course makes reference to the warfare that exists between the Kingdom of Christ on the one hand and the kingdom of Satan on the other. That warfare continues to the end of time in one sense. Revelation 19, therefore, describes the conclusion of that warfare as a great battle. The battle will be Judgment Day, when all of Christ's enemies are judged and removed into hell.

The end of the war also refers to the cross, for it was at the cross that Christ defeated Satan. Hebrews 2:14 declares that Christ by His death destroyed Satan. At the end of the world we will see Satan and all his kingdom completely destroyed.

Now you are beginning to wonder, "What about the seventieth seven?" Let us go on with the study and see how that period of seven years fits into place.

Christ Confirms His Covenant

Let us begin to unravel verse 27 of Daniel 9. There God declares that He shall confirm the covenant with many for one week or one seven. How are we to understand this phrase? Who is "He"? What covenant is it that He will confirm? Who are the many with whom He will confirm this covenant?

Many theologians stumble on this verse. They suggest that the "he" is the antichrist, who will make a covenant with the Jews. Moreover, they insist that this verse is concerned with the tribulation period that must come, as prophesied in Matthew 24:21.

In Daniel 9, verses 25 and 26, we saw that God was talking about the Prince who was to come, who could be only the Messiah. Therefore, the antecedent of the "He" that shall confirm the covenant can be only the Messiah of verses 25 and 26. There is no suggestion in these verses that the "He" of verse 27 could be the antichrist.

Furthermore, we shall see that this verse cannot be discussing the final tribulation period because shortly we will see that sacrifice and offering ceased in the middle of the week, and that can refer only to the time when Christ was hanging on the cross. It was at that time that He completed the ceremonial laws and ended sacrifices and offerings.

The Covenant of Salvation is in View

Ordinarily in the Bible when God is speaking of a covenant, He has in view God's covenant of grace or redemption that He made with believers. The word "covenant" in the Old Testament is the Hebrew word "berith." It is found some 280 times in the Old Testament. Sometimes it is translated "league," as for example when one political nation makes a league with another nation, but more than 87% of the time that it is used in the Old Testament, it definitely relates to the covenant of grace or the covenant of salvation. It actually is a word that is synonymous with the word "Gospel."

In the New Testament the word "covenant," which is also translated "testament," is the Greek word "diatheke." It is found thirty-three times in the New Testament, and in every instance it relates to the covenant of salvation.

> *Christ went to the cross so that*
> *God's covenant of grace or salvation*
> *might become effective for all who*
> *would believe on Him.*

For example, when Jesus instituted the Lord's Supper, He declared in Matthew 26:28, "For this is my blood of the new testament." In Romans 11:27 God quotes from the Old Testament as He explains why a remnant chosen by grace was coming into the body of Christ from national Israel. There He declares, "For this is my covenant unto them, when I shall take away their sins." Hebrews 12:24 declares, "Jesus the mediator of the new covenant." Again, Hebrews 13:20 speaks of the "blood of the everlasting covenant." These references to the covenant can be speaking only of Christ, who went to the cross so that God's covenant of grace or salvation might become effective for all who would believe on Him.

When Jesus stood on the shore of the River Jordan, John the Baptist looked at Him and said, "Behold the Lamb of God, which taketh away the sin of the world" (John 1:29). Christ came as the Lamb to confirm the covenant.

Going back to Daniel 9:27, God indicates that He shall confirm the covenant with many. The many for whom Christ came to confirm His covenant of salvation are those He came to save: "Thou shalt call his name JESUS: for he shall save his people from their sins" (Matthew 1:21). "For even the Son of man came . . . to give his life a ransom for many" (Mark 10:45).

From the above we can see that the phrase we are studying has no Biblical validation for the suggestion that it is antichrist who will make some kind of covenant. Moreover, we see that it emphatically relates to the covenant of grace, which is the theme of the whole Bible.

As we have seen, the end of the sixty-second week of Daniel occurred in 29 A.D., when Jesus was baptized. It was at that time, as the Holy Spirit came upon Him, that He was officially anointed High Priest; He was officially declared to be the Messiah. It was also that year that became the beginning of the seventieth week. Therefore, we see that everything is fitting into place exactly as it should.

Thus we must come to the conclusion that when verse 27 declares, "he shall confirm the covenant," the "he" is the Lord Jesus Himself. The covenant is the covenant of grace, and, of course, He came to give His life a ransom for many (Matthew 20:28). Therefore He confirmed the covenant for many.

What about the rest of the seventieth seven? If we go from 29 A.D. for seven years, we end up at about 36 or 37 A.D., but the Bible tells of nothing significant happening in these years. Maybe we are on the wrong path after all. Let us continue to study verse 27 and see.

Sacrifice and Offering have Ceased

The Bible says, in the second phrase of Daniel 9:27, "And in the midst of the week [that is, for half of the seven] he shall cause the sacrifice and the oblation to cease." This is a tremendous statement, which offers a clue that we are on the right path. God is declaring by this language that in the midst, or in the middle, or for half of the seventieth seven, sacrifice and offering will cease. This important piece of information must be faced in any possible solution to the seventy sevens of Daniel 9.

> *There is only one time in history when sacrifice and offering ceased, and that was when Jesus hung on the cross.*

Consider: There is only one time in history when sacrifice and offering ceased, and that was at the cross. When Jesus hung on the cross, the veil of the temple, that huge veil some fifty feet high and several inches thick, which separated the holy of holies from the holy place, was rent in two from top to bottom. That is, it was rent by God. Never again would the holy of holies be a place where only the high priest could go to meet God. The whole business of sacrifices ended. The whole Old Testament priesthood ended with Christ going to the cross. Never again would there be blood sacrifices. Oh, it's true that the Jews for a number of years after this continued to offer blood sacrifices, but insofar as God's plan is concerned, these sacrifices had no meaning whatsoever.

Sacrifices were offered almost from the beginning of time: Abel offered a blood sacrifice; Noah offered a blood sacrifice. It was further articulated on Mount Sinai when God gave all the commands about blood sacrifices and burnt offerings. All these sacrifices were pointing to "The Sacrifice," the Lord Jesus Christ Himself. By His death, He completed all the burnt offerings and blood sacrifices. Never again would the sacrifice of any animal or a burnt offering have meaning in God's timetable. Christ completed all of this. Never again will we come under the ceremonial law.

Therefore, when Daniel 9:27 indicates that for half the week, or in the midst of the week, sacrifice and offering will cease, we know that 33 A.D. is in view. But 33 A.D., the spring Passover Day when Christ hung on the cross, when sacrifice and offering ceased, was three and one half years later than 29 A.D. Remember it was 29 A.D. when the sixty-two sevens ended, and Christ was officially designated as the Messiah, as John the Baptist declared, "Behold the Lamb of God, which taketh away the sin of the world" (John 1:29).

---

*The seventieth seven began with
Christ's baptism in 29 A.D.*

Can you see, dear friend, that the seventieth seven began with Christ's baptism in 29 A.D., and three and one half years later, at the end of the first half of the seventieth seven, sacrifice and offering ceased because Christ hung on the cross? Therefore, we now have a very clear path from the giving of the law in 458 B.C., when Ezra went to reestablish the law, that is, to rebuild the spiritual city, right to the cross, insofar as the first sixty-nine and one half sevens are concerned.

The End of the Seventieth Week

What about the last half of the seventieth seven? Let us read again Daniel 9:27:

> And he shall confirm the covenant with many for one week: and in the midst of the week he shall cause the sacrifice and the oblation to cease, and for the overspreading of abominations he shall make it desolate, even until the consummation, and that determined shall be poured upon the desolate [or upon the desolator].

Of what is this speaking? It is giving us information that after the cessation of sacrifice and offering, which would have to be 33 A.D., there would be a time of the overspreading of abominations. That sounds like the events that will occur just before the end of time. When we study the Bible we find that near the end of time Satan is loosed to deceive the nations (Revelation 20). At the end of time, the rebellion comes. We read about this in II Thessalonians 2, in relation to the man of sin, who takes his seat in the temple. Jesus tells us in Matthew 24 that at the end of time wickedness will multiply. This is the time of the overspreading of abominations. This is the time of the final tribulation that we have been studying.

> *The last half of the seventieth seven goes from the cross to Judgment Day and the end of time.*

The overspreading of abominations is to be followed by the consummation. It will be followed by the determined end, the determined decree, that shall be poured upon the desolator. It is at the end of time that Judgment Day will come, at which time God's judgments are poured out upon the unsaved and upon Satan. This is the consummation, the time of the decreed end. Therefore, God is declaring here that the last half of the seventieth seven goes all the way from the cross, when sacrifice and offering ceased, to Judgment Day itself, at the end of time.

The Prerogative of God to Use Numbers as He Desires

We might begin to argue right at this point, "Now wait a minute! You just can't do that! It's one thing to try to see a jubilee year as a solution to the first seven weeks. And it is possible to see a spiritual building as a solution to the language relating to the building of Jerusalem. However, to use literal years from the commandment to Ezra until Jesus' death on the cross, and then call the whole New Testament period, from the cross to Judgment Day, a period of three and one half years, that is asking too much. To go from literal years to some kind of symbolical use of numbers all in the same passage, that does not seem believable."

Indeed, our human logic may say all of this, but we must remember it is God who wrote the Bible. I did not write the Bible and neither did any other human speaker or teacher or preacher write the Bible. We have to sit very humbly under the teaching of the Bible and let God show us what He had in mind.

As a matter of fact, you will notice in Daniel 9:24-27 that God does not say there are seventy weeks of *years*. Rather, He says there are seventy weeks. He is not indicating whether they are years or some other unit of time. While it is true that in the first path we followed in going from Ezra to the cross, seventy weeks was indeed a period of 490 years; in the second path we followed the initial period was a jubilee period. This was so, as we have seen, inasmuch as a jubilee period comes after each and every seven weeks or forty-nine years. Thus God points us to a jubilee period by the reference to seven weeks. Therefore, the actual transpired time before the sixty-two weeks began was the period 458 B.C. to 407 B.C., which is a period slightly longer than that which would result if we were to stay strictly with years.

Likewise, as we look at the last half of the seventieth week, we are under no stricture insofar as the language of Daniel 9:27 is concerned to insist on literal years. Rather, we have to search the Bible to let it tell us what this period is. As we have seen, verse 27 clearly shows that it is the period 33 A.D., when Christ hung on the cross, to Judgment Day at the end of time. Later we will see that God reinforces the fact that the last half of the seventieth week is indeed the New Testament period. This will be seen by the language found in Revelation 11 and 12.

Judgment Day is the End of the Seventy Weeks
In order to arrive at the two ends of time under the figure of seventy weeks, one at the cross and one at Judgment Day, obviously, God has to do something special with the numbers. It is God's province, it is God's prerogative, it is God's right to take the last half of the seventieth seven and make it cover the whole New Testament period.

> *To arrive at the two ends of time . . . God has to do something special with the numbers.*

We know this last half of the seventieth seven must begin at the time of the cross because that is when sacrifice and offering ceased. This path must go from the cross all the way to the end of time because Daniel 9:27 declares that the seventieth seven ends with the time of the overspreading of abomination and the determined end, or the decreed end, being poured out upon the desolator or the desolate. That time is Judgment Day and the end of time.

Judgment Day Signifies that the Atonement has been Completed
The end of time, when Judgment Day occurs, is also the time when our salvation is completed. Remember, verse 24 speaks about seventy sevens that begin with the building of Jerusalem and end with

the finishing of transgression, the end of sins, the making of reconciliation and the bringing in of everlasting righteousness. Christ completes our salvation when He returns in judgment.

> *The Bible says that we are saved, but the Bible also says that we will be saved.*

       The Bible says that we are saved, but the Bible also says that we will be saved. We are saved in the sense that we have received our resurrected souls, but we have not yet received our resurrected bodies. That will occur at the completion of our salvation. Then He will have finished transgression in a total way. Then He will have made an end of sins in a total way - not only an end of our sins but also an end of the sins of the unsaved - in that they will have been cast into hell. Then He will have made reconciliation for iniquity, not in the sense that He went to the cross, but in the sense that He will have given us our redeemed bodies. He will have reconciled the rest of us to Himself. Our bodies, as they go into the grave, are unsaved, but they will be resurrected perfect spiritual bodies. This is the ultimate completion of what God has in view. Therefore, we see that both paths fit all the language of Daniel 9:24-27.

Further Evidence

       When we study Revelation 11 we find further evidence that shows us that the period of time from the cross to Judgment Day is symbolized in the Bible by the figure of three and one half years. We might recall that in Daniel 9:27 God is saying that the last half of the seventieth seven is the whole New Testament period, from the cross until Judgment Day, or until the return of Christ on the last day. One half of seven years is three and one half years, which God speaks of spiritually as 1260 days. That is precisely the time period that Revelation 11:3 is talking about: "And I will give power unto my two witnesses, and they shall prophesy a thousand two hundred and threescore days, clothed in sackcloth."

       Study of these two witnesses shows that they must be the New Testament church because Revelation 11:4 speaks of them as olive trees, a figure also found in Romans 11, where it is used in speaking of the body of Christ. Revelation 11:4 also declares that they are the two candlesticks standing before the God of the earth. In Revelation 1 and 2 God shows us that every congregation, every church, is represented in heaven by a candlestick. God speaks of two witnesses because He says: "In the mouth of two or three witnesses shall every word be established" (II Corinthians 13:1). Thus these two witnesses are a representation of the New Testament church as it brings the Gospel.

The Church brings the Gospel during the Last Half of the Seventieth Week

Because the Bible is one cohesive whole, God reaches back to Daniel 9:27 and picks up the time period that is the last half of the seventieth seven, the time period from the cross to Judgment Day at the end of time, and uses that figure here in Revelation 11:3, where He declares, "They shall prophesy a thousand two hundred and threescore days, clothed in sackcloth." This period of time as we saw from Daniel 9:27 is the whole New Testament period. Do we see the beautiful symmetry, the marvelous cohesive oneness of the Bible? It all begins to tie together, does it not? Once we find the key, the clue phrases, we see how it ties together.

> *When the temple is completed, that is, when all who are to become saved have become saved, then the end will come.*

You will remember in Daniel 9 we saw that the city and the temple refer to Christ, or to His body, the church. That is the same figure used in Revelation 11:1, where God speaks about measuring the temple of God. The temple is the body of Christ that is being measured. In Revelation 11:1 we read: "Rise, and measure the temple of God, and the altar, and them that worship therein."

Earlier in our study (page 235), we learned that this verse relates to the fact that God's time line of history is the unfolding of God's salvation plan. Thus when the temple is completed, that is, when all who are to be saved have become saved, then the end will come. It is during the 1260 days spoken of in Revelation 11:3, a period of time that is approximately three and one half years and which identifies with the last half of the seventieth week of Daniel 9, that the Gospel is sent out into all the world.

We read in Revelation 11:3 that the two witnesses are clothed in sackcloth. Even though we become kings because we have become sons of God at the time of salvation, we live on this earth as our Savior lived. We read of Him that He was meek and lowly of heart. So, too, we are to be most humble servants of God, ministering to the spiritual needs of men and women who are living under the wrath of God. To be clothed in sackcloth also emphasizes the sorrow of our hearts as we witness to a world dying in their sins. But it is a world wherein very few respond to the glorious salvation message whereby they can be rescued from eternal damnation.

Revelation 12 also Relates to Daniel 9

In Revelation 12 God again picks up the figure of a half week with the language of verse 6:

And the woman fled into the wilderness, where she hath a place prepared of God, that they should feed her there a thousand two hundred and threescore days.

The woman in view in this verse can be shown to be the believers from whom Christ was born. Christ is shown to be the man child in Revelation 12:5. There the Bible speaks of the woman giving birth to a child whom we know to be Christ. When He was caught up unto God, that is, He ascended into Heaven, the woman, whom we might also call the New Testament Church, continues in the wilderness, where she is nourished by God.

The wilderness is a figure taken from the Old Testament. You will recall that the Israelites left the land of Egypt and spent forty years in the wilderness before they entered the promised land, the land of Canaan. That wilderness sojourn again is the whole New Testament period. We will have crossed the Jordan River and entered the land of Canaan in the fullest sense of the word at the end of time when we receive our resurrected bodies. The 1260 days is the figure that God uses as being equivalent to three and one half years. God has again reached back to Daniel 9:27 to show that this is the New Testament period.

We see, therefore, in these two chapters of Revelation, that God has given us beautiful validation of the concept taught in Daniel 9:27 that the last half of the seventieth week is the period from the cross to Judgment Day.

Now we want to examine Daniel 12:12, which builds on the information we have learned from Daniel 9:24-27.

> *This verse is written in a book of the Bible that has much to say about end time events.*

The Exact Timetable of Jesus' Ministry Prophesied

In Daniel 12:12 God gives us a remarkable prophecy that we must carefully examine if we are to appreciate the information in the Bible that relates to God's timetable for His salvation plan and for the world itself. This verse declares:

Blessed is he that waiteth, and cometh to the thousand three hundred and five and thirty days.

Because this verse is written in a book of the Bible that has much to say about end time events, for years I have tried to relate this verse and its reference to 1335 days to the timing of the end. However, no matter how I tried, I was unsuccessful in relating it in any meaningful way with the end of time.

Truth concerning this verse began to dawn when I started to wonder if these verses related to the first coming of Christ. Could it be that the word "he" in this verse is a reference to Jesus Himself? He would be the blessed one. He would be the one who must wait to come.

Why must Christ *wait* to come? Couldn't He have come whenever He decided to come? The answer is No! As we have learned, God has a very carefully planned timetable for all of history. This timetable is tied very securely to God's salvation plan. The coming of Christ is the greatest event in this salvation plan, but His coming had to fit precisely into this timetable. Therefore, Jesus had to *wait* for the exact time when this timetable called for Him to come. That is why Galatians 4:4-5, which we looked at earlier, indicates that Jesus came in the **fullness of time**.

What then is the period of 1335 days for which he must wait to come? Examining the 1335 days in the light of what we know concerning the timetable of Christ's first coming, it was not difficult to see this as a possibility. In our study of Daniel 9:27, we learned that the time from the baptism of Jesus to the cross was approximately three and a half years. We learned that it was at Jesus' baptism that He officially began His work as the Messiah and that sacrifice and offering ceased in the middle of a week of seven years. We learned that the only time sacrifices ended was at the cross when Jesus sacrificed Himself for our sins. If the middle of the week meant precisely three and a half years then that equals 1279 days, but 1279 days is short of 1335 days. It is obvious that more time is required to come to 1335 days. Could it be that the middle of the week was an approximation? But then the Bible would have said "*about* the middle of the week."

Then I remembered that Jesus had one more task to do that distinctly related to the Atonement: That was the sending of the Holy Spirit. We read in John 16:7-8:

> Nevertheless I tell you the truth; It is expedient for you that I go away: for if I go not away, the Comforter will not come unto you; but if I depart, I will send him unto you. And when he is come, he will reprove the world of sin, and of righteousness, and of judgment.

The Holy Spirit was, of course, poured out at Pentecost in 33 A.D. Pentecost was fifty days after the cross. Fifty days added to an exact three and one half years gives us a span of time equal to 1329 days. This is only six days less than 1335 days. Daniel 9:27, which speaks of the Messiah being cut off, does not appear to be insisting on an exact half year of 183 days and it would appear that we have discovered what God had in mind with the 1335 days. However, by studying the Bible more carefully we will find the three and one half years are a very exact time.

If we start with the 1335 days prophesied in Daniel 12:12, we can reconstruct the timing of events that preceded Pentecost. The last fifty days of the 1335 days was the period from the Saturday of the crucifixion to Pentecost. Six days earlier than this was the Sunday we call Palm Sunday. On this day the time of the atonement was officially announced as having come. Jesus came into Jerusalem and was proclaimed a king. This precipitated all of the required events that brought Christ to the cross a few days later. Such actions as the evidences of the hatred of the pharisees and the betrayal by Judas brought to reality Christ's crucifixion. Therefore, the Sunday we call Palm Sunday and the crucifixion are inseparably connected, both occurring in the month Nisan.

Moreover, we read in Exodus 12:3 that on the tenth day of Nisan the Passover Lamb was to be selected. It was to be killed on Nisan 14. In the year 33 A.D. when Jesus became our Passover Lamb, the tenth day of Nisan began at sundown on Sunday and continued until sundown on Monday. In Mark 11:9-11 God identifies Palm Sunday with the tenth day of Nisan, which began at sundown on Sunday. Mark 11:9-11 says:

> And they that went before, and they that followed, cried, saying, Hosanna; Blessed is he that cometh in the name of the Lord: Blessed be the kingdom of our father David, that cometh in the name of the Lord: Hosanna in the highest. And Jesus entered into Jerusalem, and into the temple: and when he had looked round about upon all things, and now the **eventide** was come, he went out unto Bethany with the twelve.

Please note that the activities of Palm Sunday came to a close in the evening, thus tying the day to Nisan 10 when the Passover Lamb was selected. Therefore, Palm Sunday is intimately identified with the cross in that it was the day when Jesus effectively announced that the atonement was at hand - the Passover Lamb that was to be killed had been selected.

If we now recognize that Palm Sunday occurred exactly three and a half years after Jesus was baptized, the timetable is as follows:

1.	Jesus' baptism to Palm Sunday	3 years	=	1096 days
		½ year	=	183 days
2.	Palm Sunday to cross			5 days
3.	Cross to Saturday in tomb			1 day
4.	Saturday of crucifixion to Pentecost			50 days
			Total	1335 days

To the very day, this prophecy was fulfilled.

This 1335 days is the exact number prophesied in Daniel 12:12. To the very day, this prophecy was fulfilled.

When we examine the 1335 days we can pinpoint that period on the calendar. The end of it is as we have seen on Pentecost in 33 A.D. In an examination of the Jewish calendar for 33 A.D., we find that Pentecost was May 24. (Remember that all dates are Jerusalem time.) We know that this is an accurate date because of the great amount of Biblical evidence that points to 33 A.D. as the year of the cross. When we examine the Jewish calendar for 33 A.D., we find that the timing of the Passover agrees perfectly with the Biblical information that identifies with the timing of the Passover.

Therefore, we can be quite certain that Pentecost occurred on May 24, 33 A.D. But what date in 29 A.D. was exactly 1335 days earlier than this? It would be interesting to know if Jesus was baptized on any kind of special day insofar as new moons or other feast days are concerned.

When we attempt to use the Jewish calendar to exactly determine feast days such as the Passover and Pentecost for years other than 33 A.D., we are unable to know whether we have been given an accurate date or a date that is as much as two days off. This is because the rabbis decided that the first day of Tishri, which is the Feast of Trumpets in the Bible or Rosh Hashanah in the Jewish calendar, must be changed up to two days if it falls on certain days. The first day of Tishri, which is the seventh month of the Jewish calendar, should be a day of a new moon. This is called for in the Bible. Therefore, the Jewish calendar is a lunisolar calendar in which each month begins with a new moon. However, because there are twenty-nine and one half days in a Jewish month and this cannot be easily divided into a year of 365¼ days, each Jewish month begins on a different day of our calendar (the Gregorian calendar).

To complicate matters further, under certain circumstances, Tishri 1 was shifted as much as two days to allow for certain circumstances set forth by the rabbis. We read in a book that describes the Jewish calendar:

In addition to being neither a pure lunar calendar nor a pure solar calendar, the Jewish calendar is not a pure lunisolar calendar either. The Rabbis, in order to prevent the holiday of Yom Kippur from falling on a Friday or Sunday, to prevent the holiday of Hoshana Rabba (the 7th day of Sukkot) from falling on the Sabbath, and to fulfill their requirement that there be no less than 353 days in an ordinary year nor more than 385 days in a leap year, declared that the start of the month of Tishri (whose first day is Rosh Hashanah) can be postponed up to two days beyond the new moon of the month of Tishri.

The reason given by the Rabbis for the Friday-Sunday prohibition is to prevent a Sabbath (Yom Kippur is considered to be a Sabbath) from falling two days in a row. Moreover, the Rabbis did not want Hoshana Rabba to fall on a Sabbath because the ancient "Beating-of-the-Willows" ceremony associated with this holiday could not take place. They determined that there are five lunar events that can cause violations of these requirements. The start of Rosh Hashanah is postponed whenever a new moon of the month of Tishri occurs in one of the five following ways:

1 If the new moon of Tishri falls on a Sunday, Wednesday, or Friday of any year, then Rosh Hashanah is postponed one day.

2 If the new moon of Tishri falls at or after noontime on any day of the week, then Rosh Hashanah is postponed one day.

3 If, as a result of #2, the start of Tishri is postponed to a Sunday, Wednesday, or Friday, then Rosh Hashanah is postponed one more day.

4 If the new moon of Tishri, in a year following a leap year, falls on a Monday after approximately 9:32 A.M., then Rosh Hashanah is postponed one day.

5 If the new moon of Tishri, in a non-leap year, occurs on a Tuesday between approximately 3:11 A.M. and noon, then Rosh Hashanah is postponed two days.[3]

Obviously, therefore, we cannot obtain precisely accurate information from a Jewish calendar unless we have a very great understanding of all the above rules.

However, according to astronomical calculation we can discover precisely how accurate the Jewish calendar is. For the year 29 A.D. when Jesus was baptized, the true date of His baptism is September 28, whereas the Jewish calendar would show September 29. Therefore, to obtain true dates for 29 A.D., all of the Jewish calendar dates must be shown as one day earlier. September 28, therefore, is the date that begins the 1335 days of Jesus' ministry.

The computation of the 1335 days of Jesus' ministry works out as follows:

No. of Days in Calendar	No. of Days Toward 1335 Days
Three years: 9/28/29 to 9/27/32 inclusive	
(3 x 365.2422) = 1095.7266	1096
September 28-September 30	3
October 31 (32 A.D.)	31
November 30 (32 A.D.)	30
December 31 (32 A.D.)	31
January 31 (33 A.D.)	31
February 28 (33 A.D.)	28
March 31 (33 A.D.)	31
April 30 (33 A.D.)	30
May 1-May 24 incl. (33 A.D.)	24
	1335

Please note that three days are included for September. This is because the day of the baptism of Jesus, which was September 28, was also a day identified with Jesus' work on earth, which began with His baptism. Also the 24th of May is included because that was the date when Jesus sent the Comforter, who is the Holy Spirit.

Interestingly, September 28, 29 A.D. is a very special date. This is because September 28 is Tishri 1 and Tishri 1 is the date of the Feast of Trumpets. Concerning this day, we read in Leviticus 23:23-25:

> And the LORD spake unto Moses, saying, Speak unto the children of Israel, saying, In the seventh month, in the first day of the month, shall ye have a sabbath, a memorial of blowing of trumpets, an holy convocation. Ye shall do no servile work therein: but ye shall offer an offering made by fire unto the LORD.

We can be certain that it was on this special day of the Feast of Trumpets that Jesus was baptized.

We can be absolutely certain that it was on this special day of the Feast of Trumpets in 29 A.D. that Jesus was baptized. We can be absolutely certain because God had prophesied hundreds of years earlier in Daniel 12:12 that "Blessed is he [the Messiah] that waiteth, and cometh to the thousand three hundred and five and thirty days." How precisely the Bible gives information!

The Hebrew word in Daniel 12:12 that is translated "come" in the King James Bible is used very interestingly in another place. More common Hebrew words translated "come" are "yarad," "yatsa," "bo," "nagash," "qarab," and "alah." But the word "come" used in Daniel 12:12 is the Hebrew word "naga." The same word "naga" is translated "touch" more than ninety times in such phrases as "the soul that shall touch any unclean thing" (Leviticus 7:21) and "an hand touched me" (Daniel 10:10). But this same word "naga" is also translated "come" in a few places. One of these places is extremely interesting because it is used in connection with the observance of feast days. This citation is Ezra 3:1, where we read:

> And when the seventh month was **come**, and the children of Israel were in the cities, the people gathered themselves together as one man to Jerusalem.

The word "come" is the Hebrew "naga" even as it is in Daniel 12:12. In Ezra 3:6 God adds the words:

> From the first day of the seventh month began they to offer burnt offerings unto the LORD. But the foundation of the temple of the LORD was not yet laid.

These verses historically relate the experiences of Israel in Ezra's day. Spiritually they must point to Jesus, who laid the foundation of the spiritual temple - the whole body of believers - by going to the cross. The historical event recorded in Ezra 3 is, therefore, a portrait pointing to the baptism and announcement of Jesus as the Lamb that would take away the sins of the world. Both in Ezra 3 and in Daniel 12:12 God is focussing on Tishri 1. Three and one half years later, the foundation of the temple would be laid by Jesus experiencing God's wrath.

Since the word "come" used in both Ezra 3 and Daniel 12:12 ordinarily signifies "touch," we can know that Daniel 12:12 is teaching that Christ as the blessed one had to wait for the fullness of God's timetable before He could come to, or be in touch with, the 1335 days, which was the period of time when Jesus did all of His work as

Savior. It began on Tishri 1 or the Feast of Trumpets in 29 A.D. and ended 1335 days later on May 24, 33 A.D., when the Holy Spirit was given at Pentecost. How beautiful and harmonious is the Word of God. How trustworthy are all the prophecies and numbers of the Bible.

The Birth of Jesus

In a discussion of dates that relate to Jesus, it might be profitable to try to discover the date of the birth of Jesus. We know very conclusively that He was baptized on the day of the Feast of Trumpets 29 A.D. We know conclusively that He was crucified on Friday, Nisan 14, our April 3, 33 A.D., which was the first day of the Passover. We also know that He poured out His Holy Spirit on Sunday, May 24, 33 A.D. All of these dates are key feast days and, of course, relate to Jerusalem time.

But what about His birth? Can we learn something about that?

The Bible does not speak directly about His birth date nor about His birth year. However, we have already learned in this study that there is a great amount of circumstantial evidence that points to 7 B.C. as the year of His birth. In fact, in our earlier study of Daniel 9:25-27, we saw that the Bible says in Daniel 9:25:

Know therefore and understand, that from the going forth of the commandment to restore and to build Jerusalem unto the Messiah the Prince shall be seven weeks, and threescore and two weeks: the street shall be built again, and the wall, even in troublous times.

We learned that this first seven weeks of years was a jubilee period of fifty years, which was to be followed by sixty-two weeks of years or 434 years. We learned that it was in 458 B.C. that Ezra was commanded to bring God's Word to Jerusalem, which was the spiritual equivalent of building Jerusalem. The jubilee period that began in 457 B.C. and ended in 407 B.C. together with 434 continuous years beginning in 406 B.C. brought us to 29 A.D., when Jesus officially began His work after He was baptized.

The language of Daniel 9:25 declares that from the going forth of the command to build Jerusalem until the Messiah the Prince shall be seven weeks, which strongly implies that Jesus would be born during a jubilee year and in fact might even be born on the Day of Atonement when the jubilee year was begun. We read in Leviticus 25:9:

Then shalt thou cause the trumpet of the jubile to sound on the tenth day of the seventh month, in the day of atonement shall ye make the trumpet sound throughout all your land.

> *We might find that Jesus was born*
> *on or about the Day of Atonement*
> *that ushered in the jubilee of 7 B.C.*

Based on this information, we might even find that Jesus was born on or about the Day of Atonement that ushered in the jubilee of 7 B.C.

To begin our search we must examine the Bible to find any other verses that could possibly give us information concerning the timing of His birth.

We read in Luke 1:35-36:

And the angel answered and said unto her, The Holy Ghost shall come upon thee, and the power of the Highest shall overshadow thee: therefore also that holy thing which shall be born of thee shall be called the Son of God. And, behold, thy cousin Elisabeth, she hath also conceived a son in her old age: and this is the sixth month with her, who was called barren.

These verses suggest that Jesus was conceived about six months after John the Baptist was conceived in the womb of his mother, Elizabeth. Since the ordinary period of pregnancy is about nine months, the conception of John the Baptist was about fifteen months before the birth of Jesus. Thus if we can determine when John the Baptist was conceived, we would also have a fairly good idea of when Jesus was born.

In Luke 1:5 we read:

There was in the days of Herod, the king of Judaea, a certain priest named Zacharias, of the course of Abia: and his wife was of the daughters of Aaron, and her name was Elisabeth.

Zacharias was the father of John the Baptist, and in this verse we learn that in his priestly duties he was of the course of Abia. In I Chronicles 24 we discover that the divisions of the priests were twenty-four, that is, the priesthood was divided into twenty-four courses. In verse 10, we read: "The seventh to Hakkoz, the eighth to Abijah."

Thus Zachariah being of the course of Abia or Abijah served in the eighth course. These courses followed one another throughout the twelve months of the Jewish calendar. Since there were twenty-four courses in all, two courses would have served in each month with the eighth course ending its service at the end of the fourth month.

That we might understand this correctly, God has given us information, in I Chronicles 27, concerning the armed services. They were divided into twelve courses with 24,000 men in each course. God informs us that the captain of each course was assigned to one month's service. We read for example in I Chronicles 27:5:

The third captain of the host for the third month was Benaiah the son of Jehoiada, a chief priest: and in his course were twenty and four thousand.

Thus we are quite sure that in similar fashion the eighth course, that of Abijah, would have ended at the end of the fourth month of the Jewish calendar.

Returning to Zacharias, we read in Luke 1:23-24:

And it came to pass, that, as soon as the days of his ministration were accomplished, he departed to his own house. And after those days his wife Elisabeth conceived, and hid herself five months . . . .

This verse suggests that the conception of John the Baptist occurred shortly after the fourth month of the Jewish calendar. From Luke 1:36 we have learned that it was in the sixth month of Elizabeth's pregnancy that Mary was told that she would be with child of the Holy Spirit. Therefore, the conception of Jesus by the Holy Spirit probably took place near the end of the tenth month or early in the eleventh month of the Jewish calendar.

According to the Jewish calendar, the end of the tenth month was January 2, 7 B.C. Jesus then would have been born about nine months of our time after January 2, 7 B.C. Thus, His birth would have been late in September or early in October of 7 B.C.

A look at the Jewish calendar for the year 7 B.C. shows that the Day of Atonement was October 4. Furthermore Tishri 1 or the Feast of the Trumpets was September 24, and the Feast of Tabernacles was October 9 to October 16. Thus, Jesus could have been born on or about the Feast of the Trumpets, on or about the Day of Atonement, or on or about the Feast of Tabernacles. Because of the language of Daniel 9:25 the most likely date for the birth of Jesus is October 4, the Day of Atonement, when the Jubilee Trumpet was sounded.

We can analyze His birth date in a slightly different way. The last day of the fourth month in 8 B.C. was July 8 according to our calendar. We are probably correct in concluding that Elizabeth became pregnant soon thereafter, possibly as early as July 15. If that were the case, then her son John was born on or about April 15, 7 B.C. We know it was a full term birth because Luke 1:57 records: "Now Elisabeth's full time came that she should be delivered; and she brought forth a son."

We also know that Mary spent about three months with Elizabeth for we read in Luke 1:56: "And Mary abode with her about three months, and returned to her own house." Additionally, at the time Mary was told she would be with child by the Holy Spirit, the angel declared to her in Luke 1:36: "And, behold, thy cousin Elisabeth, she hath also conceived a son in her old age: and this is the sixth month with her, who was called barren." In verse 39 we read that "Mary arose in those days, and went into the hill country with haste, into a city of Juda" to visit Elizabeth. On the basis of these pieces of information, we suspect that Mary was close to three and one half months with child at the time she returned home from her visit with Elizabeth.

The sequence of events would have been as follows:
1. John the Baptist was conceived about July 15, 8 B.C.
2, Jesus was conceived 5½ to 6 months later or about Jan. 1, 7 B.C.
3. Mary arrived for 3-month visit with Elizabeth about Jan. 15.
4. Mary left Elizabeth after John was born, about April 15.
5. Jesus was born about 9 months after Jan. 1, which is about Oct. 1, 7 B.C.

As we have already learned, the Day of Atonement, which began the jubilee period for 7 B.C., was October 4. Therefore, Jesus would have been born on or near the Day of Atonement.

In examining the question of the birth date of Jesus, we have not tried to discover with precise accuracy the date of the Day of Atonement. This is so because we have not found sufficient information in the Bible to become that precise. We do know, however, that the Jewish calendar for 7 B.C. is within two days of being completely accurate. Therefore, we have not sought further astronomical calculation.

In any case we can understand in the historical sense why Mary and Joseph found no room in the inn. Jerusalem and all the neighboring communities were filled with Jews who had come from all over the land of Israel to celebrate the feast days of the seventh month.

I want to leave this thought with you as we talk about making reconciliation for iniquity. What about your sins? Have your sins been paid for? Have you repented of your sins and abandoned yourself to the Lord Jesus Christ, so that you know that this Gospel, which we are talking about, refers to you, too? This is a very important question, and I trust that as we continue our study, you will be so exercised that you, too, if you are not already saved, will cry out to God for His mercy.

SUMMARY

Thus far in our study of Daniel 9 we have looked at the seventy weeks referred to in verses 24-27, and we have seen that the key that unlocks the mystery of this period of time is to remember that the command to restore and build Jerusalem signified the reestablishment of the law in Jerusalem. To put it in New Testament language, it has to do with the sending forth of the Gospel. Whenever we present the Gospel to anyone, whenever we are witnessing for the Lord Jesus Christ, we are temple builders. We are city builders, building the city of God. Therefore, we should not be surprised to find in Revelation 21 that the whole body of Christ is actually pictured as the Holy City, the New Jerusalem.

When we studied Daniel 9:24-27 we saw that these verses can be understood if we realize that the beginning of the time referred to here relates to Ezra, a priest of God, who had been mandated by the Persian King Artaxerxes, in the year 458 B.C., to establish the law in Jerusalem, that is, to build the spiritual city. Exactly seventy weeks of years later, that is, seventy times seven or 490 years later, in the year 33 A.D., Christ hung on the cross. There He finished the transgressions, that is, He paid for the sins of all who believe on Him. He made reconciliation for iniquity and He brought in everlasting righteousness. Only because He went to the cross can we know everlasting life. Only because Christ went to the cross can we be covered by Christ's righteousness so that our sins no longer stand against us. So, verse 24 has given us a distinct path of 490 years, beginning in 458 B.C., to the time of the cross, which was in 33 A.D.

We saw that there is another path that goes from 458 B.C. that also brings us to Christ, but it is more complex. It began with a period of fifty years, or a jubilee period called seven sevens of years. This was followed by a period of 434 years, bringing us to 29 A.D. Thus we see that the seventieth seven, the last seven of years, began in 29 A.D., when Christ was singled out as the Lamb of God who came to take away the sins of the world. This is when Christ was baptized, and He officially began His work as Messiah.

It is imperative that we remember, as we make this study, that the Bible is its own interpreter. We must let the Bible give us the clues and the keys whereby we can understand difficult Scriptures. We cannot just look at the Scriptures and say, "Well, that looks like so and so. That seems to make sense; let's go on from there." We have to make sure we have Scriptural justification for the conclusions we believe we receive from the Bible. In this study we have seen that the Holy City is the body of Christ, or the body of believers. We have also seen that the sanctuary and the city are a picture or figure of Christ Himself. There is ample Scriptural justification for this. We have seen that, having learned this, these verses of Daniel 9 begin to open up very beautifully.

So far in our study of Daniel 9:24-27, we have seen that every phrase in this intriguing passage begins to make sense when we have the key. Once we discovered the major clue, that the city and the sanctuary discussed in these verses are not a literal city and a literal temple, these verses began to open up for us. We discovered that the city and the sanctuary refer to Christ Himself or to His body, the believers in Him who will hear the Gospel or hear the law of God and thus become saved. Once we discovered this we began to see that every phrase in this passage began to fit into place.

We see, therefore, a beautiful parallel, a beautiful cohesiveness in Daniel 9:24-27. There are two paths, both of which begin at the same point in 458 B.C. and both of which end with the coming of Christ. Both end with Judgment Day. One was the first coming of Christ and the Judgment Day at the cross, when Christ paid for the believers' sins. The second is the coming of Christ on the last day, when the unsaved and Satan and his evil hosts will be judged for their sins.

Finally, we briefly looked at Revelation 11 and 12 and saw that God used the figure of 1260 days to signify the New Testament period from the cross to Judgment Day. And 1260 days approximates three and one half years. It surely became obvious that this figure of time was taken from the last half of the seventieth week of Daniel 9.

May it be that this study will encourage us all to continue our search of the Scriptures, knowing that under God's gracious provision, truth can slowly develop for us.

NOTES

[1] Jack Finegan, *Handbook of Biblical Chronology* (Princeton, New Jersey: Princeton University Press, 1964), paragraph 425, page 273.

[2] *Ibid.*, paragraph 459, page 296.

[3] Fred Reiss, *The Standard Guide to the Jewish and Civil Calendars* (West Orange, New Jersey: Behrman House, Inc., 1986), vi.

Chapter 13
The Year of Christ's Return
Begins to Unfold

Thus far in our study we have discovered the truth that God had hidden within the Old Testament sufficient clues and guideposts so that a very careful student of the Bible, who lived decades before the birth of Christ, could have discovered the exact year that Christ was to come. We have found that the Bible has given a great abundance of clues that point to the year of Christ's first coming. Because we know when Christ did come we are able to know the validity of these clues.

> *The question that is shouting at us is: Can we know from the Bible the year that Christ will return?*

In this chapter we will pursue the logical question that is shouting at us: Can we know from the Bible the year that Christ will return? Can it be that hidden in the Bible God has given clues concerning the timing of the second coming of Christ? Certainly we have learned much about how to evaluate potential clues.

In this study we are greatly helped by what we learned from the work of our mythical Nathanael. By following the same principles we should not run the risk of abusing the Bible. Of course, because we only want truth, we know we want to let the Bible guide us. Under no circumstances do we want to force a verse to make it say something it does not.

As we continue, we will find many paths that home in on a certain year that looks increasingly like the year of Christ's return. Each of these paths is somewhat circumstantial in character. Even though they become exceedingly plausible because they constantly bring us to the same year, we would never dare to say that we have found absolute truth. We have to admit that we could have overlooked something in the Bible that could invalidate our conclusions.

There are a number of truths concerning the future that are absolute in character, and we should look at them before we proceed with our study. These truths are not debatable. We can argue about the timing of Christ's return and the end of the world, but we can not argue about these truths that are so clearly set forth in the Scriptures. They are all based on absolute declarations of the Bible. These truths alone should make every individual examine himself and his relationship with God, for every human being must face God and give an account of his life.

Absolute Truths that Must Be Remembered

When we think of the return of Jesus Christ and the end of the world, we must consider the following statements to be absolute truths.

1. Jesus is coming again. In Matthew 24:30 we read:
And then shall appear the sign of the Son of man in heaven: and then shall all the tribes of the earth mourn, and they shall see the Son of man coming in the clouds of heaven with power and great glory.

In Acts 1:10-11, the following is stated in connection with Christ's ascension into heaven in the year 33 A.D.:
And while they looked stedfastly toward heaven as he went up, behold, two men stood by them in white apparel; Which also said, Ye men of Galilee, why stand ye gazing up into heaven? this same Jesus, which is taken up from you into heaven, shall so come in like manner as ye have seen him go into heaven.

God declares to us in I Thessalonians 4:16:
For the Lord himself shall descend from heaven with a shout, with the voice of the archangel, and with the trump of God: and the dead in Christ shall rise first.

These verses together with many others guarantee that Jesus is coming again.

These verses guarantee that Jesus is coming again.
When He comes it will be the end of the world.

---

2. When Jesus comes it will be the end of the world. God declares to us in Matthew 24:29-30:

> Immediately after the tribulation of those days shall the sun be darkened, and the moon shall not give her light, and the stars shall fall from heaven, and the powers of the heavens shall be shaken: And then shall appear the sign of the Son of man in heaven: and then shall all the tribes of the earth mourn, and they shall see the Son of man coming in the clouds of heaven with power and great glory.

In II Peter 3:10 God declares:
> But the day of the Lord will come as a thief in the night; in the which the heavens shall pass away with a great noise, and the elements shall melt with fervent heat, the earth also and the works that are therein shall be burned up.

3. The New Testament era that began at Pentecost in 33 A.D. is the last era God has ordained for this world. When the New Testament era has finished its course, the end will come. God does not have another era in view, an era that will be different from this present era. We read in Hebrews 9:26:
> For then must he often have suffered since the foundation of the world: but now once in the end of the world hath he appeared to put away sin by the sacrifice of himself.

God says in I Peter 4:7:
> But the end of all things is at hand: be ye therefore sober, and watch unto prayer.

And in I Corinthians 10:11 we read:
> Now all these things happened unto them for ensamples: and they are written for our admonition, upon whom the ends of the world are come.

In this verse God uses the plural "ends" to indicate that this is the last era for everything. It is the last era for national Israel, for the New Testament external church, for the nations, for wickedness, and for bringing the Gospel.

> *When this world is no more, all the*
> *unsaved, those who have died and*
> *those who are alive, will be judged.*

4. The end of the world will be the time when all the unsaved are judged. This is true for both those who died in the past and those who are living at the time Christ returns. In John 5:28-29 we read:

Marvel not at this: for the hour is coming, in the which all that are in the graves shall hear his voice, And shall come forth; they that have done good, unto the resurrection of life; and they that have done evil, unto the resurrection of damnation.

God declares in Hebrews 9:27:

And as it is appointed unto men once to die, but after this the judgment.

Revelation 20:10-13 assures us that:

And the devil that deceived them was cast into the lake of fire and brimstone, where the beast and the false prophet are, and shall be tormented day and night for ever and ever. And I saw a great white throne, and him that sat on it, from whose face the earth and the heaven fled away; and there was found no place for them. And I saw the dead, small and great, stand before God; and the books were opened: and another book was opened, which is the book of life: and the dead were judged out of those things which were written in the books, according to their works. And the sea gave up the dead which were in it; and death and hell delivered up the dead which were in them: and they were judged every man according to their works.

5. When Christ is ready to come and end this present world's existence, it will be at a time when the world is going about its business in normal fashion. In Luke 17:26-30 we read:

And as it was in the days of Noe, so shall it be also in the days of the Son of man. They did eat, they drank, they married wives, they were given in marriage, until the day that Noe entered into the ark, and the flood came, and destroyed them all. Likewise also as it was in the days of Lot; they did eat, they drank, they bought, they sold, they planted, they builded; But the same day that Lot went out of Sodom it rained fire and brimstone from heaven, and destroyed them all. Even thus shall it be in the day when the Son of man is revealed.

God says in I Thessalonians 5:2-3:
For yourselves know perfectly that the day of the Lord so cometh as a thief in the night. For when they shall say, Peace and safety; then sudden destruction cometh upon them, as travail upon a woman with child; and they shall not escape.

6. At the time of the end the external church will have become increasingly apostate. II Thessalonians 2:3-4 speaks of the man of sin sitting in the temple at a time when there is a falling away. It can be shown that this man of sin is Satan, and that he is coming as an angel of light and will increasingly rule the congregations, although the congregations will think they are serving Christ.

II Thessalonians 2:3-4:
Let no man deceive you by any means: for that day shall not come, except there come a falling away first, and that man of sin be revealed, the son of perdition; Who opposeth and exalteth himself above all that is called God, or that is worshipped; so that he as God sitteth in the temple of God, shewing himself that he is God.

Matthew 24:24:
For there shall arise false Christs, and false prophets, and shall shew great signs and wonders; insomuch that, if it were possible, they shall deceive the very elect.

This deception, which will increasingly be in evidence, is a judgment of God on the churches, as He blinds those who have departed from truth. In II Thessalonians 2:8-11 God warns:

And then shall that Wicked be revealed, whom the Lord shall consume with the spirit of his mouth, and shall destroy with the brightness of his coming: Even him, whose coming is after the working of Satan with all power and signs and lying wonders, And with all deceivableness of unrighteousness in them that perish; because they received not the love of the truth, that they might be saved. And for this cause God shall send them strong delusion, that they should believe a lie.

And in I Timothy 4:1-2 we read:

Now the Spirit speaketh expressly, that in the latter times some shall depart from the faith, giving heed to seducing spirits, and doctrines of devils; Speaking lies in hypocrisy; having their conscience seared with a hot iron.

7. Not only will the churches be departing from the truth but the world will become increasingly wicked. In the first chapter of Romans, God sets forth the ugly truth of the wickedness of mankind. In Romans 1:18-32, we read these indictments.

For the wrath of God is revealed from heaven against all ungodliness and unrighteousness of men, who hold the truth in unrighteousness; Because that which may be known of God is manifest in them; for God hath shewed it unto them. For the invisible things of him from the creation of the world are clearly seen, being understood by the things that are made, even his eternal power and Godhead; so that they are without excuse: Because that, when they knew God, they glorified him not as God, neither were thankful; but became vain in their imaginations, and their foolish heart was darkened. Professing themselves to be wise, they became fools, And changed the glory of the uncorruptible God into an image made like to corruptible man, and to birds, and fourfooted beasts, and creeping things. Wherefore God also gave them up to uncleanness through the lusts of their own hearts, to dishonour their own bodies between themselves: Who changed the truth of God into a lie, and worshipped and served the creature more than the Creator, who is blessed for ever. Amen. For this cause God gave them up unto vile affections: for even their women did change the natural use into that which is against nature: And likewise also the men, leaving the natural use of the woman, burned in their lust one toward another; men with men working that which is unseemly, and receiving in themselves that recompence of their error which was meet. And even as they did not like to retain God in their knowledge, God gave them over to a reprobate mind, to do those things which are not convenient; Being filled with all unrighteousness, fornication, wickedness, covetousness, maliciousness; full of envy, murder, debate, deceit, malignity; whisperers, Backbiters, haters of God, despiteful, proud, boasters, inventors of evil things, disobedient to parents, Without understanding, covenantbreakers, without natural affection, implacable, unmerciful: Who knowing the judgment of God, that they which commit such things are worthy of death, not only do the same, but have pleasure in them that do them.

In Jeremiah 17:9 we read:
The heart is deceitful above all things, and desperately wicked: who can know it?

> *Human kindness and other commendable character traits have been a result of God's restraint on the inherent wickedness of mankind.*

The fact that throughout history human kindness, generosity, honesty, and other commendable character traits have been seen can be only a result of God's restraint on the inherent wickedness of mankind. Given the indictment of Jeremiah 17:9, if mankind were allowed to live in his natural wickedness for any period of time, he would self destruct. But God, to accommodate His plan to have the world continue to a predetermined time, restrains sin.

However, when God gives men up to sin, as we read in Romans 1, then God allows mankind to go deeper into sin, thus preparing the world for Judgment Day. In II Timothy 3:1-5, we are warned:

This know also, that in the last days perilous times shall come. For men shall be lovers of their own selves, covetous, boasters, proud, blasphemers, disobedient to parents, unthankful, unholy, Without natural affection, trucebreakers, false accusers, incontinent, fierce, despisers of those that are good, Traitors, heady, highminded, lovers of pleasures more than lovers of God; Having a form of godliness, but denying the power thereof: from such turn away.

Moreover, God speaks of the fact that at Christ's return the world will be as it was in the days of Noah. We learned earlier that this indicates that it will be business as usual until Jesus returns. It also indicates that the world of Noah's day had become increasingly wicked. We read in Genesis 6:5-7:

And God saw that the wickedness of man was great in the earth, and that every imagination of the thoughts of his heart was only evil continually. And it repented the LORD that he had made man on the earth, and it grieved him at his heart. And the LORD said, I will destroy man whom I have created from the face of the earth; both man, and beast, and the creeping thing, and the fowls of the air; for it repenteth me that I have made them.

Since the world at the return of Jesus will be as in the days of Noah, we can expect that even as the world was becoming increasingly wicked when the flood came, the world will be increasingly wicked near the end.

> *Every unsaved person will be judged*
> *and found guilty and cast into hell.*

8. At the time of the end, not only will each and every unsaved person be judged but he will be found guilty and be cast into hell where he will eternally suffer the wrath of God in payment for his sins. The Bible declares in Matthew 13:40-43:

As therefore the tares are gathered and burned in the fire; so shall it be in the end of this world. The Son of man shall send forth his angels, and they shall gather out of his kingdom all things that offend, and them which do iniquity; And shall cast them into a furnace of fire: there shall be wailing and gnashing of teeth. Then shall the righteous shine forth as the sun in the kingdom of their Father. Who hath ears to hear, let him hear.

And in Matthew 13:49-50:

So shall it be at the end of the world: the angels shall come forth, and sever the wicked from among the just, And shall cast them into the furnace of fire: there shall be wailing and gnashing of teeth.

9. The punishment for sin shall go on forevermore. Revelation 14:10-11 tells us:

The same shall drink of the wine of the wrath of God, which is poured out without mixture into the cup of his indignation; and he shall be tormented with fire and brimstone in the presence of the holy angels, and in the presence of the Lamb: And the smoke of their torment ascendeth up for ever and ever: and they have no rest day nor night, who worship the beast and his image, and whosoever receiveth the mark of his name.

In Matthew 25:46 Jesus declares concerning the unsaved: And these shall go away into everlasting punishment: but the righteous into life eternal.

The Last Era

Many people have the idea that this world can go on and on. Even many believers have been led to believe that this world is presently in the church age but that God has planned for a future golden age, which will be followed by the end of the world. When we carefully read the Bible we will find clear statements that we are in the final era of this world's existence. This era began with Pentecost in 33 A.D. and will end with the return of Christ and the end of the world.

In Acts 2:1-6 and 17, explaining the phenomena that took place on that Pentecost Sunday, Luke declared, under the inspiration of the Holy Spirit:

Acts 2:1-6: And when the day of Pentecost was fully come, they were all with one accord in one place. And suddenly there came a sound from heaven as of a rushing mighty wind, and it filled all the house where they were sitting. And there appeared unto them cloven tongues like as of fire, and it sat upon each of them. And they were all filled with the Holy Ghost, and began to speak with other tongues, as the Spirit gave them utterance. And there were dwelling at Jerusalem Jews, devout men, out of every nation under heaven. Now when this was noised abroad, the multitude came together, and were confounded, because that every man heard them speak in his own language. Acts 2:17: And it shall come to pass in the **last days**, saith God, I will pour out of my Spirit upon all flesh: and your sons and your daughters shall prophesy, and your young men shall see visions, and your old men shall dream dreams.

> *The last days have come and . . . every believer is mandated to be a prophet.*

God is indicating that the last days have come and during these last days it is God's program to evangelize the world by commissioning, qualifying, and mandating every believer to be a prophet. Why would He call this era of evangelization the "last days"? The obvious answer is that the term "last days" indicates that there is not another to follow insofar as this present world is concerned.

When we study the Bible we find that the history of the world can be divided into several distinct eras. The first era is the 6023 year period from creation to the flood of Noah's day. The second is the period from the flood to the confusion of the languages, which probably happened with the division of the continents. The Bible informs us that the division of the continents occurred in the days of Peleg, who lived from 3153 to 2914 B.C., and since the flood came in the year 4990 B.C., the era between these two events was about 1900 years.

The third era the earth experienced was the era that ended with the circumcision of Abraham in the year 2068 B.C., when God officially began the nation of Israel. The era from the division of the earth to the beginning of the nation of Israel was about 1000 years. The next era was that of the nation of Israel being altogether prominent in God's dealing with the earth. The era began with the circumcision of Abraham and ended when Christ hung on the cross in 33 A.D. Therefore, that era was exactly 2100 years in duration. Pentecost in 33 A.D. began the last era of this earth's existence. There is no era left in God's plan that is to follow this present era. The Bible teaches that when this era has come to an end, this world and the whole universe is to be destroyed. We read in II Peter 3:10:

> But the day of the Lord will come as a thief in the night; in the which the heavens shall pass away with a great noise, and the elements shall melt with fervent heat, the earth also and the works that are therein shall be burned up.

We read in Matthew 24:14:
And this gospel of the kingdom shall be preached in all the world for a witness unto all nations; and **then shall the end come.**

When the era of preaching the Gospel is finished, then the end will come.

God is indicating by this statement that when the era of preaching the Gospel that began at Pentecost in 33 A.D. is finished, then the end will come. What follows is a new heaven and a new earth, which is entirely different from the present universe. We read in II Peter 3:13, "Nevertheless we, according to his promise, look for new heavens and a new earth, wherein dwelleth righteousness."

References to the present era as the last days are found in a number of verses. Hebrews 1:2 declares:
Hath in these last days spoken unto us by his Son, whom he hath appointed heir of all things, by whom also he made the worlds.

In I Peter 1:20 we read:
Who verily was foreordained before the foundation of the world, but was manifest in these **last times** for you.

God further states in I John 2:18:
Little children, it is the last time: and as ye have heard that
antichrist shall come, even now are there many antichrists;
whereby we know that it is the **last time**.

In Hebrews 9:26 God approaches this truth with slightly
different language. We read:
For then must he often have suffered since the foundation of the
world: but now once in the **end of the world** hath he appeared
to put away sin by the sacrifice of himself.

> *The era of national Israel ended*
> *when Christ hung on the cross.*

In this passage God is teaching that the cross was in the era of
the end of the world. The era of national Israel ended when as Christ
hung on the cross the veil of the temple was rent. With the tearing open
of that huge curtain that separated the Holy of Holies from the holy
place, the temple was no longer the holy place and Jerusalem was no
longer the holy city. A new era, the last era, had begun.
In I Peter 4:7 God speaks of this last era by declaring:
But **the end of all things is at hand**: be ye therefore sober, and
watch unto prayer.

And in I Corinthians 10:11 we read:
Now all these things happened unto them for ensamples: and
they are written for our admonition, upon whom **the ends of
the world are come.**

The Bible clearly teaches that the end of this present era is the
end of the world. The question is: How long will this era continue? It
already has encompassed more than 1950 years.

Which Century Will End This Last Era?
In what century are we to look for the return of Christ? If we
know this we will be saved from looking at dates in directions where
truth cannot conceivably be.

The answer to the question of what century is remarkably easy. Jesus gave us the answer in Matthew 24:32-33 where He speaks of the sign of the fig tree in leaf as a sign that Christ is at the very gates. This passage tells us:

> Now learn a parable of the fig tree; When his branch is yet tender, and putteth forth leaves, ye know that summer is nigh: So likewise ye, when ye shall see all these things, know that it is near, even at the doors.

Never in the history of the world has a nation been destroyed and scattered and then reconstituted almost 2000 years later.

The return of Israel to their land in 1948 was an event that could be called almost miraculous. Never in the history of the world has a nation been destroyed and scattered as Israel was in 70 A.D. by the Roman Titus and then become reconstituted as a nation almost 2000 years later. This did happen to Israel, and this return was fully anticipated in Matthew 24:32-33.

We thus see that in order for Biblical prophecy to work out God can guide the miscalculations of a monk as he prepares a calendar and He can guide the affairs of a scattered people so that after almost 2000 years they again become a nation among the nations of the world.

National Israel - The Fig Tree

When we look at Matthew 24:32-33 carefully we see two truths that relate to our study. The first is that it speaks of a fig tree with leaves. The second is that this fig tree is a sign that the end of the world is at hand.

It should be pointed out that in the Bible, with one exception, the fig tree can be a figure only of national Israel. This is seen in such statements as Hosea 9:10:

> I found Israel like grapes in the wilderness; I saw your fathers as the firstripe in the fig tree at her first time: but they went to Baal-peor, and separated themselves unto that shame; and their abominations were according as they loved.

We also read of Israel as typified by a fig tree in Joel 1:7:

> He hath laid my vine waste, and barked my fig tree: he hath made it clean bare, and cast it away; the branches thereof are made white.

These passages can be speaking only of national Israel.

> *No nation at any time in history fulfills the Biblical typology of the fig tree except the nation of Israel.*

To approach the question from another direction we might ask: What nation other than national Israel could be in view? We know that God uses the figure of a cedar in speaking of heathen nations, but never does He use the figure of a fig tree. Moreover, He cannot have had the Israel of God, the whole body of believers in view. This is so because when Jesus cursed the fig tree He declared, in Matthew 21:19: "Let no fruit grow on thee henceforward for ever." Thus we know the New Testament church was not in view in any sense, for it has been bearing fruit ever since the cross. In fact, no nation at any time in history fulfills the Biblical typology of the fig tree except the nation of Israel. Significantly, national Israel has never borne fruit to the present day. Oh, yes, there is a remnant chosen by grace that comes from national Israel, and how we praise God for these believers, but as a nation they are as adamant in their rejection of Christ as the Messiah as they have ever been.

When we examine all the passages that relate to a fig tree we find that it signifies that which was under the curse of God. Mark 11:21 emphasizes this, "The fig tree which thou cursedst." There is one who came from that nation who Himself became a curse on behalf of all of us who believe on Him. That is, of course, the Lord Jesus Christ. He, therefore, is also typified by a fig tree in such passages as Micah 4:4 and Zechariah 3:10. He is called the fig tree because in bearing our sins He came under the curse of God, even as the nation of Israel came under the curse of God.

This is why Matthew 24:32-33 speaks of a fig tree in leaf. It is a nation that has equal standing with other political nations of the world, but there is no fruit. That is, there is no assent to Jesus as their Messiah. They as a nation will not acknowledge Jesus because they have come under God's curse.

This stubborn continued refusal to recognize Jesus as their Messiah is in itself a remarkable situation. Every political nation is only too proud and happy to acknowledge those people of their nation who have made significant contributions to the welfare of mankind.

> *It cannot be denied: No one has had a greater impact on the world than Jesus.*

While the Lord Jesus and His Kingdom have had many critics, it cannot be denied that no one has had a greater impact on the world than Jesus. Therefore, because He is a Jew, one would think that the nation of Israel would be proud and happy to acknowledge Him as their favorite son. Even more so when we consider the intense sufferings the Jewish nation has undergone during the last 2000 years - and more especially during the last sixty years - one would think that they would cry out to the God of the Bible for His mercy.

The fig tree bears leaves without fruit. There is no national recognition of Christ as their Savior. There is no pleading and beseeching with Jehovah God for His mercy in a way that accords with Bible truth, and all of this was predicted in the Bible. The fig tree was never again to bear fruit (Matthew 21:19). Most of the nation would remain in blindness until the last of the Gentiles would come in (Romans 11:25). The fig tree is in leaf and after more than four decades in their own land there is not the slightest inclination for them as a nation to turn to Christ.

The Fig Tree Is a Sign

There is a second truth that bears heavily on our study. The fig tree with leaves is a sign. It is a sign that summer is nigh. Jesus declares in Matthew 24:33, "So likewise ye, when ye shall see **all these things**, know that it is near, even at the doors." What are "these things"? In the previous verse Christ had been speaking of the very act of His return immediately after the tribulation. This event cannot be in view by the phrase "these things" because "these things" refer to events immediately before the return of Christ, at which time Christ will be at the doors; that is, He will be ready to make His appearance.

There are two things in view by the use of the term "these things" in verse 33. The first is that the church will become heavily apostatized as indicated by the language of Matthew 24:15; and the second is that the fig tree will be in leaf (verse 32). When these two events occur we will know that Christ is at the door: The return of Christ and the end of the world is imminent.

It is this truth that tells us which century we are to look at for the return of Christ, and that century is our century. The fig tree is in leaf. Almost miraculously after nearly 2000 years it is in leaf.

> *The abomination of desolation is increasingly standing in the holy place, where the true Gospel is normally found.*

Moreover, the churches and denominations that normally have been reasonably true to the Word of God are being assaulted by other gospels, which are not the true Gospel. The abomination of desolation - Satan coming with false gospels that look like the true Gospel - is increasingly standing in the holy place, where the true Gospel is normally found.

We know from the Bible that the last event this world faces before the return of Christ is the final tribulation period. We studied this in great detail earlier (see Chapters 2 and 3).

Jesus says in Matthew 24:21:
For then shall be great tribulation, such as was not since the beginning of the world to this time, no, nor ever shall be.

Then He declares in verses 29-31:
Immediately after the tribulation of those days shall the sun be darkened, and the moon shall not give her light, and the stars shall fall from heaven, and the powers of the heavens shall be shaken: And then shall appear the sign of the Son of man in

heaven: and then shall all the tribes of the earth mourn, and they shall see the Son of man coming in the clouds of heaven with power and great glory. And he shall send his angels with a great sound of a trumpet, and they shall gather together his elect from the four winds, from one end of heaven to the other.

The duration of this tribulation period is 2300 evening mornings or 2300 days. Do you recall that we found this truth in Daniel 8?

Since 2300 days is a little more than six years (about six years, four months), we can expect two dates to surface as we seek clues concerning the timing of the end of time. Since we are working only with years we would expect these dates to be separated by the duration of the final tribulation period, that is, six years and four months, which rounds off to six years.

The Earth's Timetable Governed by God's Salvation Plan

In Deuteronomy 32:8 God sets forth a provocative declaration:

When the Most High divided to the nations their inheritance, when he separated the sons of Adam, he set the bounds of the people according to the number of the children of Israel.

> *The eternal children of Israel are determinative insofar as when this world will come to an end.*

The first meaning of this verse surely must be that the timetable of the earth's existence is not determined by the number of unsaved people who are to be born into the world. Rather, God is teaching that the elect of God who are the eternal children of Israel, are determinative insofar as when this world will come to an end. This verse restates the principle that we have been emphasizing in this book: The time line of history is the unfolding of God's salvation plan. Thus, when the last of the elect have become saved, then the end will come. Matthew 24:14 also emphasizes this principle:

And this gospel of the kingdom shall be preached in all the world for a witness unto all nations; and then shall the end come.

It is also implied by other passages, such as II Peter 3, where God teaches that He is patient with mankind because He does not want any of God's elect to perish.

There is a second meaning to Deuteronomy 32:8. In Job 14:5 we read, "Seeing his days are determined, the number of his months are with thee, thou hast appointed his bounds that he cannot pass." In this verse God clearly indicates that the bounds are related to time - to days and months. In Deuteronomy 32:8 God declares that the bounds were according to the number of the children of Israel. Again this brings us back to the first meaning; namely, that the children of Israel are those who have experienced salvation, those who have received eternal life.

The children of Israel are also the tribes of national Israel who typified the body of believers. If the tribes are in view in any sense we immediately wonder: How many tribes were there? The answer is there were thirteen tribes. While Jacob had twelve sons, each of whom became the progenitor of a tribe, one of his sons, Joseph, was given a double inheritance. Joseph's two sons, Ephraim and Manasseh, each became a tribe equal to any of the other eleven tribes.

If, therefore, God is determining the bounds of time for this world by the number of tribes, then one would expect the time duration to be 1300 years, 13,000 years, or 130,000 years, as the tribes were thirteen in number. However, as this study shows, only 13,000 years is possible. Interestingly, while the Old Testament church was found mainly under the heading of the tribes of Israel, we find the New Testament church under the heading of the apostles. And even as there were apparently twelve tribes but actually thirteen, so, too, there were apparently twelve apostles but there were actually thirteen (Judas, who betrayed Christ, was replaced with Matthias). This is so because Paul insisted that he was an apostle particularly called of God to be an apostle (I Corinthians 15:9).

> *The Bible apparently assures us that the duration of the earth is to be 12,000 years.*

Likewise, the Bible apparently assures us that there are to be 12,000 years in the duration of the earth. That is, creation occurred 11,000 years (remember 11,000 + 6 years) before Christ. And Revelation 20:1-3 teaches that Satan was to be bound "a thousand years." Since it can be readily shown that Satan was bound at the cross so that Christ would not be frustrated in His program of salvation for the world, the duration of the earth should be 11,000 plus this apparent 1000 years for a total of 12,000 years. Moreover, you will recall that God says in Genesis 6:3:

> And the LORD said, My spirit shall not always strive with man, for that he also is flesh: yet his days shall be an hundred and twenty years.

While this 120 years could be the 120 years during which Noah constructed the ark, it apparently could also be a reference to the fullness of time for all mankind. The number twelve does signify the fullness of whatever God has in view. Then the 120 years could also signify 1200 years or 12,000 years or 120,000 years for the duration of man's existence on earth. Given all the other information in the Bible, we know that 12,000 years is the only number that can relate.

But the New Testament period has continued for almost 2000 years, so the following interesting parallels are suggested:

Apparently	*Actually*
12 tribes	13 tribes
12 apostles	13 apostles
12,000 years	13,000 years

Now we should broach the question: Where does 13,000 years bring us? This is easily answered. Creation occurred in the year 11,013 B.C. (see page 295 ff). Exactly 13,000 years later brings us to 1988. This was the thirteen thousandth anniversary of the history of the world.

13,000 Years According to Joshua 6

In Joshua 6 we read the interesting account of the destruction of Jericho. Jericho was a Gentile city that was marked for total destruction because of its wickedness. Its destruction typifies the destruction of the world at its end. The curious fact was that the army of Israel was to march around the city once a day for six days and then seven times on the seventh day. We read in Joshua 6:3-5:

> And ye shall compass the city, all ye men of war, and go round about the city once. Thus shalt thou do six days. And seven priests shall bear before the ark seven trumpets of rams' horns:

and the seventh day ye shall compass the city seven times, and the priests shall blow with the trumpets. And it shall come to pass, that when they make a long blast with the ram's horn, and when ye hear the sound of the trumpet, all the people shall shout with a great shout; and the wall of the city shall fall down flat, and the people shall ascend up every man straight before him.

Indeed on the seventh day the city was destroyed exactly as God predicted. Two significant facts stand out: The people marched around the city for a total of thirteen times, then they blew the trumpet and shouted. Are these actions to remind us of the 13,000 years from the beginning of time to Judgment Day? Are the blowing of the trumpets and the shout of the people to remind us of Judgment Day? God describes the end of the world in I Thessalonians 4:16:

For the Lord himself shall descend from heaven with a shout, with the voice of the archangel, and with the trump of God: and the dead in Christ shall rise first.

1988 is exactly 13,000 years after the year of creation.

Thus we see another focus on the year 1988, which is exactly 13,000 years after the creation year 11,013 B.C.

13,000 Years According to Genesis 47

Another intriguing account is found in the Bible in connection with Jacob's family coming into Egypt to escape the famine. Remember Jacob's son Joseph had become the prime minister of Egypt. Jacob's other name was Israel. He, therefore, was a figure or type of the Israel of God. Joseph was a type of Christ in that he was the son of Israel (remember Jesus came from the nation of Israel), and in that he was taken from prison and had come to rule over Egypt as Christ came from the prison of God's wrath to become ruler of everything (Ephesians 1:19-22).

Especially interesting is Jacob's age when he came under the care and protection of Joseph. When Pharaoh asked his age, he answered in Genesis 47:9:

And Jacob said unto Pharaoh, The days of the years of my pilgrimage are an **hundred and thirty years**: few and evil have the days of the years of my life been, and have not attained unto the days of the years of the life of my fathers in the days of their pilgrimage.

We cannot help but see the parallel between this account and the pilgrimage of believers in this world. When do we escape the evil days of this earth? In one sense we escape them when we become saved, but the final escape is the end of the world. Could God be pointing to that by the 130 years? We see again how 13,000 years or the year 1988 stands out as the end of the world.

Surely 1988 is a very important year.

Does that mean that we could have expected the year 1988 to be a candidate for the year of Christ's return? Surely it must be a very important year, but we know it cannot be the year of the end of the world because we have already passed the year 1988.

Remember that when Nathanael was seeking the timing of the first coming of Christ he discovered that epochal events were separated by even thousands of years plus the time required for the final tribulation period of 2300 days or twenty-three years. He had found that:

1) from the year of creation (11,013 B.C.) to the flood (4990 B.C.)
= 6,000 + a tribulation period time (23 years)

2) from the flood (4990 B.C.) to the cross (33 A.D.)
= 5,000 + tribulation period time (23 calendar years)

3) from creation (11,013 B.C.) to the birth of Christ (7 B.C.)
= 11,000 + tribulation period time (2300 days or 6 years)

Even so we would expect that the duration of time from creation (11,013 B.C.) to the second coming of Christ would be 13,000 plus the tribulation time of either 2300 days or twenty-three years. If this is so, since 1988 is the 13,000 year end, then six years later would bring us to 1994 as the year of Christ's return, and twenty-three years later would bring us to the year 2011 as the year of Christ's return.

If we are on the right track, 1988, which is the 13,000th anniversary of the world, was the beginning of the final tribulation period.

To summarize, if we are on the right track, we would expect that the year 1988, which is the 13,000th anniversary of the world, was the beginning of the final tribulation period spoken of in Matthew 24:15-29. We know from Daniel 8 that the final tribulation period will be 2300 days, which is six years. Therefore, six years later than 1988 (actually 2300 days), Christ would return and we would be at the end of this world's existence. That is the year 1994.

But we need far more information from the Bible than what we have discovered thus far. Surely this information is not conclusive.

Number Two and the End of the World

Actually there is more - much more. Let us continue our search as we discover how God uses the number two in the Bible.

The number two in the Bible, if it has any spiritual significance, is the number of the church. The disciples went out two by two. The seventy went out by twos. The two witnesses of Revelation 11 represent the New Testament church as it brings the Gospel.

Remember when Nathanael was puzzling over the number 2000, he discovered that one path that brought him to the time of the coming of the Messiah was the 2000 years from the birth of Jacob (2007 B.C.) to the jubilee year when Christ was born (7 B.C.). This 2000 year period in a real sense represented the period of the Old Testament church. Jacob fathered the tribes of Israel. These tribes became the nation of Israel, which was the Old Testament church.

---

*The Old Testament church is represented
by the period from 2007 B.C. to 7 B.C.
And 1994 A.D., 2000 years later, may
be a candidate for the year of
Christ's return.*

While the official ending of the nation of Israel as the representation of the Kingdom of God on this earth occurred at the cross when the veil of the temple was rent, in another sense we could say that their era ended with the birth of Christ, just as the era of the New Testament church in one sense began with the birth of Christ. So we see the Old Testament church is represented by the period from 2007 B.C. to 7 B.C. And 1994 A.D., which is 2000 years later, is the year we have already seen as being a candidate for the year of Christ's return.

We should recognize that the 2000 years in another sense could be after 33 A.D., when Christ was crucified, which would bring us to the year 2033 A.D. This, therefore, should also be considered as an outside possibility for the timing of Christ's return.

About 2000 Cubits and Crossing the Jordan River

While we are looking at the number 2000, do you recall that Nathanael puzzled about the fact that there were to be about 2000 cubits between the priests and the children of Israel as they approached the Jordan River? The priests with the ark are a picture of Christ. The Jordan River was a figure of hell that we (or Christ on our behalf) must endure before we can be right with God. To go through the Jordan River on dry ground as Israel did is a dramatic picture of believers passing through hell - that is, paying for their sins in hell - because only if the penalty for our sins has been fully paid can we enter heaven. Hell as the water of the Jordan River has not touched us because Christ has been our stand-in or substitute in paying that penalty. Surely we can see the possible suggestion that the 2000 cubits represent the time that God has scheduled to bring in those who become saved. Thus they could represent the time between the first coming of Christ and the second coming of Christ, when the salvation of all believers will have been completed.

The Biblical account of the 2000 cubits is in Joshua 3:3-4:

And they commanded the people, saying, When ye see the ark of the covenant of the LORD your God, and the priests the Levites bearing it, then ye shall remove from your place, and go after it. Yet there shall be a space between you and it, about two thousand cubits by measure: come not near unto it, that ye may know the way by which ye must go: for ye have not passed this way heretofore.

An important word in these verses is the word "about." Between Israel and the ark there shall be "about two thousand cubits." This means that 2000 cubits is an important number but not an exact number. Thus, since the priests and the ark went into the Jordan River ahead of Israel and represent Christ, who endured hell on behalf of all believers, it is altogether valid to see the 2000 cubits as a picture pointing to the 2000 year period either from the birth of Jesus to His second coming or from the baptism of Jesus to His second coming. We should take note of all three of the following years.

1. 2000 years from birth of Jesus   which is 1994
2. 2000 years from baptism of Jesus which is 2029
3. 2000 years from the cross   which is 2033

About 2000 Swine

Interestingly and perhaps significantly we find the same phrase "about two thousand" used in connection with the pigs that plunged into the sea when they were filled with evil spirits (Mark 5:1-17). Without question the pigs represent the unsaved who are ruled over by Satan. The sea is a picture of hell. Both the unsaved and the devils will be cast into hell when Jesus comes again (Revelation 19:20 and 20:15). Therefore, the destruction of the 2000 pigs could be pointing to Judgment Day at the end of time.

Spiritually the basis for this victory over Satan is the fact that Christ came. He vanquished Satan at the cross. If the citation in Mark 5 indicated simply "two thousand swine" and if any kind of time reference were in view, we would know this reference could be pointing to 33 A.D. plus 2000 years = 2033. However, even as the 2000 cubits of the Joshua 3:3-4 citation are given as "about two thousand cubits," so, too, the citation in Mark 5 is "about two thousand" swine. Therefore, we know that God is not pointing to the year of His return as being exactly 2000 years after the cross. Rather it is *about* 2000 years. Thus, it could also refer to 2000 years after Christ's birth in 7 B.C., which brings us to 1994 A.D. or it could refer to 2000 years after the baptism of Jesus, which brings us to 2029 A.D. In any case we have learned that as we looked at time references relating to Christ's first coming, each time reference began at a significant year that in itself related to some aspect of the Gospel. The only significant years that occurred about 2000 years ago are the years in which Jesus was born (7 B.C.), the year He was baptized (29 A.D.), and the year He was crucified (33 A.D.).

Therefore, even as was the case when we examined the "about two thousand cubits" reference of Joshua 3, so that we saw the reference could be to an end in the year 1994 or 2029 or 2033 A.D., so, too, the reference to the 2000 swine could also point to any one of these three years. However, because of the word "about" we can be fairly certain that it refers to an inexact period of time. Thus, since 2033 A.D. is exactly 2000 years after the cross, we can be quite certain that this is not the year to which these references to "about two thousand" point. That leaves 1994 and 2029 A.D. as possibilities.

About 200 Cubits

While we are considering these references to "about two thousand cubits" and "about two thousand" swine we should also consider another "about" reference. In fact, it is an "about" reference used in connection with the distance reference of 200 cubits. We read in John 21:8:

> And the other disciples came in a little ship; (for they were not far from land, but as it were two hundred cubits,) dragging the net with fishes.

And in John 21:11:

> Simon Peter went up, and drew the net to land full of great fishes, an hundred and fifty and three: and for all there were so many, yet was not the net broken.

> *Our salvation will be complete when*
> *we receive our resurrected bodies at*
> *the return of Jesus.*

Earlier in our study we learned that the 153 fish represented all believers, those who will become saved. The sea is a picture of hell from which we are rescued. The net is a picture of the Gospel as it is applied by the Holy Spirit to the lives of those who are rescued into salvation. The shore or land is a picture of the Kingdom of God, which we have entered into when we become saved. Our salvation will be complete when we receive our resurrected bodies at the return of Jesus.

Thus we can see that the 200 cubits could represent the entire New Testament era. It officially began at Pentecost in 33 A.D. when the Holy Spirit was poured out and it continues until the last of the elect have become saved and our salvation is completed upon Christ's return. Each cubit, therefore, equals ten years. But the Bible says "as it were two hundred cubits." The phrase "as it were" can also be properly translated "about." Therefore, these "about two hundred cubits" could represent about 2000 years from the cross, as the end of the Gospel era. For the same reasons just indicated in connection with the "about two thousand" swine, we believe we should look at 1994 or 2029 A.D. as the end of the world.

The Prophet Ezekiel - A Picture of Israel

In Ezekiel 4 God gave the prophet Ezekiel a strange command. He was commanded to take a clay tile and iron pan and use these articles to simulate God's wrath against Jerusalem. Furthermore, he was to lie on one side for a period of 390 days to simulate that God is pouring out His wrath against Israel upon Ezekiel. He then was to repeat this by lying on his other side for forty days to simulate God's wrath on Judah. In other words Ezekiel becomes a symbol of Israel and Judah. That this is so is clearly seen in the language of Ezekiel 24:24. This verse informs us:

> Thus Ezekiel is unto you a sign: according to all that he hath done shall ye do: and when this cometh, ye shall know that I am the Lord GOD.

> *The procedure of making the prophet a picture or symbol of God's intentions was frequently used by God.*

This procedure of making the prophet a picture or symbol of God's intentions with nations was frequently used by God. For example, God wished to describe the adulterous character of Israel in the days that Hosea was prophet. He, therefore, instructed Hosea to marry a harlot. The harlot was a picture of Israel while Hosea was a picture of God. Hosea's marriage to a harlot typified God's marriage to adulterous Israel (Hosea 1:2).

Likewise, at another time God wished to show Egypt that they would be conquered by Assyria. He, therefore, instructed the prophet Isaiah to typify the conquered Egypt. Isaiah 20:3-4 describes this action by the words:

And the LORD said, Like as my servant Isaiah hath walked naked and barefoot three years for a sign and wonder upon Egypt and upon Ethiopia; So shall the king of Assyria lead away the Egyptians prisoners, and the Ethiopians captives, young and old, naked and barefoot, even with their buttocks uncovered, to the shame of Egypt.

In similar fashion in Ezekiel 4 God is indicating He has plans for judgment against Israel, and He is using the prophet Ezekiel to typify Israel. For 390 days, Ezekiel is to lie on his left side and have bread and drink water that has been carefully measured out. Thus Ezekiel is to typify Israel, for Ezekiel 4:4-5 tells us:

Lie thou also upon thy left side, and lay the iniquity of the house of Israel upon it: according to the number of the days that thou shalt lie upon it thou shalt bear their iniquity. For I have laid upon thee the years of their iniquity, according to the number of the days, three hundred and ninety days: so shalt thou bear the iniquity of the house of Israel.

Ezekiel 4:16-17 describes this punishment on Israel, typified by Ezekiel, by declaring:

Moreover he said unto me, Son of man, behold, I will break the staff of bread in Jerusalem: and they shall eat bread by weight, and with care; and they shall drink water by measure, and with astonishment: That they may want bread and water, and be astonied one with another, and consume away for their iniquity.

After Ezekiel had lain on his left side for 390 days, he was to lie on his right side for forty days. This is to typify God's judgment on Judah. Verse 6 declares:

And when thou hast accomplished them, lie again on thy right side, and thou shalt bear the iniquity of the house of Judah forty days: I have appointed thee each day for a year.

What judgment on Israel and Judah could God have in view? The last half of verse 6 gives us a partial clue. There God declares that each day of the forty days represents a year. And in verse 5 God indicates that each day of the 390 days represents a year. Thus, it appears that a period of 390 years of judgment is to be suffered by Israel and forty years by Judah.

What period of time could Ezekiel have in view? Let us briefly examine God's dealings with Israel.

You will recall that in 931 B.C. the nation of Israel was divided into two nations. The southern kingdom with its capital in Jerusalem was called Judah because its dominant people were of the tribe of Judah. The northern kingdom with its capital in Samaria consisted of ten of the tribes, so it was called Israel.

Israel was destroyed by the Assyrians in 709 B.C. (about 120 years before Ezekiel is prophesying) and has never again been restored as a nation of ten tribes. Judah was destroyed and brought into captivity in 587 B.C. by the Babylonians. This was about the time that Ezekiel was prophesying. They began to return to Jerusalem forty-eight years later in the year 539 B.C. In the year 458 B.C., Ezra came to Jerusalem to reestablish the law. The last noteworthy date connected with Israel's restoration was 445 B.C. when Nehemiah rebuilt the wall of Jerusalem.

Those dates are recited because Ezekiel 4 is picturing God's judgment on Israel as a period of 390 days or 390 years - and on Judah forty days or forty years. However, regardless of how we look at Israel or Judah we find no identification with a period of forty years or 390 years; none of the key numbers 709, 587, 539, 458 or 445 appears related in any way to the numbers forty or 390. We almost begin to wonder if God has made an error.

> *God has not made a mistake. God is always accurate.*

But God has not made a mistake. God is always accurate in everything declared in the Bible. We must look more carefully at Ezekiel 4 to determine its meaning.

A Day for a Year

The first clue that helps us is found in verse 6 where God converts days into years - a day for a year. Thus we are instructed to look at years rather than days. Moreover, we discovered that God is punishing Israel for their iniquity during these periods of time.

How long would God punish Israel for their continuing rebellion against God? In Mark 11 Jesus cursed the fig tree and declared that it never again was to bear fruit. In Romans 11:25 God informs us that blindness in part has come upon Israel until the fullness of the Gentiles come in. That is, as long as one person anywhere in the whole world remains unsaved and who is to be saved (that is, he is one of God's elect), Israel as a nation will remain in unbelief. It must be emphasized that in Romans 11 God is also pointing out that as long as Gentiles are being saved, a remnant chosen by grace from national Israel also is becoming saved. Praise God for this trickle of believers that is coming out of national Israel even as there is a remnant coming from every other political nation.

> *God's judgment on Israel goes all the way to the end of time.*

The point, however, that we cannot miss is that God's judgment on Israel goes all the way to the end of time, for when the last of God's elect have become saved, the end will come.

If God's judgment remains on Israel until the end of time, it means that the end of both the 390 days and the forty days must also be the end of time. This means that in Ezekiel 4 God is giving us a very significant time clue concerning the end of the world. That is, it would be a time clue if we could find the beginning points of the forty days and 390 days.

390 Days Equals 3900 Years

Let's examine the 390 period first to discover what we can from this number. Remembering that we must look at years rather than days, we have before us 390 years or 3900 years. As we have already seen in looking at other numbers in the Bible that give us clues concerning the end of time, God frequently multiplies by ten, by one hundred, or 1000 to give us the answer. To indicate this principle in another way: The addition of zeroes to a number does not change the essential meaning or purpose of the number.

When we look at a time span of 390 years that ends with the end of the world we find nothing that is significant. If we are very close to the end of time, 390 years earlier brings us to a time in which can be found no significant date that identifies with Biblical language.

> *In a sense, Jacob being renamed Israel was the beginning of Israel.*

On the other hand, when we study a period of 3900 years we find something very interesting. The most significant event pertaining to Israel about 3900 years ago was the event when Jacob's name was changed to Israel. This event is recorded in Genesis 32:28. Jacob had been wrestling with God at the River Jabbok. In this significant context God changes Jacob's name to Israel - a name that means prince of God. This is the first time the name Israel is used concerning the nation of Israel that would spring from the loins of Jacob, for we will recall that Jacob fathered twelve sons who became the twelve tribes of Israel. Thus, in a sense, Jacob being renamed Israel was the beginning of Israel. This is so even though in fact the Jewish nation began in 2068 B.C., when Abraham was circumcised.

> *This tremendous experience took place in 1907 B.C., when Jacob was 100 years old, and 3900 years added to 1907 B.C. brings us to 1994 A.D.*

When did this event occur? Remember, we saw earlier that this tremendous experience of Jacob took place in the year 1907 B.C. Jacob was 100 years old at the time. And 3900 years added to 1907 B.C. brings us to - yes! - it brings us to the year 1994 A.D.

Now we might protest. True, 3900 years added to 1907 B.C., when Jacob's name was changed to Israel, conveniently comes to 1994 A.D. But in Ezekiel 4 God teaches that His judgment is on Israel for 390 days or 3900 years. Is it true that God's judgment was on Israel throughout its history?

How do we know that the beginning of the 3900 years was the time when Jacob's name was changed to Israel? Why, for example, couldn't the beginning of the 3900 years have been the year 1877 B.C. when Israel entered Egypt? Then 3900 years would bring us to the year 2024 for the end of the world.

These are fair questions, so let us try to answer them. Let us look at the second question first. How can we be sure that 1907 B.C. was the beginning of the 3900 year period? This will be answered quite conclusively when we look at the forty days of Ezekiel 4. Remember, it, too, was the period when God's wrath was on Israel. It, too, is a period that must end on Judgment Day for the same reasons that the 390 days must end on Judgment Day

Forty Days Equals 4000 Years

When we seek a solution to the forty days it must be a period that begins at a significant moment in the history of Israel and ends forty years or 400 years or 4000 years later in the same year that the 3900 year period ends. We shall see that the year 1994 satisfies this requirement. Thus, we will know for certain that the year 1907 B.C., when Jacob became Israel, is the beginning of the 3900 years.

The first question must now be answered. Does the Bible teach that during its entire history, God's wrath was on national Israel? Were they not God's chosen people who received multitudinous blessings from God?

> *Israel briefly experienced great blessings, for example, during the reign of Solomon.*

It is true that there were brief moments when Israel experienced great blessings, for example, during the reign of Solomon. However, when we look at the approximately 4000 years of the existence of Israel, we find that normally they were under God's judgments.

This was already in evidence in Jacob's lifetime. He had to go to Egypt to escape the grievous famine that was in the land of Canaan. At the time he came to Egypt he confessed to Pharaoh, in Genesis 47:9, "Few and evil have the days of the years of my life been."

In Egypt they were oppressed, but there, too, they were under God's wrath because of their constant rebellion. Ezekiel 20:8-9 records:

> But they rebelled against me, and would not hearken unto me: they did not every man cast away the abominations of their eyes, neither did they forsake the idols of Egypt: then I said, I will pour out my fury upon them, to accomplish my anger against them in the midst of the land of Egypt. But I wrought for my name's sake, that it should not be polluted before the heathen, among whom they were, in whose sight I made myself known unto them, in bringing them forth out of the land of Egypt.

During the forty years in the wilderness, as Israel journeyed from Egypt to Canaan, the same conditions prevailed. Ezekiel 20:13-14 states:

> But the house of Israel rebelled against me in the wilderness: they walked not in my statutes, and they despised my judgments, which if a man do, he shall even live in them; and my sabbaths they greatly polluted: then I said, I would pour out my

fury upon them in the wilderness, to consume them. But I wrought for my name's sake, that it should not be polluted before the heathen, in whose sight I brought them out.

As a matter of fact, most of Israel perished in the wilderness because of unbelief.

So it was throughout the history of Israel. They were oppressed by the Moabites, by the Canaanites, and by the Syrians because of their unbelief. Finally, in the days of Isaiah a few decades before the ten tribes were to be destroyed by the Assyrians, God declared in Isaiah 6:9-12:

And he said, Go, and tell this people, Hear ye indeed, but understand not; and see ye indeed, but perceive not. Make the heart of this people fat, and make their ears heavy, and shut their eyes; lest they see with their eyes, and hear with their ears, and understand with their heart, and convert, and be healed. Then said I, Lord, how long? And he answered, Until the cities be wasted without inhabitant, and the houses without man, and the land be utterly desolate, And the LORD have removed men far away, and there be a great forsaking in the midst of the land.

God is declaring that Israel as a nation will never respond to the Gospel.

By this language God is declaring that Israel as a nation will never respond to the Gospel. Because their continued rebellion brought judgments upon them, we are not surprised that God's judgments have continued to come. They were destroyed by the Assyrians in about 710 B.C., by the Babylonians in 587 B.C., and by the Romans in 70 A.D. We know that today they continue in their rejection of Christ the Messiah.

Later in our study when we look at the 1290 days of Daniel 12, we will see that they cover a period that begins with judgment (the daily was taken away, which we will see signifies the beginning of the silencing of the Gospel), and ends with Judgment Day. The beginning of this period was 1877 B.C., just thirty years after 1907 B.C. when Jacob became Israel. Thus in Daniel 12 God was also to some degree characterizing Israel as a nation under judgment.

We, therefore, can be assured that we are on very solid ground when we look at 3900 years of Israel's history as a period when God's judgment was upon them so that repeatedly they experienced God's wrath.

We are assured that our treatment of the 390 days as representing the 3900 year history of Israel, beginning with the changing of the patriarch Jacob's name to Israel in 1907 B.C., is valid.

It might be noted in passing that Jacob's name was changed to Israel when he was 100 years old. Do you remember that the number one hundred signifies the completeness of whatever is in view? Therefore, in the completeness of time (Jacob is 100 years of age) Israel begins. They continue for 3900 years to the end of time - 1994 A.D.

Let us return to the forty days of Ezekiel 4. This is the period of time Ezekiel was to lie on his right side because God's judgment was on Judah. Judah was another name for the nation of Israel. In fact, the name Jew, which identifies with all blood descendants of Abraham, comes from the name Judah.

Forty years or 400 years or 4000 years is to be the duration of time that Judah is to bear their iniquity. When we looked at the 390 days we found that the period of time ended with Judgment Day. For the same reasons we know that the forty, 400, or 4000 year period must end with Judgment Day.

Therefore, for the same reasons that the 390 day period signified 3900 years, we can know that the forty days signify 4000 years. So we wonder what event was of such importance that it signified the beginning of this 4000 years.

> *In 2007 B.C., Jacob the progenitor*
> *of the nation of Israel was born,*
> *thus in a sense the nation of Israel*
> *was born.*

Indeed a noteworthy event did occur about 4000 years ago. It was the year 2007 B.C. In that year Jacob was born, and since Jacob was the progenitor of the nation of Israel, in a sense 2007, the birth year of Jacob also marked the birth year of Israel. That is, at least in the sense that God's judgments were upon national Israel.

From the day that Jacob was born there was rebellion. Jacob was the second born of the twins, Esau and Jacob. As a babe in the womb he was not satisfied with this God-ordained arrangement. He, therefore, came forth from his mother's womb clutching the heel of Esau (Genesis 25:26). His very name Jacob means "supplanter" or "deceiver." This, too, suggested a man who fundamentally was under God's wrath and would be under God's judgments.

We find that at the age of 60 he conned his brother out of his birthright and then wilfully and drastically lied repeatedly to his blind father Isaac in order to have the blessing that Esau, who was older, was entitled to have. Small wonder Jacob told Pharaoh, "Few and evil have the days of the years of my life been" (Genesis 47:9).

> *Jacob was born 2007 B.C., and 4000 years later is 1994 A.D.*

So we see that 2007 B.C. when Jacob was born is indeed a very significant day insofar as being a beginning for 4000 years. And 2007 B.C. followed by 4000 years ends on - yes, that's right - on the year 1994 A.D. How significantly every path we follow using the prophetic numbers of the Bible focuses on 1994 A.D.

We have thus seen that the 390 days during which Ezekiel was to be a type or figure bearing the wrath of God is pointing to the 3900 year period beginning in the year 1907 B.C. when Jacob's name was changed to Israel and continuing to 1994 A.D. On the other hand the forty days Ezekiel was to be a type or figure bearing the wrath of God is pointing to the 4000 year period beginning in the year 2007 B.C. when Jacob was born and also continuing to 1994 A.D.

> *The 390 day prophecy and the forty day prophecy must end at the same time - Judgment Day.*

The fact that both the 390 day prophecy and the forty day prophecy must end at the same time - Judgment Day - gives us vast assurance that we understand the Scriptures correctly when we see the end as 1994 A.D. Let us explore this a moment longer.

Do you recall that when we looked at the 390 days we raised the question: Why couldn't the 3900 year period have begun, for example, in 1877 B.C. when Jacob went into Egypt? We will see why 1877 could not have been the year. Thirty-nine hundred years after 1877 would bring us to the year 2024 A.D. If this were indeed Judgment Day, then 4000 years earlier than 2024 A.D. must also be a very significant year. That would be 1977 B.C., when Jacob was 30 years old. But there isn't the slightest hint or suggestion in the Bible of any importance being placed on 1977 B.C. Therefore, the year 2024 A.D. cannot be the end of time.

Moreover, there is no combination of years that satisfies the requirements of both the 390 days and the forty days of Ezekiel 4, that is, except for the solution we have come to in this study. Indeed we see that 1994 looks more and more like a candidate for the year of Christ's return.

We see that 1994 looks more and more like a candidate for the year of Christ's return.

---

390 + 40 = 430

One other possibility is suggested. The 390 years of Israel's punishment added to the forty years of Judah's punishment make a total of 430 years. We are attracted to the 430 years Israel was in Egypt (Exodus 12:40-41). This period was between the years 1877 B.C. and 1447 B.C. and was called the period of bondage or being in the iron furnace. It began and ended hundreds of years before Ezekiel's prophecy.

Yet we are drawn to this period. Not only does the 430-year period equal the 430 years of Ezekiel 4, but there are two other characteristics about the number 430 that suggest we look at it a bit longer.

The first characteristic is that in Ezekiel 4:6 it is declared that a day shall equal a year. The only other place in the Bible that declares this is in reference to the forty years in the wilderness. There too the reference is that a day shall equal a year.

Numbers 14:34: After the number of the days in which ye searched the land, even forty days, each day for a year, shall ye bear your iniquities, even forty years, and ye shall know my breach of promise.

We have learned how forty years is a figure of the 4000 years that began with the birth of Israel in 2007 B.C. and possibly will end precisely 4000 years later.

The second characteristic of the 430 years is that in Exodus 12:40-41 language is employed to indicate that the 430 years was an exact period of time to the very day.

Exodus 12:40-41: Now the sojourning of the children of Israel, who dwelt in Egypt, was four hundred and thirty years. And it came to pass at the end of the four hundred and thirty years, even the **selfsame** day it came to pass, that all the hosts of the LORD went out from the land of Egypt.

The other place in the Bible where this same language is employed is in relation to the forty years in the wilderness.

Joshua 5:11: And they did eat of the old corn of the land on the morrow after the passover, unleavened cakes, and parched corn in the **selfsame** day.

We therefore see that God has definitely related the period of 430 years to the period of forty years.

Another 430 year period in the dates listed might assist us (see page 309 ff). The foundation of Solomon's temple was laid in 967 B.C. The command to rebuild the temple was given by Cyrus in the first year of Cyrus king of Persia in 537 B.C.

According to the Biblical record, Israel would be in bondage seventy years. That bondage began in the year 609 B.C. when the last God-fearing king, Josiah, was killed. It ended seventy years later when Babylon was conquered by the Medes and Persians in 539 B.C. Incidentally, according to very adequate secular records this occurred in October of 539 B.C. Jack Finegan[1] wrote:

The biblical references to the first year of Cyrus when he made the proclamation which allowed the Jewish exiles to return from Babylon to Jerusalem (II Ch 36:22f; Ezr 1:11ff.) are presumably stated in terms of his reign in Babylon since they deal with an event in that city. According to the cuneiform evidence and the Babylonian calendar, Babylon fell on Tashritu 16 = Oct 12, 539 B.C., and Cyrus entered the city two and one-half weeks later on Arahsamnu 3 = Oct 29. His Babylonian regnal years began, therefore, as shown in Table 77.

Table 77. Babylonian Regnal Years of Cyrus
at the Beginning of His Reign

Accession	539/538
Year 1	538/537
Year 2	537/536

Accordingly his first year, in which he made the proclamation, was 538/537 B.C.

A year in the Babylon calendar covered the period from March/April of one year to February/March of the next year. Therefore, the freeing of Israel from Babylonian rule definitely occurred in 539 B.C. According to the above information, the first year of Cyrus fell in the years 538 and 537 B.C. Therefore, the decree given by Cyrus in his first year to allow the exiles to return could have been given either in our year 538 B.C. or in our year 537 B.C. We will learn that 537 B.C. fits very precisely into the Biblical chronological framework.

As was indicated the foundation of Solomon's temple was laid in the year 967 B.C. Thus a period of 430 years transpired between 967 B.C. and 537 B.C. How is this 430 year period related to our question? Let us look at Cyrus in the context of the entire Bible.

Cyrus - My Shepherd

The Bible teaches that in a real sense Cyrus is a type of Christ in His second coming. Note these verses of Isaiah.

Isaiah 44:28: That saith of Cyrus, He is my shepherd, and shall perform all my pleasure: even saying to Jerusalem, Thou shalt be built; and to the temple, Thy foundation shall be laid.

Isaiah 45:1-6: Thus saith the LORD to his anointed, to Cyrus, whose right hand I have holden, to subdue nations before him; and I will loose the loins of kings, to open before him the two leaved gates; and the gates shall not be shut; I will go before thee, and make the crooked places straight: I will break in pieces the gates of brass, and cut in sunder the bars of iron: And I will give thee the treasures of darkness, and hidden riches of secret places, that thou mayest know that I, the LORD, which call thee by thy name, am the God of Israel. For Jacob my servant's sake, and Israel mine elect, I have even called thee by thy name: I have surnamed thee, though thou hast not known me. I am the LORD, and there is none else, there is no God beside me: I girded thee, though thou hast not known me: That they may know from the rising of the sun, and from the west, that there is none beside me. I am the LORD, and there is none else.

Note, too, the following passages of Isaiah 13, which speak of Judgment Day and of the Medes in this context. Cyrus and Darius were the kings of the Medes and the Persians who conquered the nation of Babylon in 539 B.C.

Isaiah 13:9-11: Behold, the day of the LORD cometh, cruel both with wrath and fierce anger, to lay the land desolate: and he shall destroy the sinners thereof out of it. For the stars of heaven and the constellations thereof shall not give their light: the sun shall be darkened in his going forth, and the moon shall not cause her light to shine. And I will punish the world for their evil, and the wicked for their iniquity; and I will cause the arrogancy of the proud to cease, and will lay low the haughtiness of the terrible.

Isaiah 13:17-20: Behold, I will stir up the Medes against them, which shall not regard silver; and as for gold, they shall not delight in it. Their bows also shall dash the young men to pieces; and they shall have no pity on the fruit of the womb; their eye shall not spare children. And Babylon, the glory of kingdoms, the beauty of the Chaldees' excellency, shall be as when God overthrew Sodom and Gomorrah. It shall never be inhabited, neither shall it be dwelt in from generation to generation: neither shall the Arabian pitch tent there; neither shall the shepherds make their fold there.

Note too that in Revelation, Babylon is used as a figure of the world during the final days, when it is under the domination of Satan. It is to be destroyed at the return of Christ.

Revelation 17:4-5: And the woman was arrayed in purple and scarlet colour, and decked with gold and precious stones and pearls, having a golden cup in her hand full of abominations and filthiness of her fornication: And upon her forehead was a name written, MYSTERY, BABYLON THE GREAT, THE MOTHER OF HARLOTS AND ABOMINATIONS OF THE EARTH.

Revelation 17:18: And the woman which thou sawest is that great city, which reigneth over the kings of the earth.

Revelation 14:8: And there followed another angel, saying, Babylon is fallen, is fallen, that great city, because she made all nations drink of the wine of the wrath of her fornication.

Revelation 16:19: And the great city was divided into three parts, and the cities of the nations fell: and great Babylon came in remembrance before God, to give unto her the cup of the wine of the fierceness of his wrath.

The entire eighteenth chapter of Revelation uses Babylon as a figure of the world coming to judgment.

The same idea is paralleled in Jeremiah 25:17-18:
Then took I the cup at the LORD'S hand, and made all the nations to drink, unto whom the LORD had sent me: To wit, Jerusalem, and the cities of Judah, and the kings thereof, and the princes thereof, to make them a desolation, an astonishment, an hissing, and a curse; as it is this day.

And in Jeremiah 25:26-27:

And all the kings of the north, far and near, one with another, and all the kingdoms of the world, which are upon the face of the earth: and the king of Sheshach shall drink after them. Therefore thou shalt say unto them, Thus saith the LORD of hosts, the God of Israel; Drink ye, and be drunken, and spue, and fall, and rise no more, because of the sword which I will send among you.

> *Cyrus came to destroy Babylon and rebuild the temple, and Christ will come to destroy this sinful world and bring in the perfect sanctuary.*

So even as Cyrus came to destroy Babylon and rebuild the temple, so Christ will come to destroy this sinful world and bring in the perfect sanctuary, which is Himself dwelling among men. This ideal temple is symbolized by the construction outlined in the last eight chapters of Ezekiel. These eight chapters must be considered as symbolical in the light of Revelation 21:22: "And I saw no temple therein: for the Lord God Almighty and the Lamb are the temple of it."

Turning again to the 430 years, we see a distinct 430 year period beginning with the construction of the temple in 967 B.C. and ending with the command to rebuild the temple in 537 B.C. We thus must ask: If Cyrus as destroyer of Babylon is a type of Christ as destroyer of the sinful world, and builder of the perfect temple, His church at His second coming, isn't it significant that this rebuilding of the temple occurred exactly 430 years after construction of the first temple was begun? We begin to sense that God is telling us that even as the forty years or 4000 years apparently are exactly related to Christ's second coming, so the 430 years must be equally related to His second coming.

Looking again at the dates listed we note another interesting period.

Entrance into Egypt	1877 B.C.
Exodus	1447 B.C.
Time elapsed	430 years

Entrance into Egypt	1877 B.C.
Destruction of Jerusalem	587 B.C.
Time elapsed	1290 years

This 1290 years is significant for two reasons. The first is that it is directly related to the 430 years we are presently studying. Three times 430 = 1290.

1290 Brings Us to the End of Time

The second reason for the significance of the number 1290 is that Daniel speaks of 1290 days in the context of the closing events of the world.

Daniel 12:11: And from the time that the daily sacrifice shall be taken away, and the abomination that maketh desolate set up, there shall be a thousand two hundred and ninety days.

Because we have seen that the 430 years are probably somehow related to Christ's return and a day was employed in Ezekiel 4 to represent a year, we could no doubt safely assume that Daniel's 1290 days also represent 1290 years. In fact, the period from 1877 to 587 B.C., which equals 1290 years, is at least a shadow or foretaste of fulfillment of Daniel's prophecy. Let us see why this is so.

In 1877 B.C., Israel and his family were saved from starvation by coming under the care and keeping of that great type of Christ, Joseph. This was surely a reflection of Christ's salvation for Israel, His church, which was effected on the cross. However, the event of Israel entering into Egypt in 1877 B.C. can be considered another way.

> *The land of Canaan is a picture or type of the homeland of the residents of the Kingdom of God.*

In the Bible, God uses the land of Canaan as a picture or type of the homeland of the residents of the Kingdom of God. The inhabitants of the Kingdom of God are those who have become saved. They are typified by national Israel as that nation, which began with Abraham, dwelt in the land of Canaan.

On the other hand, God ordinarily uses Egypt to typify a situation of being in bondage to sin, of being under the wrath of God, of being ruled over by Satan. We read in Deuteronomy 5:6: "I am the LORD thy God, which brought thee out of the land of Egypt, from the house of bondage."

When God warns of judgment coming upon the church because of apostasy, He declares, for example, in Deuteronomy 28:27:

> The LORD will smite thee with the botch of Egypt, and with the emerods, and with the scab, and with the itch, whereof thou canst not be healed.

And in Deuteronomy 28:68 He warns:

> And the LORD shall bring thee into Egypt again with ships, by the way whereof I spake unto thee, Thou shalt see it no more again: and there ye shall be sold unto your enemies for bondmen and bondwomen, and no man shall buy you.

> *The two witnesses represent the church as they send forth the Gospel throughout the New Testament period.*

In Revelation 11 God speaks of the final tribulation as a time when the two witnesses are killed. These two witnesses represent the church as they send forth the Gospel throughout the New Testament period. The fact that they are killed is emphasizing that the light of the Gospel is no longer shining. This is increasingly the situation during the final tribulation period. In this connection we read in Revelation 11:8:

> And their dead bodies shall lie in the street of the great city, which spiritually is called Sodom and Egypt, where also our Lord was crucified.

This verse speaks of the city where our Lord was crucified. Jesus was crucified outside the gates of Jerusalem, and Jerusalem is a type or picture of the body of believers, which is the church. Now Jerusalem - that is the church - has become Sodom and Egypt. It has become subject to judgment as ancient Sodom was and it has come under bondage to sin, which is typified by Egypt.

How does all of this relate to the 430 years of Ezekiel 4 and the prophecy of Daniel 12:11 where 1290 days are specified? We will find a very significant relationship.

When we look closely at Daniel 12:11 we see that it speaks of two events. The first is that the daily shall be taken away. The second is that the abomination that makes desolate will be set up. The way this verse is written appears to indicate that these two events will occur simultaneously. They are then followed by a period of 1290 days or whatever the 1290 days signify.

Let us look at the first event, the daily being taken away. Please note that the word "sacrifice" is *italicized*. This indicates it was not in the original Hebrew text. Both in this verse and in Daniel 8:11 where this phrase appears the word "daily" probably refers to the candlestick that burns continuously in the temple. We read in Leviticus 24:2-4:

> Command the children of Israel, that they bring unto thee pure oil olive beaten for the light, to cause the lamps to burn continually. Without the veil of the testimony, in the tabernacle of the congregation, shall Aaron order it from the evening unto the morning before the LORD continually: it shall be a statute for ever in your generations. He shall order the lamps upon the pure candlestick before the LORD continually.

These lamps burning continuously were a portrait of the light of the Gospel giving light in the spiritual temple - the body of believers. When the daily is taken away it means that the churches have become increasingly apostate. They are no longer light bearers of the Gospel.

They have begun to bring false gospels so that it is Satan who rules in their church.

The event of the abomination of desolation being set up is also speaking of churches that have become apostate. While they should be ruled over by Christ as they preach the true Gospel, in reality they have begun to bring false gospels so that it is Satan who rules in the church even though the deceived congregation thinks that they are serving Christ. Both events are taking place during the final tribulation period when the true Gospel is increasingly pinched off.

There are two other times in history when these conditions were sufficiently in view that they typified what would happen during the final tribulation. One of these times was during the twenty-three year period that extended from the death of King Josiah in 609 B.C. until the destruction of Israel by the Babylonians in 587 B.C. inclusive. Earlier we learned that this twenty-three year period is a type or picture of the 2300 days of the final tribulation.

Another time when the taking away of the daily candlestick signified the final tribulation was the year 1877 B.C., when Israel went into Egypt. Israel remained in Egypt for 430 years and was freed from Egypt in the year 1447 B.C. It was the year 1447 B.C. that God brought salvation to national Israel. That is, the literal, physical freeing of them from the land of Egypt is a tremendous picture or figure of salvation, when the believer is freed from the tyranny of sin and Satan: This salvation will be completed on the last day. Thus the going out of Egypt in the year 1447 B.C. points to the end of the world.

Another time that typified the end of the world was the year 587 B.C., at the end of the twenty-three years of tribulation that Israel experienced. The judgment upon Israel was a type or figure of the end of the world when the churches will be judged. So we see a very insistent relationship between the 430 years in Egypt, the 430 years in Ezekiel 4, and the 1290 days of Daniel 12.

More must be said - All of the questions are not answered. Daniel 12:11 is speaking of the abomination that makes desolate. The focus of this verse is the end of the world. Therefore, even as the 430 years in Egypt ended with judgment on Egypt and salvation for the Israelites, so the 430 year period is related to the timing of Christ's return. Even as the time period of 430 years from Solomon's temple foundation in 967 B.C. to the command by Cyrus to rebuild the temple in 537 B.C. is a type of Christ in His return, so we sense some function of 430 must end at Judgment Day. Even as Daniel's 1290 days were prefigured by Israel's going into Egypt and ended with judgment on Judah 1290 years later, so we must conclude the 1290 years are somehow related to the end of time.

An additional clue to a possible solution is offered by the one-to-three relationship of the 430 years to the 1290 years. This is a rather common occurrence in God's plan as revealed in the Bible. Moses' life was divided into three periods of forty years. When he was 40 years old, he was ready to bring deliverance to the Israelites.

Acts 7:23-25: And when he was full forty years old, it came into his heart to visit his brethren the children of Israel. And seeing one of them suffer wrong, he defended him, and avenged him that was oppressed, and smote the Egyptian: For he supposed his brethren would have understood how that God by his hand would deliver them: but they understood not.

When Moses was 120 years old, he brought them to the threshold of Canaan. Their deliverance to the promised land had practically been accomplished. Forty years is, of course, one third of 120 years.

In Zechariah 13:8-9 God utilizes a one third-two thirds relationship in a most interesting way. He divides the whole human race symbolically into two groups. We read:

And it shall come to pass, that in all the land, saith the LORD, two parts therein shall be cut off and die; but the third shall be left therein. And I will bring the third part through the fire, and will refine them as silver is refined, and will try them as gold is tried: they shall call on my name, and I will hear them: I will say, It is my people: and they shall say, The LORD is my God.

When God finally allowed Israel to have kings rule over them, He again utilized three divisions of equal length.

Saul was the first king to rule over the twelve tribes. He reigned for forty years (Acts 13:21). He was removed because of disobedience.

I Samuel 13:13-14: And Samuel said to Saul, Thou hast done foolishly: thou hast not kept the commandment of the LORD thy God, which he commanded thee: for now would the LORD have established thy kingdom upon Israel for ever. But now thy kingdom shall not continue: the LORD hath sought him a man after his own heart, and the LORD hath commanded him to be captain over his people, because thou hast not kept that which the LORD commanded thee.

David followed Saul, with a forty-year reign. Following David, Solomon reigned for forty years. At Solomon's death the major part of the nation of Israel was removed forever from God's chosen line of kings. This is shown to us by the language of I Kings 11:31-32:

And he said to Jeroboam, Take thee ten pieces: for thus saith the LORD, the God of Israel, Behold, I will rend the kingdom out of the hand of Solomon, and will give ten tribes to thee: (But he shall have one tribe for my servant David's sake, and for Jerusalem's sake, the city which I have chosen out of all the tribes of Israel:).

Similarly there were 480 years from the time when Israel was freed from Egyptian bondage in 1447 B.C. until the beginning of the construction of the temple in 967 B.C. The temple was a dramatic picture or representation that pointed to the sending of the Gospel into all the world. In the year 7 B.C., just 960 years after the temple, Christ was born as the true temple. The one-to-three relationship of the 480 years to the 1440 years is obvious.

Returning to the 430 years, we saw a one-to-three relationship of the 430 years to the 1290 years. The 430 years began in 1877 B.C. at the entrance into Egypt and ended with judgment on the Egyptians in 1447 B.C. The 1290 year period ended in 587 B.C. with judgment on the nation of Israel.

This does not fulfill or complete the prophecy of the 430 years or the 1290 years. We saw that somehow the end of those two periods must coincide with Christ's return. Does the one-to-three relationship offer a solution? Let's begin again at 1877.

> 1877 Israel enters Egypt
> <u>1447</u> Israel leaves Egypt
> 430

> 1877 Israel enters Egypt
> <u>587</u> Judgment on Israel
> 1290   (3 x 430) = 1290

Now suppose that we multiply the 1290 years by three to establish the next one-to-three relationship. Three times 1290 equals 3870 years. Since the 1290 period began in 1877 we must find the year that is 3870 years after 1877 B.C. That is the year - yes, it is 1994 A.D.

1994 A.D.
<u>1877 B.C.</u>
3871
<u> - 1 year,</u> subtracted when going from B.C. to A.D.
3870 years

Returning now to Daniel 12:11, you will recall that God declared that from the taking away of the continual and the abomination that makes desolate there would be 1290 days. Employing a year for a day as instructed in Ezekiel 4 and seeing the pattern of the one-to-three relationship, we have seen a very precise path from the time Israel entered into Egypt until the end of Israel in 587 B.C. and the end of the church age when Christ returns in 1994 A.D.

$$
\begin{aligned}
1877 - 1447 &= 430 \text{ years} \\
3 \times 430 &= 1290 \text{ years} \\
1877 - 587 &= 1290 \text{ years} \\
3 \times 1290 &= 3870 \text{ years} \\
1877 \text{ B.C.} - 1994 \text{ A.D.} &= 3870 \text{ years}
\end{aligned}
$$

The year 1877 B.C. ended the 430 years of Egyptian bondage.

The year 587 B.C. is 1290 years after Jacob entered Egypt and also is the end of the last 23 years of Israel before they were destroyed by the Babylonians.

The end of the 3870-year period after Jacob entered into Egypt appears to point to the end of the final tribulation period, which will coincide with Christ's return.

> *Repeatedly the year 1994 A.D.*
> *appears to be a likely candidate*
> *for the year of the end*
> *of history.*

Surely these time relationships cannot be coincidental. We are finding that repeatedly the year 1994 A.D. appears to be a likely candidate for the year of the end of history.

God's Plan Suggested by Jesus

One other passage comes to mind that in some degree appears to corroborate the evidence presented in this chapter. We have discovered that there is substantial reason to believe that Christ will return six years after the end of 13,000 years and exactly on the end of 4000 years. A statement in Matthew reinforces this timetable. In Matthew Jesus spoke to the scribes and pharisees as follows:

> Matthew 23:29-36: Woe unto you, scribes and Pharisees, hypocrites! because ye build the tombs of the prophets, and garnish the sepulchres of the righteous, And say, If we had been in the days of our fathers, we would not have been partakers with them in the blood of the prophets. Wherefore ye be witnesses unto yourselves, that ye are the children of them which killed the prophets. Fill ye up then the measure of your fathers. Ye serpents, ye generation of vipers, how can ye escape the damnation of hell? Wherefore, behold, I send unto you prophets, and wise men, and scribes: and some of them ye shall kill and crucify; and some of them shall ye scourge in your synagogues, and persecute them from city to city: **That upon you may come all the righteous blood shed upon the earth, from the blood of righteous Abel unto the blood of Zacharias son of Barachias,** whom ye slew between the temple and the altar. **Verily I say unto you, All these things shall come upon this generation.**

Jesus accuses the Jewish leaders of all the righteous blood shed on earth from Abel to Zechariah. Abel was of course the son of Adam who was killed by his brother Cain, but he lived thousands of years before there were any Jews. On the other hand, the Zechariah who was murdered between the sanctuary and altar lived in all probability during the reign of King Joash, 800 years before Christ. Inasmuch as many prophets were killed during this 800 years and many during the New Testament period, one wonders why Christ mentions Zechariah. He speaks of **all** the righteous blood shed upon earth and reaches all the way back, eleven millenniums, and appears to indicate that all the righteous blood is to be understood in a very universal sense, beginning at creation and ending at the end of the world. But the murder of Zechariah is foreign to the concept of this all-of-history-embracing responsibility by these leaders. That is, unless we are to understand something different in regards to the reference to Zechariah. Let us look for a moment at II Chronicles 24 where the incident of the murder of Zechariah is recorded.

II Chronicles 24:15-25: **But Jehoiada waxed old, and was full of days when he died; an hundred and thirty years old was he when he died.** And they buried him in the city of David among the kings, because he had done good in Israel, both toward God, and toward his house. Now after the death of Jehoiada came the princes of Judah, and made obeisance to the king. Then the king hearkened unto them. And they left the house of the LORD God of their fathers, and served groves and idols: and wrath came upon Judah and Jerusalem for this their trespass. Yet he sent prophets to them, to bring them again unto the LORD; and they testified against them: but they would not give ear. **And the Spirit of God came upon Zechariah the son of Jehoiada the priest,** which stood above the people, and said unto them, Thus saith God, Why transgress ye the commandments of the LORD, that ye cannot prosper? because ye have forsaken the LORD, he hath also forsaken you. **And they conspired against him, and stoned him with stones at the commandment of the king in the court of the house of the LORD.** Thus Joash the king remembered not the kindness which Jehoiada his father had done to him, but slew his son. And when he died, he said, The LORD look upon it, and require it. **And it came to pass at the end of the year, that the host of Syria came up against him: and they came to Judah and Jerusalem,** and destroyed all the princes of the people from among the people, and sent all the spoil of them unto the king of Damascus. For the army of the Syrians came with a small company of men, and the LORD delivered a very great host into their hand, because they had forsaken the LORD God of their fathers. **So they executed judgment against Joash.** And when they were departed from him, (for they left him in great diseases,) **his own servants conspired against him for the blood of the sons of Jehoiada the priest, and slew him on his bed, and he died:** and they buried him in the city of David, but they buried him not in the sepulchres of the kings.

In this passage Zechariah is recorded as being the son of Jehoiada while Jesus talks about Zechariah the son of Barachias. That this is the same Zechariah is indicated by the parallel language of II Chronicles 24:19 with Matthew 23:34 and II Chronicles 24:21 with Matthew 23:35. There is no conclusive evidence that Jehoiada is the immediate father of Zechariah. The language of the Bible would permit him to be grandfather or great-grandfather with Barachias being the immediate father, or Barachias could have been the father or grandfather of Jehoiada. Why Christ emphasized the name Barachias is another question, which does not appear to be germane to our present discussion.

If we look closely at this passage in II Chronicles we see that Jehoiada was a priest of God who had been given the responsibility of guiding the leadership of the nation of Judah. When the crown prince Joash was seven years old, Jehoiada arranged for him to be crowned king. The queen mother, Athaliah, who had murdered all of the royal family except Joash (he was hidden by Jehoshabeath the wife of Jehoiada), was killed by order of Jehoiada, and the kingdom made secure for Joash. Joash did what was right in the eyes of the Lord all the days of Jehoiada the priest (II Chronicles 24:2).

Notice the age of Jehoiada at death. He was 130 years old, the same age as Jacob when he was saved by Joseph. Even as Jacob's 130 years are a parallel to the 13,000 years from Adam to Christ's second coming, we wonder - is Jehoiada (which means Jehovah knows) and his 130 year life span symbolic of the 13,000 years of God's care over His people?

Notice what happens after Jehoiada's death. Joash killed Zechariah, but at the end of the year (II Chronicles 24:23) Joash was killed. Since Joash reigned forty years (II Chronicles 24:1), Zechariah was apparently murdered in Joash's fortieth year. How interesting that we have two numbers in this passage that have been very important in our determination of the year of Christ's return. We saw that the 13,000 years ended at the end of 1988. This is to be followed by the tribulation of 2300 days or six years after which Christ is to return in 1994, at the precise end of 4000 years. During this tribulation, which is the period of the final tribulation when Satan is assaulting the church, the last of the prophets will be killed. Thus Zechariah, who preached after the 130 years of Jehoiada and before the conclusion of the forty years of Joash, is a type or is symbolic of those prophets who will be killed during the last tribulation when the man of sin (Satan) reigns.

Jehoiada's 130 years point to the 13,000 years of God's protection over His people, 11,013 B.C. to 1994 A.D. Joash's forty years point to the last 4000 years of the church, beginning with the birth of Jacob in 2007 B.C. and ending with the return of Christ in 1994 A.D.

> *Jesus is speaking of the whole generation*
> *of evil, which is guilty of killing the*
> *prophets from the beginning of time*
> *through the final tribulation.*

During the last year of Joash's reign, Zechariah was killed, which points to the final tribulation, which begins when the 13,000 years have ended. It is during the final tribulation that God declares that the church, typified by Joash killing Zechariah, kills the prophets. The generation Jesus is speaking of is the whole generation of evil, which is guilty of killing all the prophets from the beginning of time, when Abel was killed, up to and including the killing of the prophets, typified by Zechariah, during the final tribulation. Remember earlier in this study we learned that killing the prophets had to do with believers being driven from the congregations and other means of subverting the Gospel.

400 Years Equals 4000 Years
The Bible has more to say to us in connection with the number forty. In Genesis 15:13-14 God prophesied to Abraham:

> And he said unto Abram, Know of a surety that thy seed shall be a stranger in a land that is not theirs, and shall serve them; and they shall afflict them four hundred years; And also that nation, whom they shall serve, will I judge: and afterward shall they come out with great substance.

In this cryptic statement God is speaking first of all of Israel being oppressed for 400 years in the land of Egypt. They actually were there 430 years (Exodus 12:40-41), but they were not oppressed the entire 430 years. It was not until a pharaoh came to power who did not know Joseph that the oppression became severe.

Nevertheless, God speaks of this oppression as a period of 400 years because it symbolically points to someone other than Israel. We will see who this is in a moment. Israel came out of Egypt with great possessions, as Genesis 15:14 teaches. We read that they plundered the Egyptians in Exodus 12:36:

> And the LORD gave the people favour in the sight of the Egyptians, so that they lent unto them such things as they required. And they spoiled the Egyptians.

The going out of Egypt was simultaneous with God's judgment on Egypt. It was at that time that all of the firstborn of Egypt were killed.

It was also at that time that the Passover was instituted. This historical event that was anticipated by the language of Genesis 15:13-14 was pointing to the great event of salvation. Israel's presence as slaves in Egypt is a picture of those who are to be saved, who begin as slaves to sin and Satan. The Passover, which was instituted when Israel went out of Egypt, was a beautiful type or figure of Jesus, who is the Passover Lamb, who was slain to save us.

The salvation provided by Christ is a two-part event. At the moment a believer experiences salvation he receives his eternal resurrected soul. He is freed from the dominion of Satan, and he becomes a son of God. He retains an unsaved body that continues to lust after sin, and since his body is an integral part of his very being, his salvation will not be complete until his body, too, has become saved.

Therefore, his salvation will not be complete until he experiences the resurrection of his body. This great and wonderful event will occur on the last day when Christ comes on the clouds of glory. It is then that the believer receives his eternal inheritance in the fullest sense of the word. He will receive his resurrected body, and he will become owner of the new heaven and new earth. This earth, which is presently owned by the peoples of this earth - most of whom are unsaved - will be taken from the unsaved and as a new earth it will become the eternal habitation of the saved. The unsaved will be judged and removed into hell.

> *This earth, which is presently owned by the peoples of the earth, will be taken from the unsaved and as a new earth will become the eternal habitation of the saved.*

Thus we see the following parallels in view in Genesis 15:13-14.

	Historical Reality:	*Pointing To:*
1. Abram's seed	National Israel	Believers in Christ
2. Strangers in a land that is not theirs	National Israel in Egypt	God's elect living in present world
3. Shall serve them	National Israel slaves of the Egyptians	a. God's elect, slaves of sin before salvation and still subject to sin after salvation b. God's elect subject to the political governments of the world
4. They shall afflict them	National Israel afflicted by their Egyptian masters	God's elect experiencing the tribulation of this world (John 16:33)
5. That nation whom they shall serve	The firstborn of Egypt killed	The unsaved of the world judged on the last day
6. They shall come out	National Israel comes out of Egypt	The believers' salvation is on the last day
7. With great substance	National Israel plunders the Egyptians (Exo. 12:36)	The believers receive the new heaven and new earth

In this outline we have covered all of the phrases of Genesis 15:13-14 except one, and that is 400 years. As we have already seen, historically this refers to part of the 430 years that national Israel was in Egypt.

How does this point to the salvation of the elect? Since all of the other phrases in these verses do so, we know this period of 400 years must also refer to the elect. But in what manner?

We will find our answer if we realize that there is another Israel in the Bible besides national Israel, and that is the Israel of God, which is made up of all believers in the Lord Jesus Christ. Galatians 3:29 teaches: "And if ye be Christ's, then are ye Abraham's seed, and heirs according to the promise."

> *Both national Israel and the Israel of God received the name Israel from the patriarch Jacob.*

Both national Israel and the Israel of God received the name Israel from the patriarch Jacob, whose name was changed to Israel at the time he wrestled with the Lord at the River Jabbok. Concerning the elect of God, the Bible teaches in Romans 9 that Jacob is used as an example of those who are saved. Romans 9:8-13 declares:

That is, They which are the children of the flesh, these are not the children of God: but the children of the promise are counted for the seed. For this is the word of promise, At this time will I come, and Sarah shall have a son. And not only this; but when Rebecca also had conceived by one, even by our father Isaac; (For the children being not yet born, neither having done any good or evil, that the purpose of God according to election might stand, not of works, but of him that calleth;) It was said unto her, The elder shall serve the younger. As it is written, Jacob have I loved, but Esau have I hated.

Please note that in these verses God declares that "the children of the promise are counted for the seed." Then He indicates that the children of the promise include the son of Sarah - Isaac - and the son of Rebecca - Jacob. These men are types or figures of all who are children of the promise - the elect. Thus we are not surprised that not infrequently when God uses the name Israel, He is talking about the whole body of believers - the Israel of God. Likewise we are not surprised when God uses the name Jacob to speak of the whole body of believers - the Israel of God.

How does this relate to the 400 years of Genesis 15:13-14? Does the whole body of believers live as strangers in this world for 400 years? We know that is an impossible idea. Believers have lived in this world for 13,000 years. We do know that insofar as the 400 years relate to the spiritual Israel, which consists of all believers in Christ, the end of the 400 years must be their salvation.

> *Believers are typified by Jacob and*
> *are called Jacob in the Bible . . . and*
> *become a part of the spiritual Israel.*

We also know that because believers were typified by Jacob, and indeed sometimes are called Jacob in the Bible, the birth of the patriarch Jacob is also a picture of the believer as he comes into this world or of the believer as he becomes saved and becomes a part of the spiritual Israel. Therefore, we can expect that 400 years or 4000 years (remember we saw earlier that adding another zero to a number does not change the meaning or intent of the number), before the end of the world - Jacob was born. That is, symbolically the nation of believers, typified by Jacob, was born or came into being 4000 years before the end of the world.

We know, of course, that Jacob was born in the year 2007 B.C. Four thousand years after 2007 B.C. would point to 1994 as the end of the world. The parallelism would look like this.

Gen. 15:13-14	*Historical Reality*	*Pointing to*
400 years	National Israel (Jacob) in physical bondage in Egypt	The Israel of God (all of the elect) under affliction during the period symbolically running from the birth of Jacob (the new birth of each believer) to end of world

We can see why God used the number 400 years when speaking of the bondage of Israel in Egypt. As we saw earlier, it was a somewhat awkward figure when identified with national Israel; that is, unless this servitude began as early as some forty years before the death of Joseph. It becomes a significant number when the 400 years are related to the elect of God who are typified by Jacob who was born exactly 4000 years before the end of the world.

We will summarize what we have discovered thus far.

1. The restoration of national Israel as a political nation fulfills the prophecy that the fig tree was to be in leaf as a sign that Christ's return was imminent. This assures us that we are very close to the end of time.

2. 11,013 B.C. (creation) + 13,000 years   = 1988
         13 tribes, 13 millenniums
         13 times around Jericho
         Jacob 130 years old

3. 11,013 (creation) + 13,000 years + 2300 days   = 1994

4. 11,013 (creation) + 13,000 years + 23 years   = 2011

5. 2007 B.C. (Jacob born) + 4000 years   = 1994

6. 1907 B.C. (Jacob's name becomes Israel) + 3900 years
                                          = 1994

7. 1877 B.C. (Israel entered Egypt) + 3 x 1290 years
                                          = 1994

8. 7 B.C. (Jesus born) + 2000 years   = 1994

Indeed 1994 is beginning to establish itself as a possible year for the return of Christ. Increasing evidence indicates that the year 1988 was the beginning of the 2300 day final tribulation. The year 2011 must also be kept in mind.

What About National Israel?

Before we continue we should look once more at the birth of Jacob in 2007 B.C. Since Jacob was the twin brother of Esau, Esau also was born in the year 2007 B.C. Interestingly, Jacob became the progenitor of the nation of Israel; Esau and Ishmael (the latter was born to Hagar by Abraham), became the progenitors of the Arab nations. Rebecca, the mother of Jacob and Esau, was troubled by the conflict that was going on in her womb, as we read in Genesis 25:22-23:

> And the children struggled together within her; and she said, If it be so, why am I thus? And she went to inquire of the LORD. And the LORD said unto her, Two nations are in thy womb, and two manner of people shall be separated from thy bowels; and the one people shall be stronger than the other people; and the elder shall serve the younger.

The year 1994 A.D. will mark
4000 years of conflict between
Jews and Arabs.

The conflict between Jews and Arabs continues today. The year 1994 will mark 4000 years of this conflict. It appears that the year 1994 will mark the end of this conflict because Christ will return.

It is indeed interesting and surely significant that national Israel, which in many ways typified the New Testament church, will come to its end at the same time that the church comes to its end at the conclusion of the final tribulation.

Returning to the question of the end of national Israel, one cannot help but wonder about the 400 men who came with Esau to meet Jacob when he returned to Israel after having fled from Esau's wrath forty years earlier (see Genesis 33). Could this relate to the 4000 years of hostility between the Jews and the Arabs?

God has dealt constantly with the nation of Israel in intervals of forty or 400 days or years. These were periods of testing. A few examples are given.

1. 40 years in the wilderness
2. 40 days when Moses was on Mount Sinai
3. 400 years from leaving Egypt in 1447 B.C. until Saul was crowned king in 1047 B.C.
4. 40 years under Saul as king to please them rather than God

In each instance Israel failed the test. Sin always won out.

In Luke 13:6-9 God speaks of Israel as a fig tree that was tested three times and did not bear fruit and therefore should be cut down. Then it was given one more opportunity to bear fruit. If it did not it was to be cut down.

Israel bore little or no fruit in the wilderness journey.

Israel bore little or no fruit when in the land of Canaan.

Israel bore little or no fruit when Jesus was among them.

Then in 1948 Israel again became a nation. They again were being tested. Would they bring forth spiritual fruit? The year 1988 was the fortieth year. They should have been destroyed because there was no fruit, but God allows them to go to the end of another forty. This forty is multiplied by one hundred (the number that signifies completeness) to give the number 4000. The year 1994 is exactly 4000 years after the birth of Jacob, the progenitor of Israel. They will be cut down at the end of 4000 years because it appears that that year is the end of the world.*

NOTES

[1] Jack Finegan, *Handbook of Biblical Chronology* (Princeton, New Jersey: Princeton University Press, 1964), 170.

* See Appendix I for additional discussion of the future of national Israel..

Chapter 14
The Year of Christ's Return
Continues to Unfold

We are not dealing with a question wherein idle speculation can have a part. Nor can this be a study based on a premonition or the belief that some supernatural sign has been given. The Bible is our only source of divine truth. We must, therefore, limit our investigation to Bible information.

Admittedly any study is subject to error, but when the same year for Christ's return begins to surface from many Biblical vantage points, then we can know that there is an increasing likelihood that we are on the right track.

> *Select any year other than 1994 and*
> *then try to find Biblical support for*
> *that year.*

One might try to argue that the Bible can be interpreted in many different ways. Therefore, given a predisposition to look for a particular end-time year, substantial support for that year could be found by "manipulating" the Biblical data. It is true that some support might be found for an anticipated date, but substantial and increasing evidence pointing to that assumed date will not be found. I encourage any reader who uses this argument to select any year other than 1994 and then try to find Biblical support for the year selected. If it is the true date, then we know it is God's date and the Bible - God's Book - will support that date.

That is, the Bible will support that date if it were God's purpose to hide supporting evidence within the Bible. Because in the earlier chapters of this study we discovered tremendous evidence that God had hidden within the Bible the timing of Christ's first coming, we have been vastly encouraged that likewise God has hidden within the Bible major clues concerning the timing of His second coming.

The Number Three Points to Christ's Return

The number three, or thirty or 300, is a number that teaches an important spiritual concept; namely, it represents the purpose of God. When this concept is realized we will see that the number three also guides us to the year 1994 as the year of Christ's return. Let us see why this is so.

When Jesus was in Gethsemane He prayed three times that the cup might pass from Him. Because it was the purpose of God that He drink the cup of God's wrath on behalf of those who were to be saved, Christ did not pray a fourth time. God's purpose was clearly seen when no response came from God after our Savior had prayed three times.

Likewise, the Apostle Paul prayed three times that the thorn in the flesh be removed. God's purpose was that Paul was to bear it because God's grace is sufficient (II Corinthians 12:8-9). Paul did not pray a fourth time because the answer that established God's purpose for Paul was given in response to three times of prayer.

Gideon was to fight the Midianites. God winnowed down Gideon's army of 32,000 men to a small band of 300 men, which in turn was divided into three companies (Judges 7). It was God's purpose that God would give the victory. God did not require the might of men to achieve success. His purpose is clearly seen in God's use of the number three.

Another example of the importance of the number three is that Joseph was 30 years old when he became prime minister of Egypt (Genesis 41:39-46). It was God's purpose that Joseph serve as a figure or type of Christ who officially began His redemptive work and in a sense ascended the throne of Israel when He was about 30 years of age.

John the Baptist not only introduced Jesus as the Lamb that would take away the sins of the world, he also announced that the kingdom of heaven was at hand (Matthew 3:2). In fact, when Jesus began to preach, He, too, declared, "The kingdom of heaven is at hand" (Matthew 4:17). A kingdom requires a king to rule over it. It was a kingdom at hand because Jesus, the King, had come. Even though He was born a King (John 18:37), He was not announced as the Messiah, the King, until He was **about 30 years old** (Luke 3:23). Thus He was typified by Joseph and David, both of whom also began to reign at the age of 30 years.

The proclamation of Jesus as King will not be recognized by the whole world until Judgment Day. Then Jesus will come as King of kings and Lord of lords (Revelation 19:16). Then every knee shall bow and every tongue shall confess that He is Lord (Philippians 2:10-11).

When is Judgment Day? We have already seen that 1994 is the probable year. It is amazing that 1994 is exactly 3000 years after David's coronation in 1007 B.C. Christ who is seated on David's throne will be acclaimed King by the whole world (obviously the unsaved will not do so gladly), exactly 3000 years after David was made king. Surely we see God's magnificent purpose of redemption in this 3000 years.

We are astounded how the year 1994 appears again. Surely we must be going in the right direction in our study.

But there is more.

Abraham Purchased a Cemetery

In Genesis 23 God uses the whole chapter to record a most unusual purchase. The Bible tells us in Hebrews 11:9 that Abraham, "sojourned in the land of promise, as in a strange country, dwelling in tabernacles with Isaac and Jacob," and in Hebrews 11:13, "confessed that they were strangers and pilgrims on the earth." Therefore, Abraham, though he lived one hundred years in the land of Canaan, never built a city, and he never owned any land, that is with one exception. The Bible records in Genesis 23 that when his wife Sarah died at the age of 127 years, Abraham bought a field that had a cave in the end of it. In this cave not only was Sarah buried but Genesis 49:31-50:13 records that three patriarchs: Abraham, Isaac, and Jacob, together with wives Rebecca and Leah, were also buried there.

After Sarah died Abraham located the owner of the field and cave and in the presence of all the people of the land, engaged in a curious conversation as he purchased the cave for a sepulchre. The owner was Ephron the son of Zohar. He was a Hittite while all the people of the land were Canaanites. Both the Hittites and the Canaanites are representative of the nations of the world who have no regard for Jehovah, the true God.

When Abraham made known to Ephron his desire to purchase the cave, Ephron declared in Genesis 23:10-11:

And Ephron dwelt among the children of Heth: and Ephron the Hittite answered Abraham in the audience of the children of Heth, even of all that went in at the gate of his city, saying, Nay, my lord, hear me: the field give I thee, and the cave that is therein, I give it thee; in the presence of the sons of my people give I it thee: bury thy dead.

In reply to the offer of the cave as a gift, Abraham declared in verse 13:

And he spake unto Ephron in the audience of the people of the land, saying, But if thou wilt give it, I pray thee, hear me: I will give thee money for the field; take it of me, and I will bury my dead there.

Verses 14 and 15 give us Ephron's strange reply.

And Ephron answered Abraham, saying unto him, My lord, hearken unto me: the land is worth four hundred shekels of silver; what is that betwixt me and thee? bury therefore thy dead.

In this reply the value of the land and cave is given as 400 shekels of silver. Verses 16-18 declare that Abraham paid this amount to obtain ownership. Again the emphasis is made that all of this transaction was done in the audience of the sons of Heth and in the presence of the children of Heth, before all that went in at the gate of his city.

While the language employed by Ephron and Abraham in completing this transaction may have been commonly used by people of that day, God had to have a very special reason to record it for us. To my knowledge there is no other buy and sell language that is similar in nature in the Bible. In fact, it is also unique that the life span of Sarah is given. The Bible nowhere records the life span of any other woman. It is also odd that whereas Abraham lived as a stranger, in death he wanted to have a permanent location. This passage is unique in that:

1. Sarah's life span is given as 127 years.

2. Abraham purchased land and a cave to be used as a sepulchre for the burial of the patriarchs. Did he think his descendants would own that land until the end of the world?

3. The transaction was completed in the presence of all the people of the land, who were Canaanites.

4. A sum of 400 shekels of silver was paid.

5. It was emphasized that this price meant nothing between Abraham and the seller.

In looking for the spiritual Gospel meaning of this curious account we know that it occurred in the year 2030 B.C., because Genesis 17:17 records that Abraham was ten years older than Sarah. Since Abraham was 100 years of age in 2067 when Isaac was born, Sarah was 90 years old. Thus, Sarah's death thirty-seven years later would have been in the year 2030 B.C. Why does God record a price of 400 shekels of silver? Why the disclaimer that this was nothing between the buyer and seller? Why the repeated reference that this was done in the presence of all the Canaanites?

We are helped by the Biblical reference to another burial. In John 11 we read of the death of Lazarus, verse 39: "for he hath been dead four days," and verse 17 declares: "Then when Jesus came, he found that he had lain in the grave four days already."

We wonder, why does it say four days *already*? We can make sense of this if we tie the raising of Lazarus to the purchase of the cave in which Sarah was buried. The common denominators are *burial in a cave* and the number *four*. Remember that the Bible declares that a day is as a thousand years, and remember that Jesus raised Lazarus after he had been in the tomb four days *already*, and then we can understand that it is as if Lazarus had been in the tomb 4000 years and now it is time for him to be raised.

According to God's plan believers are strangers and pilgrims on this earth. When they die, in their soul existence they leave this earth and go to live with Christ in heaven, but their bodies cannot go into heaven until they experience the resurrection that will occur at the end of the world. Therefore, their bodies have to be on this earth until the end of the world.

The payment of 400 shekels of silver that Abraham paid was made to make the cave secure. It did not guarantee that Abraham's seed would possess that particular site until the end of the world. However, the payment symbolically looked towards the resurrection at the end of the world. This is proven by the use of the number four in connection with the raising of Lazarus. He was not raised until his body had *already* been in the grave for four days.

In the Book of Esther, King Ahasuerus, who typified God as the supreme ruler of the world, ruled over 127 provinces (Esther 1:1). The number 127 is the age at which Sarah died and was buried. Thus we may conclude that she represented all believers over whom God reigns. They are strangers and pilgrims but at death must leave their bodies on this earth. The 400 shekels, like the four days in which Lazarus was in the tomb, point to the day of resurrection and the certainty of the resurrection of our bodies, which, of course, comes at the end of the world.

The purchase of the cave by Abraham was done publicly, in the presence of the people of the land of Canaan. Likewise, the burial of the believers are public events, that is, they are done in the presence of the unsaved of the world.

We do wonder why such emotional language is featured in the John 11 account: Mary wept and the Jews wept. Even Jesus wept. Jesus groaned and was troubled. If the 400 shekels, like the four days, symbolize being in the tomb until the resurrection, and since when Jesus came to Bethany Lazarus had *already* been in the grave four days, then the next citation emphasizes the joy of resurrection as opposed to the extreme sorrow of having to be part of death.

> *The raising of Lazarus points to the*
> *spiritual resurrection we receive*
> *when we become saved.*

God has many reasons for writing the Bible precisely the way it was written. Certainly one grand truth that shines through in the raising of Lazarus is that it is pointing to God's method of saving people. Before we are saved we are spiritually as dead as Lazarus was physically dead. When we are spiritually dead, our loved ones ought to be weeping over us because we are on our way to eternal damnation. God Himself, the Bible records, has no pleasure in the death of the wicked (Ezekiel 33:11). The raising of Lazarus therefore points to the spiritual resurrection we receive when we become saved.

There may be an additional reason why the Bible records this extreme sorrow: Just prior to the resurrection of the last day, there will be the final great tribulation. It is a time of great sorrow for the believers as they see their loved ones snared into false gospels, as they see their church fall away from truth, as the believers must leave or are driven away from their church.

With this in mind we should note a very interesting situation. As we saw earlier, Sarah was buried in the year 2030 B.C. The 400 shekels like the four days must point to 4000 years. A time period of 4000 years plus the time of the final tribulation would then place the end of the world at either 4023 years after 2030 B.C. or 4006 years after 2030 B.C. Remember, the final tribulation should be twenty-three years long but could be shortened to 2300 days. Checking each computation we find the following:

2030 B.C. + 4000 years + 2300 days (6 years+) = 1977 A.D.
2030 B.C. + 4000 years + 23 years = 1994 A.D.

Are we surprised that 1994 A.D. again comes into view? Surely this must be an important year in God's timetable.

God uses the number seven to illustrate and emphasize the perfection of God's plan.

The Number Seven Points to Christ's Return

The number seven is a very important number that God uses to illustrate and emphasize the perfection of God's plan. In speaking of the perfection of the Holy Spirit, God speaks of the seven Spirits before the throne (Revelation 5:6).

The dragon of Revelation 13 has seven heads, which indicates the perfection of God's plan that allows Satan to rule the hearts of unsaved men.

The ark was seven months in the hands of the Philistines, which indicates the perfection of God's plan insofar as apostasy and rebellion will persist in the church.

Other examples, such as the seven churches of Revelation 2, the seventy weeks of Daniel 9, the seventy years of II Chronicles 36:21 and Daniel 9:2, all indicate the symbolic use of the number seven in the Bible.

We can find all kinds of illustrations in the Bible that appear to relate to a 7000-year history of the world. For example, please take note of the following.

1. Enoch was raptured seven generations after Adam (Genesis 5:23-24 and Jude 14). Will the church be raptured seven millenniums after Noah?
2. Noah entered the ark seven days before judgment began. Was this prophetic of the seven millenniums that would pass until final judgment?
3. The Feast of Tabernacles that commemorated the Israelites' wilderness sojourn lasted seven days with the eighth day being a day of solemn rest. Do we have an illustration here of the church in its wilderness sojourn of seven millenniums to be followed by its eternal rest in the new heavens and the new earth?
4. Pentecost followed seven weeks. Is Pentecost, when the firstfruits of the harvest were offered and when the Holy Spirit was given as a guarantee of our salvation, an illustration of the new heavens and new earth following seven millenniums?
5. The leprous person was pronounced cleansed on the eighth day. Is this related to seven millenniums followed by total cleansing in heaven where righteousness dwells?
6. The year of jubilee followed seven weeks of seven years. It was the fiftieth year. Is this a parallel to heaven following seven millenniums?
7. Nebuchadnezzar acknowledged God as ultimate ruler of the universe after seven times passed over him (Daniel 4:23). Is this typical of the nations of the world acknowledging Christ as King of kings at the end of seven millenniums?
8. After seventy years, Tyre as a figure of the earth will be dedicated to the Lord (Isaiah 23:15-18). After 7000 years will the earth, too, be the new heavens and the new earth?
9. After seventy years (Jeremiah 25:11-13), the whole land will become a ruin and a waste and Babylon will be punished eternally. Babylon is given here as a figure of the world under Satan's domination. Will Satan and the nations of the world be punished eternally after 7000 years?

Surely, we expect that the number seven, or seventy, or 700, or 7000 must have something to say concerning the timing of the return of Christ. Let us examine this possibility. In doing so we will again see that the year 1994 comes into view in a most interesting fashion.

We know, of course, that in studying the number seven we cannot begin with creation. Creation was the year 11,013 B.C. No number system could begin with that date and relate to the number seven.

The Bible Divides History into Two Major Parts

While the earth has a total history of about 13,000 years, God has divided this time span into two major epochs. In II Peter 3:5-7 we read:

> For this they willingly are ignorant of, that by the word of God the heavens were of old, and the earth standing out of the water and in the water: Whereby the world that then was, being overflowed with water, perished: But the heavens and the earth, **which are now**, by the same word are kept in store, reserved unto fire against the day of judgment and perdition of ungodly men.

The first world was destroyed by water. . . . The present world will be destroyed by fire.

In these verses, the Bible emphasizes that there was a world that had previously existed, and there is a world that now is. The first world was destroyed by water - the flood of Noah's day. The world that now is will be destroyed by fire at the end of time.

The first world existed for slightly more than 6000 years - 6023 years to be exact (11,013 B.C. - 4990 B.C.). How long will the present earth last? If God is using the number seven to indicate the perfection of God's plan, we would logically assume that the earth that began after the flood in 4990 B.C. would have its end exactly 7000 years later. That would bring us to the year 2011 A.D.

That 7000 years is to be expected is especially suggested by the awkward language of Deuteronomy 15:1-2. These verses read:

> At the **end of every seven years** thou shalt make a release. And this is the manner of the release: Every creditor that lendeth ought unto his neighbour shall release it; he shall not exact it of his neighbour, or of his brother; because it is called the LORD'S release.

This language, which in the original Hebrew is definitely *end of seven years*, is very hard to understand. Its historical meaning appears to be this: Every seventh year the land was to lay fallow. That is, no seed was to be sown and no crops were to be harvested. Exodus 23:10-12 records:

> And six years thou shalt sow thy land, and shalt gather in the fruits thereof: But the seventh year thou shalt let it rest and lie still; that the poor of thy people may eat: and what they leave the beasts of the field shall eat. In like manner thou shalt deal with thy vineyard, and with thy oliveyard. Six days thou shalt do thy work, and on the seventh day thou shalt rest: that thine ox and thine ass may rest, and the son of thy handmaid, and the stranger, may be refreshed.

The phrase "let it rest" in these verses is the same Hebrew word as "release" in Deuteronomy 31:10-11, which we will look at presently. The word is rarely found in the Bible. By means of the general subject matter of these three passages as well as the unique use of the Hebrew word that is translated "let it rest" or "release" we know that these three passages are intimately associated with each other.

The apparent teaching for ancient national Israel was that during the seventh year, when no crops were harvested, creditors who had loaned money at interest to fellow Israelites were not to charge interest during that seventh year. A reasonable explanation seems to be that because no income was available from harvested crops, no interest was to be charged.

The difficulty arises when we read in Deuteronomy 15:1, "At the **end** of every seven years thou shalt make a release." Surely it would make more sense and be a more easily understood command if God had instructed that **during** the seventh year there was to be a release.

To complicate matters even more Deuteronomy 31:10 declares:

> And Moses commanded them, saying, At the end of every seven years, in the solemnity of the year of release, in the feast of tabernacles.

As noted earlier this verse uses the same language as Deuteronomy 15:1-2. It also speaks of the year of release, and significantly it also uses the same phrase "the **end** of seven years." But the end of the Jewish year was in the spring, fifteen days before the Passover; the Passover was observed during the first month of the year.

However, in Deuteronomy 31:10 the end of the year is spoken of as the Feast of Tabernacles. The Feast of Tabernacles was in the seventh month of the Jewish calendar, and the seventh month is nowhere near the end of the year. Therefore, we see another awkward time relationship. The Feast of Tabernacles is not the end of the year. How this was resolved in the historical situation we do not know, but that question is relatively unimportant. God has carefully chosen the language of these verses so that truth might shine through, which is more important than the historical event.

In the Bible, the phrase "the end" is commonly associated with the end of time. Moreover the Feast of Tabernacles was a feast observed at the completion of the harvest. It is also called the Feast of Ingathering in the Bible (Exodus 23:16, 34:22). It therefore signifies the harvest at the end of the world. Jesus warns in Matthew 13:39, "The harvest is the end of the world."

Therefore, the "release" of Deuteronomy 15:1-2 and Deuteronomy 31:10 point in some way to the end of the world. Perhaps the releasing by the lender is a parallel concept to that found in connection with the jubilee year. At that time all property went back to its original owners and other debts were forgiven. Certainly it is pointing us to the conclusion of our salvation when God's grace is manifested to us in the highest possible degree and we receive our resurrected bodies.

In these verses the references to the end of the seventh year could mean no more than the fact that at the end of time the perfection of God's plan of salvation will be realized. On the other hand, we cannot help but wonder if this is also some kind of time clue.

That brings us back to our question: Does the number seven give us a clue concerning the timing of the end? The flood occurred in 4990 B.C. Seven thousand years later brings us to 2011 A.D. This year had support from only one other Biblical reference. That was when we added a possible twenty-three year tribulation period to an even 13,000 years to arrive at a total number of years for the history of the world. It may look like the number seven has symbolical importance but is not to be considered a time reference.

But wait. There is more information we must consider. Jesus says in Matthew 24:21-22:

> For then shall be great tribulation, such as was not since the beginning of the world to this time, no, nor ever shall be. And except those days should be shortened, there should no flesh be saved: but for the elect's sake those days shall be shortened.

In these verses Jesus is speaking of the final tribulation period, which is to come just before the return of Christ and Judgment Day. We read in Matthew 24:29:

> Immediately after the tribulation of those days shall the sun be darkened, and the moon shall not give her light, and the stars shall fall from heaven, and the powers of the heavens shall be shaken.

Let's go back to the 7000 years that we have been examining. The first world lasted 6023 years without God's salvation plan being realized in its fullness. God begins again with the world. This time God's salvation plan will go to perfection. Not only is it typified by the number seven, but it is to have its perfection by being completed during a period of 7000 years.

The last event of this 7000-year
period is the final tribulation period.

The last event of this 7000-year period is the final tribulation period. The Bible is entirely clear that this sad event must be experienced.

The Days of the Final Tribulation Will Be Shortened

Now we come to the intriguing information. We have read in Matthew 24:21-22 that for the sake of the elect those days of the final tribulation period will be shortened. That is, God appears to be declaring that this final tribulation period should be a certain length of time. If it were that length of time, it seems it would fit perfectly with God's perfect plan of 7000 years. Judgment Day would be in the year 2011 A.D.

But for the sake of the elect those days will be shortened. As we saw earlier in our study, during the final tribulation period the Gospel will be increasingly pinched off so that fewer and fewer become saved.

We must conclude that the return of Christ will not be 2011 A.D. but some years before this. How much earlier than 2011 A.D. Jesus will come depends entirely on how much God shortens the final tribulation period.

We will now look at the timetable of the final tribulation period to discover, if we are able, how long it should be. Since we already know its duration is to be 2300 evening mornings (Daniel 8:13-14), which is about six years, once we know how long the final tribulation period should have been we will be in a position to know the possible date of Christ's return based on the number seven. By subtracting the difference between the expected length of the final tribulation period and 2300 days from 2011 A.D. we should arrive at the expected year of Christ's return.

We will now pursue the question of the normally expected time duration of the final tribulation period.

Remember earlier in our study we learned that the final tribulation period could be either seventy years or twenty-three years in duration. The three and one half days of Revelation 11 are far too short to be understood in any way except symbolically. Thus we wonder which time period should have been the one expected just before the end of the world. According to the information we presently have it should be shortened to 2300 days and the end of the 2300 days will coincide with the end of the world.

If we try to place seventy years into this arrangement we find it will not compute. Seven thousand years after 4990 B.C. brings us to 2011 A.D. as we have seen. Subtracting seventy years from 2011 A.D. brings us to 1941 A.D. Adding 2300 days to this would bring us to the year 1947 A.D. Since that year is long past we know that a seventy year period of tribulation is not to be expected.

Twenty-Three Years - The Expected Time Duration

When we place into the time arrangement an expected tribulation period of twenty-three years we begin to find harmony. If we subtract twenty-three years from 2011 A.D. we come to 1988 A.D. Adding 2300 days to this brings us to 1994. Isn't it remarkable! The very years that continually have come to our attention are again before us. Surely this could not be coincidental. Surely we must be finding truth.

Now we should carefully examine another question. Why would God shorten the final tribulation period from twenty-three years to 2300 days? Can we find some answers to this?

Let us return to the citations in Matthew 24 and Mark 13, which refer to this shortening. Both in Matthew 24:22 and in Mark 13:20 the reason given for the shortening is that it is done for the sake of the elect inasmuch as no flesh can be saved if it continues the full length. We read in Mark 13:20:

> And except that the Lord had shortened those days, no flesh should be saved: but for the elect's sake, whom he hath chosen, he hath shortened the days.

How are we to understand this verse? It will become more clear to us if we remember that this sin-cursed world continues as long as it does so that all those who are to be saved will indeed become saved. In II Peter 3, for example, God is discussing the longsuffering of God toward this world of sin. He then declares in II Peter 3:9:

> The Lord is not slack concerning his promise, as some men count slackness; but is longsuffering to us-ward, not willing that any should perish, but that all should come to repentance.

> *If the world came into judgment too early, God's salvation plan would be frustrated.*

God is teaching that He patiently endures the wickedness of mankind because there are those who must become saved. If the world came into judgment too early, God's salvation plan would be frustrated. Every single individual elected to salvation must first become saved. Jesus says in John 6:37 and 39:

All that the Father giveth me shall come to me; and him that cometh to me I will in no wise cast out. . . . And this is the Father's will which hath sent me, that of all which he hath given me I should lose nothing, but should raise it up again at the last day.

> *Once the last elect individual has*
> *become saved, the end will come.*

The Saving of the Last One of the Elect - The End

Once the last elect individual has become saved the end will come. In Matthew 24:14 we read:

And this gospel of the kingdom shall be preached in all the world for a witness unto all nations; and then shall the end come.

In Revelation 11:1-2 God declares:

And there was given me a reed like unto a rod: and the angel stood, saying, Rise, and measure the temple of God, and the altar, and them that worship therein. But the court which is without the temple leave out, and measure it not; for it is given unto the Gentiles: and the holy city shall they tread under foot forty and two months.

In this interesting passage God is measuring the temple and those who worship in it. The temple is the body of believers. It is constructed as people become saved. It is measured, that is God has a concern for its size and shape. That is where God's chief interest is. On the other hand, the court of the Gentiles is not measured. The word "Gentiles" in this verse is speaking of the unsaved of the world. God is showing that the number of the unsaved or the length of their time on earth is not God's chief concern. The duration of this earth must be long enough so that everyone who is to become saved does become saved.

Earlier in our study we looked briefly at Deuteronomy 32:8:

When the Most High divided to the nations their inheritance, when he separated the sons of Adam, he set the bounds of the people according to the number of the children of Israel.

> *The timetable of the earth's existence*
> *is not determined by the number of*
> *unsaved people who are to be born.*

From this verse we learn that the timetable of the earth's existence is not determined by the number of unsaved people who are to be born. Rather it is the total number of the body of believers, the elect of God, the eternal children of Israel, that is determinative of when this world will come to an end. This accords perfectly with the principle we have reiterated many times: The timetable of history is the unfolding of God's salvation plan. Therefore, when God has saved each and every one who is to be saved, God's salvation plan has been fulfilled. There no longer exists any other purpose for the world to continue. Thus, God immediately ends history by bringing the world to its end.

This principle is also taught by the language of Revelation 6:9-11:

> And when he had opened the fifth seal, I saw under the altar the souls of them that were slain for the word of God, and for the testimony which they held: And they cried with a loud voice, saying, How long, O Lord, holy and true, dost thou not judge and avenge our blood on them that dwell on the earth? And white robes were given unto every one of them; and it was said unto them, **that they should rest yet for a little season, until their fellowservants also and their brethren, that should be killed as they were, should be fulfilled.**

The implication of these verses is also that Judgment Day will come as soon as all of the believers have been saved. For the sake of the elect this world will come to an end as soon as the last of the elect are saved. It is not God's intention that believers are to live in this sin-cursed world any longer than that.

> *The world has continued as long as
> it has so that all of the elect could
> become saved.*

The problem that must be faced then is that in order to come to a perfect 7000 years, seventeen more years must elapse after the 2300 day tribulation period. Those seventeen years added to the 2300 days would result in a twenty-three year tribulation period, which, as we have seen, agrees with much Biblical data concerning the length of the final tribulation period. It also agrees perfectly with a 7000 year span of time from the flood to the end of time. These last seventeen years would be a time when no one would become saved because all who were to become saved had become saved before this seventeen year period began. The world has continued as long as it has so that all of the elect could be saved. Once they are, for the sake of the elect, God must end the world. Therefore, to do this the final tribulation will not continue twenty-three years but only 2300 days. Thus the 7000 years also must be shortened by seventeen years. Thus we can understand the meaning of Mark 13:20.

The Number Seventeen Identifies with Heaven

We are going to discover that in the Bible if God uses the number seventeen symbolically to present spiritual truth, it is used to identify with heaven. Let us look at a few examples. Once we understand this we will find how beautifully it fits into God's arrangement for the end of the world.

In Genesis 37 we have the account of Joseph who dreamed that He would rule over his brothers. His dreams about this are recorded in verses 7-10.

> Genesis 37:7-10: For, behold, we were binding sheaves in the field, and, lo, my sheaf arose, and also stood upright; and, behold, your sheaves stood round about, and made obeisance to my sheaf. And his brethren said to him, Shalt thou indeed reign over us? or shalt thou indeed have dominion over us? And they hated him yet the more for his dreams, and for his words.

And he dreamed yet another dream, and told it his brethren, and said, Behold, I have dreamed a dream more; and, behold, the sun and the moon and the eleven stars made obeisance to me. And he told it to his father, and to his brethren: and his father rebuked him, and said unto him, What is this dream that thou hast dreamed? Shall I and thy mother and thy brethren indeed come to bow down ourselves to thee to the earth?

In these dreams he was unknowingly anticipating the time when he would be prime minister of Egypt and in this office he would rule over his brothers. In this he was to serve as a great figure of Christ who saves us from spiritual hunger and becomes Lord and King over us.

A curious piece of information concerning these dreams of Joseph is that God tells us how old Joseph was when he dreamt these dreams. Genesis 37:1-2 declares:

And Jacob dwelt in the land wherein his father was a stranger, in the land of Canaan. These are the generations of Jacob. Joseph, **being seventeen years** old, was feeding the flock with his brethren; and the lad was with the sons of Bilhah, and with the sons of Zilpah, his father's wives: and Joseph brought unto his father their evil report.

Why would God tell us the age of Joseph at this time of his life? There may be a number of reasons but surely one of them is because in the dreams that he experienced at this age, he is a picture of our Savior, who sat at the right hand of God to rule in His Kingdom. To reign over his brethren is surely a picture of Christ reigning over His Kingdom. Christ reigns from heaven as King of kings and Lord of lords; therefore, we can see that the number seventeen, Joseph's age at this time, may be identified with heaven. At least we see that the number seventeen and reigning are in a close relationship to each other. We know that Christ, who is definitely typified in many ways by Joseph, reigns from heaven.

Let us look at another seventeen. A few years after Joseph's dreams, he became ruler in Egypt, second only to pharaoh. Then his father, Israel, came under Joseph's care and keeping to escape a severe famine. Jacob was 130 years of age when he was saved by Joseph. Jacob, also named Israel by God, is a picture of all who have been saved by the Lord Jesus Christ, who in turn was typified by Joseph. Significantly, Jacob being saved by Joseph gives us the truth that the number seventeen points to heaven. Then we read in Genesis 47:28: "And Jacob lived in the land of Egypt seventeen years: so the whole age of Jacob was an hundred forty and seven years."

This indeed is interesting information. God wants us to know that Jacob (Israel) lived in Egypt for seventeen years, under the care and keeping of Joseph. Now we must ask: "How long are we under the care and keeping of Jesus once we are saved?" Or: "How long after our salvation is completed at the end of time do we remain under the care of our Savior?"

> *The seventeen year period of Jacob under the care of Joseph becomes equivalent to us spending eternity under the care of Christ.*

The answer to our questions is: "Forever." Throughout eternity we are under the care of our Lord. Therefore, we can see that the seventeen year period of Jacob under the care of Joseph becomes equivalent to us spending eternity under the care of Christ. For the second time we see that the number seventeen typifies heaven.

One other illustration should be offered to show that the number seventeen typifies heaven. In the Book of Jeremiah we discover that God is declaring to Israel that they are to be driven from their land. They are to go into captivity because of their repeated rebellion against God. In this sad context Jeremiah was told to buy a field. We read in Jeremiah 32:8:

So Hanameel mine uncle's son came to me in the court of the prison according to the word of the LORD, and said unto me, Buy my field, I pray thee, that is in Anathoth, which is in the country of Benjamin: for the right of inheritance is thine, and the redemption is thine; buy it for thyself. Then I knew that this was the word of the LORD.

Jeremiah wondered why he was to buy this field at a time when Judah was to be destroyed by the Babylonians. He, therefore, inquired of the Lord concerning this in verses 16-25. Jeremiah 32:25 summarizes his question to the Lord concerning this:

> And thou hast said unto me, O Lord GOD, Buy thee the field for money, and take witnesses; for the city is given into the hand of the Chaldeans.

In other words Jeremiah is implying by this statement that the purchase of a field is altogether inconsistent with the fact that Judah is to be destroyed by the Chaldeans (another name for the Babylonians). God answers him in verses 26-44 and indicates that Jeremiah's purchase of the field is a sign that God would bring Israel back to its land. Jeremiah 32:44 summarizes this promise:

> Men shall buy fields for money, and subscribe evidences, and seal them, and take witnesses in the land of Benjamin, and in the places about Jerusalem, and in the cities of Judah, and in the cities of the mountains, and in the cities of the valley, and in the cities of the south: for I will cause their captivity to return, saith the LORD.

God's promise of a return to the land points not to the physical land but to salvation, signified by the land of Canaan. Verses 38-40 show this very clearly.

> Jeremiah 32:38-40: And they shall be my people, and I will be their God: And I will give them one heart, and one way, that they may fear me for ever, for the good of them, and of their children after them: And I will make an everlasting covenant with them, that I will not turn away from them, to do them good; but I will put my fear in their hearts, that they shall not depart from me.

The words "they may fear me for ever" and "I will make an everlasting covenant with them" can have fulfillment only in the arena of salvation. It could never relate to a physical land because this world is to be destroyed by fire. Moreover, the phrase of verse 44, "I will cause their captivity to return" is a clue phrase that always relates to salvation.

Thus we see that the purchase of the land by Jeremiah relates to our salvation and the fact that we inherit the new heavens and the new earth. Now we might ask, "What does all of this information have to do with the number seventeen?" Actually, very much. In Jeremiah 32:9 we read:

And I bought the field of Hanameel my uncle's son, that was in Anathoth, and weighed him the money, even **seventeen shekels of silver.**

In other words the value of our spiritual inheritance is typified by the price of seventeen shekels of silver. Again, even as we saw by other examples, the number seventeen is signifying heaven.

One Hundred and Fifty-Three Fish

Before we finish with the number seventeen as it relates to the timing of Christ's return we must look at one other Biblical seventeen. In John 21:3-11 we read that after Jesus arose from the dead, seven of the disciples went fishing. When Jesus told them to cast their net on the other side of the boat they "drew the net to land full of great fishes, an hundred and fifty and three."

Verse 8 of John 21 gives the information that they were about 200 cubits from shore. What does this incident represent? Remember that earlier in our study we learned that the fish represent the believers, those who become saved. Jesus said, "I will make you fishers of men" (Matthew 4:19). The sea represents hell, from which we are taken when we become saved. Every human being is under the wrath of God until he becomes saved. The wrath of God eventuates in hell, which is eternal damnation. The shore represents the safety of salvation and being brought into the Kingdom of God. Earlier we also learned that the about 200 cubits was a distance looking to the period of time from the first coming of Christ to His second coming.

> *It must be an important fact that is being presented when God gives us the precise number of fish that was caught.*

What about the number of fish? Surely it must be a very important fact that is being presented when God gives us the precise number of fish that was caught. Remember we learned earlier that in the Bible there are numbers that are outstandingly important because of special characteristics they have. For example, we saw that the special number 276 was given to us in Acts 27 to represent the fullness of believers who will remain safe when judgment falls on the church during the final tribulation period. It is a number made of two numbers, 12×23. Twelve is the number signifying the fullness of God's plan or if it were further broken down it could signify God's purpose for the true believers. Also $3 \times 4 \times 23$, which signifies God's purpose all over the world. We saw that the number twenty-three, which signifies God's judgment, is unique in that the sum of all the digits before and including the number twenty-three add up to 276:

$$1 + 2 + 3 \ldots + 22 + 23 = 276.$$

God is focusing very earnestly on the number twenty-three.
        Returning to the 153 fish we find that it is made of the numbers:

$$3 \times 3 \times 17 = 153.$$

        Again God brings a very sharp focus on the number seventeen inasmuch as:

$$1 + 2 + 3 \ldots + 15 + 16 + 17 = 153$$

As noted earlier, the number three signifies the purpose of God whereas the number seventeen signifies heaven. Thus we can learn that the purpose of God is to bring all believers, who are "caught" by the Gospel, into heaven. It is amazing and yet not at all amazing as we see the harmony of the Word of God even through the numbers of the Bible.
        Returning now to the perfection of God's plan of salvation for the earth, signified by the number seven, we have learned:
        1. God's plan for the world that began after the flood of Noah's day, 4990 B.C., called for a perfect 7000 years until its end. This would have to be the year 2011 A.D. It was typified by the language of Deuteronomy 15:1 that at the end of seven years there was to be a release, language that points to the end of the world when the world will be released from its bondage of decay and the believers will be released from this world to enjoy the new heavens and the new earth.

2. The last twenty-three years of this 7000-year period is to be a time of great tribulation and during this time, God will pour out His judgments on the church for its growing apostasy.

3. The twenty-three year tribulation period, however, was reduced in length by seventeen years to bring it down to a period of 2300 days. This is so because by the 2300th day the last of the elect will have become saved.

4. Because God's timetable for the existence of the earth is tied to the time required to save all of the elect, the world will be brought to an end seventeen years earlier than 2011 A.D. This avoids the possibility of the earth continuing beyond the time required to save the elect. For the sake of the elect the perfect 7000 years will be reduced by seventeen years because there will be no one left who is to become saved during those seventeen years.

5. Effectively then for the believers, the perfect 7000 years is made up of two parts. The first part runs for 6983 years from 4990 B.C. to 1994 A.D. The last seventeen years of the perfect 7000 years are in the new heavens and the new earth. Of course, since the number seventeen signifies heaven and that continues forevermore, the last seventeen years of the 7000 years continue forevermore.

Two Times Seventeen and the End

Before we leave the number seventeen we might look at one other bit of curious information. We must remember that God sometimes doubles numbers without changing their meaning. Remember, for example, we saw in the early part of our study that seven, the number signifying perfection, was doubled to fourteen to point to the 1400 years from the entrance of Israel into the land of Canaan in 1407 B.C. to 7 B.C. when Jesus was born. Likewise when we double the number seventeen we discover a very interesting piece of information.

The entrance of Israel into the land of Canaan in 1407 B.C. typified the believers' entrance into salvation or into the new heavens and the new earth. Doubling the number seven to 1400 years brought us to 7 B.C. and the birth of Christ who came to provide entrance into salvation, into the new heavens and the new earth.

Let us now travel two times seventeen or 3400 years down through time starting with the same year 1407 B.C. Yes! We come to the same year we have seen repeatedly. We come to the year 1994. Indeed heaven was anticipated in 1407 B.C. when Israel entered Canaan. Heaven is symbolized by the number seventeen or by the doubling of the number seventeen to 3400. Heaven is signified in its fullest degree when we travel 3400 years from 1407 B.C. to 1994 A.D. Indeed we are seeing that 1994 A.D. must be the year of Christ's return.

We are not finished with our examination of the Biblical data that suggest the year of Christ's return. Before we look at the most dramatic information of all let us review what we have thus far discovered.

First, we are working with information that is drawn from the Bible. We have carefully stayed away from speculation and any evidence from sources other than the Bible.

Second, we have found that the time line for the history of the world is God's plan of salvation for the world. Therefore, when the last of the elect are saved, the world will come to an end.

Third, we have found a number of paths that all conclude at one year - the year 1994.

Fourth, each path begins at a different point in history.

Fifth, each path begins at a point in history that is of intense importance in relation to God's salvation plan.

Sixth, each path travels from a beginning point with Biblical validation that the numbers used symbolize God's salvation plan.

Seventh, we have found abundant evidence in the Bible that by following the methodology employed in this study, an Old Testament believer could have determined the year of Christ's first coming strictly from the Old Testament data.

Let us summarize this information.

Beginning Point	_Path_	_Conclusion_
1. Creation, 11,013 B.C.	-13,000 years + tribulation period (2300 days = 6+ yrs) later -13 tribes -Israel saved by Joseph when Jacob was 130 yrs old	1994 A.D.

Beginning Point (Continued)	_Path_	_Conclusion_
2. The world begins again after the flood of 4990 B.C.	-7000 years later (the perfection of God's timetable) less the shortening of the tribulation period (17 yrs, which = heaven)	1994 A.D.
3. Jacob born 2007 B.C.	-4000 yrs later based on 40 yrs of Eze. 4	1994 A.D.
4. Jacob's name changed to Israel 1907 B.C.	-3900 yrs later based on 390 years of Eze. 4	1994 A.D.
5. Israel entered Egypt in 1877 B.C.	-1290 called for in Dan. 12 -3x430 (1877 - 1447) =1290 1877 - 1290 = 587 B.C. -3 x 1290 = 3870: (1877 - 3870) =	1994 A.D.
6. Israel enters Canaan 1407 B.C.	-3400 years later -2 x 17 the number of heaven	1994 A.D.
7. David becomes king over Israel 1007 B.C.	-3000 years later -3 = purpose of God	1994 A.D.
8. Jesus' birth, 7 B.C.	-2000 years later -2 = number of the church -2000 cubits between ark and people -2000 swine cast into sea	1994 A.D.

Virtually every Biblical date of any importance has been found to be related to these time clues. Notable exceptions are the circumcision of Abraham in 2068 B.C. and the crucifixion of Christ in 33 A.D. As we saw earlier the years 2068 B.C. and 33 A.D. identify in a marvelous way with the first coming of Christ. Later we will see how beautifully 33 A.D. fits into the data showing us the timetable of Christ's return.

This study may have pressed an idea here or there a bit heavily, but when eight separate paths, each beginning at a different point in history, each path utilizing a different number that signifies one aspect of God's salvation plan, and each path arrives at the same date, then we must conclude that the year 1994 has a great possibility of being the year of Christ's return.

There is more. As we continue our study we shall look at the most significant evidence of all that 1994 may be the year to expect Christ's return and the end of the world.

> *Our study of the Bible concerning the year of Christ's return has encompassed a great amount of Scripture . . . and we have found tremendous harmony between the Scriptures.*

Our study of the Bible to discover clues concerning the year of Christ's return has encompassed a great amount of Scripture. Indeed we have found tremendous harmony between the Scriptures that assures us that we may have uncovered God's blueprint for the earth.

Now we will search for the year of Christ's return by examining the jubilees of the Bible. We will be amazed at what we find.

> *In the New Testament era, we find that the year 1994 is a jubilee year.*

The Jubilee Year

In our study of Daniel 9:25-27 we discovered that every fiftieth year was a jubilee year. We learned that the Bible directs us to the fact that 457 B.C., 407 B.C., 357 B.C., etc., were jubilee years. Thus the year 7 B.C., to which all of the evidence points as the year Jesus was born, is also a jubilee year. If the jubilee periods are projected into the New Testament era the next jubilee year, after 7 B.C., was fifty years later, the year 44 A.D. Remember that when we move from B.C. to

A.D. we must subtract one year inasmuch as there is no year 0. Thus 7 + 44 - 1 = 50 years. **Continuing in the New Testament era we find that the year 1994 is also a jubilee year.** This is the year that so much Biblical information points to as the possible year of Christ's return.

When we read in the Bible about the purpose of the jubilee year, we find that the language points to His return at the end of time.

In Leviticus 25:9-10 we read concerning the jubilee:

> Then shalt thou cause the trumpet of the jubile to sound on the tenth day of the seventh month, in the day of atonement shall ye make the trumpet sound throughout all your land. And ye shall hallow the fiftieth year, and proclaim liberty throughout all the land unto all the inhabitants thereof: it shall be a jubile unto you; and ye shall return every man unto his possession, and ye shall return every man unto his family.

Verse 13 adds: "In the year of this jubile ye shall return every man unto his possession." From this information we know that it was a year that dramatically points to the end of the world. It is at that time that every believer comes into his own land and possession. That is the new heaven and new earth that God will create after this earth is destroyed. The believers will live there forever as the family of God.

> *The end of the world is intimately associated with the jubilee.*

Likewise all of the unsaved will be gathered together into the land in which they will live forever. Unfortunately that is hell, where they will experience eternal damnation. The end of the world is therefore intimately associated with the jubilee.

The jubilee year 1994 A.D. is particularly significant. According to Leviticus 25:2-9, the first jubilee year was to be observed fifty years after Israel entered the land of Canaan. That was the year 1357 B.C. The year 1994 A.D. is then the sixty-eighth jubilee year. The number sixty-eight is made up of the numbers 2 x 2 x 17 or 4 x 17. As we discovered earlier in our study, the number two is repeatedly identified with the church while the number four is identified with the whole world or universality. We might also recall that the number 17 is repeatedly identified with heaven. Thus 2 x 2 x 17 = 68 points to the church as it comes into heaven. Likewise 4 x 17 emphasizes that heaven has come to the world. In either case the number 17 signifies that heaven is very important.

There is another important feature in the fact that 1994 is a jubilee year. When we studied the seventy sevens of Daniel 9:25-27, we found that God points to the commandment to restore and to build Jerusalem as the beginning of seventy sevens of years. We discovered that that command was fulfilled by Ezra when he came to Jerusalem to bring the law of God. We learned that the spiritual city, Jerusalem, is built by bringing the Gospel, which is the law of God.

We also learned that there were two paths of seventy times seven or 490 years both of which go to Judgment Day. The first path was exactly 490 years after Ezra arrived in Jerusalem in 458 B.C. Because there is no year 0 in going from an Old Testament event to a New Testament event, we add the Old Testament years to the New Testament years and subtract one. The period of 490 years thus brings us to 33 A.D. when Christ suffered for our sins. Thus, Judgment Day was experienced by Christ as He bore the wrath of God for those He came to save. This Judgment Day took place in 33 A.D. Add 458 Old Testament years to the thirty-three New Testament years and subtract one year and we obtain 490 years or seventy sevens of years.

We also learned that Daniel 9:25-27 presents another path to Judgment Day and that is the Judgment Day at the end of time when there will be the consummation and God's wrath will be poured upon the unsaved. We learned that this path also began with Ezra in 458 B.C., but this path included a reference to a jubilee period. It speaks of seven sevens, which is forty-nine years. This is the time between two jubilee years. We discovered that the first jubilee was in the year 457 B.C. Thus, as we extended the jubilee periods into the New Testament era, we discovered that 1994 is also a jubilee year.

---

*1994 A.D. is the fiftieth jubilee year since the
beginning set forth in Daniel 9:25-27.*

It is an especially significant jubilee in that it is the fiftieth jubilee since the beginning set forth in Daniel 9:25-27. **It is in reality a jubilee of jubilees inasmuch as forty-nine jubilees have gone before it.**

---

*We have discovered many paths that
lead to 1994 A.D. as the end of time.*

The year 1994 is indeed a significant year. Not only have we previously discovered many paths that lead to 1994 as the end of time, but now we have learned that it is a jubilee year. The jubilee has everything to do with the end of time. Moreover we have learned that it is a very special jubilee year in that it is the sixty-eighth (4 x 17) since the beginning of jubilee years, and it is also a jubilee of jubilees in that it follows the forty-nine jubilees that began with the rebuilding of the temple as declared in Daniel 9:25-27.

1955 Years

Now we should focus on another aspect of the timetable that leads to the end of time. Earlier in this study we found that much Biblical information focuses on the year 1988 A.D. We also came to realize that the last event prior to the return of Christ was the final tribulation period. We learned that in all likelihood it was to be a period of 2300 days as taught by Daniel 8:13-14. When 2300 days, which is a little longer than six years, is added to 1988 we come to 1994, which could well be the year of our Lord's return.

> *Christ paid for the sins of believers*
> *in 33 A.D., 1955 years earlier than*
> *1988 A.D., which is the period when*
> *Satan was bound.*

We also realize that the first coming of Christ was to pay for the sins of the believers, which He did on the cross in the year 33 A.D., which is 1955 years earlier than 1988 A.D. This is the period when Satan has been bound so that people from every nation could be saved.

The number 1955 is a most interesting number. It is made up of three numbers:

$$5$$
$$17$$
$$23$$
$$5 \times 17 \times 23 = 1955$$

All three of these numbers have intense spiritual significance.

The number five is used repeatedly in the Bible to indicate both the spiritual quality of grace and redemption as well as the spiritual quality of God's judgment and God's wrath on the unsaved. Significantly, both these qualities will be in abundant evidence when Christ returns. On the one hand He will complete the salvation of the believers by giving them their resurrected bodies. On the other hand He will come to judge the unsaved.

Even more importantly, during the entire 1955 years from Pentecost in 33 A.D. until the beginning of the final tribulation period, the Gospel has gone forth as a two-edged sword into all the world. Believers who wield this sword are spoken of in the Bible as the savour or fragrance of life unto life as well as death unto death (II Cor. 2:15-16). Thus the number five intimately identifies with the sending forth of the Gospel as it has gone forth during the New Testament era.

The second number that is a factor of the number 1955 is the number seventeen. Earlier in our study we learned that the number 153 is unique and therefore of great importance because it is not only made up of $3 \times 3 \times 17 = 153$, but also the sum of all the integers going before and including seventeen equals 153. Thus $1+2+3\ldots+16+17=153$. Earlier in our study we learned that God especially called attention to this number in connection with the 153 fish caught by the disciples (John 21:11). Remember we learned that these 153 fish represent all those who are to be saved during the New Testament era. It is made up of $3 \times 3 \times 17 = 153$. The number three focuses on the purpose of God and the number seventeen focuses beautifully on heaven, which is the destination of all believers. Therefore it is extremely significant and wonderful to find that the number seventeen is an integral part of the time span from Pentecost in 33 A.D., when God began His plan to evangelize the world, to 1988, which appears to be the year that Satan is loosed so that he can hinder the Gospel and so that wickedness will multiply as God begins to prepare for the final judgment and the end of the world.

The number seventeen found as an integral part of the years God has ordained for the sending forth of the Gospel surely stresses that believers are saved so that they become citizens of heaven. This is parallel to the 153 fish which also features the number seventeen in connection with those whose destination is heaven.

The third number that makes up the number 1955 is the number twenty-three. It, too, is part of a very rare number. Remember the 276 people who were saved when the ship in which they were travelling was completely wrecked? You may also remember that, like the number 153, the number 276 is a rare number in the Bible in that it features the number twenty-three in the same manner that the number seventeen is featured as part of the 153 fish. Earlier in our study we learned that the number twenty-three is related to judgment. We have already seen that the Gospel is sent forth into the world and is used by God not only to save those who believe but it is also a judgment upon those who will not believe.

These numbers point to Christ's return when He will complete the salvation of the believers and bring God's wrath on the unsaved.

These three very significant numbers point to Christ's return when He will complete the salvation of the believers and bring God's wrath on the unsaved. **We should be astonished to find these three**

numbers in the period during which God evangelized the world,
but then we should not be at all astonished for the timetable of history
is entirely of God's making.

> *We find these three numbers in the*
> *period of the evangelization of the*
> *world. The timetable of history is*
> *entirely of God's making.*

When we look more carefully at this 1955 year period we find
something else that is astonishing until we realize that God is in control
of these matters. The evangelization of the world began with Pentecost
in 33 A.D. Pentecost was a feast day celebrated by Old Testament
Israel. God selected this feast day to pour out His Spirit and to indicate
the beginning of God's plan to evangelize the world (Acts 2).

As we learned earlier, the year 33 A.D. is accurate insofar as
the Jewish calendar is concerned. Remember when we were unravelling
the 1335 days of Daniel 12:12, that the end of the 1335 days was
Pentecost in 33 A.D. The date was May 24 according to our calendar.
Remember the 1335 days accurately encompassed the ministry of our
Savior from the time He was baptized on the first day of the seventh
month of 29 A.D. until Jesus returned to heaven and fulfilled His
promise to send the Comforter. Remember the Comforter is the Holy
Spirit, sent by Christ to evangelize the world. Therefore, we would
logically conclude that if the 1335 day period of Daniel 12:12 ended at
Pentecost (May 24, 33 A.D.), then Pentecost would mark the beginning of the 1955 year period from 33 A.D. to 1988 A.D.

If the 1955 year period ended sometime in 1988, it would be
followed by the 2300 day final tribulation period that must end
sometime in the jubilee year 1994. We will now undertake to see what
we can discover concerning this time sequence.

First of all we should discover the timing of the special Biblical
feast days that can be projected from the Old Testament into the present
day. We do this because earlier in our study we learned that God had
unfolded His salvation plan with great identification with the Old
Testament feast days. We have also learned from our study that:

1. Jesus was born in a jubilee year.

2. Jesus was announced by John the Baptist as the Lamb of God which takes away the sin of the world on Tishri 1, which is known theologically as the Feast of Trumpets.

3. Jesus was crucified on Nisan 14, the Passover Day, while the priests were sacrificing the passover lambs in the temple.

4. The Holy Spirit was poured out, that is, God began His program to evangelize the world on the day of Pentecost.

5. By projecting the Old Testament jubilee years into the New Testament era, we learned that 1994 A.D. is a jubilee year, .

When we examine the year 1988 A.D., we discover that both the Jewish calendar and the astronomical calendar give the following dates that may be of interest to us. Remember that all dates are Jerusalem time.

September 12 = Tishri 1 = Feast of Trumpets
May 22 = Pentecost

Previously we learned that Pentecost of 33 A.D., when God began His plan to evangelize the world was May 24. Then for 1955 years (remember 5 x 17 x 23), the Gospel went out into all the world. The day of Pentecost in 33 A.D. signalled God's intention to evangelize the world, and each year thereafter, Pentecost Day was in a sense a reaffirmation of God's Gospel intent.

Then we came to the year 1987. Pentecost Day again reaffirms that God will continue to send forth the Gospel into the world. But when the time of Pentecost came in 1988 there was no such plan. We learned that 1988 was the year when the final tribulation was to begin. And so in a real sense, the day of Pentecost of 1988, which should have taken place on the Jerusalem date of May 22, did not take place because the final tribulation, the falling away, the loosing of Satan had begun.

We, therefore, should be quite accurate in saying that the New Testament era of sending forth the Gospel officially came to an end on May 21, 1988 - the day before Pentecost; that is May 22 is the day Pentecost should have come in the year 1988. Thus, May 21 was also the day the 2300 days of the final tribulation were to begin. As we learned earlier, this does not mean that no one could be saved after May 21, 1988. Rather it means that the assault of Satan on the churches had officially begun. It means that increasingly at a very rapid rate churches and denominations will become apostate.

Continue 2300 days from May 21, 1988, and we arrive at September 6, 1994. What day is that in relation to the Jewish calendar? Earlier we had found that somehow the Jubilee, which officially begins on the Day of Atonement, may be intimately related to the return of Christ. We also learned that the Feast of Tabernacles might somehow be related to the end of the world. We wonder where these feast days occur in 1994.

Follow the same procedure that we employed in determining the accurate date for Pentecost in 1988, and we discover that the first day of the seventh month, which is Tishri 1, is September 6 in 1994. Both the astronomical date and the Jewish calendar date are in agreement with this.

We have already learned that September 6 is the 2300th day if we begin with May 21, 1988. The dating is as follows:

	Days in Month or Year
May 21 - May 31, 1988 incl	11
June, 1988	30
July, 1988	31
August, 1988	31
September, 1988	30
October, 1988	31
November, 1988	30
December, 1988	31
1989	365
1990	365
1991	365
1992 (leap year)	366
1993	365
January, 1994	31
February, 1994	28
March, 1994	31
April, 1994	30
May, 1994	31

Days in Month or Year (Continued)	
June, 1994	30
July, 1994	31
August, 1994	31
September 1-September 6, 1994 inclusive	6
	2300 days

In the year 1994 it appears that He will again be announced on the first day of the seventh month.

Amazingly - or maybe it is not at all amazing - Jesus in His first coming was announced on the first day of the seventh month, which was the day of the Feast of Trumpets (see Chapter 12). On that day He officially began His ministry as the Lamb of God to take away the sins of the world. And 1965 years later in the year 1994 it appears that He will again be announced **on the first day of the seventh month, which is the date of the Feast of Trumpets**. Isn't it remarkable how God uses the Old Testament feast days as markers for His New Testament salvation plan? Or possibly it is not remarkable at all considering that the same God who created this complex universe is the God of salvation.

The Date of The End

We have learned that the first day of the seventh month, September 6, in the year 1994, is the end of the 2300 days of tribulation. Could that also be the date of the end of the world and Christ's return? The answer must be negative. One of the dominant reasons for considering 1994 as the year of the end is that it is a jubilee year, but on September 6, the year of the 1994 jubilee has not yet begun. We read in Leviticus 25:8-12:

> And thou shalt number seven sabbaths of years unto thee, seven times seven years; and the space of the seven sabbaths of years shall be unto thee forty and nine years. Then shalt thou cause the trumpet of the jubile to sound on the tenth day of the seventh month, in the day of atonement shall ye make the trumpet sound throughout all your land. And ye shall hallow the fiftieth year,

and proclaim liberty throughout all the land unto all the inhabitants thereof: it shall be a jubile unto you; and ye shall return every man unto his possession, and ye shall return every man unto his family. A jubile shall that fiftieth year be unto you: ye shall not sow, neither reap that which groweth of itself in it, nor gather the grapes in it of thy vine undressed. For it is the jubile; it shall be holy unto you: ye shall eat the increase thereof out of the field.

These verses teach that a jubilee year does not officially begin until the tenth day of the seventh month, the Day of Atonement, which is September 15 in the year 1994. Thus one would suspect that Christ will not return at least until September 15.

Earlier in our study we saw that there were three especially important feasts for which all the men of Israel were to go to Jerusalem. We read in Deuteronomy 16:16:

Three times in a year shall all thy males appear before the LORD thy God in the place which he shall choose; in the feast of unleavened bread, and in the feast of weeks, and in the feast of tabernacles: and they shall not appear before the LORD empty.

The first feast was the Feast of Unleavened Bread, which was the time of the Passover (Deuteronomy 16:2-3).

The second was the Feast of Weeks, which came seven weeks later (Deuteronomy 16:9-10). This feast is called Pentecost in the New Testament because it came fifty days after the Passover.

The third feast was the Feast of Tabernacles, which is also called the Feast of Ingathering (Exodus 23:16). It was observed beginning five days after the Day of Atonement, which announced the jubilee year.

> *The first feast - the Passover - was being observed by national Israel on the day that Jesus, who was the Passover Lamb, was hanging on the cross.*

Very significantly, the first feast - the Passover - was being observed by national Israel on the very day that Jesus, who was the Passover Lamb, was hanging on the cross.

Moreover, on the very day that the Jews were observing the Feast of Weeks, when they brought in the firstfruits of their labors, on the day called Pentecost, that is the very day that God poured out His Holy Spirit and began His program to evangelize the world. This is especially remarkable because it occurred seven weeks into the New Testament side of the cross.

With the above information in mind, we begin to wonder whether either the Day of Atonement or a day during the Feast of Tabernacles might be the actual day of Christ's return. Let us look at both possibilities as we continue our study.

The Day of Atonement

As we have learned, the Day of Atonement, the tenth day of the seventh month Tishri, was a very important day. In Leviticus 23:27-28 God declares:

> Also on the tenth day of this seventh month there shall be a day of atonement: it shall be an holy convocation unto you; and ye shall afflict your souls, and offer an offering made by fire unto the LORD. And ye shall do no work in that same day: for it is a day of atonement, to make an atonement for you before the LORD your God.

It was only on the Day of Atonement that the high priest went behind the curtain that separated the Holy of Holies from the holy place (Leviticus 16). On this day he sprinkled blood on the mercy seat that covered the ark of the covenant. This act pointed beautifully to the sacrifice of Christ as He paid for our sins during the Passover of 33 A.D.

Since our salvation will be completed when our Lord returns, we can understand why God would identify the beginning of the jubilee year with the Day of Atonement.

We read in Leviticus 25:9-10:

> Then shalt thou cause the trumpet of the jubile to sound on the tenth day of the seventh month, in the day of atonement shall ye make the trumpet sound throughout all your land. And ye shall hallow the fiftieth year, and proclaim liberty throughout all the land unto all the inhabitants thereof: it shall be a jubile unto you; and ye shall return every man unto his possession, and ye shall return every man unto his family.

Note that on this day the sound of the trumpet was to be made throughout the land. When we search the Bible we do not find another day after this when the trumpets were to be blown. In I Corinthians 15:51-53 God prophesies:

> Behold, I shew you a mystery; We shall not all sleep, but we shall all be changed, In a moment, in the twinkling of an eye, **at the last trump: for the trumpet shall sound,** and the dead shall be raised incorruptible, and we shall be changed. For this corruptible must put on incorruption, and this mortal must put on immortality.

The sound of the last trumpet could identify with the blowing of the seventh trumpet, which is spoken of in Revelation 11:15:

> And the seventh angel sounded; and there were great voices in heaven, saying, The kingdoms of this world are become the kingdoms of our Lord, and of his Christ; and he shall reign for ever and ever.

Or it could identify with the blowing of the trumpet at the beginning of the jubilee year. Obviously it would identify with both of these events if Jesus returns on the Day of Atonement, September 15, which will be the day that begins the 1994 jubilee year.

We learned earlier in our study that Jesus was born on or about the Day of Atonement (see page 418). Since in a spiritual sense He is our Jubilee in that all of the blessings of the jubilee year are completed in Him, it would have been very appropriate if He had been born on the beginning day of a jubilee year. In fact, there is at least an implication of this in the language of Daniel 9:25, "From the going forth of the commandment to restore and to build Jerusalem unto the Messiah the Prince shall be seven weeks . . . ." We learned that this first seven weeks is a jubilee period and the fifty years added to the years that followed in this verse come to the time of the cross in 33 A.D. Nevertheless in this language there is at least an intimation that Jesus might have been born during a jubilee year. We have learned that undoubtedly He was born in the jubilee year 7 B.C. We also saw that even though God does not precisely detail the timing of Jesus' birth, it had to be fairly close to, and could have been on, the Day of Atonement, 7 B.C., which is within the possibilities allowed by the Scriptures.

> *If this is true, then His second coming on the Day of Atonement, September 15, 1994, is entirely reasonable.*

If this is true, then His second coming on the Day of Atonement, September 15, 1994, is entirely reasonable. This will be precisely, to the very day, forty jubilee periods after His birth.

For all these reasons we wonder if September 15 is the date of His return. However, a day during the Feast of Tabernacles is also a distinct possibility. Let us see why.

Could Jesus Return during the Feast of Tabernacles?

In Exodus 23:16, where the Feast of Tabernacles is called the "feast of ingathering," God speaks of it as being the "end of the year." Exodus 23:16:

> And the feast of harvest, the firstfruits of thy labours, which thou hast sown in the field: and the feast of ingathering, which is in the end of the year, when thou hast gathered in thy labours out of the field.

This is further indicated in Exodus 34:22 where we find the phrase, "and the feast of ingathering at the year's end." That this "feast of ingathering" is the same feast that is called the "feast of tabernacles" can be seen by comparing the language of Exodus 23:14-17 with that of Deuteronomy 16:16. Exodus 23:14-17 declares:

> Three times thou shalt keep a feast unto me in the year. Thou shalt keep the feast of unleavened bread: (thou shalt eat unleavened bread seven days, as I commanded thee, in the time appointed of the month Abib; for in it thou camest out from Egypt: and none shall appear before me empty:) And the feast of harvest, the firstfruits of thy labours, which thou hast sown in the field: and the feast of ingathering, which is in the end of the year, when thou hast gathered in thy labours out of the field. Three times in the year all thy males shall appear before the Lord GOD.

Deuteronomy 16:16 likewise tells us:

Three times in a year shall all thy males appear before the LORD thy God in the place which he shall choose; in the feast of unleavened bread, and in the feast of weeks, and in the feast of tabernacles: and they shall not appear before the LORD empty.

Why is the Feast of Tabernacles or the Feast of Ingathering spoken of in connection with the *end* of the year? We know that it was to be observed from the fifteenth to the twenty-second day of the seventh month of the Jewish calendar. Perhaps historically it was spoken of as the end of the year meaning the end of the growing year, which signified that all the harvest had been completed. We can speculate about that but in any case God does assign the phrase "end of the year" to this feast.

> *This feast signified their arrival in the land of Canaan after spending forty years in the wilderness.*

We know that this feast signified two experiences of ancient Israel: First, their arrival in the land of Canaan after spending forty years in the wilderness; second, the completion of the harvest each year. We read about both of these events in Leviticus 23:39-43:

Also in the fifteenth day of the seventh month, when ye have gathered in the fruit of the land, ye shall keep a feast unto the LORD seven days: on the first day shall be a sabbath, and on the eighth day shall be a sabbath. And ye shall take you on the first day the boughs of goodly trees, branches of palm trees, and the boughs of thick trees, and willows of the brook; and ye shall rejoice before the LORD your God seven days. And ye shall keep it a feast unto the LORD seven days in the year. It shall be a statute for ever in your generations: ye shall celebrate it in the seventh month. Ye shall dwell in booths seven days; all that are Israelites born shall dwell in booths: That your generations may know that I made the children of Israel to dwell in booths, when I brought them out of the land of Egypt: I am the LORD your God.

From these verses we know that this feast identified with the completion of the harvest. The Bible speaks of the end of the world as the harvest. In the parable of the tares Jesus tells us in Matthew 13:38-42:

The field is the world; the good seed are the children of the kingdom; but the tares are the children of the wicked one; The enemy that sowed them is the devil; the harvest is the end of the world; and the reapers are the angels. As therefore the tares are gathered and burned in the fire; so shall it be in the end of this world. The Son of man shall send forth his angels, and they shall gather out of his kingdom all things that offend, and them which do iniquity; And shall cast them into a furnace of fire: there shall be wailing and gnashing of teeth.

This harvest is also spoken of in the ominous language of Revelation 14:15-19:

And another angel came out of the temple, crying with a loud voice to him that sat on the cloud, Thrust in thy sickle, and reap: for the time is come for thee to reap; for the harvest of the earth is ripe. And he that sat on the cloud thrust in his sickle on the earth; and the earth was reaped. And another angel came out of the temple which is in heaven, he also having a sharp sickle. And another angel came out from the altar, which had power over fire; and cried with a loud cry to him that had the sharp sickle, saying, Thrust in thy sharp sickle, and gather the clusters of the vine of the earth; for her grapes are fully ripe. And the angel thrust in his sickle into the earth, and gathered the vine of the earth, and cast it into the great winepress of the wrath of God.

> *The land of Canaan can signify the fact of our salvation and the completion of our salvation.*

Returning to Leviticus 23:39-43, we find that these verses also speak of dwelling in booths or tents to commemorate the forty years in the wilderness. At the end of these forty years they crossed the Jordan River and came into the land of Canaan. The land of Canaan is a Biblical figure of the Kingdom of God, which we enter into when we become saved. Thus, the land of Canaan can signify not only the fact of our salvation but also the completion of our salvation, which we will obtain when Christ comes and gives us our resurrected body.

In this connection we might recall Jesus' words found in Luke 4:18-19:

The Spirit of the Lord is upon me, because he hath anointed me to preach the gospel to the poor; he hath sent me to heal the brokenhearted, to preach deliverance to the captives, and recovering of sight to the blind, to set at liberty them that are bruised, To preach the acceptable year of the Lord.

In these verses it surely appears that God is equating the time for preaching the Gospel with a year. Thus, the end of the year would identify with the phrase, "the feast of ingathering, which is in the end of the year" (Exodus 23:16).

Moreover, Revelation 12 speaks of the earth as a wilderness in which the Christian dwells. We read in Revelation 12:6:

And the woman fled into the wilderness, where she hath a place prepared of God, that they should feed her there a thousand two hundred and threescore days.

Remember when we studied the seventy sevens of Daniel 9:24-27 and we learned that the 1260 days is a figure that identifies with the bringing of the Gospel throughout the whole New Testament era? Therefore when Israel came into the land of Canaan it could be said that they had come to the end of the "acceptable year of the Lord" (Luke 4:19), that is, they had come to the end of time, which will occur when the preaching of the Gospel has been completed. The end of the world can be intimately identified with the Feast of Tabernacles.

Remember that the term "last day" is found only eight times in the Bible. Four of these occurrences are in the sixth chapter of John, where we read of the resurrection of believers on the last day (verses 39, 40, 44, 54), and it is found once in John 11:24, where Martha confidently asserted that her dead brother would rise in the resurrection of the last day.

The sixth place the term "last day" is found is John 12:48, where we read:

He that rejecteth me, and receiveth not my words, hath one that judgeth him: the word that I have spoken, **the same shall judge him in the last day.**

All six of these citations identify with the end of the world, which must come on the last day of the world's existence. Amazingly, or maybe not so amazingly, the two remaining citations are both used in connection with the Feast of Tabernacles. In John 7:2-10, we read of Jesus attending the Feast of Tabernacles in Jerusalem. Then we read in John 7:37: "In **the last day**, that great day of the feast, Jesus stood and cried, saying, If any man thirst, let him come unto me, and drink."

In Nehemiah 8 we read of Israel celebrating the Feast of Tabernacles under the leadership of Ezra. The Bible declares in Nehemiah 8:18:

Also day by day, from the first day unto the **last day**, he read in the book of the law of God. And they kept the feast seven days; and on the eighth day was a solemn assembly, according unto the manner.

We, therefore, must consider the possibility of Christ's return on one of the days of the Feast of Tabernacles for the year 1994, which will be the period from September 20 to September 27.

It is true that I Corinthians 15:52 identifies the resurrection of the dead with the sounding of the last trump; and the Bible does not speak of the sounding of the trumpet in connection with the Feast of Tabernacles. But, of course, this does not necessarily imply that the Bible is teaching that the trumpet will not be sounded in connection with a day of the Feast of Tabernacles, should that day be the last day.

To summarize our conclusions we can be fairly sure of the following:

1. The last day cannot be earlier than the jubilee day, called the Day of Atonement, which occurs September 15, 1994.

2. The last day will probably not take place later than September 27, which is the eighth day of the Feast of Tabernacles of 1994.

3. The last day could possibly take place any time between September 15 and September 27, 1994.

4. Even though we have abundant evidence that in all likelihood the last day will occur in 1994, we definitely cannot know the day nor the hour of our Savior's return.

The Day When Christ Is Announced Is Not the Day of His Return

Now we must face another problem. We have very carefully calculated by the Biblical evidence that the tribulation period of 2300 days ends precisely on the first day of the seventh month, which is sometimes called the Feast of Trumpets. That date in 1994 is September 6. We have also discovered that the last day will take place on a day between September 15 and September 27. Are we becoming confused? How can we reconcile September 6 with a date that may be as long as three weeks later? The solution to this apparent dilemma can be found as we continue to search the Bible. We should look at several verses in Luke 21. In Luke 21:25-28 we read:

> And there shall be signs in the sun, and in the moon, and in the stars; and upon the earth distress of nations, with perplexity; the sea and the waves roaring; Men's hearts failing them for fear, and for looking after those things which are coming on the earth: for the powers of heaven shall be shaken. And then shall they see the Son of man coming in a cloud with power and great glory. And when these things begin to come to pass, then look up, and lift up your heads; for your redemption draweth nigh.

The statement "for the powers of heaven will be shaken" is also found in Matthew 24:29-30:

> Immediately after the tribulation of those days shall the sun be darkened, and the moon shall not give her light, and the stars shall fall from heaven, and the powers of the heavens shall be shaken: And then shall appear the sign of the Son of man in heaven: and then shall all the tribes of the earth mourn, and they shall see the Son of man coming in the clouds of heaven with power and great glory.

In Mark 13:24-27 we have more information.

> But in those days, after that tribulation, the sun shall be darkened, and the moon shall not give her light, And the stars of heaven shall fall, and the powers that are in heaven shall be shaken. And then shall they see the Son of man coming in the clouds with great power and glory. And then shall he send his angels, and shall gather together his elect from the four winds, from the uttermost part of the earth to the uttermost part of heaven.

This citation speaks of "those days, after that tribulation," which indicates that there will be a period of some days between the official end of the final tribulation (September 6) and Christ's return. These days must be the brief period from September 6 until a day between September 15 and September 27.

It is obvious that the days that begin September 6 will be days of stark terror for the inhabitants of the world. No wonder we read in Revelation 6:15-17:

> And the kings of the earth, and the great men, and the rich men, and the chief captains, and the mighty men, and every bondman, and every free man, hid themselves in the dens and in the rocks of the mountains; And said to the mountains and rocks, Fall on us, and hide us from the face of him that sitteth on the throne, and from the wrath of the Lamb: For the great day of his wrath is come; and who shall be able to stand?

Because of the terrible nature of those days the Lord assures the believer in Luke 21:28:

> And when these things begin to come to pass, then look up, and lift up your heads; for your redemption draweth nigh.

Wonderfully, the awful days just before the end of the world will be blessed days for the believer. He will know that at any moment he will receive his glorified spiritual body and will be caught up to be with Christ. He will know that the time of the creation of the new heavens and the new earth has come. That is why it is so important that we know **now** that we are saved. It is important because during the final days it will be too late for salvation.

SUMMARY

We now should summarize our findings. We have discovered that God had developed a very interesting and harmonious chronology for the earth. From our very superior vantage point, of being near the end of time, we can see how it all goes together.

One striking fact is how God divides time into blocks of even thousands of years or even hundreds of years. Each period of time begins with a significant event that relates to the unfolding of God's salvation plan and ends with another event that is completely involved with God's salvation plan. The reason for this is that the time line of history is governed by the unfolding of God's salvation plan. The even thousands of years are frequently modified very **slightly but always with the same three numbers.** These numbers are completely interrelated. Two of the numbers are those which signify tribulation or judgment. They are 2300 days (a bit more than six years) and twenty-three years. The third number is the difference between these two numbers. It is the number seventeen years, which is used in the Bible to signify heaven. These three numbers figure prominently in the chronology God has established.

Thus we have found that there are:

*13,000 years from creation to the beginning of the final tribulation period - 11,013 B.C. to 1988 A.D.

*13,000 years plus 2300 days (6 years) that encompass all of history - 11,013 B.C. to 1994 A.D.

*11,000 years plus 2300 days (6 years) that encompass the period from creation to the birth of Christ - 11,013 B.C. to 7 B.C.

*6000 years plus 23 years that encompass the history of the first world - 11,013 B.C. to 4990 B.C.

*7000 years less 23 years plus 2300 days (6 years), which equals 7000 years less 17 years, that encompass the second period of this earth, beginning with the flood in 4990 B.C. and continuing to 1994 A.D.

*2000 years from the first coming of Christ to His second coming - 7 B.C. to 1994 A.D.

*4000 years from the birth of Jacob and Esau, an event that marked the beginning of the rivalry between the Jews and the Arabs, and the end of both these nations - 2007 B.C. to 1994 A.D.

*4000 years from the birth of Jacob, which in a sense points to the birth of the body of believers, and the end of the believers on earth - 2007 B.C. to 1994 A.D.

*5000 years less 23 years plus 2300 days (6 years), which equals 5000 years less 17 years, from the beginning of the second world to the first coming of Christ - 4990 B.C. to 7 B.C.

*4000 years, typified by the 4 days Lazarus was already in the tomb (cave) and by the 400 shekels paid by Abraham in the year 2030 B.C. for the purchase of the tomb (cave) in which Sarah was buried, plus 23 years goes, to the resurrection in 1994 A.D.

2030 plus 4000 years plus 23 years = 1994 A.D.

*1000 calendar years from the laying of the temple foundation until the cross when the spiritual foundation was laid - 967 B.C. to 33 A.D.

*2100 years from the official beginning of the nation of Israel and their end as God's special people - 2068 B.C. (Abraham circumcised) to 33 A.D. (the cross).

*3000 years from the anointing of the literal King David and the coming of the King of kings, Jesus, who was typified by David - 1007 B.C. to 1994 A.D.

*1000 years from the anointing of King David and the coming of King Jesus to this earth - 1007 B.C. to 7 B.C.

*1440 calendar years from Israel's entrance into the land of Canaan, which signified the believers' entrance into the kingdom of heaven, and the cross where Jesus made provision for the believers to enter heaven - 1407 B.C. to 33 A.D.

*1440 years from the time Israel was freed from bondage in Egypt to the coming of Christ who came to free men from spiritual bondage (spiritual bondage is typified by Egypt) - 1447 B.C. to 7 B.C.

*3900 years from the giving of the name Israel to Jacob and the completion of making the believers the spiritual Israel - 1907 B.C. to 1994 A.D.

*1100 years from the loss of the ark until Jesus, who was typified by the ark, endured hell for our sins - 1068 B.C. to 33 A.D.

*1100 calendar years from the recovery of the ark until Jesus arose from the grave, which indicated His victory over hell - 1067 B.C. to 33 A.D.

We discovered, too, that there is a very precise timetable covering Christ's ministry.

Event	*Time*
Christ is announced as the Lamb of God to take away the sins of the world and is baptized	Feast of Trumpets Sept. 28, 29 A.D.
Christ presents Himself to be crucified exactly 3½ years after His baptism	Feast of Trumpets Sept. 28, 29 A.D. to triumphal entry Sunday, March 29, 33 A.D.
Christ crucified	Friday, April 3, 33 A.D.
Christ sends the Comforter, the Holy Spirit, exactly 1335 days inclusive from His baptism	Feast of Trumpets, Sept. 28, 29 A.D. to Pentecost May 24, 33 A.D.
The Gospel era - 1955 years (5 x 17 x 23)	Pentecost May 24, 33 A.D. to May 21, 1988 A.D.
The Final Tribulation 2300 days inclusive period from end of Gospel era to announcement of Jesus' second coming	May 21, 1988 A.D. to Sept. 6, 1994 A.D. (Feast of Trumpets)

Last Day and return of Christ sometime on or between:

September 15, 1994: Beginning of 1994 Jubilee year,

and

September 27, 1994: Last Day of Feast of Tabernacles

One last thought as we complete our study.

Do you remember that we learned that Jonah warned that in forty days Nineveh was to be destroyed? Do you also recall that the number forty is that of testing? Nineveh's testing time was forty days. They repented and were not destroyed.

Likewise Israel was forty years in the wilderness. Remember in Revelation 12 the wilderness represents the time believers are in this world on their way to heaven. Israel failed the test and most of them perished in the world because of unbelief.

Remember we learned that in a real sense the Israel of God began in 2007 B.C. when Jacob was born. The 4000 years from 2007 B.C. to 1994 A.D. when Christ returns are, therefore, representative of the testing that mankind endures on this earth. If he fails the test by not believing in Christ, he is subject to the wrath of God, which is typified by the Israelites dying in the wilderness. If he trusts in Christ as his Savior, he enters the Kingdom of God, having been given eternal life. This was typified by the Israelites who crossed the Jordan River into the promised land.

The testing period of 4000 years is almost over. Have you failed the test? Or have you trusted in our Lord Jesus Christ as your Savior and Lord so that you know that when He comes, you will be with Him forevermore?

CONCLUSION

The material set forth in this book has been researched with great care. Care was constantly exercised to make sure that no Biblical data was forced or fudged to make it fit into a preconceived idea. Every attempt was made to be faithful to the Bible. The results of this study indicate that the month of September of the year 1994 is to be the time for the end of history.

We must be cautious. There could be something that has been overlooked. In view of the many paths that I have found that focus on 1994 it seems extremely unlikely that we have overlooked something. However I modestly and humbly acknowledge that such a possibility exists.

The fact that readers can call on the Open Forum program (see Appendix II), which is aired Monday through Friday for one and one half hours each evening, should be very helpful. Questions can be answered and additional information that either supports or contradicts the information offered in this study can be aired. Those of us who are sincerely interested should faithfully and diligently pray that truth will be served.

In I Thessalonians 5:2 we read:

For yourselves know perfectly that the day of the Lord so cometh as a thief in the night.

The coming of our Lord on the last day will be a complete surprise to the unsaved of the world because they do not trust the Bible. On the other hand, we read in I Thessalonians 5:4:

But ye, brethren, are not in darkness, that that day should overtake you as a thief.

While this verse can be understood to teach that a believer is always ready for Christ's return because he already has eternal life, it can also embrace the meaning that the believer has learned much from the Bible concerning the timetable of Christ's return. We are reminded again of Daniel 12:4 where God indicates that at the time of the end, "knowledge shall be increased." Concerning this knowledge, God declares in Daniel 12:10, "none of the wicked shall understand; but the wise shall understand."

At the beginning of this study I said that during the last twenty years I have answered the question concerning the end of the world with the statement, "I will be very surprised if we reach the year 2000 A.D." After having done this study I now say equally carefully, "I will be surprised if we reach October 1, 1994."

The conclusion that we are only months away from the end of the world and Judgment Day is, of course, super awesome. **Suddenly more than five billion people individually must face the fact that very soon they will stand before God to give an account of their lives.** Wonderfully, those who believe they are saved have a little time to examine themselves in the light of the Bible teachings to make sure that they truly are saved. If there were ever a time for self-examination, it is now.

Anyone who looks with longing eyes on the material things, on the pleasures of this world, and knows that he does not want to give up these things, will come under judgment. Remember Lot's wife, who perished because she looked back to Sodom where her material possessions were. You must quickly assess your life to determine where your priorities are.

Anyone who decides that he does not believe the fact that the end is so close can do so, but he will be like the proverbial ostrich that sticks his head in the sand. His unbelief will not in any way change the reality of the fact of Christ's return.

By God's mercy there are a few months left. However, if this study is accurate, and I believe with all my heart that it is, there will be no extensions in time. There will be no time for second guessing. When September 6, 1994, arrives, no one else can become saved. The end has come.

If you, dear reader, are not saved, there is still a little time to cry to God for mercy. Look in your Bible at the reaction of the Ninevites to the proclamation of Jonah that in forty days Nineveh was to be destroyed. Nineveh was a wicked and godless city, in complete rebellion against the God of the Bible. Yet they repented and from information found in the New Testament, we can know that many became saved. Let me quote a few verses that God records for us in the Book of Jonah. In Jonah 3:4-9 we read:

> And Jonah began to enter into the city a day's journey, and he cried, and said, Yet forty days, and Nineveh shall be overthrown. So the people of Nineveh believed God, and proclaimed a fast, and put on sackcloth, from the greatest of them even to the least of them. For word came unto the king of Nineveh, and he arose from his throne, and he laid his robe from him, and covered him with sackcloth, and sat in ashes. And he caused it to be proclaimed and published through Nineveh by the decree of the king and his nobles, saying, Let neither man nor beast, herd nor flock, taste any thing: let them not feed, nor drink water: But let man and beast be covered with sackcloth, and cry mightily unto God: yea, let them turn every one from his evil way, and from the violence that is in their hands. Who can tell if God will turn and repent, and turn away from his fierce anger, that we perish not?

The God of heaven who spared the Ninevites is the same God who will spare you from this impending judgment if you cry to Him for mercy.

It should be emphasized that this is not a time for theological debate. Someone may say, "I don't believe it will happen because this is not what we Baptists or Methodists or Presbyterians or whatever teach." The time for that kind of argumentation is long past. The only thing to do is carefully check out these things using the Bible alone as your guide. There is no time left to trust your pastor or your church. You must trust only the Bible.

My earnest prayer and desire is that somewhere in the world there may be one or more people who are brought face to face with their lost condition and who by God's mercy become saved. That is finally the purpose of publishing this book.

Addendum

While there is no Biblical sanction for this addendum and therefore, it carries no weight whatsoever, there is a very curious fact that shows up. During the twentieth century there are only six years that have the unique distinction of having the sum of the integers adding up to the number twenty-three. These are 1949, 1958, 1967, 1976, 1985, and 1994.

$$1 + 9 + 9 + 4 = 23$$

Curiously the next year that has this characteristic is the year 2399, which is more than 400 years from now.

It is indeed curious, and probably not significant at all, that the number twenty-three is so deeply entwined with history and surfaces for the last time in connection with the expected year of our Lord's return and Judgment Day.

Appendix I
The Future of National Israel

A Biblical citation that is frequently used to prove that God still has a glorious future for national Israel is Romans 11:25-26. These verses inform us:

> For I would not, brethren, that ye should be ignorant of this mystery, lest ye should be wise in your own conceits; that blindness in part is happened to Israel, until the fulness of the Gentiles be come in. And so all Israel shall be saved: as it is written, There shall come out of Sion the Deliverer, and shall turn away ungodliness from Jacob.

Many theologians read these verses and are convinced that they do indeed teach that God is promising great blessings for national Israel. Doesn't this passage declare that while blindness is now upon national Israel, the time will come when all Israel will be saved? And since this great event has never happened in the past, surely it will happen in the future. The very fact that Israel is again in its own land surely anticipates a future spiritual restoration of national Israel.

While these ideas may appear attractive for one reason or another, they are not even suggested by these verses. The fact is, these verses teach us exactly the opposite; namely, that there never will be spiritual restoration of national Israel. Let us look at these verses very carefully to discover in detail what they teach.

In Romans 11:7-9 God is teaching that national Israel is divided into two parts. We read:

> What then? Israel hath not obtained that which he seeketh for; but the election hath obtained it, and the rest were blinded (According as it is written, God hath given them the spirit of slumber, eyes that they should not see, and ears that they should not hear;) unto this day. And David saith, Let their table be made a snare, and a trap, and a stumblingblock, and a recompence unto them.

The one part, which consists of the elect, is a very small part of the nation, for Romans 11:5 speaks of the elect as a remnant: "Even so then at this present time also there is a remnant according to the election of grace."

In Elijah's day this remnant was included in the "seven thousand men, who have not bowed the knee to the image of Baal" (verse 4). It also included the Apostle Paul (verse 1) in his day.

The other part of national Israel consisted of those who were blinded. This includes the major part of national Israel at any time in its history.

Today we see this division of national Israel in the same two parts. While there is a trickle of believers in the Lord Jesus Christ found amongst those who are blood descendants of Abraham, sadly we see that the vast majority remains in unbelief.

In Romans 11:25 God again makes reference to the part of Israel that remains in blindness. Indeed, He tells us how long this condition of blindness will prevail in national Israel. We read there that "blindness in part is happened to Israel, until the fulness of the Gentiles be come in." This statement not only tells us how long this blindness will continue on the one part of Israel but it also implies that during the same period a remnant chosen by grace will continue to come in. As we continue our study we will see what a blessed promise this is to those who are Abraham's blood descendants.

How long will this blindness continue? Verse 25 declares "until the fulness of the Gentiles be come in." The phrase "fulness of the Gentiles" would have to include every Gentile in the entire world who was chosen by God to be saved. If the fullness of the Gentiles had come in, it would mean that nowhere in the world could there be one more person who, as one of God's elect, was still to be saved. Thus, this verse teaches us that as long as there remains one Gentile in the world to be saved, we can expect that the greater part of national Israel will remain in their blindness.

This means that Israel as a nation will never turn to the Lord. Matthew 24:14 teaches, "And this gospel of the kingdom shall be preached in all the world for a witness unto all nations; and then shall the end come."

Many theologians envision an eschatological program in which at some time in the future national Israel is supposed to evangelize the world. Romans 11:25 teaches, in a very definite way, the incorrectness of such an eschatological scheme. God is declaring emphatically and specifically that we must recognize, sorrowfully, that as long as one Gentile anywhere in the world remains to be saved, the greater part of national Israel will remain in spiritual blindness.

All Israel to be Saved

Does Romans 11:26 promise that "**all** Israel shall be saved"? Indeed it does. But who is all Israel? Israel has existed as a people for over 4000 years. All who are blood descendants of Abraham are a part of national Israel. Surely no one who lived in previous generations and who died in unbelief can be saved. Yet they are just as much a part of Israel as the blood descendants of Abraham who are living today. Therefore, if all Israel is to be saved and yet there exists this vast part of Israel that lived and died without becoming saved, then surely we can see that we have to look for a meaning of the term "all Israel" other than the one that includes every blood descendant of Abraham. Let us, therefore, look at the phrase "all Israel" more closely.

The key word is **all**. When we use the word all in ordinary speech we normally use it in an all-inclusive sense. That is, if we were told that all the people in a particular room were wearing shoes, we would rightly assume that no one in the room had bare feet. But when the Bible uses the word **all**, its meaning is conditioned by the context in which it is found.

For example, in Acts 2:17 God declares that He will pour out His Spirit on **all** flesh. Does this mean that every person in the entire world will experience the pouring out of the Spirit in his life? No, we know from other parts of the Bible that only those who become believers in Christ experience the pouring out of the Spirit in their lives. Thus God is effectively teaching in Acts 2:17 that He will pour out His Spirit on all flesh (whom God intends to save). Only God's elect will experience this wonderful event, that is, when one of the elect becomes saved, he experiences it. Thus in this verse the word all does not mean the entire human race. Rather it includes all in the human race whom God planned to save.

Likewise in I Corinthians 15:22 God states, "For as in Adam all die, even so in Christ shall all be made alive." From information given elsewhere in the Bible, we know that the first *all* includes each and every human being that has ever lived on this earth. The Bible tells us that there is "none righteous, no, not one" (Romans 3:10).

If the second *all* of this verse included each and every person in the entire human race, God would be teaching universal salvation by means of this verse, for the phrase "be made alive" means, in this context, to be saved. But universal salvation is not suggested anywhere in the Bible. The fact is, the Bible offers many statements that tell us that hell will be heavily populated. The only way we can look at this verse so that it harmonizes with everything else in the Bible is to realize that it is teaching, "so in Christ shall all be made alive" (all whom God intends to make alive - that is, God's elect). Again the *all* is conditioned by other Bible truths.

Let us return now to Romans 11:26, where God declares, "all Israel shall be saved." We know from verse 25, which we have just examined in detail, that at any time in the history of Israel, right up to the time when even one Gentile in the entire world remains to be saved, most of Israel will remain in unbelief. Therefore, "all Israel" must refer to all Israel who are to be saved. That is, even as "all flesh" of Acts 2:17, and "all be made alive" of I Corinthians 15:22, refer to the totality of God's elect who are to be saved, so in Romans 11:26 the term "all Israel" must refer to the totality of God's elect who are to be saved from within national Israel. We should therefore read verse 26a this way: "And so all Israel (who are the remnant of the election of grace) shall be saved."

But aren't we missing something? Doesn't Romans 11:26 teach that **after** the fullness of the Gentiles comes in then all Israel shall be saved? Cannot "all Israel" refer to all who are national Israel living at the time the fullness of the Gentiles will have come in? Couldn't there be a massive turning of national Israel to Christ **after** the last of the Gentiles who are to be saved have become saved?

SO Does Not Mean THEN

As a matter of fact, many theologians change the word "so" in Romans 11:26 to the word "then" or the word "after." You can check any number of books that teach the premillennial view and find that this is the case.

The word "so," which in its Greek form is found more than 150 times in the Bible, is **never** translated "then" or "after." In a few places it is translated "in this manner," but it is never translated to indicate a chronological event. Romans 11:26 in no way suggests that **after** the fullness of the Gentiles come in **then** all Israel will be saved. Rather it is teaching that blindness will continue to be on the major part of national Israel right to the end. This means that there always will be that other part of national Israel - the remnant chosen according to the election of grace. As long as one Gentile remains to be saved, there is the remnant, the trickle of God's elect, in national Israel who will be saved. And so, that is, in this manner, all Israel who are to be saved will be saved.

So we see that Romans 11:25-26 is teaching exactly the opposite of that which is taught by many people. Not only is it **not** teaching a future glory for national Israel, but the passage is teaching the sad fact that there **will not** be a future glory for national Israel. These verses, therefore, bring us precisely the same truth that we discovered in all of our previous study. They reinforce our conviction that we correctly understand the Bible insofar as God's dealings with national Israel are concerned.

Before we leave these verses, we should comment on the last half of verse 26 and all of verse 27, where we read:

... as it is written, There shall come out of Sion the Deliverer, and shall turn away ungodliness from Jacob: For this is my covenant unto them, when I shall take away their sins.

Whether they realize it or not, those who teach that Romans 11:25-26 are proof texts that there will come a time when all of national Israel will become saved are effectively teaching two salvation programs. The first is that which has been in effect until the present time, wherein believers come one by one into the Kingdom of God; the second is a program wherein a whole nation will come in. According to their understanding of Romans 11, the whole nation cannot come in until the deliverer shall come out of Zion, who shall turn away ungodliness from Jacob and shall take away their sins.

Some even believe that the deliverance of Romans 11:27 is a political deliverance. This idea, however, is altogether without possibility in view of the phrase, "when I shall take away their sins."

In other words, according to some theologians' understanding of these verses, the Savior must still come to save national Israel. Apparently, the fact that Christ has already come as Savior is not sufficient. This teaching in a real sense denies the atonement. Why is this so? Does the Bible in any way teach two salvation programs: one for all believers throughout time, including the remnant chosen by grace from national Israel who have lived and died during the last 4000 years, and the other for the whole nation of Israel that might exist at some future time?

Surely the Bible does not teach two salvation programs. Moreover, when Jesus came as the Savior, to whom did He come? Did He come to the Chinese? To the Egyptians? To the North American Indians? Indeed not. He came to **national Israel**. Jesus was a Jew. He was born in a Jewish city, Bethlehem. He grew up in a Jewish city, Nazareth. He was baptized by a Jewish prophet, John the Baptist, in the River Jordan, which flowed through the land of the Jews. He preached for more than three years in Jewish cities such as Capernaum, Jericho, Bethany, and Jerusalem. All of His disciples were Jews as were His personal friends, such as Mary, Martha, and Lazarus.

Indeed, Jesus **has already come** as the Deliverer from Zion to take away the sins of those He came to save out of national Israel. Because He came as the Deliverer to take away sins, we rejoice that it is possible that individuals out of national Israel, as well as out of every other political nation of the world, can be saved. To suggest that Jesus must still come to save national Israel is to deny all that the Bible teaches concerning the first coming of Christ.

Moreover, to teach that God has a different plan of salvation for a future generation of national Israel, whereby they as a whole body will be saved, is to deny a fundamental principle wherein God declares He is not a respecter of persons.

Are there other statements in the Bible that relate to national Israel of today? Indeed there are.

In Isaiah 6 we read of the commissioning of Isaiah to be a proclaimer of the Gospel to the Israel of his day. But when he is prepared to go forth with the Gospel, he is told in Isaiah 6:9-12:

And he said, Go, and tell this people, Hear ye indeed, but understand not; and see ye indeed, but perceive not. Make the heart of this people fat, and make their ears heavy, and shut their eyes; lest they see with their eyes, and hear with their ears, and understand with their heart, and convert, and be healed. Then said I, Lord, how long? And he answered, Until the cities be wasted without inhabitant, and the houses without man, and the land be utterly desolate, And the LORD have removed men far away, and there be a great forsaking in the midst of the land.

These terribly negative words were written more than 700 years before Christ. Already in that day God was underscoring the same principle we saw emphasized in Romans 11:7 that, except for a remnant chosen by grace, the rest of Israel would remain blinded. This relationship of Isaiah 6 to Romans 11 is proven dramatically as Romans 11:8 quotes Isaiah 6:9 in support of the proposition that most of Israel remained in unbelief even during the Apostle Paul's day.

According to the language of Isaiah 6, how long is Israel to remain blinded? Isaiah 6:11 declares, "Until the cities be wasted without inhabitant, and the houses without man, and the land be utterly desolate." This sounds like the condition of blindness will continue until the end of time. Certainly it cannot refer to any desolation experienced by Israel between the time of Isaiah and the New Testament period when God wrote through the Apostle Paul, for Romans 11:8 is not the only verse that quotes Isaiah 6 in regards to the continuous unbelief of Israel. Jesus quotes the same words in Matthew 13:14-15 and the Apostle Paul, near the close of his ministry, quoted them again in Acts 28:25-26.

The Fig Tree - Cursed Forever

In Mark 11 Christ alludes to the sad future of national Israel in very specific language, in connection with a fig tree. Do you recall that we discovered that the fig tree relates to national Israel? In Mark 11:12-14 we read:

And on the morrow, when they were come from Bethany, he was hungry: And seeing a fig tree afar off having leaves, he came, if haply he might find any thing thereon: and when he came to it, he found nothing but leaves; for the time of figs was not yet. And Jesus answered and said unto it, No man eat fruit of thee hereafter for ever. And his disciples heard it.

Why did Jesus curse this innocuous fig tree? Mark 11:20-21 records:
And in the morning, as they passed by, they saw the fig tree dried up from the roots. And Peter calling to remembrance saith unto him, Master, behold, the fig tree which thou cursedst is withered away.

Why did Jesus come seeking figs when it was not the time for figs? Didn't Jesus, who is eternal God, who created the world, know it was not time for figs? And why does the Bible say that He was hungry?

Only if we begin to see that this fig tree represents national Israel and that Christ cursed the fig tree to teach something concerning national Israel does the cursing of the fig tree have any meaning. Let us examine this passage carefully to discover the deeper spiritual meaning that it conveys.

Verse 12 declares that Jesus was hungry when He came seeking for fruit from the fig tree. Did Jesus have an earnest desire that national Israel might bear fruit, that is, that they would respond to Him as Messiah? Indeed He did. In Matthew 23:37-38, Christ declares:

> O Jerusalem, Jerusalem, thou that killest the prophets, and stonest them which are sent unto thee, how often would I have gathered thy children together, even as a hen gathereth her chickens under her wings, and ye would not! Behold, your house is left unto you desolate.

Do you recall the words of Luke 19:41-44 where our Lord weeps over Jerusalem as He prophesies the impending doom of Jerusalem?

> And when he was come near, he beheld the city, and wept over it, Saying, If thou hadst known, even thou, at least in this thy day, the things which belong unto thy peace! but now they are hid from thine eyes. For the days shall come upon thee, that thine enemies shall cast a trench about thee, and compass thee round, and keep thee in on every side, And shall lay thee even with the ground, and thy children within thee; and they shall not leave in thee one stone upon another; because thou knewest not the time of thy visitation.

While it was not God's sovereign plan to save a great number from national Israel, nevertheless, God has no pleasure in the death of the wicked (Ezekiel 33:11). The desire of God is the obedience of His creatures. Only because God has elected some of mankind to salvation and then proceeds to incline their wills and hearts to Him does anyone become saved.

This is why the Bible records that Jesus was hungry and He came seeking figs when He obviously knew there were no figs. He is expressing His desire that national Israel would respond to the Gospel even though He knew that they would not turn to the Gospel. How could He know that they would not turn to the Gospel? Remember Mark 11:13 records it was not time for figs. Jesus knew of God's curse on national Israel as recorded in Isaiah 6. Remember, in Matthew 13:14-15 He quotes from Isaiah 6 to give the reason for the adamant unbelief of Israel of His day. As Jesus came to this fig tree with leaves so that from a distance it looked like it might be bearing fruit, Jesus knew there would be no figs. Likewise, as we look at Israel in the days of Jesus, it looked very much like it should bear spiritual fruit. The leaves were there. It was a nation in its own land - a remarkable fact considering the terrible devastation of Israel in 587 B.C. by the Babylonian empire.

But it was a nation that could not be expected to bear spiritual fruit. Because of their constant unbelief and rebellion down through the centuries, already more than 700 years earlier, in the days of Isaiah, God had pronounced the curse of Isaiah 6:9-12 that they would be blinded (that is, except for the remnant chosen by grace spoken of in Romans 11:5).

And so it was not the season for fruit. Christ's curse of the fig tree becomes a reiteration, an underscoring of the curse already given in Isaiah 6.

Now the question arises: In the record of the cursing of the fig tree, is there any clue as to how long this curse will apply - how long will national Israel as a nation not bear spiritual fruit? We found that Isaiah 6 intimated that this could be the condition of national Israel all the way to the end of time.

When we look at Mark 11:14 carefully, we discover that indeed God is declaring that it is His expressed intention that national Israel would never again bear fruit. He pronounced, "No man eat fruit of thee hereafter for ever." Forever! Never again would this fig tree bear fruit. No wonder today we see national Israel opposed to Jesus as Messiah.

Can you see that in Mark 11 we have in another form a repetition of the words of Isaiah 6? Can you see the perfect agreement between Mark 11 and Romans 11:25? In this passage from Romans God declares that blindness will continue on the major part of national Israel until the fullness of the Gentiles comes in, that is, until the end of time. Surely we are finding complete agreement with the sad principle that national Israel will never respond to Christ as Messiah.

From our superior vantage point of living almost 2000 years after Christ went to the cross, we see the dramatic fulfillment of this prophecy. Israel does exist as a nation but as a nation they are as negative toward Christ as they ever have been. There is a trickle of believers, a remnant chosen by grace. Indeed, all of God's prophecies concerning national Israel have come to fulfillment. See *The Fig Tree* (available from Family Radio, Oakland, CA, 94621), for additional discussion on the future of national Israel.

Appendix II
Family Radio Stations and
"Open Forum" broadcast times

Alabama 9:00-10:30 pm
Birmingham WBFR 89.5 FM

Arizona 8:00-9:30 pm
Phoenix KPHF 88.3 FM

California 7:00-8:30 pm
Chico KHAP 89.1 FM
El Cajon KECR 93.3 FM
El Cajon KECR 910 FM
Eureka 103.1 FM
Fresno KFNO 90.3 FM
Le Grand KEFR 89.9 FM
Long Beach KFRN 1280 AM
Palm Springs 105.5 FM
Paso Robles 105.5 FM
Sacramento KEBR 1210 AM
Sacramento KEBR 89.3 FM
San Luis Obispo 94.3 FM
San Francisco KEAR 106.9 FM
Santa Maria 104.9 FM
Santa Cruz 89.3 FM
Santa Barbara 92.7 FM
Stockton 88.1 FM
Ukiah KPRA 89.5 FM

Connecticut 3-4:30 pm
Vernon WCTF 1170 AM

Florida 10:00-11:30 pm
Jacksonville WJFR 88.7 FM
West Palm Beach WWFR 91.7 FM
Okeechobee WWFR 91.7 FM
Okeechobee WYFR Shortwave
    5985 kHz
    9505 kHz
    (heard all over the United
    States and Canada)
St. Petersburg WFTI 91.7 FM

Georgia 10:00-11:30 pm
Columbus WFRC 90.5 FM

Illinois 9:00-10:30 pm
Chicago WJCH 91.9 FM
Joliet WJCH 91.9 FM

Iowa 9:00-10:30 pm
Ames 89.1 FM
Cedar Rapids 95.1 FM
Des Moines KDFR 91.3 FM
Fort Dodge 89.1 FM
Iowa City 93.1 FM
Shenandoah KYFR 920 AM

Continued next page

Maryland 10:00-11:30 pm
Annapolis WFSI 107.9 FM
Baltimore WFSI 107.9 FM
Washington WFSI 107.9 FM
Hagerstown 93.5 FM

Massachusetts 10:00-11:00 pm
Boston WEZE 1260 AM

Michigan 9:00-10:30 pm
Grand Rapids WFUR 1510 AM

Nebraska 9:00-10:30 pm
Omaha KYFR 920 AM

New Jersey 10:00-11:30 pm
Atlantic City 89.3 FM
Camden WKDN 106.9 FM
Newark WFME 94.7 FM

New York 10:00-11:30 pm
Albany 90.7 FM
Buffalo WFBF 89.9 FM
New York WFME 94.7 FM
Poughkeepsie 90.5 FM
Smithtown WFRS 88.9 FM
Webster WFRW 88.1 FM

Ohio 10:00-11:30 pm
Cuyahoga Falls WCUE 1150 AM
Toledo WOTL 90.3 FM
Youngstown WYTN 91.7 FM

Oregon 7:00-8:30 pm
Eugene KQFE 88.9 FM
Grants Pass 97.7 FM
Medford 107.1 FM

Pennsylvania 10:00-11:30 pm
Erie WEFR 88.1 FM
Johnstown WFRJ 88.9 FM
Philadelphia WKDN 106.9 FM
Pittsburgh 97.7 FM

South Carolina 10:00-11:30 pm
Charleston WFCH 88.5 FM

Texas 9:00-10:30 pm
Beaumont KTXB 89.7 FM

Utah 8:00-9:30 pm
Salt Lake City KUFR 91.7 FM

Washington 7:00-8:30 pm
Kirkland KARR 1460 AM
Longview KJVH 89.5 FM

Wisconsin 9:00-10:30 pm
Milwaukee WMWK 88.1 FM

Scripture Index

About the Author

Harold Camping was born in Colorado and at an early age moved with his family to California. He earned a B.S. degree in civil engineering from the University of California at Berkeley in 1942. In 1958 he helped found Family Radio and some years later gave up a successful construction business to devote full time to the Christian radio ministry, which now broadcasts worldwide. He and his wife, Shirley, have raised seven children; they make their home in the San Francisco Bay area. He is the Family Radio president and general manager and participates in the broadcasts by teaching on the Family Bible Study program and by serving as host of the Open Forum, a live call-in program. A forty-year student of the Bible, he has been steadfast in his attempts to provide Biblical answers to questions posed by Open Forum listeners.

He has written other books and booklets, including *Adam When?*, "The Biblical Calendar of History," *Feed My Sheep, The Fig Tree, The Final Tribulation, First Principles of Bible Study*, "Galatians Chapter One," "Galatians Chapter Two," "Galatians Chapter Three," "The Glorious Garden of Eden," "God's Magnificent Salvation Plan," *The Gospel: God's Covenant of Grace*, "Let the Oceans Speak," "The Seventy Weeks of Daniel 9," "Sunday: The Sabbath," *What God Hath Joined Together*, "What Is The True Gospel," and "When Is The Rapture?" These publications are available from Family Radio, Oakland, CA 94621.

Readers with questions or comments may call during the Open Forum program, which is aired weekday evenings on Family Radio stations (see Appendix II). The toll-free number is 1-800-322-5385.